Conflict and Peacemaking in Multiethnic Societies

Conflict and Peacemaking in Multiethnic Societies

Edited by
Joseph V. Montville

Lexington Books
An Imprint of Macmillan, Inc.
New York

Maxwell Macmillan Canada
Toronto

Maxwell Macmillan International
New York   Oxford   Singapore   Sydney

Lexington Books
An Imprint of Macmillan, Inc.
866 Third Avenue, New York, N.Y. 10022

Maxwell Macmillan Canada, Inc.
1200 Eglinton Avenue East
Suite 200
Don Mills, Ontario M3C 3N1

Macmillan, Inc. is part of the Maxwell Communication Group of Companies.

Printed in the United States of America

printing number
    3   4   5   6   7   8   9   10

Library of Congress Cataloging-in-Publication Data

Conflict and peacemaking in multiethnic societies / Joseph
  V. Montville, editor
        p.   cm.
    ISBN 0-669-21453-1 (alk. paper)
    ISBN 0-669-28106-9 (pbk : alk. paper)
    1. Ethnic relations — Congresses. 2. Culture conflict — Congresses.
3. Conflict management — Congresses. I. Montville, Joseph V.
II. Center for the Study of Foreign Affairs.
GN496.C65   1989   89-12581
                                CIP

*To Judith, Shannon,
Clea, and Doris*

Contents

III   Sri Lanka in the Southern Asian Context   239

IV   Sudan in the African Context   341

Preface

B eyond the threat of global annihilation by nuclear weapons, there are very good statistical reasons why war, the roots of political violence, and the challenges of peacemaking have become major preoccupations of the academic, government, policymaking, and international security affairs communities. Since 1700 A.D., there have been 471 wars in which at least 1,000 people were killed. Ninety percent of the approximately 100 million deaths recorded in these wars occurred after 1900. And there is a new trend evident. Since the end of World War II, there has been only one "war"—the Soviet-Hungarian conflict in 1956—in Europe. But as of February 1989, some nineteen wars (1,000-plus deaths) are being fought in the Third World; and regardless of the ideological dressing many of these conflicts wear, most have a strong ethnic and/or sectarian base.

Vietnamese ethnic consciousness was a major factor not only in the wars with France and the United States but also in the subsequent battles with China and Cambodia. Muslim Afghans fought (mostly) Slavic Soviets; and within Islam, a Sunni Arab, Semitic regime in Iraq engaged in a bloody war with the Shiite, Aryan government in Iran. The enduring conflict among Israelis, Palestinians, and other Arabs is a constant concern, not only because of the victims but also because of the broader regional and global strategic implications. The Lebanese state has been torn apart in sectarian killing. Black–white tension persists in South Africa. And these are only the headline stories.

It was with these facts in mind that Hans Binnendijk, then director of the Center for the Study of Foreign Affairs at the Department of State's Foreign Service Institute, decided to mount a major conference series on conflict and peacemaking in multiethnic societies. The meetings took place on February 18–19 and May 4–6, 1987, at the Foreign Service Institute in Arlington, Virginia. The Center for the Study of Foreign Affairs, now directed by Dr. Michael Vlahos, is the Institute's bridge to the academic and professional world outside of government, where new perspectives developed in the nongovernmental sector can be combined with the practical experience gained by foreign affairs professionals.

This volume is made up of essays produced by conference members after the February and May meetings so that they could employ insights generated in the deliberations by the representatives of the several social science disciplines represented, including history, political science, political economy, international relations, international law, sociology, area studies, psychoanalysis, and political conflict resolution. Several conference participants who did not produce essays added commentary that enriched the proceedings. These participants included Ambassador Eamon Kennedy of Ireland; W. Kendall Myers and Peter Bechtold of the Foreign Service Institute's School of Area Studies; Professor Edward Azar, University of Maryland; Jerrold M. Post, M.D., George Washington University; and David Throup. Former deputy assistant secretary of state for inter-American affairs, Paul D. Taylor, and Professor Howard Wriggins, Columbia University, also made valuable contributions. The editorial skills of Diane Bendahmane have contributed greatly to the lucidity of the chapters.

A debt is owed to the United States Institute of Peace, Washington, D.C., which funded the conferences, essays, and editorial preparation of this volume. The views expressed herein are solely those of the authors and do not represent the views of the Center for the Study of Foreign Affairs or the Department of State.

I
The Varieties of Ethnic Conflict Analysis

As the table of contents indicates, this volume, though divided into five parts, actually comprises three segments. Part I reviews the history and nomenclature of ethnic conflict, with special perspectives from the developed West and traditional societies of the Third World. It then presents a selection of ways to look at ethnic conflict, not only as a reflection of profound yet predictable psychological motives in given ethnic groups, but also as a challenge to the arts of social and political engineering. Parts II through IV offer case studies of so-called hot ethnic conflicts—in Northern Ireland, Sri Lanka, and Sudan—that have continued to defy the efforts of would-be peacemakers. But these sections also examine conflicts within the geographic and/or cultural regions of the hot conflicts and offer clues and precedents as to how governments and peoples managed to keep political violence within acceptable bounds or avoid it altogether. The final segment (part V), on lessons drawn, was written by scholars who participated in all of the case study presentations and were asked to reflect on the insights thus gained.

Perhaps unique in the analytical mix presented herein is the attempt to integrate explicitly empirical and theoretical contributions from the scientific study of individual and group behavior into politics—or, more simply, political psychology. The theme here is that in the most grievous and historically bloody ethnic conflicts, there are specifically psychological tasks to be performed at the same time as or, more likely, before some of the more creative schemes of constitution drafting and political institution building described in this book can be fruitfully undertaken.

To start off part I, Uri Ra'anan provides an impressively informed review of the history of ethnic consciousness in politics, which could very well be subtitled "The History of Mankind to Date." It is offered as an antidote to what Ra'anan contends is the both liberal and Marxist tradition that holds that modernization causes ethnic consciousness simply to wither away along with other primitive or superstitious characteristics of traditional culture. In his stimulating assessment, the idea of modern nation-state turns out to be something of an intellectual conceit.

In a complex and erudite essay, Martin Heisler explains why ethnicity as manifested in the modern Western state is of a significantly different quality than that seen in traditional societies. He contends that ethnicity is likely to become noteworthy in an industrialized democracy only after religious, social, and economic divisions and needs for political participation have been met. In a modern state, where civilization may have its discontents, ethnicity may be something of a psychological haven. The rise of ethnic consciousness is, in fact, associated with the success of modern industrial states in meeting material and security needs and in enhancing civil liberties and income equity.

Milton Esman provides the first assessment in the classic political science tradition of the causes of ethnic conflict, using examples drawn from modern and traditional societies. He walks us through a variety of analytical hypotheses and offers some practical guidelines for the formulation of conflict management strategies. For his part, Remi Clignet presents a functional analysis of the conditions in family relationships, the ecology of survival, such as the availability of water or fertile land; the role of territoriality; and other environmental factors that affect both *intra-* and *inter*ethnic tensions and conflict. He provides an extremely valuable template with which to assess traditional and modern versions of the frustration/aggression dyad in the economic and social context.

Vamık D. Volkan, a medical doctor, psychiatrist, and psychoanalyst introduces political psychology as a critical analytical tool in political conflict analysis. His contribution is a primer on basic concepts from depth psychology that explain how the human psyche is a fundamental actor in the surface phenomena of politics. He explains the developmental basis of hostility and its externalization on "enemies," the link between the individual self and the person's ethnic identity, the elusive functions of leadership, and the necessity for traditional politicians and diplomats to learn about and accommodate the hidden human agenda. As noted in the table of contents, I return to this theme in my epilogue (chapter 29).

It will soon be apparent to the reader that the theory of power-sharing—the elaboration of political institutions in ethnically, linguistically, and religiously fragmented states that generate a sense of relative political, economic, and social justice among the various groups—is a recurrent subject in this volume. First introduced into the political science literature by Arend Lijphart as "consociational democracy," power-sharing is a concept under constant discussion in South Africa, Northern Ireland, and many other states and regions where ethnic conflict is endemic. In his essay, Kenneth D. McRae provides a very useful and fresh critique of power-sharing theory, including its applicability in Third World situations. Jürg Steiner discusses the issue in the specific context of Swiss power-sharing, pointing out that the ability of Switzerland to develop institutions to manage ethnic conflict results not from Swiss genetic superiority but from a history of bloody warfare and lessons learned the hard way. He recommends that those who would apply the Swiss model elsewhere take great care to assess the feasibility of the transfer to the receiving political culture.

Donald L. Horowitz's chapter on the comparative politics of ethnic conflict management is a goldmine of information on how states from Canada to Malaysia have successfully used a great variety of constitutional, political, and structural mechanisms to reduce, redirect, envelop, and dissipate existing or potential ethnic violence. The essay reflects the broad objective of this volume: to be much more than the traditional academic compendium of description and analysis but to be, also, a practical handbook for foreign ministries, national and provincial governments, journalists, research institutions, universities, nongovernmental leaders in nonprofit and commercial enterprises, and citizen diplomats alike, literally around the world.

1

The Nation-State Fallacy

Uri Ra'anan

Toward a New Typology: Semantic Barriers

It has been one of the fallacies of contemporary political thought, particularly in the West, to assume that the international arena of the twentieth century is occupied largely, if not almost exclusively, by nation-states or nation-states-to-be. (The term *nation-state* is either tautological or, if it is to be lucid and coherent, presumably would have to refer to a polity whose territorial and juridical frontiers coincide with the ethnic boundaries of the national entity with which that state is identified, frequently by its very name.)[a] To be sure, protagonists of the nation-state view will usually admit that one portion of the globe—the so-called developing areas—does not quite fit their conceptual framework. However, they will quickly add that in these areas, a process is under way, subsumed under the facile heading "nation building," that will result almost inevitably in the area's "normalization"—its *Gleichschaltung* with the rest of the world.

Those who hold this view will dismiss as tribalism any rejoinders pointing out that these areas already comprise many genuine national entities—such as the Yoruba, Ibo, Ewe, and others—frequently numbering millions of members and possessing a well-developed culture, language, and historical consciousness, but that the arbitrary boundaries of the postcolonial states usually cut across or ignore these ethnic units. Consequently, the attempt to "build nations" on the basis of the current artificial frontiers and states actually may undermine or destroy existing nationalities. Most of the advocates of the prevailing trend in political thought will regard such arguments, at best, as anachronistic and likely to hamper their streamlined models of modernization and the economic and functional efficiency to be implemented by highly centralized states and their bureaucracies.

Adapted from Uri Ra'anan, "Ethnic Conflict: Toward a New Typology," in Uri Ra'anan, ed., *Ethnic Resurgence in Modern Democratic States: A Multidisciplinary Approach to Human Resources and Conflict* (New York: Pergamon Press, 1980). Reprinted with permission.

The better informed of these analysts perhaps will allow that, in addition to not applying to the developing areas, their theory also does not provide an entirely appropriate description of conditions within the successor states of the three former great polyglot dynastic entities of Southeastern, Eastern, and Central Europe—the Ottoman, Romanov, and Hapsburg empires. Generally, however, they will downplay these anomalies by categorizing the current nationality conflicts of that part of the world as mere minority problems.

The rest of the globe (approximately the region known as the West) is viewed predominantly in contemporary thought as the very birthplace of the modern nation-state and its primary showcase.

The Nation-State: A Negligible Minority

On the political map of the world, the territorial frontiers of the state and the ethnic boundaries of the constituent nation rarely coincide. Iceland, metropolitan Portugal, Norway, and a few others are the exceptions among the approximately 170 more-or-less sovereign countries existing today. In very many cases, the state is larger than the "nation"; that is, the juridical limits of the state extend well beyond the area settled by its *Staatsvolk* (that is, the ethnic group that created the state, is largely identified with it, constitutes the bulk of its elite, and is the source of the predominant culture). For instance, Great Russians make up only half the population of the U.S.S.R., and even if, by a very wide stretch of the political imagination, one were to accept as "co-*Staatsvölker*" of the U.S.S.R. the fourteen other national groups for which the various constituent Soviet republics were named, the boundaries of the Soviet Union would still embrace some 26 million additional citizens (almost one-tenth of the population) who belong to "other" or "minority" ethnic entities and occupy considerable portions of the country. Similarly, in the Yugoslav case, the original *Staatsvolk,* the Serbs, make up little more than 40 percent of the inhabitants. Even if Croats, Slovenes, Macedonians, and Montenegrins, whose names the other Yugoslav republics bear, were to be regarded in the same light as the Serbs, this would still leave Yugoslavia with other or minority nationalities amounting to nearly one-fifth of its total citizenry and inhabiting sizable stretches of its territory.[b]

Nor is the West exempt from such situations. France, *the* classical nation-state of the political textbooks, contains, adjacent to its outer limits, German-speaking Alsatians; Italian-speaking inhabitants of the eastern Riviera and Corsica; Catalans and Basques at either end of the Pyrenees; Celtic Bretons; and Flemings southwest of the Belgian frontier—amounting altogether to nearly one-tenth of metropolitan France's citizens, without even counting the population of French "overseas departments" or the large number of foreign laborers in the country, North Africans and others. In the Canadian case, even if one regarded as *Staatsvölker* the descendants of settlers both from the

British Isles and from France (Quebecois and Acadians), each in their respective sections of the country, one would still be left with a "third Canada"—including Scandinavians, Germans, Dutch, Ukrainians, Poles, Jews, Italians, Indians, and Eskimos—exceeding one-fourth of Canada's citizens and inhabiting considerable stretches of its territory, especially in the prairies, the north, and the northwest.

In the Far East, even the island state of Japan, despite its long history of relative isolation, is far from homogeneous. It includes not only a sizable Korean minority but also the aboriginal Ainus, who persist tenaciously in the country's northernmost reaches.

If in these and at least 100 other instances the state is larger in size than the area inhabited by the nation or *Staatsvolk,* there are, conversely, quite a few cases in which the boundaries of the nation exceed the territorial limits of any one state. There is a German nation, but, until recently, there were several German states (the German Federal Republic, The German Democratic Republic, possibly West Berlin—if it could be regarded as a separate state—and perhaps even Austria). Switzerland, Liechtenstein, and Luxembourg, although a majority of their inhabitants speak German and/or German dialects, presumably would not be considered German states by most analysts. A Korean and a Vietnamese nation exist, but each has been divided into two separate, more-or-less sovereign states (one of which, South Vietnam, subsequently was eliminated by conquest). Quite a few observers, within and outside the Middle East, argue that in spite of some historical, ethnic, linguistic (dialectical), and religious differences, the various Arab groups constitute one single nation, whereas currently there are twenty-one Arab states. There is a Jewish state, but it contains less than one-fourth of the Jewish people, as well as a sizable Arab minority.

There is a Hungarian state, but the frontiers imposed upon it by the post–World War I and II settlements exclude nearly 3 million Magyars from the motherland (in Transylvania, southern Slovakia, and the Vojvodina), not to speak of the many hundreds of thousands in the New World who are of Magyar descent. There are two Chinese states (actually there are three, if one regards Singapore from the ethnic point of view), but they do not include either the Chinese inhabitants of Hong Kong or the millions of "overseas Chinese" in Southeast Asia and in the Western Hemisphere. Even in relatively homogeneous Scandinavia, the Swedish state fails to include half a million Swedes in neighboring Finland, right across the Gulf of Bothnia, not to mention the millions of ethnic Swedes in North America. These are but a few of the scores of examples in which the ethnic limits of the nation transcend the territorial frontiers of one particular state.

Thus, in well over 90 percent of the independent countries existing today, the state either is considerably larger or much smaller than the area inhabited by the corresponding nation or *Staatsvolk.* Nation-states, far from constituting the rule on the contemporary political map, remain a very exceptional phenomenon—if a high degree of ethnic homogeneity and congruity between the geographic outlines of the state and nation are regarded as the primary criteria of the nation-state. (If these are not the criteria, then little, if any, real meaning attaches to the term.)

If this is true today, how much more was it the case during earlier decades and centuries? After all, only in the second, third, and fourth quarters of this century has it become customary to attempt to "clean up" the ethnic map. This has included genocidal measures: against Jews and Gypsies under Hitler; Crimean Tatars, Volga Germans, and Chechen-Ingush under Stalin; Ibos in Nigeria; southern blacks in the Sudan; both Tutsi and Hutu in Rwanda and Burundi; Armenians in Anatolia; overseas Chinese in certain parts of Southeast Asia; and Kurds in Iraq. Peoples have been expelled: Asians from Uganda and Germans from most of East-Central Europe. Populations have been exchanged through agreement, by semivoluntary moves, as a result of fear, or in the wake of unilateral measures: Hellenes from Turkey and Turks from Greece; Macedonian Bulgars from Greece and Hellenes from Bulgaria; Turks from Bulgaria and Bulgars from European Turkey—all in the 1920s; most Hindus and Sikhs from Pakistan and many Muslims from India; practically all Jews from the Arab countries and about three-fourths of the Arabs from the area that became Israel in 1948–49; and some of the few Ukrainians and Belorussians still remaining in truncated post–World War I Poland and many ethnic Poles from former Polish territories annexed to the U.S.S.R.

Despite all these ethnic clean-up measures, genuine nation-states have remained the exception on the political landscape, as has been noted. Obviously, there were even fewer instances of ethnic homogeneity in the period that preceded these measures—that is, up to 1920—not to mention the fact that until the two Balkan wars and World War I, there were three great multinational states: the Ottoman, Hapsburg, and Romanov empires (only the last of these was succeeded by an equally polyglot state—the U.S.S.R.). Moreover, during the first half of the nineteenth century, there were thirty-nine separate German and nine Italian states. Nation-states, therefore, not only are very much in the minority on the contemporary political scene but have been even more exceptional in history.

Multiethnic States and Nationalism

Thus, multiethnic polities have constituted the norm across the ages and still do today. Despite this prevalence of polyglot entities—or perhaps because of it—*nationalism* (that is, the self-assertion of ethnic groups, ranging from primary cultural, religious, and educational endeavors, via political organization, to the ultimate step of struggling for territorial or state power) has been a highly significant phenomenon throughout most of recorded history. Many contemporary Western political scientists deny this and trace "true" nationalism, which they regard as a "modern ideology," no further back than the French Revolution or, at most, the absolutist centralized states of the seventeenth century. Of course, anyone acquainted with the paeans to England and the English in Shakespeare and to the concept of Italy in Dante—not to speak of the lyrical and epic portrayals of the struggles for cultural and religious self-expression and national survival of the Hellenes and the Hebrews in the Greek classics and in the Bible—will wonder if this view is not somewhat simplistic.

It is not difficult to grasp the reason for the apparent paradox that multi-ethnic states, rather than posing an obstacle, constitute a breeding ground for the growth of nationalistic manifestations. An awareness of national differences and a perception of the incompatibility of interests are far less likely to develop in ethnically homogeneous societies, where individuals usually do not encounter in their daily lives problems caused by the need to function (during study, work, or litigation) in a language other than their mother tongue, to adjust to unaccustomed and incomprehensible cultural traditions, or to compete economically and socially with personalities molded by an entirely different background and heritage. Conversely, the sudden impact of one ethnic group on another—whether because of invasion, annexation, migration, or simple fluctuation in the language or cultural frontiers between two peoples—cannot but give rise to some, most, or all of these problems, which are likely to be aggravated if the nationalities concerned find themselves within the frontiers of a single state. In that case, they are likely to seek satisfaction of their aspirations through a struggle for political control of the whole country or, at least, portions of it.

Thus, it is symptomatic that the center of French separatism in Canada is to be found not in the solidly French Quebec hinterland but in multinational Montreal. Similarly, the focus of the Belgian nationality conflict is bilingual Brussels, not the homogeneously Flemish farmland of the north or the overwhelmingly Walloon coal areas of the south.

One can, of course, discover instances in which distinctly nationalistic tendencies have become evident even in apparently homogeneous countries, but closer investigation usually will reveal that in these cases, extraneous ethnic elements actually have impinged on the native population. For example, Iceland, an almost "pure" nation-state, recently has shown signs of somewhat strident nationalism. In fact, this new nationalism is largely due to the situation on the sea surrounding the island, where a large proportion of this nation of fishermen spends its working days and has to compete with trawlers from Britain and other countries. In a sense, therefore, Iceland is ethnically homogeneous only on land, not on the equally important adjacent waters.

Pathetic Fallacies

Perhaps the argument presented so far should not be regarded as particularly revolutionary, as it is based on data with which at least historians of the period 1806 to 1939 have long been acquainted. However, for some reason, quite a few adherents of other disciplines, particularly Western economists and some political scientists, recently seem to have discovered—with surprise and sometimes with shock—that even contemporary Western societies contain mutually competing, often antagonistic, culturally, religiously, and/or linguistically distinct ethnic groups that regard themselves as nationalities or even as nations-to-be and struggle for political and/or territorial power.

It may be useful to review the origins and antecedents of the still-fashionable misapprehensions of such analysts and observers. One of the pathetic fallacies of the period that began in the closing stages of World War II was to assume that the great wave of nationalism, which had swept across Europe between the Napoleonic and Hitlerian eras, had fulfilled its aspirations through the creation of a series of supposed nation-states and would somehow ebb away. The futuristic literature of the period was full of patent panaceas, such as the common expectation that federalism would dominate the post–World War II world and fuse the remnants of nationalism into some higher, supranational amalgam, embodied in various large federations of states.

It was taken for granted, moreover, that national fervor had begun to fade away in an easterly direction. After all—so most economic and political planners of the time argued—the concept of the modern nation-state was born during the sixteenth and seventeenth centuries in the bureaucratically centralized, postmedieval societies of Western Europe: Britain, France, and the Netherlands. By the nineteenth century, so they claimed, following the French revolutionary elaboration of the idea of *la nation* and in reaction to the Napoleonic expansionist drive for conquest, nationalism had reached Central Europe, leading eventually to the formation of unitary states in Germany and Italy, and then had moved eastward to the Balkans and East-Central and Eastern Europe, which became known, par excellence, as the hotbeds of national strife. By the twentieth century, the wave was said to have moved still further east to the so-called Middle East, eventually reaching the rest of colonial Asia and Africa.

By this time, the West (that is, Western Europe and the Western Hemisphere), where so-called nation-states had been established centuries ago, was supposed to have recovered from, or even to have proved immune to, the "infantile malady" that was now ravaging less-fortunate lands. This was believed so firmly that Western states such as Switzerland, France, and the United States were held as the classical examples of societies that had solved the "national problem."

Events in recent years, of course, have demonstrated that these obituary notices for Western nationalism were, to put it mildly, premature. Belgium has become the arena of revived Flemish and Walloon separatism, and the end is not in sight. France has been confronted by national movements of the Bretons, the Corsicans, and the Basques, and Spain by movements of the Basques and Catalans. The growth of French separatism in Quebec appeared meteoric until recently. The United States has come to acknowledge that it is striving for a pluralistic society rather than a melting pot. Then there is, of course, Ulster, not to mention the rise of Welsh and Scottish nationalism in the United Kingdom. Finally, in the classical home of supposed national resolution, Switzerland, a very sharp conflict has exacerbated relations between the German Protestant majority of the canton of Berne and the predominantly Catholic and overwhelmingly French population of the Jura, in the north of the canton. The secession of the northernmost portion of the Jura from Berne has not resolved the problem.

Why have the prophets of the 1940s and 1950s turned out to be so mistaken? The reasons, apparently, include academic prejudice and wishful thinking. As has been pointed out, many of the would-be prophets have been economists or adherents of certain categories of political science, especially those with a functionalistic bias. Professionally, they have tended to be enamored of sheer size, "efficiency," and "viability." To most of them, it has appeared axiomatic that large territorial units, with rich, variegated resources, would prove to be more competent and effective members of the global community than their smaller, poorer counterparts. Consequently, these prophets have been prejudiced in favor of sizable federations and other large polities and have tried to convince themselves and others that existing states (however arbitrarily their frontiers might mutilate ethnic units) are, in fact, nation-states or nation-states-to-be.

In contrast, most historians and anthropologists have been inclined to doubt whether, even under modern (that is, postmedieval) conditions, artificial nation building really has been successful to any degree, except perhaps temporarily in a couple of West European instances and in some immigrant societies. Moreover, historians have been well aware that the sultans in five centuries were unable to build an Ottoman nation out of Turks, Arabs, Armenians, Kurds, and Greeks; the tsars in several centuries could not build a single nation out of Great Russians, Ukrainians, Belorussians, Poles, Finns, and Georgians; nor could the Hapsburg emperor-kings, in a similar time span, build one nation out of Germans, Hungarians, Czechs, and Croats. There is no indication that these large, polyglot but ramshackle empires, beset by unending struggles for self-government of the subject nationalities, really were more efficient, stable, or happy societies than those of their much smaller successor states that were reasonably homogeneous ethnically, such as Estonia and Lithuania (states that were destroyed subsequently not by internal conflict but by Soviet imperialism).

Admittedly, for a brief period after World War II, it appeared as if the advocates of mass, size, and federation might have a point. The European Economic Community (EEC) was founded; unions between Mali and Senegal and between Egypt and Syria (the United Arab Republic) were established. However, the latter two unions quickly broke up, and although the EEC has grown in size and economic stature, Europe's political reality remains de Gaulle's "l'Europe des patries," rather than a true European federation whose members really have merged their individual sovereignties and foreign policies.

Moreover, centrifugal tendencies quickly became apparent and spread within existing states between Slovaks and Czechs; Croats, Macedonians, and Serbs; Ukrainians, Georgians, Lithuanians, Jews, and Great Russians; Walloons and Flemings; Basques and Castilians; Francophones and Anglophones in Canada; Kurds and Arabs in Iraq; black Africans and Arabs in the Sudan; Ibos, Yorubas, and Hausa-Fulanis in Nigeria; and Bengalis and Biharis in East Pakistan (Bangladesh). Thus, if anything, the trend has been toward the breakdown of existing polities into still-smaller entities rather than their merger into larger units.

The survival of so-called regional organizations in Africa, the Arab world, and Latin America in no way contradicts this trend, as these structures remain mere sounding boards and are not evolving as supersovereignties. This is quite evident from the continued hostility between Ethiopia and Somalia within the Organization of African Unity and between Syria and Iraq and Algeria and Morocco within the Arab League.

Three Concepts of Nationality

Conceivably, current misapprehensions might not have persisted but for the well-nigh impenetrable semantic confusion, especially in the West, that has enveloped the whole topic of nationality and nationalism because of a failure to recognize that there are at least three distinct meanings, with entirely different connotations, in various regions of the world.

The Western View

In the West (that is, roughly, Europe west of the Rhine and the Western Hemisphere), a primarily territorial concept of nationality (having much in common with the legal concept of jus soli) has developed during the modern era. Western Europe was one area where classical feudalism really flourished. Historical myth notwithstanding, feudalism of this type did not necessarily breed anarchy but rather provided, in several cases, a congenial environment for the growth of centralization and bureaucratic statehood, as evidenced by the history of the early Norman-Angevin monarchy, from William I to Henry II, and that of Norman Sicily.

On the basis of this heritage, the postmedieval, absolutionist Western

European monarchies of the Tudors and the Valois were able to establish modern, bureaucratic, centralized states. In these instances—and perhaps in these instances alone—some degree of nation building can be demonstrated to have occurred. In a sense, it was these new *states* that assisted the process of creating the modern French and English *nations,* rather than the other way around (although, as has already been pointed out, even in these cases, this process, extended over generations, has not been completed to this very day).

Therefore, allegiance to the state, residence therein, and submission to its jurisdication are the hallmarks of the Western idea of nationality—to the point where, in American English, one speaks of a *national* of a country when one actually means a *citizen.* The two terms have become synonymous. It is an individual's place of residence and his passport that largely determine his nationality in the West; that is, the criteria are primarily territorial and juridical, precisely as in the case of jus soli. For the same reasons, the concepts of state and nation have tended to converge in the English language, to a degree that causes many to refer to *national interests* when, in fact, they mean *state interests,* while others speak simplistically of a world of nation-states.

As already demonstrated, however, there are rather few instances in which the limits of the state and those of its constituent nation really coincide. Loyalty and commitment to the state and to the nation often not only are not synonymous, but may be mutually incompatible. In order to unite a nation split asunder by official boundaries or to win independence for a nationality that lacks sovereign territory, individuals sometimes feel impelled to fight the states in which they dwell and whose formal citizenship they hold. In the pre-1938 Austrian Republic, being a nationalist meant supporting an *Anschluss* between Austria and the German Reich—that is, attempting to obliterate the republic and submerge it in a greater Germany. Thus, *nationalist* and Austrian *patriot* were antithetical terms. The interests of the state and the nation simply were incompatible. The same was true, of course, of any of the particularist German and Italian states in the first half of the nineteenth century.

Similarly, being a Jordanian or Lebanese patriot and being a pan-Arab nationalist who happens to be a citizen of Jordan or Lebanon are antithetical concepts. The creation of a pan-Arab empire, probably ruled from Cairo or Damascus, effectively would mean the end of independent Jordanian and Lebanese states (to the extent that Lebanese independence can be regarded as meaningful while Lebanon is still under virtual Syrian occupation). In multinational states, it maybe possible to be a patriot and a nationalist simultaneously—provided one happens to be a member of the *Staatsvolk.* It is hardly feasible, however, for minorities. In Czechoslovakia, a Czech can, at one and the same time, support his state and his nation (or at least he could under Eduard Beneš and Alexander Dubcek). However, an ethnic Magyar from southern Slovakia cannot simultaneously and without contradiction support the Czechoslovak state, whose passport he holds, and the aspirations of the Magyar nation, which presumably would lead to the eventual separation of Magyar-speaking southern Slovakia from Czechoslovakia and its reunion with the Hungarian motherland.

Because the identification of state and nation occasionally has rested on some degree of reality in Western history, most Westerners assume that it prevails today throughout most of the world. Actually, it has been, and remains, a very exceptional phenomenon. The contemporary Western political glossary suffers considerably from the semantic confusion that derives from this misapprehension.

The fallacious assumption that certain Western concepts actually have universal application has led Westerners and many Western-educated Africans and Asians to think and speak in such terms as *nation-building,* the fallacies of which were discussed earlier.

The Eastern and Southern Views

In a majority of ancient communities, as in most contemporary non-Western societies, the criteria that determine a person's nationality were derived not from jus soli but rather from jus sanguinis. According to the latter concept, it is not *where* an individual resides and which state has jurisdiction over him that determines his nationality, but rather *who* he is—his cultural, religious, and historic identity—that is, his ethnicity, the heritage received from his ancestors and carried with him, in mind and body, irrespective of his current domicile. Jus sanguinis is a personal (as opposed to the Western territorial) criterion of nationality.

For instance, following the Germanic invasions of various provinces of the Roman Empire, there lived—side by side in the same territory and under the sway of the same "barbarian" ruler—ex-Roman citizens and members of one of the Germanic tribal confederations (such as Goths, Vandals, Burgundians, Franks, and Lombards). Yet in most cases, and over a considerable period of time, the two groups remained distinct entities and, before the law, what mattered was who the defendant was, not where he was living. Usually, Romans were judged by Roman law and the new Germanic settlers by their own Germanic customary law. Both groups regarded this practice as proper and, indeed, as a precious safeguard of their respective rights and privileges.

It is from this general model that two current, slightly differing, but related non-Western concepts of nationality are descended: the Eastern (approximately covering Europe east of the Rhine) and the Southern (roughly covering the southern and eastern rims of the Mediterranean—that is, the successor states of the Ottoman Empire). Both are based on personal rather than territorial criteria, but the Eastern approach tends to focus on cultural touchstones of ethnicity (including ancestral language and name), whereas in the

Southern view, religion is one of the primary hallmarks of nationality, so that the existence of a separate religious community frequently is a precondition for the successful development of full-fledged nationhood.

Cultural Touchstones. The Eastern concept, of course, long antedates the rise of Communist regimes. In the democratic Czechoslovak Republic under Thomas Garrique Masaryk and Eduard Beneš (1919–38), for example, Czechoslovak citizenship was quite distinct and separate from nationality. There was no "Czechoslovak nationality." In the Czechoslovak census, Czechoslovak citizens regarded themselves, and were regarded by others, as belonging to one of seven primary nationalities (Czechs, Slovaks, Sudetengermans, Magyars, Ruthenes, Jews, and Poles) and registered accordingly—for example, citizenship, Czechoslovak; nationality, Magyar; religion, Catholic; marital status, single; and so forth. The Czechoslovak state, at least in theory and to some extent in practice, recognized the right of each of the nationalities to its own educational, linguistic, and other facilities (in order to preserve its distinct identity), as well as to a reasonably proportionate share of official appointments, particularly in the respective areas in which the population of each of the ethnic groups was concentrated.

Again, in the U.S.S.R. today, although there is Soviet citizenship, there is no Soviet nationality. The Soviet census (and the Soviet internal passport or identity card) requires the registration of each citizen as a member of one of the more than 100 separate nationalities—Great Russian, Ukrainian, Belorussian, Uzbek, Georgian, Armenian, Jewish, and so forth. Regrettably, in the Soviet case, unlike pre-1938 Czechoslovakia, such identification does not necessarily ensure the grant of the corresponding cultural and national privileges, although they are promised in the Soviet constitution. On the contrary, national identity frequently becomes the basis for discrimination. However, the analysis here is concerned primarily with describing political concepts, not with deciding whether they are currently abused rather than implemented.

Acknowledging that various separate nationalities exist side by side with a single citizenship is in line with the historic traditions of the region, dating back many centuries. According to the personal rather than territorial touchstones embodied in these traditions, a Georgian who lives in Moscow—and perhaps was even born there and speaks Russian more fluently than his ancestral Georgian tongue—will still regard and register himself, and be regarded by others, as a Georgian rather than as a Great Russian. What matters is not where he resides nor even necessarily which language he now speaks best, but what his ancestry and cultural heritage is—who he is or, rather, who he perceives himself to be and who others perceive him to be.[c] In recognition of this aspect, the Soviet census contains a special category comprising members of ethnic groups who no longer speak the ancestral language of their nationality—presumably because they are dispersed—but have adopted another tongue, usually Russian. They are still registered as Ukrainians, Georgians, and so on, but with a comment to the effect that they now command a language other than the mother tongue of their nationality. The percentage of such persons is particularly high among Poles, Germans, and Jews in the U.S.S.R.

The nineteenth-century cultural and political history of many of the "revived" nationalities of East Central and Southeastern Europe probably reinforced the tendency to apply personal rather than territorial touchstones. Peoples whose state had disappeared from the map as a sovereign entity centuries earlier and whose national tongue had degenerated into a peasant dialect without a literature, because it had been superseded as the elite form of written and spoken communication by the language of the conquerors, usually initiated their national renaissance by resuscitating their ancient language in a modernized and literary form. In many cases, this cultural thrust, as well as the subsequent moves to ignite the spark of national insurrection, emanated not from the segments of the population that had remained settled on the soil of the old homeland, but rather from individual members of the intelligentsia who were living abroad in the diaspora.

Modern Greek language and literature owed much to a few Hellenic writers living in Italy, and the Panhellenic movement originated with the sons of Greek merchants in Odessa and those of Phanariotes in Bucharest. The modern Serb language and literature was largely the creation of a handful of Serbs in the Hapsburg Empire, and the Bulgarian uprising was initiated by members of the Bulgarian diaspora in Odessa and Bucharest. Similarly, the revival of Hebrew as a modern spoken tongue with a secular literature and the establishment of a Jewish national movement, Zionism, were the products of the diaspora of Eastern and East Central Europe.

In all of these instances, individuals who were imbued with national sentiments helped to resuscitate an ancient language and culture and then to organize a national movement, thus reviving the nation as a whole, which in turn proceeded to recreate the old national state. In other words, whereas in the West, there were some cases in which a state created a nation, in the East, individuals sometimes revived nations, which then recreated states. It is a reasonable assumption that these factors played a role in accentuating the personal criteria of the Eastern—as opposed to the territorial criteria of the Western—concept of nationality.

Religious Touchstones. In the areas south and east of the Mediterranean, formerly dominated by the Ottoman Empire, a third, Southern view of nationality prevails. It bears close resemblance to the Eastern approach insofar as it stresses on the individual's heritage and personal identity rather than his domicile or passport. However, according to the Southern concept, a more significant role in determining national identification is played by religion than by other cultural factors.[d] A very important cause for this phenomenon may be found in the history of the Ottoman institution known as the *millet*. For centuries after their appearance on the political scene, the Ottoman Turks regarded themselves essentially as an army engaged in an ongoing holy war that had settled down temporarily during one of the truces, rather than as a normal, permanent state. Consequently, their ideas of governance were rather rudimentary. They were interested mainly in collecting from the conquered peoples financial contributions for the upkeep of the Ottoman armed forces as well as an occasional tribute of male children to be converted to Islam and to serve as recruits in the elite corps of those forces. As far as administration was concerned, the Ottoman sultans were content to set up a skeleton framework in which their authority was exerted by nominated representatives (whose positions in remote areas tended to become semiautonomous and even hereditary). These representatives dispensed the sultan's justice mainly in accordance with Koranic precepts, but those among the conquered who were regarded as non-Muslim "infidels" were allowed largely to see their own internal civil governance in line with their respective religious canons. Since the aristocracy and warrior castes of the various subject peoples often had been decimated during the course of the Ottoman conquest, the only group left with the necessary literacy and experience to cope with juridical and organizational functions usually was the clergy.

Consequently, the limited civil law autonomy of the conquered peoples became, de facto, a form of clerical and religious self-government, applying canon law—particularly with respect to matters of personal status, such as marriage, divorce, and inheritance. Under this *millet* system (as under the Eastern concept of nationality), what mattered was not where an individual lived but who he was. Members of the Armenian Orthodox *millet* (that is, community) paid certain taxes to its clergy, elected its officials, and were judged by it in civil matters—primarily, personal status issues—irrespective of whether they lived in the predominantly Armenian-populated provinces of eastern Anatolia or as a scattered minority in the large Turkish cities. As a result of the *millet* system, national identity in the regions south and east of the Mediterranean eventually became almost synonymous with religious identity. Thus, the Armenians are simultaneously a distinct nationality and a distinct religion (disregarding the small minority of Armenian Catholics), and the same is true of the Jews, the Druzes, and, to some extent, the Maronites, the Greeks, the 'Alawites, and others.

It is not widely realized that several Middle Eastern states have inherited and incorporated into their system of government various aspects of the *millet* concept; for instance, it constituted the key to Lebanon's ingenious internal "compromise" until the recent tragic events and Syria's subsequent domination of the country. According to the compromise, the president, premier, and speaker of the house were chosen from the Maronite, Sunni, and Shiite *mil-*

lets, respectively, and a fixed proportion of members of parliament represented each of the various *millets.* Israel, via the British Palestine Mandate, has inherited another aspect of the Ottoman *millet* system—the exclusive jurisdiction of the various *millet* religious courts over questions of personal status, such as marriage, divorce, and inheritance. Yet Zionism in the nineteenth century started as a predominantly secular national movement, modeled on the Italian *Resorgimento* and the Polish, Greek, and Hungarian national revivals. In other words, a movement that originally developed in harmony with the overtones of the Eastern approach to nationality eventually reached fruition in an area permeated by the Southern view.

Atomistic and Organic Views of Nationality

To summarize briefly, there are essentially three major approaches to the nationality question: the Western territorial concept and the Eastern and Southern personal concepts, with East and South respectively emphasizing different criteria of nationality. Some writers, however (mostly from that great experimental laboratory of national conflict resolution—the late Hapsburg Empire)—particularly Karl Renner (*Das Selbstbestimmungsrecht der Nationen*)—have proposed a somewhat different analytical schema. In Renner's typology, there is an *atomistic* view, according to which the only legally and constitutionally recognizable entities (with the possible exception of the economic field—that is, corporations and trade unions) are the indivisible, centralistic state as a whole and the various individual citizens, who have no collective status but merely form an unconnected, haphazard, atomized aggregate of persons. There is no intermediate, constitutional entity between these individual parts and the state as a whole.

According to Renner, opposed to this atomistic concept is an *organic* view, which gives legal and constitutional recognition to politically intermediate units (frequently of an ethnic nature) between the state and the individual citizen. Proponents of the organic approach may be divided, in turn, into two groups: those who advocate the *territorial principle* and those who advocate the *personal principle*. Under the territorial principle, autonomy may be granted to a specific administrative area (province, canton, or, as in the United States, state) that has a separate historic identity and tradition of its own or, preferably, that is populated predominantly by a single ethnic group. These autonomous areas are then constitutionally recognized as legal entities and are linked to each other by bonds of federation or confederation.

Under the personal principle, individual members of an ethnic group, irrespective of their domicile and without regard to whether they constitute a regional majority or are living as a dispersed minority throughout the state as a whole, are joined together in an autonomous organization (not unlike the *millet*) that is then also constitutionally recognized as a legal entity.[c] The autonomous organizations of the various nationalities coexist with the central government of the state and its local administration but have the special constitutional prerogative and duty to carry out certain functions (or to act as monitors and ombudsmen over their implementation by the regular central and local government organs).

Such functions presumably would include the establishment, maintenance, and development of the appropriate educational and cultural institutions and facilities through which the ethnic group in question, irrespective of its size, may preserve and enhance its particular linguistic, historical, cultural, and religious heritage. Also involved would be the implementation of measures to ensure that, in their contact with judicial, administrative, and other facets of regular government and in their dealings with general public institutions, no individuals of any ethnic group should be disadvantaged by regulations or practices that take insufficient account of their linguistic preferences and abilities and their cultural and religious customs.

As may be gathered from the many instances of ethnically centrifugal tendencies in multiethnic states cited earlier, it is entirely conceivable that the trend toward separatism may become so strong that the multiethnic societies may have difficulty coping with the next century. Whatever the future may hold, it is hoped that some of the extant semantic and conceptual confusion may be dispelled, at least in part, by the attempt here to present two mutually compatible typologies, one of the author's own making and the other distilled from the work of Karl Renner (and Otto Bauer). Without minimal theoretical clarity and consistency, practical attempts at ethnic conflict resolution would appear to be foredoomed.

Notes

a. In this chapter, the following terms are employed more or less interchangeably: *nationalities, national entities, ethnic units, ethnic entities, ethnic groups, peoples,* and the like. Similarly, *ethnicity* and *nationality* are used in some contexts with roughly the same connotation. The terms *nation, constituent nation,* and *Staatsvolk* are usually employed to denote an ethnic group that currently controls power in at least one state or has controlled state power in the past.

b. The author is concerned with conceptual and semantic lucidity, and no normative implications should be read into the points made in this chapter concerning renewed ethnic self-assertion and accelerating centrifugal trends within existing states. No plea is intended in favor of "redrawing the map" as such. The study attempts merely to discern significant phenomena and to evaluate their impact on the political environment.

c. In the current Soviet practice it is, in fact, the bureaucracy that implements the census or issues internal passports that decides such questions, rather than the individual citizen who responds to the questionnaire. There are, for instance, specific official instructions on how children of ethnically mixed marriages are to be registered. Moreover, if a citizen with a typically Jewish or Polish family name or patronymic were to declare himself a Great Russian or a Ukrainian, the bureaucrat who filled in the official form probably would register him as Jewish or Polish anyhow or would ask to see the internal passports of his parents to verify how their nationality had been registered.

d. There is considerable overlap along the frontiers between the Eastern and Southern views of nationality. It must be recalled that at one stage, Ottoman rule extended to the Carpathians and to the lower Dnieper and Don, embracing not only the Balkans but even portions of the Ukraine (borderland). Under the influence of Panslavism and other eighteenth- and nineteenth-century ideologies, these regions eventually became "Europeanized" and part of the Eastern zone in terms of the nationality question. However, there are distinct remnants of the Southern (Ottoman) approach, which focuses on religion as an important criterion of nationality. For instance, Bosnian *Muslims,* who speak the same language and are of the same ethnic descent as their Orthodox or Catholic Serbo-Croatian neighbors, simply having been converted to Islam under Ottoman rule, now are recognized in the Yugoslav census as a separate nationality, Yugoslav *Muslims.* For that matter, Serbs and Croats are essentially one ethnic group, speaking practically the same language. The main difference is that the Serbs are Orthodox, employing the Cyrillic alphabet (reflecting their Byzantine heritage), while the Croats are Catholic, employing the Latin alphabet (reflecting their Roman heritage). Yet the Yugoslav census and constitution treat them as separate nationalities. Until recent years, the Orthodox Ukrainians and the Ruthenes, the western branch of the Ukrainian people—of the same ethnic stock and speaking the same tongue—were regarded as different nationalities because the Ruthenes had become Uniates (Greek Catholic) while under Polish rule. For a long period, the Bulgars and their Pomak kinsmen were treated as distinct ethnic groups, merely because the Pomaks, although perfectly good Bulgars, had been converted to Islam during the period of Ottoman domination.

e. Much of what follows in this paragraph represents not only Renner's approach but the refinements conceived by his Social-Democratic colleague, Otto Bauer (*Die Nationalitätenfrage und die Sozialdemokratie*). Dissatisfied with his party's 1899 nationality program, which in paragraph 4 called simply for "national minority rights," Bauer demanded that it be expanded to read: "Within each region of self-government, the national minorities shall form corporate entities with public juridical status, enjoying full autonomy in caring for the education of the national minority concerned, as well as in extending legal assistance to their co-nationals vis-à-vis the bureaucracy and the courts."

2
Ethnicity and Ethnic Relations in the Modern West

Martin O. Heisler

C oncerns about ethnic relations are ubiquitous today. They engage all sorts of countries—Western and non-Western, large and small, democratic and nondemocratic, rich and poor—even those with no ethnic minorities. Since the early 1960s, troublesome issues centered on ethnocultural distinctions have arisen in many modern societies in the West, once considered free of—or no longer susceptible to—politically significant ethnicity. And the presence of large numbers of migrants and refugees has added multiethnic dimensions to previously homogeneous societies. This is mirrored by new concerns in the countries of emigration, because many of their citizens have become ethnic minorities elsewhere.

Predictions of the fading importance or even disappearance of ethnic division in modern societies—common in the literature of the social sciences since the 1920s—were mistaken or, at least, shortsighted.[1] Although modernization has substantially attenuated historical patterns of ethnicity, the conditions of modernity have created seemingly similar phenomena. Those predictions were cast in a positive mode. Ethnicity was seen as premodern—primordial, parochial, an impediment to progress and conducive to conflict—and its evanescence was welcomed as a felicitous by-product of modernization. The recent rise of ethnic politics to salience in the West may seem ironic in this light, as it reflects the symptoms of modernity.

The Scope and Varieties of the Problem

The incidence and range of concerns about ethnic differences are nearly as great in the West as in any other part of the world. Objectively, however, the problems in the West are much less severe than those in Africa, Asia, and the Middle East; and there are more instances of peaceful management of ethnic differences. Further, there are reasons to think that what we see in the West today is essentially different from ethnicity and ethnic relations in less-developed, non-Western societies or in the West in earlier times, where politically charged ethnicity has been associated with civil strife, international conflict, dislocation, and the threat of instability.

The rise of ethnicity to salience in the West during the past quarter-century likely follows from the opposite conditions. In most cases, it is associated with the successes of advanced industrial democracies in providing material and physical security for their populations, maintaining political stability, extending and institutionalizing civil rights and liberties, and making measurable progress toward status and income equality—and in building expectations for more progress along these lines.

In the past twenty-five years, demands ranging from greater attention from government or more extensive representation in it to partial or, rarely, complete autonomy have been voiced in fourteen of the twenty-two countries of interest here.[a] Such demands made in the name of ethnic groups have been especially notable in seven of the countries, with leaders mobilizing considerable support among ethnic populations, organizing and sustaining their positions over time, and eliciting concerted responses from central governments: the United Kingdom (regarding Northern Ireland, Scotland, and Wales), Spain (mainly in the Basque provinces and Catalonia), Belgium, Canada, France, Switzerland, and Italy. Ethnic parties have entered the political arenas of these countries and a few others, though not all have persisted.

In six cases, ethnic demands have sometimes been accompanied by violence; but only in two, Northern Ireland and Spain, has violence been substantial and protracted. About 3,000 people have died in such conflicts since the mid-1960s in the West (in a population of more than 600 million), almost all of them in Northern Ireland and Spain. That is a great and lamentable human loss; but the contrast with the non-Western world, where ethnic conflict has led to several million deaths in the same period, is striking.[2]

There have been political reactions to the new minorities in most of the dozen receiving countries, including some with small numbers of foreigners. Parties or movements that appeal to xenophobia have come into being in places as different as France, with about 4 million immigrants on indefinite sojourns, and Denmark, where a few thousand refugees are present but not settled. "Mainstream" parties have also engaged issues centering on both foreign and indigenous minorities.

Few consistent relationships can be discerned between such reactions to foreigners and their numbers or the degree of their "alienness"—or even their presence. Thus, for example, there are neither foreigners nor indigenous minorities in Iceland's population of less than a quarter-million, yet Iceland has often shown concern for the "cultural integrity" and composition of its population. In contrast, Luxembourg, with 370,000 people the second smallest Western state, seems sanguine about the presence of 100,000 foreigners (the largest proportion of such "semisettled" people in Europe), most of them culturally and some of them racially very different from its natives.

Portugal has no ethnic divisions; but because more than one in four Portuguese lives abroad, the Portuguese government, economic institutions, and people must cope with many problems related to ethnicity—albeit not traditional ones.

Ethnic tensions may spill over borders, posing problems for the governments of neighboring states; and they often involve culturally integral groups split by international borders.[b] Thus, the Irish Republic has been chronically entangled in the cultural strife of adjoining Ulster, and the issue of South Tyrol affects Italian–Austrian relations. The internationalization of ethnic problems in the West, though not as significant as in many other parts of the world, sometimes damages otherwise good relations between neighbors. The actions of Spanish Basque separatists have done so recently, for instance, as they challenge French laws and engage French Basques across the border.

The Aims of this Chapter

Concerns related to ethnicity can arise in any country in the late twentieth century, regardless of the sizes of minorities or the sorts of differences between them and the rest of the society—or, for that matter, regardless of whether there are any minorities within its borders. (Japan, one of the more homogeneous countries, exhibits more anxiety about ethnic purity and the presence of even very small numbers of foreigners and more sensitivity in its policies and publicly sanctioned social closure than many markedly heterogeneous countries. It has erected obstacles to the "permanent" settlement of even third- and fourth-generation descendants of immigrants.)[3] If ethnicity can affect any state, would it not be better to concentrate on what it means—how and why it appears, what the consequences are, and how it is dealt with—than on whether it matters?

Such questions motivated this chapter, and two propositions form its core. First, I believe that ethnicity in the West differs from seemingly similar phenomena elsewhere, as well as from traditional scholarly perspectives on the subject. I stress these differences throughout, because ethnic phenomena in the modern West vary in kind, not just in degree, and they can only be understood if they are treated on their own terms. Historically significant elements, such as the ascriptive and subjective ties that bind groups and the "objective" markers of individuals—physical appearance, language, and religion—are less important. Combined with new or newly consequential factors, they make for politically and socially salient ethnicity that is different from that in other places and times. Three such factors stand out: (1) some aspects of social and psychological modernity; (2) the nature of the modern Western state, including the political ethos and policies of democratic regimes; and (3) new developments in international and transnational relations.[c]

Second, the politics of contemporary ethnicity and ethnic relations derive more from the nature of the modern democratic state and its political styles than from qualities indwelling ethnicity or the dynamics of ethnic groups. Altered forms and meanings of ethnicity and ethnic relations imply that the tasks of managing problems associated with them are also likely to differ. For historical reasons—especially differences in the timing and rates of modernization—issues that are important in mobilizing ethnic sentiments and demands often cluster around regional differences in the distribution of economic conditions and life chances. But in most Western states, inequities are more readily approached at the individual than the group level.[4]

To understand such differences, the analysis of ethnicity and ethnic relations—including conflict—must first be put in context. We must differentiate the settings of ethnic phenomena in today's Western democracies from other settings. The main distinctions are introduced in the next section; forms of ethnicity are then arranged in a developmental taxonomy. The aim is not only to highlight and reason through such distinctions but also to bound the venerable concepts and theories more clearly by limiting their use to appropriate domains. Finally, some of the politically salient manifestations of ethnicity are considered in their contexts, with particular attention to the newly important factors.

What Ubiquity Masks: Concepts in Search of Meanings for the Modern West

Social scientists have long cherished the cliché that "most" societies are multiethnic. If this was ever accurate, it is now misleading. To posit two classes of societies—one that is susceptible to ethnic problems and, residually, another that consists of a small number of homogeneous states not prone to such problems—puts a premium on finding similarities and discourages a disciplined search for social, psychological, institutional, political, economic, and international relations–associated distinctions between what we already know and what we should come to know on its own terms.

The classic conceptions and explanations of ethnicity and ethnic relations were developed by social anthropologists working in small, simple societies early in this century. They were and remain appropriate for studying structurally integral, functionally comprehensive ethnicity—that is, where ethnic groups form whole social systems and comprise the basic social, political, and economic environments for their members' lives. But their uncritical application to the modern West—where, instead of such integrity and comprehensiveness, we find predominantly symbolic or utilitarian modes of ethnicity—creates serious problems. Among these are two related pitfalls, which Giovanni Sartori termed "conceptual stretching" and the "travelling problem."[5]

Traditional scholarship looked to a society's cultural distinctiveness, ethnic composition, and boundaries for its points of departure. This leads one to expect that the import of ethnic differences will vary with readily discerned characteristics of the population.[d] In many cases it does not, however, because of institutional differences and policy intervention and because individuals may have considerable latitude in *choosing* the extent to which they assume or emphasize ethnic roles.

Individual Choice

In less modern settings, people are socialized into their ethnic identity from infancy. In the classic view, ethnicity is largely a self-concept derived from a culturally coherent and insulated environment. In a sense, people are born into it; and the ethnic collectivities to which they belong reinforce their boundaries by molding individual identity. Individuals have little or no meaningful choice as to who or what they are in ethnic terms. In the modern West, however, most people have choices in some form and degree.[6] Although there is generally little or no choice among ethnic identities, people can modulate the level of salience accorded ethnicity in their conceptions of themselves.

Without belaboring the now-commonplace observation of the presence of choice, we should strive to understand why and in what circumstances ethnic affiliation and identity are chosen by those who have alternatives. As the philosopher David Kolb noted in his recent treatise on modernity, the availability of choice is commonly taken to characterize the ideal of being modern: "A [modern] person is defined in a way that separates the process of choice from the content chosen."[7] With Kolb, I believe that we must also consider the content of what is being chosen and why.

An understanding of the contemporary West will emerge from the consideration of developmental contexts for ethnicity and the examination of psychological modernity and the nature of the modern democratic state, to be discussed later. Here, I note some of the influences on the relative ease of the exercise of choice: the structure of modern society; the legal, constitutional, and policy frameworks of the state; the ideological ethos of the regime; and the consequent psychological responses and calculations of self-interest of individuals. Ethnicity becomes less comprehensive and continuous than it is in less-developed settings, and people gain the possibility of emphasizing or deemphasizing their ethnic affiliation.

In general, the availability of choice reflects a twofold condition. It is a function of social, political, economic, and psychological modernity—a concomitant of particular stages and forms of development, not perforce a "Western" quality. And for most of the countries of interest here, it is also a product of the broad, diffuse normative dispositions found in liberal democracies.

It is difficult to demarcate liberal democracy precisely and succinctly, but its apposite aspects can be noted.[8] The individual is the primary bearer of rights and status in the eyes of the state. If collectivities are accorded rights and status, these are generally functionally limited and specific, and the internal structures and operations of such groups are expected to conform to the normative templates of the regime. Thus, if particular liberties are assured for all citizens, groups cannot legitimately deny them to their members; if they do, the state is expected to intervene on the individual's behalf. In liberal democracies, political authority derives from popular consent; and in the late twentieth century, egalitarian values and practices are institutionalized and civil liberties formally assured. Although they differ in many respects, the English-speaking countries, West Germany, the Low Countries, the Nordic states, France, and Switzerland all have liberal democratic regimes. In short, the part of the world of concern here is virtually coextensive with the universe of liberal democracies today.[e]

Two important distinctions between the less-developed settings and the modern West are now evident. In the former, ethnicity means belonging and is essentially a given, whereas in the latter, it is more akin to a chosen affiliation. Consequently, ethnic groups in the modern West hardly resemble the functionally and structurally comprehensive, inclusive societal divisions they constitute in other settings. Groups and relations between them reflect social, economic, and political forces characteristic of the type of state, rather than particular traits indwelling ethnicity.

The cliché that most societies are multiethnic arose from and reinforces a labeling, counting, and mapping view of ethnicity and its political import. It encourages the view that "ethnics" and the ethnic structures of societies are readily recognizable; and that view, in turn, leads to the treatment of the identifying boundaries of individuals and the structural boundaries of groups as real and clear-cut. Such a view is associated with a set of fallacies that I shall call *ethnic nominalism*. It is related to the problems of "conceptual stretching" and "travelling" about which Sartori cautioned; and in today's West, it can occasion serious analytical and policy errors.

Ethnic Nominalism

Ethnic nominalism[9] is the assignment of ethnic labels to aggregates without commensurate, specific evidence regarding the nature, intensity, comprehensiveness, and continuity of individual identity and group structure. It treats *all* who share *some* of the markers of an ethnic group—residents of a particular region or users of a language—or who sometimes, for some purposes, identify or associate with such a group as if they were members of a continuous, comprehensive, and structurally integral social entity. But in the modern West, neither individual identity nor the structure of the collectivity is likely to be based, in its essence, on ethnicity. In sum, ethnic nominalism imbues the fragmented, intermittent ethnic dimensions of individual and group life in modern societies with an integrity and a salience they may not possess.

Ethnic nominalism obscures and obfuscates the meaning of ethnicity for both individual and group. It reifies and magnifies ethnicity and reinforces the illusion of the appropriateness of the traditional concepts and theories of ethnicity for understanding it in modern societies. It may be appropriate for the analyst to treat all members of a small, preliterate tribal society as ethnics and to view the collectivity as an ethnic group—because there is a strong likelihood that they are, empirically. But to assume such uniformity and monolithic traits in modern, advanced industrial societies is, minimally, to make a priori judgments in lieu of empirical tests and, thus, to risk making errors of inference.

Ethnic nominalism may also make the task of managing group-based demands appear deceptively simple; and it often serves the interests of political actors who claim to speak for ethnic groups. If policies that favor members of some groups—such as quotas or affirmative action programs—are in place, they may also benefit individuals. But where it is used as the basis for rigid compartmentalization by some nominal trait (language in Belgium or race in South Africa, for example), it may diminish venerable personal prerogatives and civil liberties. Ethnic nominalism sometimes carries heavy normative freight as well as analytical risk.[10]

Ethnicity in the modern West is rarely as clear-cut or significant or continuous as it appears to the ethnic nominalist. Its forms and meanings vary greatly from one setting to another, and so might the means appropriate for coping with it. Some of these problems are apparent in the ways the notion of ethnic conflict is commonly used.

Ethnic Conflict

The term *ethnic conflict* shows the blurring of meaning and loss of analytical insight exacted by general explanatory concepts and conceptual stretching. The two words occur together with such frequency and casualness in the literature that, as with that other twinned term, *sex and violence,* a conscious effort must be made to remember that it is no more necessary for conflict to be associated with ethnicity than for violence invariably to accompany sex.

Ethnic conflict is more metaphorical than real in most of the West today. Contention and competition are better characterizations of the dynamics of ethnic relations. Peaceful contention for status and resources is usually channeled through legitimate political activity, legally sanctioned cultural expression, and acceptable private behavior. Even massive demands tend to be dealt with through policy responses, bargaining, or negotiated institutional or constitutional adjustments—within frameworks suited to the orderly management of issues and claims in dispute.[11]

The political import of ethnicity in the West does not reside, in the main, in conflict or even contention between ethnic groups—or between them and the country as a whole. It entails, more centrally, individual mechanisms for coping with some of the stresses and frustrations found in postindustrial society; the pursuit of such values as equality and equity; the efficacy of parties and other political channels in dealing with cultural as distinguished from economic or class aspirations; ways for governments to circumvent or amend principles of legitimacy regarding distributional policies; and myriad other factors.[12]

Virtually never is one whole, organized cultural entity pitted against another in the clear-cut fashion of the classic paradigms of ethnic conflict. Instead, claims are made by some political actors in the name of groups. Nor have ethnic differences led to extensive and protracted violence, except in the two cases noted earlier; and it is not a coincidence that, in comparison with other Western societies, those cases are in relatively underdeveloped settings.

The structures of ethnic groups in the West are much less coherent and comprehensive than those in traditional conceptions and theories. In his well-known propositional inventory of the functions of social conflict (building on Georg Simmel's theoretical work), Lewis Coser noted that "in groups that appeal only to a peripheral part of their members' personality, . . . conflicts are apt to be less sharp and violent than in groups wherein ties are diffuse and affective, engaging the total personality of their members."[13] Ethnic groups in advanced industrial societies are predominantly of the first sort. Many in less-developed societies are of the second kind; and Coser's "Tenth Proposition" can be seen to operate in them: "Conflict with another group defines group structure and consequent reaction to internal conflict."[14] A modicum of this has occurred in the West—mainly in Northern Ireland, the Basque provinces, Belgium, and Quebec—but it is not common.

Grounds for Skepticism Regarding the Revival Thesis

Seeing recent ethnic phenomena in the West as revivals of age-old ethnicity may stem from excessive, uncritical concentration on the similarities and not enough attention to the differences.[15] Several critical differences can be discerned if conceptual stretching and ethnic nominalism are avoided. Changes in the meanings of ethnic identity and its functions for individuals in the post–World War II period become apparent. In most cases, the functions and forms of ethnic conflict are close to the diametric opposites of what they used to be in the West and what they may be elsewhere today. Many of the goals of "ethnics" now relate to greater access to societal institutions and more equitable distribution of status and resources, in terms of societywide or even transnational standards of equity. Ethnic contention is more likely to be focused on greater integration into the larger society than on the reinforcement of group boundaries and distinctions, as is generally the case in premodern settings.[f]

Discontinuities have intervened between earlier and current manifestations in both individual-level ethnicity and the organization of collectivities. Such pervasive and prolonged processes as the formation of modern states and the age of nationalism did more than simply attenuate or interrupt historical ethnicity. Ethnic identity, solidarity, and organization were thoroughly vitiated—disrupted and often delegitimized—over several generations in most of the societies that became Western democracies.

The burden of demonstrating that ethnicity was merely dormant during that long period, only to rise to salience recently, is a heavy one; ultimately, the choice between following that view or treating what we see now as distinct phenomena may have to remain a judgment call. The developmental taxonomy to be presented here supports the argument that the changes and discontinuities in ethnicity over time and from setting to setting are important, even if it falls short of incontrovertibility.

The Modern West in Context

There are many ways to classify and contextualize patterns of ethnicity. The taxonomy given here serves three purposes. First, it locates the seminal concepts and theories formulated by anthropologists and sociologists in the 1920s and 1930s in the contexts in which they were developed. Second, the discontinuities can be gleaned from the developmental patterns and changes in the nationalism phase, when many of the fundamental elements of ethnicity and the bases of its legitimacy were fractured or greatly attenuated. Finally, analytical delineation of the present setting provides a clearer view of the nature of modern ethnicity and clues to its recently increased political salience. Contrasts between the least modern contexts and the contemporary West suggest the inaptness of classic conceptual and theoretical notions for considering current manifestations. The developments in the third context bear on the cogency of the ethnicity revival thesis.

Four Settings of Ethnicity in Developmental Perspective

With the ever-present risks of oversimplification and excessive generalization that attend such undertakings, I suggest that there are empirically and analytically important and theoretically consequential differences in ethnicity and ethnic relations across four settings:

1. The small, preindustrial, preliterate, functionally comprehensive and usually isolated social systems studied by social anthropologists.

2. Larger, more complex, multiethnic or "plural," but still preindustrial societies, where most people live in ethnic groups relatively isolated from

others (the few remaining are found in parts of Africa, Asia, the Near East, the Arctic, and the South Pacific).

3. Nations in nineteenth- and twentieth-century terms: politicized, mobilized, state-controlling or state-seeking, large, culturally conscious groups that comprise most of the population of a countrywide society.

4. The modern societies of industrialized Western democracies, past the peak of the nationalist era—with marked functional specialization; structural differentiation and economic and political integration through roles, institutions, laws, programs, and policies; and expectations that cut across ethnic distinctions.

The Origins of Concepts of Ethnicity in Small, Primitive Societies

The core concepts of ethnicity were derived from small, primitive societies. Ascription—self-definition through belonging—and subjective identity, or a "we-feeling," were very strong, and they bound the group in a fashion that was essentially an extension of kinship. Such settings were also characterized by substantial "objective" similarities in the population, and government played a relatively unimportant part in binding individuals to the group or in determining the content or intensity of ethnic identity.

Individuals hardly had choices in these respects. The opportunity to choose to establish, reject, or increase or decrease the intensity or the continuity of ethnic identification was nonexistent or trivial. Acceptance or rejection were not options, because the group and the society were one; therefore, choice would have meant accepting or rejecting the social system. Cross-societal mobility was virtually nil, and no plausible alternatives to one's ethnic group and identity existed or could be imagined. The focus, forms, and intensity of ethnic identification were products of the individual's status and role sets, socialization, and social relationships—not something he or she could modulate unilaterally. Sociocultural—rather than governmental—incentives, values, and sanctions were most relevant in shaping individual identity and its salience as well as intergroup dynamics.

Preindustrial, Plural Societies and Traditional Notions of Ethnic Relations

Although, in the abstract, there was marginally more choice regarding the focus and intensity of identity in larger, complex, but still premodern societies, in practice it was still closely circumscribed. Ethnic identity was largely a function of the same factors as in the first context. It was defined to an important degree by the dynamics of intergroup relations—the extent and nature of contact and conflict. If "objective" factors (such as race, language, or other highly visible traits) were not significant in differentiating populations, movement across group boundaries became a possibility for a few; but it served to bind most even more closely. In terms of Fredrik Barth's theory, contact at the boundaries reinforced—in some cases, even established—identity.[16] The roles of government in conditioning identity, shaping and maintaining group boundaries, and structuring relations among groups varied substantially. Constitutional, legal, and policy measures (or their functional equivalents) may have exerted some influence. But since the scope of government was slight compared with that of modern states, such influence was not likely to be great.

The Integration of Modern States, Nationalism, and the Attenuation of Classic Ethnicity in the West

Nationalism imparted political (rather than sociocultural) salience to ethnicity, and it contributed to transmuting ethnicity from traditional to current Western forms. In conjunction with the formation of modern states, it served to disconnect the present from the past, rather than serving as an evolutionary bridge. Mass mobilization and the politicization of culture became means for attaining political autonomy vis-à-vis out-groups and, simultaneously, for organizing and legitimizing (more or less) popularly based government. At the same time, social differentiation, urbanization, and industrialization in the extended, national society shifted individual statuses and roles away from the smaller, ascriptive, *Gemeinschaft*-like communities found in the first and second contexts toward large, achievement-oriented, *Gesellschaft*-like societies, organized and institutionalized on the basis of specific roles and discrete statuses.[17]

The bases of legitimacy changed drastically. Postfeudal patterns of organization lost their legitimacy; and the ground was prepared for the modern state, with universalistic bases of citizenship—legal standing, responsibilities, entitlements, and foci of loyalty. In most states that were to become Western democracies, these processes were accompanied by the dislocations that Corrigan and Sayer associated with cultural revolution in eighteenth-century England:

> To define "us" in national terms (as against class, or locality, or ethnic group, or gender, or religion, or any other terms in which social identity might be constructed and historical experience comprehended) has consequences. Such classifications are means for a project of social integration, which is also, inseparably, an active *dis*integration of other focuses of identity and conceptions of subjectivity. They provide a basis for construction and organization of collective memory—the writing of history, the manufacture of "tradition"—which is inseparably an active organization of forgetting.[18]

Ascriptive bonds shared by the entire society are the hallmarks of nationality. They differentiate societal—*national*—groups from one another, consistent with Barth's and Simmel's ideas regarding the bounding and binding functions of contact and conflict, by asserting the greater similarities of members to each other compared to the differences between them and those outside the nation. (In this sense, the nation should be seen as a large, society-encompassing ethnic group.) The state's drive to render its population governable drove what John Armstrong called the *mythomoteur* that undermined the legitimacy of subnational solidarity groups: the articulation, selective construction, embellishment, or partial or even wholesale invention of the ascriptive and subjective bonds of that population.[19]

Thus, ethnic groups did not give way to nations spontaneously, through integration or modernization. Although those processes contributed appreciably to their attenuation, their delegitimation by the state was a more important factor. The institutions, laws, programs, and policies of the state created an alternative, societywide locus of belonging and focus for loyalty. Again, Corrigan and Sayer's characterization of the process in eighteenth-century England has broad relevance:

> What state activities above all regulate into silence are precisely identifications in terms of, and expressions of the experience of, differences—. . . that which materially (as opposed to ideologically) makes us what we are. These are systematically and concertedly ruled out by the integrative categories of official discourse: the citizen, the voter, the taxpayer, the consumer, the parent, the "man in the street."[20]

Although virtually nowhere was this process wholly completed, it created powerful and lasting, normatively and instrumentally superordinate alternatives to ethnic identity. The institutional and legal frameworks of modern states—reinforced by industrialization, urbanization, and economic, social, and political mobilization—exerted a strong centripetal pull. The cosmopolitan nation became a rewarding alternative for individual identification, especially as it was reinforced by incentives and sanctions from the state.

Most people responded, at least in some measure. They paid taxes and obeyed and were judged by central laws,[g] served in the nation's military,[h] pursued their political goals through parties and the vote, pursued their economic interests through functionally organized interest groups, and were linked to the state through secular administration. As economic mobilization progressed, formerly mainly rural populations moved to cities and larger towns and experienced more and more intense transactions with people from different regions and subcultures. Education strongly reinforced and extended these integrative effects of expanding central institutions, bureaucracy, industrialization, mobilization, and urbanization. The history that children were taught emphasized national commonalities at the expense of subnational—

regional or ethnic—heritage.[i] They identified with the institutions and symbols of the state in increasing degrees and with regard to more and more aspects of their lives.

The population of the state became the most inclusive social setting and focus of identification with regard to the outside world—that is, in relations among states; and it also militated in favor of the assimilation of immigrants. Economic—and, later, political and social—integration was considerable, even where assimilation was not achieved. The pattern of sojourners who indefinitely eschew assimilation and citizenship and remain largely unintegrated—common and widely tolerated today—would have been anathema in the nationalist era.

But although these integrative forces were powerful, ethnic attachments and social structures did survive on the peripheries and in the interstices of the national state. Political and economic integration did not permeate regions with low levels of mobilization; and discrimination by dominant groups through the central institutions they controlled insulated peripheral subcultures. Such discrimination reflected the great gaps still to be bridged by the application of egalitarian democratic norms and universalistic criteria of inclusion for citizens. Some of these vestiges became the nodes of ethnic identity and ethnic group–based politics recently, especially where marked discrepancies in economic conditions and life chances were perceived between the center and ethnically distinct peripheries.[21]

But the boundaries between peripheries and centers remained at least partly open; and the attractions of the cosmopolitan cores grew steadily—particularly from the perspectives of the remaining "ethnics." In most places, these attractions did not abate until after World War II—and then, ironically, mostly for the more acculturated.

In most cases, only partial, structurally fragmented ethnic identity and group organization survived the dual thrust of modernization and the increasingly pervasive, centripetal state. The possibility of entering the sphere of the center through some roles meant that *ethnicity no longer demarcated people but only some aspects of their lives.* Ethnic identity came to be based on the residual aspects of life and ideation.[j] It became intermittent as well as partial, and that, in turn, led to the possibility of "nesting" identification.

Thus, although it is true, as Arend Lijphart pointed out, that "ethnic loyalties show remarkable resistance to efforts aimed at their destruction,"[22] the advent of national identities and integrated states changed the meaning and importance of those foci of identification it did not eradicate. Some dimensions of life were redirected toward the center, while others remained locally focused.[23] One could become a loyal Briton without ceasing to be a Scot or a Yorkshireman; and such nesting of identities made possible the retention of more parochial identities. As Donald Horowitz has noted, "ethnicity in the West typically does not displace all other forms of group difference."[24]

However, nesting loyalties were acceptable only as long as the state was the unchallenged cardinal focus. Combined with economic integration, urbanization, and other forces, this political development and the growth of more powerful central governments reshaped ethnic loyalties, individual identity, and group structures. Where ethnic ties were not destroyed, they were transformed as social, psychological, political, and economic facts and emerged from the age of nationalism and modernization with radically changed import.

Such social and identificatory restructuring continues, but the thrust of public policies and legislation has been bifurcated in recent times. Although most states continue to underline the primacy of the center, some now accord recognition and at least contingent forms of legitimacy to subsocietal groups—including those that seem to be more or less like ethnic groups. These macro-level changes, coupled with some of the consequences of social and economic modernity for individuals, to be discussed later, point up the differences in the current phase.

The Modern West

The predominant pattern today is *post*nationalist, indicating passage through the nationalist phase. Although nationalism ebbs and flows in Western societies, virtually nowhere has it been a salient force since World War II.[k] Such societies are much nearer the *Gesellschaft* than the *Gemeinschaft* pole of the classic continuum. Their modernity is evident in the vast numbers of collectively comprehensive societywide (sometimes transnational) institutions, laws, communication networks, and cultures, as well as high degrees of specialization, role differentiation, achievement-oriented (rather than parochially ascriptive) bases of individual identification, and other qualities. The contours and content of this setting are examined in the next section, but one important feature of the postnationalist phase should be considered here.

If cultural distinctiveness gives rise to demands for group autonomy today, these demands are much more likely to be for limited autonomy than for complete independence or full self-determination.[25] This change from earlier periods is largely due to three developments. First, economic integration, incomplete though it is in many places, has so bound the fortunes of peripheral populations to the center that in most cases, the costs of going it alone would far outweigh those of accommodation in the framework of the existing state.[l] Second, especially in Western Europe, the institutionalization of liberal democratic norms has vitiated many of the grounds for political separation commonly cited one or two generations ago. The extension of civil liberties to individuals and civil rights to groups has not rendered ethnically based grievances moot;[m] but the delegitimation of discrimination has made accommodation more attractive to status minorities.

Finally, some governments have responded to, or anticipated, desires for greater local autonomy by decentralizing some functions—particularly those with high cultural loading—thereby muting popular concerns. This policy approach often marginalizes political entrepreneurs who are seeking to mobilize mass support within ethnic groups by making their claims appear more extreme. (The Spanish government, by granting considerable local autonomy to the Basque and Catalan provinces in 1980, achieved such results in part.[n])

Self-determination is less attractive than it was a few generations ago, but the goal of independence has not disappeared entirely. Besides being the goal of the hard cores of the Basque and Catalan movements, it is voiced by substantial numbers of well-organized Corsicans (who want independence from France) and by some Quebecois, as well as by small but committed groups in the "Celtic fringe"—Scotland, Wales, and Brittany. From the center's perspective, demands for moving from one state's jurisdiction to that of another are akin to demands for self-determination. Militant Catholics in Northern Ireland and a small minority of German-speakers in South Tyrol have the goal of unification with Ireland and Austria, respectively. But the latter—like very small numbers of ethnic Germans and Danes who live on the "wrong side" of the border between those two countries or French citizens with Flemish antecedents who live adjacent to Belgium—have decreasing prospects of gaining sufficient local support to make political headway in the foreseeable future.

More limited demands for some form and degree of autonomy for regions populated by culturally distinct populations are widespread. Since the early 1960s, they have been most evident in the Swiss Jura; in Canada's Maritime Provinces (and for shorter periods and perhaps less seriously, in the western mineral- and oil-producing provinces); in Occitanie, Alsace-Lorraine, and the Basque region in the Pyrenees in France; in South Tyrol; and on both sides of the "linguistic frontier" that has divided Flemings and Walloons since the early Middle Ages—more than a thousand years before Belgian independence.

If other movements—such as the Frisian in the Netherlands, the Andalusian and Galician in Spain, the Catalan and Bordelais in France, and the Cornish in England—have been less audible, it is because they have had less success in mobilizing their regional populations. There are several reasons for this lack of success. Political entrepreneurs have not been able to capture and hold the attention of their prospective constituents by elevating cultural issues above those involving economic security and other more tangible considerations. Also, central governments have been responsive to regional and subcultural concerns.

Foreigners on indefinite stays confront a different situation. Rights and status in the modern state derive from citizenship; and very few of the more than 15 million foreigners living in Western Europe seem inclined to adopt their host countries formally.[26] This is especially true where such a decision necessitates giving up one's original citizenship. This ambivalence is fostered by the governments and by a wide array of private and quasi-public organizations in the home countries, which want these people to retain their ties to their homelands and, specifically, to eschew citizenship in the host countries.[27]

If traditional ethnicity, group structures, and ethnic relations have been vitiated by the development of modern societies, states, and economies and yet there are widespread concerns with ethnic phenomena in the contemporary West, what is the situation that we now see?

New Influences and Patterns of Politics in the West

New elements account for the main distinctions between traditional forms of ethnicity and recent phenomena in the West. Moving from the lowest level of analysis to the most inclusive, the most crucial among these elements are (1) the psychological responses of individuals to modernity; (2) normative and structural characteristics of modern Western states; and (3) new patterns in international relations and transnational culture. The first element helps to explain why people who are historically and socially removed from a life centered on ethnicity and ethnic group organization might choose to emphasize those dimensions in a modern setting. The second element provides clues to differences in patterns of ethnic relations, deriving from the key factors in the political structures of contemporary Western states. The third element suggests reasons for such novel aspects of ethnicity and ethnic relations in the contemporary West as the prolonged semisettled condition of migrants, heightened regional assertiveness, and—in the opposite direction—the further erosion of historically distinct cultural and subcultural boundaries. Taken together, these factors point to the continued relevance of ethnicity in modern societies; but they also suggest a protean future for it: The character and import of ethnicity will be shaped more by political and economic circumstances than by the social dynamics traditionally associated with ethnic phenomena.

Ethnicity as Psychological Haven

Modern, industrialized societies are often psychologically unsatisfying, inhospitable, or worse. The organization of social and economic life and the high degree of role specialization in them tend to fragment the persona and lead to alienation. This alienation can affect the affluent and politically efficacious, not just the poor or ill-adapted.[28] Where vestigial or even artificial ethnic foci for identification exist, people may turn to them for amelioration.

More specific reasons derive from the unsurprising observation that in societies premised on achievement, most people will not succeed in socially sanctioned, psychologically satisfying ways and degrees. With generally lower-class barriers in modern Western societies, people are now socialized early in life to strive to reach the top rungs of occupational, economic, and social status ladders. Most will not, of course; they cannot.[29] If a focus for subsocietal ascriptive identification is available, the propensity to turn to it increases in some proportion to the importance attached to "failure" by the individual.[30]

That focus need not be ethnic. Religious groups that require more intense commitment than the norms for religious identification and association in the society—cults or fundamentalist sects, for example—can serve the same function, and so can other types of ascriptive groups. The psychological gains from such affiliation are evident. In addition to the succor provided by ascriptive ties, the individual can externalize the causes of his or her "failure" through group affiliation. Failure can be attributed to discrimination or to the characteristics of the group.

Affiliating with "people like oneself" in ascriptive havens does not preclude continuing participation in the modern sector. Such participation and affiliation—pursuing a sense of belonging—are not either-or or zero-sum in nature. Movement across roles in daily life, going from ascriptive family and home to achievement-oriented job and back again, is easy and common; and it is protected by an umbrella of modern notions and practices of privacy. Movement can occur even within the same role, as ethnic, racial, and other solidarity-based cohorts in the workplace show.

Rational calculations of self-interest and policy-related aspects of politics in the modern democratic state have parallel, often reinforcing effects on ethnic affiliation.° It may pay to emphasize individual ethnic identity and to organize along ethnic lines for political purposes. Theoretical rigor calls for an eventual answer to the question of which comes first—alienation and frustration in reaction to certain aspects of life and work in modern industrialized societies or politically motivated ethnic identification—but it cannot be provided here (if at all). However, it seems reasonable to aver that the salience accorded ascriptive choices—and perhaps the choice itself—is affected by psychological concomitants of modernity. In sum, in this view, recent manifestations of ethnicity are reactions to precisely those consequences of modernization that were long predicted to make them obsolete; and rational calculations of self-interest may provide an impetus in the same direction. This view is reinforced by a consideration of politics in modern democracies.

The Political Arena

Some time ago, I sought to show that ethnicity is likely to become salient in an industrialized democracy only after religious and socioeconomic class divisions and demands for basic political inclusion have been managed.[31] If this is so, it brings us back to our focal questions, in somewhat altered forms. Are ethnicity and ethnic politics substantially different in form where societal cleavages no longer threaten the integrity of state and society from where such cleavages are still unmanaged? What difference might the acceptance of cohabitation—working at problems arising from ethnic pluralism in the political arena—make for ethnics and the state? How might the political processes and structures through which sectarian and class divisions are managed influence the forms and dynamics of ethnic politics?

Ethnicity and ethnic politics *have* been affected by political changes associated with the prior management of other cleavages. Several factors have been especially, though not equally, important in most countries: the ethos of liberal democracy; impacts of the welfare state; and certain forms of group-based political bargaining.

The Liberal Democratic State. The normative templates of liberal democracy do not fit ethnic distinctions. In liberal democracies, the prerogatives, protections, and political standing of individuals are accorded on universalistic grounds and are extended through citizenship. They apply to ethnics in the same fashion as to all others. Indigenous minorities can and usually do participate in politics in a "normal" fashion. The high voter turnout in national elections in Western states, with the exception of the United States and Switzerland, is a simple, albeit weak, indication that the minorities neither are excluded from fundamental political activity nor exclude themselves. They have learned to work within and through the regime.

But the prevalent political processes serve functional and class-based interests much better than those premised on ethnic or regional commonalities. This is due less to formal discrimination than to biases in the political ethos and structures of liberal democracies. Where individuals are the bearers of rights and the norms of universalistic citizenship do not sanction the exclusion of citizens on the basis of ethnic distinctions, it is also difficult to justify special treatment on such grounds.

People in some subcultures and regions *were* systematically disadvantaged in the course of modernization. Peripheral populations modernized later, and in some places their material conditions and opportunities still lag behind national averages. Such developmental lags had an impact on ethnicity and ethnic relations in some subcultures or regions. But although this may have been important in the reinforcement—in some cases, the advent—of feelings of being targets of discrimination and of salient ethnicity in some Western societies, the onset of prolonged slow growth and the inaptness of political structures were probably more important.

It is rare for real or imagined ethnic problems to be directly acknowledged, given the dearth of legitimate means for equalizing the standing of members of groups as such. Incomes and life chances were substantially equalized between the end of World War II and the mid-1970s in most Western societies, but mostly on the basis of individual circumstances and universalistic considerations. Where the conditions of members of disadvantaged groups were addressed directly (most notably in the United States), the reigning liberal democratic norms made it difficult to legitimate opportunity-equalizing remedial policies.[p]

Bringing the material conditions and life chances of individuals in historically disadvantaged groups up to the levels enjoyed by other citizens posed fewer problems for regimes dedicated to the general leveling of gross income and wealth differentials than for those with more laissez-faire fiscal and social policies. Probably not coincidentally, the former have been more common in more homogeneous societies than in those with pronounced ethnic and regional divisions. Thus, the welfare state and tax and wage policies helped to equalize incomes and wealth considerably in the 1960s and 1970s in the Nordic countries, West Germany, Austria, the Netherlands, and New Zealand and moderately in France, Italy, Belgium, Canada, and Australia. There was notably less progress in this regard in the United States, Britain, and Spain.

Macroeconomic Conditions and the Welfare State. Leveling of differentials between peripheral populations and national means was often contingent on sustained economic growth, even where ideological commitments to the leveling were strong. Economic growth from the postwar recovery to the mid-1970s had notable positive consequences. But it also masked important structural realities regarding ethnic relations; and by stimulating the importation of workers, it contributed to new ethnic problems in much of the Western world.

On the positive side, most people found themselves on ascending escalators. Personal incomes rose dramatically—both directly, through wages and profits, and indirectly, through greater publicly provided benefits; the creation of jobs in the modern sectors of the economy heightened expectations for the future; and economic expansion both stimulated and was fueled by the development of previously lagging regions. Ethnics and populations in peripheral regions benefited, generally at the same rates as societies at large (sometimes more, as the economic modernization and attractiveness for investments of formerly backward areas tended to create booming conjuncture). In addition, sustained growth generated huge fiscal dividends for governments: Tax revenues increased as a consequence of greater economic activity. This made possible spending more for social and income-equalizing policies and launching new programs, without either cutting into established programs or raising taxes.

Fiscal dividends also provided opportunities for buying ethnic peace. Governments could address resource-related claims—and they could try to convert status demands into economically treatable and, therefore, more tractable issues—through what in more stringent times might be deemed politically unacceptable profligacy. The conflict management functions of public policies could be accorded priority over strict cost-accounting criteria of efficiency while the economic going was good. (In Belgium, for instance, programmatic redundancy was created in culturally sensitive policy areas— education being the most notable—by absorbing huge costs that would not have been economically or politically tenable in times of severe macro- economic scarcity, such as have prevailed since the mid-1970s.)[32]

The impacts of the comprehensive welfare state on ethnicity and ethnic relations are often overlooked. The welfare state is a new type of state that was institutionalized in most Western democracies during the period of sustained growth that ended (at least for the time being) in the mid-1970s.[9] It unites citizens through the programs, policies, bureaucracies, and macro- economic conditions they share. *But this is a political and material bond, not an identitive or emotional one.* Culturally distinct peoples are linked through the state; but such ties are between individuals or households on the one hand and the state on the other, not between "ethnics" or groups and the society.

Welfare state entitlements were extended with relative ease during the long period of economic growth. While this growth lasted, it was not necessary to make or even reaffirm the risky, often conflictive partisan, normative commitments that had been required to establish the programs and policies we call the welfare state. In the recent era of relative security, political leaders and publics may have lost the values and skills that were instrumental in building this sort of state and in eroding actual or potential social divisions through ever-widening circles of inclusion by citizenship. As a result, both the leveling of inequalities and the management of conflict and contention have become problematic under the prevailing economic conditions.

The structural reality hidden by beneficent economic times may be more conflict-laden—as regards class, regional, and ethnic interests—than the positive-sum conditions of the expanding welfare state has allowed us to see. Undertaking the building of egalitarian societies fosters expectations of continuing equalization of life conditions; and if resource constraints—coupled with a lack of political commitment or skill—lead to pulling up short or veering from such a course, people whose prospects of catching up are dimmed may react. Mobilization along ethnic or regional lines would be one predictable reaction.

In many states, the escalator has been halted or even reversed by macro- economic travails. The gap between the better-off and the less well-off has grown in several countries during the 1980s. (This trend has been particularly pronounced in Britain and the United States.) Redistribution has become politically as well as economically difficult. The illusion of a free lunch, engendered by prolonged growth and large fiscal dividends, has been shattered.

The harsh political consequence predicted by Rose and Peters in 1978 has materialized: Governments have found themselves in a political bind—either curbing the social expenditures and redistributive efforts associated with the welfare state or raising taxes, or both.[33] In such circumstances, it should not be surprising if culturally distinct, materially disadvantaged populations that had played by the rules of liberal democratic regimes—articulating demands as individuals or households or through functionally rather than ascriptively organized groups—become disenchanted with the regime's rules of the game (not just with economic and governmental performance) and turn to ethnic solidarity as a political medium.

Group-Based Political Structures. Distinctions between politics based on ascriptive ties and politics based on functional organization are mimicked by aspects of the two preeminent theories in the comparative study of politics in Western states—"consociational democracy" and "corporate pluralism."[34] They share a central concern with group structures and patterns of elite relationships that parallel and complement electoral participation. The most vital difference between them for our purposes is that the former has been more important in dealing with ascriptively arrayed segments, the latter with the politics of functional or interest groups. These theories and the research they have inspired cannot be examined here, but a few observations may shed light on ethnic relations and their management.

One of the most important contributions in the body of Arend Lijphart's distinguished work is to demonstrate the limitations of and alternatives to straightforward majority rule in plural societies.[35] In simple terms, where the boundaries between minorities and dominant majorities are relatively rigid—as where classic ethnic, racial, or religious solidarity groups are present—unbridled majority rule carries serious long-term disadvantages. It is inimical to political stability (because permanent minorities would be alienated from the regime) and inconsistent with at least two basic norms of democracy: the protection of the policy interests as well as the civil rights of minorities and the opportunity for a minority to become the majority someday by winning over some of the majority's adherents.

Lijphart has suggested several ways for dealing with this problem, many of which can be summarized under his rubric "consensual democracy"—a complex framework with wider application than the consociational democracy model but entailing a few of the same assumptions. Key from our perspective is the assumption of clear, more or less fixed boundaries between minority groups and the general society. Consociational democracy depends on the segmentation of society into vertical groups. Thus, groups divided by cleavages are not in constant contact with one another in matters in which their differences would lead to conflict. Only their leaders interact, when they bargain at the level of the state; and they are guided by shared, overarching interests in cohesion, stability, and governmental efficacy. The relevant aspects of consensus democracy also seem to hinge (although perhaps less centrally) on a clear delineation of subsocietal groups: People are in groups or are separated by formal (for example, federal) boundaries in an unambiguous and continuous fashion.

The consensual and consociational democracy models help to explain the success of several cases of cohabitation by politicized ethnic groups. Belgium, deemed by Lijphart "the most thorough example of consociational democracy, the type of democracy that is most suitable for deeply divided societies"[36] and a fairly good example of a consensual democracy as well,[37] satisfies the criterion of clear group boundaries (though not without impinging on the civil liberties and political preferences of some of its population sufficiently to cause the downfall of the last two governments). Another instance of such a felicitous outcome is Switzerland, "the consensual prototype."[38] Relations between French-speaking and English-speaking Canadians are also moderated by federalism.

Lijphart terms these three cases "incongruent federations"—federal regimes in which ethnic and other forms of cultural similarities are greater within constituent units of the federation than across them.[r] If there were sufficient congruity (using the term in its ordinary sense, with apologies to Lijphart for reversing his terminology) between governmental jurisdictions and the identifying and transactional boundaries of ethnic groups in multiethnic societies, then perhaps many of the problems associated with ethnic diversity could be managed by converting them into more manageable tasks in intergovernmental relations. This would approximate the segmentation of society into vertical groups; and the leaders of the homogeneous units could then bargain at the level of the state, like elites in consociational democracies.

Power-sharing and divisions of jurisdiction are the key features of such arrangements. The first circumvents the automatic attachment of invariably losing positions to ethnic and other culturally distinct populations. The second permits minorities some form and degree of autonomy, particularly in matters of great cultural sensitivity. Although the distribution of ethnic populations does not yield such congruity in all cases, most of the important recent manifestations of ethnic assertiveness have geographic cores. In addition to the aforementioned three countries, *some* of the members of *some* cultural minorities in Spain (Catalonia, the Basque country, Galicia, and Andalusia), France (particularly Britanny, Corsica, Occitanie, and the Basque region), Great Britain (particularly Scotland and Wales), Italy (South Tyrol), Finland (its Swedish-speakers), and Friesland in the Netherlands are clustered in relatively homogeneous areas. The Danish minority in Germany and the German minority in Denmark also live in relatively compact, contiguous areas near the border between the two countries.

But even if geographic contiguity were more common and complete, several significant problems would remain. First, in most of the West today, ethnicity lacks sufficient structural integrity, functional comprehensiveness, and continuous saliency to serve as an adequate basis for encapsulating people in governmental jurisdictions. Doubtless some do hold steadfastly to ethnic values and associations; these concerns are continuously salient for them. But most Europeans are integrated in the larger society with respect to important aspects of their lives and aspirations. Liberal democratic values militate in favor of personal mobility with regard to identity as well as geography or sub-state governmental units. Forcing the permanent salience of ethnicity on individuals who have not embraced it unequivocally would strain the legitimacy of any but the least mature democracies. Put more strongly, it is difficult to justify normatively the redrafting of fundamental social contracts on the basis of ethnic nominalism.

Second, given the commitment to reduce inequalities in opportunities and life conditions—and because "inequalities tend to be greater among than within sovereign states, and in federal than in unitary states"[39]—making good on the promises of the welfare state could become problematic politically if jurisdictions were drawn on the basis of nominal ethnicity. The leveling of individual differences would be impeded; and perhaps more seriously, disparties in the material conditions of groups would require explicit transfers across jurisdictions. Under most macroeconomic conditions, but especially in hard economic times, such redistributive tasks would present elites at the state level with monumental political difficulties.

Third, it is difficult to find legitimate ways of organizing and representing people in terms of ascriptive ties, given the integration of Western states in the nationalist phase, the establishment of societywide rights, and criteria of equity and inclusion through citizenship. In all but the strongest, most clear-cut cases of ethnoregional cohesion, the social contract between individuals and the state preempts as well as supersedes a putative social contract between modern ethnics and ethnic groups.

The fourth problem concerns the difficulty of representing—that is, speaking for—Frisians, Alsacians, or Welshmen. The first stage of demands based on ascriptive ties focuses on grievances about discrimination, inequality of status and material conditions, and political inclusion. The second stresses the culturally distinctive values and character of the subsocietal group. Most people in the category can relate to first-stage demands, even if they have no immediate experience with the discrimination at issue. Representation and organization in the second phase are more problematic, however, because they require agreement on the substance of the demands, the priorities attached to them, and the forms the responses should take. For example, a statement such as "Frisian should be the language of instruction in the schools of Friesland" may not represent a valid collective choice, as some Frisians may prefer to have their children educated in standard Dutch, some may have other priorities, some may be Hollanders working for national firms in the province, and some may not care.

Finally, although ethnic nominalism is not an issue for most of the 15 million semisettled foreigners in Europe, neither power-sharing nor jurisdictional autonomy holds much promise for addressing their concerns. Noncitizens without permanent commitment to their host societies have limited rights and claims on resources. Given the developmental history and rationale of the welfare state, foreigners are not, in fact, parties to or descendants of the struggles and bargains such a state represents.[40]

These reservations regarding the management of ethnic relations through the assignment of jurisdictions to collectivities stem from the character of ethnicity and ethnic groups in the modern, democratic societies depicted in earlier sections of this chapter. The partial, part-time nature of ethnic identification, its intermittent salience, the integrative promises and dynamics of the welfare state, the problems attending ethnic nominalism, and other factors engender reservations about any approach to managing ethnic relations in the modern West that entails the treatment of ethnics as formal group actors. For them (as well as for many indigenous ethnic populations), some form of corporate pluralist or interest group–based activity may be more effective, since it is less formal and less rigid than the devolution of authority by jurisdictions.

If corporate pluralism is viewed as a legitimized style of representation and policymaking common to many Western states (rather than as some formal theory with stringent criteria), it offers promise—especially where groups lack clear bounding and territorial contiguity. Corporate pluralism is akin to classic interest group politics, with two differences.[41] In most Western polities (the United States is a notable exception), interest groups have access to the policy process as a matter of course in an aboveboard, legitimate fashion. And such groups can be intermittent—becoming more active as issues on the policy agenda or the concerns of their constituents dictate. Their constituency may ebb and flow, depending on the extent of the mobilization of the populations they claim to speak for.

Myriad problems accompany the structuring and internal operation of such interest groups. Nonetheless, and even though they are not consistent with the norms of "pure" liberal democracy,[42] such groups have proved effective almost everywhere in linking the status and resource concerns of minorities—including those of semisettled migrants—to the values of the regime and in conveying demands into the policy process. It is through such channels that the concerns of minorities have penetrated policy agendas in most Western states; and they account for many of the successes of culturally distinct populations in terms of the equalization of status and economic conditions achieved in recent times.

However effective such means may be in the long run, they seldom produce swift, dramatic results. For that reason, and because they reflect ordinary—routinized—forms of political participation, they may not satisfy the symbolic aspects of demands associated with cultural movements. And because the ability of ethnic political entrepreneurs to mobilize their populations is affected by responses to ethnic claims from the "central establishment," the interest group channel may impinge on the effectiveness of such leaders.

Incremental gains made through such activity make it difficult to hold the commitment of marginal ethnics to the group; the constituency from which political support for ethnic demands or action is drawn may shrink. Granting partial autonomy to the Basque and Catalan provinces in Spain; giving formal status to regions in France; efforts by the Italian government to address some of the structural economic problems in South Tyrol; the eventual success of the referendum on canton status for Jura; the increasing attentiveness of governments in Canada and elsewhere to both extreme and moderate demands—all these actions have served to weaken group cohesion and to marginalize ethnic issues, at least for some.

Foreigners have also been represented through interest groups—indeed, often in a strictly corporate pluralist fashion—by organizations in the host societies. Labor unions, churches, social service providers, and other corporate actors have regularly championed their interests. In this way, and because of the various forms of support they receive from organizations in their homelands, the positions of these newest ethnic minorities in the West have been ameliorated.[43] Their circumstances resemble, in some ways, those of indigenous peripheral minorities prior to the generalization of citizenship rights, the leveling impacts of the democratic welfare state, and the advent of an ethos of greater social tolerance.

Conclusion

The ubiquity of concerns about ethnic phenomena and the manifestations of politics presented in ethnic terms is undeniable; but ethnicity and ethnic relations—and their political import—vary sufficiently to warrant some categorical distinctions. Although the presentation of such differences may appear excessively categorical to some, it is necessary to emphasize them near the beginning of a volume with global scope. Ethnicity and ethnic relations in the contemporary West differ in meaning and form from what is found in most of the rest of the world; and they differ as well from what obtained in the West in the past.

Ethnic identity in the part of the world surveyed here tends to be a partial, part-time aspect of people's self-concepts. Care should be taken to avoid classing all those who display some concern with or interest in the ethnic dimensions of their personae as "primordial ethnics," for ethnic groups are generally not integral social systems with functionally comprehensive, structurally discrete character. Virtually nowhere do they pose a credible challenge to the integrity of the states in which they live. Ethnic relations, with two important exceptions, are not conflictive. Instead, in most cases, they reflect contention and competition over values enmeshed in public policies, the equitable administration of those policies, and questions about the proper role of the state in maximizing preferred values in the realm of private (as distinguished from governmental) relationships.

The modern Western state—generally anchored by liberal democratic principles, adorned by a panoply of social programs and more or less egalitarian policies, and operating in terms of universal inclusion through citizenship—is an arena for both group and electoral politics. Some groups and some electoral activities are based on ascriptive concerns, but few political actors or issues are purely, entirely based on them. Indeed, the multiplex nature of life in modern societies militates against the perfect mobilization of people in terms of any single dimension of their lives—no matter how basic or primordial it may seem. People in such settings are not essentially ethnic; and the political goals and actions of very few are determined purely by such concerns.

But there is much in the politics and social relationships of most Western societies that is significantly influenced by cultural or ethnic considerations. In nearly two-thirds of the countries within the purview of this chapter, issues related to ethnic or cultural concerns are currently on the political agenda. This is important not only because it shows the prevalence or salience of those concerns but also because it suggests that polities are now so structured that they are able, at least, to attempt to address such concerns.

This is perhaps the most fundamental difference between the modern West and most of the rest of the world with regard to ethnic relations. Although ethnic issues are important in many Western democracies, they are generally dealt with—with greater or lesser success—as issues and democratically. The difference between the setting depicted in this chapter and most others is that in most other settings such issues tend to be life-defining, whereas in the setting presented here they revolve more around life-styles.

Contrasts abound in policy approaches to ethnic issues; but that is not new. Fifty years ago, the government of one of the most important European countries—Germany—undertook to exterminate some of its minorities as well as those of surrounding states it controlled; in contrast, for seventy years, one of its small neighbors—Denmark—has been gradually, humanely, but steadily assimilating its largest minority, eroding virtually all distinctions between society and minority.[44] Although the Nazi horrors have not been replicated, large-scale, protracted ethnic violence—group against group or, more often, state against ethnic group—is not uncommon in the late twentieth century. The Danish pattern is more representative of ethnic relations in the West today, at least with regard to its pacific, politically democratic approach. It is hard to overstate the importance of these differences.

Notes

a. For the purposes of this chapter, the Western world is composed of Western and Central Europe, North America, Australia, and New Zealand—twenty-two countries, ranging in size from Iceland and Luxembourg to the United States. The passing of the Portuguese, Spanish, and Greek dictatorships in the mid-1970s means that all have democratic regimes now—a significant factor in ethnic relations. I have omitted Israel and Japan because, with regard to ethnic relations, they are unlike Western democracies in nontrivial respects, and I have added Spain, Portugal, and Greece.

b. Sometimes an ethnic conflict thousands of miles away has such effects. Refugees from conflicts in Asia, Africa, and the Middle East have sought haven in the United States, West Germany, Scandinavia, Britain, Australia, and elsewhere in the West in considerable numbers since the mid-1970s. Britain's circumstances are complicated by the family ties of many refugees to immigrants who entered earlier from Commonwealth and former Commonwealth states. Most of these countries were willing hosts for a time; but as the numbers increased, their hospitality ebbed. As demand for long-term or permanent asylum grows, resistance to it has hardened in the late 1980s.

c. Following conventional usage, *international* refers to relationships between governments, *transnational* to relations between nongovernmental actors (such as labor unions, church organizations, and cultural federations).

d. In the modern West, such an expectation is often misleading. Switzerland, for instance, is divided by ethnocultural, religious, and linguistic cleavages; yet except for the now-resolved Jurassien movement for a canton separate from Berne—a goal which, notwithstanding difficulties in mobilizing the population in the presence of crosscutting religious and linguistic cleavages, was achieved—it has long been relatively free of such conflict.

e. For reasons elaborated in another chapter, Belgium's approach to managing ethnic differences may have moved it some distance from the liberal democratic model. Liberal democracies are readily recognized in contrast to other types of regimes. Thus, we should not expect to find these traits in most Asian and African societies or Eastern European countries—or in any authoritarian regimes or most premodern polities.

f. It is a given in sociological and anthropological theories that ethnic conflict has two fundamental functions: delineating ethnic identity and groups (boundary making) and shaping the internal structures of such groups.

g. The constituent units of federations often retained distinctions in legal systems, as in Canada and Switzerland; but in most cases, central constitutions, laws, and institutions were preeminent. Further, those units rarely coincided perfectly with the boundaries of ethnic groups, and there was usually considerable cross-jurisdictional movement. There were even fewer exceptions in unitary states, Scotland being perhaps the most notable.

h. There have been few exceptions. French-Canadians, not sharing English-Canadian support for British interests in international relations, were not willing to die for what they saw as the majority's concerns. A policy of no overseas service for conscripts was adopted in the two world wars.

i. Again, there were exceptions, and some of them are interesting in terms of recent manifestations of ethnicity. A majority of Flemish children in Belgium have historically attended Catholic rather than state schools; provincial responsibility for education in Canada, coupled with Catholic schooling, insulated children in Quebec;

and cantonal organization in Switzerland and regional jurisdictions elsewhere also muted the integrative thrust of education. In the United States, segregated schools—coupled with the "neighborhood school" principle, which reinforced effects of residential segregation—had similar impact, particularly regarding black children. This can be compared with attempts to compel use of the dominant, state-controlling group's language, which frequently produced backlash and demands for autonomy. Spanish policies in the Basque provinces and in Catalonia, especially during the first two decades of the Franco regime, provide an example.

j. This development accounts in large part for my criticisms of ethnographic positivism and ethnic nominalism. Compare Gellner's argument that in modern, industrialized societies, ethnic distinctions are likely to be eroded by "entropy," while racial differences are more lasting bases of disadvantages and discrimination. See Gellner, *Nations and Nationalism,* ch. 6 (cited in note 17).

k. A controversial judgment underlies this usage. *Nationalism* is used here only in reference to a societywide phenomenon, whereas some see the recent rise to salience of ethnic demands as a manifestation of subsocietal nationalism. Walker Connor, for instance, terms it "ethnonationalism"; see for example, "Ethnonationalism in the First World" (cited in note 15). But historians have long recognized multifarious and profound differences between the two levels. For example, in his meticulous study of nationalism, John Breuilly devotes his chapter on "separatist nationalism in the developed nation states" to those differences, because "these new nationalist movements are very different from those of the nineteenth century"; see *Nationalism and the State* (Chicago: University of Chicago Press, 1985), ch. 14 (the quotation appears on p. 279).

l. Exceptions exist where the resources commanded by peripheral groups are substantially greater than those of the society as a whole and where, consequently, political autonomy promises economic betterment as well. Independence for the Basque provinces and Catalonia from Spain and for Scotland from the United Kingdom held such prospects for some in the 1970s. Since then, responses by the centers and changed national and global circumstances (such as the advent of a democratic regime in Spain or, for Scottish aspirations, the drop in the price of oil) have altered economic expectations and muted such demands.

m. Such democratization has arguably stimulated the grievances of ethnic groups in some places, as the translation of such values into practice often lags behind raised expectations and elevated standards of treatment—thereby fueling perceptions of discrimination. See Arend Lijphart, "Political Theories," pp. 61–62 (cited in note 1).

n. Nationwide referenda in 1979 overwhelmingly approved "home rule" for these provinces, effective January 1, 1980. Although the well-organized Basque independence movement has continued to engage in both terrorist attacks on central institutions and suasion toward cohesion and "loyalty" inside the Basque country, its base appears to have shrunk.

o. Cf. Nathan Glazer's observation: "One doesn't know whether the group pressing for autonomy or more central government funds feels deprived because of an ethnic difference, or because of regional discrimination. The group has a choice as to which basis of deprivation it will emphasize" (American Pluralism: Voluntarism or State Action?" p. 233 (cited in note 10.)) A discussion of rational choice perspectives of ethnicity and ethnic relations would have to be prefaced by an orientation to that frame of reference, precluded here by limited space. For a theoretical foundation, see Ronald Rogowski, *Rational Legitimacy* (Princeton, NJ: Princeton University Press, 1974). See, also, Michael Banton, *Racial and Ethnic Competition* (Cambridge: Cambridge University Press, 1983).

p. The arguments about affirmative action—"reverse discrimination" to some— are too well known and too intricate to rehearse here. The clash of such policies with the general tenets of liberal democracy in the United States is explicated, rather one-sidedly, by Nathan Glazer, *Affirmative Discrimination* (New York: Basic Books, 1975) and *Ethnic Dilemmas,* ch. 9–11, 16 (cited in note 10).

q. Although social programs and policies were initiated in many European countries in the nineteenth century, a wide range of programs and comprehensive coverage were not instituted until much later in most countries. With other observers of the welfare state, I see the United States, Switzerland, Ireland, and Japan as laggards in some degree. If they are not full members of the club, then Greece, Spain, and Portugal are not yet serious candidates for membership. These generalizations are applicable only to the remaining fourteen of the twenty-one countries of concern here.

r. *Congruence* reflects parallels in the ethnic or cultural composition of the populations of the constituent units and the federation as a whole; *incongruence* means differences by unit boundaries. See Lijphart, *Democracies,* pp. 179–83 (cited in note 35).

References

1. For excellent analyses of both the misleading theoretical assumptions that led to predictions of the evanescence of ethnic divisions and the developments that have made such divisions newly salient, see Arend Lijphart, "Political Theories and the Explanation of Ethnic Conflict in the Western World: Falsified Predictions and Plausible Postdiction," in Milton J. Esman, ed., *Ethnic Conflict in the Western World* (Ithaca, NY: Cornell University Press, 1977), pp. 46–64.

2. This gross approximation is based on data in Christopher Hewitt, "Majorities and Minorities: A Comparative Survey of Ethnic Violence," *Annals* 433 (September 1977): 150–60—expanded to include cases from Africa and elsewhere and updated from news accounts.

3. See James Fallows, "The Japanese Are Different from You and Me," *Atlantic Monthly* (September 1986): 37–41.

4. See, for example, Vernon Van Dyke, "The Individual, the State, and Ethnic Communities in Political Theory," *World Politics* 29, no. 3 (April 1977): 343–69; Frances Svensson, "Liberal Democracy and Group Rights: Individualism and Its Impact on American Indian Tribes," *Political Studies* 27, no. 3 (September 1979): 421–39; and Vernon Van Dyke, "Legitimacy in Plural Societies," *Politikon* 10, no. 2 (December 1983): 6–25.

5. Giovanni Sartori, "Concept Misformation in Comparative Politics," *American Political Science Review* 64, no. 4 (December 1970), 1033–53.

6. See Ronald Cohen, "Ethnicity: Problems and Focus in Anthropology," *Annual Review of Anthropology* 7(1978): 379–403; Nathan Glazer and Daniel P.

Moynihan, "Introduction," in Glazer and Moynihan, eds., *Ethnicity: Theory and Experience* (Cambridge, MA: Harvard University Press, 1975), pp. 1–26; and Orlando Patterson, "Context and Choice in Ethnic Allegiance: A Theoretical Framework and Caribbean Case Study," *ibid.*, pp. 305–49.

7. David Kolb, *The Critique of Pure Modernity: Hegel, Heidegger, and After* (Chicago: University of Chicago Press, 1986), p. 6. For a model of the modern individual, operationalized for the study of those who are becoming modern, see Alex Inkeles, *Exploring Individual Modernity* (New York: Columbia University Press, 1983), especially pp. 7–10.

8. See Anthony Arblaster, *The Rise and Decline of Western Liberalism* (Oxford: Basil Blackwell, 1984); and Kenneth Dyson, *The State Tradition in Western Europe* (New York: Oxford University Press, 1980). See, also, note 4 and, for an early consideration of the normative implications of liberal democracy for subcultural identity and groups, William Sharp McKechnie, *The State and the Individual* (Glasgow: James MacLehose and Sons, 1896), ch. xiv–xx.

9. Cf. Henri Tajfel, *Human Groups and Social Categories* (Cambridge: Cambridge University Press, 1981), p. II.

10. Cf. Nathan Glazer, "American Pluralism: Voluntarism or State Action?" in Nathan Glazer, ed., *Ethnic Dilemmas, 1964–1982* (Cambridge, MA: Harvard University Press, 1983), especially pp. 126–30. My normative perspectives on this issue diverge from Glazer's.

11. See Giovanni Sartori, *The Theory of Democracy Revisited* (Chatham, NJ: Chatham House, 1987), pp. 89–92.

12. See Daniel Bell, "Ethnicity and Social Change," in Glazer and Moynihan, *Ethnicity,* pp. 147–48; Cohen, "Ethnicity: Problem and Focus in Anthropology;" Lijphart, "Political Theories," pp. 62–63; and Martin O. Heisler, "On the Political Salience of Ethnic and Territorial Identity in Modern, Western Societies: The Convergence of Economic and Ascriptive Factors," paper presented at the Joint Sessions of Workshops of the European Consortium for Political Research, Brussels, April 1979.

13. Lewis Coser, *The Functions of Social Conflict* (New York: Free Press, 1956), p. 68.

14. *Ibid.,* pp. 95–104.

15. Walker Connor has made the most sweeping argument in this regard. See "Ethnonationalism in the First World: The Present in Historical Perspective," in Esman, *Ethnic Conflict in the Western World,* pp. 19–45, especially pp. 41–43; "Self-Determination: The New Phase," *World Politics* 20 (October 1967): 30–53; and "The Politics of Ethnonationalism," *Journal of International Affairs* 27, no. 1 (1973): 1–21. Arend Lijphart also makes such an assumption in "Political Theories" but in a more balanced fashion. For a nuanced, contextually sensitive discussion of "a resurgence of ethnic identification as the basis for effective *political* action," see Bell, "Ethnicity and Social Change." (The quotation appears on p. 141.)

16. Fredrik Barth, ed., *Ethnic Groups and Boundaries: The Social Organization of Culture Differences* (London: Allen & Unwin, 1969).

17. The literature on this point is vast and diverse. For what I have in mind, see Ernest Gellner, *Nations and Nationalism* (Ithaca, NY: Cornell University Press, 1983), pp. 63ff., and the quotations from Corrigan and Sayer that follow.

18. Philip Corrigan and Derek Sayer, *The Great Arch: English State Formation as Cultural Revolution* (Oxford: Basil Blackwell, 1985), p. 195. Milan Kundera, the Czech novelist, is the source of the concept in the final phrase.

19. John A. Armstrong, *Nations before Nationalism* (Chapel Hill: University of North Carolina Press, 1982), pp. 9, 129–67, 293.

20. Corrigan and Sayer, *The Great Arch*, p. 198 (italics omitted).

21. Jack E. Reece, *The Bretons Against France: Ethnic Minority Nationalism in Twentieth-Century Brittany* (Chapel Hill: University of North Carolina Press, 1977), pp. 227–28; and Martin O. Heisler and B. Guy Peters, "Scarcity and the Management of Conflict in Multicultural Polities," *International Political Science Review* 4 (September 1983): 327–44. These facts are at the heart of Michael Hechter's thesis in *Internal Colonialism: The Celtic Fringe in British National Development, 1536–1966* (Berkeley and Los Angeles: University of California Press, 1975).

22. Lijphart, "Political Theories," p. 49.

23. Stein Rokkan, "Dimensions of State Formation and Nation-Building: A Possible Paradigm for Research on Variations in Europe," in Charles Tilly, ed., *The Formation of National States in Western Europe* (Princeton, NJ: Princeton University Press, 1975), pp. 562–600.

24. Donald L. Horowitz, *Ethnic Groups in Conflict* (Berkeley: University of California Press, 1985), p. 19.

25. See Martin O. Heisler, "Ethnic Conflict in the World Today: An Introduction," *Annals* 433 (September 1977): 2–4. Cf. Lijphart's discussion of the impacts of Third World movements toward self-determination (decolonization) on Western societies ("Political Theories," p. 63).

26. See Rosemary Rogers, "The Transnational Nexus of Migration," *Annals* 485 (May 1986): 38–50, especially pp. 41–42.

27. *Ibid.* and Barbara Schmitter Heisler, "Immigrant Settlement and the Structure of Emergent Migrant Communities in Western Europe," *Annals* 485 (May 1986): 76–86.

28. W. Simon and J.H. Gagnon, "The Anomie of Affluence: A Post-Mertonian Conception," *American Journal of Sociology* 82 (September 1976): 356–78.

29. See Jürgen Habermas, *Technik und Wissenschaft als "Ideologie"* (Frankfurt: Suhrkamp, 1968), especially 39–41; *Erkenntis und Interesse Theorie* (Frankfurt: Suhrkamp, 1968); and Richard J. Bernstein, ed., *Habermas and Modernity* (Cambridge, MA: MIT Press, 1985).

30. Cf. Cohen, "Ethnicity," pp. 400–402. There may be the appearance of intellectual incest here: Cohen cites discussions with me as the source for his information; however, he uses my ideas obliquely and builds a tangentially related case, partly independent of my argument.

31. Martin O. Heisler, "Institutionalizing Societal Cleavages in a Cooptive Polity: The Growing Importance of the Output Side in Belgium," in Martin O. Heisler, ed., *Politics in Europe: Structures and Processes in Some Postindustrial Democracies* (New York: David McKay, 1974). See, also, Lijphart, "Political Theories," pp. 59–61; J.R. Rudolph, Jr., and R.J. Thompson, "Ethnoterritorial Movements and the Policy Process," *Comparative Politics* 17 (April 1985): 292; and M.O. Heisler, "Managing Ethnic Conflict in Belgium," *Annals* 433 (September 1977): 32–46.

32. Heisler and Peters, "Scarcity and the Management of Conflict."

33. Richard Rose and Guy Peters, *Can Government Go Bankrupt?* (New York: Basic Books, 1978).

34. Arend Lijphart introduced the notion of "consociational democracy" in two seminal articles: "Typologies of Democratic Systems," *Comparative Political Studies* 1 (April 1968): 3–44; and "Consociational Democracy," *World Politics* 21 (January 1969): 207–25. The "new corporatist" theories date from the publication of Martin O. Heisler, with Robert B. Kvavik, "Patterns of European Politics: The 'European Policy' Model," in Heisler, ed., *Politics in Europe*, pp. 27–89; and Philippe C. Schmitter, "Still the Century of Corporatism?" *Review of Politics* 36 (January 1974): 85–131.

35. See, especially, Arend Lijphart, *Democracies: Patterns of Majoritarian and Consensus Government in Twenty-One Countries* (New Haven, CT: Yale University Press, 1984); *Democracy in Plural Societies* (New Haven, CT: Yale University Press, 1977); and *Power-Sharing in South Africa* (Berkeley: University of California, Institute of International Studies, 1985), ch. 4.

36. Arend Lijphart, "Introduction: The Belgian Example of Cultural Coexistence in Comparative Perspective," in Arend Lijphart, ed., *Conflict and Coexistence in Belgium: The Dynamics of a Culturally Divided Society* (Berkeley: University of California, Institute of International Studies, 1981), p. 1.

37. Lijphart, *Democracies,* p. 217.

38. *Ibid.*

39. See Lijphart, "Political Theories," p. 59, and the article cited there: David R. Cameron and Richard I. Hofferbert, "The Impact of Federalism on Education Finance: A Comparative Analysis," *European Journal of Political Research* 2 (September 1974): 225–58.

40. Gary F. Freeman, "Migration and the Political Economy of the Welfare State," *The Annals* 485 (May 1986): 51–63; M.O. Heisler, "Transnational Migration as a Small Window on the Diminished Autonomy of the Modern Democratic State," *The Annals* 485 (May 1986): 153–166.

41. Gabriel A. Almond, "Corporatism, Pluralism, and Professional Memory," *World Politics* 35 (January 1983): 245–60.

42. See Theodore J. Lowi, *The End of Liberalism,* 2nd ed. (New York: W.W. Norton, 1979).

43. Barbara Schmitter Heisler, "Immigrant Settlement."

44. Jörgen Elklit and Ole Tonsgaard, "The Policies of Majority Groups Towards National Minorities in the Danish-German Border Region: Why the Differences?" *Ethnic and Racial Studies* 6 (October 1983): 477–91; and "Elements for a Structural Theory of Ethnic Segregation and Assimilation," *European Journal of Political Research* 12 (March 1984): 97–99.

3
Political and Psychological Factors in Ethnic Conflict

Milton J. Esman

Defining the Concept

A necessary condition for the occurrence of ethnic conflict is the coexistence of two or more culturally differentiated communities under a single political authority. Cultural differentiation can result from religion, language, race, national experience, or combinations of these factors, which are almost always ascriptive. These collective identities are activated by the presence of one or more communities of strangers—other ethnic groups—as actual or potential competitors within the relevant political or economic space of the ethnic group. In the contemporary world of territorially defined political authorities, ethnic conflict occurs within the framework of a single state. Conflicts between states, even when they are articulated in ethnic terms—as, for example, between French and Germans or Japanese and Chinese—are defined as conflicts between two separate political authorities and are regulated normatively by international law.

Tensions and disputes between ethnic groups within the same state occur under a great variety of conditions and manifest themselves in complex patterns that have defied attempts at simple generalization or classification. Ethnic communities that have long been identified with and have established themselves in a particular geographic area encounter different problems from those of recent immigrant groups. The structure of the polity is also an important variable. Federal systems provide different opportunities for conflict management from those provided by unitary states; "open" polities that permit relatively free political association and participation produce a different environment for ethnic politics from that produced by "closed" polities that severely restrict and punish political organization and expression.

Political Mobilization

One point of departure for the analysis of contemporary ethnic conflict is the concept of political mobilization. The mere presence of two or more ethnic communities in the same political space does not necessarily signify conflict; indeed, ethnic communities, for various reasons, may remain passive and unmobilized for long periods of time. However, if they wish to make sustained and consequential claims on other ethnic groups or on the state, they must mobilize their resources for collective action. What, then, precipitates ethnic mobilization?

The presence of grievances alone does not seem to be sufficient, as many ethnic groups experience, often over long periods of time, grievances and discontents that do not trigger a political response. The most likely cause of ethnic mobilization is a serious and manifest threat to the vital interests or established expectations of an ethnic community, to its political position, cultural rights, livelihood, or neighborhoods. For example, the previously passive Malays mobilized immediately and decisively when the British colonial authorities threatened to eliminate their "special position" as the indigenous people and to confer equal political rights and status on the immigrant Chinese and Indians. Mobilization by one community may then activate responsive countermobilization by others, who sense that the defense of their legitimate interests in a politicized environment requires collective action on their part. Thus, the Chinese and Indians in Malaya felt compelled to mobilize defensively to counteract the fresh assertiveness of the Malays, which they regarded as a potential threat to their interests.

Though defense against threats accounts for many instances of mobilization, it cannot explain others. The second factor associated with mobilization is the collective recognition of fresh opportunities. In the absence of apparent threats, openings may appear in the political environment that afford opportunities for collective benefits if the group can organize itself to claim them. With prodding and inspiration from new claimants to leadership, members of the community may find reasons to reassess their expectations, producing the frequently observed combined phenomena of rising expectations and relative deprivation; even as objective conditions improve, individuals become increasingly dissatisfied because their individual or collective sense of entitlement has risen faster than it has been fulfilled. To realize and struggle for these emergent possibilities, ethnic groups mobilize for collective action.

A dramatic example was the mobilization of American blacks during the late 1950s as a result of such domestic factors as an expanding economy, a more supportive federal judiciary, and growing support among whites for civil rights, as well as the international demonstration effect of the emergence of independent African states. Although their objective conditions were improving, their progress lagged behind their rising expectations by a large margin, producing unprecedented political mobilization and activation on their part. To symbolize this transformation in their collective identity and expectations, they shifted their designation from *Negro* to *black*.

Several variable factors affect the ability of ethnic groups to assert their claims convincingly. Among these factors are the resources these groups have available and are able to commit to the common struggle, including their numbers; their geographic distribution—concentrated or dispersed; their organizational, economic, and communications skills; their financial capabilities; and their prestige within the larger society. Equally important are the abilities, commitment, and coherence of the political entrepreneurs who organize and guide the struggle and the activists or cadres who provide ongoing links with the mass of their ethnic community. The leaders formulate and articulate the agenda that defines the issues and maintains the organization that aggregates and deploys the human and material resources available for the struggle.

And herein lies a problem, because no ethnic group ever maintains a monolithic position, even in the face of extreme adversity—for example, the violently contending factions in the Palestine Liberation Organization and among the oppressed blacks in South Africa. Ethnic groups tend to be fragmented along class, ideological, extended kinship, and other lines; internal politics can be intense and violent, even as they face off against common enemies; and the most frequent expression of internal politics involves the right to control the common resources of the ethnic organization and to speak authoritatively for the group in its relations with outsiders, including the state.

One function of leadership is to establish and propagate the goals of the ethnic movement: long-term goals such as hegemony (domination of the state), self-determination (regional or cultural autonomy or even independence), or equitable inclusion for the collectivity or for individuals in the polity and the economy. Conflicts and organizational cleavages may emerge over long-term goals and especially over the more immediate objectives and tactics of struggle. Much of the energy of ethnic group leaders must often be committed to managing and conciliating these internal tensions and conflicts in order to maintain control of their constituency and to battling opponents within the ethnic community. One frequent issue of contention relates to the tactics of struggle—working within the rules of the system to achieve incremental progress peacefully or resorting to confrontation and violence to produce fundamental changes.

The course of ethnic mobilization depends not only on factors internal to the group itself, as already indicated, but also on the political environment it encounters. That environment may offer some opportunities and impose some limitations for promoting claims on behalf of a mobilized ethnic community. It therefore conditions goals and especially tactics. In a relatively open system, it is more likely that the authorities will attempt to deflect, coopt, or mitigate ethnic claims and that violent tactics are unlikely to be required or to command the support of most members of the ethnic community. In relatively closed systems—South Africa, for example—violent tactics may appear to be the only recourse available to aggrieved ethnic groups. But even in relatively open systems, such as Northern Ireland or the Basque country, ethnic extremists may succeed in outbidding moderate leaders who are prepared to compromise with the state or with competing ethnic groups; violent and extremist minorities may then attempt to intimidate, neutralize, or even eliminate moderates within their own community. Virtually every Palestinian leader who has attempted to initiate negotiations with the Israelis has been assassinated by one or another faction of the PLO.

Ethnic Solidarity

The discussion of mobilization, which is a precondition for sustained ethnic conflict, raises a prior question: What is there about ethnicity that produces emotionally grounded and politically significant solidarity? Why should and why do people identify and mobilize for collective action along ethnic, rather than class, occupational, residential, or ideological lines? It is clear that ethnic identity and solidarity differentiate groups in terms of perceived common interests and destiny, creating we–they, insider–outsider bonds that are seen to determine the security and life chances of the individual and the competitive status and opportunities of the ethnic collectivity.

But why is there solidarity along ethnic lines? The dominant political and social philosophies of the past century and a half—democratic market-oriented liberalism and Marxian socialism—despite their fundamental disagreements on many basic issues, have consistently denigrated ethnicity as a basis for personal identity, especially for political and social action. Democrats regard the free-standing individual as the appropriate moral unit of value, ascriptive ethnicity being the residue of less enlightened stages of historical development, while Marxists regard economic class as the sole objective basis for social differentiation, ethnicity being an expression of "false consciousness" that divides and weakens the productive classes in their struggle for a more just, progressive, and efficient social order. Thus, the persistence and even the resurgence of ethnicity as a political force, even in advanced industrial societies, has raised afresh the question: Why ethnic solidarity? What is there about ethnicity that maintains its salience for political mobilization in such a great variety of societies, from Fiji to Spain and the Soviet Union, from Canada and India to Belgium, from Sudan and Ethiopia to Northern Ireland and Lebanon?

Indeed, it appears that in the present era, ethnic solidarity has become a politically more significant differentiator and basis for social action than ever before. The most persuasive and all-inclusive explanation is the emergence of the modern state. The era, since the mid-eighteenth century, of industrialization, rapid urbanization, secularization of belief systems and practices, and confidence in the transforming powers of science and technology has witnessed the parallel development of democratic and egalitarian thought and the emergence of the modern territorial state as the universal structure for political authority. These concomitant macrohistorical changes have been characterized by many social theorists as "modernization." From their eighteenth-century origins in Western Europe, these economic forces and the political models and ideologies that reinforce modernization have been carried by Western trade and investment, colonial expansion, and information systems to all corners of the world. Though the ability and the willingness of non-Western societies to absorb and incorporate the institutions, practices, and ideas associated with modernization have varied greatly, one element from Western experience that has become universalized is the modern bureaucratic state, claiming the capacity to enforce its rule on all the societies under its territorial jurisdiction.

Ethnicity and the Modern State

During earlier epochs, except for extracting taxes and performing limited services, central political authorities interfered little in the lives of their subjects. Although ethnic communities competed among themselves on their boundaries, sometimes violently, there was little need to mobilize for collective political action. The dominant expectation of students and devotees of the idea of modernization—a view to which many continue to adhere—was that modernization would gradually erode ethnic identities and solidarities and render them useless to society and to the individual as well. Modernization would liberate the individual from dependence on traditional societal structures—such as ethnic groups—because rewards would flow according to the universal and objective criteria of individual achievement and performance, rather than because of ascriptive group membership. As the needs and aspirations of individuals, regardless of their ethnic backgrounds, became similar under the impact of modernization, they would be incorporated as individuals into a common urban-industrial, secular culture. Ascriptive loyalties, no longer functional to modern man, would wither away—and the sooner the better. Through processes of "nation building" engineered by the modernizing elites of the political center, individuals would learn to identify with and relate to the state in place of their inherited ethnic communities, which would gradually be reduced to sentimental and folk memories. Patriotism, nationalism, and eventually universalism would supplant parochial group allegiances.

This prediction has proved to be only partly true—and for many countries, essentially false. Instead, during the twentieth century, the modern state has become the principal arena of competition for access to and control of the scarce resources for which members of society compete; and they tend to compete less as atomized individuals or as members of social classes or ideological associations and more as adherents to ethnic communities. Traditional ethnic solidarities have not been supplanted; they have, instead, become modernized. They have become efficient vehicles for the articulation and promotion of values that are important in contemporary societies. In many countries, people are more readily mobilized for the promotion and defense of collective interests defined along ethnic lines than by other categories of collective identity. Thus, unexpectedly, modernization and the concomitant need to compete for resources controlled by the modern state have actually stimulated mobilization and collective action and have increased the likelihood, the frequency, and the intensity of conflict derived from ethnic solidarities. Ethnicity in a modern guise has emerged as a powerful group mobilizer and weapon of social conflict, not only in most Third World societies but also in the Soviet bloc and in many advanced industrialized countries.

With their enhanced capacity to tap financial resources from indigenous and foreign sources and their increased ability to maintain civil and military bureaucracies and, thus, to penetrate, regulate, and serve society, taking from some and distributing to others, even relatively weak contemporary states become consequential in the lives of their subjects. For in large measure, it is the state that determines who gets what; this occurs in states as "weak" as Burma and Ethiopia or as "strong" as Belgium, Malaysia, and the U.S.S.R. Ethnic affinity becomes a powerful—though not the exclusive—mobilizer and promoter of collective interests; and it is only mobilized collectivities that can effectively participate in the fierce and unremitting competition for the resources at the disposal of the state. Thus, modernization has witnessed the competitive mobilization of ethnic communities to capture and hold the machinery of the state, to claim their fair share of the resources deployed by government, or to demand autonomy from the reach of unfriendly political authorities.

What Ethnic Groups Contest

The modern state establishes and enforces the formal rules and the informal practices that determine who gets what—the relative power and status of ethnic communities and, thus, the opportunities and life chances of their individual constituents. An outline of the main values allocated by the modern state indicates how consequential they may be:

1. *Political participation.* Who, in terms of ethnic membership, is eligible to hold office? How are office-holders selected? Who may take part in the choice of office-holders? To whom and in what ways are office-holders accountable? What rights and opportunities are available for political association, for the assertion of group interests, and for making claims on the state?

These are the critical questions about who holds the keys to the political kingdom. Participation in government can decisively affect the relative power, status, and influence of competing ethnic communities, including the ability to make and enforce the rules that determine cultural status and that allocate economic resources and opportunities.

2. *Cultural status.* What rights and symbolic dignity are accorded by the state to a group's language or religious beliefs and practices? Is education available in the group's language, and up to what level; or must children study and compete academically in the language of a more privileged ethnic group? What is the official status of the group's language? What is the working language of government? Are public services available in the group's language? (Language rights are often a good indicator of the relative status of an ethnic group and of the competitive opportunities of its members.) Does public policy legitimize, dignify, and reward ethnic pluralism; or does it encourage cultural and social assimilation of minorities into the dominant community; or does it enforce legal or de facto inequality in status and in treatment?

3. *Economic opportunities.* By what rules and practices are jobs allocated in the military, the police, and the various government bureaucracies? As government and parastatal jobs in most societies confer power, prestige, and secure incomes and pension rights, they are especially important to the more educated segments of ethnic communities, the strata from which leaders and activists are disproportionately drawn. Access to wealth, including land, capital, credit, foreign exchange, and business licenses; eligibility to compete for government construction and supply contracts; and opportunities for employment in the private sector—these are frequently regulated by rules or informal practices enforced by the state and its officials. The distribution of public services—such as housing, agricultural inputs and marketing, health facilities, development projects, and local public works such as roads, water supply, and electricity—may be determined by government action. Because all of these benefits and many of their costs are divisible, they are frequently distributed by rules and practices that, by design or effect, have substantially differential impacts on competing ethnic communities. The relative benefits and costs may be perceived, by the various ethnically sensitive actors, to be distributed unfairly and inequitably. When this is the case, the threats and the grievances at the root of ethnic conflict are exacerbated.

Perceived Biases as Precipitators of Ethnic Conflict

States frequently behave—by the rules they establish or enforce or by their actual practices—in ways that are biased to the advantage of some ethnic groups and at the expense of others. Even when states adopt what their officeholders regard as fair and equitable arrangements, the arrangements are often not perceived as fair and equitable by some of the states' ethnic constituents. Some measures may be overtly preferential and discriminatory; others may be seen by some participants as discriminatory in their effect (and, by inference, in their intent). Meritocratic competition through objective examination procedures—for university admission, government employment, or public contracts, for example—may appear entirely fair and objective to ethnic groups that are equipped to perform well in such competitive examinations but unjust and illegitimate to those whose members perform poorly under these apparently impartial rules. The latter judgments are based not on the formal equity of the procedures but on the interethnic distribution of results. Where policies such as affirmative action or group proportionality are instituted to produce more equitable results, the stronger competitors are likely to be aggrieved by what they regard as reverse discrimination—allocations by ethnic group politics rather than by objective individual performance. *Backward regions*—often a surrogate term for territorially based ethnic communities—demand a disproportionate share of public investment to spur their economic development, whereas advanced regions, which contribute most of the revenues, insist on investments that yield the highest economic returns, meaning allocations to their region.

In countries where politics are already polarized along ethnic lines, the competition for favorable rules and allocations by government virtually ensures that ethnicity will remain an important criterion for political organization and that ethnically based claims will maintain a prominent place on the agenda of the state. Where ethnic mobilization has been weak but ethnic identity and solidarity are latent forces waiting to be activated, there are strong incentives for political entrepreneurs to identify instances of neglect or injustice to their ethnic brethren by the authorities and to mobilize along ethnic lines—under their leadership, of course—to overcome these injustices by impressing their particular needs on the public agenda, promoting and defending their just claims, and combating the unjust and threatening action of ethnic enemies or the state apparatus.

Success in this endeavor inevitably stimulates countermobilization by other communities, laying the groundwork for ethnic conflict of the kind that pervades the modern world. The issues over which they contend may be political, cultural, or economic, in a wide array of combinations. Sometimes they spill over state borders to the international arena. Because the modern state is the principal theater in which contemporary ethnic conflicts are played out, the burdens of conflict management fall mainly on the state and its senior officials.

Rational Political Actors

Within the framework of the state, ethnic groups are mobilized by political entrepreneurs to promote and protect their collective interests. One school of writers—and I identify personally with this approach—perceives interethnic conflict as the rational pursuit of organized group interests. Peaceful coexistence can be achieved by negotiation, accommodation, and compromise resulting from hard bargaining through political processes that do not, at least in the short run, eliminate or "resolve" conflict, but prevent the competition from erupting into destructive violence. A number of structural and procedural arrangements and allocative mechanisms have proved successful in controlling ethnic conflict.[1]

Though the cultivation of friendly attitudes, mutual respect, and accommodative practices facilitates conflict management, in the short run, at least, the parties do not necessarily learn to like or even respect one another or the state that enforces these arrangements. Nor must they regard these arrangements as entirely fair or satisfactory, but they manage to coexist, compete, and carry on their lives relatively peacefully. As there can be no assurance that these arrangements will not break down, the potential for violence is always present, and its prevention requires continuous surveillance and management by public authorities. This approach to conflict management is essentially political. Its initial presumption is that the ethnic disputants are behaving as rational actors, deploying their resources to promote and defend group interests that are real, not illusory, even when the specific positions they take on goals or tactics may be ill-advised, unfeasible, or perverse.

Psychiatric and Conflict-Resolution Approaches

Another school of writers focuses on the potential for ethnically based conflicts to lead to extreme and dangerous polarization, with high potential for disruptive violence.[2] They attribute ethnic violence—and social violence in general—to aggressive impulses activated by societal stress, such as rapid urbanization, economic depression, or frustrated expectations. They look upon manifestations of ethnic conflict beyond the most restrained and civil as essentially irrational and pathological because of the destructiveness and damage to all participants, including many innocents, that results from its potential for unrestrained and escalating violence. They would hope to head off such violence, to restrain and eventually to resolve these conflicts by processes of mediation that help the conflicting parties to recognize and act on their common long-term interests in survival, progress, and civil coexistence. These common interests, they believe, are far greater for all parties than the short-term advantages that any party might realize from continuing conflict and violence. These processes of intermediation must help the parties to perceive their genuine and overriding common interest in a peaceful settlement from which all of them mutually benefit. When this degree of understanding has been achieved, practical compromises become possible. These methods of mediation draw on experiments with group therapy, inspired by psychiatric and sociopsychological perspectives.

These two perspectives, political and psychiatric, differ in their diagnoses of the fundamental roots of ethnic conflict. They differ also in their prescriptions for the processes needed to moderate and manage the milder conflicts that persist in the Malaysias, Belgiums, and Yugoslavias of this world, as well as the brutal and intractable ethnic civil wars that rage in such places as Sri Lanka, Sudan, Northern Ireland, South Africa, and the Punjab.

External Intervention

Inherent in ethnic conflicts is the propensity to attract and involve external actors and foreign interventions. External parties may choose to intervene for purely strategic reasons. For example, the Israelis assist the southern Sudanese against a common enemy, the Arab-Muslim regime in Khartoum, and India helps the ethnic Bengali revolt in order to dismember their common enemy, Pakistan. Outsiders may also intervene in response to domestic pressures based on sentimental ethnic affinity—for example, India's support for the struggle of Sri Lanka's Tamil minority and Saudi assistance to fellow Arabs and Muslims in Eritrea against the Christian and, later, the Marxist Ethiopian state. Sometimes the participants actively invite sympathetic external intervention in the form of material or diplomatic support to strengthen their competitive position. External intervention has become a common reality in interethnic conflict, much of it mischievous, cynical, and purely self-interested.

What may prove to be more constructive in mitigating and eventually settling such conflicts is the possibility of external intervention by disinterested voluntary agencies, governments, or multilateral organizations to assist the conflicting parties in finding formulas for terminating their conflicts and evolving patterns for mutually beneficial coexistence. There is a brief history of relatively disinterested initiatives by such outsiders. These have included many failures—in Northern Ireland, South Africa, and Israel–West Bank— and also a few conspicuous successes, including the Addis Ababa agreement that ended for a time the brutal seventeen-year civil war in Sudan in 1972.

The possibilities for constructive external intervention into ethnic conflicts have been underplayed in the academic treatment of the subject. Part of the intellectual equipment that disinterested outsiders may bring to these efforts is an appreciation, based on comparative analysis, of the origins of these disputes; the processes of collective mobilization; the dynamics of escalating conflict; the salience of the modern state as the principal rule-maker and allocator of values that the parties involved perceive to be distributed inequitably; and the practical possibilities, limitations, and strategic timing for effective external mediation. There has recently emerged a cumulative body of knowledge about ethnic conflict, an incipient science, which can be brought to bear by those who are committed to efforts at mediation. Their point of departure, in my opinion, should be the assumption that mobilized ethnic parties are attempting—perhaps unwisely, perhaps even destructively—to promote and defend real group interests as they define them. Rather than attempting to transform attitudes and perceptions, external mediation should search for practical structures and procedures that may accommodate these divergent interests and enable the parties to the dispute to practice coexistence as an alternative to mutual destruction.

Ethnic solidarities, especially those that survive bitter conflicts, are certain to persist into the future, and ethnic parties will insist on the continuing reality of group interests and their right to assert and protect them. It is unlikely, in the short run, that these group interests can be transcended by any mediation-induced perception of common interest, beyond peaceful coexistence on mutually tolerable terms. These negotiated terms cannot be expected to please any party entirely, and certainly not all their factions, but they are vastly preferable to continuing destruction and violence. With experience, accommodative practices may become institutionalized, as they have in Switzerland, but they may also break down and reignite violence, as has happened again in southern Sudan. Ethnic conflict requires continuous and vigilant management.

Reconciling the Psychological and the Political

Serious conflicts involving the state and mobilized ethnic communities can seldom be "resolved" or settled in the short run. The best that can be hoped for is that they be successfully managed so that violence can be prevented as mutual trust develops. Conflict management that is not based on state-imposed coercion must be grounded in practical arrangements—structures such as regional or cultural autonomy, procedures such as proportionality or minority guarantees—that represent expedient, consensual adjustments in the normal and ongoing pursuit of group interest. Recent experience demonstrates, however, that the pursuit of ethnic group interests may break out of rational control and lapse into mindless violence that develops its own destructive momentum. When this occurs, the processes of reconciliation may depend on patient timing, on isolating and discrediting the extremists on both sides, and on producing an environment for mediation that enables the parties in conflict to negotiate a political settlement. It is at this point that the psychological and the political approaches to conflict regulation converge. In my opinion, the main potential for sociopsychological insights is to produce the atmospherics of mediation that are needed to facilitate negotiation and hard bargaining. From these processes may then emerge the practical and expedient political compromises that can reconcile previously antagonistic ethnic group interests, thereby terminating violence and laying the groundwork for civil coexistence.

References

1. Donald Horowitz, *Ethnic Groups in Conflict* (Berkeley: University of California Press, 1985).

2. John W. Burton, *Conflict and Communication* (New York: Free Press, 1969); and John E. Mack, "Nationalism and the Self," *Psychohistory Review* 2, no. 2–3 (Spring 1983), pp. 47–69.

4
Conflict and Culture in Traditional Societies

Remi Clignet

D uring the recent past, the incidence of guerrilla activities, involving the terrorist destruction of public or private property, has markedly increased in comparison to classic warfare. Yet there are increased variations in this particular form of collective violence. Intra- or interethnic strife plagues industrialized nation-states as often and as threateningly as it affects developing societies. Further, ethnic strife seems to be caused as much by domestic as by international conflicts. Correspondingly, if it is tempting to view distinct instances of new forms of institutionalized violence as caused by analogous social and economic disorders, it is equally tempting to impute them to diffusion—the terrorists of one particular nation-state and their hunters borrowing their strategies from external sources. To understand the upsurge in guerrilla activity, it is necessary to ascertain whether intra- or inter-societal conflicts represent merely a reactivation of latent contradictions among the various segments of the same nation-state or among the nation-states themselves.

This chapter explores the two sets of competing hypotheses concerning the origin and the latent properties of inter- and intraethnic conflicts. As latent contradictions may affect primarily the various basic cultural units of modern nation-states, the first part of the chapter is devoted to an examination of the variety of tensions experienced by the familial units that constitute each tribe or ethnic group. The second part lifts the level of analysis to identify the variety of conflicts among the tribes or ethnic groups that make the same nation. As intra- and interethnic tensions represent dynamic processes, the last part of the chapter seeks to identify the short- and long-term forces that activate latent contradictions to endow them with a virulent and dramatic form.

Tension among Familial Units

The cohesiveness of an ethnic group depends on the impact of the prevailing modes of subsistence on the relations that successive generations develop with one another and on the alliances that familial groups can forge within the same ethnic group. Thus, the material conditions of social life affect the nature of the conflicts that occur both within and between familial groups and, notably, the disruptive role played by gender or generation. More specifically, these conditions affect the profiles of the protagonists, the objects of the challenges, their frequency, and the arenas within which the tensions are expressed and dealt with.

The Effects of Modes of Production

Each mode of subsistence has its own requirements. While horticulture and intensive agriculture, based on the constant use of the same land, generate elaborate patterns of division of labor among age groups and between genders, they also foster an acute sense of spatial boundaries and an extensive elaboration of the distinction between insiders and outsiders. Further, this mode of subsistence operates within two conflicting demographic constraints. At the lower end of the demographic continuum, the survival of the group is jeopardized whenever the sex ratio of the adult population falls below a critical threshold or whenever dramatic disparities appear in the relative numerical importance of distinct age groups. In such a situation, there are not enough people to obtain the optimal yields from the land available. At the upper end of the continuum, however, returns on investments decline markedly whenever the density of exploitation of the soil exceeds a critical threshold, with a subsequent accentuation of disparities in the life chances of individual familial groups.

The histories of the Bamileke in Cameroon and the Kabre in Togo offer cases in point. These two peoples, who have settled in regions that do not lend themselves easily to itinerant modes of agricultural production, are characterized by high fertility rates. As a result, they must "export" migrants from their natural habitat whenever they are too numerous in relation to the productivity of the soil of their native land. The emigrating segments of these two ethnic groups retain a tight-knit social organization, which helps them to be successful economically and therefore visible, and this visibility stirs the jealousy of the other inhabitants of the communities to which they have moved.

Alternatively, pastoralists, peoples who practice an itinerant type of agriculture or rely on long-distance commercial activities, have a different sense of space. For them, the notion of territory is closely intertwined with the cycle that underlies the use of such crucial facilities as wells and pastures. Specifically, it is related to the drying up of wells or springs or to overgrazing and the depletion of available pastures. In this mode of subsistence, the notion of territory is intermittent and is related to acute crises. Further, the necessities of the division of labor practiced within such groups renders the notion of territory more abstract, as the control that men or adults exert on women or dependents is looser. Because of the distance separating familial actors from one another in their daily lives, the ideologies that underlie the division of labor and power along sex or age lines may stand in conflict with the actual autonomy that individual women or children enjoy in their daily activities.

The Nupe of Nigeria offer a case in point. Despite the preeminence of the social status assigned to males, the long-haul commercial activities of Nupe women enable them to enjoy greater autonomy than that spelled out by the model of familial relations to which both Nupe males and females subscribe. Consequently, the entire Nupe population harbors feelings of jealousy and uncertainty toward Nupe women.

Differences in the material basis of economic life are paralleled by contrasts in the size of familial groups and in the frequency of contacts between individuals both within and across such groups. Because of corresponding variations in modes of socialization, the incidence, the intensity, and the objectives of conflicts also differ within or among such familial groups. To come back to the Nupe example, disparities between familial ideologies and practices are associated with skews in the distribution of witchcraft accusations. Contradictions between the rules that govern division of authority along gender lines and the actual autonomy enjoyed by females are such that the Nupe view witchcraft as an exclusive character of women. Although this use of women as targets of collective aggression reflects the centrifugal forces at work in Nupe society, it may also hold other forms of collective violence in check.

The Effects of Rules of Descent

There are sharp contrasts in the tensions typical of matrilineal as opposed to patrilineal societies and in the solutions these societies adopt to cope with the corresponding conflicts.

Among matrilineal peoples such as the Agni or the Baoule of the Ivory Coast, the Akan of Ghana, or the Kerala of India, there are inconsistencies between lines of descent and lines of authority. Lines of descent run through females, lines of authority through males. Although all familial positions are defined in terms of the distance that separates individuals from their common female ancestor, only males are entitled to control individual beliefs and practices. All the members of a matrilineal family group are subordinate to the oldest mother's brother. The corresponding arrangements generate recurrent tensions between affines (in-laws)—that is, between the wife-mother's relatives and her husband and his family. These tensions, which result from the uncertainties surrounding the obligations and rights of women and their children toward their family of origin and their family of destination, are manyfold. The tenuous character of conjugal loyalties is such that wives are often accused of unfaithfulness. Should they be divorced, their offspring are most likely to live with maternal uncles. Although children are legally subordinate to their maternal uncles—to whom they owe respect, for whom they should work, and from whom they expect to inherit—they often maintain affectionate and informal ties with their fathers.

Because of the centrifugal social pressures generated by conflicts among brothers-in-law, wives, and husbands, or between children and their maternal uncles, familial groups in matrilineal societies tend to be concentrated in relatively large communities. The size of these communities dilutes interfamily feuds in a larger context. Further, not only does the pattern of settlements most typical of matrilineal societies increase the frequency of contacts among the most significant familial protagonists, but it is also conducive to the creation of suprafamilial agencies of a political or religious nature, which arbitrate domestic feuds.

Conversely, for patrilineal peoples, the parallels that exist between lines of descent and lines of authority might be expected to lower the frequency and the incidence of conflicts between affinal groups. In contrast to the necessary homogeneity of the sociopolitical profile of matrilineal ethnic groups, patrilineal societies enjoy more degrees of freedom in their social organization and, notably, in their modes of subsistence. In turn, differences in the economic activities of patrilineal peoples are associated with parallel contrasts in the number and significance of the obligations that men and women must satisfy as a result of marriage. The resulting differences in the tensions that pit spouses and their respective relatives against one another or children against their parents are associated with parallel contrasts in the mechanisms used to manage and regulate such tensions.

To conclude, there are contrasts both in the central tendencies and the dispersion of the distribution of familial conflicts of matri- and patrilineal cultures. In addition, these two kinds of cultures do not respond similarly to social change. The effects of urbanization and industrialization or of a cash-crop mode of agriculture are more disruptive in matrilineal than in patrilineal societies. For example, modernizing ideologies assign the responsibility of the costs of formal schooling to fathers, but they also emphasize the benefits that the fathers might derive from the social success of their offspring. Since maternal uncles rely on tradition to demand their share of the profits resulting from the formal schooling of their nephews or nieces, modernization exacerbates the latent conflicts between in-laws. Further, as the processes of modernization entail patterns of individual migration, they lower the efficiency of existing tension-reducing mechanisms. The growing number of unsolved conflicts impedes the relative economic development of matrilineal peoples and makes them more critical of their own institutions.

Aside from the distinction between matrilineal and patrilineal lines of familial organization, ethnic groups also differ from one another in terms of their commitment to an impartible or partible mode of inheritance. In the first case, testators provide their male children with specific bequests as a function of their respective *identity*. In the second context, the testators are expected to give the same amount to each of their male children and to respect the principle of *equality*. Impartible modes of inheritance are supposed to generate recurrent tensions between individual testators and the totality of their heirs. In addition, as such modes facilitate out-migration, they turn aggression outside the immediate community. In contrast, societies dominated by partible rules of succession are more often torn by conflicts among individual heirs or among neighboring families.

The Effects of the Structure of Matrimonial Exchanges

Human societies conceive marriage in various economic terms. Some of them view marriage as obliging the bride's family to lose a source of labor and emotional support. Therefore, they consider that a marriage requires the bridegroom or his male relatives to pay a compensation, the form of which varies across cultures. Insofar as the bride's male parent uses the resources accumulated through the institution of bride price or bride wealth to marry off his male children, there is a long-term balance in the economic relations that familial groups develop with one another. The underlying principle of reciprocity facilitates matrimonial mobility (divorce and remarriage) of both men and women.

In contrast, other human societies associate the institution of marriage with the obligation for the bride's family to provide the newlyweds with a dowry. This obligation represents a potential source of intra- and interfamilial feuds. Within the family, the dowry presupposes that the father is allowed to control the romantic attachments of his daughters. The drama of Romeo and Juliet stems from the contradictions that oppose individual feelings to the alliances and interests of familial groups. Further, familial groups do not necessarily have the resources sufficient to constitute the dowries that must accompany the marriages' of all daughters, some of whom are doomed to remain spinsters. The absence of models to identify which daughter is entitled to marry first as a function of the familial resources available at the time causes tensions that may easily degenerate into open conflicts. The absence of sons may present the same disruptive potential. The eventual adoption of sons-in-law (notably, in China)—who, almost by definition, come from more modest circumstances than their brides—ensures the continuity of the brides' familial groups. However, it also creates invidious comparisons and feelings of mistrust.

Between families, the institution of the dowry does not raise significant problems so long as brides and grooms belong both to the same geographic and socioeconomic environment. But Molière's comedies illustrate the conflicts, between genders and between social classes, that mobility provokes concerning the payment and the upkeep of dowries. Further, in France and elsewhere, the domestic conflicts that surround dowries result less from discontinuities in the diffusion of a progressive and feminist ideology than from the loss of control over their sons-in-law that the brides' fathers experience in social contexts characterized by high rates of change and mobility.

The Effects of Modes of Political Integration

While human societies differ from one another in terms of the protagonists and the objective of the conflicts that occur both within and among familial groups, they also differ in terms of their political integration and, hence, the mechanisms that might be used to adjudicate the corresponding feuds. These mechanisms may be local or cosmopolitan. They may also be internally or externally induced.

At the lower end of the continuum of political integration are *acephalous societies,* where political mechanisms are not centralized and where familial groups justify their cooperation on the basis of sharing the same residence and, hence, the same ancestor. The Tonga of Zambia, the Lugbara of Uganda, and the Bete of the Ivory Coast provide examples. In all of these cases, cooperation is associated with significant taboos, notably with regard to intermarriages. Because marriages act as rationales for political alliances, they must involve strangers.

Chieftain societies are characterized by the development of a leadership ideology that extends beyond local settlements and generates loyalties based on the sharing of a common language or a common set of religious principles or beliefs, even though there is no centralized bureaucracy to embody and reinforce the unity of the beliefs and practices. The Alur of the southern part of Sudan and the Nyamwesi and the Lake Victoria provide cases in point. In short, the political frailty of such societies results from the disparities between the scope of their ideological orientations and the weakness of the underlying institutional support.

At the upper end of the political integration continuum are *centralized states,* such as the Bornu of Northern Nigeria, the Gonja of Northern Ghana, and the Mossi of Upper Volta. Such states present two qualities that differentiate them from the types of societies already reviewed. First, they comprise social categories with differing obligations and privileges; and second, the interrelations among these categories are mediated by a corporate entity that transcends them and represents all of them in dealing with the outside world.

Variations in the form and the extent of political integration should be associated with parallel differences in the frequency and severity of conflicts that ethnic groups experience. Among ethnic groups with low political integration, internal tensions are more likely to result from the difficulties caused by sharing access to the same scarce resources. In contrast, in more complex, highly politically integrated societies, such tensions are more frequently generated by the misunderstandings associated with the exchanges of labor, services, and goods across social groups.

Variations in political integration are also associated with parallel contrasts in the mechanisms that are used to adjudicate internal and external conflicts. The greater the political integration of the society at large, the more likely it is that there will be full-time judges who base their decisions on a body of fully elaborated legal principles. Similarly, the greater the political integration, the more likely the society is to have a full-time army whose mission is to maintain order within the national territory and to protect external boundaries from outside aggressors.

Conflict among Tribes or Ethnic Groups

There are significant variations in the processes that regulate the emergence of citizenship. Indeed, there are marked contrasts in the processes that underlie the geographic and functional scope of the interactions that ethnic groups develop with one another.

Sharing the Same Terrritory

Interethnic contrasts within the same territory raise the question of the criteria used by each group to legitimize its claims. In the Ivory Coast of forty years ago, a number of Mossi migrants to cocoa and coffee farms were often tempted to save their earnings and buy land from their Bete employers. For the Mossi, the transaction was a property transfer entirely dictated by a cash economy. For the Bete, such a transaction could never be a sale, as the land belonged to the community as a whole and therefore could not ever be sold. In their eyes, the transaction could be, at best, a long-term lease, which, negotiated on a personal basis, required the payment of a regular rent and could not be transferred to the leaser's heirs. In short, the Bete based their legal claim on the legitimacy they derived from having occupied the land before the Mossi.

Alternatively, newcomers may take advantage of their greater political integration and wealth to push the original settlers to a less appealing area. As an example, the pagan peoples of Northern Cameroon were chased from the plains to adjacent hills by the pastoralist Fulani and the trader Hausa, who took advantage of their long-learned mobility to claim the most profitable land. As we shall see, the claims of legitimacy based on the priority of settlement in an area may also depend on the presence of more powerful and more encompassing third parties. Thus, the rights of the initial occupants of the capital cities of the Ivory Coast and Ghana (the Ebrie in Abidjan, the Ga in Accra) were protected by colonial authorities, who felt that the limited numbers of these peoples would restrict the claims they would make in the relevant real estate negotiations. In short, neither differential dates of settlement nor differential size are necessary and sufficient conditions to legitimize the claims made by two distinct ethnic groups over the same territory.

The Effects of Interethnic Marriages

Although interethnic marriages contribute to the incorporation process of initially distinct peoples in the same nation-state, the extent of their influence depends on the interaction between ethnic and gender stratification. The contribution of interethnic marriages to nation building is maximal when the spouses originate from peoples who enjoy roughly the same status in the ethnic hierarchy, or when differences in ethnic status do not prevent a similar frequency of interethnic marriages for men and women.

Alternatively, there are two types of asymmetric interethnic marriages. In one case, the men of dominant ethnic groups compete successfully with their counterparts of a subservient ethnic status to gain access to eligible women. The dominant men marry women from a lower ethnic origin but prevent their sisters or daughters from marrying outsiders. The Romans adopted this behavior toward peoples they conquered. It represents a case of assimilation whereby the subservient group is condemned ultimately to disappear altogether. In the other case, men who come from "marginal" ethnic groups take advantage of their economic success to marry women who are located higher in the ethnic hierarchy. In Yaounde, the capital city of Cameroon, a relatively large number of economically successful Hausa take Ewondo women as junior co-wives in order to accelerate their own integration into the social fabric of the city. In this case, national integration reflects complex patterns of exchange between the economic success of the husband and the prestige enjoyed by the ethnic group from which the wife originates.

Ethnic, Residential, and Occupational Differentiation

Insofar as interethnic conflicts depend on the differential visibility of the ethnic groups that comprise the society at large, they are also contingent on the relationships among ethnic, residential, and occupational modes of differentiation. In medieval Europe, Jews were segregated in neighborhoods where they exerted a monopoly on the banking operations of the community at large. Similarly, the Hausa of many West African countries are predominantly concentrated in urban areas where they are engaged in trading activities that benefit the community as a whole. The same pattern characterizes Chinese immigrants, who live in neighborhoods dubbed Chinatowns. In these three instances, ethnic identity is highly correlated with both occupational specialization and residential segregation. Insofar as these high correlations symbolize the high visibility of the peoples to whom I allude here, they explain why the peoples become scapegoats whenever the society at large experiences a political or economic crisis.

Yet the influence of occupational specialization on the relative visibility of a particular ethnic group might be more diffuse than it appears at first glance. Strangers located at the two ends of the occupational hierarchy may become the targets of hostility and resentment. At the lower end of the continuum, unemployment accentuates the visibility and the vulnerability of migrant workers brought to jobs that the local population was initially unable or unwilling to perform. The histories of migrations to the mining centers of South Africa, Zambia, and Zaire provide examples. At the upper end of the continuum, the descending phases of the economic cycle in the Ivory Coast, for example, often tend to accentuate the visibility of the Dahomeans or the Togolese (the Dagos), whose earnings are judged to be disproportionate to those of the local populations, regardless of their respective occupational roles. When this happens, the Dagos are the targets of popular hostility. Their fate is particularly striking because the expatriated Senegalese are frequently able to avoid the same difficulties, in spite of the higher position they have traditionally occupied in the socioeconomic hierarchy. Indeed, as contrasts in the treatment meted out to the two groups seem to reflect differences in their respective absolute numbers, in the rates at which these numbers have grown in the period preceding the crisis, and in their residential isolation, they suggest that the effects of occupational specialization are mitigated by other forces. Thus, in such complex societies as modern France, the same core of French people displays, simultaneously and selectively, their hostility toward some successful minorities (Jews) and some components of unskilled workers (black or North Africans, rather than Turks or Portuguese). Finally, the effects of the links among ethnic identity, occupational specialization, and residential segregation are minimal when occupational interdependence binds two easily identifiable groups and only those two. In Nigeria, for instance, Hausa herdsmen have privileged relations with Kanuri butchers.

The Effects of Social Boundaries

In both so-called traditional and complex societies, ethnic visibility and the feelings it fosters depend on the criteria used by the various components of the society at large to define their boundaries. The effects that both differences and similarities in outlook have in this regard are more complex than it appears at first glance. First, as noted by the German sociologist George Simmel, strangers stir ambivalent feelings and are able to induce their hosts to give confidences they would refuse to give to their friends, without experiencing the desire to become more intimate with those who share their secrets.[1]

Second, notwithstanding Heider's assertion that similarity causes sympathy, a closer look at available evidence suggests that similarity also breeds competition and hostility and, hence, amplifies whatever feelings exist between interlocutors.[2] Thus, at the familial level, sororal polygyny is the only form of plural marriage that certain ethnic groups allow, convinced as they are that having the same familial background reduces jealousy. However, it is the only form of polygyny that is condemned by some other peoples, as they fear the effects of the intensity of the competition between sisters on the functioning of the new household. At a higher level of analysis, parallels in the economic orientations and opportunities of modern French, German, and British societies explain why the alternatively positive and negative feelings of French citizens toward their western and eastern neighbors are more intense than their feelings toward Spaniards or Italians. In short, one might suspect that the chances of integration of two distinct peoples in the same political entity probably follow curvilinear (convex) patterns, both extreme similarity and extreme dissimilarity between these two peoples being inimical to their cooperation.

Third, similarities and dissimilarities may be defined in relation to a third party or a set of extraneous conditions. Thus, patterns of interaction between certain ethnic groups may be defined in terms of common fate and, more specifically, of the bonds they have with an internationally defined organization. Such bonds may be sources of integration or disintegration. Both languages and religions may help the integration of ethnic groups that are otherwise highly different from one another. Yet it should still be noted that the integrative effects of lingua francas or of "catholic" (that is, universalist) religions are contingent on a number of intervening factors. The diffusion of a lingua franca may result from the sheer demographic weight of the peoples who are interacting with one another. It may also result from the development of commercial networks, as has been the case for Swahili in East Africa and Diula in West Africa. The use of these languages may have represented a strategic weapon that limited the intervention of colonial powers in the transactions that involved primarily differing components of the colonized society.

An analysis of the diffusion of Islam in French-speaking West Africa would reveal analogous processes. Initially facilitated by French administrators, who saw in Islam a beneficial centralizing force that would cut the number of relays in the local political structures, the diffusion of Islam later on was instrumental in regrouping, through a common hatred of European colonialism, West African peoples who were subject to the centrifugal forces of diverse economic or familial structures. Indeed, the integrating power of universalist religions varies with the extent to which they are reinterpreted by local cultural entities. As an example, regardless of the claims of the Catholic Church to universalism, there are variations in the behaviors, attitudes, and beliefs of Polish, Irish, German, Italian, and Latin American Catholics in North America. The coexistence of these distinct forms of Catholicism results both from the residential segregation of these various peoples and from their commitment to maintain parishes staffed with priests of their own national origin.

Common fate may also exaggerate the centrifugal forces already exerted on patterns of interaction among independent cultural units. As an example, the cleavage between Protestant and Catholic ideologies replicates and confirms already existing modes of distinction between existing ethnic groups in the context of both colonizing and colonized societies. The map of the borders between Catholic and Protestant cultures in Zaire overlaps the maps that separate key local peoples from one another as well as those that distinguish the territories assigned to Walloon and Flemish missionaries. Indeed, in their own metropole, Flemish and Walloon peoples are increasingly unclear as to whether the tensions between them result from their linguistic or religious differences or whether such differences simply represent more intense contrasts in the demographic and economic trajectories of the regions from which the two peoples originate. The same disintegrating effects of universalist religions intervene in Southeast Asia, where the differentiation between Islam and Buddhism supersedes and masks contrasts in the economic and political organization of local peoples. In the Middle East and in parts of Asia, the growing differentiation between Shiites and Sunni within Muslim communities interacts with the contrasting economic opportunities enjoyed by local peoples as well as with their respective patterns of social stratification.

Finally, the common fate experienced by adjacent but distinct cultural units may disrupt the existing hierarchies both within and between such units. *Within* cultural units, the introduction of formal schooling has often been initially defined as irrelevant to the functioning of existing hierarchies. In certain European countries, formal schooling was the plum that parents used to compensate younger children for being barred from the major part of the assets to be transferred to key heirs. In certain African countries, elites sent their slaves or their distant relatives to school, because they initially viewed formal education as inimical to the perpetuation of their power. Both in Europe and Africa, the rewards derived from schooling ended up reversing existing patterns of stratification.

In terms of hierarchies *between* ethnic groups, sociologists Nimkoff and Middleton suggested some twenty years ago that "hunting and gathering peoples chase game and berries in the same way that the workers of postmodern or post-industrial societies chase their jobs."[3] As the requirements of these sets of activities are symbolically equivalent—notably, with regard to mobility—hunters and gatherers may adapt more successfully to social change than sedentary agriculturalists, whose familial organizations involve complex networks of interactions among individuals. As a result, colonization may alter the political rank-ordering and the differential clout of hunting and gathering peoples and societies whose survival involves sedentary forms of agriculture.

To conclude, the significance of the notion of common fate as a determinant of the patterns of interaction among preexisting ethnic groups, castes, or social classes highlights the insufficient character of the concept of modernization, or Westernization. Each ecumenical power—whether political, religious, or linguistic—tends to reproduce its own specific traits in its modes of diffusion. As a result, there are significant differences in the stimuli that correspond to the political style of French as opposed to British colonial administrators and of Vietnamese as opposed to Japanese technical assistants, or to the missionary activities of Protestant as opposed to Catholic or Muslim missionaries. Moreover, the effects of these different stimuli are paralleled by variations in both the intensity and the form of the responses of the distinct components of social systems to such stimuli.

Ethnic Differences and the Role of Time

Thus far, the analysis has been presented as if the frequency of interethnic contacts and their effects on national integration were independent of time dimensions. Yet the centripetal and centrifugal pressures exerted on the various types of social units are always contingent on *specific* circumstances. The role played by circumstances in this regard highlights the significance of analytical distinctions between historical and sociological time and between modern and traditional time.

Historical versus Sociological Time

Historical time refers to discontinuities in the changes typical of the phenomena under study. These discontinuities might be the result of natural catastrophes (flood, drought, earthquake, and the like) or a selective distortion in the social distribution of responses to the stimulus. In contrast, sociological time suggests that the effects of urbanization, industrialization, or any other form of modernization are uniform, additive, and cumulative.

As an illustration of the importance of the distinction between the two terms, the unexpected nature of the drought that plagued Africa during the 1970s may have reactivated or transformed latent conflicts that tend to place pastoralist in opposition to agriculturalist societies or, among the pastoralist societies, place familial groups that own a large herd in opposition to those with much more limited means of survival. The question is whether such an accident has confirmed the existing mode of stratification (sociological time) or has been conducive to a reversal in the existing rank-ordering of genders, of co-wives in polygynous households, and of age groups, social classes, or ethnic groups at the level of the society at large.

As another illustration, the Breton, Corsican, Catalan, or Basque nationalisms have recently experienced intense revivals in France, in spite of the continuous and cumulative properties of the actions taken by French educational and cultural authorities to eradicate progressively any form of particularism and to achieve national unity. These revivals may have been provoked by the emergence of disparities between the educational and occupational opportunities offered to the successive generations of individuals in such provinces; they may also be the result of reversals in the social mobility that individuals could expect in view of the career profile of the preceding generations. One thing is sure: In the long term, centralized Jacobinism seems to provoke effects that run against the expected results.

One can find parallel examples in the African context. Thus, even though one can expect that interethnic differences in educational enrollments and attainments parallel the differential distance that separates each group from the coast from which modernization processes originate—or the differential duration of their respective exposure to the messages of European administrators, missionaries, teachers, and traders—the effects of sheer duration (sociological time) are often transformed by the differential vulnerability of these various peoples to exogenous sources of change. In the case of Cameroon, the rate of educational or occupational success of the Bamileke deviates significantly from what one might expect from their location and the relatively infrequent and superficial character of their interactions with colonizers (historical time). Indeed, the pressures exerted by demographic growth on the soil of the Bamileke have rendered members of this ethnic group more prone than other Cameroonian peoples to migrate and enter new occupational niches. In the same way, even though there tends to be a close relationship between increases in overall school enrollments and the sex ratio of student populations, increases in the number of female students are higher among the Baoule than among other peoples of the Ivory Coast, who have yet been more durably and intensely exposed to the influence of missions and schools. The weight of historical rather than sociological time introduces discontinuities in the ethnic distribution of changes in female enrollments.

To conclude, the distinction between sociological and historical time makes it easier to ask more focused questions regarding the sequence and the timing of events that trigger or stop the reactivation of latent conflicts between the components of the same ethnic group or between ethnic groups.

Traditional versus Modern Times

Individuals are tempted to locate themselves, alternatively, in the time defined by the traditions of their ethnic group of origin or in the time typical of a modern social and cultural order. Their choices in this regard depend on the rewards they anticipate. As a first example, African male students tend to reject the traditional institution of bride price (the payment of money or services to the bride's male relatives), which, they argue, is incompatible with the ideal of romantic and modern love. However, they favor the perpetuation of traditional divorce procedures, which minimize the obligations they would owe to their former wives. In a symmetrical way, even though their female counterparts acknowledge the traditional character of bride wealth, they see it as protective of modern female individuality and consider that it is compatible with a modern form of divorce.

In a similar vein, American newspapers recently reported the case of an unmarried older Zambian female student, pregnant by her European lover, who tried to convince a customary or traditional court to oblige him to pay the compensation fixed by her ethnic group. To be a university student, to choose to remain single (the normal age at first marriage is way below twenty), to be told by her lover that he did not want her to have a child—all these traits point toward a "Western" definition of female individualism. Alternatively, the choice of tribal judges and the desire to obtain the sums of money or services fixed by the tradition to compensate young women and their families for the disgrace brought by pregnancies out of wedlock constitute as many components of a traditional framework. In the contemporary world, the emergence of interethnic conflicts is often related to the inconsistencies between the temporal components of self-identity in a traditional as opposed to a modern context.

As a last and similar example, the same American newspapers have commented on the conflict between a Kikuyu widow and officials of the Luo peoples in Kenya as to the most appropriate burial of her deceased husband. Officials wanted the corpse to be returned to Luo land in order to appease the ancestors' spirits, thereby asserting the continuity of the ethnic group and the need for individuals to display their subservience to the material manifestations of the ideal that intergenerational solidarity represents. The widow retorted, not without reason, that ghosts should not control human beings and that she was entitled to give a modern and, hence, individualized burial to her former husband. Here is another illustration of how individuals rely on the continuity of traditional time and the discontinuity of modern time to legitimize their respective self-interests, which are themselves derived from the interplay of gender and ethnic stratification.

Conclusion

The purpose of this chapter has been to show the relativity of the political principle *Divide ut regnas*. Even though the very survival of this principle in its original Latin form suggests that it is valid in various settings and circumstances, the thrust of the argument presented here has been to identify the variety of forces that prevent or facilitate the multifaceted integration of individuals into their familial groups, of these familial groups into larger cultural units, and of these larger units into the society at large.

But the forces that facilitate integration or conflict at these various levels represent only potentials. Thus, it remains necessary to identify the conditions under which these potentials are activated, remain dormant, or are reactivated. In this regard, it is important to underline why the effects of any policy of integration or destabilization, far from being cumulative, are contingent on specific historical circumstances that bring about reversals, accelerations, or slow-downs in the expected processes. It is equally important to underline how interethnic relations induce individual actors to base the legitimacy of their respective actions on the merits of both traditional and modern time. In short, the problematic nature of the expression *Divide ut regnas* results as much from the uncertainties underlying its effectiveness as from its dubious morality.

References

1. George Simmel, *The Sociology of George Simmel* (Glencoe, IL: Free Press, 1950), p. 127.

2. As quoted by Roger Brown, *Social Psychology* (New York: Free Press, 1965), p. 575.

3. Meyer Nimkoff and R. Middleton, "Types of Family and Types of Economy," *American Journal of Sociology* 66 (1960): 215–25.

5

Psychoanalytic Aspects of Ethnic Conflicts

Vamık D. Volkan

Externalization, Projection, and Displacement

In clinical practice, one often sees patients who are strongly prejudiced against the members of some ethnic group other than their own and who share stereotyped views of this scorned group with their fellows. Still more often, however, the exaggerated dislike the patient exhibits is the end result of his attempt to resolve his personal psychic problems. The scorned group is perceived either as the enemy or as an unacceptable aggregation of persons who must be kept at an emotional and physical distance. Concepts of ethnicity or nationality are associated with the identification of enemies and allies.

Clinicians with a psychoanalytic or psychodynamic orientation can help the patient who has pathological and obsessional views of other ethnic groups by bringing to light previously unconscious mental conflicts and the mechanisms of externalization, projection, and displacement with which the patient has attempted to deal with these conflicts. These three mechanisms—externalization, projection, and displacement—are the chief psychological defense mechanisms that contribute to the establishment of prejudice.

Externalization, a primitive form of projection, is the process of transferring an aspect of oneself—a devalued self-image, for example—onto another person or thing, or onto another group of persons in the case of ethnic distaste.[1] A child, abashed at falling down, may say that it was not he who fell but his doll; by externalizing his "fallen self"—by indicating that his doll was clumsy—he tries to make his sense of self more cohesive and acceptable to his ego. In this event, the only responsibility the doll bears is that of being present in the environment. This same kind of externalization is exhibited by an individual who believes that any member of a particular ethnic group to which the individual does not himself belong is poorly endowed intellectually, however lacking any evidence of this deficiency may be in reality.

Psychologically, *projection* is a more sophisticated mechanism than externalization. Projection becomes available to a child at a further stage of his development than that in which he depends on externalization. In projection, unacceptable unconscious impulses, attachments, and thoughts—after under-going a certain degree of distortion—enter an individual's consciousness in the form of external perceptions. Another person or group, such as an ethnic group, is then perceived as the "container" of the individual's previously unconscious unacceptable psychic content. He seeks targets tinged with what Freud called "kernels of truth" when he uses projection, looking for some con-gruity between the projected psychic material and the targets that will receive it. It is hard to modify some of these projections because of this fit. The person who projects unconsciously expects what he has projected to return to himself and, thus, fearfully seeks to distance himself from the other individual or group. Paradoxically, however, he remains preoccupied with his relationship with the target of his projection. Jaffe discussed this ambivalent relationship: The projection mechanism is used with the aim of destroying the container while at the same time preserving the tie to it.[2] A person may, for example, hold Arabs or Jews or Americans to be "unclean" when he projects his "unclean" psychic content onto them. Meanwhile, he is obsessed with a search for Arabs, Jews, or Americans in his everyday life in order to avoid them so that he can be sure that the "uncleanliness" will not move back to its original source. Some individuals use some targets as containers for both projections and externalizations; when this occurs, although the individual experiences discomfort, he finds the object indispensable. He tries to stabilize his projec-tions and externalizations in order to protect what he wants to keep within.

Displacement is investing feelings about one person in another person, thing, or group. For example, a person might feel toward his employer or an ethnic group the hatred evoked by his father.

All people use such mechanisms, but clinicians are concerned with their pathological, maladaptive use. Many developmental events in an individual's life lend themselves to the natural utilization of the three mechanisms just described. It can be said that the first individualized enemy is the mothering person who cannot respond to the infant's need for immediate gratification. There is a striking biological upsurge in a child's innate aggressive drive at about nine months of age, and he is forced to channel or master it. At this time of his life, he is dependent on his mother and her love, and the upsurge of his aggression signals danger if it is turned toward her. Among the mecha-nisms he then uses, as Parens demonstrated, is the displacement of destructive cathexis, a defense that may become a source of prejudice that appears later.[3] For example, at the time of toilet training, the child begins to develop unconscious symbolic meanings associated with his feces.[4] Later, such devel-opments, if not sublimated, may be echoed in ethnic relations; the darker skin of a member of the "enemy" group may stimulate unconscious association with feces.

Bengt Herulf, a Swedish psychoanalyst, told of a middle-aged man whose main interest, besides his profession and his family, was the pacifist movement. However, the symptoms he exhibited, such as a phobia about handling knives, indicated that he had another side, which he was avoiding. Once in analysis, he became aware through recurring dreams of being engaged in battle with an aspect of himself that he named "War Monster."[5] Through treatment of this patient and others with similar clinical characteristics, Herulf focused on the developmental psychological battles of preadolescence, during which the youngster struggles internally to free himself from being unconsciously bound to his parents. Herulf concluded that when there are developmental difficulties, these internal battles leave scars, of which the War Monster is an example. Individuals like this patient harbor a lust for destruction and war, either openly or in hidden ways. The Dragon Mother or the Devil Father who must be destroyed may be displaced; or the youngster may externalize his War Monster and then have to fight the object of his externalization in order to keep the War Monster out. Herulf noted that the sound of martial drums or some charismatic leader who is obsessed by war can easily arouse such persons against an ethnic or national group.

To understand ethnic conflicts as part of the global political scene, it is necessary to look at the behavior of groups, not just single individuals, however powerful they may be as political figures. It is certain, however, that since groups of any size are made up of individuals, the psychodynamics of individual persons find an echo in group relations.

When such mechanisms as externalization, projection, and displacement are used by large groups—an ethnic population, for example—the large group, once formed, develops its own identity and psychological processes. Under economic, political, or military stress, and when there is no clear leadership, a large group is more likely than an individual to regress; and the mobilization of externalization and projection is immediate and more powerful in the regressed group. Moreover, large groups are fickle in their likes and dislikes.

An attempt to gain a psychological understanding of ethnic relations and conflicts requires an examination of individualized prejudices and their derivative operations in the large group. Also required, if one wishes to go further, is a search for the beginning of the development of targets for externalization, projection, and displacement that the youngster *shares* with the fellows of his ethnic group, since this sharing creates a bond among them.

Shared Targets

I have written elsewhere of the details of a developmental event that occurs at about thirty-six months of age, at a time when, I believe, the psychological foundation of the concept of shared enemies and allies is laid and when the associated concepts of ethnicity and nationality become part of the developmental process.[6]

According to present knowledge, a child's development of a sense of self (his unconscious as well as conscious collection of perceptions, sensations, thoughts, and affects that permit construction of his self-image) and a sense of others is a very gradual process. The infant does not at first know where he ends and other people begin. Because he lacks the ability to integrate pleasurable and unpleasurable experiences with his environment, he can form only fragmented images of himself and others. Clinical observations show that at about thirty-six months of age, the child becomes able, after many trials and tribulations, to develop a cohesive sense of self that integrates the wanted with the unwanted, the pleasurable with the unpleasurable. He can then also maintain others in his environment as "gray" entities, rather than seeing them as "all black" or "all white." However, the task of crystallizing a cohesive and integrated self-representation and a similarly accurate representation of others is never altogether complete; black and white fragments remain and must be dealt with lest they threaten the cohesion of the child's sense of himself.

Under the influence of his parents, a child uses what Mack called "cultural amplifiers"; they are employed as containers to receive externalizations of unintegrated images of himself and others.[7] These amplifiers are usually inanimate or nonhuman entities, such as ethnic food, colors, or geographic locations. At this point in his development, a child experiences the cultural amplifiers as though they held some psychological magic; for example, an ethnic soup given to an ailing child is experienced as an extension of the all-good, always-caring mother. For an American child, a cowboy hat becomes a reservoir of a "good" fragment of the self, and wearing it provides external support to the sense of self. For Finnish children, the sauna contains aspects of their own pleasurable selves as well as the image of a warm mother—or an angry, hot father.[8] Children learn to take satisfaction in the properties of their own ethnic group—and to consider what is shared by those of another ethnic group as "bad." In Cyprus, for example, a Greek Orthodox church may seem to a Turkish child a container of his own bad aspects.[9]

Since such cultural amplifiers, or *suitable targets of externalization,* are shared by important parenting figures in any given ethnic or national group, the children of that group share them also. Bad suitable targets of externalization become the psychological foundation of the concept of enemy in a social and political sense. As the child grows, he becomes involved in abstracting a meaning from such shared targets, developing such sophisticated concepts as ethnicity or nationality and giving specific names to such concepts—Turkishness or Greekness, for example. Although they absorb new symbolic meanings as the child develops, some suitable targets of externalization—such as a national flag—remain inanimate throughout life. But in some instances, involvement in the abstract idea of ethnic and national identity is superimposed on the expectation of getting magical help from an ethnic song or feeling unique by putting distance between oneself and another ethnic group and its cultural amplifiers.

Under the stress of military involvement, for example, the members of an ethnic or national group may revert to original, childish ways of binding with one another and may return to employing inanimate or nonhuman objects. Palestinians in the occupied Gaza Strip carry small, inanimate objects with Palestinian national colors in their pockets, through which they unconsciously construct a network with other Palestinians. When Cypriot Turks were obliged between 1963 and 1968 to live in enclaves surrounded by Cypriot Greeks, they turned to a shared hobby—raising parakeets in cages. By externalizing their confined and needy selves onto these birds, they could psychologically feel cohesive as individuals and as members of their own kind. The birds, an adult version of suitable targets of externalization, helped the Cypriot Turks, at a most difficult time in their history, to maintain their individual as well as their group identities.

The psychological magic felt to reside in a variety of inanimate objects has been well studied by psychoanalysts. Such objects appear on a spectrum and at different levels of human development; adults and children are likely to attach different meanings to the same object. These meaningful objects could be transitional objects—the teddy bear or security blanket, fetishes, or mementos kept obsessionally and ambivalently by a mourner to provide a locus for the self-image to meet that of the loved/hated one who is lost.[10] The suitable target for externalization is an important inanimate or nonhuman object that is contaminated with our human aspects. The targeting serves as a precursor of ethnic and national differentiation and is involved in the formation of the concept of shared enemies or allies in the political and social sense.

Identifications

The developing child takes part in other psychological phenomena that help him to form sophisticated and deep-rooted concepts about "belongingness"; to make abstractions of and name his suitable targets of externalization; and to experience his ethnic and national identity. One of these psychological maneuvers is identification—an unconscious mechanism of the ego whereby one assimilates the functional images of another within himself. Through identification, one person comes to resemble another in some way. In different phases of life, people identify with different aspects and functions of others. In identifying with fellow members of one's group, one identifies with their investment in ethnicity and other related issues and shares in differentiating those who are unlike the group and inimical to it.

I consider that a child has only *traits* of ethnicity or nationality until he goes through adolescence; these traits may be strongly felt in childhood, but they do not comprise a full-blown view of the other group as a common enemy in the social and political sense. Going through adolescence, the child experiences inescapable turmoil in loosening his internal ties to the images of his parents and to the images of the suitable targets of externalization that belong to his childhood. The targets and their derivative concept—ethnicity and nationality—are reestablished at the end of the passage through adolescence. Since the youngster is at this time feeling peer-group pressure and has become part of a larger external world, the newly established sense of ethnicity and nationality has a firmer and larger foothold in the youngster's interaction with his environment. This is not to say that early parental influence disappears; under peer pressure, the adolescent is likely to rediscover most of the original, parent-directed targets, although they may now be disguised or bear new names. As his horizons expand beyond the family and neighborhood, the adolescent observes and internally experiences the world as larger and from a new point of view. At this point, identifications have lasting effects on his involvement with ethnicity and nationality. If the love partner chosen in late adolescence or adulthood is from the same ethnic background, there is a tendency to invest further in shared ethnic symbols and traditions.

Definitions of Ethnicity and Related Concepts from a Psychoanalytic Perspective

Ethnicity, like nationalism, changes its scope and substance according to the discipline by which it is being studied. Political scientists and historians state that in the late nineteenth and early twentieth centuries, the terms *ethnicity* and *nationality* took on new meanings quite different from those of classical Greek thought. We can refer to historical events or social components in describing any ethnic phenomenon. Physical anthropologists focus on cranial dimensions, nasal profiles, and the like. Horowitz, who is a professor of law as well as a political scientist, suggested that the concept of ethnicity must be somewhat elastic.[11] Descriptive studies of ethnicity and nationality refer to descent from a putative ancestor and the sharing of a common territory, history, language, religion, or way of life. Psychological descriptions can also be given.

The psychoanalytic view of ethnicity described here is based on the inescapable processes of human development. Group formation—whether in clans, tribes, or national or ethnic groups—includes the intertwining of the sense of self with the identity of the group at primitive levels. Belonging to such groups is not the same as belonging to clubs or professional organizations, as the former groups are tinged with raw and primitive affects that pertain to one's sense of self and its protection. We are gratified when fortune smiles on our own ethnic groups, and under certain circumstances we would rather die than change our ethnic identity; such a change is tantamount to a kind of death of the sense of self. We may actually die—or kill our enemy—rather than permit the loss of this sense of self. "It is better to be dead then Red" has a certain psychological validity.

In times of peace, sharing ethnicity within a group may have a healing and supportive effect, as it draws emotional borders that protect the sense of self of both the individual and his group from injury. However, because people have ethnicity or nationality, they have at least a potential need to have enemies. When one ethnic group becomes the enemy of another, both are tied together through externalization and projection. In such a case, the enemy's existence is its opponent's necessity. The enemy group may or may not be truly dangerous, but every enemy absorbs from its opponent group certain psychological phenomena that further complicate the dealings between the two parties. As Stein indicated, "Enemies are neither 'merely' projections, nor are they merely 'real.' "[12]

Because the human mind is at least partly responsible for creating enemies, humankind must develop ways to deal with them—on a spectrum from adaptive-peaceful to maladaptive-destructive. One way to cope is to create rituals between ethnic groups or other related large groups. All such groups need leaders to play a central part in such rituals.

Leaders

Freud believed that because a herd instinct is innate, all human beings are either leaders or followers.[13] Followers, obviously in the majority, require an authority to make decisions for them, and they are tied not only to one another but also to their idealized leader. The same phenomenon is apparent in ethnic relations. For example, even untrained eyes can often see how an ethnic group identifies its members and expresses devotion to a common leader. Kracke, a psychoanalytic anthropologist, studied the leader–follower relationship outside the higher-level societies found in Europe and elsewhere and stated that even in an Amazon society, the headman or leader promotes group continuity and serves as a buffer between the social structure and the individual.[14] Whether he uses force or persuasion, the leader plays a key role in actualizing the social structure. Kracke found that when anger and resentment toward the leader develop, such feelings are dealt with by displacement.

Like any political leader, the ethnic leader continually updates and modifies the conscious and unconscious needs of his followers, assessing—not always consciously—his effect on them and their degree of devotion to him. In a two-way interaction, although the needs of his followers influence the leader's position, his own personality makeup gives them direction. Some writers from different disciplines divide political leadership, including ethnic group leadership, into two types.[15] One type is characterized by a transforming leader, the other by an "in-between" leader.

The first type provides a large and visible stage for the ethnic targets of externalization and manipulates them to influence societal change. An example would be today's leadership in Iran, where certain objects, such as the *chador,* are shared by Iranian women as a symbol of a new sense of being Iranian.

The second type of leader helps his group to absorb, discard, or modify changes that took place under the direction of the transforming leader. Peaceful—or warlike—rituals of treating another ethnic group are also filtered through the point where the leader–follower interaction takes place.

Rituals

Because an ethnic group is tied to opposing groups through externalization, projection, and displacement—above and beyond any real-world issues that involve them—there is a potential for the eruption of conflict between ethnic groups. Most of the wars or warlike situations that exist in the world today are based on or at least tinged with ethnic differences.

Psychoanalysis has shown that wars themselves are considered rituals, although some people do not want to believe that something in the human mind and development causes humankind to make war. However, rituals between opposing groups are not always warlike; the mind is endowed not only with aggressive drives but also with libidinal drives, and the rituals between ethnic or national groups can be seen on a spectrum ranging from peaceful ones to war. Ethnic groups do compete, reflecting the competition of Oedipal-phase children for the favor of the parent of the opposite sex. However, in psychologically pre-Oedipal preoccupation with an enemy, there are two major, basic principles that govern enemy–ally relations between one large group and another.

The first principle deals in a paradoxical way with a *sameness* between ourselves and our enemies, between their ethnic group and ours. As the opposing ethnic group is a reservoir of our own unwanted psychic material, besides being opposed by realistic considerations, there is an unconscious perception of a certain likeness. Such likeness must be denied and never permitted to enter our consciousness, in order to keep our projections, externalization, and displacements stable and the identity of ourselves and our group cohesive.

The second principle concerns the need for a psychological gap between rival groups. Such a gap may be considered a necessity, but its existence establishes a connection in a negative way. One group is obsessed with the other's (the enemy's) presence and seeks information about it urgently—because of unconscious processes as well as real circumstances. However, when such information points to a sameness between groups, it is often distorted.[16]

A phenomenon known in psychoanalysis as the *narcissism of minor differences* clearly explains the preoccupation of ethnic groups with these two principles. When two such groups live side by side, for example, they do not want to acknowledge a total likeness, so they focus on—or create—minor differences that, in time of peace, they exhibit in rituals, such as dress, dances, speech patterns, and the like. In times marked by hostility, these minor differences assume a major and stubborn emotional importance; some people have even given up their lives rather than abandon them.

Horowitz reported that during the riots of 1958, Sinhalese mobs methodically searched out men who wore their shirts *over* their *vertis;* this identified Tamils—who could not be identified by different skin color and the like—and enabled the Sinhalese to victimize them.[17] In a time of peace, a minor difference in another group's manner of dress would unconsciously be felt to enhance the individual's personal and group sense of identity.

When some warlike situation comes about because of events in the real world or because of emotional issues, an ethnic group perceives the enemy group more and more in a stereotyped way in order to protect itself from contamination by the possible boomeranging of psychic content. At the threat of war, the enemy group can even be dehumanized and seen as monstrous. In this manner, the suitable targets of externalization that were used in childhood are recreated. At the same time, fear grows with the threat that the likeness and distancing principles may not be stabilized. Paradoxically, people fight wars to modify emotional borders in order to stabilize the emotional principles that exist in ethnic or national relations. The dominant psychological aim of war is to establish new psychological borders that will effectively keep the dehumanized enemy out or modify it. It seems that anxiety over the threat of losing the identity of oneself or one's group because of the possibility that externalizations and projections will return is greater than the fear of dying in battle. Therefore, from a metapsychological viewpoint, wars have "therapeutic" aspects. The trouble is that they cause so much destruction and have, in the nuclear age, the potential of annihilating humanity.

The Psychology of Mourning

Mourning is the human reaction to loss, change, and the threat of loss or change; it is a key concept in large-group interaction. Obviously, war brings mourning; the fallen and lost territories are mourned, and any new land gained cannot be "owned" until a reaction like mourning takes place. One can also see mourning at the negotiation table at which representatives of opposing ethnic or other large groups meet. This process consists of surrendering demands previously made as well as changing emotionally tinged positions and perspectives.

I suggest that the training of diplomats should include a study of the ramifications of the mourning process and of the ways in which an inability to mourn becomes a political determinant. This inability can change ethnic identity in an ethnic conflict, because if a group cannot mourn, it cannot accept real change. Mythologized as well as realistic memories of hurts and psychological wounds of one generation are conveyed to the next generation,[18] which, consciously or not, tries to recreate a version of the event in which the self-esteem of individuals or their group was damaged. The hope is to gain a new ethnic or national identity that is infused with enhanced self-esteem. The histories of ethnic groups should be studied by taking into consideration psychological processes, especially complications in group mourning.

Conclusion

The psychoanalytic perspective on ethnic conflicts suggests that there are inevitable developmental processes involved. Wallas, an English political scientist—and, later, Lasswell—suggested that political processes are not rational exercises and that they cannot be fully understood by rational thought processes.[19] I have reviewed here, however briefly, some of the general psychological formulations reflected in ethnic relations, which underlie the "irrational" aspects of the political process.

A description of interethnic conflict from the psychoanalytic viewpoint does not analyze away the importance of economic, military, and historical issues. However, to minimize the psychological processes involved in conflict is to rule out the elucidation of deadlocks, particularly those that are chronic. Like Dorn and Sigall, I call for interdisciplinary research using psychoanalytically informed alternative methods to deal with ethnic conflicts when the usual official diplomacy fails.[20] Elsewhere, I have described the psychological concepts involved in one such alternative approach (Track II Diplomacy).[21]

References

1. J. Novick and K. Kelly. "Projection and Externalization," *Psychoanalytic Study of the Child* 25 (1970): 69–95.

2. D.S. Jaffe. "The Mechanism of Projection: Its Dual Role in Object Relations," *International Journal of Psycho-Analysis* 49 (1968): 662–77.

3. H. Parens. *The Development of Aggression in Early Childhood* (New York: Jason Aronson, 1979).

4. L.S. Kubie, "The Outgoing of Racial Prejudice," *Journal of Nervous and Mental Diseases* 141 (1965): 265–73; and J.W. Hamilton, "Some Dynamics of Anti-Negro Prejudice," *Psychoanalytic Review* 53 (1966): 5–15.

5. B. Herulf, "The War Monster and Its Lust for Destruction and War," Paper presented at the 35th Congress of the International Psychoanalytic Association, Montreal, July 29, 1987.

6. V.D. Volkan, *The Need to Have Enemies and Allies: From Clinical Practice to International Relationships* (New York: Jason Aronson, 1988).

7. J.E. Mack, working paper entitled "Cultural Amplifiers," presented at the Committee on International Affairs at the Fall Meeting of the Group for the Advancement of Psychiatry, White Plains, New York, November 10–12, 1984.

8. V. Tähká, E. Rechart, and K.A. Achté. "Psychoanalytic Aspects of the Finnish Sauna Bath," *Psychiatrica Fennica* 2 (1971): 63–72.

9. V.D. Volkan, *Cyprus: War and Adaptation* (Charlottesville: University Press of Virginia, 1979).

10. P. Greenacre, "The Fetish and the Transitional Object," in P. Greenacre, ed., *Emotional Growth,* Vol. 1 (New York: International Universities Press, 1971), pp. 315–34; D.W. Winnicott, "Transitional Objects and Transitional Phenomena," *International Journal of Psycho-Analysis* 34 (1953): 89–97; and V.D. Volkan, *The Linking Objects and Linking Phenomena* (New York: International Universities Press, 1981).

11. D.L. Horowitz. *Ethnic Groups in Conflict* (Berkeley: University of California Press, 1985).

12. H.F. Stein. "On Professional Allegiance in the Study of Political Psychology," *Political Psychology* 7 (1986): 248.

13. S. Freud, "Why War?" (1932), in J. Strachey, ed. and trans., *The Standard Edition of the Complete Psychological Works of Sigmund Freud,* Vol. 22 (London: Hogarth Press, 1961), pp. 197–215.

14. W.H. Kracke. *Force and Persuasion: Leadership in an Amazon Society* (Chicago: University of Chicago Press, 1978).

15. J.M. Burns, *The Power to Lead: The Crises of the American Presidency* (New York: Simon & Schuster, 1984); and A. Zaleznik, "Charismatic and Consensus Leaders: A Psychological Comparison," in M.F.R. Kets de Vries, ed., *The Irrational Executive* (New York: International Universities Press, 1984).

16. Volkan, *The Need to Have Enemies and Allies.*

17. Horowitz, *Ethnic Groups in Conflict.*

18. R.R. Rogers. "Intergenerational Exchange: Transference of Attitudes Down the Generations," in J. Howells, ed., *Modern Perspectives in the Psychiatry of Infancy* (New York: Brunner/Mazel, 1979), pp. 339–49.

19. G. Wallas, *Human Nature in Politics* (Lincoln: University of Nebraska Press, 1908); H. Lasswell, *Psychopathology and Politics* (Chicago: University of Chicago Press, 1980).

20. R.M. Dorn and M.W. Sigall, "Political Science and Psychoanalysis," *Psychoanalytic Review* 64 (1977): 299–309.

21. V.D. Volkan, "Psychological Concepts Useful in the Building of Political Foundations between Nations (Track II Diplomacy)," *Journal of American Psychoanalytic Association* 36 (1988): 109–41; and Volkan, *The Need to Have Enemies and Allies.*

6
Theories of Power-Sharing and Conflict Management

Kenneth D. McRae

The Rise of a New Political Concept

This chapter concerns one particular line of thought that has been prominent in the study of comparative politics for just over two decades. I am referring to the concept usually known to political scientists as "consociational democracy," which is the rather technical term proposed by Arend Lijphart to denote a model of democracy and certain existing democratic systems that seek to resolve political differences by techniques of consensus rather than majority rule. The word *consociation,* or rather the Latin *consociatio,* has an honorable though minor role in the history of political thought.[a]

To understand the consociational idea, it is important to note the intellectual setting within which it developed two decades ago. The decade of the 1960s saw a major debate among political scientists over the question of how far the stability of political regimes requires a homogeneous or integrated political culture. For a discipline in transition from a primary concern for political institutions to an increasing concern for political behavior, the dominant tendency was to associate stability with party systems and the social systems underlying them. The prevailing view saw the "Anglo-American" model of a two-party system with a majority government as inherently stable and efficient. In contrast, the "continental" European model of democracy, as exemplified by France, Italy, or the short-lived Weimar Republic of Germany, with its multiparty systems and coalition ministries, was seen as inherently weak and unstable. Although some scholars conceded that the differences might arise in part from the different electoral systems on the Continent, instability was more often attributed to the more fragmented social structures of the countries in question.

At the time, this debate about stability had a practical importance far beyond academic circles. In dozens of newly independent states emerging from colonialism, new governmental structures were being built on societal foundations that were even more diversified and fragmented than those of the familiar Western European examples. Many social scientists had a major concern for the viability and political stability of these new states. Perhaps too much influenced by the Western examples that they knew best, they saw ethnic diversity in the new states as a serious barrier to stable and effective government, which in their view could develop only in a politically integrated society.[b] Thus, they saw ethnic and cultural diversity as an automatic recipe for social conflict. The remedy, they thought, would come from massive nation-building efforts to overcome "primordial" loyalties and to create a more homogeneous political culture. Social engineering on such a scale posed an enormous challenge.

In 1967, these academic perspectives began to change. At the World Congress of the International Political Science Association, held in Brussels in September of that year, two papers challenged the basic linkage between political stability and social structure. Working independently of each other and building on their previous work, Arend Lijphart and Gerhard Lehmbruch pointed to major anomalies in the then-current classifications of political systems.[1] As Lehmbruch phrased it, his paper analyzed

> . . . a type of political systems that has hitherto been rather neglected in comparative research: we speak of systems in which political groups like to settle their conflicts by negotiated agreements among all the relevant actors, the majority principle being applicable in fairly limited domains only.[2]

To illustrate this principle, Lehmbruch described the decision-making process in Switzerland and Austria, on which he had just published a short research monograph,[3] and he added a third example that would shortly afterward move from among the more successful to among the less successful cases of conflict resolution—Lebanon.

Arend Lijphart had written, but in 1967 had not yet published, a study of the political system of the Netherlands. His paper presented at the Brussels meeting reviewed existing literature on the classification of political systems and proposed a more comprehensive set of categories that would make room for apparently deviant cases—such as the Netherlands—that exhibited simultaneously both high social fragmentation and obvious political stability. For this new category, which had hitherto been either ignored or dismissed by theorists as anomalous, Lijphart proposed the term *consociational democracy*. Its distinguishing feature is the ability of the leaders of the contending subcultures to avoid the dangers of intergroup conflict through cooperation.

Competing Explanations of Consociationalism

On the central point of interelite cooperation, the papers by Lehmbruch and Lijphart coincided very closely. However, the two authors diverged in their explanations of why elite cooperation may arise in some fragmented societies but not in others. Lehmbruch pointed to the specific political culture of the country concerned, "the fact that peculiar norms of conflict management develop under specific historical circumstances."[4] In this view, he was followed by another early contributor to the consociational democracy concept, Hans Daalder, who saw both the Netherlands and Switzerland as historically predisposed toward consociational politics, primarily as a result of "older traditions of elite accommodation" that were well developed in both countries before the French Revolution.[5] For both Lehmbruch and Daalder, the main concern of consociational theory was to explain why some of the smaller Western European democracies (most obviously Austria, Belgium, the Netherlands, and Switzerland) had developed clear traditions of accommodative elite behavior, whereas other, larger countries with similar levels of social fragmentation (most obviously France and Italy) were characterized by more sharply polarized political systems.

Lijphart found the primary explanation in the capacity of the elites themselves to appreciate the dangers of social fragmentation, to transcend barriers of hostility, and to devise appropriate compromises on political issues. In addition to these political skills, he argued, elites must also be sufficiently positively motivated toward the political system. His original theoretical paper of 1967 listed several conditions favorable to the development of consociational patterns but did not include an earlier historical tradition of elite cooperation in the list. The contrast between Lijphart and Lehmbruch is perhaps best illustrated by their differing interpretations of the Austrian case. Whereas Lijphart saw the post-1945 grand coalition of the Second Republic as a conscious and innovative response to the dangers and ultimate collapse that befell the first Austrian Republic, Lehmbruch saw this same coalition as founded on "rules of the parliamentary game" and "political usages" developed for rather different purposes during the last years of the Hapsburg Empire.[6]

In several later writings, Lijphart refined and elaborated on his ideas on consociational democracy, most notably and most thoroughly in his book *Democracy in Plural Societies*. This volume listed and examined nine conditions favorable to the development of consociational politics. In this expanded list, he considered the question of prior historical traditions, particularly as posed by Lehmbruch and Daalder, and concluded that an earlier tradition of elite accommodation might indeed be a "favorable condition for consociational democracy" and "even of greater importance than the other factors, but it is not a prerequisite."[c] He underlined the voluntaristic aspects of his theory by continuing as follows:

> It is particularly important to stress the voluntary, rational, purposive, and contractual elements of consociational democracy because the discussion of

the consociational model as a normative model in later chapters presupposes that consociationalism is an example that can be freely and deliberately followed.[7]

It is this voluntaristic, open-ended quality of Arend Lijphart's version of consociational democracy that generally gave the idea a worldwide currency and at the same time attracted a corresponding volley of criticism and dissent. The Lijphart message was an exciting one because of its fundamental optimism. It offered a normative model that could be tried in a wide variety of situations of intergroup conflict, even when prospects for success appeared bleak. Its only apparent limits lay in the capacity and the will of the leaders of the groups involved to understand the situation and devise appropriate solutions by negotiation. Since these limits can never be known in advance, the consociational approach can lay claim to a very broad mandate. In a more sober vein, Lijphart assessed the prospects for success of consociational democracy as a set of probabilities: When societal pluralism is low, the majoritarian model of democracy is likely to be superior; as pluralism increases, the consociational model is more likely to succeed; when societal pluralism becomes more extreme, the chances for consociational democracy will also diminish toward zero.[8] The ultimate claim of Lijphart's variant of consociational democracy is that even when the chances of success are quite remote as a result of extreme fragmentation, no other form of democracy can do better.

favorable or advantageous position or chance against one's opponent

Criticisms of Lijphart's Theory

The broad claims of Lijphart's theory and the preeminence they have been given in recent political science have made the theory a target for numerous critics, who have attacked from many vantage points. One approach has been to criticize the *quality* of democracy that consociationalism delivers—its supposed requirement of mass deference to elite decisions, its need for secrecy in bargaining, its supposed extra costs or inefficiencies, and its alleged inflexibility and low capacity for innovation. Among some Marxists, consociationalism is seen as a form of social control that helps to divide the working class on religious-ideological lines and to perpetuate bourgeois rule. Another set of criticisms rejects the consociational model as an accurate description of political life in the Netherlands or in Switzerland, or else proposes an alternative model—for example, of a neocorporatist type—as a better explanation for the working of Dutch or Austrian pluralism. Still others question the causal relationships or the timing sequences in Lijphart's model.

Other critics have focused on Lijphart's methodology. Some have questioned the classification of entire systems as either majoritarian or consociational, calling for a more refined classification of decision making that recognizes variations within a given system. Still others have deplored the absence of necessary relationships or "laws" in the consociational paradigm, with the consequence that it cannot be rigorously tested and either confirmed or invalidated by the absence or presence of a single deviant case.

Most of these dissenting opinions are not directly relevant to the question of ethnic conflict.[9] Certain other criticisms, however, are directly relevant to the multiethnic society and the problem of ethnic conflict. Though expressed in many different ways, these criticisms can conveniently be reduced to three questions: First, can the consociational idea be imported or adapted in other previously nonconsociational countries as a remedy for ongoing conflicts? Second, can it be used effectively for racial, ethnic, linguistic, or religious-communal conflicts? Third, can it be transplanted from the older political systems of Western Europe, where democracy is well entrenched, to the more fragile political regimes of the Third World? In one sense, the second and third questions are logically included in the first, but they serve here to highlight points that have been singled out as special difficulties in the academic literature. A brief description of each of these questions is therefore in order.

Can Consociationalism Be Imported?

Lijphart is quite clear in stating that consociational democracy may be attempted in virtually any society, regardless of the degree of societal pluralism. With high pluralism, the chances of success diminish. However, no other form of democracy has a better chance, and nondemocratic regimes are also unstable. In any case, success is never guaranteed, even under the most favorable conditions, because so much depends on the unmeasurable factor of elite skills and motivation. In contrast to Lijphart's position, Lehmbruch and Daalder held that consociational decision making in the cases that we know best is the product of specific historical circumstances in specific countries. Although this view does not reject the idea that consociational methods might be transplanted to other settings, it does suggest that the success or failure of the transfer may depend on the specific political culture to a degree that Lijphart was reluctant to recognize. There is the further, more practical consideration that once any conflict has reached a high level of intensity, it may be extremely difficult to achieve conditions favorable to meaningful negotiation, but this is a problem common to all conflict situations, not just to the consociational model.

What Kinds of Conflicts Can Consociationalism Remedy?

There can be no doubt that consociational party politics in each of the four "classic" European cases—that is, Austria, Belgium, the Netherlands, and

Switzerland—emerged from divisions over religion and class. This double cleavage engendered strong Catholic-conservative, liberal, and socialist subcultures in all four countries. For the critical period, Austria's only significant political parties stemmed from these ideological foundations, as did those of Belgium until the linguistic tensions of the 1960s. The Netherlands and Switzerland each added one more distinct subculture to the basic three—Dutch Protestants and Swiss agrarians, respectively. The question then arises as to whether the success of consociational politics in bridging these religious-ideological cleavages can be equally applicable to the supposedly more intense and irreconcilable differences over race, ethnicity, language, or religious fundamentalism that lie at the root of many contemporary conflicts.[d]

For Lijphart this was not a problem, because he treated different kinds of political segmentation on exactly the same basis. Further, he noted that some analysts have come to almost exactly opposite conclusions regarding whether consociationalism is more appropriate for religious conflict or for ethnic conflict, and that in certain cases (such as Lebanon), this distinction may be difficult to draw.[10] My own work on linguistic divisions in two of the four classic European cases of consociationalism at least partially supports Lijphart, in the limited sense that a country exhibiting consociational patterns around one kind of cleavage tends to develop similar patterns around new issues or new cleavages as they arise. Thus, the demand for a separate new canton in the Bernese Jura district of Switzerland was handled—mainly at the cantonal level—by procedures that were clearly consociational.[11] Similarly, the appearance of increased linguistic conflict in the Belgian political system during the 1960s was marked by an obvious continuation and even reinforcement of consociational political processes, which were implemented, however, through major changes in political institutions.[12]

Is Consociationalism Relevant in the Third World?

The relevance of consociationalism in the Third World has been discussed less frequently. For one thing, many Western social scientists consider that classifications based on geographic categories such as Western or non-Western are unhelpful and unscientific. Lijphart himself noted the "mistaken view" of some critics who have rejected a consociational solution for South Africa *because of* the concept's supposed Western origins.[13] Nevertheless, in his earlier *Democracy in Plural Societies,* there is an entire chapter that discusses the applicability of the consociational model to the developing world. In that chapter, he traced the mixed record of consociational democracy in Lebanon, Cyprus, and Malaysia, concluding with a "general appraisal" of conditions that increase or decrease the likelihood of success of consociationalism in the Third World. Some of these conditions are favorable—for example, precolonial traditions of collective decision making. However, among "unfavorable factors," he noted an additional "set of developmental factors" arising from the "developmental dynamics of Third World societies"—stagnant political development, loss of deference to elites, increasing cross-cultural contacts through urbanization, rising expectations, fading memories of the shared liberation struggle—factors that need not be elaborated here. The point is that in spite of repeated reminders that individual Third World countries differ greatly among themselves, Lijphart found some *additional* conditions linked to the processes of development that appear to make the Third World setting *generally* different from that of the developed world.[14] One must add that this did not dissuade him from his basic position that the consociational model still offers the best hope for political stability and economic development for the plural societies of the Third World. Nevertheless, Lijphart's analysts in *Democracy in Plural Societies* leaves a distinct impression that even under equivalent structural conditions, a developing society may face obstacles arising from the dynamics of development that are not present in more developed societies.

An Alternative Model of Power-Sharing: The Control Model

The concept of consociational democracy—especially the voluntarist version developed by Lijphart—rapidly became part of the intellectual tool kit of students of comparative politics. It soon found applications and modifications far removed from the Western European settings in which it had first been developed. In the fertile interplay between Lijphart's model and the complexities of the real world, another young political scientist took note of another anomalous case that departed radically from the favorable conditions for consociationalism but nevertheless stood out as a case of relative political stability. Ian Lustick's case study concerned the Arab minority in Israel; and in the course of explaining the paradox of stability in a society as deeply divided as Israel, he developed an alternative theoretical model to Lijphart's consociational theory, which he called a control model.[15]

Essentially, the control model is another formula for political stability, but it operates differently than consociational politics and in settings where the conditions for successful consociational politics may be deficient. In particular, it may occur in settings where one majority segment dominates and reduces any other segment to a position of subordination (that is, where Lijphart's favorable condition of an intersegmental balance of power is lacking). In his development of a general theoretical model for a society with two segments, Lustick listed seven basic divergences between consociationalism and control, which may be abridged and summarized as follows:

1. *Resource allocation* in the consociational model is made in the interests of both segments by the elites of both groups; in a control model, allocation is made in the interests of the dominant group by its own elite.

2. *Linkages between segments* in the first model are effected through negotiation and compromise; in the second, they are exploitive or "penetrative."

3. *Hard bargaining* between elites is normal in consociational systems, whereas in control systems, it is a sign of dysfunction or breakdown.

4. The *official regime,* represented by the bureaucracy, the courts, the armed forces, and so on, in a consociational model acts as a neutral umpire among the segments; in a control system, it is the administrative arm of the majority segment.

5. *Legitimation of the political order* in the first case is based on the common welfare of all groups; in the second, it is founded on the interests and needs of the majority segment.

6. The *central strategic problem* for subcultural elites in a consociational model is both symmetrical for all groups and oriented in two directions, requiring both successful interelite bargaining and internal group discipline to implement decisions; in control systems, the strategic problem for the elites is asymmetric, but for both majority and minority elites, interelite relations are more of a problem than maintaining group cohesion.

7. The *visual metaphor* for a consociational system is "a delicately but securely balanced scale," whereas that for a control system is "a puppeteer manipulating his stringed puppet."[16]

It is important to understand clearly the original relationship between the consociational model and the control model. As elaborated by Lustick, the control model was developed primarily for analytical purposes, not as a normative goal. It was developed to *explain* political stability in certain "deeply divided" societies, where the conditions for consociational politics plainly were not present. It was devised not as a critique of consociational theory but as an explanatory alternative to it. In normative terms, the control model is a "second-best" alternative. Lustick explicitly admitted the superiority of the consociational model when it can be used successfully; however, a control model "may be preferable to the chaos and disorder that might accompany the failure of consociationalism," as in the case of Lebanon.

> In deeply divided societies where consociational techniques have not been, or cannot be, successfully employed, control may represent a model for the organization of intergroup relations that is substantially preferable to other conceivable solutions: civil war, extermination, or deportation.[17]

The control model has a middle position in the normative hierarchy: It is inferior to consociational democracy, but it stands above several more repressive alternatives. Further, it delivers benefits (though in all probability not equal or proportional benefits) to both dominant and subordinate groups.

Lijphart's View of the Control Model

Arend Lijphart included a short discussion of the control model in his *Power-Sharing in South Africa,* though he erred momentarily in listing it among the "critiques of consociational democracy." He basically agreed with Lustick that as an "alternative to consociational democracy," the control model is not attractive because of its intersegmental inequalities, instead of the "basically equal segments in consociational systems." But his argument then took a more dubious turn. In addition to segment inequality, "control is not an equal contender with consociationalism because it usually entails a political system that is not democratic. The only exception is the case of a majority segment which controls one or more minority segments in a majoritarian democracy." The "classic example" of this, he argued, is Northern Ireland, where Protestant majority control preserved "both peace and democratic institutions from the 1920s to the 1960s" but then "turned into civil war." Lijphart did not refer at all in this brief discussion to the example that gave rise to Lustick's model—the state of Israel and its Arab minority—perhaps because at this point, he was comparing the consociational and majoritarian models of democracy. Further, he suggested that even the exceptional, democratic case of the control model—the unequally segmented majoritarian democracy—is not genuine democracy, because "majority-control democracy spells majority dictatorship" in such a setting.[18]

These comments seem too hasty a dismissal of the control model. It is by no means obvious that control systems are "usually . . . not democratic," though the control model clearly does seem to be applicable in nondemocratic settings. Far from being unusual or rare in democratic settings, one can think of Lustick's model as being applicable in a descriptive sense to a great many situations in the real world where distinct ethnic, racial, or religious minorities face a repressive or merely a dominant host society. That this control may be exercised less obtrusively than in Israel does not necessarily make the model irrelevant; the mark of an efficient control system is its relative invisibility or low salience. To cite only one category of examples, the past and present situations of aboriginal peoples in many parts of the world seem to be described all too accurately by the control model, even in countries that have been models of democracy for their other citizens.

The Two Models Compared

The examples of control extend beyond these obvious cases and challenge us to a more thorough analysis. In particular, there is a need for closer study of the relationship between consociational and control models and the ways in which they differ at a practical or applied level. My own recent work leads me to suggest that both these models can occupy places in a unified typology of political regimes, and that for more detailed analysis, it may be useful to visualize consociationalism and control not as discrete models but as end-points of a continuum that allows for various intermediary positions along the scale.[19]

A full consideration of the theoretical issues that arise in developing such a typology of regimes would go beyond the intended scope of this chapter, but the range of possibilities that comes into view in relating consociational and control models may be illustrated by a few specific situations and examples. First, a country may exhibit consociational patterns or practices among some groups while simultaneously displaying a control relationship with respect to another group. As Lustick recognized, this is the case in Israel.[20] Second, a regime may evolve over time from control to consociationalism, or vice versa. In Switzerland, the radical hegemony in the nineteenth century evolved gradually into the very stable consociational coalition system of the last few decades, whereas the quasi-consociational system of the United Province of Canada after 1840 gave way after 1867 to a federal regime that Gordon Cannon presented persuasively as an example of a control model.[21] Third, in a federal system, with its multiple political arenas, any given group may be simultaneously in subordinate, equal, and superordinate positions in different cantons or provinces and at the federal level. Both Canada and Switzerland exhibit examples of this, and the analysis may be applied separately to the linguistic and religious dimensions. Finally—and in this fourth category the argument must be more nuanced—a country that is consociational in some policy areas might be closer to a control model in others. Thus, one can argue that the Swiss political system is more visibly consociational in matters of language and culture than it is in questions of economic policy, which tend to reflect more directly the financial predominance of Zurich and the industrial heartland.

What seems to be missing in our analytical resources at the moment is a capacity to assess just when a consociational arrangement should be attempted and when its probability of success becomes so low that other strategies become more attractive. Arend Lijphart's stance on this question has been unhesitating: Even if the chances of success are quite remote, no alternative solution has any better chance of success; therefore, there is little or nothing to lose by attempting a consociational solution. Others have argued against this position, on the ground that the risks and costs of a failed consociational experiment may be high enough to make alternative strategies preferable if they hold out a higher probability of success.

Two hypothetical examples will illustrate the dilemma more clearly. One of Lijphart's structural conditions favorable to consociationalism is that no segment should be in a majority or dominant position; but in situations of ethnic or linguistic conflict, such majority–minority situations occur quite frequently. This does not automatically preclude a consociational relationship, but it does make it more difficult to establish and maintain. Such a system may require special institutional arrangements or better-than-average attitudinal patterns (or both) to be successful. The greater the disparities of resources among segments, the more difficult may be the preservation of a consociational system and the more probable that it will tend to develop at least some features of a control system.

Another example relates to values. For Lijphart, successful consociational systems result from the capacity and the willingness of elites of different sectors to negotiate intergroup compromises that are acceptable to all segments. But what if the leadership of any segment is simply *unwilling* to maintain the system in any form or is committed to its overthrow or to secession? If the elites of any nondominant segment are insufficiently committed to maintaining the political system, the control model may have more chance of success than the consociational model, at least in the short run. Such temporary success may buy time for conditions to emerge that are more favorable to consociational solutions.

One may tentatively summarize this question by saying that consociationalism may succeed even when structural and attitudinal factors are moderately unfavorable; but without certain *minimal* conditions (as yet unidentified), the chances of success are infinitesimal. In particular, if the consociational process is to succeed, the elites of the groups in question must have some minimal level of commitment to dialogue and negotiation, on the one hand, and probably also to at least some shared objectives with other groups. This minimal shared outlook could arise from loyalty to the political system, from perceptions of group interest, from fear of violence, or from other factors, but if it is absent, the management of ethnic conflict may call for strategies other than consociationalism. The control model is one of these possible alternatives, and there are doubtless others that fall outside the scope of this chapter.

The Two Models and the World of Political Action

In reflecting on our current levels of understanding of ethnic conflict, I am led to stress the advantages of closer study of these two models that we now have. The consociational model has been well researched and very broadly applied in a wide variety of settings. It has yielded many fruitful insights in comparative politics, though this does not necessarily mean that all of its implications for ethnic relations and ethnic conflict have been fully explored. The control model is less fully developed and has been less studied, perhaps because it has been less attractive from a normative standpoint. Nevertheless, I suspect that the control model is important for the frequency of its occurrence, often in not easily identifiable forms. From the standpoint of ethnic relations, there are undoubtedly far more examples of control, in one form or another, than of balanced consociational systems. Further, there is some evidence that in the harsher conditions of the real world, consociational systems often stand quite close to control systems and may sometimes cross the invisible theoretical line that sets them apart. But this somber conclusion also contains a note of optimism, because it implies that with sufficient insight and cooperation at the elite level, a control system may likewise be made less onerous and may even cross the boundary in the other direction to become recognizable as a consociational system.

If the reformer's task is not to understand the world but to change it, the social scientist would be well advised to understand first just what is going to be changed. The picture suggested by the juxtaposition of the two theoretical models is clear enough. Essentially, the problem is how to convert a relationship of intergroup domination to one of equality. When the models are brought closer to the real world, however, the images become more blurred; and at this level, most political changes in a positive direction are, at best, incremental. The social scientist who is aware of these limits can cooperate with the politician (who knows their nature all too well) to set an itinerary toward a new destination. To recall a metaphor already used in the earlier literature, the problem is one of social engineering.[22] But the immediate task of the social (or consociational) engineer—to alter the original metaphor—is to move the train along the axis that runs from the control model toward the consociational model, remembering that the roadbed may be rough and broken and taking care that the coaches do not become uncoupled along the way.

Notes

a. The political concept of *consociatio* was developed by Johannes Althusius in his *Politica methodice digesta* (Herborn, 1603). The word appears earlier in Joannes Bodinus, *De republica libri sex* (Paris, 1586), and it also occurs, though infrequently, in classical Latin, most notably in Cicero.

b. This idea was not new. As early as 1861, John Stuart Mill had expressed doubts about the capacity of plural societies, especially multilingual societies, for representative government: "Free institutions are next to impossible in a country made up of different nationalities. Among a people without fellow-feeling, especially if they read and speak different languages, the united public opinion, necessary to the working of representative government, cannot exist." A.D. Lindsay, ed., *Utilitarianism, Liberty and Representative Government* (London and New York: J.M. Dent and E.P. Dutton, respectively, 1947), p. 361.

c. The other favorable conditions listed in this volume relate primarily to factors of social structure (a balance of power among subcultures, smallness in size, the type and pattern of cleavage structure, the relationship of the party structure to cleavage structure, possibilities of reducing conflict through federalism or decentralization or other forms of encapsulation) and also to another aspect of the value system (overarching loyalties to the nation or state). In a more recent formulation developed in relation to the case of South Africa, Lijphart modified this list in minor ways but also added to it one important new condition: socioeconomic equality among the segments. See his *Power-Sharing in South Africa* (Berkeley: University of California, Institute of International Studies, 1985), pp. 119–26, and compare with his *Democracy in Plural Societies,* pp. 53–99 and 173–74 (cited in note 7).

d. Among other critics, Brian Barry has warned of the danger of extending the consociational "formula" from divisions over church and state or social class "to other divisions and in particular those involving ethnic identity." See his "Political Accommodation and Consociational Democracy," *British Journal of Political Science* 5 (1975): 502–5.

References

1. For the published versions of these two papers, see Arend Lijphart, "Typologies of Democratic Systems," *Comparative Political Studies* 1 (1968): 3–44; and Gerhard Lehmbruch, "A Non-Competitive Pattern of Conflict Management in Liberal Democracies: The Case of Switzerland, Austria, and Lebanon," in K.D. McRae, ed., *Consociational Democracy* (Toronto: McClelland and Stewart, 1974), pp. 90–97.

2. Lehmbruch, "A Non-Competitive Pattern," p. 91.

3. Gerhard Lehmbruch, *Proporzdemokratie: Politisches System und Politische Kultur in der Schweiz und in Oesterreich* (Tübingen: Mohr, 1967).

4. Lehmbruch, "A Non-Competitive Pattern," p. 93.

5. Hans Daalder, "On Building Consociational Nations: The Cases of the Netherlands and Switzerland," reprinted in McRae, *Consociational Democracy,* p. 113.

6. Lijphart, "Typologies," p. 18; Lehmbruch, "A Non-Competitive Pattern," p. 93.

7. Arend Lijphart, *Democracy in Plural Societies* (New Haven and London: Yale University Press, 1977), p. 103.

8. *Ibid.,* pp. 236–38.

9. Lijphart himself listed most of the critics in a comprehensive bibliography on consociationalism in his *Power-Sharing in South Africa* (Berkeley: Institute of International Studies, University of California, 1985), pp. 137–71. In chapter 4 of this work, he replied to many of them, though his organizational scheme differed from the one presented here.

10. *Ibid.,* pp. 96–98.

11. Kenneth D. McRae, *Conflict and Compromise in Multilingual Societies: Volume 1. Switzerland* (Waterloo, Ontario, Canada: Wilfrid Laurier University Press, 1983), pp. 185–213.

12. Kenneth D. McRae, *Conflict and Compromise in Multilingual Societies: Volume 2. Belgium* (Waterloo, Ontario, Canada: Wilfrid Laurier University Press, 1986), especially pp. 124–73.

13. Lijphart, *Power-Sharing in South Africa,* p. 97. He noted the consociational elements clothed in other terminology in Sir Arthur Lewis, *Politics in West Africa* (London: Allen and Unwin, 1965).

14. Lijphart, *Democracy in Plural Societies,* pp. 164–76.

15. I. Lustick, *Arabs in the Jewish State: Israel's Control of a National Minority* (Austin: University of Texas Press, 1980). The theoretical model was developed in his article "Stability in Deeply Divided Societies: Consociationalism versus Control," *World Politics* 31 (1979): 325–44.

16. These seven conditions are spelled out more fully in Lustick, "Stability in Deeply Divided Societies," pp. 330–32.

17. *Ibid.,* p. 336.

18. Lijphart, *Power-Sharing in South Africa,* pp. 101–2.

19. This notion was developed further in Kenneth D. McRae, "Consociationalism and Control as Alternative Models of the Plural Society," Paper presented at the Canada-Israel Round Table on the Experience of Multi-Ethnic Societies, Jerusalem, 1985.

20. Lustick, "Stability in Deeply Divided Societies," pp. 335–36.

21. G.E. Cannon, "Consociationalism vs. Control: Canada as a Case Study," *Western Political Quarterly* 37 (1982): 50–64. In turn, he saw developments in Quebec after 1960 as a breakdown of the control model and a search for a new, more egalitarian relationship.

22. Lijphart referred to "consociational engineering" as a form of "political engineering." See his *Democracy in Plural Societies,* ch. 7.

7

Power Sharing: Another Swiss "Export Product"?

Jürg Steiner

Switzerland offers to the world a few export products of high quality. Recently, there has been some talk that political power-sharing as practiced in Switzerland may be another "export product" for the many troubled multiethnic societies around the world. Exactly what is meant by power-sharing in Switzerland, and to what extent can the concept be applied elsewhere?

How the Power-Sharing System Works

At the most visible level, Swiss power-sharing means that each of the three major language groups has a share in the Federal Council, the seven-member executive body of Switzerland. Currently, there are four German-speakers, two French-speakers, and one Italian-speaker in the Federal Council. This distribution corresponds approximately to the population share of the three language groups (70 percent German, 20 percent French, 10 percent Italian). Romansh is a fourth official language, but it is spoken by less than 1 percent of the population and consequently is not usually represented in the Federal Council.

Executive power-sharing by language groups is a custom rather than a constitutionally or legally mandated rule. Therefore, the system can be practiced with some flexibility. The Italian-speakers, for example, occasionally have no federal councilor because, with only 10 percent of the population, they have no numerical claim for a permanent representation in a seven-member body.

The Swiss manage to avoid the tricky question of which language group the prime minister belongs to by having no prime minister at all. The Federal Council is led, instead, by a chairperson; the position rotates every year according to seniority. During his or her year in office, this person has the title "federal president," which can easily be misleading for someone who does not know that the president is only primus inter pares in a strictly collegial body.

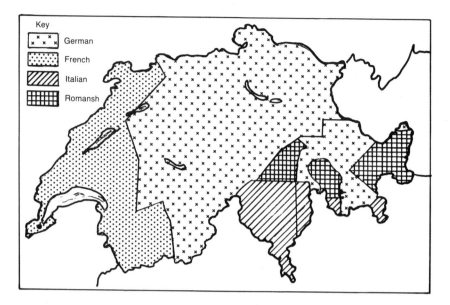

Figure 7–1. Switzerland: Cantons and Languages

Each federal councilor heads a department, such as foreign affairs, defense, or interior. Although some departments may sometimes be more desirable than others, in principle they are all of the same status. The federal president, like the other councilors, also heads a department. The collegial structure of the Federal Council makes it easy to share executive power among the language groups, because the problem of how to distribute ministries of unequal importance is avoided.

The principle of power-sharing among language groups applies not only to the Federal Council but also to Swiss society as a whole. For example, the army, at its highest level, has seven three-star generals, who are selected in such a way that there are usually four German-speakers, two French-speakers, and one Italian-speaker. The postal service is headed by three directors, nearly always two German-speakers and one representative of the linguistic minorities. Power-sharing among language groups is also practiced in private associations. For example, it is unimaginable that the executive committee of the Swiss Soccer Association would consist of German-speakers only.

Switzerland is about half-Catholic and half-Protestant, and power is shared between these two groups, too. In the Federal Council, an attempt is always made to have a rough balance between the two religious denominations. In the army, too, a great effort is made to guarantee that Protestants and Catholics are approximately equally represented among the top officers.

Finally, there is power-sharing with regard to party affiliation. The Federal Council is composed according to the so-called magic formula: two Free Democrats, two Christian Democrats, two Social Democrats, and one representative of the Swiss People's party. This distribution among the four leading parties exactly corresponds to their strength in parliament. Party affiliation is also important for the three directors of the postal service, where one seat is usually reserved for a Social Democrat.

American readers may wonder whether Swiss power-sharing amounts to a quota system, which would be unconstitutional in the United States. In the context of affirmative action programs, American courts do allow the setting of goals but not of quotas. Switzerland, however, does indeed operate to a large extent by a quota system, and the courts do not intervene. According to Swiss political thinking, not only individuals but also groups have rights. French-speakers, for example, should have the right to be represented among the top army officers. When a French-speaking three-star general retires, the search for his replacement is practically limited to French-speakers. But what about a German-speaker who may be more qualified than the top French-speaking candidate? The former is indeed discriminated against on the basis of his language affiliation. This is the price that the Swiss are willing to pay for their system of power-sharing. This price, however, should not be exaggerated. In the foregoing example, the highly qualified German-speaker simply has to wait until a three-star general of his own language group retires. Sometimes, of course, bad luck may strike; no opening may occur when someone is the "ideal" age for a particular position. For example, a German-speaking Free Democrat of Catholic faith, regarded as a top candidate, may never make it to the Federal Council, because during his prime political years, his particular combination of attributes may never be demanded.

Filling the various top positions in Swiss society is often like solving a difficult puzzle, but as already mentioned, the system is flexible. For example, if a particular government commission does not have enough French-speakers, at a later time or on another commission, French-speakers may be overrepresented as compensation. It is also important to note that a group's right of representation cannot be enforced in court. In Switzerland, power-sharing is a political rather than a legal system. If the Italian-speakers do not get a position to which they think they are entitled, they must take up the fight politically, not through the courts.

Power-Sharing and Power-Competition

Power-sharing differs substantially from power-competition, the prevailing model in the United States. In a system where groups compete for power, the basic assumption is that the best-qualified individual should always get the powerful position. For the presidency, for example, there is no rule that different groups—blacks, Hispanics, and so forth—should get their turn. The candidate who competes most successfully gets the job, whatever his or her group affiliation may be.

But if one looks closer, there are also some elements of power-sharing in the United States. Each administration makes an effort to have at least one or two blacks in the cabinet. The informal rule to have a black on the Supreme Court seems to have developed as well. The Democratic party has gone a long way toward recognizing group rights in the reforms of its party convention, where certain groups have guaranteed rights of representation. Despite these elements of power-sharing in the United States, competition for power is clearly the dominant mode. This explains why sports jargon is so often used to describe American politics, which is seen as a highly competitive game. Usually, there are clear winners and losers; and whoever loses has no right to exercise power.

In Switzerland, the notion of winning and losing is much less prevalent in politics. In the Federal Council, the French-, Italian-, and Romansh-speakers would always lose if the German-speakers used their voting strength. But usually an outcome is sought in which the linguistic minorities reach some gains, too.

Power-sharing and power-competition can be seen as the polar ends of a continuum. Although Americans often think of democracy exclusively in terms of power-competition, the example of Switzerland shows that power-sharing may serve as another model of democracy, and it is a model that may serve the needs of the many troubled multiethnic societies of this world better than the power-competition model. History has shown that power-competition often leads to instability and chaos. If there are two ethnic groups in a country—one of, say, two-thirds of the population and the other of the remaining third—election competiton always gives the victory to the larger group, and the minority group suffers permanent frustration. This is the tragic story in Northern Ireland, where the Catholic minority is no longer willing to tolerate the constant election victories of the Protestant majority. In such a case, power-sharing might lead to a better result.

Lessons from Swiss Power-Sharing

The Need for Development Time

The experience of power-sharing in Switzerland demonstrates, first, that it may take a long time for a country to develop a culture of power-sharing. One may despair at the hatred among the various cultural groups in Lebanon, for example. How could such groups ever share power? Similar hatred, however, can be found in Swiss history. Catholics and Protestants, in particular, were hostile for a long time. They battled each other not less than four times in bloody civil wars from the sixteenth to the eighteenth centuries. The language groups have never actually fought each other, but relations have often been quite tense. For example, during World War I, German-speakers supported Germany and French-speakers supported France.

Looking at Switzerland today, one may come to the conclusion that its people are by nature particularly peaceful, but there is no evidence at all for such a conclusion. There is nothing special about the genes of the Swiss that predisposes them to practice power-sharing. Rather, the current pattern of decision making is the result of a long learning process. The Swiss learned that if power is shared among the various groups, their country is more stable and prosperous. Some Swiss historical heroes symbolize this message; for example, Swiss history tells how the monk Brother Klaus mediated between feuding rural and urban cantons in the fifteenth century. In countries such as South Africa, Lebanon, and Northern Ireland, there are no such generally recognized symbolic figures of mediation. In those countries, there is no precedent for power-sharing. Perhaps matters have to become worse before the leaders will begin to realize that the sharing of power may be the only path to peace and prosperity in their deeply divided countries. This was the experience of Austria, which had to go through a civil war before its leaders were willing to share power in the grand coalition of Conservatives and Socialists after World War II. Traumatic memories of the atrocities of the past certainly contributed to this change in Austrian history. Examples such as Switzerland and Austria indicate that civil war may someday be followed by power-sharing in other countries, also. Current hatred is not a necessary obstacle to such a development.

Equality of Economic Status

Power-sharing is easier to arrange if the economic statuses of the various groups are about equal. This condition is largely fulfilled for Swiss language groups. With regard to banking, for example, the important centers are not only German-speaking Zurich but also French-speaking Geneva and Italian-speaking Lugano. Similarly, all three language groups are confronted with the problem of poor mountain farmers. If banking were concentrated in one language area and poor mountain farming in another, conditions for power-sharing would be much more difficult. With regard to religion, however, conditions are somewhat less favorable. Catholic regions are generally less affluent than Protestant areas, which helps to explain why, historically, it has been more difficult to introduce power-sharing among religious groups than among language groups.

Most difficult of all is power-sharing between the bourgeois parties and the socialists in Switzerland. The latter often complain that they are coopted into a capitalistic system in which the interests of the working class are sold out. There is a vocal minority in the Socialist party that would like to break with the prevailing system of power-sharing. This minority argues that power-sharing protects the interests of the haves against the have-nots. This is exactly what many black leaders argue in South Africa, and correctly so. Genuine power-sharing will not be possible in South Africa unless the white population accepts a much more equal distribution of economic wealth. The whites have to agree to a dramatic affirmative action plan to improve the economic situation of the black population. If the whites are not willing to move quickly in this direction, all talk of power-sharing is mere window dressing. In Switzerland, incidentally, a new test for power-sharing will come with the many nonwhites who arrive as refugees or foreign workers in the country. Will Switzerland include this new group of immigrants into its system of power-sharing? Are the Swiss willing to let nonwhite immigrants rise in economic and social status so that power-sharing will not be merely symbolic?

The so-called Jura problem helps to illustrate the two lessons discussed so far. The Jura problem arose in the bilingual Bern canton, which, at the outbreak of the crisis, was 85 percent German-speaking and 15 percent French-speaking. Many French-speakers, concentrated in the Jura districts, felt discriminated against and demanded separation from the Bern canton and the establishment of their own Jura canton. The handling of this demand did not go smoothly at all, and there were even some incidents of violence. Thus, the Jura problem reinforces the argument that the Swiss are not by nature more peaceful than other people. If the appropriate structural conditions are absent, the Swiss may resort to violence even today.

What were the underlying structural problems in the Jura districts? The separatist movement had its stronghold in the three most northern districts of the Jura. The people in these districts were in a disadvantaged position in three important ways. First, along with the people of the three southern districts of the Jura, as French-speakers they were in a minority position, not only in Switzerland at large but also in their own canton. Second, the three northern Jura districts were Catholic, whereas the three southern Jura districts, alone with the German-speaking part of the canton, were Protestant. Third, located at the periphery of the canton on the border with France, the three northern Jura districts were economically deprived.

Given these cumulative disadvantages, it is understandable that it was difficult for the three northern Jura districts to participate fully in the power-sharing arrangements of the canton. This refers exactly to the second lesson from Swiss power-sharing: Unequal status makes power-sharing difficult. With regard to the Jura problem, only a spark was necessary to make the situation explosive. This spark was set off in 1947 when a Jurassian member of the cantonal executive cabinet was denied, because of his language, the important Department of Public Works. There was an uproar in the Jura, and

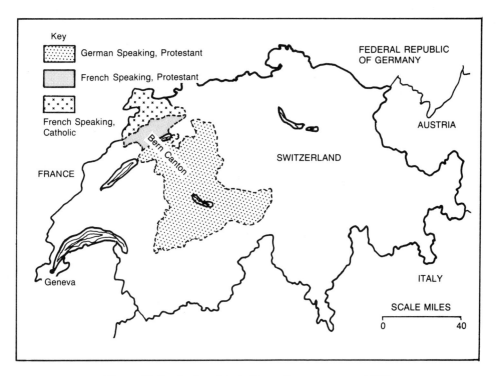

Figure 7–2. Switzerland: Bern Canton up to 1978

a long list of grievances was put forward to the Bernese authorities. On January 1, 1979, after a long and intricate struggle—which included several referenda—the three northern districts of the Jura got their own canton. But as of today, the question is still not settled; there is continued controversy over which canton some border communes should belong to. More important, the new Jura canton claims the three southern, Protestant districts of the Jura region. These southern districts are internally split. Is their main identity with their fellow French-speakers in the north, with whom they differ religiously, or with the German-speakers in the south, with whom they share the same religion? Again, if the structural conditions are not favorable, the Swiss, too, have their difficulties with linguistic and religious diversity.

Neutrality in Foreign Policy

A third lesson from Switzerland is that power-sharing is helped by a foreign policy of neutrality. In a culturally diverse society, there is always the risk of severe splits over foreign affairs, because the individual groups may have different sympathies for foreign countries. In Switzerland, this danger arose most dramatically in World War I, when, as already noted, most German-speakers supported Germany and most French-speakers supported France. It was only the policy of neutrality that held the country together.

What could have happened to Switzerland in World War I is happening today to Lebanon. Until the mid-1970s, power-sharing worked reasonably well in Lebanon, because the country had a relatively neutral position on the Middle East conflict. The tragedy of Lebanon is that it suddenly got involved in the intricacies of the Middle East conflict. As might be expected for a culturally diverse country, the various groups took sides with different countries, and this opened the door for the invasion of Lebanon by foreign troops. The same danger also exists for South Africa, with the potential that the superpowers will become involved. South Africa certainly has a better chance of internal power-sharing if it is allowed to stay out of the superpower confrontation.

Use of the Referendum

Power-sharing must be institutionally combined with a strongly developed referendum so that rule by an elite cartel can be prevented. If competition for power is replaced by the sharing of power, relations among the elites may become too cozy. Control must then be exercised by the people themselves. A referendum gives them the means for such control. In Switzerland, each constitutional amendment must be submitted to a popular referendum. For laws, a referendum is required only if those requesting it gather 50,000 signatures on a petition. In addition, through a popular initiative, 100,000 persons can propose a constitutional amendment, which must then be submitted to a vote of the people.

Of all the Western democracies, Switzerland uses the referendum by far the most often. Usually four times a year, the Swiss people are called to the voting booth to decide a variety of questions at the federal, cantonal, and communal levels. The strong use of the referendum compensates somewhat for the lack of importance accorded parliamentary elections. With the system of power-sharing, elections do not offer the possibility of replacing one set of leaders with another. Whatever the election results, the major parties continue to form the executive cabinet. Changes in electoral strength result, at most, in minor adjustments in the distribution of cabinet seats; and not even such minor changes have taken place for more than twenty-five years. During that time, the seven-member Federal Council has always contained two Free Democrats, two Christian Democrats, two Social Democrats, and one representative of the Swiss People's party. Given this stability, it is essential that the referendum give some control to the people. It was the lack of a referendum that made power-sharing so problematic in Austria and the Netherlands in the 1950s and 1960s.

8
Ethnic Conflict Management for Policymakers

Donald L. Horowitz

I n severely divided societies—the Lebanons, Malaysias, and Nigerias of this world—it is possible to manage or reduce ethnic tensions. It is not possible to obliterate those tensions—that is fanciful—and it is even more fanciful to pretend they are not there, as a great many first-generation leaders of such countries did.[a]

Buried in this assertion are two assumptions, which I shall mention but not discuss further. The first is that it is good to limit ethnic conflict, that the benefits that accrue from the limitation of ethnic conflict outweigh any disadvantages. The second is that more drastic solutions may not be feasible.

Ethnic conflict is intractable, partly because it is highly conducive to zero-sum outcomes—I win, you lose. It has high symbolic content. Back in the 1960s, in Kuala Lumpur in Malaysia, there was a big neon sign on the top of an office building that said, "Jayakan Bahasa Kebangsaan," which, translated, means, "Glorify the national language"—which means, in turn, "Glorify the Malay language" and, by extension, "denigrate the other languages." In glorifying the Malay language, one implicitly denigrates the Chinese language, the Tamil language, and also English, which a good many non-Malays prefer to Malay. There is no way to compromise on whether or not Malay is to be glorified. Glorification is indivisible. The symbolic side of the conflict is prevalent, and it is not amenable to the manipulation of material benefits that so often constitutes the stuff of modern policymaking.

In addition, ethnic conflicts have an ascriptive character; that is, they relate to birth. The birth character of ethnic affiliations sometimes clashes with the institutions of the modern state, which are premised on choice. Elections provide an example; the word *elect* means to choose. Assume that there are two groups in a hypothetical state: one (group A) is 60 percent of the population; the other (group B) is 40 percent. Assume, further, that party A has the loyalty of the A group and party B the loyalty of the B group and that the parties and their supporters are distributed so that party A will control 60 percent of the constituencies elected in single-member districts on a first-past-the-post or plurality system (the way the members of the U.S. Congress are elected, for example) and party B will control 40 percent of the constituencies. It is easy to see that party A will win the election. As a matter of fact, it will win all elections in the future, assuming constant rates of population increase between the two groups. This is not an election at all, but a census. Group A voters uniformly choose party A, and group B voters uniformly choose party B. The modern election presupposes floating voters, but significant numbers of floating voters between party A and party B do not exist in most severely divided societies. In such cases, one group is permanently excluded and, not surprisingly, resorts to a number of extralegal strategies, typically involving violence. Riots may be the first immediate effect. If group B is territorially concentrated, it may opt for secession. If it is disproportionately represented in the officer corps of the armed forces, it may attempt a coup. In these ways, ascriptive voting creates major problems for democracy. It is not the Westminster system that causes the problem in such societies, but the Westminster system coupled with ethnically based parties.

There are variations on this permanent majority–permanent minority theme, but many of them end up resembling the A–B case. For example, suppose that there are six groups—A, B, C, D, E, and F—of roughly equal size. Suppose that A, B, and C are in the north and D, E, and F are in the south. Groups A, B, and C have a little more in common with one another than they have with groups D, E, and F, and vice versa. These six groups are quite likely, given the incentives of the Westminster system, to congeal into two supergroups, two parties, two clusters, on a 51–49 basis, and exactly the same result will follow: inclusion and exclusion. That, in fact, describes Nigeria and several other African states in the 1960s quite nicely: clustering and bifurcation of groups.

Incentives for Moderation

What can be done about tensions that result from the creation of permanent majorities and minorities? It might be suggested that conflict reduction is a superfluous exercise in such cases, because political leaders do not want to reduce ethnic conflict. Most of the time in severely divided societies, there is much more to be gained by pursuing the conflict than by reducing it. But there are certain times that are propitious for conflict reduction. At those times, it is important to know what strategies, techniques, and policies might be used.

When are those times? It is difficult to specify them all, but I think I can specify some of them. Let me advance a few categories and examples, all of them cast in terms of political incentives for accommodation. Before I do so, let me on this particular point contrast consociational theories. Consociational theories tend to assume that motives for conflict reduction already exist among the leaders of the groups.[1] Thus, they assume this problem away, and it is not a trivial problem. It is a very serious problem, appropriately cast in terms of political incentives. Casting the problem in this way, I would like to use several concrete cases, extracting from each a slightly more general category.

A few examples of cases in which ethnic conflict was reduced show that a number of different situations create incentives for accommodation. The first case is Nigeria in 1978. Having ruled steadily since 1966, the military was turning power back to the civilians. The civilians concluded that they did not want to go back to the old Westminster arrangement, for they were conducive to the polarization that Nigeria underwent in the 1960s, which had led to the Biafra war. It was largely a polarization of north against south, of Hausa against Ibo. By 1978, all the political parties said, in essence, "Never mind who wins, who loses, who gains, and who does not gain. Extreme conflict is really bad for all of us, partly because we cannot tell in advance how we are going to come out of it." Anybody who has read John Rawls will notice some analogies here.[2] "If we come out on the short end, we shall really be hurt. Since we do not know how we are going to come out, let us assume that we shall get hurt, and let us devise institutions to prevent it from happening." In other words, despite the possibility of gains under the Westminster system, the players prefer a system in which low conflict is more likely.

Bitter experience—experience that is bad for everybody—gives rise to the notion that change is necessary. Lebanon and Sri Lanka may ultimately come to this position, although neither one of them has as yet. But bitter experience in which some have gained more than they have lost, or anticipated bitter experience in which one group thinks it is likely to come out ahead, is not likely to give rise to conflict-reducing motives.

One such case is Sri Lanka. In the 1950s, Sri Lanka experienced a good deal of Sinhalese–Tamil conflict. The Sinhalese came out ahead in the short run. Sinhala became the official language. As a result, there were very bloody riots all over Sri Lanka in 1956. In 1957, the then-prime minister, S.W.R.D. Bandaranaike, and the leader of the Tamils, S.J.V. Chelvanayakam, got together and drafted the B-C Pact, as it was called. The pact did not endure. Sinhalese opinion was against it, because the Sinhalese thought that there were further gains to be made by pursuing the conflict. Thus, even though leaders of the two main groups wanted to reduce the conflict, they could not.

A second case that illustrates propitious timing for accommodative arrangements is Lebanon in 1943. When other objectives, often international objectives, cannot be obtained without an agreement to reduce conflict, then conflict reduction measures may be brought into play. In the Lebanese case, it was a question of expelling the French. The French were weak during World War II. The Lebanese wanted independence but could not agree on terms until they realized that having independence was more important than transitory gain for one or another party. The governmental system they established lasted forty-two years. In a country like Lebanon, if peace can be maintained for forty-two years, the participants are doing well. It is important to judge these matters not retrospectively, but prospectively.

In a number of their colonies, the British conditioned the grant of independence on multiethnic political organization, which was equally a kind of incentive for leaders to get together. They provided for their colonists the incentive the Lebanese discerned for themselves. Achieving some other objective that overrides the conflict-pursuing objectives can result in accommodation.

The third case is Malaysia in 1952—five years before its independence in 1957. I choose that year because the formative events in Malaysian interethnic cooperation occurred in 1952, not in 1957. Before 1952, the Malaysians had never had an election. The British decided that the right way to start was from the bottom up—actually quite a typical British assumption. Starting from the bottom up, with town council elections, was intended to prepare the way for a parliamentary election. As it happened, the town councils represented the urban population, and the urban population was disproportionately Chinese. The only way that the leading Malay party, the United Malays National Organization (UMNO), could have a chance of winning such an election was to link up with a Chinese organization. Non-Malay—that is, Chinese—votes were so crucial that a multiethnic alliance was formed, and it won elections all over the peninsula. To keep the alliance going, conciliatory policies were adopted. As the alliance gained strength, Malay and Chinese extremist parties got in place on the flanks, so there was no longer any advantage for UMNO to appeal to extreme Malay opinion. Constrained by its partnership with non-Malay parties, UMNO could hardly adopt a pro-Malay line as hard as the line adopted by the exclusively Malay party on the flank. The multiethnic alliance and the flank parties got locked in place as a result of these formative elections.

Electoral incentives can actually be a source of motives for conflict reduction. As I shall show later, electoral incentives can also be a *technique* of conflict reduction.

The fourth case is Sudan in 1972. A civil war had been raging for about a decade, and suddenly it ended. How did that happen? Both sides suddenly found that they were weaker than they had been the day before. In the case of the northern Sudanese, Jaafar Nimeiri, the president, had just uncovered a very dangerous coup plot against him, largely communist-inspired, and he had executed a large number of participants in the plot. This was a major undertaking. Nimeiri also had some special difficulties with the Ansaris, an Islamic sect that was not favorably disposed toward him. Suddenly, he realized that he would risk his survival by fighting a war in the south. On the other side, the southern Sudanese rebels had been getting their supplies through Idi Amin's Uganda, but by about 1972, Idi Amin had rediscovered his Muslim identity and had also discovered that there was money in Libya.

As a result, the Israeli arms that were coming to the southern Sudanese through Uganda were suddenly cut off. For this reason, the Anyanya rebels in the south concluded that it would be better to end the war. So, simultaneously, both sides suddenly looked weaker. Needless to say, if only one side looks weaker, the chances of accommodation are slim.

These are some of the "windows of opportunity" for accommodation. No doubt there are others that could be mentioned, and they need to be mentioned, because it is a mistake to assume that conflict-reducing motives are present automatically—that they already exist among the leaders of conflicting groups.

Timing is important. The earlier a country starts working on interethnic accommodation, the better. Take the case of Nigeria. By 1978, the Nigerians were up against a large and entrenched military, for the most part as a result of ethnic conflict and the civil war. At the end of 1983, the armed forces took power back from the civilians and undid everything that Nigerian statesmen had done so well in 1978–79. Had the 1978 institutions been in place at independence in 1960, there is a good chance that the conflict-producing events of the 1960s might not have occurred. Had they not occurred, the Nigerian military might not have been in a position to upset the accommodative arrangements that were finally instituted in 1978–79. Similarly, from 1977 through 1980, Sri Lanka adopted a number of highly effective conciliatory policies, but unfortunately, by then, the government of Sri Lanka was up against an entrenched terrorist guerrilla movement in the north, which was quite unimpressed with these conciliatory policies, because the Tamils had already suffered a full seven years of Mrs. Bandaranaike's discriminatory polices. Had the sequence been reversed—that is, had the conciliatory policies of the Jayewardene government been put into effect in 1970—there might not be any fighting in Sri Lanka today.

There are two different approaches to the process of interethnic accommodation: negotiation or reciprocity, on the one hand, and legislation or public policymaking, on the other. Reciprocity means exchange; each of the conflicting groups gives the other something. On the other hand, in public policymaking, the conflicting groups assemble and agree on appropriate policy outputs, sometimes embodied in constitutional provisions. It is true, to some extent, that every time a body assembles and adopts a constitution, it is engaged in exchange. And vice versa: reciprocity, repeated often enough, creates policy. The products of recurrent exchanges become a kind of constitution for the parties. Nevertheless, there is something to the distinction. If groups come together only to exchange—only to trade horses, not to make ostensibly neutral rules—they are likely to run into certain pitfalls. Such pitfalls are less likely, on the whole, if the approach is public policymaking rather than mere exchange.

One such pitfall is the *incommensurables* pitfall, whereby apples and oranges are traded but eventually spoil at different rates. For example, in Malaysia, around the time of independence, the Chinese wanted above all to be citizens. Most did not have citizenship at that time. For their part, the Malays wanted a number of things, among them economic advancement. The per capita income of Malays was much lower than the per capita income of Chinese. As part of a much larger trade of incommensurables, these two were exchanged: the Chinese were to get jus soli citizenship—that is, citizenship as a result of being born in the country; and the Malays were to get, by some vague and unspecified means, some degree of economic advancement. Citizenship was just a stroke-of-the-pen thing, but economic advancement for an ethnic group was by no means a stroke-of-the-pen thing, and the Malays did not get what they thought they had bargained for. As a result, about ten years later, many Malays argued that there had been what the lawyers would call a failure of consideration. The quid was there, but there was no quo. "We gave you citizenship," said the Malays, "but we did not get our economic advancement. We should revoke your citizenship." The Malaysian government had a lot of trouble with this. Indeed, eventually, in 1970, a constitutional amendment was passed forbidding anybody from advocating the revocation of Chinese citizenship.

A number of other such pitfalls inhere in the exchange method of accommodation, because the process requires that some decisions be taken that would not be taken in the ordinary course of public policymaking. In general, therefore, I prefer the use of public policymaking; but it is not always possible to operate that way.[3]

The Range of Options: The Extremes

What policies have been or might be used to foster accommodation? There are quite a number at the extremes. Secession or partition is one of separating antagonists; each involves homogenization. If two groups cannot live together, perhaps they should get a divorce.[4] Another way is homogenization by means of assimilation—that is, literally, the loss of group identity. (I mean to distinguish assimilation from acculturation, which is altogether different.) There is also, of course, homogenization by extermination.

Secession or partition is the least bad alternative in a few cases, but it is generally not a very good alternative. Those who think it is have not looked closely enough at what has happened in such cases. Typically, remnants of each group are left on the wrong side of the border. Prospects are also ripe for irredentas—claims to retrieve land and people on the other side of the border. Partition creates boundaries that are not satisfying. If the boundaries do not really apportion ancestral lands correctly, then there will be attempts to rectify the boundaries.

Partition, because it puts an international boundary between the contenders, converts what was domestic ethnic conflict into often more dangerous international ethnic conflict. There are some telling examples of how much more dangerous this is, as in the case of India and Pakistan.

Furthermore, new forms of ethnic conflict emerge from partition or secession. Separating out one group does not separate out all the groups. If Biafra had succeeded in its secession attempt, there also would have been the Rivers people to take care of. The Ibo wanted self-determination for themselves *and* for the other people who lived in eastern Nigeria. That is the first of the ethnic composition problems, but there is another one. Ethnic identity is heavily contextual. In what was the Eastern Region of Nigeria, an Ibo may be, for example, an Owerri Ibo or an Onitsha Ibo. In Lagos, he is simply an Ibo. In London, he is a Nigerian. In New York, he is an African. If a putative country like Biafra were to become genuinely independent, the level of conflict in the state would drop down to lower (subethnic) levels but would not necessarily decrease in intensity. Some of these subethnic divisions are extremely intense. Moreover, in the rump state—that is, in what would have been left of Nigeria—there would have been very intense conflict among three categories of people remaining there: the Hausa-Fulani of the north; the northern, largely Christian, "Middle Belt" minorities; and the Yoruba of the west. Occasionally, partition is necessary, but it is not as attractive an option as it appears. It should be a policy of last resort.

Assimilation—changing group boundaries by incorporating a group or amalgamating with it—is a long-term business that takes decades or centuries. It is not a good short-term policy, and—it must be underscored—the short term is what policymakers should care about, because what severe ethnic conflict puts at risk is the short- and medium-term survival of a country. Most countries do not have in the short and medium term the formidable coercive resources to bring about the kind of assimilation that would reduce ethnic conflict substantially. And when they try it, they typically produce a separatist reaction among such groups as the Basques and the Kurds. Assimilationist policies tend to backfire.

The remaining techniques of accommodation are much less sweeping and intellectually less satisfying, both because the categories are less clean and neat and because the successes are less dramatic. Still, that is where emphasis ought to be concentrated—on the murky business of what can be done to reduce conflict and to limit and control it.

Structural Techniques

Structural techniques change the institutional format in which conflict occurs, thereby altering the structure of incentives for political actors without making any promises about ethnic outcomes. The main structural techniques have to do with the apportionment of territory—typically, federalism and regional autonomy—and electoral systems. Both territorial and electoral systems are very important levers of policy. Both are promising and prominently used techniques of conflict reduction. Another set of prominently used techniques are distributive policies, which attempt to alter the ethnic balance of rewards and opportunities. Typically, these involve preferential policies of recruitment in the public or private sector, business licenses, contracts, and share ownership; the list is almost endless.[5] Distributive policies entail the ethnically skewed direction of the rewards and opportunities available in a society, and that is not what I shall focus on here.

It is particularly important to note that structural techniques have some efficacy. Such a conclusion is quite contrary to the common assertions that developing countries have little leeway to manage ethnic divisions in a democratic setting. In reality, there is room for quite a lot of constructive innovation, and some countries have begun to move in such a direction. The institutions and the policies differ from country to country. Some use territory, and some use elections; some involve the creation of homogeneous states, and some involve the creation of heterogeneous states. Some involve one mode of election, and some have to do with another mode. But wherever these techniques succeed, there are two main underlying mechanisms at work. First, a given device creates incentives for cooperative interethnic relations—that is, it makes it pay to be cooperative across ethnic boundaries. Alternatively—and these are not mutually exclusive alternatives—a given device may exacerbate intraethnic (within-group) conflict at the expense of interethnic conflict.

The two mechanisms are related, because interethnic cooperative links are more likely among portions of ethnic groups than among cohesive and undivided groups. Why should group A, with 60 percent of the population, cooperate with group B, with 40 percent? There is not much incentive for the A majority to be concerned with accommodating group B. But suppose that group A is divided into two parties, each representing 30 percent. Now there is an incentive for one of the A parties to be cooperative with the B group. It is often—though not always—easier to cooperate across ethnic lines if intraethnic divisions are present. So, the two mechanisms can work together.

Territorial Innovations

Nigeria's federal experiment demonstrates the uses of territorial innovations in conflict reduction. The Nigerians had two differently designed systems, separated by thirteen years of military rule, so it is possible to trace causal relations. Nigeria has had two fresh beginnings (and will soon have a third), one at independence in 1960 (which lasted six years, until the military coup of January 1966) and another in 1979 (which lasted four and a half years, until the end of 1983).

These two periods were dramatically different, largely because territory was carved up differently. In the First Rebublic, the country was divided into three main regions, each controlled by a single ethnic majority and a party representing that majority. These three regions were used as springboards for the three main groups—Hausa, Yoruba, and Ibo—to fight for power at the center. In each region, and especially in the north, the regional majority was overrepresented in politics, largely as a result of first-past-the-post elections. The Hausa-Fulani, about half of the north's population, had three-quarters of the regional assembly seats from 1961 to 1965. The Northern Peoples' Congress (NPC), the party controlled by the Hausa, won nearly all of the northern seats in the federal house, although, again, the Hausa comprised only about half of the population of the north. Minority parties, needless to say, were underrepresented and basically suppressed. In the north, it did not pay to belong to a minority party. If all of the patronage opportunities in the region were to be controlled by the NPC, it made much more sense to adhere to it. The same situation existed in the east and the west, and that led to a struggle among the three parties: Hausa, Yoruba, and Ibo. Eventually, it was simply Hausa versus Ibo, because the Yoruba proved to be the least cohesive of the three groups, and they split. One segment went with the Hausa and the other with the Ibo. This bifurcation or polarization led to the Biafra war.

In the Second Republic, the situation was different. In 1967, the military government divided the country into twelve states. In 1976, seven additional states were added. The Hausa were divided among six states, the Yoruba among five, the Ibo between two. What effect did this have? First, it created a new, lower, less-dangerous level at which ethnic conflict occurred. Since half of the states were homogeneous, the conflict in those states was intra-ethnic. If it is thought that intraethnic divisions might mitigate interethnic divisions, one way to foster intraethnic divisions is to create homogeneous states. People will struggle for power within those homogeneous states.

Elsewhere, the conflicts were interethnic; that is, the states were ethni-cally heterogeneous, and there was interethnic conflict in those states. But such conflicts did not necessarily replicate the lines of interethnic conflict at the national level of politics, because there were many local groups competing with one another as well. And there were also interstate conflicts, which fre-quently pitted one Yoruba state against another Yoruba state, one Ibo state against another Ibo state, one Hausa state against another Hausa state. Occa-sionally, too, there was interstate conflict in which ethnicity played no part. For example, when a decision had to be made about how to divide up oil revenue, states advocated alternative formulas that benefited them. Oil-rich states argued for revenue allocation by location of the resource; others wanted allocation by population.

The proliferation of states at the national level had far-reaching electoral consequences. In the Second Republic, there was basically a recrudescence of the same three parties that had prevailed in the First Republic. The Ibo and

Yoruba parties won almost all of the votes in their states in the 1979 elections; but in the Muslim north, the creation of a half-dozen states breathed new life into what had been impotent northern opposition parties based on ethnic and subethnic divisions. For example, the Kanuri, who are Muslims but not Hausa, now had their own state and their own party, and their party controlled the state. Previously, it had made no sense to support a party that would be consigned to futile and punishing opposition in the undivided north, but now the electoral incentives were transformed. The divided Northern Region provided ten states, ten legislatures, ten governors, and fifty federal senators. As a result, there were incentives to organize on a subregional level; a group with no chance to control the old Northern Region could now control a single state. The former minority parties in the Northern Region became the majority parties in the new states, and two former opposition parties controlled four of the ten states. The old NPC gave rise to a successor, the National Party of Nigeria (NPN), which controlled only six of the ten states. Ethnic parties were not abolished, although that had been the hope of the framers of the arrangements. The effect of the new federalism was different. The power of largely ethnically based parties was simply made a little bit more proportional to their underlying ethnic group strength.

In other words, federalism operates like an electoral reform, like proportional representation. Federalism can set one arena off from another, making and remaking legislative majorities and minorities by adjusting the territories in which their votes are to be counted. So the rule of decision is no longer "Winner take the whole region," because there is no whole region anymore. The undivided region had given an enormous bonus to the Hausa-Fulani–dominated NPC. The ten states created, in this case, five parties instead of the former three, because the two former northern minority parties suddenly become important factors. So, federalism can foster multiparty fluidity, depending on how electoral arenas are demarcated. Then the question becomes: Can multiparty fluidity be preserved? That is what was operating in the Second Republic, a quite fluid system.

I should make one more point about Nigeria before considering electoral devices explicitly. The reduced strength of the successor to the NPC in the north—the NPN—gave that party a powerful incentive to do what the new electoral arrangements for president (which I shall come to in a moment) also encouraged it to do—namely, to appeal to ethnic groups outside its core area. In the First Republic, the NPC was just looking for power on its own; the NPN in the Second Republic could not do that. It therefore had every reason to reach out and line up with some groups outside its core region. In other words, there were incentives for interethnic cooperation. As a matter of fact, the NPN presidential candidate won the election of 1979 precisely because he was more successful than the other candidates in reaching out across ethnic boundaries to non-Hausa voters.

Electoral Innovations

In considering electoral systems and conflict reduction, it is necessary to keep one salient fact prominently in mind. In severely divided societies, political parties tend to break along ethnic lines. Given this fact, there are at least five goals that can be pursued profitably through the electoral system.

The first involves the A–B, 60–40 problem. In such a case of bifurcation, it is tempting to try to fragment the support of the majority group in order to prevent it from achieving permanent domination. Can group A be fragmented through use of the electoral system? And does it make sense to do so?

Second, one might wish to induce an ethnic group, especially a majority group, to behave moderately toward another group and engage in interethnic bargaining. This does not necessarily entail fragmenting its support but merely requires providing incentives to moderation.

Third, one might wish to encourage the formation of multiethnic political organizations—either parties that span ethnic groups or coalitions that do so. This is related to the second objective of inducing a party to behave moderately, because without interethnic moderation, interethnic political coalitions will quickly fall apart.

Fourth, one might wish to preserve a measure of fluidity or multipolar balance among several groups to prevent bifurcation. If there are six groups, A, B, and C might crystallize and form one group, and D, E, and F might crystallize and form another. Then the A–B, 60–40 problem would be present. Avoiding bifurcation by preserving fluidity is an objective the electoral system might foster.

Finally, in some situations, it might be advisable to reduce the disparity between votes won and seats won, so as to reduce the possibility that a minority or a plurality could gain a majority of seats. When a group with less than a majority gains the largest number of seats in a parliamentary system, that is a prescription for warfare. Imagine a country with two main ethnic groups. Group A is divided into two parties, each with 30 percent support, but group B, with 40 percent support, is not divided. Suppose that all over the country, three-way contests are held under a first-past-the-post system. Group B will end up with a majority in parliament—at least 51 percent, probably more. A minority, group B, will control parliament, and members of group A, a majority, will consider that control illegitimate. Can such a disparity between votes won and seats won be reduced, so as to reduce the chance that such an illegitimate minority regime will emerge?

Most of these goals can, indeed, be attained. The first objective—fragmentation—is the most difficult to attain through the electoral system. It was tried in Guyana in 1964, where the East Indian political party, the People's Progressive Party (PPP) had previously won 57 percent of the seats with 42 percent of the vote. For a number of reasons, the British attempted, in the last election of the colonial period, to break up the solid support of the PPP. Proportional representation by party lists was adopted in lieu of the first-past-the-post system by constituencies. The hope was that the East Indian supporters of the PPP would divide up into Hindus and Muslims, but they did not. Muslim parties sprung up and entered the contest, but they all lost their deposits; they were completely unsuccessful, even though, in principle, proportional representation ought to provide abundant incentives for party fragmentation. In fact, the British had adopted the Israeli list system of proportional representation, with no minimum requirements for legislative representation. Even that was not enough to induce separate parties to form. So, fragmentation is difficult to accomplish, even by draconian means.

Federalism, however, may succeed in achieving the goal of fragmentation. What cannot be done through the electoral system can sometimes be done through the territorial system. In northern Nigeria, that is precisely what happened in the Second Republic. Group A, the Hausa, were fragmented because people who had earlier voted for the Hausa party voted for other parties in the Second Republic, after the north had been divided into ten states. To put the point differently, party *structure* may be hard to change by electoral reform, but party *posture* may be easier to change through the electoral system. That is, a party that is extreme today may become moderate tomorrow because of incentives for interethnic coalition.

Can moderation, the second goal, be achieved? The Lebanese system of 1943 made moderation mandatory. There were common-roll elections; everybody got to vote for everybody, but all the offices and seats were reserved, and mixed lists were put up, often in multimember constituencies. What this meant was that a Sunni had to run for a Sunni office against another Sunni; a Maronite had to run for a Maronite office against another Maronite; and a Shiite had to run against another Shiite. And in legislative elections, because there were multimember contituencies, there were mixed tickets for these various offices for the electorate as a whole to vote for. If candidate X was a Maronite and candidate Y was a Shiite, there was no point in their being antagonistic to each other. They might as well join hands and form part of the interethnic ticket that was required. They could then exchange the votes of their supporters, for these were *common-roll elections for reserved seats.* Executive offices—such as the presidency (a Maronite position) and the prime ministership (a Sunni position)—were also reserved in the same way as legislative seats were. This system put a premium on interethnic moderation at the expense of intraethnic division. Fortunately for the Lebanese, Lebanon is very well endowed with subethnic distinctions around which these intraethnic divisions could crystallize.

The Nigerian Second Republic presidential electoral scheme is another example of how incentives for moderation can be built in. A candidate could not become president of Nigeria even if he had the largest number of votes unless he also had at least 25 percent of the vote in no fewer than two-thirds of the then nineteen states. That meant that even if he had the support of any two of the three major groups, he could not become president of Nigeria. He had to have some minority support or the support of all three major groups. Because of the distribution requirement, he had to reach out and conciliate and propitiate the interests of groups other than the ones he was accustomed to appealing to. The system worked brilliantly. The Nigerian legislature was a hothouse of ethnic claims, and its presidency was a panethnic office.

The second preference system for the election of the president in Sri Lanka ought to have the same moderating effect as the Nigerian scheme had. In Sri Lanka, every voter has to indicate second and third preferences for president. If no candidate secures a majority, then the second preferences are reallocated to form the majority. That means that in a competition between two closely matched Sinhalese parties, which is usually the case, Tamil voters may decide the election. The Tamil voters' first choice will be for a Tamil candidate. However, the question is not who their first choice is; he cannot get elected. The question is who their second choice is. Is it going to be the Sinhalese candidate of the Sri Lanka Freedom party or the Sinhalese candidate of the United National party? The Sinhalese parties, then, must bid for Tamil second preferences—a system well designed for interethnic moderation.[b]

The third goal is the formation of multiethnic parties and coalitions. Multiethnic parties are very difficult to form in severely divided societies. The Nigerians did about as good a job as possible, using the distribution requirement. The NPN began to bring under its wing members of groups other than the Hausa. But truly multiethnic parties are intrinsically almost impossible in severely divided societies. Multiethnic *coalitions* are much less difficult to form. Here it is important to distinguish two types of multiethnic coalition, only one of which is conducive to moderation. Unfortunately, the type of coalition that is conducive to interethnic moderation is the more difficult to form.

Suppose that there are three contesting parties and none gets a majority of seats in a parliamentary system, so a coalition must be formed. Two of the parties exchange seats—the A party contributes 40 percent and the B party contributes 20 percent. The two then have 60 percent and have beaten the C party, which has 40 percent. The A–B coalition organizes the government. This is a coalition of convenience; it comes into being only to form a government. When parties are organized ethnically, that motive is not enough for moderation, particularly because such coalitions tend to be formed between parties that have no competitive overlap in the electorate. If the A party and the B party are going to form a coalition, they are most likely to form it if they are not competing for the same votes. Then there is no need to worry about what is going to happen next time around. If, however, the two parties are competing for the same votes, the coalition makes the next election awkward and demoralizes lower-rank party functionaries, who see the other party as the electoral enemy. The absence of competitive overlap among coalition parties also means that there will be little or no agreement between the parties on the main contentious ethnic issues in the society.

The result is that because parties with ethnically polar positions end up in coalitions, these coalitions do not last, and they dissolve acrimoniously. Typically, the larger partner edges out the smaller one—buying over some members of the legislature, inducing them to cross the aisle—and forms a government alone. The smaller partner then goes into opposition. There are many examples of this.

The other kind of coalition makes more sense for interethnic conciliation. This is a coalition of commitment, so called because it entails a commitment to interethnic accommodation on the part of the partners. This kind of coalition is formed by pooling not just seats in parliament but also popular votes. Suppose that there are two constituencies. In one constituency, party A, representing group A, is close to having a majority of voters but not close enough to win by itself; but party B, representing group B, has no hope of getting a majority in that constituency. In the other constituency, where B is close to a majority of voters and A has no hope of winning, there is mutual advantage in making a deal. Party B will throw its few voters in party A's almost-majority constituency to party A if party A will do the same for party B in the constituency in which party B is favorably placed. The two will pool votes. In other words, wherever party A has a chance of winning and party B does not, party B's voters vote for party A, and vice versa. Vote pooling is conducive to political accommodation, because neither party can make a vote-exchange deal with the other unless it can tell members of its ethnic group that the other party is moderate on the issues that concern them.

Unfortunately, not enough has been done in the developing world to facilitate this sort of arrangement, so there are many more coalitions of convenience than coalitions of commitment. But the Malaysian Alliance, now the National Front, is based fundamentally on the principle that in marginal constituencies where the Malay candidate would lose but for the Chinese votes, the Chinese votes are forthcoming. Incidentally, this includes the constituency of the prime minister of Malaysia, who is dependent on Chinese votes for his survival. Similarly, there are even more constituencies in which the Chinese candidate cannot win without Malay votes supplied by the United Malays National Organization. Both Chinese and Malay candidates run on a common coalition ticket.

Can one induce coalitions of commitment? Yes. Alternative voting is one way to do it; heterogeneous constituencies in a situation of party plurality is another way. And there are other ways; Lebanon's mixed lists were yet another way to achieve this objective. It is not sufficiently appreciated how important this objective is in interethnic accommodation.

The fourth goal is fluidity. Whether or not multipolar fluidity can be created comes down to whether or not groups can be fragmented by the electoral process, and that is a very difficult objective to achieve. But once there is fragmentation, it is possible to prevent crystallization into a bifurcated system, into A and B. The Lebanese system prevented the crystallization of allegiances into overarching Muslim and Christian divisions. In the 1950s, it was perfectly plausible for Muslims to go one way in Lebanon and Christians to go another. But the Lebanese system, with its sectarian division of offices, seems to have entrenched lower-level sectarian affiliations as against overarching Christian or Muslim affiliations. It is possible that there are other ways of doing the same thing. As a matter of fact, in the Second Republic system in Nigeria, the combination of federalism, with some states that could be controlled by particular minority groups and parties, and plurality election (not majority election) for national legislative office tended to encourage this kind of fluidity. The presidential system, on the other hand, tended to encourage party consolidation.

Two of the goals may work against each other. The goal of cross-ethnic distribution, which is conducive to moderation, works in favor of party consolidation and against multipolar fluidity. Therefore, it is important to decide whether the avoidance of crystallization into two parties is the major objective—because of the fear of ethnic bifurcation—or whether multiethnic support for parties is the major objective. Both may help ethnic accommodation, but they are alternative, somewhat incompatible means to that end.

Finally, the fifth goal is proportionality. Can one prevent the B party from taking power with a minority of votes but a majority of seats? The Guyanese elections of 1964 proved that proportionality works to this end. What happened in the 1964 Guyanese election was that the PPP, with a plurality of votes, was thrown out of office. In 1961, the PPP, as I said earlier, had 42 percent of the votes under a first-past-the-post system and 57 percent of the seats—a 15 percent disparity between seats and votes. In 1964, under proportional representation, the PPP had roughly 45 percent of the votes and roughly 45 percent of the seats. The other parties were equally proportionate. The result was that the PPP, with only 45 percent of the seats, went into opposition, and two other parties formed a coalition. This was, incidentally, a coalition of convenience, which eventually fell apart.

Innovation, Timing, and Deflection

The accommodative impact of most of these innovations has proved to be rather short-lived. The Guyanese innovation achieved its objective, but that objective was not really moderation or interethnic coalition—just proportionality—so it is not by itself a test of accommodation. The Lebanese devices lasted for decades. Nigeria was done in by a coup in 1983. Sri Lanka has been done in—and I think will be done in for some time—by separatist violence that began soon after the accommodative arrangements were adopted. Because the Nigerian coup had nothing to do with ethnicity, the case of Nigeria may simply prove that accommodative arrangements cannot solve all of the political problems of developing countries, particularly when the innovations come so late that they are up against enormous problems created by earlier arrangements that fostered conflict. If the arangements in Sri Lanka had been put into place before the Bandaranaike government took power in 1970, it is very unlikely that the Bandaranaike government would have engaged in the kind of discrimination that has produced such a powerful reaction among the Tamils. If that is true, the likely success of accommodative innovations turns on questions of sequencing. It is not that innovations like those in Nigeria and Sri Lanka do not work; they do work. The problem is that they are not adopted until it is too late or until they are likely to be deflected from achieving their purpose. In addition to choosing appropriate techniques, those who wish to institute structures for ethnic accommodation are up against separate problems of leadership motivation, of timing, and of deflection.

Notes

a. Most of the matters discussed in this chapter can be found in more detail in my book *Ethnic Groups in Conflict* (Berkeley and Los Angeles: University of California Press, 1985).

b. A more detailed consideration of Sri Lankan and Malaysian electoral systems and their consequences is contained in my other contribution to this volume, chapter 25.

References

1. See, for example, Arend Lijphart, *Democracy in Plural Societies* (New Haven, CT: Yale University Press, 1977).

2. John Rawls, *A Theory of Justice* (New York: Oxford University Press, 1971).

3. For a further discussion, see Donald L. Horowitz, *Ethnic Groups in Conflict* (Berkeley and Los Angeles: University of California Press, 1985), pp. 584–88.

4. Samuel P. Huntington, "Foreword," in Eric A. Nordlinger, *Conflict Regulation in Divided Societies* (Cambridge, MA: Harvard University Center for International Affairs, 1972).

5. See Horowitz, *Ethnic Groups in Conflict,* ch. 16. See, also, Myron Weiner, "The Political Consequences of Preferential Policies: A Comparative Perspective," *Comparative Politics* 16 (October 1983): 35–52.

II
Northern Ireland in the Western Context

With the commencement of the case studies, there is little need for extended introductory comment. Each chapter is the work of an internationally respected expert, the result of an extensive talent search for the original conferences that resulted in this volume. And although, as always, political events have marched on in each of the countries profiled, the essays were crafted with a view to timelessness. The historical consciousness in which each essay is rooted represents an interpretive background against which new developments can be continually assessed.

Like the other "hot" cases—Sri Lanka and Sudan—Northern Ireland presents political analysts with a particularly difficult challenge. The Protestant–Catholic, unionist–nationalist conflict produces new victims with regularity. And repeated efforts of the United Kingdom government to resolve the political dispute have failed. In the following chapters, Richard Rose reviews the twentieth-century history of the Northern Ireland conflict, which, in fact, goes back at least four centuries.

John Darby offers some thoughts on how the practical need to get along in communities and the workplace, if and when Catholics and Protestants do meet, contributes functionally to the relatively low level of intercommunal violence.

Padraig O'Malley considers efforts at compromise and reform since the modern wave of "troubles" began in 1969, with special emphasis on the impact of the Anglo–Irish Agreement of 1985, which gave the Irish Republic a say in the affairs of the Catholic minority in Ulster. His is an intricate analysis that highlights the seemingly intractable suspicions and fears found on both sides, but especially on the part of the unionist political leaders.

All three of these essays provide evidence that traditional methods of conflict analysis and conflict resolution strategies could benefit significantly from an understanding of the psychological tasks that must be addressed. The reader need not wait to finish the entire volume before reviewing the Volkan essay (chapter 5) and reading the epilogue (chapter 29).

Each in its own way, Heisler's chapter on Belgium, McRae's on Canada, and Gunther Eyck's on the South Tyrol reinforce the hope that devoted, hard-working, and mature political leadership—combined with pragmatism and imagination in the building of institutions and electoral arrangements—can and does work in multiethnic societies. In each case, leaders in a position to do so have found ways to recognize the identity and specific cultural needs of minority communities and to make the compromises on language, education, and other issues necessary to meet these needs. And even though the conflict management work in Belgium, Canada, and the South Tyrol is never completed, requiring constant vigilance and labor, it is important for communities and states elsewhere that suffer from ethnic violence to know that there are cases that justify optimism.

9

Northern Ireland: The Irreducible Conflict

Richard Rose

Northern Ireland is a challenge to the comforting belief that describing a situation as a problem guarantees the existence of a solution. In this strife-torn land where the United Kingdom meets the Republic of Ireland, there is no solution—if a solution is defined as a form of government that is consensual, legitimate, and stable. This situation is not unique to Northern Ireland; many member states of the United Nations lack consensus and legitimacy and are of doubtful stability. Unlike most nonconsensual regimes, however, Northern Ireland suffers from a lack of authority (that is, the ability to maintain public order) yet maintains democracy (there is freedom of speech and there are free elections, with proportional representation that ensures one person, one vote, one value).

Northern Ireland has been governed without consensus for many centuries. Before the arrival of forces of the English Crown in the late twelfth century, Ireland was, like neighboring Scotland, an unsettled place, and no one clan leader could enforce central authority throughout the island. The sixteenth-century Reformation divided the indigenous population of Ireland, which remained Catholic, from newly Protestant England and Scotland. The threat this posed to the Crown[a] was met by the plantation of Protestants from Scotland and England in Northern Ireland at the same time and by a similar legal formula as the plantation of Virginia and other American colonies. The resulting battles were concluded in 1690 by the unification of the whole of Ireland under the authority of the Crown. When the Irish uprising succeeded in creating a separate Dublin-based state in 1921, the Protestant majority in six counties of Northern Ireland succeeded in remaining within the United Kingdom, but the Catholic minority there continues to aspire to unification with the twenty-six counties of the Republic of Ireland.

In Northern Ireland, bullets as well as ballots are used to express political dissent and to pursue conflicting political goals. In 1912, Protestants organized the illegal and armed Ulster Volunteer Force to express their opposition to a home rule bill that Westminster Parliament in London was considering, a bill that would have placed the Protestant counties under a Dublin parlia-

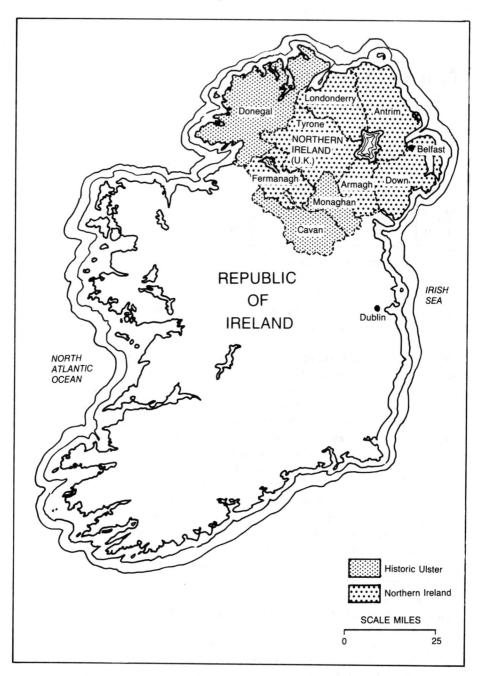

Figure 9–1. Northern Ireland Showing the Nine Counties of Historic Ulster

ment. The 1916 Easter rising by the illegal Irish Republican Army (IRA) in Dublin inaugurated a five-year internal war, which ended with a treaty recognizing an independent Irish government for twenty-six counties. This was not accepted by all Irish republicans, and a bloody civil war followed. The tradition of armed resistance to "illegal" laws (that is, measures that deny a group's claim to nationality) actively persists to the present.

In such circumstances, the immediate objective of politicians is not a long-term "solution," but containment of the conflict that faces them. When some elected politicians regard abstention as a normal tactic and unelected politicians regard violence as normal, management of public order is not just a parliamentary problem. Whereas the goal of the British government was once described as maintaining "an acceptable level of violence," the illegal IRA wants to maintain a level of violence so *unacceptable* to the British government that it will withdraw from Northern Ireland, leaving its future government to be fought out within the island of Ireland.

Multiple Divisions

The United Kingdom versus the Republic of Ireland

The fundamental conflict in Northern Ireland is about the boundaries of the state. Two member states of the United Nations—the United Kingdom and the Republic of Ireland—each claim the six counties of Northern Ireland. Article 2 of the Constitution of the Republic of Ireland lays claim to "the whole island of Ireland." The United Kingdom asserts contingent sovereignty; it is committed to Northern Ireland's remaining a part of the United Kingdom as long as a majority of its population so wishes.

Within Northern Ireland, the million Protestants have consistently voted to remain under the Crown, whereas most of the half-million Catholics aspire to being unified in an all-Ireland republic. When the British government held a referendum on this issue in 1973, 98.9 percent of those voting favored remaining part of the United Kingdom. Only 1.1 percent of the votes were against, because the Catholic third of the population abstained en bloc, reflecting the belief that the only valid test of opinion about Irish unity would be a ballot held throughout the island of Ireland, where the overwhelmingly Catholic electorate of the Republic would outnumber Protestant voters by a margin of about three to one.

The two sovereign states that lay claim to Northern Ireland usually agree to disagree amicably. The British government has no positive attachment to Northern Ireland. Ulster's[b] population is less than 3 percent of the United Kingdom; the economy is less prosperous; the political parties fighting elections are local to Ulster; and the Conservative, Labour, and Social and Liberal

Democratic parties do not contest elections there. The fighting that has kept British troops continuously in action in Northern Ireland since 1969 is regarded as a painful duty, not as a battle to maintain the British Parliament at Westminster. When violence erupts on mainland Britain (the term used to describe the larger island of the United Kingdom), public opinion often manifests a readiness to "hit" the IRA and then to pull out of Northern Ireland. Many British cabinet ministers over the years have publicly or privately endorsed the idea that the eventual resolution of the Northern Ireland problem can come only through the unification of Ireland. Moreover, by agreeing to a referendum in which the people of Northern Ireland could choose whether or not they wished to remain in the United Kingdom, the British government has granted Northern Ireland, under specified circumstances, the unilateral right to secede.

The Republic of Ireland is ambivalent about its claim to authority over Northern Ireland, as stated in Article II of its constitution. Article III of its constitution recognizes that special arrangements need to be made "pending the re-integration of the national territory." The 1985 Anglo–Irish Agreement gave de facto acceptance by the Dublin government to the nonintegration of the island of Ireland until such time as a majority in Northern Ireland give their consent. The Republic's government has been harsh in opposing violence by the IRA within its twenty-six-county boundaries. But because the state was created by armed revolt against the Crown, and because it shares with the IRA the goal of national unity, it is less prepared to countenance measures that it regards as unfair or oppressive against republican violence in Northern Ireland. The Dublin government has refused to extradite to Northern Ireland Republicans who face murder charges there, on the grounds that they are being accused of a "political" crime.

Protestants versus Catholics

Disagreements between Protestants and Catholics within Northern Ireland have been expressed by both ballots and bullets. From 1921 to 1972, Northern Ireland was governed by a democratically elected Parliament at Stormont, a suburb of the capital of Belfast. The outcome of each election was never in doubt: The Ulster Unionist party always won, fighting on a single issue—the maintenance of the union of Northern Ireland with Great Britain. Some of the members of Parliament elected by the Catholic minority abstained from participation, on the grounds that Northern Ireland was illegitimate. For that reason, Catholic voters saw nothing illogical in voting for Republicans who had been convicted of violent crimes, as violence against the British was a recognized way of seeking Irish unity, and the enforced abstention of a prisoner was no different from abstention by a politician who was not in jail. Those Irish nationalist M.P.s who did attend Parliament refused to accept the title of Her

Majesty's Loyal Opposition, in order to emphasize their *dis*loyalty to the Crown. The Protestants considered that a group that was politically disloyal had few claims on the state and that the majority could therefore govern as it wished. As the English Bill of Rights is about the authority of Parliament and does not confer justiciable rights on individuals along the lines of the American Bill of Rights, the Catholic minority effectively lacked the recourse to courts that blacks in the American South used to good effect.

Over the years, IRA groups conducted a sporadic military campaign against the Northern Ireland government. To defend its regime, Stormont relied on the Royal Ulster Constabulary and the all-Protestant Ulster Special Constabulary. It also had emergency powers to ban demonstrations and to intern suspected Republicans without trial. Until 1969, few lives were lost in such campaigns, and the mass of the population was unaffected. However, the campaigns fueled Protestant suspicions of Catholic disloyalty and encouraged Catholics to endorse illegal actions in defiance of Stormont's authority.

In 1968, Catholics organized marches to protest against discrimination in allotting public housing and jobs in favor of Protestants and against gerrymandering in some local government councils.

Since 1969, Ulster politics has been subject to continuous violence, euphemistically described as "the troubles." The immediate trigger was the use of force by the Royal Ulster Constabulary to suppress street demonstrations by Catholics and Protestants in August 1969. When Catholics began forming armed defense groups, the IRA began recruiting members to advance its cause by attacking the British Army as well as the Royal Ulster Constabulary. The IRA is now split into three different groups: the Provisional IRA, the Official IRA, and the Irish National Liberation Army (INLA). As British discipline of Ulster defense forces increased, Protestants began forming illegal defense forces to attack Catholics. Notwithstanding thousands of arrests and prison sentences, the violence has continued since.[1]

The violence takes many forms: the killing of Ulster policemen and British Army forces by the IRA and the shooting of IRA suspects by official security forces and illegal Protestant forces; bombings of military targets, public places, and individual homes and random bombings intended to induce a general sense of terror; and more or less spontaneous fighting between Protestants and Catholics. Since 1969, more than 2,500 people have been killed, more than ten times the number of British lives lost in the Falklands war. Given that the population of Northern Ireland is only about 1.5 million, the death toll is the equivalent of more than 90,000 people killed in Britain or 400,000 killed in the United States. It is important to emphasize that the death toll is *not* comparable to deaths resulting from motor accidents or antisocial crime. Violence in Northern Ireland is *purposeful*—part of a war about maintaining or undermining the authority of the state.

The parties to political debate in Ulster are not only the vote-seeking organizations familiar to American politicians; there are also paramilitary organizations, which use violence to force attention to their demands. Moreover, although the names of parties and other groups often change, many of the faces behind them are familiar from past activities. The small scale of Ulster society means that politicians are thrown into frequent contact with one another on the street, in pubs, and in meetings. Politicians rub shoulders with clergymen and members of paramilitary organizations, as well as with ordinary constituents looking for help with personal problems. They have a good idea about what their coreligionists and the other side are doing to maintain or subvert civil government and public order. A number of elected politicians have been murdered during the current round of troubles, including two Westminster members of Parliament. A third, an IRA member, killed himself by fasting to death in prison as a political protest.

The Ballot box Versus Armed Struggle

Political organizations within Northern Ireland are divided along two dimensions: The first is the sectarian divide between the Irish Catholics and the Protestants who identify with Britain; the second is a division between those who compete at the ballot box and those who fight through the use of military weapons (see figure 9–2). Nine-tenths of the electorate casts votes for a party whose appeal is confined to a single religion. The Alliance party of Northern Ireland, which appeals to Catholics as well as Protestants, has tested the appeal of the "moderate" policies typically endorsed by outsiders; the Alliance wins only a tenth of the Ulster vote. In effect, electoral competition in Northern Ireland is competition between the Official Unionists and the Democratic Unionists for the votes of Protestants who oppose a united Ireland, or between the Social Democratic and Labour party and the Provisional Sinn Fein for votes of pro–Irish unity Catholics (see table 9–1).[c]

The weight of armed groups in Ulster politics is out of all proportion to the numbers on active service or in prison. The percentage that actively sup-

	Protestant	Catholic
Competes at elections	Ulster Unionists Democratic Unionists	Social Democratic and Labour party (SDLP)
Uses force	Ulster Volunteer Force Ulster Defence Association	IRA (three groups)

Source: Richard Rose, *Northern Ireland: Time of Choice* (Washington, DC: American Enterprise Institute, 1976).

Figure 9–2. Divisions within Northern Ireland

Table 9–1
Votes for Northern Ireland Parties, 1987 United Kingdom
Parliamentary Election

	Votes		Seats	
	Number	*Percent*	*Won*	*Contested*
Unionist and Protestant	380,292	52.0	13	17
Official Unionists	276,230	37.8	9	12
Democratic Unionists	85,642	11.7	3	4
Popular Unionists	18,420	2.5	1	1
Irish Unity and Catholic	256,770	35.1	4	14
Social Democratic and Labour party	154,087	21.1	3	13
Sinn Fein	83,389	11.4	1	14
Workers' party	19,294	2.6	0	14
Others	93,090	12.8	0	17
Alliance party of Northern Ireland	72,671	10.0	0	16
Others	20,419	2.8	0	3

ports paramilitary groups is a small minority in each of the two communities, but a much larger fraction is prepared to excuse or tacitly accept the use of violence on its own side, while criticizing violence by the other side. Sinn Fein actively exploits this ambivalence, campaigning for support with the cry that Irish unity can be won with a ballot in one hand and an Armalite (a weapon favored by IRA snipers) in the other. In the 1987 United Kingdom general election, Sinn Fein secured almost one-third of the Catholic vote. Protestant armed groups see themselves as an alternative to electoral politics, whether in the form of Dr. Ian Paisley's Democratic Unionist party or the previously dominant Official Unionist party. The existence of multiple paramilitary organizations within the Catholic and Protestant communities reflects disagreements about how to deal with the troubles and sometimes leads to bloody internecine disputes.

Every elected Ulster politician is immediately under pressure from two sides. First, there is pressure to justify reliance on elections rather than physical force. As the outcome of an election is a foregone conclusion, with Protestants always winning a majority of seats in Northern Ireland because they constitute two-thirds of the electorate, Catholic politicians have particular difficulty in explaining to their followers why yet another defeat will help their cause. Even more, there is difficulty in explaining why winning a handful of seats in a British Parliament with 650 members will advance the cause of Irish unity. As long as Stormont was in existence, Protestants could be urged to vote to maintain their control of government locally. Now that government is in the hands of resident British ministers elected by voters from mainland Britain, Ulster Protestants have no more hope than Ulster Catholics of influencing the government by their votes.

In a world in which pacifists are relatively few and no government renounces the use of force, proponents of armed force invoke a variety of arguments to justify their actions. The IRA can point out that without a violent uprising, the Republic of Ireland would not have come into existence so soon. Ulster Protestants can claim that if the Crown ignores their views, they have just as much right to local self-determination as American colonists did in 1776. Because Northern Ireland itself is the battleground, armed groups are peculiarly dependent on local support for their survival. Locals will react against a group that perpetrates a particularly vicious act of terror, and even more against a group that invites retaliation against its community. The average Ulster citizen probably accepts the need for such groups as a "last resort" defense against being deserted by the British or Irish government in a time of need.

Censorious visitors to Ulster may tell the residents: "Don't you understand? It can't happen here." People who have lived through the troubles are likely to reply in a slow Ulster drawl: "But it has."

Incentives to Action and Inaction

Given the insoluble nature of the Northern Ireland political conflict, both the British and the Irish governments had no difficulty in justifying to themselves a policy of studied avoidance from the end of the Irish troubles of the 1920s until the recent troubles. The creation of a Northern Ireland Parliament that was responsible for maintaining law and order in Ulster protected the British government at Westminster from involvement in the exercise of its nominal responsibility. British ministers could dismiss awkward questions about activities in Ulster with the statement that this was not their responsibility.

Because Dublin's acceptance of the partition of the island of Ireland was challenged in a bloody civil war in the 1920s, it had no wish to agitate an issue that represented its failure to secure Irish unity. The Dublin government first turned inward, seeking to differentiate itself from Ulster as well as from Britain by developing a society that was Catholic and Gaelic, and then turned outward, hoping that economic development would stop massive postwar emigration.

Within Northern Ireland, there was a lopsided stalemate. Protestants saw no need to modify the Stormont regime, for it gave them all the powers of a Westminster-type parliamentary government, unchecked by an American-style bill of rights. Catholics saw no hope of modifying a regime in which they were an electoral minority. Only in a united Ireland could they exercise influence at the ballot box. The failure of IRA campaigns to change the government, and the inevitable police actions that the campaigns invited, made physical force unpopular, too. Catholics favored insubordination, but not violent rebellion. Protestants favored an order that placed power in their hands.[2]

Optimism created the first cracks in the status quo. In the early 1960s, a new generation of politicians had come forward in Northern Ireland who were not interested in fighting again the troubles of the 1920s. Terence O'Neill, who became unionist prime minister at Stormont in 1962, believed that economic development was desirable in itself for the material benefits it would bring. He also believed that economic change would reduce the communal divide: "If you give Roman Catholics a good job and a good house, they will live like Protestants because they will see neighbours with cars and television sets."[3] O'Neill was prepared to shake hands with the premier of the Irish Republic in pursuit of good relations between Ireland north and south. But the Ulster unionists were not prepared to shake hands with Ulster Catholics, nor were the Catholics seeking integration in a state that they rejected on principle. Politically, the biggest effect of O'Neill's quasi-ecumenical politics was to divide Protestants and give an opening to Dr. Ian Paisley to enter politics by raising the cry that O'Neill was giving an opening to "home rule and Rome rule" (that is, a united Ireland government).

A group of first-generation Catholic university graduates believed that civil rights movements worldwide were creating a climate in which they could advance demands peacefully and to some advantage through street marches and petitions. The marches they organized in 1968 attracted worldwide attention—and sympathy, too, when marchers were clubbed down by the Royal Ulster Constabulary. The British government pressed the O'Neill government to concede on matters such as the elimination of archaic and discriminatory franchise laws for local government elections. O'Neill's responses were too little and too late for the demonstrators, but too much for hardline Protestants. The civil rights groups soon lost control of events, as suppression of demonstrations by the Royal Ulster Constabulary rekindled republican sentiments.

In August 1969, a Protestant–Catholic confrontation during traditional Protestant parades in Londonderry was followed by violence throughout the province in which eight people were killed. Under duress, the British government committed troops to restore public order. Initially, the troops were welcomed by the Catholics. The Irish government offered verbal reassurances to the Catholics, who feared sectarian violence. The IRA cited the violence as evidence of the need for armed protection by IRA forces.

The introduction of troops in August 1969 was the product of pessimism, not optimism. With the local police out of control, the death toll rising, and uncertainty about what the Dublin government might do, there was an imperative need for action. The involvement of the British government in Ulster marked the destruction of its traditional policy of benign neglect. From then on, it would be immediately responsible for government. The only question was: How?

Governing without Consensus: Variations on a Theme

Governing with consensus is far easier than governing without it; a fully legitimate government is foolproof, whereas a government that lacks full legitimacy can be destabilized by the shortcomings of its governors as well as by the actions of its opponents. The history of government in Northern Ireland since 1969 is the story of a forlorn search for consensus. The British government had little grounds for believing consensus possible, but it had short-term political incentives for putting an overly optimistic gloss on a discouraging situation. Because the conflict was occurring within the United Kingdom, rather than in some remote colonial setting, the government could not easily dismiss difficulties as of no concern at Westminster, nor could it easily withdraw from a part of its home territory.[d]

In the distinctive circumstances of Northern Ireland, the only stable form of government would be one supported by a concurring majority, based on agreement freely given by four groups: a majority of Ulster Protestants, Ulster Catholics, the British government, and the Irish government. The British and Irish governments would almost certainly endorse any form of government that Ulster Protestants and Catholics jointly agreed to. However, these two groups consistently fail to concur. Even when some Protestants and some Catholics agree, divisions within their own communities mean that such agreement can be shot down, figuratively or literally, by others in their communities. In consequence, each group prefers to look for allies outside: The Ulster Protestants turn to the British government and the Ulster Catholics to the Irish government and, through it, to Irish influence further afield—for example, in the United States.

Although people on other continents can easily recommend what ought to be done about Northern Ireland, the British government, as the nominally sovereign power, has had the unique and daunting experience of trying to put its recommendations into effect. Whatever criticisms may be made of the British role in Northern Ireland, consistently following a single course of action is not one of them. By turns, the British government has sought to appeal to every group within Ulster; unintentionally if not intentionally, it has alienated every group or at least has planted seeds of suspicion that can sprout when the political temperature rises. The very different initiatives it has taken are described in the following sections.

Backing the Stormont Regime to the Hilt

When British troops went into Northern Ireland in 1969, they were acting in defense of the civil power. As long as the Stormont Parliament remained in being, this was the government that Ministry of Defense forces were defending. This was not the position desired by the Labour government, whose sympathies were with the Catholic minority. But neither Prime Minister Harold Wilson nor Home Secretary James Callaghan had any means of ordering the elected government of Northern Ireland to act. Their ultimate weapon—invoking the authority of the British Parliament to suspend the Northern Ireland Constitution—was described by ministers as "like the hydrogen bomb," having terrible consequences if used, for it would dump at the feet of the British cabinet the responsibility for everything that happened in Ulster.

The British government succeeded in extracting sufficient concessions from unionist prime ministers to split the Unionist party, for what was deemed a minimum move in London was regarded as going too far by many unionists. In consequence, Terence O'Neill and his successor, James Chichester-Clark, each had to resign as prime minister. However, the concessions were inadequate to appeal to Catholic electorate politicians. Moreover, the IRA used the violence of 1969 as an opportunity to build up substantial forces within Ulster, and by the spring of 1971, it had started the calculated killing of British soldiers and of Royal Ulster Constabulary policemen.

In August 1971, the British government accepted the logic of the IRA attack and counterattacked. The British Army was used in aid of the Stormont civil power to enforce internment—the arrest and detention of more than 300 Catholics suspected of alleged Republican activities. Internal war broke out with a vengeance, as internment mobilized the Catholic community in active support of the IRA. On January 30, 1972, British paratroopers fired on a nonviolent Catholic march in Londonderry, killing thirteen men.[4] These shootings, known as Bloody Sunday, prompted worldwide protests and an embarrassed silence by the British government. In Dublin, demonstrators attacked and burned the British embassy.

Repudiating the Stormont Regime

Within eight weeks of Bloody Sunday, the British government had ended the Stormont regime, deposing unionist Prime Minister Brian Faulkner. The powers of the popularly elected Northern Ireland Parliament were transferred to a British cabinet minister, the secretary of state for Northern Ireland, initially William Whitelaw. As a politician responsible to a British, not an Ulster constituency, the new Northern Ireland secretary was not so vulnerable to internal political pressures as the Stormont politicians had been. On the other hand, he had no electoral base whatsoever in Northern Ireland. Moreover, control of the day-to-day operations of government in Ulster remained in the hands of the established departments and agencies of the Stormont government. The new Northern Ireland Office brought in a top layer of British civil servants, with special concern for political and security initiatives. Because direct rule operated without any accountability to locally elected politicians, it thus had something in common with a colonial administration in the days of the British Empire.

The system of government established in 1972 was aptly described as "temporary direct rule." The British government was directly responsible, without the complications of a Parliament controlled by Ulster Unionists. Rule was meant to be temporary, for no cabinet member wanted to be permanently responsible for the government of a region whose troublesome nature was now exposed for all the world to see. Having gotten in, the aim of temporary direct rule was to get the British government out.

The violence in the province—in 1972 there were more than 10,000 shooting incidents, 1,300 explosions, and 467 killed—was an incentive to prompt action, but it gave no grounds for optimism. The Catholic Social Democratic and Labour party was moderately encouraged, for Stormont, the Protestant Parliament for a Protestant majority, was now gone. Bloody Friday—twenty-two coordinated IRA bomb attacks in public places in Belfast that killed nine bystanders in one afternoon in July 1972—temporarily undermined support for the IRA. The Protestants were demoralized and confused. They did not like the loss of their own government, but they could not, in principle, attack the British government for asserting its sovereignty. Criticism was directed at its failure to finish the IRA.

Coerced Power-Sharing

In place of the political vacuum created by suspending Stormont, William Whitelaw prescribed a "power-sharing" executive based on concurring majorities of Protestant and Catholic politicians. Such an administration could have been created by using the secretary of state's appointive powers. But then it would have had no claim to represent the population of Northern Ireland and no hope of substituting electoral politics for violence in the streets. The power-sharing executive was meant to be constituted by politicians elected to a new Northern Ireland assembly. Candidates and the electorate were informed that a Northern Ireland executive would be created only if Protestant and Catholic politicians were prepared to sit in it together.

The British government took a double gamble. First, it gambled that Ulster voters would elect to the new assembly a majority of politicians who were prepared to accept the terms of power-sharing. It could do nothing to influence the choice of candidates or the votes cast. Second, it gambled that the politicians elected would be willing to make common cause in office and, while doing so, could retain the support of their followers in the streets as well as at the ballot boxes.

The British government did not describe its policy as one of coercion, but it made clear to everyone concerned that it was not prepared to accept an elected Ulster body that would not support power-sharing. When the people of Ulster twice elected bodies that rejected power-sharing, each time the British government used its power of coercion to dismiss a freely elected representative body.

The power-sharing executive installed in January 1974 had the full backing of the Catholic Social Democratic and Labour party (SDLP) and of a part of the Ulster Unionists led by Brian Faulkner. The SDLP support was premised on the fact that the British government had coerced the Unionists to accept a vaguely defined "Irish dimension" in the new system of government. This was also the cause of Unionist divisions. As IRA violence continued, Protestant anxieties rose. In May 1974, the Ulster Workers Council, a Protestant body with strong ties to trade unions as well as to parliamentary groups, called a general strike in support of a demand for a new election to test whether or not the power-sharing executive represented a majority of the Northern Ireland people. The British government refused this request, but the British Army was unwilling to try breaking the strike. As the strike intensified to extend to essential services, the power-sharing executive fell. The British government had succeeded in coercing the Faulkner-led Unionists, but Faulkner could not coerce the Protestant electorate.[5]

In response to this new vacuum, the British government called an election for a constitutional convention to recommend a new instrument of government for Northern Ireland. But it also sought to coerce the convention by stipulating that it was prepared to accept only a power-sharing constitution. The majority of representatives elected to the convention were opposed to power-sharing. The respect of the convention majority was dismissed out of hand, *because* it represented the views of the anti–power-sharing majority of the Northern Ireland people. Killings escalated.[6]

"Chatting Up" Gunmen

Having failed to coerce elected politicians, the British government then briefly pursued a strategy of trying to "chat up" (that is, win the goodwill and confidence of) IRA and Protestant paramilitary organizations. Ever since 1969, political representatives of the British government had sought to open lines of communication with illegal forces, while the British Army sought to suppress those forces. The intensification of violence and the demonstrated power of the Ulster Workers' Council to bring down an elected assembly encouraged those engaged in British special operations to think that it might prove easier to deal with spokesmen for physical force.

In an effort to win the goodwill of the gunmen, the British government gave the Ulster Volunteer Force legal status in 1974. At the end of the year, the Provisional IRA proclaimed a cease-fire following talks at Feakle, in the Republic of Ireland. The British government recognized Sinn Fein "incident centers," where aggrieved Catholics and British officials could try to resolve specific disputes without resorting to violence, so that Sinn Fein, the electoral arm of the Irish republican movement, could work with the British Army to prevent unplanned disruptions of the cease-fire. The Social Democratic and Labour party decried this step, which undercut its standing in the Catholic community. The British government valued an agreement with Sinn Fein *because* it could speak for the IRA. As the British ambassador to Dublin put it, "Nobody was fooled by the switching of civilian hats and military caps."[7] The cease-fire soon collapsed, and the number of deaths by political violence rose in 1975 and 1976.

Direct Rule Takes Root

After the dismissal of the Northern Ireland constitutional convention in March 1976, the British government accepted that although direct rule was in form temporary, it was going to be around a long time.[8] The Labour Northern Ireland secretary, Roy Mason, formerly the minister of defense, backed the use of covert special forces in armed antiterrorist activities and also favored the "Ulsterization" of the conflict—that is, replacing British Army personnel by full-time and part-time Ulster Protestants in the Royal Ulster Constabulary and the Ulster Defense Regiment.[e] The total number of people killed in political violence fell below 100 in 1978, the first time this had happened in nearly a decade. Civil servants were encouraged to find ways of demonstrating that even though direct rule was not representative government, it was "good government," as that term is used by apolitical administrators.[9]

Within Northern Ireland, the continuance of direct rule was not unwelcome to Protestant politicians, for it confirmed the status of the province as a part of the United Kingdom. It was unpopular, however, with all kinds of Catholic political groups and with the Republic of Ireland, to which it offered no political advantages. The evident failure of contesting elections forced the Social Democratic and Labour party to become more aggressive in advocating steps to link Northern Ireland and the Republic. In 1981, a smaller, more experienced, and hardened IRA struck in a new direction: It called a hunger strike by republican prisoners jailed for violent crimes. By the time the hunger strike ended later in the year, ten IRA members had starved themselves to death in protest against British policy.

The hunger strike mobilized massive Catholic support for the republican cause. The first hunger striker, Bobby Sands—standing as a parliamentary candidate while in a prison cell—was elected as a member of the British Parliament in a by-election that was held in Fermanagh shortly before his death. Each death was followed by a public and highly political funeral. The days leading up to the deaths were closely watched in Northern Ireland. Ulster Protestants watched, too, declaring that the British government should not give in to intimidation by people pledged to overthrow by force the government of their part of the United Kingdom. Within Ulster, the hunger strike succeeded in the Sinn Fein aim of polarizing political opinion.

Talking to the Politicians Again

James Prior was made Northern Ireland secretary in September 1981, because the prime minister wished to remove him from a post where he had a right to comment on economic policy. Prior pronounced direct rule an unsatifactory, second-best solution. In its place, he proposed "rolling devolution"—in effect, an attempt to introduce power-sharing on a step-by-step basis. An assembly was elected in 1982 with only the right to scrutinize and question Northern Ireland officials. It was promised additional powers if there was a concurring majority of Protestant and Catholic members in agreement about a formula for power-sharing. There was no mention of an Irish dimension. This infuriated the Social Democratic and Labour party, which contested the assembly election but abstained from taking the seats it won there, as did Sinn Fein. The assembly failed to roll; it had collapsed from inanition before the end of its one and only term.

Agreement among Non-Ulstermen

The Anglo–Irish Agreement signed in November 1985 between the British and the Irish governments reflects the fact that non-Ulstermen find it far easier to agree about Northern Ireland than Ulster people do. The agreement is based on a coincidence of interests. Each government wishes to be seen by its own electorate as achieving progress about—if not actually in—Northern Ireland. Evidence of progress is also useful diplomatically, particularly in the United States, where the British government is fighting a defensive operation against American congresspersons who support Irish unity and the Irish government is contending with IRA spokesmen for the sympathies of Irish-Americans from Boston to San Francisco.

The Anglo–Irish Agreement was a great symbolic innovation. Although previous British initiatives had paid lip service to an Irish dimension, they had always included Ulster politicians and excluded direct involvement by the government of the Republic of Ireland. As appropriate for an international agreement, this initiative involved only the heads of the sovereign states affected. But Ulster politicians were not treated equally in the process of exclusion. The Social Democratic and Labour party was formally excluded but, in fact, had an important hand in the discussions. The Dublin government could hardly sign a document if it was not acceptable to the largest Catholic party in Northern Ireland. Ulster Unionists and Democratic Unionists were excluded from the discussions because the British government knew they would not like the result and did not consider their opposition to be very significant.

In form, the agreement established the Intergovernmental Conference in Belfast, with a small staff of British and Irish civil servants, to discuss a range of policies, including security and the administration of justice; it also pledged efforts at increased cross-border cooperation. Although the responsibility for administering the government remained with Britain, the Irish government was given the right to put forward proposals and to comment on matters of interest to the Catholic community. The agreement also pledged to diminish the role of the Intergovernmental Conference if Protestants and Catholics agreed to participate in a power-sharing administration for Northern Ireland.

In an unusual show of unity, Protestant politicians joined in opposition to the Anglo–Irish Agreement. The fact that it was signed by the British and Irish prime ministers, meeting in Northern Ireland without any representative of Ulster present, was interpreted as the denial of self-determination by the Ulster majority. Unionists paid more attention to clauses put in to mollify the Social Democratic and Labour party than to clauses put in to mollify themselves. From their reading of the agreement, they concluded that it was a step toward a united Ireland: Exclusion from deliberations was regarded as part of a deliberate British plan to "sell out" the Protestant majority. Deprived of a forum, the unionists fulminated. There was no acceleration of violence on the Protestant side—and no deceleration on the IRA side.

Conclusions

While unionists continue to proclaim that "Ulster says no" to the 1985 agreement, the Social Democratic and Labour party still awaits the next stage in its long-term goal of Irish unity. The symbolic nature of the accord means that there is no immediate impetus to further action. But Ulster politics, as this review has emphasized, is dynamic, not static. For two decades, periods of seeming quiet have been times when one or another group has organized to take an initiative intended to introduce a new form of destabilization. The object of political groups within Ulster is not to accept the status quo but to stimulate change by whatever means they have at hand.

Meanwhile, the British and Irish governments are satisfied that they have achieved a "temporary" Anglo–Irish Agreement to complement "temporary direct rule." Whereas direct rule is a tangible expression of Britain's authority in Northern Ireland, the agreement is a symbolic expression of the Republic's permanent aspiration for Irish unity. As long as there is no sign of a concurring majority, the Irish government has the easier task, maintaining its symbolic commitment to unity, while the British government has the hard task, governing without consensus.

Notes

a. The term *Crown* is used here to refer to the government that has been known since 1921 as the United Kingdom of Great Britain and Northern Ireland, now under Queen Elizabeth II. Until the Act of Union of Great Britain and Ireland in 1801, Ireland was a separate kingdom of the Crown.

b. Ulster is the name for a historic nine-county province of Ireland. In 1921, six of its counties—Antrim, Down, Armagh, Londonderry, Tyrone, and Fermanagh—formed Northern Ireland; three other predominantly Catholic counties—Donegal, Cavan, and Monaghan—became part of what is now the Republic. For euphony, the term *Ulster* is often used as a synonym for Northern Ireland.

c. Although political parties do not like being described by the religion of their voters, the fact remains that the support of each of the four parties named is almost exclusively from one religion. Opinion polls indicate that there are a minuscule number of Protestants who support Irish unity and a limited but significant minority of Catholics who are prepared to remain within the United Kingdom—albeit not on terms acceptable to the two unionist parties.

d. Nor has the Dublin government made realistic preparations to take over responsibility for governing Northern Ireland, for it fully realizes that doing this would leave it with the problem of coercing 1 million Protestants.

e. The forces were open to Catholics, and the British government actively sought to recruit Catholic members after 1969, but few came forward to join; and Catholic members of the security forces have been vulnerable to being murdered by the IRA, just as Protestants are.

References

1. For a guide to the various paramilitary organizations and statistics of violence (and for much other useful information), see W.D. Flackes, *Northern Ireland: A Political Directory* (London: BBC Publications, 1983).

2. For a survey of attitudes at this time, which also emphasizes the many nonpolitical similarities between Protestants and Catholics, see Richard Rose, *Governing without Consensus: An Irish Perspective* (Boston: Beacon Press, 1971).

3. Quoted in Rose, *Governing without Consensus,* p. 301.

4. For the British justification, see *Report of the Tribunal,* chaired by Lord Justice Widgery, HC 220 (London: HMSO, 1972). For an independent assessment of the same evidence, see the report prepared by the American lawyer Samuel Dash (sub-

sequently special prosecutor for Watergate), *Justice Denied* (New York: International League for the Rights of Man, 1972).

5. For an informed and detailed account of this unusual event, see Robert Fisk, *The Point of No Return: The Strike Which Broke the British in Ulster* (London: Andre Deutsch, 1975).

6. On the events leading up to the constitutional convention and the outcome, see Richard Rose, *Northern Ireland: A Time of Choice* (Washington, DC: American Enterprise Institute, 1976).

7. Sir John Peck, *Dublin from Downing Street* (Dublin and London: Gill and Macmillan, 1978), p. 20. See, also, Flackes, *Northern Ireland,* pp. 91–94; and Richard Rose, "Is the United Kingdom a State?" in P. Madgwick and Richard Rose, eds., *The Territorial Dimension in United Kingdom Politics* (London: Macmillan, 1982), pp. 100–136.

8. For a detailed analysis of the evolution of the institutions of direct rule, see Derek Birrell and Alan Murie, *Policy and Government in Northern Ireland* (Dublin: Gill and Macmillan, 1980).

9. For an analysis of steps taken, see P.N. Bell, "Direct Rule in Northern Ireland," in Richard Rose, ed., *Ministers and Ministries* (Oxford: Oxford University Press, 1987), pp. 189–226.

10

Northern Ireland: The Persistence and Limitations of Violence

John Darby

The Irish conflict, it has often been observed, is a very contrary one. Every time the English find an answer, the Irish change the question. One of the central paradoxes of the conflict in Northern Ireland is the apparent contradiction between its two dominant characteristics—its persistence and its relatively low level of violence. These two phenomena help to define it as an essentially limited and controlled conflict, unlikely to be eliminated and unlikely to become significantly worse. Together, they provide insurance that the level of conflict will not become intolerable and set up an obstacle to radical approaches.

Seventeenth-Century Roots

It is easier to demonstrate the persistence of the Irish conflict than to explain its low level of violence. The arrival of Scottish and English planters in the early seventeenth century provided the demographic basis for the conflict in Ulster, which was to concentrate the native Irish in areas separate from those of the colonizing Scots and English. The newcomers differed significantly from the native Irish in religion, language, social customs, and economic status. Nevertheless, despite attempts to maintain these distinctions, there was considerable mixing from the start, and soon after the plantation, the attempts to retain demographic segregation were informally abandoned.

Violence was a central feature of the conflict between the dominant planters and the subordinate Gaels, but its motives and forms of expression were inconsistent. Collective rural violence was a bewildering confusion of faction fighting, grievances about land, political protest, and "elements of carnival."[1]

The Persistence of Violence

In Ulster, where the balance between Protestants and Catholics was closer than in other parts of Ireland, rural violence was also fueled by sectarian rivalry. "The sectarian divide was too functional to be permitted to disappear."[2] Changes in land ownership and tenancies were the measure of success or failure and were tenaciously resisted or sought. Although the intensity of sectarian violence fluctuated greatly, it exerted a pervasive influence on the day-to-day living of many communities in nineteenth-century Ulster.

With the growth of industrial Belfast from the early nineteenth century, sectarian violence became increasingly an urban phenomenon. Between 1835 and 1935, there were eight periods of serious rioting in Belfast (1835, 1857, 1864, 1872, 1886, 1898, 1920–22, and 1935 are years in which some disturbances were recorded). There were also two serious riots in Londonderry (1869 and 1884).

The current period of violence, which has been uninterrupted, except for variations in form and intensity, since 1969, is the longest and most sustained of all. It followed a period when all signs appeared to indicate an end to the sectarianism of the past.

Why this persistent violence? The first of two possible explanations is essentially an ethnic analysis, which points to a consciousness of collective identity as the prime moving force in Irish history. As early as 1814, a parish minister from County Antrim put it plainly: "The inhabitants of the parish are divided into two races of men as totally distinct as if they belonged to different countries and religions. These may be distinguished by the usual names of Scotch and Irish."[3] In particular, the nationalist ideal of Irish unity has provided the furniture for ideology—the dates, the heroes, the heroic deeds recorded in song and poetry, the language, the culture; and the British and the unionists have been obstacles in the way of achieving the great vision of a united Ireland. The removal of these obstacles has been the task taken on by the Irish Republican Army (IRA) since its formation. Nationalists regard the unionists as heretics, to be consigned to whatever fate their heresy deserves. For their part, the unionists have to live with the paradox of maintaining an ideology rooted in British values while distrusting British governments. Their loyalty is to union with a Britain that is patently impatient with their intransigence. Nationalists, by definition, threaten this union and so are viewed by unionists as traitors with whom compromise is impossible.

It has often been pointed out that the historial roots of both ideologies are suspect and, particularly, that the doctrine of nationality is historical nonsense invented in the nineteenth century. Even the notion that Irish unity has been handed down from generation to generation as a holy grail is doubtful. However, it is aspiration that counts, not whether the ideologies are legitimate.

The other main explanation for the persistence of the conflict is based on economics. The first official inquiry into the present violence, the 1969 Cameron Report, came out with a comforting two-word analysis: "jobs and houses."[4] According to this liberal analysis, there is nothing wrong that

50,000 jobs would not cure. It would certainly provide some comfort if the Irish conflict could be identified with economic deprivation. The problem is that there appears to be no historical relationship between general economic conditions and the tendency toward rioting. Violence has broken out apparently randomly during periods of prosperity and depression.

A more sophisticated economic analysis looks to the specific grievances of the Catholic minority, rather than to general economic depression. The disparity between the Catholic and Protestant communities has remained remarkably stubborn despite reforms since 1969. At present, the unemployment rate for Catholic males is 2.5 times that of Protestant males, and the rate for Catholic females is 1.5 times that of Protestant females. A government discussion paper published in 1986 confirmed that "between 1971–85 the Catholic community's disadvantage in employment remained both quantitative and qualitative, obtained throughout the province and persisted despite progressive convergence of educational attainment between the two communities."[5] The disparity cannot be satisfactorily explained by educational, cultural, or demographic characteristics. Direct discrimination also seems to be a minor factor. The inequality rests primarily on historical discrimination perpetuated through current employment practices—the inertia factor.

There is no doubt that the relative deprivation of the minority community is a cause of alienation and discontent. It is less easy to show a correlation between unemployment and involvement in violence. The avowed aims and targets of the IRA do not aim at removing such disparity or providing jobs. On the contrary, its bombing campaign has reduced jobs, at least in the short term. Nor is it easy to see any relationship between the removal of Catholic grievances about housing and a reduction of violence or support for the IRA.

The Low Level of Violence

It is important to remember that this persistent antagonism has been between two ethnic groups, not between hostile neighboring countries. The distinctions between ethnic conflicts and international wars are significant. In ethnic conflicts, the combatants permanently inhabit the same battlefield. It is not possible to terminate hostilities by withdrawal behind national frontiers. Even during tranquil periods, their lives are often intermeshed with those of their enemies. As a consequence, intercommunity conflict is often characterized by internecine viciousness, rather than by the more impassive slaughter of a war.

In such circumstances, community conflicts, unless arrested at an early stage, tend to develop along predictable lines: They expand to involve a greater number of activists, disputing a greater number of issues; disagreement grows into antagonism; enemies become more efficiently organized under more implacable leaders; and the restraints on decent behavior are weakened as the dangerous elements overwhelm the more moderate.

Against this general pattern, consider the conflict in Northern Ireland. Its origins, depending on one's political perspective, have been traced to various points between the twelfth century and 1969. Since 1969, it has been persistently violent. There has certainly been ample time for the dangerous elements to drive out the restraining ones.

During the early 1970s, many observers believed that the upsurge of violence could only lead to one of two outcomes: The belligerents would either be shocked into an internal accommodation or propelled into genocidal slaughter. Neither occurred. More than a decade later, a settlement seemed further away than ever, and the level of violence, though remarkably persistent, had not intensified.

On the contrary, there is evidence that community violence has diminished rather than increased in intensity at both provincial and local levels. Having reached a peak of 468 in 1972, annual casualty figures declined to 64 in 1984. The proportion of civilian, as opposed to admitted combatant, deaths diminished, and the number from direct violence between the communities almost disappeared. By 1984, it was difficult to find any examples of the sectarian rioting that had been the main form of violence in 1969 and 1970. Why weren't the two communities drawn into more violent confrontation?

There are three principal reasons for this low level of violence. The first is to be found in the dynamic of the violence itself. Since 1970, its main form has changed from sectarian rioting into a guerrilla war between republican paramilitaries and the British Army. More recently, it has been predominantly a struggle between the IRA and the security forces. In any case, the conflict was increasingly fought through surrogates and became somewhat ritualized. This allowed many people from both sides to maintain their sympathies but to withdraw from direct involvement in violence.

The second reason is the manner in which the military activities have been conducted. Engagements between the IRA and the British Army have been carried out within limits defined by the IRA's own choice. There have certainly been plenty of civilian and accidental casualties; however, the IRA's concept of limiting violence to "legitimate targets" has reduced casualties by applying limitations to the conduct of the war. It is undeniable that the definition of *legitimate* has been constantly changing. It came to include civilian workers and caterers in army camps, as well as policemen who had resigned from the force. In 1987, it allowed the shooting of a part-time prison instructor on a campus of the University of Ulster and the bombing of a judge and his wife. Nevertheless, whether the application of the concept is dictated by altruism or necessity, it is, in effect, an artificial, self-imposed constraint by combatants on their activities.

Mechanisms to Regulate and Control Violence

Although the foregoing reasons help to explain the reduction in violence in Northern Ireland, the fundamental reason for the low level of violence arises from the relationships between Protestants and Catholics within their local communities. According to Shibutani and Kwan, the most important factors in determining the course of a conflict are the peculiar interrelationships between the combatants: "What each side does is a response to the actual or anticipated moves of its opponents; thus the course of events is built up by social interaction."[6] This process often intensifies the conflict by creating a spiral toward unrestrained violence. In Northern Ireland, however, the same reciprocal process has controlled rather than stimulated the spread of violence. The long duration of the conflict between Catholics and Protestants over three centuries has led to the evolution of social mechanisms to regulate and control their relationships. The two hostile groups that inhabit what A.T.Q. Stewart called the same "narrow ground," though unwilling to assimilate and unable to remove each other, gradually evolved forms of relationships that regulated rather than resolved their antagonisms.[7] Each mechanism was appropriate to a particular setting, varying between urban and rural conditions and in accordance with the religious ratio peculiar to each locality. The mechanisms were not always successful.

The most significant of these mechanisms are avoidance, situational variations in relationships, and functional integration.

Avoidance

In some parts of Northern Ireland, Catholics and Protestants have effectively avoided conflict by avoiding each other. In urban areas, especially those that experienced intimidation and enforced population in the early 1970s, the boundary between the Catholics and the Protestants is often marked by physical barriers requested by the inhabitants. It is ironic that "successful" intimidation in 1971, by reducing the number of minority families and, hence, the occasions for tension in urban communities, helped to account for the virtual disappearance of intimidation by 1975. Segregation has often reduced violence.

Situational Variations in Relationships

Complete avoidance between Catholics and Protestants is impossible in most parts of Northern Ireland. Most people may "mingle with a consciousness of the differences between them,"[8] but they do mingle. In most places, it is possible for members of the two groups to develop relationships without abandoning their separate basic allegiances. They may drink in the same pubs, use the same shops, work together, and belong to the same clubs. Much depends on the demographic mix in the neighborhood, or even on the setting. In his novel *No Surrender* (1960), Robert Harbinson described how, although he shunned and feared Catholics during his childhood in Protestant Sandy Row, it was possible for him to become friendly with a Catholic family while on holidays in another part of the province.

The advantage of these situational variations is that they permit changes to evolve at their own speed. Even during periods of tension, it is possible for a Protestant and a Catholic, each of whom would regard the other with suspicion if seen in his district at night, to suspend animosities and continue to work at the same workbench during the day. The limits to the relationships are determined by the context, and the context itself has varied through time.

Functional Integration

Although relationships between members of the two communities may vary with circumstances, certain groups in any community are more disposed toward cooperation than others. Protestants and Catholics from the middle classes are much more likely to be in contact than those from the working classes, through common membership in clubs and societies. There is also plenty of evidence that common material or social interests can overcome sectarian suspicions.

"Reconciliation groups," whose objective was to bring together Catholics and Protestants, have been much less successful. In districts that had experienced sectarian violence, the argument that people should get together because they had been hostile toward one another was not persuasive.

All these mechanisms act as restraints on the conduct of the two conflicting communities. They demonstrate that there is a wide spectrum of intergroup relationships. At one end is a highly polarized, potentially violent relationship; at the other is a high level of cooperation and interaction. Individuals and communities throughout Northern Ireland differ as to where they are on this spectrum. Nor is the spectrum itself static; it has altered through time, and the alterations have accelerated most dramatically in times of community violence.

Controls and Communities

The cumulative effect of so great a variety of microcontrols also constitutes a macrocontrol. In effect, the control mechanisms prevent absolute group cohesion in both communities, thereby standing in the way of a more extreme and genocidal form of conflict.

The variety of local relationships has produced, within each religious group, a gap between the members at the center and those at the periphery. At the center is the person who lives in the heart of his own group and whose contact with the other religious group is minimal. His political and cultural attitudes are not contaminated by the views or desires of his opponents, because he does not know what they are. He is relatively untouched by either the ties or the fears of his coreligionists who live among members of the other group. The problem seems uncomplicated and the solution—"Smash the IRA" or "Brits out"—simple. All that goes on around him, even internal disputes, confirms him in the uncompromising purity of his position.

On the periphery is the person who lives in a more or less integrated area. He shares cultural connections with the other side, which create an obligation of decent behavior. His friends and workmates are likely to include members of the other religious group. If he belongs to the local minority, he may be aware of his vulnerability if violence should spread to his locality. Consequently, both his inclinations and his apprehensions are more likely to urge him toward accommodation and compromise. In the view of his coreligionists at the center, he is a "trimmer."

The Northern Ireland problem has often been described as a conflict between two communities. In another sense, it is a conflict between two different concepts of community. On the one hand, most people in Northern Ireland, whether they wish it or not, recognize that they are born into a Catholic or Protestant community that shares beliefs, culture, and problems, but not a geographic base. They are also born into a geographic community, a small localized territorial group defined as a unit by its members. Both carry obligations and loyalties.

Both concepts of community might be regarded as magnets that exert pull on the loyalty of the individual. In less dramatic times, the strength of the ethnic magnet is determined by a number of factors, including local religious ratios, previous experience of violence, and distance from the ideological heartlands. In times of extreme tension and violence, the attraction of the ethnic magnet becomes more powerful. During the Ulster Workers' Council strike in 1974, for example, many Protestants felt the need to demonstrate their membership in the Protestant community by participating in demonstrations or manning barricades, even at the price of antagonizing or frightening their Catholic friends. Seven years later, the hunger strikes had a similar effect on many Catholics, and Protestants were alarmed by the number of previously nonpolitical Catholics who attended the funerals of dead hunger-strikers. Even districts that took pride in their long history of good community relations were affected by the pull. Ethnic identities, like seeds, can lie inert for decades and still retain their fertility. They are activated, not by the duration of the conflict but by its periodic eruption into spasms of intense violence. In the final analysis, however, the more violent the conflict becomes, the more likely are the outlying members of the group to be pulled toward positions defined by the center. The controls provide no guarantees.

The Way Ahead

Even if it is agreed that the controls of the conflict are effective, few would accept that the endemic violence in Northern Ireland is tolerable. Indeed, the more efficient the controls, the less the incentive to confront the problem and seek a "solution." Richard Rose, another contributor to this volume, has little sympathy for such a search. Instead, he believes that the problem is that there is no solution.[9]

This gloomy view has a positive as well as a negative side. If it is accepted, the consequence is that it may be more sensible to seek to improve the situation, rather than to "solve" the problem. The emphasis should be shifted, at least in the short term, away from a vain search for a political solution toward more concrete, and perhaps more realizable, objectives. How might those mechanisms be supported which have preserved for most people a relatively normal life despite the persistence of violence? How can the economic and social inequalities that led to the outbreak of violence in the 1960s be removed? Is it important to support the new integrated schools that have developed so rapidly since 1980? In other words, given the apparent political stalemate, is there not a strong case for introducing internal reforms that will remove minority, and majority, grievances?

An awkward problem lurks in the interface between the use of violence and the demand for reform. It is often assumed that the first arises from the second. Certainly, it seems likely that a long-term easing of violence depends on the removal of legitimate grievances. However, as already mentioned, there is no evidence that one directly affects the other, at least in the short term. Neither is there convincing evidence that the perception of relative deprivation by Catholics has increased support for the IRA.

In Northern Ireland, demands for socioeconomic reform have been expressed mainly through legal processes, and demands for British withdrawal and Irish unification have been expressed through violence.

In the meantime, I take my stand with Arthur Koestler's plea for pragmatism:

> What we need is an active fraternity of pessimists. They will not aim at immediate radical solutions, because they know that these cannot be achieved in the hollow of the historical wave; they will not brandish the surgeon's knife at the social body, because they know that their own instruments are polluted. They will watch with open eyes and without sectarian blinkers for the first sign of the new horizontal movement; when it comes they will assist its birth; but if it does not come in their lifetime they will not despair. And meantime their chief aim will be to create oases in the interregnum desert.[10]

References

1. P. Townsend, *Political Violence in Ireland* (New York: Oxford University Press, 1983), p. 46.

2. *Ibid.*

3. Quoted in *Community Forum* 4 (1974) (journal of the Northern Ireland Community Relations Commission, Belfast, now defunct).

4. Cameron Committee, *Disturbances in Northern Ireland* (Belfast: Her Majesty's Stationery Office, 1969).

5. Northern Ireland's Department of Economic Development, *Equality of Opportunity in Employment in Northern Ireland* (Belfast: Her Majesty's Stationery Office, 1986), p. 5.

6. T. Shibutani and K. Kwan, "Changes in Life Conditions Conducive to Interracial Conflict," in G. Marx, ed., *Racial Conflict* (Boston: Little, Brown, 1971), p. 135.

7. A.T.Q. Stewart, *The Narrow Ground* (London: Faber and Faber, 1977).

8. J.C. Beckett and R. Glasscock, eds., *Belfast: The Origin and Growth of an Industrial City* (London: BBC Publications, 1967), p. 188.

9. R. Rose, *Northern Ireland: A Time for Choice* (Washington, DC: American Enterprise Institute 1976).

10. A. Koestler, *The Yogi and the Commissar and Other Essays* (London: Macmillan, 1965).

11

Northern Ireland: Political Strategies for the Management of Conflict

Padraig O'Malley

British Political Initiatives: 1972–84

In March 1972, the British government prorogued the Stormont Parliament and instituted direct rule. During the next thirteen years, the government launched five political initiatives that were designed to bring some measure of self-government to Northern Ireland.

The first white paper on Northern Ireland's constitutional future appeared in March 1973.[1] It proposed a new, seventy-eight member assembly for Northern Ireland, elected by proportional representation. The assembly would take over the day-to-day government of Northern Ireland, though Westminster would retain control over security. The white paper also advanced the idea of power-sharing to guarantee minority representation in the government. Elections for the new assembly were held in June 1973, and after five months of wrangling, the Social Democratic and Labour party (SDLP), the Unionist party, and the Alliance party agreed to form a power-sharing executive.

Within a month, the three parties met with the British and Irish governments at Sunningdale, England, to work out the political framework in which the new government would operate. The Irish government, for the first time, recognized the de facto existence of Northern Ireland when it agreed to the stipulation that a change in the constitutional status of Northern Ireland would require the consent of a majority of the people there. For its part, the British government gave a positive expression of its willingness not to stand in the way of a united Ireland if consensus for one did emerge, and the Northern Ireland executive, under pressure from Westminster and the SDLP, agreed to a council of Ireland to give institutional expression to the "Irish dimension." The council was to have two tiers. The first tier, a council of ministers, would have consisted of seven ministers from both Dail Eireann and the Northern Ireland assembly, and decisions would have required a unanimous vote. The second tier, a consultative assembly made up of sixty members—thirty from each side, elected by members of both parliaments—would have an advisory role.

The new arrangements were short-lived; indeed, the Irish dimension aspect of the agreement never moved beyond the blueprint stage. Rather than face down the militant Ulster Workers' Council strike, called in May 1974 to protest the proposed council of Ireland, the newly elected Labour government stood aside, thus ensuring the collapse of the agreement and the experiment in power-sharing. For nationalists, the government's actions had more than a touch of familiarity. In their view, Britain's failure to take a stand was part of a historical pattern, no different from its reneging on home rule in 1914 when it appeared that militant unionists were prepared to take up arms against the Crown. The lesson then—and again in 1974—was clear: The British government would back down in the face of the threat of unionist violence.

Thereafter, the "initiatives" were, for the most part, an exercise in form. The constitutional convention of 1975–76 was an elected conference of Northern Ireland parties that tried to come up with a form of government for Northern Ireland that would command widespread community acceptance. A majority of the seats in the convention were held by unionists, and the report submitted to Westminster at the end of 1975 recommended a return to majority rule, albeit with a committee assignment system that was weighted somewhat in favor of nationalists—a measure that was sufficient, in the eyes of unionists, to safeguard minority rights. Not surprisingly, this proposal was rejected by the British parliament, and although the convention was recalled at the start of 1976 to reconsider its findings, it ended its sittings in March of that year without reaching any agreement acceptable to Westminster. Unionists remained adamant: Majority rule was democratic rule.

A framework for an interim form of devolution was the brainchild of the fourth secretary of state, Roy Mason, in 1977–78. His call for negotiations was rejected, however, by both the SDLP and the Official Unionist party. In 1980, the fifth secretary of state, Humphrey Atkins, produced yet another white paper, setting out two options for safeguarding the interests of the minority, but his negotiations with the political parties simply petered out.[2]

Next it was the turn of the sixth secretary of state, James Prior, who came up with still another variation of the power-sharing/constitutional convention formula. His plan called for "rolling devolution"—a seventy-eight member assembly that would determine how power should be exercised, the crucial requirement being that the assembly's recommendations would have to command "widespread acceptance throughout the community."[3] To ensure this, up to 70 percent of the members would have to agree on how devolved power should be exercised. Devolution could be either total or partial—that is, on a department by department basis—and it could be revoked: hence the appellation "rolling devolution." But even if devolution failed to "roll," the assembly would have powers to "debate, vote and report" on impending legislation and other matters and to have its reports laid before Westminster. It would also have a system of committees that would "monitor and scrutinize the work of the departments," thereby allowing it "to influence the development of policy from the onset of the Assembly's life." No specific provision was made on the question of an Irish dimension, although the white paper did acknowledge that "the difference in identity and aspiration" that lay at the heart of the problem "could not be ignored or wished away."

The SDLP and the Dublin government of Charles Haughey rejected the white paper out of hand: the SDLP because power-sharing was not being offered as a right but "only on the basis of it being granted by Unionists" and because "there was no provision for a very strong and positive and concrete expression of Irish identity"; the Haughey government because it viewed Prior's proposal as a measure to resuscitate once again, by artificial means, "a failed political entity."

Elections for the assembly were held in October 1982, and although the SDLP contested them, it did so on a manifesto that it would boycott the assembly. Sinn Fein, the political party of the Irish Republican Army (IRA), having seen the effectiveness of electoral intervention during the hunger strikes in 1981, also contested the elections on an abstentionist platform and secured 33 percent of the nationalist vote—occasioning at least slight tremors of apprehension among government officials in Dublin and London and raising questions regarding the continued viability of what appeared to be a somewhat divided and dispirited SDLP.

The new assembly met at Stormont for the first time on November 11, 1982, with only members of the Democratic Unionist party, the Official Unionist party, and the Alliance attending. For a period during 1983 and 1984, the Official Unionist party boycotted it—not that the party's absence made any difference. From the start, the assembly was stillborn—a talking shop for unionists—and the government unceremoniously wound it up when its first term expired in October 1986.

Despite the lack of success that attended the attempted political initiatives throughout this period, the basis for a political formula remained in place. Successive Irish governments accepted that the status of Northern Ireland would not change without the consent of a majority of the people there, and successive British governments acknowledged that an Irish dimension existed and that a devolved government would have to have the support of the nationalist community.

In two crucial respects, however, the capacities of both governments, but especially the British government, to translate good intentions into political actions were severely circumscribed by the entrenched, unmovable positions of their respective clients. The unionists, secure in their constitutional position under the Northern Ireland Constitution Act of 1973 and tenacious in their belief that their numbers alone exempted them from being coerced into any form of devolved government that did not countenance majority rule—or any north–south relationship that involved more than mere "neighborliness"—

were in a position to veto every proposal. Moreover, since their position on an Irish dimension was absolute, the fact that it was associated with devolution made any progress on devolution impossible. Devolution would require their making concessions on the sharing of power with the Social Democratic and Labour party, and an Irish dimension would involve their making concessions to the south. On the nationalist side, the refusal of the SDLP to enter into any discussion of devolution without a prior undertaking that an Irish dimension was an issue of at least equal standing gave it, too, a veto power that led to paralysis. Accordingly, the British government's power to move the political parties in the north in the direction of an accommodation was severely curtailed. It was a zero-sum game: Anything that appeared to be acceptable to unionists was a sufficient reason for its rejection by nationalists; and conversely, anything that appeared to be acceptable to nationalists was a sufficient reason for its rejection by unionists.

The Anglo–Irish Agreement: Sharing the Responsibility

The Anglo–Irish process, initiated in May 1980 by Irish Prime Minister Charles Haughey and British Prime Minister Margaret Thatcher, resulted in a series of summit meetings in December 1980, November 1981, November 1983, and November 1984 between the prime ministers of both countries. The communique following the December 1980 meeting set the broad frame of reference. It called for bilateral meetings to give "special consideration to the totality of relationships within these islands" and commissioned "joint studies on a range of issues including possible new institutional structures." In November 1981, both governments agreed to establish an Anglo–Irish intergovernmental council to give institutional expression "to the unique character of the relationship between the two countries." The council met on a regular basis—indeed, in one eighteen-month period, November 1983 to March 1985, it met on no less than thirty occasions.[4] In short, the basis was laid for an institutional framework within which the Irish and British governments could accommodate their mutual interests and debate their often not inconsiderable differences on a whole range of matters, including Northern Ireland. Such institutional relationships, it was clear, was not subject to the veto powers of the northern parties. The Anglo–Irish process, therefore, was the first step in shifting the framework for a solution out of the narrow confines of Northern Ireland and making it the shared responsibility of the two sovereign governments.

The summit held at Hillsborough Castle, County Down, on November 15, 1985—at which British Prime Minister Thatcher and her then Irish counterpart, Garret Fitzgerald, affixed their signatures to the Anglo–Irish

Agreement—was, according to the communique that followed it, "the third meeting of the Anglo–Irish Intergovernmental Council to be held at the level of Heads of State."

The agreement—which was ratified by Dail Eireann on November 21 by 88 votes to 75 and by the House of Commons on November 27 by 473 to 47, and which was registered under Article 102 of the Charter of the United Nations on December 20—effectively gave Dublin a consultative role in the governing of Northern Ireland.

The agreement was succinct, its brevity almost concealing the craftsmanship that went into its wording.[5] First, both governments affirmed that any change in the status of Northern Ireland would come about only with the consent of a majority of the people of Northern Ireland. Both governments recognized that at present, the unionist majority wished for no change in the status of Northern Ireland. And both governments promised to introduce and support in their respective parliaments legislation to secure a united Ireland if, in the future, a majority of the people in Northern Ireland clearly wished for and formally consented to the establishment of a united Ireland.

Second, the two governments agreed to set up the Intergovernmental Conference, which would be jointly chaired by the British secretary of state for Northern Ireland, currently Tom King, and a "Permanent Irish Ministerial Representative"—at present, the minister for foreign affairs, Brian Linehan. The functions of the conference would pertain both to Northern Ireland and to the Republic of Ireland, specifically with regard to political matters, security arrangements, the administration of justice, and the promotion of cross-border cooperation. A provision specifying that "determined efforts shall be made through the Conference to resolve any differences"—a binding legal obligation with precedent in international law—ensured that the Irish government's role would be more than merely consultative (though less than fully executive).

Third, both London and Dublin supported the idea of a devolved government, to deal with a range of matters within Northern Ireland, that would command "widespread acceptance throughout the community." Should this occur, Dublin would, nevertheless, retain a say in certain areas affecting the interests of the nationalist minority (such as security arrangements and human rights). If devolution were not to come to pass, then Dublin would continue to have a say in all matters that affect nationalists. Finally, the agreement specified that after three years, the workings of the conference would be reviewed "to see if any changes in the scope and nature of its activities is desirable."

The logic of the agreement and the ordering of the priorities was as follows: First, work out the relationships between the two governments on a government-to-government basis; develop a set of institutional arrangements that are not susceptible to the shifting vagaries of political actions in the north; and then look for an internal settlement within Northern Ireland. Thus, because widespread unionist opposition to the agreement was anticipated, it provided an inducement to encourage unionists to negotiate an acceptable form of devolution with nationalists. On the one hand, there is the carrot: The more willing unionists are to share power with nationalists, the smaller the role of the conference and, hence, the smaller the role of the south in the affairs of the north. On the other hand, there is the stick: The longer unionists refuse to share power, the larger and more long-lasting the role of the south in the affairs of the north. In this sense, the agreement was designed to undermine unionist intransigence.

The Anglo–Irish Agreement initially brought together strange bedfellows. Fianna Fail, Sinn Fein, and the unionist parties opposed it with varying degrees of vehemence; the Social Democratic and Labour party, the Alliance, and the coalition parties in the Republic (Fine Gael and Labour) supported it with various degrees of enthusiasm. The British political parties, in a rare display of unanimity—and being more than willing to have Britain's Ireland problem become, in some small and more obvious measure, Ireland's problem—gave it their unconditional imprimatur.

In Northern Ireland, most nationalists enthusiastically supported the agreement and all unionists overwhelmingly rejected it—and that broad equation of support and rejection has generally remained in the same balance to the present, reflecting, perhaps, the conflict's zero-sum attributes. In part, nationalist support for the agreement continues to remain strong because unionists continue to oppose it strongly. Nationalists, it seems, are disposed to believe that there must be something in the agreement for them, if only because unionists reject it so completely.

In fact, the agreement has not been a cure-all for nationalist grievances, and its tangible benefits are few. Many of the achievements attributed to it— such as repeal of the Flags and Emblem Act; the decision to abolish the Divis, Unity, and Rossville flats; the greater powers police have to control parades; reforms in the Emergency Laws, reducing the maximum period police can hold suspects from seventy-two to forty-eight hours; the atrophy of the super-grass system; the proposals to tackle job discrimination; a new code of conduct for the Royal Ulster Constabulary; and better procedures for handling complaints against the police—would probably have come about even in the absence of the agreement, though not, perhaps, as expeditiously.

The agreement has had no significant impact on the level of violence—the numbers of killings in 1986 and the first part of 1987 were above 1985 levels. The IRA still strikes randomly, ruthlessly, and with little regard for life; the loyalist paramilitaries can ply their deadly trade with an enthusiasm that sometimes borders on the pathological; and the divisions between the two communities remain as great as ever. So, in terms of facts and figures and the more obvious measurements of progress—and always bearing in mind that what is progress to one community is more often than not anathema to the other—the agreement has hardly lived up to its early billing.

Indeed, in terms of the extent to which the agreement has achieved one of its principal aims—that is, the extent to which it has promoted peace and stability in Northern Ireland (where some 16,000 British troops are now stationed, and political violence has claimed more than 2,600 lives during the past eighteen years) and helped to reconcile the unionist and nationalist communities—it must be considered a failure.

However, to judge the agreement in these terms alone would be to misunderstand its real purpose and the profound impact it has had on the unionist psyche.

The Historic Significance of the Anglo–Irish Agreement

There can be no doubting the agreement's historic significance. For the first time since 1920, when the partition of Ireland occurred, the British government has explicitly recognized that the Republic of Ireland has a role to play in the governance of Northern Ireland—a far cry from the Downing Street declaration of 1969 that "responsibility for affairs in Northern Ireland is entirely a matter of domestic jurisdiction," or from the 1982 declaration by the Foreign Office that Britain considered itself "under no obligation to consult the Dublin government about matters affecting Northern Ireland." Giving Dublin a role in Northern Ireland constitutes an implicit acknowledgment by Britain that the partition of Ireland, in political and social terms, has been a failure. For its part, the Irish government has explicitly accepted the fact that Northern Ireland will remain within the United Kingdom as long as that is the wish of a majority of the people there. This amounts to an implicit acknowledgment that unification is an aspiration, not an inevitability. The agreement, therefore, is a quid pro quo of sorts. In exchange for the Irish government's recognition that unionists have the right to say no to a united Ireland, the British government was prepared to give the Irish government a role in Northern Ireland in areas relating to the aspirations, interests, and identity of the nationalist minority. It was prepared to give concrete institutional expression to an Irish dimension.

Accordingly, the status quo that had existed from 1920 to 1985 was destroyed with two strokes of the pen; and if the Union as unionists knew it was over, so, too, were the fanciful notions, so earnestly and witlessly promulgated in the south for sixty years, that only Britain's presence in Northern Ireland stood in the way of Irish unity. In this sense, the old order is dead, the agreement being, on the one hand, the plug that was pulled on the artificial, political-life-support systems that were sustaining Northern Ireland and, on the other hand, a shock to the body politic itself.

It is not important, therefore, whether the agreement has a list of accomplishments to its credit that can be ticked off to show that it has made good on its promise. Even in the absence of line-item successes, there is no going back to preagreement assumptions or political arrangements. The agreement will survive arguments—even disagreements over extradition, reform of the single-judge, no-jury Diplock courts, the administration of justice, or security arrangements—because, ultimately, these issues will continue to be addressed within the framework of the new institutional arrangements created by the agreement. These institutions will continue to exist: The forum for discussion will remain intact even if the issues discussed there are not adequately resolved.

The Process of Creating a New Environment

There are yardsticks for measuring the efficacy of the agreement. The processes it has set in motion have created a political environment that will either facilitate or further hinder political dialogue between the two communities within Northern Ireland. If, at the end of these processes, dialogue is less possible than in the past, then the Anglo–Irish Agreement will have failed—these processes will not have created an environment conducive to political bridge-building.

The three major ingredients of that process, which have yet to work themselves out, will be discussed one by one in the following sections.

The Unionist Predicament

Unionists have been unable to develop a coherent political response to the agreement. While they rant and rage and threaten, they are unable to come to grips with how the agreement has affected their real position within the Union, unable to evaluate their options, and unable to determine how to get themselves back into the political process without losing both face and credibility.

The unionist campaign to smash the agreement, which at best was ill-planned and at worst was simply a primeval response to a perceived threat, has collapsed in unholy disarray. Nothing has worked—not the special by-elections the unionists forced when they resigned their seats in the Westminster Parliament, nor their "Days of Action" when they called one-day strikes to shut down Northern Ireland, nor the sporadic disorganized street violence, nor the intimidating power of their parades, nor their withholding of local rate, nor the abstention of their councilors from local government bodies and their members of parliament from Westminster, nor their refusal to talk with British government officials, nor their 400,000-signature petition to the queen.

The British government, with the full backing of the Irish government, has made it clear that it will not entertain, under any circumstances, the demand of the unionists that the agreement be suspended before they engage in talks with nationalists about future governance arrangements for Northern Ireland. The agreement is simply nonnegotiable as a precondition for talks.

Nor has the efforts of the task force set up by the two unionist political parties to assess the effectiveness of their campaign gotten Unionists out of the corner into which they so successfully had painted themselves.[a] The report of the task force (*An End to Drift*) called on the two party leaders, Ian Paisley and James Molyneaux, to open "without prejudice" discussions with the British government, a suggestion the two leaders are pursuing with less than wholehearted enthusiasm.[6]

The Official Unionist party is hopelessly split between integrationists and devolutionists. Neither wing trusts the other, and the inability of the party to reconcile the two means that the policy stalemate will continue and effective leadership will not emerge. Molyneaux's minimalist "do-nothing" politics are as much a product of strategy as of paralysis, predicated on the belief—or hope—that, ultimately, the agreement's internal contradictions will bring it down.

Within the Democratic Unionist party, matters are not much better. Ian Paisley is a prisoner of Paisleyism. Having dominated unionist politics for close to twenty years and having climbed to his position of preeminence over the political carcasses of the unionist leaders he destroyed when they tried to reach an accommodation with the nationalists, he now finds himself facing the step that might lead him to join them on the refuse heap of unionist has-beens. Absolute positions cannot appear to be less than absolute; otherwise, they are not positions at all. "No surrender" cannot accommodate "not too much surrender." "Not an inch" cannot subsume "no more than an inch."

Misjudgment, the absence of a coherent strategy, and their own rather naive belief that the British government would back down, as it had in 1912 and 1974, in the face of the threat of loyalist violence, all played a part in contributing to the collapse of the unionists' campaign. The main reason for the paralysis of will, however, is their inability to reach a consensus on where they are going and how they are going to get there. In short, the Anglo–Irish Agreement has precipitated a unionist identity crisis.

Unionists, despite the fact that the agreement explicitly states that there will be no change in the status of Northern Ireland as part of the United Kingdom without the consent of a majority of its people, believe that the Union—that is, the connection between Northern Ireland and Great Britain dating from 1920 and beyond that to 1801—is over. They further believe that the agreement gives the Irish government a toehold in the north that is, in their view, the first step on the "slippery slope" to unification.

These perceptions have undermined one component of their identity—their Britishness. This, in turn, has aggravated the enduring tension within unionism itself between those whose primary interest lies in maintaining the connection with Britain and those whose primary concern lies in not becoming part of an all-Ireland state. For the latter, loyalty to Britain is conditional on Britain's looking after their interests—that is, keeping them out of an all-Ireland state. The agreement has undermined the basis of that loyalty.

Before unionists can engage in substantive talks with nationalists about power-sharing or any other matter, they must decide what their relationship to Britain means to them and what the continuing form and extent of that relationship is to be: whether they want to patch up the marriage, work out a new relationship, or settle for a divorce—whether they are willing, in the words of the task force, "to accept the Anglo–Irish Agreement as the price for the Union or to negotiate a new constitutional basis for Northern Ireland." It may be a long, painful, and ultimately even an unsatisfying process, but until the unionists resolve these questions, the issue of talks with the Catholics is moot. The agreement, therefore, is a catalyst that—by requiring unionists to redefine their relationship to Britain—will, by necessity, require them to redefine their relationship with the rest of Ireland.

The task force report was one small step in the direction of acknowledging the new realities, to the extent that it could refer to "the SDLP's participation in the government of Northern Ireland (on a basis other than majority rule) provided the Social Democratic and Labour party agreed to forfeit the role of the government of the Republic of Ireland as custodians of the Nationalists interest." Meanwhile, however, unionists struggle on, not yet willing to come to terms with the unpalatable options they face: either to do nothing and watch the agreement take greater institutional hold or to do something and admit that the agreement is a fact of life.

The Social Democratic and Labour Party's Agenda

The Anglo–Irish Agreement calls for many of the functions of the conference to be transferred to a power-sharing government in Northern Ireland whenever the two communities agree on the form of governance. The assumption here is that the Social Democratic and Labour party wants power-sharing and believes that it can work. However, the SDLP "has no ideological commitment to devolution." Moreover, at the moment, there is no indication that it has any real idea of what power-sharing arrangements it might find acceptable in terms of the powers and functions it would be prepared to assume, the responsibilities it would be required to share, and the trade-offs it would be called on to make in the form of a lesser involvement on the part of the Republic, a diminution in the authority of the Intergovernmental Conference, and the possible removal of the conference secretariat, with its complement of Irish civil servants, from Belfast. The SDLP, therefore, has to settle on an agenda that spells out what it wants and what it will settle for in terms of participation in the governance of Northern Ireland vis-à-vis its aspiration to Irish unity, and it must develop a policy that balances its requirements for power-sharing with its commitment to Irish unity and the expression of that commitment in the form of the Irish dimension.

The impact of the SDLP in recent years—whether convincing the political parties in the Republic to participate in the New Ireland Forum[b] or as adviser to the Irish government during the two governments' negotiations with the British government that led to the Anglo–Irish Agreement—has been mainly passive-aggressive. Both these initiatives were attempts, in one way or another, to shore up constitutional nationalism (that is, the SDLP) in the north. Thus, to a considerable extent, the SDLP's successes have been the product of the efforts of others in circumstances in which the process itself was more important than the outcome. However, if the unionists ever make it to the negotiating table, the SDLP will have to deal in terms of outcomes rather than processes, a situation that will call for the kind of policy debate the SDLP has avoided in recent years and one that it may not be able to withstand, given the many hues of green—united only by their opposition to the violence of militant republicanism—that come under its broad umbrella. Accordingly, if future talks with the unionists are to go anywhere, the SDLP will have to develop skills that are germane to outcome-oriented negotiation rather than to process-development mediation. And so, for the SDLP, too, the costs of not talking at present may be far less than the benefits of talking. The SDLP may simply allow things to stand for the time being—the preferred behavior of the passive-aggressive—so that the conference institutionalizes itself in the form of a de facto joint authority: an administrative solution to their quandary that would embrace elements of one of the options of the New Ireland Forum report.

Mr. Haughey's Agenda for Northern Ireland

Irish Prime Minister Haughey has moved from outright opposition to the agreement and a questioning of whether it did anything to improve the lot of nationalists in Northern Ireland, which he expressed when he was in opposition, to an endorsement, or at least a reluctant acceptance, of the agreement, albeit with the continuing caveats that progress has been difficult and disappointingly slow, which he articulates as leader of the government.

Over the years, however, Prime Minister Haughey has remained remarkably consistent in this analysis of the conflict: Northern Ireland is a failed political entity that cannot be resuscitated. At this point, just where he would stand on talks between unionists and nationalists that would have as their frame of reference the resuscitation of that entity is as yet unclear. In other words, even if the Social Democratic and Labour party were able to agree on the forms of power-sharing it would find acceptable, it is not clear whether

Haughey would regard these arrangements as just one more formula to breathe life back into a failed political entity. It might well be that he would find that the aspiration to Irish unity, which is the raison d'être of Fianna Fail—the largest political party on the island of Ireland and the voice of the Irish nationalist tradition—is better served through his government's continued direct input via a strong, vigorous, and increasingly powerful Intergovernmental Conference than through the relegation of the conference to a secondary position. Or Prime Minister Haughey might conclude that his interests are better served by using the occasion for the review of the workings of the conference, which the agreement calls for after three years, to open the process to unionists. He could agree to what would amount to a de facto suspension of the agreement in return for unionist agreement to participate, together with the two governments and the other constitutional political parties in Northern Ireland, in an all-party conference to discuss "the totality of relationships" between the two islands. It would be a bold, imaginative gesture and probably too much, too soon for the unionists. The point, however, is that in the Irish government's perspective, Fianna Fail is a national party, the Social Democratic and Labour party is a regional one, and their respective agendas are not necessarily the same.

There are, of course, other considerations: whether Sinn Fein will continue to hold its share of support in the nationalist community, whether the IRA can be contained to an extent that the level of violence will begin to drop below its 1985 level, and whether unionist alienation will begin to assume more forbidding forms. Ultimately, however, the success of the Anglo–Irish Agreement will be measured in terms of the extent to which it facilitates a resolution of the often-conflicting agendas it poses for the major constitutional players. It may fail to do so. The extent of the segregation of the two communities in Northern Ireland is almost total; the agreement, at best, treats the symptoms, not the causes of that segregation; and the best-intentioned structures developed and imposed from without cannot substantially alleviate the wellsprings of a seemingly intractable and immutable communal division that emanates from deep within. But even if it does fail, it has altered the context for all future policy action. Its enduring importance, therefore, is the fact that it was implemented in the first place.

Postscript: Events in 1988

A string of extraordinary events at the beginning of 1988 brought Anglo–Irish relations to their lowest level in years. The Stalker-Sampson investigation into allegations that the Royal Ulster Constabulary had engaged in a shoot-to-kill policy in the early 1980s was completed. However, the British attorney general, Sir Patrick Mayhew, announced in Parliament that the report would not be made public and that eleven senior constabulary officers, said to have been named in the report for perverting the course of justice, would not be prosecuted for national security reasons. Dublin, which was not consulted beforehand about these decisions, strongly protested both the decisions themselves and its total exclusion from the process that led to them.

The Court of Appeal rejected the plea by the Birmingham Six,[c] and the House of Lords refused to hear the case. Dublin and London wrangled over extradition—Dublin insisting that London was still sending extradition applications without evidence, despite new extradition requirements; London denying the charges and citing its full adherence to procedure.

Aidan McAnespie, a twenty-four-year-old native of Monaghan, a town across the border in the Republic, was shot dead at a border checkpoint in Aughnacloy by a British soldier stationed at a lookout post, who claimed that his weapon accidentally discharged itself; the Republic's government appointed the deputy commissioner of the Garda (police) to inquire into the killing, rather than using the Intergovernmental Conference to express its concerns. The anger over McAnespie's death was compounded when it was learned that Private Ian Thain, the only British soldier ever convicted of killing a civilian in Northern Ireland, had been released after only twenty-six months of a life sentence for the murder of Thomas Reilly in West Belfast and had returned to his regiment.

Three unarmed members of the IRA were shot dead by British security forces in Gibraltar, raising new questions about shoot-to-kill policies. Two off-duty British soldiers were savagely beaten by a nationalist mob and then shot to death by the IRA mob when their car accidentally found itself in the middle of the funeral procession for an IRA volunteer, one of three people shot dead days earlier by a Protestant gunman who opened fire on the mourners at the funerals of the three IRA volunteers shot in Gibraltar.

Nonetheless, despite these incidents and the outcry in the minority community in the north and the distress of the government in the south over the British government's handling of the Stalker-Sampson affair, both Prime Minister Haughey and Prime Minister Thatcher reaffirmed their commitment to the Anglo–Irish Agreement. Special meetings of the Intergovernmental Conference were called to resolve differences. Meanwhile, John Hume, leader of the SDLP, and Gerry Adams, leader of Sinn Fein, engaged in talks. Hume did so ostensibly for the purpose of persuading Sinn Fein to call on the IRA to order a cease-fire that would open the way to "a permanent cessation of all military and violent activity." Adams did so to try and initiate an overall nationalist political strategy that would "examine ways in which conditions for peace could be established."

Molyneaux, leader of the Official Unionist party, appeared for a brief moment to suggest that he would be willing to talk with Prime Minister Haughey about the "totality of relationships." His use of the phrase that

Haughey had employed to describe the scope of his summit meeting with Thatcher in 1980 encouraged wild speculation that Molyneaux had somehow been converted to the wisdom of some new north–south relationship to take the place of the Anglo–Irish Agreement. Haughey indicated his eagerness to talk; Molyneaux, however, quickly put distance between himself and the suggestions. Meanwhile, the Paisley–Molyneaux "talks about talks" with Tom King, the Northern Ireland secretary of state for Northern Ireland, continued, seemingly ad infinitum.

By the end of the summer of 1988, the principals on all sides had more or less ended up at the points from which they had started. The unionist parties reiterated their refusal to engage in talks about devolution while the agreement remained in place; the proposals they put to King addressed administrative rather than legislative devolution; Paisley reiterated his opposition to power-sharing for the umpteenth time; both the SDLP and Haughey's government distanced themselves from devolution; and the Sinn Fein–SDLP talks had come to a halt without resolution of any of the questions they were to address.

A poll taken shortly after the imbroglio over the Stalker-Sampson report and the rejection of the Birmingham Six's appeal found that only 16 percent of Catholics believed that the agreement had benefited the minority community, whereas an overwhelming 81 percent of Catholic respondents could find no benefit to their community from the agreement. Protestants, of course, found even less in the agreement with which they could identify: 88 percent of Protestant respondents believed that Protestants had not benefited from the agreement, and only a miniscule 4 percent could detect any benefits to their community from the agreement.

Notes

a. In February 1987, James Molyneaux, leader of the Official Unionist party, and the Reverend Ian Paisley, leader of the Democratic Unionist party, jointly established the Unionist Task Force to evaluate the extent of support within the unionist community for the campaign against the Anglo–Irish Agreement and to ascertain what consensus, if any, existed about alternatives to the agreement. The task force had three members: Harold McCusker, deputy leader of the Official Unionist party; Frank Millar, chief executive of the Official Unionist party; and Peter Robinson, deputy leader of the Democratic Unionist party.

b. The four major constitutional nationalist political parties on the island (Fianna Fail, Fine Gael, and Labour from the Republic and the SDLP from Northern Ireland) participated from May 1983 through May 1984 in the New Ireland Forum. The forum, which published its report in May 1984, set out the constitutional nationalists' analysis of the Northern Ireland problem and outlined their views on the direction possible accommodations might take. Their preferred solution was for a unitary all-

Ireland state. However, they also indicated that they would be prepared to consider a federal/confederal state or joint authority. See *New Ireland Forum Report,* Dublin, May 1984.

c. Six Irish nationals had been tried and convicted on a number of charges arising out of two pub bombings in Birmingham on November 2, 1974, in which nineteen people died. Subsequently, sufficient evidence of their innocence turned up to warrant a court review of the case.

References

1. United Kingdom, Parliament. *Northern Ireland: Constitutional Proposals,* Cmnd. 5259 (London: Her Majesty's Stationery Office, March 1973).

2. United Kingdom, Parliament. *The Government of Northern Ireland: Proposals for Further Discussion,* Cmnd. 7950 (London: Her Majesty's Stationery Office, July 1980).

3. United Kingdom, Parliament. *Northern Ireland: A Framework for Devolution,* Cmnd. 8541 (London: Her Majesty's Stationery Office, April 1982).

4. Paul Arthur, "The Anglo–Irish Agreement: Events of 1985–86," *Irish Political Studies* 2 (1987): 99–107.

5. For a comprehensive review of the Anglo–Irish Agreement and its background, see Padraig O'Malley, "The Anglo–Irish Agreement," Occasional Paper No. 7, (Washington, DC: U.S. Department of State, Foreign Service Institute, Center for the Study of Foreign Affairs, January, 1987).

6. Unionist Task Force report, *An End to Drift* (an abridged version of the report presented to Mr. Molyneaux and Dr. Paisley), Belfast, June 16, 1987.

12

Hyphenating Belgium: Changing State and Regime to Cope with Cultural Division

Martin O. Heisler

In 1830, with Belgium on the threshold of independence, the French statesman Talleyrand justified designs on a part of it by asserting that "there are no Belgians, there never have been, there never will be. There are Frenchmen, Flemings . . . and Germans."[1] Although wrong in important respects, the statement was not merely hyperbole. For although effective governmental, political, and economic institutions were built in a framework of unitary, constitutional monarchy, a broad and deep national solidarity proved elusive. Consociational and corporatist structures and practices made it possible to cope with religious and class differences for over a century. But the country that came into being through a "union of oppositions" and adopted "Union makes strength" as its motto could not manage its profound ethnic division—evident before independence, but salient only since about 1960—without fundamentally altering the state.

Belgium has been regionalized—in effect, transmuted into a federation—in the past twenty years. Three "cultural communities" and three regions have been created through constitutional engineering. The institutions, jurisdiction, and responsibilities of the state have been altered, and the ways in which citizens relate to one another through the state have also been changed profoundly.[a] Less formal but no less vital changes have occurred in the regime—the institutions and rules of politics; and some basic individual rights historically associated with liberal democracy in Belgium and elsewhere have been affected. It is no longer possible to be simply Belgian.

One must now be a member of a Dutch- or a French-language cultural community (the latter includes more than three-quarters of Brussels' residents) or the small German-speaking minority. Parliament divides into legislatures for those communities on the basis of language when dealing with culturally or regionally sensitive issues. Regional governments—with executive, legislative, and administrative agencies addressing important social and economic as well as cultural functions—are in place in Flanders, Wallonia, and Brussels. Complex, detailed provisions have been made for the protection of minorities, defined in political as well as cultural terms. Thus, 150 years after Talleyrand's cynical gambit, Belgium is populated by Dutch-speaking Flemings and French-speaking Walloons and Brusselers (and a few German-speakers). By law, all Belgians are now hyphenated.[b]

But hyphens connect as well as separate. In important respects, the regionalized state and its political processes link Belgians more effectively than the unitary state did. Collectively, the central, regional, and local governments of Belgium may possess greater legitimacy than the unitary state would have.

Background

An old country in a relatively new state, Belgium was ruled from Madrid, Vienna, Paris, or The Hague for several centuries. A collection of fiefdoms,

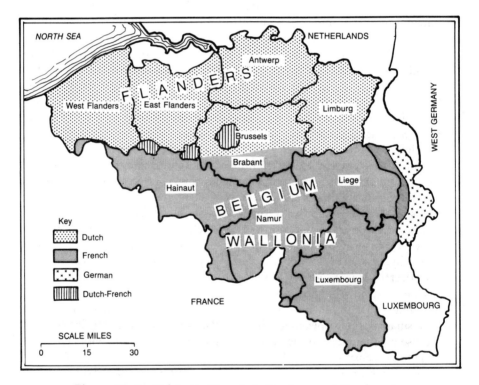

Figure 12–1. Belgium: Linguistic Regions and Provinces

Belgium was always an unintegrated periphery of some distant dynasty. A "linguistic frontier," running west to east, has demarcated the Flemish north and the Walloon south since Roman times.[2] Although never a closed boundary, first acquiring administrative status in the 1820s and legal and political meaning only recently, it has long separated culturally as well as linguistically different populations. Transactions within groups remain far more numerous than transactions among them.[3]

There was a marked asymmetry across regions in economic, political, and social terms at independence. Parts of Wallonia and Brussels were among the first thoroughly industrialized areas in the world, whereas Flanders, the heart of the northern renaissance 350 years earlier, was an economic and social backwater. By the 1840s, an enlightened constitution assured civil liberties for all. But because participation was limited to propertied elites— essentially French-speaking upper and upper-middle classes—Flemings could not convert their numbers into power. The numerical majority was a status minority, politically and economically disadvantaged and culturally stigmatized.

Partly because of structural economic changes that affected them differently, the positions of the regions and groups have been reversed dramatically in the past forty years.[4] Inequalities in political status and economic circumstances have been greatly reduced by the thoroughly democratic, egalitarian welfare state. Because of their numbers, Flemings are now preeminent in politics, as well as in many other aspects of the society's life. They can now advance in public life and in national and multinational firms without shunting their own language and culture.

French-speaking Belgians began to exhibit fears of *minorisation* soon after World War II. Francophones—richer, more progressive, and more powerful until then—declined politically, economically, and in self-confidence, both in absolute terms and in relation to Flemings. The areas that were first to industrialize have experienced deindustrialization, whereas long-backward Flanders has enjoyed sustained economic development.[5] Constitutional changes and the new political equations accompanying regionalization and harsh economic times have rendered Brussels, the erstwhile center of "Belgianness," relatively impotent and peripheral.

The "linguistic question"—a euphemism for cultural and regional contention, as well as the most obvious marker of ethnic difference—has dominated most aspects of political life since the early 1960s. It often casts ideological, economic, and even foreign policy issues into a framework of confrontation among the cultural groups.[6] It has exacted costs in governmental efficiency and money and, in nontrivial ways for some, traditional individual and family prerogatives,[7] *but not in lives or civil order,* when compared with other deeply divided societies.[8]

The Aims of This Chapter

This chapter focuses on four aspects of the Belgian case. First, the changing contexts of ethnic relations—the effects of asymmetric development and the shifts in such asymmetries—are examined. Second, the impacts of those shifts on political parties are analyzed, along with the roles of the consociational and corporatist practices, organizations, and norms that have long characterized Belgian politics. The party system and the consociational-corporatist political style are keys to understanding the transformation of the regime and why and how regionalization was used to cope with ethnic division. Third, constitutional and institutional changes are briefly assessed. And finally, some of the ramifications of regionalization for governance, party politics, values, and ethnic relations are noted in the conclusion.

Shifting Asymmetries and Contexts of Differentiation

Development usually affects parts of a society unevenly in the short to medium term, especially in the presence of marked cultural differences. From long before independence until World War II, most political and economic development in Belgium redounded in favor of French-speakers, and disadvantages accrued to Flemings. This asymmetry was converted into rigid, structured disparities and was embedded in the regime. For over a century, the institutions, practices, and norms of that regime not only reflected but legitimized self-sustaining inequalities between the major segments of the population. The reversal of those asymmetries brought pressures for change. The combination of structural economic malaise and the fear of the conversion of numerical minority into permanent minority status that mobilized Walloons in the 1950s led to significant changes in regime and state.

Structured Francophone Preeminence and Flemish Minority Status

During the latter part of the colonial period, political, commercial, and intellectual elites tended to be Francophone and to exhibit a bourgeois culture, later most closely identified with Brussels. French rule between 1792 and 1814 spurred industrial development in the south, reinforced that elite's predominance, and implanted both ideas and institutions for a strong central government and standardization—including a single state language.[9] Dutch rule (from 1815 to independence) reinforced the trend toward political centralization. And although it encouraged use of the Dutch language and gave it a role in administration (especially in the Flemish provinces), it did not diminish the preeminence of the Francophone upper classes.

The new state continued these trends and legitimized them.[10] Flemings could raise their material, political, and social status by using French and adopting the life-styles of the Francophone bourgeoisie; and many did. This path of mobility and integration had profound implications for ethnicity at the individual level and for the structure of group relations. It engendered perceptions and norms that linked becoming Belgian with embracing the dominant group's language and some of its culture—at least in public (whence the adage: "Flemish in the kitchen, French in the parlor"). One writer put it more strongly: "Tout Flamand qui voulait arriver devait se servir du français; comme on l'a dit: pour devenir Belge, il fallait cesser d'être Flamand. (If he wants to succeed, a Fleming has to do it in French; as the saying goes, to become a Belgian one must stop being a Fleming.)"[11]

These traits of the first regime had profound and lasting effects on ethnic relations: the acceptance by many Flemings, not just most Francophones, of the normalcy of "Belgianization"; the fostering of resentment and a sense of second-class citizenship among Flemings;[12] and the cooptation and acculturation of many of the more educated, ambitious and resourceful among them.[c] Coupled with asymmetric development, this led to reinforcing (rather than crosscutting) relationships among the socioeconomic, religious and ethnic cleavages—contrary to conventional scholarly wisdom about cleavage patterns.[d]

Thus, for more than a century after independence, the dynamics of social and economic mobility had the effect of concentrating in Flanders a large proportion of those who were less well-off, less mobile, less secularized, and less Belgian.[e] Being ethnic tended to mean being Flemish. Although Walloons were also ethnics in most senses of the term, the French language and earlier modernization opened the doors to integration wider for them.[13]

Regime Stability and the Primacy of Economic and Political Issues

Concerns with economic welfare began to mobilize and politicize Flemings in the mid-nineteenth century as much as or more than the culturally unpalatable paths to integration did. The transformation of the essentially literary, folkloric Flemish movement into a political one was triggered by "disastrous economic deterioration [in the 1850s], comparable to Ireland's."[f] The direction of these energies toward economic goals and greater political participation was an indication of the strength of the regime. Collective action led to political successes: the legalization of collective bargaining, the formation (in 1885) and subsequent rise of the Belgian Workers' (later Socialist) party in the political arena, the achievement of one *man*–one vote between 1894 and 1919 (women were not enfranchised in national elections until after World War II), and the launching of the welfare state. Mass action—Flemish and Francophone—was channeled toward economic improvement and political access. The political structure, characterized by the consociational rule of party leaders and the roles of corporatist organizations in forming and implementing policy,[g] was effective in dealing with economic and participatory demands.

The regime worked on what it did best; and its successes in managing issues so tailored strengthened it. There were periodic confrontations—working-class demands for inclusion and socioeconomic justice, church–state relations—but managing these crisis-framed issues helped to extend the viability of the regime by decades.[h] Ethnic relations were rarely addressed directly and never in a concerted fashion until the rapid, quite sudden rise of the cleavage to saliency, between 1958 and 1961.[14] Although the regime began to erode in the late nineteenth century, as it evolved toward electoral democracy, it retained its essential character long enough to launch regionalization in the 1960s.[15]

By the late 1940s, universal political participation, progress toward equity among classes, and the comprehensive welfare state had largely redressed the political and economic imbalances underlying the old, asymmetric relationship between Flemings and Francophones.[16] This was accomplished in a framework of liberal democracy: The pursuit of equality was justified on universalistic and individualistic grounds—all Belgians had equal entitlements, based on citizenship. Discrimination against less-integrated Flemings survived into the era of political democracy; but it became an informal, social disposition, with little or no support from state and regime. Structured inequality across ethnic groups had lost its legitimacy by the late 1950s.

The regime prepared the way for the reversal of the historical asymmetries through its policies; but the reversal itself was triggered by events that began in the last months of World War II. In one of the ironies affecting relationships among Belgium's population groups, the early industrialization of portions of Wallonia that had undergirded Francophone preeminence became a disadvantage in the aftermath of the war.

Reversed Asymmetries and the Rise of the Ethnic Cleavage

Belgium was liberated so swiftly after D-Day that its industrial plant was liberated essentially intact. But much of what was liberated intact dated from the nineteenth and early twentieth centuries and was obsolete. Consequently, the south's industries were very unfavorably positioned after the war. They had to compete not only with newly built or rebuilt—more modern and efficient—

West German and Dutch facilities but also with the Flemish north. Flanders enjoyed several competitive advantages, including large, modern ports. More important, because it was much less industrialized than the Borinage and other areas of Wallonia, its labor relations were free of the "distributive coalitions" that Mancur Olson has associated with low productivity and slow growth.[17] Thus, it attracted a disproportionately large share of both domestic and foreign investment after the war. By the late 1950s, Flanders' growth rate was substantially higher than that of the country as a whole, while the Walloon economy was contracting.[18]

Labor shortages developed in the north, while Wallonia, with its less and less productive coal mines (vital to much of its industry) and obsolete plants, began to experience massive structural unemployment. Three factors militated against a rationalization of this asymmetry in the labor market: Strong unions demanded relief for local economic conditions from government and resisted relocation and retraining for their members; social programs and unemployment benefits made unemployment financially tolerable for most; and linguistic and cultural differences made the prospect of Walloons commuting even short distances to Flanders very unattractive, in a country where distances are relatively short and daily commuting to Brussels and regional centers is a way of life for many.[19]

Walloon politicians wanted relief for the region, not rationalization through market forces at the national level. They saw connections between regional economic decline and political eclipse. The formation of the Mouvement Populaire Wallon in 1960–61 and the emergence and success of a regional political party, the Rassemblement Wallon, in 1968, reflected rapidly increasing Walloon mobilization. In 1963–64, a new party was born in Brussels: the Front Démocratique des Francophones, an ideologically mixed, militantly Francophone party focused on the city's interests. These developments indicated a widespread, substantial reorientation of political loyalties and activity by Francophones. They were the most important early steps toward restructuring the regime and the state. The Volksunie (VU), a militantly Flemish regional party, antedated the Walloon and Brussels-based parties by a decade; but the advent of the Francophone parties was more significant, for it signaled the end of national, "Belgian" integration as a norm. The Francophone parties represented movement away from the regime by those whose values and aspirations had been most directly reflected in it until the 1960s.

The Transformation of the Party System and the Fading of the Old Regime

The rise of regional parties eroded the near-monopoly of the three major parties—Christian Social (read Christian Democrat or Catholic), Socialist, and Liberal—in the electoral and parliamentary arenas. Among them, they received more than 95 percent of the vote in 1958 but less than 74 percent by 1971. Their ability to manage the regime in a consociational fashion declined sharply. At least as important was the push toward linguistic issues, exerted on the traditional parties by their new competitors. As in the building of the welfare state, the established parties sought to steal the thunder of the newcomers and, by acting on the ethnic-regional issues, to preserve as much of their rapidly shrinking electoral base as possible.[20] They held on only long enough to launch regionalization.

The traditional parties split into Flemish and Francophone wings, and these soon became separate parties. Common ideological denominators proved insufficient in the face of ethnic and regional pressures. And once they were organized regionally, differences in the values of the parties' more homogeneous regional constituencies further eroded their cohesion. The proliferation of parties—two Christian Social, two Socialist, two Liberal (for a while three, with one for Brussels), and the Volksunie, Rassemblement Wallon, and Front Démocratique des Francophones—made stable coalitions and the continuation of a regime built on effective bargaining among leaders problematic. By the late 1960s, when revision of the constitution was broached, the two-thirds majorities required for constitutional changes (in Parliament, sitting as a constituent assembly after new elections) could be obtained only if either both the Flemish and the Francophone wings of all traditional parties concurred or if five of the six of these parties and at least two of the "linguistic" parties were in agreement. Since the latter were deemed hostile to the regime and demanded more radical regionalization than the old parties wanted, the revision of the constitution was undertaken by the former.[21]

The fragmentation of the party system is key to understanding why federalization was used to deal with the ethnic cleavage once it became salient. The leaders of the traditional parties could manage societal divisions as long as those parties had an effective monopoly of votes among them, for they could claim to aggregate and represent the political preferences of constituencies held together by more than just agreement on the issues of the day. The Christian Social, Socialist, and Liberal parties reflected, in Val R. Lorwin's terms, three "religious, socioeconomic, and political affiliations, . . . segments . . . *Weltanschauungsgruppen* (or *familles spirituelles*)."[22, i]

Such segments were built on vast networks of organizations and interest groups: labor unions, building societies, employers' federations, youth groups, and a variety of social service and insurance programs. Each segment offered a more or less comprehensive framework for association for those identified with it, with the parties as the principal political channels. Although there were nontrivial differences in the religious and socioeconomic positions of Flemings, Walloons, and Brusselers, consociational decision-making styles and corporatist administration sufficed to cement the segments until the rise of the ethnic cleavage.

The religious, socioeconomic class, and ethnic cleavages that succeeded one another to the fore in Belgian politics during the past 160 years were dealt with by bargaining, compromise, and power-sharing. Four elements of this style stand out, and their vestiges are evident in the structuring of the new regime and the regionalized state. First, newly mobilized groups could gain ready access to the political process. Just as the working class entered through labor unions and the Workers' party late in the last century, "linguistic" parties followed in the 1960s and ecological movements gained entry in the 1980s. Second, as in the Netherlands and other consociational democracies, governmental and party leaders strove to preserve common interests when faced with particularistic demands. They sought to build the broadest possible consensus without excessively diluting the policies at hand. Most factions became sharers in policy (not winners or losers, as they might have become in the United States or Great Britain). Third, detailed formulas were often devised for public policies, to achieve both the substance and impression of fairness.ʲ Finally, in quintessentially Belgian fashion, agreements and assurances worked out by the leaders of major parties—often in great detail—were usually encoded in laws and constitutional provisions, to reinforce public trust, which might falter in the presence of profound divisions.

In sum, the reversal of historical asymmetries generated regional and ethnic demands, particularly from Walloons, who previously had been relatively sanguine about the integrative thrust of the old regime. Legislation governing language usage above and below the linguistic frontier and in mixed areas, enacted in 1962–63, signaled the shift. Although Flemings had made dramatic gains in political and economic terms in the previous fifteen years, the cultural pull of the Francophone center and of the French language worked against social and cultural equality and acted as a magnet for the upwardly mobile. Parents often saw greater opportunities for their children if they were educated in French. An important purpose of the legislation governing the use of languages was to stem such acculturation.

The "linguistic question" was now on the agendas of the traditional parties; and it quickly became the cardinal issue, affecting many other matters. The language usage laws enhanced and began to legitimize notions of division along ethnic lines; and they politicized the issue in a way that made it difficult for those who might have preferred to ignore it to continue to adhere to a Belgian identity. (Many Flemings were satisfied with their progress within the existing political and economic frameworks, and many Walloons felt that their civil and political rights were reasonably secure with ascendant Flemish influence in the state.[23]) The rise of regional parties forced the traditional elites to broach and then to embrace ethnic and regional issues. This led to a fragmentation of the party system and, in turn, greatly weakened the regime—opening the door to the transformation of the state.

Changing the State to Manage the Ethnic Cleavage

The revision of the constitution between 1967 and 1971 had three major aims: (1) to institutionalize Flemish political gains; (2) to provide formal protections to Francophones, thus allaying their concerns about becoming a permanent minority and about "revanchism" by Flemings—"getting even" for historic grievances; and (3) to mute the pressures for more radical separation—federalism—emanating from the linguistic and regional parties on both sides of the linguistic frontier.[24] (It is because such regional parties as the Volksunie and the Rassemblement Wallon used the language of federalism in their rhetoric that that term has been eschewed by moderates, especially in the traditional parties.)

Five provisions of the new constitution stand out. The three regions (and a special district for the German cantons in the east) already identified were created, ostensibly on the basis of language, with Brussels mandated to be bilingual. Second, Parliament was to divide into cultural councils for the Dutch-language and French-language communities when it acted on culturally or regionally sensitive issues. Third, added protections were provided for the civil liberties of ideological, as well as cultural, minorities. Next, "alarm bell" provisions were added to the operation of the Parliament and the legislature of the Brussels agglomeration, to be triggered by a three-quarters majority of the representatives of either cultural group should they feel that the group's rights were in jeopardy through action contemplated by the body.[k] Finally, and critically important for the governance of the country and Brussels, a power-sharing formula was devised—and written into the constitution—regarding the distribution of executive positions by language: Except for the prime minister, there would be equal numbers of Dutch-speaking and Francophone members of the cabinet, as well as in the executive of the government of the Brussels region. The prime minister could come from either language group. In practice, this has meant that the prime minister is likely to be Flemish, reflecting the country's Flemish majority. Since 1971, only one short-lived government was headed by a monolingual Francophone. Conversely, the executive of the Brussels agglomeration is invariably headed by a Francophone, given the jurisdiction's substantial French-speaking majority.

A Device for Conflict Management or Polarization?

Given that the effectiveness of the consociational and corporatist modes of managing religious and class cleavages was based, in large measure, on the insulation of the populations divided by them, the creation of the regions and cultural communities could be regarded as an attempt to encapsulate ethnically distinct groups. This aim has been achieved to a considerable degree. Most Flemings and Walloons are substantially insulated from each other by the new structure. Where they do come into contact, their relationships and anxieties are bounded by relatively clear, depersonalized institutional markers. Whereas the historic "spiritual families"—Catholics, socialists, and liberals—had corporatist associations through which many social activities and services were conducted, now the regional governments perform similar functions for the linguistically arrayed population groups, as they are becoming increasingly important in the administration of economic and social programs. Flemings have fewer attractions and even fewer opportunities to drift toward the historically predominant Francophone culture. And Francophones' fears of *minorisation* are allayed in some measure by the aforementioned constitutional provisions.

But whereas the consociational-corporatist style of conflict management in the old regime relied on a command of bargaining across groups by party or factional elites, the fragmentation of the party system and the formalization of relationships among the cultural groups in the new regime severely limits both the power and the freedom of action of elites. A major difficulty arises from the proliferation of parties and functional interest organizations, caused by the aforementioned divisions along linguistic or regional lines. The multiplicity of organizational actors has greatly increased decision costs, in that it is much harder to reach agreement among many relatively small groups than it was among three parties and a few labor union, professional, and employers' federations.[25] This makes governance in general more difficult (as noted later), but in the presence of pressures from regional parties that are more militant on culturally or regionally sensitive issues, it especially impedes the ability of leaders of the more mainstream parties to negotiate without confrontation. Thus, formal rules are increasingly more important and informal bargaining less effective.

Regionalization, by extensively formalizing the ethnic cleavage, has made it more difficult to avoid zero-sum confrontations—or at least the perception of zero-sum game relationships—among the cultural groups. Such relationships exist when one group believes that any gains realized by the other must, perforce, come at its expense. Belgians had effectively avoided such confrontations in the old regime; indeed, avoiding actual or perceived zero-sum game relationships is a sine qua non of consociational regimes.[26] If ethnic peace between Flemings and Francophones is enhanced by regionalization on "low politics" issues or in everyday relationships, confrontation may be displaced to the central decision-making level or to "high politics." Two issues, one with great intrinsic importance, illustrate this consequence of the restructuring of the state.

The Problem of Brussels and a
Village Mayor's Linguistic Predilections

Francophones have more places on the national executive than their numbers would warrant, to allay their fears of the consequences of their minority status. In exchange for this overrepresentation for French-speakers at the national level, Brussels' minority of Flemish-speakers was accorded parallel overrepresentation in the city-region's government. Two factors accounted for this bargain. First, Flemings argued that, particularly in light of their national majority, they were entitled to "feel at home" in their country's capital. They needed to protect their rights there; and the many ethnic Flemings who had come to use French in their working lives needed to have the opportunity to reassume their heritage. Second, the bargain was made by Flemish and Walloon political leaders, with little representation for the approximately 7 percent of the Belgian population constituted by Francophone Brussellers. Thus, the latter's interests hardly received support.

In the view of one of its prominent Francophone politicians:

> [Brussels] is a city of largely French-speaking cosmopolitans—comprising most of the truly Belgian population—surrounded and under siege by Flemings, some of whom are undermining it from within. It cannot grow or even breathe; it cannot flourish like other great cities. And its destiny is controlled by unsympathetic outsiders with interests of their own.[27]

The future of the city is likely to remain the most troublesome unfinished business in managing the ethnic cleavage through regionalization. Any apparent solution would conflict with the democratic prerogatives of either the Flemish majority at the national level or the Francophone majority of the city. The latter is already compromised, if viewed in terms of the prerogatives of majorities. But even in a consensual rather than majoritarian democratic perspective,[28] the power-sharing formula for Brussels has made the implementation of regional government for the capital problematic and its legitimacy tenuous in the eyes of the majority of the city's population. The most likely course for the foreseeable future is continued temporizing by national governments and continuing malaise within Brussels.

Except for some small Flemish communities adjacent to Brussels—into which many French-speakers moved in the course of suburbanization, and which have special constitutional provisions for "minority facilities" for Francophones—the regions were quite homogeneous when the language laws were enacted and regional boundaries were drawn. Thus, few lives were affected directly and significantly, except in a few rural boroughs with small populations that were transferred from one region to another. But because language carries most of the emotional and political freight of the ethnic cleavage, some exceptions have acquired dramatic importance.

There has been a particularly troublesome, protracted conflict over six villages in the Voer district (Fourons in French, with a combined population of 4,300) on the German border that were transferred from the Walloon to the Flemish region twenty-five years ago.[29] The conflict brought down the government in late 1987 and necessitated parliamentary elections, but it continues to elude solution. The immediate issue has mainly symbolic significance: The head of a municipal council (in effect, the mayor) refuses to be certified in Dutch, thus defying constitutional law and goading Flemish sensibilities. (The underlying issue is less trivial: A plurality of the area's population would prefer being reattached to the province of Liège, on the Francophone side of the linguistic frontier—making it politic for the mayor to continue his recalcitrance.) The Fourons crisis is symptomatic of the divisive potential of the ethnic cleavage in relations among parties—including the regional wings of the traditional, ideologically based parties—as well as in governance in matters of "high politics."

Summary and Conclusions

The transformation of the Belgian state has made possible the preservation of social order despite the ethnic cleavage. The group violence found in many other divided societies has been avoided. Despite the devolution of many governmental functions to the new regions, public business is conducted relatively effectively and in keeping with democratic norms—except, in some respects, with regard to Brussels and a few pockets of tensions, such as the Voer district. A high standard of living has been maintained. Unemployment and domestic and foreign debt have been uncomfortably high in the 1980s; but a program of austerity begun in 1982—together with a fiscal conservatism now common to many Western countries—has gained the confidence of voters and investors, as election and investment data indicate.

The main difficulties in governance stem from three sources, two of them direct consequences of the ethnic division. The general economic downturn that began in the mid-1970s has had deep and lasting effects because of very heavy dependence on international trade and imported oil. Belgium has fared about as well or as badly as any welfare state in which the population has come to expect substantial public benefits and predictable economic growth. In most such states, bad economic times tend to be blamed on the government of the day, almost without regard for what it actually does.

Regionalization led to administrative redundancy and measurable inefficiency in public expenditures. Until the mid-1970s, sustained and substantial economic growth provided a fiscal dividend for the government—added revenues without higher taxes—which could be used for the purposeful redundancy of services and programs associated with regionalization.[30] When the fiscal dividend vanished, such policies had to be sidetracked or paid for by funds taken from established and popular programs—or by higher taxes. None of these alternatives was popular with voters or politicians; and ethnic peace and the general ability to govern suffered.

In party politics, regionalization has transmuted historically conservative tendencies in Flanders and more progressive inclinations in Wallonia into another problem at the national level. The Socialist party tends to be first in the south; the Christian Social party dominates in Flanders. The ideological distance between them is generally great enough to make effective coalitions difficult. The most workable coalitions from the standpoint of agreement on issues are likely to include only lesser parties from one region or the other, leaving either the Flemish or the Francophone electoral plurality out. This makes legitimizing policies across the country more difficult. The increasingly important tasks of the regional governments are also made harder—and unevenly so—when the dominant party in Flanders or Wallonia is a major force in the national coalition, while its counterpart is in opposition. In turn, that may increase perceptions of unfairness and exacerbate tensions between the ethnic groups.

But perhaps most troubling is a product of regionalization virtually ignored by scholars and not often discussed in Belgium: the cost of ethnic peace in terms of legislative constraints on individual and family freedom. Linguistic homogeneity in the two larger regions has been achieved more by mandate than by public consensus. Although the means used in the constitutional and legislative processes were consistent with consociational democratic practice in Belgium (in that they entailed negotiation by party elites, acting constitutionally), the "pillars" or spiritual families on which the old regime was based did not preclude individual choice and movement across segments in the formal fashion and to the extent that the regionalized state now does. The Belgian solution illustrates ethnic nominalism in a striking degree.

No firm conclusion is as yet possible regarding the long-term efficacy of that solution. Two factors—one involving relationships with neighboring countries, the other substantially extraneous to the ethnic relationship and largely outside the country's control—may contribute to the outcome. The culturally autonomous regions are free—whereas the unitary state was not, given the sensitivities of Dutch- and French-speaking citizens—to develop supportive links with the Netherlands to the north and France to the south. Such cultural ties have been established, although those between Francophone Belgians and France are not yet robust. Second, given the economy's great reliance on external transactions, the course of the international economy will continue to effect the country's fortunes strongly. The performance of Belgian governments, like those of other advanced industrial democracies, is a crucial determinant of public assessments of their efficacy. Thus, in gross terms but to a significant extent, economic conditions are likely to affect the viability of the new regime—as they would have the old regime—and this will have at least indirect effects on the ethnic relationship.

Notes

a. Many of these institutions, with more limited functions and jurisdictions, also exist for the small German-speaking minority along the German border. But because they do not figure noticeably in the politics, the ethnic relations, or the transformation of the Belgian state, I do not treat them specifically on every point.

b. Politicized by the rise of ethnic cleavage, language statistics have been problematic since the 1947 census. See Paul M. G. Lévy, *La querelle du recensement* (Brussels: Institute Belge de Science Politique, 1960). There are two kinds of data. One *assumes* that all of a region's population uses its official language. This overestimates linguistic homogeneity by at least 4 percent for Flanders and 1 to 2 percent for Wallonia. Far fewer than half the residents of the Brussels agglomeration can or actually do use both languages. With this caveat in mind, there are 57.5 percent Dutch-speakers (Flanders); 32.6 percent French-speakers (in Wallonia); and 9.9 percent officially bilingual (Brussels) by region. Scholarly surveys and other modes of sampling of first or only language actually used indicate 59 percent Dutch, 41 percent French, and 0.7 percent German. See Kenneth D. McRae, *Conflict and Compromise in Multilingual Societies: Volume 2. Belgium* (Waterloo, Ontario, Canada: Wilfrid Laurier University Press, 1986), pp. 35–53. This very thorough and balanced study is the best single source on the country.

c. This fostered the Flemish movement and, simultaneously, by drawing off some of the most capable potential leaders, made it less effective. It clearly impeded the attainment of equal status by Flemings who sought to stay within their language and culture.

d. Social scientists have long maintained that cleavages are most likely to be destabilizing and lead to conflict where distinctions of class, religion, and such other divisions as ethnicity or language coincide—thus reinforcing one another. Crosscutting, whereby those divided along one dimension are on the same side of another dimension, is expected to moderate the effects of cleavages. See, for example, Gabriel A. Almond, "Comparative Political Systems," *Journal of Politics* 18 (August 1956): 391–409. For a fine analytical and theoretical discussion and application, see Arend Lijphart, *Democracy in Plural Societies* (New Haven, CT: Yale University Press, 1977). His theory of consociational democracy—political stability in the presence of societal divisions—not only does not rely on extensive crosscutting but is based on segmentation or encapsulation of population groups, which is consistent with reinforcing cleavage patterns.

e. This may seem, at first, to be at odds with established scholarship. In fact it is not, because whereas most empirical studies of cleavage patterns in Belgium address the *nominal condition* of the population at a given time, my concern is with *percep-*

tions and dynamics—forces of development and change. Ethnic identity was likely to be less ambivalent and more salient for Flemings who were not able or willing to become "Belgian," especially when combined with perceptions of lower political efficacy and being poorer and more devout than Francophones and acculturated Flemings. See, for example, Lijphart, *Democracies*, especially pp. 71–81; and cf. Zolberg, "Belgium," pp. 120–29 (cited in note 4), and "The Making of Flemings and Walloons: Belgium, 1830-1914," *Journal of Interdisciplinary History* 5 (1974): 179–235.

f. Zolberg, "Belgium," p. 121. The similarity extended to the occurrence of a potato famine in Flanders. Such economic malaise influenced the growth and politicization of the Walloon Movement after the Second World War, as we shall see. Some Walloons voiced cultural and even separatist demands as early as the mid-nineteenth century. See Rigo De Nolf, "XIXe Eeuwse Voorlopers van de Federalistische Gedachte in België, 1842–1900" ["Nineteenth Century Forerunners of Federalist Thought in Belgium"], *Res Publica* 7, no. 2 (1965): 141–64. But there was no important Walloon movement in the political arena until after World War II. Cf. Lorwin, "Belgium," p. 171 (cited in note 13).

g. An illustration of the early importance of corporatism was "the government's strategy of subcontracting the administration of social welfare to 'responsible' associations" (Zolberg, "Belgium," p. 121).

h. Belgian political history is replete with "crises"—at least in Belgians' terms of reference. Seen from afar and with the perspective of time, however, most appear as spurs to action on difficult problems over which politicians might otherwise have temporized. The regime's career is better characterized as "punctuated evolution" than as plagued by revolutionary discontinuities. See Martin O. Heisler, "Institutionalizing Societal Cleavages," pp. 189–209 (cited in note 4).

i. The Dutch term *verzuiling* (pillarization) likewise denotes such segmentation. It is an underpinning of consociational democracy in Arend Lijphart's early formulation. See his "Consociational Democracy," *World Politics* 21, no. 2 (January 1969): 207–25.

j. Resource allocation poses problems, because any formula must be seen as fair in all parts of the country. Flanders has the largest population; but since many programs are affected by territory and distance, per capita allocations might be unfair to Walloons, with a larger, less densely populated region. Brussels faces special problems as a large city and as the site of governmental and international agencies that pay few or no taxes but place heavy demands on services. A combination of criteria is used to achieve a sense of fairness in the eyes of residents of each region. Cf. Luc Huyse, "Political Conflict in Bicultural Belgium," in Arend J. Lijphart, ed., *Conflict and Coexistence in Belgium*, p. 125 (cited in note 6).

k. These "alarm bells" consist of a temporary halt in proceedings—to permit public discussion, the mobilization of public opinion, and the intervention of judicial organs. They have been invoked once as of this writing. See McRae, *Belgium,* pp. 183, 340.

References

1. Talleyrand expressed such views several times in 1830. See, for example, G. Lacour-Gayet, *Talleyrand,* vol. 3 (Paris: Payot, 1932), ch. 22.

2. See Charles Verlinden, *Les Origines de la Frontière Linguistique en Belgique et la Colonisation Franque* (Brussels: La Renaissance du Livre, 1955); J. D'Hondt, *Notes sur l'Origine de la Frontière Linguistique* (Brussels: La Renaissance du Livre, 1952); and Jean Stengers, *La Formation de la Frontière Linguistique en Belgique, ou de la Légitimité de l'Hypothèse Historique* (Brussels: Latomus, 1959). Historically predominantly Flemish but with a large French-speaking majority in modern times, Brussels is just north of the linguistic frontier, abutting the Walloon part of Brabant province.

3. Martin O. Heisler, *Political Community and Its Formation in the Low Countries* (Ann Arbor, MI: University Microfilms, 1970), ch. III.

4. See Kenneth D. McRae, *Conflict and Compromise in Multilingual Societies: Volume 2. Belgium* (Waterloo, Ontario, Canada: Wilfrid Laurier University Press, 1986), ch. 2 and 3. See, also, Aristide R. Zolberg, "Splitting the Difference: Federalization without Federalism in Belgium," in Milton J. Esman, ed., *Ethnic Conflict in the Western World* (Ithaca, NY: Cornell University Press, 1977), ch. 5; and "Belgium," in Raymond Grew, ed., *Crises of Political Development in Europe and the United States* (Princeton, NJ: Princeton University Press, 1978), ch. 3; and Martin O. Heisler, "Institutionalizing Societal Cleavages in a Cooptive Polity: The Growing Importance of the Output Side in Belgium," in M.O. Heisler, ed., *Politics in Europe* (New York: David McKay, 1974), ch. 5; "Managing Ethnic Conflict in Belgium," *Annals of the American Academy of Political and Social Science* 433 (September 1977): 32–56, and "Belgium: Stability and Progress from Division," in Robert Rinehart, ed., *Global Studies: Western Europe* (Guilford, CT: Dushkin, forthcoming).

5. For the data, see McRae, *Belgium,* pp. 77–84.

6. Lode Claes, "The Process of Federalization in Belgium," *Delta* 6, no. 4 (1963–64): 43; McRae, *Belgium,* pp. 110–24. See, also, Heisler, "Institutionalizing Societal Cleavages," pp. 179–80; and Zolberg, "Splitting the Difference," pp. 103–4. Cf. Luc Huyse's interesting notion that communal conflicts in Belgium may be "camouflage" for partisan political interests: "Political Conflict in Bicultural Belgium," in Arend J. Lijphart, ed., *Conflict and Coexistence in Belgium: The Dynamics of a Culturally Divided Society* (Berkeley: University of California, Institute of International Studies, 1981), pp. 118–24.

7. Crude approximations of the costs of providing separate facilities in education and linguistic balance in some public agencies for 1963–73 are given in Martin O. Heisler, "Ethnic Division in Belgium," in Daniel J. Elazar, ed., *Self Rule/Shared Rule* (Ramat Gan, Israel: Turtledove Publishing, 1979), pp. 147–48. For more precise data, focusing on expenditures for higher education in 1971–81, see Martin O. Heisler and B. Guy Peters, "Scarcity and the Management of Political Conflict in Multicultural Polities," *International Political Science Review* 4, no. 3 (1983): 333–36.

8. See Zolberg, "Splitting the Difference," pp. 103–4, and "Belgium," p. 134. Observers are evenly divided in attributing one or two deaths to the ethnic cleavage since 1960.

9. Zolberg, "Belgium," pp. 103ff.

10. See Reginald De Schryver, "The Belgian Revolution and the Emergence of Belgium's Biculturalism," in Lijphart, ed., *Conflict and Coexistence in Belgium,* pp. 25–27.

11. Carl-Henrik Höjer, *Le Régime Parlementaire Belge de 1918 à 1940* (Uppsala: Almqvist and Wiksells, 1946), p. 7.

12. This was manifested in the Flemish movement. The most comprehensive

work in English remains Shephard B. Clough, *A History of the Flemish Movement in Belgium: A Study in Nationalism* (New York: Octagon Books, 1968; first published in 1930). The best works are in Dutch: H.J. Elias, *Geschiedenis van de Vlaamse Gedachte*, 4 vols. (Antwerp: Nederlandsche Boekhandel, 1963–65); Leo Picard, *Evolutie van de Vlaamse Beweging van 1795 tot 1950*, 3 vols., 2nd ed. (Antwerp: Standaard-Boekhandel, 1963); and A.W. Willemsen, *Het Vlaams-Nationalisme: De Geschiedenis van de Jaren 1914–1940*, 2nd ed. (Utrecht: Ambo, 1969).

13. Val R. Lorwin, "Belgium: Religion, Class, and Language in National Politics," in Robert A. Dahl, ed., *Political Oppositions in Western Democracies* (New Haven, CT: Yale University Press, 1966), pp. 171–172.

14. There is general agreement on when the cleavage became salient. See Heisler, "Institutionalizing Societal Cleavages," pp. 198–201. For a synopsis of its development and politics, see, also, Jules Gérard-Libois and Xavier Mabille, "Belgian Electoral Politics" in Lijphart, ed., *Conflict and Coexistence in Belgium*, pp. 131–32.

15. Heisler, "Institutionalizing Societal Cleavages," pp. 198–208.

16. For a clear picture, see McRae, *Belgium*, pp. 80–87, tables 18–21. For analyses of the institutional and political dynamics, see Martin O. Heisler and B. Guy Peters, "Comparing Social Policy across Levels of Government, Countries, and Time: Belgium and Sweden since 1870," in Douglas E. Ashford, ed., *Comparing Public Policies: New Concepts and Methods* (Beverly Hills, CA: Sage Publications, 1978), ch. 8; and A.-P. Frognier, V.F. McHale, and D. Paranzino, *Votes, clivages sociopolitiques et développement régional en Belgique* (Louvain, Belgium: Vander, 1974).

17. Mancur Olson, *The Rise and Decline of Nations: Economic Growth, Stagflation, and Social Rigidities* (New Haven, CT: Yale University Press, 1982), especially pp. 43–47. On Belgium, see J.L. Litt, "Structures sociales régionales et développement économique: la population active en Belgique de 1880 à 1961," *Mutation et Région* (1972): 3; Insitut Nationale de Statistique, "Les Investissements Industriels des Régions Linguistiques de 1955 à 1969," *Etudes Statistiques* 27 (1972): 17–34; Fernand Baudhuin, *Belgique 1900–1960: Explication Économique de Notre Temps* (Louvain, Belgium: Institut de Recherches Economiques et Sociales, 1961), pp. 263–66. Cf. Michel Quévit, *Les Causes de Déclin Wallon* (Brussels: Editions Vie Ouvrière, 1978).

18. T. Palasthy, "Indices bruts de prospérité régionale," *Mutation et Région* (1972): 1–2; Baudhuin, *Belgique 1900–1960*.

19. McRae, *Belgium*, pp. 75–77.

20. Heisler, "Institutionalizing Societal Cleavages," pp. 204–8; McRae, *Belgium*, pp. 142ff.

21. See McRae, *Belgium*, pp. 142–48.

22. Val R. Lorwin, "Segmented Pluralism: Ideological Cleavages and Political Cohesion in the Smaller European Democracies," *Comparative Politics* 3 (January 1971): 141.

23. See the interview data and analysis in Heisler, "Institutionalizing Societal Cleavages," pp. 201–4 and tables 7–10.

24. For an excellent, detailed analysis of this subject, see McRae, *Belgium*, pp. 156–73.

25. Cf. *Ibid.*, pp. 145–48.

26. See Martin O. Heisler, with Robert B. Kvavik, "Patterns of European Politics: The 'European Polity' Model" in Heisler, ed., *Politics in Europe,* pp. 27–89, *passim.*

27. Confidential interview with a regional party leader who has also served in Parliament and in the agglomeration's executive council, July 1984, Brussels.

28. For the distinctions, see Arend Lijphart, *Democracies: Patterns of Majoritarian and Consensus Government in Twenty-One Countries* (New Haven, CT: Yale University Press, 1984), especially ch. 1 and 2. See, also, chapter 27 in this volume.

29. For a detailed, more balanced discussion, see McRae, *Belgium,* pp. 285–93.

30. Heisler and Peters, "Scarcity and the Management of Political Conflict."

13

Canada: Reflections on
Two Conflicts

Kenneth D. McRae

I t would be relatively easy to present the Canadian case as a linguistic conflict that became prominent in the 1960s, peaked in the 1970s, and then
declined in the 1980s. Such a straightforward scenario, however, would
not be the most helpful way to develop a comparison with Northern Ireland,
nor would it explain all aspects of the Canadian case. To develop the comparative dimensions most relevant to the Irish context requires a closer look at
Canadian history, which soon reveals two dimensions of persistent cultural
cleavage in addition to the usual clash of economic interest groups: the one
religious, the other ethnolinguistic. From a French-Canadian vantage point,
these two lines of cleavage have normally coincided, but this has not been the
case for other groups, nor has the double cleavage worked in the same way
in every province. The tensions and conflicts stemming from religion and language in Canada have differed in their geographic patterns, in their chronolo-
gies, and in the institutional arrangements for their management.

Catholics and Protestants

When France formally ceded New France to Britain in 1763, three future lines
of cleavage in Canadian politics were born simultaneously. A colony of
France founded on the Roman Catholic religion, the French language, and the
civil law of Paris was annexed to a British Empire founded on a Protestant
establishment of religion, the English language, and English common law. In
the aftermath of the conquest, the most noteworthy concerns were religious
and legal. After a decade of uncertainty, the Roman Catholic religion and the
French civil law received guarantees in the Quebec Act of 1774, which, in
turn, stands as one of the imperial acts that precipitated the American Revolution. American independence, in its turn, had consequences for the old prov-

I thank my colleague Alain Gagnon for suggesting several corrections, clarifications, and
improvements to the original draft of this chapter.

ince of Quebec, for it introduced a new population of refugees from the
United States that was mainly English-speaking and Protestant.[a] A much
larger influx came after 1815, however, when massive emigration from the
British Isles brought dramatic population growth in the Canadas and in other
parts of British North America. In the 1830s and 1840s, a very considerable
proportion of this immigration originated from Ireland—above all during the
famine years of the late 1840s, when the Irish rural population was decimated
by failure of the potato crops.

Resemblances to Ireland

One effect of these demographic changes was that by mid-century, the structure of social cleavages in the Canadas[b] bore an ominous resemblance to that

Figure 13–1. Canada: Provinces and Territories

in Ireland. As French civil law and English common law had effectively been institutionalized through the territorial division of Upper and Lower Canada, the most salient social cleavage of the period was the religious division between Catholics and Protestants. Hereditary levels of mistrust between these groups were heightened by the activities of the Orange Order. Originally imported into Canada by Irish Protestant immigrants, Orangeism soon spread without hindrance to non-Irish Protestants, and the development of ultramontane Catholicism in Europe and in French Canada evoked strong Protestant reactions. Just as in Ireland, the Protestant element of Canada around 1850 was numerically in a minority position but dominant from a socioeconomic standpoint. Nevertheless, both French-Canadians and Irish Catholics were well organized and capable of mobilization for political action when necessary. Consequently, the history of Canada in the nineteenth century was marked by extensive electoral violence, religious riots, a major political assassination (cabinet minister Thomas D'Arcy McGee, by a Fenian), a political execution (Louis Riel, the leader of two western Métis rebellions), and major controversies over issues of church and state. On occasion, religious conflict spilled over into language conflict, so that when Roman Catholic schools were barred from public funding in Manitoba in 1890, another provincial act in the same session dropped French as an official language.

What seems evident from a broad comparison of Canada and Ireland in the nineteenth century is that many of the ingredients for escalating religious conflict were present in roughly parallel form in the two countries. Both societies were in a dependent status, and in some respects at least, the raw frontier society of Canada was no less turbulent than that of Ireland. The key question that we may ask, then, is why Ireland in the twentieth century has been marked by civil war, partition, and recurrent political violence, while Canada, despite a major twentieth-century upheaval of its own, has largely escaped the level of acute political violence that has afflicted Ireland for the past seven decades.

Tension-Reducing Factors in Canada

At this very broad level of comparison, any answer to this all-important question must be subjective and speculative. Nevertheless, one can identify several factors in the Canadian context that have helped to reduce the intensity of religious and linguistic tensions. First, the Canadian political system since 1967 has been a federal one, which means that some elements of intergroup conflict (whether religious or linguistic) could be relegated to various provincial arenas or tackled simultaneously at both federal and provincial levels. Second, this federal system has provided a substantial political separation between a primarily French-speaking Catholic Quebec and several primarily English-speaking Protestant provinces, though significant religious and linguistic minorities have continued to exist on both sides. Third, in most of rural

Canada, the Francophone and Anglophone populations have been separated as a result of divergent settlement patterns; and in most regions, this has reduced levels of daily contact. Fourth, although the Protestant–Catholic religious division in Canada did not follow such a sharp territorial separation, both groups tended in the nineteenth century to develop fairly complete networks of welfare facilities, hospitals, schools, and even their own newspapers. Fifth, the working of the federal and provincial political process normally involved three major groups, rather than two: Francophone Catholics, Anglophone Catholics, and Anglophone Protestants. In this process, English-speaking Catholics often played a bridging and mediating role between the other two groups, which sustains the familiar proposition of political science that cross-pressures arising from crosscutting cleavages help to reduce intergroup tensions. Finally, the Canadian economic setting during much of the period in question has been one of abundance and rapid growth, at least in contrast with the more modest economic situation of Ireland.

One may argue that these factors helped to defuse or moderate both religious and linguistic conflict in post-Confederation Canada, but for the longer term, the situation was not wholly favorable to conflict management. The segmentation of social institutions along religious lines also meant institutionalization of economic inequalities. As in Ulster, segmentation came to represent a certain Anglo-Protestant dominance in the economic sector, which was facilitated and perpetuated by a religiously divided educational system but which was, at the same time, mitigated by the normal participation of Roman Catholics in the political system. Canadian federalism also had its negative aspect, for in preserving French-Canadian autonomy in a strong province of Quebec, it also fostered defensive strategies of agrarian traditionalism, Catholicism, and antimaterialism as the most appropriate social milieu for French Canada. One result of such strategies was that when industrialization and urbanization came to Quebec early in the twentieth century, they produced an urban working world that was linguistically and ethnically stratified, to the severe detriment of that province's traditionalist French-speaking majority.

While Ulster moved from four decades of Protestant domination to increased Protestant–Catholic tensions in the early 1960s, the evolution of intergroup relations in Canada was subtly different. Religious conflict slowly waned, but linguistic sensitivities increased. The strength of Orangeism, which persisted stubbornly in municipal politics into the 1950s, ebbed in the 1960s but left residues of feelings and attitudes that exacerbated linguistic quarrels in the same decade. Indeed, one can argue plausibly that much of the virulence and simple intolerance of the language fight in Canada represents a continuation, in disguised form, of nineteenth-century religious conflict. Nevertheless, the language fight differed from the earlier religious one in another essential respect: Its territorial epicenter was the province of Quebec.

Further, the upheaval in Quebec that has been rather deceptively labeled the Quiet Revolution (*la Révolution tranquille*) took place in an atmosphere of rapid deconfessionalization and Christian ecumenism, which served to blunt the edge of Protestant opposition and to make the results of the revolution more widely acceptable in English Canada.

Quebec and Canada

The so-called Quiet Revolution was more than a straightforward linguistic or ethnic conflict, though it had clearly discernible linguistic and ethnic dimensions. Its many-sidedness makes it difficult to present briefly and especially to explain its causes. Even a generation later, the explanatory literature remains diffuse and unsatisfactory. Moreover, this revolution has had a profound impact not only on Quebec society but on the Canadian political system as a whole. [*]

Even the starting point of the revolution is open to argument. According to one view, the changes were inspired and unleashed by the Liberal victory at the 1960 provincial election; others see a slow but steady buildup of forces for change beginning soon after 1945 but held in check for a time by the paternalistic conservative regime of Premier Maurice Duplessis.[c] Was Quebec in the 1950s a quiet rural oasis walled off from modernity, or was it a powder keg ready to be touched off? Whatever one's view of the 1950s, the early 1960s established beyond a doubt that Quebec society had entered a stage of rapid and fundamental transformation.

Dimensions of the Quiet Revolution

What, then, *was* the Quiet Revolution? Even though a cohesive explanation may be elusive, one can identify and describe readily enough some of its major dimensions. First, it had a political dimension. A major thrust for rapid social change developed after the defeat of the long-established Union Nationale regime by a rejuvenated Liberal party in 1960 under the leadership of a former federal minister, Jean Lesage. A second dimension was economic development. A major program was launched, with particular emphasis on making up for the province's retarded economic development—a conscious policy of *rattrapage*. The new regime did not hesitate to make extensive use of public enterprise as the main motor of economic development, and the central and most symbolic part of this program was a vastly extended nationalization of private electric power companies to expand Hydro Quebec into a giant public corporation. In the Canadian context, such a policy was hardly revolutionary, for there were precedents dating back half a century in Ontario and other provinces for the public ownership of electrical energy resources.

A third and very important dimension of the Quiet Revolution was educational reform. The Francophone universities were vastly expanded, and an entire new stage of the educational system, the *collège d'enseignement général et professionnel* (CEGEP), was introduced between the secondary level and the universities in place of the former *collèges classiques*. One consequence was a dramatic widening of access to higher education. In turn, the expanded universities became nurseries for a wider political radicalism that quickly developed more far-reaching social goals.

While these changes were being made, the welfare system—formerly a domain of the church, the parish, and the voluntary association—was also being transformed. The Quebec government built systematic health, pension, and welfare systems in the public sector, at a time when federal–provincial negotiation was developing countrywide standards in these fields. In a parallel development, professional life and professional associations in Quebec became stronger and more organized, especially among the "newer" professions—such as teachers, health professionals, and engineers—that had blossomed as a result of the Quiet Revolution itself. This development could build on both old and new tendencies, on older Catholic corporate social theory and on newer notions of collective bargaining.

Along with expansion of the newer, secular, public sector–based activities went deconfessionalization and a waning of clerical influence. The teaching and nursing professions, once primarily a preserve of the Catholic religious orders, became predominantly staffed by lay personnel. There were sharp declines in the number of ordinations for the priesthood and in the number of people taking religious orders. The austere morality of traditional Catholicism that once dominated Quebec society became more relaxed. To cite just one example, provincial film censorship, at one time perhaps the strictest in Canada, soon ranked among the most liberal.

These processes of modernization were not the whole of the Quiet Revolution. Still another dimension was an intensified drive for the *francisation* ("Frenchification") of Quebec society. There was increased concern that the language of the factory floor should be understood—and spoken—by management; that the working language of the immigrant—and especially of the immigrant's children—should be that of the Francophone majority. There was also a growing confidence and conviction that the French language ought to become predominant at all levels of Quebec society and for all domains of discourse, including science, engineering, and technology. For this purpose, the new public corporations, in which language usage was more easily amenable to government control, afforded an appropriate arena for management of linguistic change. A common motif of change on many fronts was a new awareness of and pride in a distinctive Quebecois identity, a reassertion in modified form of the older phenomenon of French-Canadian nationalism.

The Potential for Conflict

It was not so much the drive for modernization and development as the new Quebecois nationalism that had the potential for sparking serious social conflict. From the early 1960s onward, this conflict was manifested at three different levels. First, it was evident *within* Quebec in the form of a challenge by new Francophone professional groups to established Anglophone managerial and professional elites—a challenge that forced many Anglophones either to adjust to changing linguistic norms or to move to another province. Second, there was increasing nonacceptance of Quebec's traditional position within the Canadian federal system and a sustained drive to enlarge the sphere of provincial jurisdiction. Finally, the conflict appeared at the international level as a clash between divergent foreign-policy goals of Canada and Quebec, most obviously in relation to the emergent association of Francophone countries, *la Francophonie*.

The channels for the expression of this heightened nationalism were also quite varied. In the 1960s, it found expression in Quebec's traditional political parties: the Liberals under Premier Jean Lesage and the more conservative Union Nationale headed by Premier Daniel Johnson. It was represented more stridently in the smaller nationalist parties, electorally insignificant but more radical and more independence-oriented in their programs. An event of some importance was the decision in 1967 of the prominent Liberal ex-minister René Lévesque to leave the Liberals to establish a new political movement more explicitly dedicated to the sovereignty of Quebec—the Mouvement Soveraineté-Association, which in 1968 joined the smaller nationalist groups to become the Parti Québécois. Further confrontation occurred in the field of industrial relations, where predominantly Francophone trade unions engaged in industrial and nationalist action against employers that could be seen as both Anglophone and capitalist. During the 1960s and 1970s, labor relations in Quebec were turbulent, marked by mass demonstrations and above-average levels of violence.

Beyond the mainstream of the labor movement, small fringe groups of students, intellectuals, and a few fanatics dreamed of liberation through armed revolution. By 1963, sporadic bombing incidents occurred in Montreal and elsewhere in the province, usually by individuals acting alone or in small groups. In October 1970, the kidnapping in quick succession of British trade commissioner James Cross and a provincial cabinet minister, Pierre Laporte, unexpectedly underlined the seriousness of the threat to the legal order and focused world media attention on the Quebec issue. In response, the governments concerned did not hesitate to invoke the War Measures Act and to rule by emergency powers. By means of these rather stringent measures, which were widely supported at the time by both Francophone and Anglophone opinion but later condemned by many civil libertarians as an overreaction, the October crisis receded, Cross was released through negotiations, and the killers of Laporte were apprehended. No further political kidnappings or killings have followed these two cases, and even theorists of the left have acknowledged that the use of violence in 1970 was counterproductive.[1]

It seems important to note that the extralegal revolutionary fringe of the Quebec social upheaval limited its operations to certain types of violence. Beginning in 1963, the first waves of the Front de Libération du Québec (FLQ) directed their bombs against symbolic objects (such as monuments or federal mail boxes), federal buildings and armories, a few industrial enterprises, homes of prominent individuals, and banks and businesses chosen as holdup targets to finance further activities. The bombs were numerous—and they caused a number of deaths and injuries—but with a few possible exceptions, they were not deliberately aimed at human targets, not even at police or military personnel. The two 1970 kidnappings, apparently in imitation of Third World and particularly Latin American models, represented a significant escalation and attracted media attention proportionately. When the second victim, Quebec Labour Minister Pierre Laporte, was killed by his captors on October 17, however, a strong wave of public revulsion and condemnation signaled the beginning of the end for extralegal methods. Even though the FLQ had enjoyed substantial support from groups of students still breathing the rarified atmosphere of the Paris revolt of 1968 and from some nationalist labor leaders, the hoped-for mobilization of rank-and-file workers by revolutionary action never materialized. Further, although FLQ activists often behaved in an immature or reckless fashion, they lived in a political culture that imposed social norms and limits even on their extralegal behavior.

On the other side, the much larger mainstream of the Quebec independence movement, under the leadership of René Lévesque, explicitly distanced itself from extralegal methods. The Parti Québécois remained firmly committed to parliamentary democracy and to the implementation of its goal of independence through majority decisions by the Quebec electorate. Lévesque himself is reported to have rejected offers of generous financial support for the newly founded Parti Québécois from Gaullist sources in France in 1969.[2] This distancing from insurrectionary methods bore fruit, as became evident at the 1970 provincial election, when the Parti Québécois won a substantial 23 percent of the popular vote, three times the level reached by the minor separatist parties at the previous election. In 1973, this figure rose to 30 percent, but the anomalies of Quebec electoral law held the party to seven seats in 1970 and only six in 1973, of a total of 110 in the legislature.

In November 1976, however, this same electoral law worked to the advantage of the Parti Québécois. As a consequence, a party committed to the democratic separation of Quebec from the rest of Canada was catapulted into power with 41 percent of the popular vote but a solid majority of 71 seats out of 110. Under Lévesque's leadership, the Parti Québécois would form the government of the province for the next nine years. Although it was to lose the crucial referendum calling for negotiation of an agreement of sovereignty-association with the rest of Canada in May 1980, the Parti Québécois nevertheless went on to win a second term of office at the provincial general election of April 1981. Even more than the sporadic violence of the 1960s and the 1970 October crisis, this nine-year period from 1976 to 1985, during which Quebec was governed by a legally elected regime actively committed to Quebec independence, constituted the most fundamental challenge to the Canadian federal system in this century.

The Quebec Question and the Canadian Political System

At the level of federal politics and policymaking, successive Canadian prime ministers responded to the challenge of the Quebec independentist movement in different ways. Under John Diefenbaker (from 1957 to 1963), the early stages of Quebec's Quiet Revolution were largely ignored in Ottawa. Diefenbaker's strongest political support lay outside Quebec, and his Conservative cabinets were were rather weak in Francophone representation. A few of his ministers even felt that a Conservative majority could be preserved without Quebec. At a symbolic level, the country's linguistic duality was deemphasized by an appeal to "one Canada" and by repeated reminders of the multinational origins of the Canadian population. Yet even the Diefenbaker goverment increased the practical use of French in Parliament by initiating the simultaneous translation of debates.

The two Liberal governments of Lester Pearson (from 1963 to 1968) emphasized more influential representation of Francophones at cabinet level. At the beginning of his term of office, Pearson announced a major commission of inquiry into French–English relations in Canada, the first such inquiry on this topic since Confederation—and the body so appointed, the Royal Commission on Bilingualism and Biculturalism—was established on the basis of parity between its Anglophone and Francophone members. Further, its terms of reference called for development of the Canadian Confederation on the basis of "an equal partnership" of the two major language groups. In other respects, the Pearson administration, which remained a minority government through two general elections, was notable for its tendency to allow Quebec some latitude in the form of its participation in certain countrywide social programs. The most noteworthy of these was the Canada Pension Plan, alongside which Quebec established a parallel pension fund of its own that soon became an important source of capital for provincial development.

Under Pearson's Liberal successor Pierre Elliott Trudeau, the strategy at the federal level changed significantly. As prime minister continuously from

1968 to 1984—except for one brief Conservative interlude in 1979—Trudeau faced both the 1970 October crisis and virtually the entire period of Parti Québécois rule in Québec. The hallmark of the Trudeau regime was strong Francophone representation in federal cabinets, with several of the major economic portfolios (including finance) being held by Francophones for the first time. Already known as an independent-minded intellectual and a committed antinationalist before his entry into federal politics, the prime minister vigorously opposed any form of special status for Quebec, seeking instead to make the federal administration more accessible and meaningful to the Francophone population. In more technical terms, his response to the Quebec issue leaned toward power-sharing at the center rather than decentralization. This position was supported by passage of the federal Official Languages Act of 1969, based on recommendations of the Royal Commission on Bilingualism and Biculturalism—a statute that recognized in law the legal equality of French and English as official languages of Canada and of all federal institutions. Language legislation was accompanied by a major effort to improve linguistic balance in the federal public service and to change the traditional Anglophone face of Ottawa into something more appropriate to its position as capital of an officially bilingual country.

The Federal Response to the Parti Québécois Challenge

The problem of an appropriate federal strategy concerning the Quebec issue became more acute after the Parti Québécois took power provincially in 1976. For the next nine years, the provincial government of Quebec would be committed not to making the federal system work but to demonstrating its disadvantages for the Quebecois. Trudeau's response, as a Francophone and a Quebecois with strong credentials himself, was to appeal directly to the voters of Quebec over the heads of their provincial government. This stance became particularly important during the referendum debate on sovereignty-association, when several Francophone federal ministers played leading roles in the campaign on the negative side. It is worth noting that this debate, which involved perhaps the most crucial political decision for Quebec and for Canada since 1867, was conducted under carefully devised rules concerning participation, financing, media advertising, and voter eligibility, embodied in a provincial statute. After an orderly but passionate campaign, the Quebec electorate—which is about 80 percent Francophone—voted by a three to two margin *against* giving the provincial government a mandate to negotiate sovereignty-association.

The complex constitutional reform process of the 1980s can also be seen as a federal response to the independentist challenge to Canada. In its essence, Trudeau's plan to meet that challenge involved two components. The first was the repatriation (or, strictly speaking, patriation) to Canada of the Canadian written constitution, the British North America Act of 1867 and its subsequent amendments—a step delayed for half a century owing to the failure of the federal and provincial governments to reach unanimous agreement on an acceptable amending procedure. The second was the incorporation in this constitution of a comprehensive charter of individual rights and freedoms, a project long promoted by the prime minister. Although the charter did little to recognize the claims of the Quebec government to represent the Francophone element in Canada, it did entrench French and English in the constitution as official languages, and it guaranteed certain specific rights to the use of French or English throughout the country. The completion of this package involved major federal–provincial negotiations and federal concessions. In the end, only Quebec refused to accept it, with Premier Lévesque complaining of the treachery of several Anglophone premiers who had initially sided with Quebec in opposing the Trudeau proposals. Yet it is doubtful if a Quebec government openly committed to sovereignty could have been induced at this time to support any conceivable package designed to renew federalism and to increase legitimacy for the Canadian constitution.[d]

The Meech Lake Accord

In time, Quebec's nonadherence to the new 1982 constitution proved a growing source of embarrassment; but by 1985, changes of government had occurred in both Ottawa and Quebec. The new Conservative federal prime minister, Brian Mulroney—himself a fluently bilingual Anglophone Quebecois—had won the 1984 election on a platform of conciliation of Quebec nationalism; cooperation with the Parti Québécois; and greater flexibility, rather than confrontation, in federal–provincial relations. By 1985, he faced a new Liberal provincial government that was similarly determined to negotiate Quebec's adherence to the new constitution, provided that certain Quebec objectives could be attained in doing so. The result was another complex round of federal–provincial negotiations, culminating in the so-called Meech Lake Accord of June 1987. One key provision of this agreement was an explicit recognition of Quebec as a "distinct society" within Canada. To obtain unanimous approval on this contentious point, the federal government had to concede a larger role to all the provinces in immigration matters and in appointments to the federal Supreme Court and Senate. As of September 1988, the Meech Lake Accord had been ratified by eight provinces out of ten, including Quebec.

Policies of Quebec Governments

In the Quebec responses to the Quebec question, the line of policy continuity is more discernible. Even though the degrees of commitment and methods have varied, all Quebec governments since Duplessis have shared a common goal of defending provincial interests and jurisdiction against federal encroachment. What differentiates Quebec from other provinces is that this goal has frequently taken more specific form as a defense of Francophone linguistic and cultural particularism against a heavy Anglophone preponderance in Canada as a whole and in North America. A common thread of cultural nationalism can be seen in all recent Quebec governments, despite considerable variations in how it has been articulated.

Under Premier Maurice Duplessis, it took the form of a defensive, constitutionalist, province-based nationalism, jealous to protect Quebec's constitutional powers from federal intrusion but little inclined toward legislative activism in its own right. Under Premier Jean Lesage, from 1960 to 1966, provincial legislative powers were used far more extensively to implement the Quiet Revolution and to modernize Quebec society, under the slogan "*maitres chez nous.*" With Lesage's Union Nationale successor, Daniel Johnson, the pace of internal social change was slowed down, but conflict with the federal government escalated over Quebec's role in foreign relations and Johnson's more confrontational motto: "*égalité ou indépendance.*[3] Johnson's premiership also marked the high point of external French intervention in the Quebec question, dramatized in 1967 by President Charles de Gaulle's theatrical endorsement of "*Québec libre*" in Montreal in the midst of the centennial celebrations of Confederation. The Liberal government of Robert Bourassa, badly shaken by the October crisis in its first year of office, worked in closer cooperation with the federal authorities but also introduced, in 1974, a bill to control the language of education in Quebec, requiring children of other than English-language background to attend French-language schools and declaring French the official language of the province.

Under Premier René Lévesque, after 1976, the objectives became far more radical, including nothing less than full sovereignty for the Quebec state. But this was to be accomplished gradually, by democratic methods, through a policy of winning independence in stages (*étapisme*). Before proceeding to the 1980 referendum on sovereignty-association, the Parti Québécois government developed an extensive legislative agenda on language, culture, social welfare, and industrial development that carried forward the thrust of modernization and social development begun in the 1960s. The linguistic cornerstone of this effort was Bill 101, passed in August 1977, a comprehensive language law that sought to make French the exclusive language of public signs; the normal language of industry and commerce; the language of education, except for children of parents educated in English in Quebec; and even the exclusive language of provincial legislation, the public service, and the courts. Even though some provisions have since been invalidated as unconstitutional by the courts, this law has had a profound impact on language usage in Quebec, and a promise by the Bourassa Liberal regime to modify it after the defeat of the

Parti Québécois in 1985 has encountered strong opposition in nationalist circles. There is a double, Hegelian-tinged irony here. On the one hand, the language legislation removed a major grievance of the province's Francophone population, and in all likelihood this contributed to the eventual defeat of the sovereignty-association referendum in 1980. On the other hand, the gradual undermining of this legislation in the courts, especially in cases argued under the new federal Charter of Rights, threatens to revive an almost dormant language struggle and to begin the cycle of separatism all over again.

Developments in Other Provinces

When set against the all-important confrontation between the governments of Canada and Quebec, the more modest developments in French–English relations in other provinces may appear to be a minor sideshow. Yet in the Canadian federal system, each of the provinces can be viewed as a distant political arena, and each has felt, in its own way, the reverberations of Quebec's Quiet Revolution. In turn, events in the nine predominantly Anglophone provinces are noted in the national press of both languages, so that even the most unimportant of these provincial arenas can have some effect on the evolution of public attitudes. A brief survey of the three central provinces with large Francophone minorities illustrates both the spread of a new linguistic consciousness and the variety of strategies devised for its accommodation.

In New Brunswick, symbolic recognition of linguistic pluralism came first, to be followed only gradually by implementation. In this small province, a Francophone minority—largely of Acadian rather than French-Canadian origin, and constituting about a third of the total population—had lived a somewhat marginal existence in both a political and an economic sense until the 1960s. In 1969, reflecting linguistic developments at the federal level, a provincial statute recognized the equal status of French and English as official languages of the province, though its various clauses were phased in over several years. New Brunswick further opted to entrench this official bilingualism in the new federal constitution in 1982. The province has also looked beyond individual language rights to the group rights of its component language communities. A provincial statute of 1981 officially recognized the existence of distinct Anglophone and Francophone "linguistic communities" in the province and enacted a corresponding general obligation of government to promote the cultural, economic, educational, and social development of these communities on an equal basis.[4]

By contrast, in Ontario, the emphasis has been on pragmatic, incremental improvements in favor of a French-language minority that is territorially concentrated mainly in the eastern and northern parts of the province. Symbolic recognition of the French language remains a sensitive political issue, possibly because of its perceived connections with the still-visible residues of the

Protestant–Catholic conflict and no doubt also because of a large, linguistically diversified immigrant population that outnumbers the Francophones in many cities. In the 1960s, the main thrust of reform was to transform Franco-Ontarian schools from a transitional model that prepared Francophone children for secondary schooling in English into an integrated primary and secondary system functioning in French from beginning to end. At the postsecondary level, a limited range of programs offered in French has also been developed in three universities and in provincial colleges of technology. More recently, the emphasis has shifted to development of French-language capabilities in the provincial justice system and in areas of heavy demand in the public sector; but in fields other than education, these programs are still in their initial phases.

In Manitoba, both the problem and the recent responses to it have been very different. The province had entered Confederation in 1870 with a dual confessional school system (Protestant and Catholic) and legislative equality for English and French, a small-scale replica of the Quebec model. Even though these religious and linguistic guarantees were constitutionally entrenched, both were swept away in 1890 by provincial statutes inspired by a rising tide of anti-Catholic and anti-French sentiment imported from eastern Canada. In just two decades, a consociational replica of Quebec had been refashioned into a hegemonic replica of Ontario.

Despite protracted legal and political struggles over the schools question in the 1890s, strong political forces overrode constitutional guarantees. Not until 1979, in a changed linguistic climate, did the Supreme Court of Canada consider and reject as unconstitutional the 1890 provincial language legislation, thereby calling into question nine decades of subsequent unilingual English provincial statutes. The court decision did not settle the issue. As an alternative to an expensive exercise of translation of obsolete statutes, the provincial government offered to provide some administrative services in French in return for a more flexible translation schedule for past legislation. But this plan encountered extensive grass-roots opposition from non-Francophones and could not be implemented, leaving the manner and extent of Manitoba's compliance with its own original minority guarantees to be determined in the courts rather than in the political arena.

Federal–Provincial Conferences

The federal–provincial conference is still another decision-making arena of growing importance. These periodic meetings of the federal prime minister, the provincial premiers, and their supporting officials were originally irregular and sporadic but have been increasingly institutionalized as part of the contemporary federal system. With the growth of cooperative federalism and shared programs since the 1960s, such conferences have become routine and regularized, and regular meetings are held separately by other ministers with specific portfolios such as finance, natural resources, or education. The patriation and amendment of the constitution have long been central questions on the agenda of these conferences; and from 1980 to 1982, the Trudeau proposals in particular evoked a major debate. The Meech Lake Accord, if ratified, will make an annual first ministers' conference a constitutional requirement, with certain topics guaranteed a place on the agenda. In terms of French–English relations, the representatives of Quebec have almost invariably played a leading role at both federal–provincial and interprovincial conferences, and the maturing of this institution has created another important channel for easing and managing the conflict generated by the Quebec question during the past three decades.

The Provinces and International Relations

Finally, a more contentious and less institutionalized arena for expression of the Quebec conflict is seen in Canadian activity on the international scene. Both the federal and the Quebec governments have strongly backed the formation of an association of Francophone countries, and both have seen *la Francophonie* as a balance or counterweight to Canada's previous links with the British Commonwealth. The sharpest disagreements have been over who should represent the interests of Canada and Quebec at the international level and especially in relations among Francophone countries. For more than two decades, some of the most bitter battles have been waged over the right of successive Quebec governments to conduct international relations and conclude agreements with foreign governments directly in matters of provincial jurisdiction, such as education or culture.[5, e] With the waning of the era of high confrontation, compromise solutions have included federal umbrella agreements within which individual provinces may negotiate and sign specific accords[f] and Canadian participation in international conferences through combined delegations of federal and provincial representatives. At the Francophone summit in Paris in February 1986, for example, the Canadian delegation included the federal prime minister and the premiers of Quebec and New Brunswick.

Factors Relevant to Conflict Management

When the Parti Québécois moved from government to opposition after the provincial election of December 1985, the challenge to the Canadian polity became less acute, and it then became possible to assess the crisis years more calmly and systematically. What does the Canadian experience contribute to our knowledge of the management of ethnic conflict?

Multiple Arenas for Political Decision Making

In the first place, it is clear that the Canadian federal system is based on multiple arenas for political decision making. The game of politics is played vigorously and significantly in several places simultaneously. A political party or movement that is stifled or defeated at one level may find other arenas that offer more promise of a positive response. This multiplicity of decision-making sites has important consequences. It means that victories are seldom total or defeats irretrievable. It means, also, that political compromises must often be worked out *between* arenas, even though in any individual arena the normal situation is one-party majority rule based on electoral law distortions. In more technical language, Canadian electoral laws make European-style consociational politics based on coalitions and proportionality unlikely in most circumstances, but the federal system, with its multiple arenas and alternative opportunities, provides an approximate equivalent. This need for compromises between arenas explains the growing importance of federal–provincial conferences in the system as a whole.

Further, as long as there is a possibility of exerting a significant influence in at least one arena, feelings of minority alienation or powerlessness are less likely. The Quebecois, as the Royal Commission on Bilingualism and Biculturalism observed in 1965,[6] were clearly aware that they were a strong majority in their own province, even as they articulated their deep-seated grievances about their status in Canada.[g] Finally, in a federal system that has multiple arenas, there are more opportunities for crosscutting issues to make the pattern of politics more intricate and, consequently, to blunt the intensity of ethnic or linguistic conflict.

Adherence to Democratic Political Procedures

A second important conclusion to be drawn from the Canadian experience is the level of commitment shown by both sides—and, indeed, by all but a few marginal political forces—to the rules of political democracy. Even though the Canadian polity itself was in question, the procedures for replacing or retaining it through public debate and referendum were, in their essential respects, acceptable to both sides. Further, even though the referendum procedure was confined to the electorate of Quebec, it seems likely that majority opinion in the rest of Canada would have regarded a clear-cut independentist vote in Quebec in a formal referendum as a legitimation of separation.[h]

One may argue that this strict adherence to democratic political procedures on both sides has so far been successful in minimizing either military or terrorist action. Although the army had been mobilized in some force against the kidnappings during the October crisis in 1970, it has played no visible role in domestic politics since then. Similarly, even the proponents of extraparliamentary methods sought to mobilize mass opinion rather than to seize power by force, and they discarded violence and terrorism as soon as they were shown to be incompatible with this aim.

A Balance between Power-Sharing and Decentralization

In the management of ethnic conflict, one of the most delicate issues is finding a satisfactory balance between the *sharing* of power at the center and the *decentralization* of power through group autonomy. Recent Canadian experience is interesting because it illustrates tendencies toward each of these options. Insofar as prime ministerial style could influence a complex system, the emphasis swung from Diefenbaker's vision of unity, to Pearson's reliance on diplomatic-style compromise, to Trudeau's version of a strong federal government, and on to the more cooperative stances of Clark and Mulroney.

But the motion was more than that of a simple pendulum. Trudeau's centralism, unlike Diefenbaker's, rested on stronger Francophone participation in a more linguistically balanced federal administration, and it both reflected and reinforced the dual loyalty of many Francophones as *Québecois* and *Canadiens.*[7] The strategy of Trudeau's Conservative successors, on the other hand, was to offer an alternative prospect of decentralization—cessation of federal–provincial confrontation and reconciliation with the Parti Québécois—on the premise that any opponent of one's major opponent is a potential electoral ally. There was a strong element of opportunism in this succession of policy positions, for politicians must work with the resources that they have. Nevertheless, the point to be emphasized is that both more power-sharing at the center and more decentralization to the provinces have been available policy options in recent Canadian experience, and the Quebec electorate is large enough to have a substantial influence on the choice. Indeed, voters in Quebec could simultaneously back Trudeau's call for a strong federal government in 1968, 1972, 1974, and 1980 even while electing the Parti Québécois provincially in 1976 and 1981. In spite of periodic fluctuations and gloomy prognostications from partisans on either side, the political system appears to be in approximate equilibrium on the dimension of centralization.

Economic Factors

The theoretical literature on ethnic conflict frequently suggests that economic factors are central to ethnic conflict in one way or another. One hypothesis holds that economic disparities—or perceptions of disparity—between ethnic groups are either primary sources of conflict or factors in its escalation. Another theory tries to analyze ethnic conflict as a variant of class conflict. Still another suggests a relationship between intensity of ethnic conflict and the business cycle, with ethnic demands (as a concern for symbolic goods) expanding in prosperous times and yielding to more pragmatic, "bread-and-butter" issues when the economy is in recession. The question is whether recent Canadian experience offers any support for these hypotheses.

In this context, the issue of economic disparity becomes two distinct questions: the economic position of Quebec in relation to other provinces or regions and the relative economic position of Francophones and Anglophones within Quebec. On the first question, there can be no doubt that a major legacy of the Quiet Revolution was a modernized and economically stronger Quebec. Some part of this greater prosperity may be due to the federal government's heightened concern for income redistribution from favored to less favored regions (Quebec and the Atlantic provinces) in response to the challenge to federal authority. Undoubtedly, much more is due to the increased managerial capability and commitment of successive Quebec governments since the 1960s. Ironically, the economic competence of the Parti Québécois administration from 1976 to 1985 may have contributed significantly to increasing Francophone prosperity and, hence, decreasing the attractiveness of the independence option.

The second aspect of economic disparity—income differentials between Anglophones and Francophones—was studied extensively for Quebec and other provinces by the Royal Commission on Bilingualism and Biculturalism. Its findings, based on 1961 census data, revealed a wide gap in earnings between the various linguistic groups, with Quebec Francophones earning, on average, only 65 percent of the average reported for Quebec Anglophones. Later studies have shown a significant narrowing of this gap. By 1971, for example, average Francophone earnings were 77 percent of the Anglophone average.[8] Similarly, much of the early literature on the Quebec question tended to portray the language conflict as a more or less clear-cut class struggle between a Francophone working class and an Anglophone bourgeoisie. Yet here, too, the recent evidence points to the steady expansion and diversification of an educated Francophone middle class from the traditional liberal professions—first into the administrative and technical strata of the public sector and then, more recently, into private-sector commerce and industry as well. If attitudes toward Quebec independence have changed, this may be, in part, because over three decades, increasing numbers of Quebecois have acquired a larger stake in their society.[9]

The possible link between the cycle of ethnonationalism and the business cycle is more ambiguous. It is true that the loss of momentum of the independentist movement coincided closely with the economic recession of the early 1980s, but it also followed closely the unsuccessful referendum campaign of 1980, a more plausible and more direct reason for the ruling Parti Québécois to alter course. On the other hand, the Canadian experience does not directly contradict the hypothesis that ethnic consciousness blossoms under prosperity and fades in times of economic difficulty. One must therefore regard the result as inconclusive on this point.

Lessons in Conflict Management

At this point, the "Quebec question" is far from being "resolved." In particular, there remain wide variations between alternative ethnolinguistic models of Canada, ranging from the federally oriented model of a centralized bilingual state through various intermediate positions to an independent—or at least largely autonomous—unilingual Quebec. One may forecast with some confidence that language divisions will continue to stand out as a primary cleavage in Canadian society and that a periodic resurgence of conflict above the levels of the mid-1980s is quite probable.

The claim for successful conflict management in the Canadian case up to the present can be summed up in three points. First, the level of overt violence and terrorist action remained marginal and minimal, diminishing sharply after 1970. Second, the more important and more general confrontation over Quebec sovereignty was a political battle, waged with verbal rather than military weapons, under prescribed rules, and culminating in a referendum. Finally, confrontation between the federal and Quebec governments both diminished in intensity and assumed a more complex and more indirect form after the 1980 referendum.

From a slightly different vantage point, the Quebec question is no longer at the top of the political agenda at either the federal or the provincial level. It remains highly salient, but other issues can claim comparable priority. The breakup of the Canadian Confederation—or, alternatively, the birth of a sovereign Quebec—is not an immediate prospect, though this does not imply any guarantee for the longer term.

Notes

a. One direct result of loyalist settlement was a division of the old province of Quebec into the separate colonies of Upper and Lower Canada in 1791. Upper Canada immediately reverted to English common law.

b. Upper and Lower Canada, separate colonies until 1840, were reunited as the Province of Canada from 1840 to 1867, but with differing institutions in Canada East and Canada West. In 1867, these became the provinces of Quebec and Ontario.

c. In fact, the signs of change preceded the Liberal victory. Maurice Duplessis died in September 1959, and the first wave of reform began immediately under his short-lived Union Nationale colleague and successor, Premier Paul Sauvé, who died after three months in office.

d. An important step in the repatriation process was a Supreme Court ruling in September 1981 that the package required a substantial measure of provincial consent but not unanimity. After this decision, Quebec could not maintain a claim to a veto.

e. With respect to treaties, a 1937 decision of the Judicial Committee of the Privy Council held that international agreements concluded by Canada in areas of provincial legislative competence may not be implemented by federal legislation, but only by provinces (the Labour Conventions Case). Quebec has sought the further power to negotiate and sign such accords. Other provinces have long been active on the international scene, but mainly in matters of trade or recruitment of manpower.

f. In Canadian–Belgian relations, the regional or subsystem pressures have been felt in parallel fashion on both sides. See J.H. Ballegeer, "Diplomacy in Plural Societies: The Cases of Canada and Belgium" (unpublished M.A. research essay, Carleton University, 1984).

g. Psychologically, perceptions are important. If Canada's linguistic communities can be viewed as two majorities, one could argue that Northern Ireland's Protestants and Catholics behave more like two minorities.

h. For this purpose, a second referendum was envisaged, as the first asked only for a mandate to negotiate the terms of a sovereignty-association agreement. One may note the sharp contrast here between Canadian attitudes toward the Quebec issue and American attitudes toward secession of the South in the 1860s. For the handling of the partially similar Jura question in Switzerland by a series of referenda, see K.D. McRae, *Conflict and Compromise in Multilingual Societies: Volume 1. Switzerland* (Waterloo, Ontario, Canada: Wilfrid Laurier University Press, 1983), pp. 190–95.

References

1. See, for example, Pierre Vallières, *Choose!* (trans. P. Williams) (Toronto: New Press, 1972), pp. 87–117.

2. P. Desbarats, *René: A Canadian in Search of a Country* (Toronto: McClelland and Stewart, 1976), p. 177.

3. See D. Johnson, *Egalité ou Indépendence* (Montreal: Editions Renaissance, 1965), especially pp. 109–10.

4. See New Brunswick, *Acts of the Legislature of the Province of New Brunswick,* 1969, ch. 14, and *Acts of New Brunswick,* 1981, ch. 0-1.1.

5. See J. Brossard, A. Patry, and E. Weiser, *Les Pouvoirs Extérieurs du Québec* (Montreal: Les Presses de l'Université de Montréal, 1967).

6. Royal Commission on Bilingualism and Biculturalism, *Preliminary Report* (Ottawa: Queen's Printer, 1965), pp. 110–13.

7. On the concept and measurement of dual loyalties, see Maurice Pinard, "La Dualité des Loyautés et les Options Constitutionnelles des Québécois Francophones," in *Le Nationalisme Québécois à la Croisée des Chemins* (Quebec: Centre Québécois des Relations Internationales, 1975), pp. 63–91.

8. Royal Commission on Bilingualism and Biculturalism, *Report* (Ottawa: Queen's Printer, 1969), vol. IIIA, pp. 15–24, especially tables 2 and 5; and F. Vaillancourt and P. Saint-Laurent, "Les déterminants de l'Évolution de l'Écart de Revenu

entre Canadien-Anglais et Canadien-Francais, Québec, 1961–1971," *Journal of Canadian Studies,* 15, no. 4 (1981): 69.

9. See A.G. Gagnon and K.Z. Paltiel, "Toward *Maitres Chez Nous:* The Ascendancy of a Balzacian Bourgeoisie in Québec," *Queen's Quarterly* 93 (1986): 731–49.

14
South Tyrol and Multiethnic Relations

F. Gunther Eyck

Compared to the long and troubled multiethnic relationships in such other Western countries as Belgium, Canada, and Spain—not to mention Ireland—that of the Italian- and German-speaking communities in South Tyrol is of rather recent origins. Even though their differences and rivalries may be traced to the national awakening of the nineteenth century, actual conflict arose only with the Treaty of St. Germain-en-Laye of September 1919. Up to that time, the area from the Brenner Pass south to Lake Garda formed part of the province of Tyrol, and the whole of Tyrol was part of the Austro-Hungarian Empire. That polyglot empire had a unique experience among European countries in multiethnic relations and possible conflict solutions.

The Italian minority in Südtirol (the South Tyrol) at worst suffered from benign neglect by the imperial authorities in Innsbruck and Vienna. But they also longed for ultimate union with their brethren in the kingdom of Italy. This union, to be sure, had been much promoted and aspired to by the Italian irredentist movement, an offspring of the Risorgimento—the regeneration of Italian nationhood. And the drive toward union was reinforced by the demands of Italian leaders for the attainment of the strategic Alpine frontier.

Following the outbreak of World War I, the Italian government made the acquisition of "Cisalpine Tyrol," together with the other border areas along the Austrian–Italian frontier, a condition for Italy's entry into the war. Under the Treaty of London (April 1915) and its secret provisions,[1] Italy joined the Entente powers fighting the Austro-Hungarian and German empires. And at the end of the war, Italy was not slow in presenting its claims check. Over the objections of the new republican government in Vienna and the even stronger ones of the Tyroleans, Cisalpine Tyrol and its quarter-million German-speaking inhabitants were transferred from Austrian to Italian sovereignty. In spite of reservations by Italian socialist leaders, who wished for a plebiscite, the Rome government incorporated the area by executive order.

Newly constituted as Venezia-Tridentina, the region comprised the Trentino, with an overwhelming majority of ethnic Italians, and the Alto Adige to

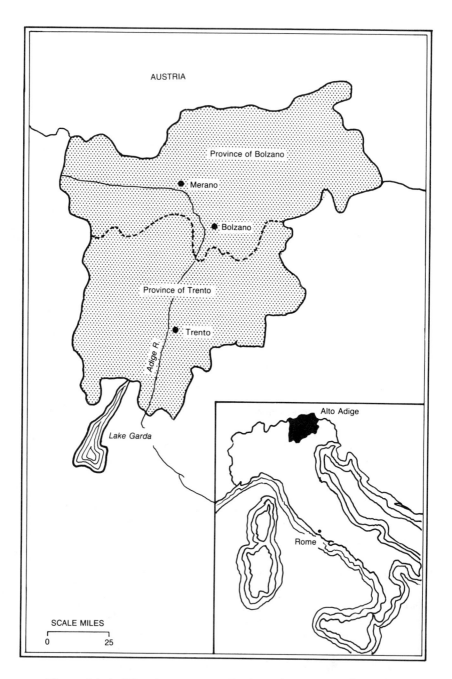

Figure 14–1. The Autonomous Region of Trentino-Alto Adige

the north. Here, the German-speaking population outnumbered the Italians at a ratio of ten to one, although a slightly better balance existed in the two major cities, Bolzano (Bozen) and Merano (Meran). In the region as a whole, however, there were almost twice as many Italians as Südtiroler. In addition, there were about 20,000 Ladins, a Celtic remnant, most of whom resided in the Alto Adige and tended to side with the German-speaking minority.

Italianization Policies

Although the pre-Fascist Italian government had allowed the region substantial autonomy, in an effort at conciliation, latent antagonism flared after Benito Mussolini became premier in October 1922. He encouraged the activities of Senator Ettore Tolomei, who acted as the principal catalyst for the *Italianita* policies of the Fascist government. Tolomei, a native of the Tyrolean–Italian border town of Rovereto, had long been a fervent spokesman for the Italianization of Tyrol up to the Brenner Pass.[2]

He now had official backing for the implementation of his proposals. On his initiative, Bolzano province was merged with Trento province into a single administrative entity with a large Italian majority. German-language instruction in public schools was banned and Italian made compulsory. German family and place names were Italianized. Südtiroler associations, including farm organizations, trade unions, and the traditional *Schützen* (sharpshooter) companies, faced dissolution.

These measures caused considerable unrest among the Südtiroler. Militants among them clashed with Fascist *squadristi* as early as 1921. The radical Andreas Hofer Bund—named after the folk hero who led the Tyrolean uprising of 1809 against the Bavarian occupiers and their French backers—became active. Its members clamored for the return of Südtirol to Austria. And the Austrian government, as well as members of Parliament on occasion, spoke passionately for their former compatriots.

The Italianization policies not only ran into increasing local resistance but also failed, above all, in inducing large-scale Italian immigration to Alto Adige. One of Tolomei's key hopes thus remained largely unfulfilled. The net increase of the Italian population in the area remained insignificant. In 1927, Mussolini allowed the reestablishment of Bolzano province in the vain expectation of furthering Italian immigration into the region.

Economic infiltration policies proved more successful, however. By the mid-1930s, car, machine, and steel industries had established, on government orders, branch factories and offices in the Bolzano area. But the decisive turn in favor of a stronger Italian presence there did not come until mid-1939. Surprisingly to many—not least to the Südtiroler—the Nazi dictator Adolf Hitler made common cause with his admired counterpart Benito Mussolini. Yet in his apparent betrayal not only of the traditional interests of the Südtiroler but also of the Nazi doctrine of unlimited support for pan-German claims, Hitler was in fact honoring a much earlier commitment to let nothing hinder Nazi–Fascist relations.

On the eve of World War II, Hitler's commitment acquired a new intensity. Since the forced *Anschluss* in March 1938, incorporating Austria into the Third Reich with Italian concurrence, only the Südtirol constituted a potential issue of tension between the two Axis partners. Two months later, during a visit to Rome, the Führer made it known that "the Alpine frontier erected between [the two countries] by nature [was] permanent and unalterable."[3]

During the first half of 1939, German–Italian discussions took place, culminating in the agreement of June 23. Under its terms,[4] a three-stage transfer of *Reichsdeutsche* and *Volksdeutsche* ("German nationals" and "ethnic Germans") was to solve the Südtirol problem once and for all. Significantly, the Nazi authorities, rather than the Italian, pressed this radical solution. Gestapo Chief Heinrich Himmler planned the resettlement of some 200,000 ethnic Germans, whereas the Italians preferred to move out only those who were strongly anti-Italian or not essential to the economic infrastructure of the province—its predominant agrarian sector almost wholly in Südtiroler hands.

On Nazi urgings, the Südtiroler were given a Hobson's choice: Either they would declare, by December 31, 1939, their readiness to leave their homes and properties and become citizens of the Third Reich within three years, or they would be left without any support or even consideration on the part of the German government. Under various kinds of pressure, almost 200,000 declared their intention to move. In actuality, however, only some 70,000 had left the area by the end of the war.[5] This was due, in part, to the exigencies of the steadily expanding world war and, in part, to rumors that once the Axis powers were victorious, as they were expected to be, the Nazi government might change its mind. The same exigencies of war were also responsible for the failure of the Italians to fill the void left by departing Südtiroler. By 1943, the ethnic Italians in Bolzano province numbered about 35,000, an increase of only 6,000 since 1939.[6]

The Nazis Take Control

Eventually, this failure proved immaterial. After the fall of Mussolini in July 1943, the Nazis immediately took control of Bolzano province and, for good measure, the Trentino and the neighboring province of Belluno as well. All were associated with Greater Germany as the *Alpenvorland* and placed under the control of the *Gauleiter* of Tyrol.

During the following twenty-two months, tensions between the two major ethnic population groups heightened dramatically. Many Südtiroler applauded the changes in administration, and a good number among them made common cause with Nazism. They served in the German armed forces, filled the ranks of newly created Südtirol police regiments, or became active members of the Nazi party, including the S.S. and the Gestapo. Only a small minority of clergy and professionals, some grouped since 1939 in the Andreas Hofer Bewegung, resisted the Nazi–Fascist resettlement deal and subsequent Nazi dominance.[7]

By contrast, the number of Italian resistants to that dominance grew steadily with the collapse of the Fascist regime. The remaining Italian Fascist officials in the area were often replaced by Nazi appointees, mainly Südtiroler. No love was lost between them, even though a semblance of cooperation was maintained as long as Mussolini's puppet republic existed by the grace of the Führer.

During the spring of 1944, the Italian partisan movement in the Trentino became increasingly active. In turn, the Nazi authorities had recourse to ever more drastic repressive and retaliatory measures, including mass executions and concentration camps. The Alto Adige, however, remained fairly quiet until close to VE-Day, when nearly two score Italians were killed while celebrating liberation.

The Paris Agreement: Coordination and Cooperation

With liberation, the contested area was returned to Italian sovereignty, but the many issues of multiethnic relations remained unresolved. Both major ethnic groups quickly asserted their claims for the governance of the Alto Adige, and each considered the other a bothersome interloper. Fortunately, wiser councils prevailed on the higher level of national governments, and a new approach to the complex problems of majority–minority conciliation was devised.

As an earnest of the projected conciliatory policies envisaged by postwar Italian political leaders, Premier Alcide de Gasperi's government engaged in a policy of "building bridges rather than barriers." And it was de Gasperi who gave shape to this policy, which was to differ so substantially from the Fascist policies of forced Italianization. The only barrier that his and succeeding Italian governments were unwilling to dismantle was the Brenner Pass frontier. Within the national borders of the new Italian Republic, however, concessions could be made and common solutions agreed upon.

In June 1946, the major Allied powers rejected Austrian demands for frontier adjustments that would have returned at least part of the Alto Adige to Austria. Instead, Austria and Italy were enjoined to cooperate. Thus, the way was also cleared for a workable relationship between the two major ethnic groups in the contested province. And on September 5, 1946, Alcide de Gasperi and the Austrian Foreign Minister Karl Gruber—both natives of the area—concluded the Paris Agreement. It was to serve as the charter of the hoped-for coordination and cooperation not only between the rivaling ethnic groups in the Alto Adige but also between the Austrian and Italian governments. More specifically, the agreement provided for administrative autonomy, linguistic and educational equality, and "a more appropriate proportion of employment between the two ethnical groups."[8]

All of these provisions were designed to benefit the Südtiroler and to ease their reservations vis-à-vis a second incorporation into the Italian state. At the same time, the Italian government wished to preserve the entire region as an integral component of the Italian Republic. For that purpose, the autonomous Regione Trentino–Alto Adige, one of five of such regions in the Republic, was created under Articles 116 and 131 of its constitution of December 27, 1947.[a]

Governmental Arrangements

To preserve both national sovereignty and regional or provincial autonomy, the Italian government promulgated a *Statuto Speciale* on February 2, 1948. The Regione Trentino–Alto Adige, unlike the earlier Venezia-Tridentina, had two constitutionally equal components: Trento and Bolzano provinces. According to the statute, each was to have a provincial assembly elected by the local adult population for a period of four years. An executive council was to be elected, in turn, by each assembly. Its head, upon election by either assembly, became the chief executive officer of the respective province. As such, he was to represent the province and chair the meetings of the executive council, composed of the departmental heads (assessors). Their stipulated powers included the administration of provincial and municipal affairs; public welfare and services; the application of laws and regulations within the regulating powers of the province; and the passage of emergency measures within the competence of the council.

The legislative and executive powers of the provinces, however, were limited and were subordinated to the national authorities in general and the regional ones in particular. The judicial and administrative functions of the region transcended those of the provinces. This arrangement was to safeguard Italian sovereignty and interests in a contested border area. A regional legislative council had an Italian majority, as elections were based on proportional representation, and ethnic Italians in the region outnumbered the Südtiroler by nearly three to one.[b]

The regional council would elect both the president and members of the regional junta, whose composition had to be proportionate to ethnic representation in the council. The responsibilities of both bodies included control of regional departments, communications, and transport; development of industrial production; regulation of banks and credit organizations; utilization of mines, forests, and public waters; health services; and tourism. Thus, essential sectors of the regional economy and infrastructure remained outside the provincial jurisdictions.

Moreover, ultimate executive power was vested in the government commissioner for the region. He coordinated "the functions of the State in the Region," supervised regional and provincial corporate bodies, and—most important—was responsible to the minister of the interior for the maintenance of public order. However, he had no responsibilities concerning the administration of justice, defense, or railroads—all of which operated directly under the control of the national government.

Minority Rights Guaranteed

To ease minority sensitivities and spur voluntary acceptance of the special statute by the majority of the Südtiroler, its drafters put into it a number of provisions that would guarantee minority rights or otherwise show a spirit of conciliation. Perhaps the most important relevant clauses dealt with linguistic safeguards. The use of German or Ladin "in public life" was guaranteed, even though Italian remained the only official language. More specifically, teaching on all levels in Bolzano province had to be in "the mother tongue of the students [and] by teachers having the same mother tongue." In dealings with government departments, residents in the province could use their native language, and replies should be in the same language. At meetings of the assemblies or in committees and other meetings of public regional, provincial, or local bodies, German could be used. German place names could be used throughout the province if their existence "has been officially ascertained and approved by Provincial law." Similar provisions were also made for the Ladin minority.

In order to assure the German-speaking population of evenhanded treatment in matters of legislative representation, the special statute stipulated that the presidents of the regional and the Bolzano provincial assemblies should hold office in rotation—first an ethnic Italian and then a Südtiroler. Moreover, the regional legislature was to meet for its first two years in Trento—as the capital of the region—and for the second two years in Bolzano.

Fiscal equity was provided under clauses that allotted nine-tenths of the revenue collected from income taxes to each of the two provinces; the same held true for real estate tax revenues. Each province, as well as the region as a whole, had to draw up its own budget. The region was also held to contribute annually, to both provinces, part of its revenue, to be calculated in proportion to the amounts collected from other taxes in the two provinces. However, the region retained the sole right to levy additional taxes or to increase existing ones. Utility taxes, too, were to be levied and collected solely by the region. And any monies channeled by the national government to the region were to be distributed at the region's discretion to the provinces.

Although the statute did make very substantial concessions to the Südtiroler, it did not go unchallenged. The intransigents among them rejected its provisions out of hand. A far larger number, represented by the Südtiroler Volkspartei (SVP), which had been founded as early as May 1945, did not so much object to the statute as criticize successive Italian governments for not carrying out all of its stipulations to the full. In the immediate aftermath of promulgation, however, the SVP chairman expressed satisfaction with the modus vivendi embodied in the statute.[9]

The Repatriation Issue

On another salient issue, the Italian government showed a similar spirit of conciliation and cooperation. Upon reasserting national sovereignty in the area in the fall of 1945, with the concurrence of the major Allies, the Italian government had to face the thorny issue of "reoption." The numerous Südtiroler who had opted for German citizenship before 1943—many of whom had not left their native soil—now had to be reconsidered for Italian citizenship.[c] The Italian government was not overly enthusiastic about taking them all back into the fold. Under Article 5 of a draft law, the government retained the right to exclude those suspected of associating with Nazi organizations and activities.

The issue was complicated by the fact that Austrian official circles pushed for the return to Südtirol of many who had moved from there to Austria as the result of the Nazi–Fascist agreement of June 1939. The underlying Austrian interest in pressuring these emigrants to return home was to increase the German-speaking population in Südtirol. After prolonged negotiations between the Austrian and Italian governments and amendments to the aforementioned Article 5, more than 200,000 Südtiroler had received or regained Italian citizenship by the end of 1952. Even though many of them probably would have preferred Austrian nationality, they realized, after the Allied powers had turned down the Austrian request for a plebiscite, that they would have to settle for the status quo ante.

Only some 4,000 Südtiroler were denied restoration of Italian citizenship because of their record as war criminals of suspects. More surprising, however, may be the fact that about 50,000 *Optanten* remained in Austria and West Germany rather than reclaim their birthright. The 20,000 who did return included an unknown number of supporters of the Südtiroler intransigents and militants.

Increase in Militancy

From the mid-1950s on, the activism and discontent of the militants increased. For one thing, they resented the increased Italian demographic presence, a concern shared by more moderate Südtiroler.[d] For another, there were increasing complaints about delays and evasions in the implementation of both the Paris Agreement of 1946 and the special statute. In the fall of 1956, the first acts of serious violence occurred. They were restricted, however, to damaging railroad equipment and power lines.

By 1957, unrest and uneasiness permeated much of the province. It was highlighted on the Südtiroler side by a mass protest meeting. In November of that year, some 35,000 people met at Schloss Sigmundskron near Bolzano. The demonstration had been triggered by the Italian announcement of a substantial government grant for the building of public housing and facilities in Bolzano City, which by that time had a nearly 80 percent majority of ethnic Italians. Rightly or wrongly, the Südtiroler assumed that this measure would benefit only the Italian population and further increase its numbers in the provincial capital.

At Sigmundskron, demands for complete separation from the Trentino could be heard. A more common theme was the charge that the special statute had been only partially implemented and the Paris Agreement honored only in the breach. And in a resolution adopted at the meeting, the Austrian government was called upon to intervene in behalf of Südtiroler claims. It lost little time in responding to this call. On several occasions, the Austrian foreign minister made strong representations to the General Assembly of the United Nations. The Italian government, in turn, preferred to lay any controversial issues pertaining to the Alto Adige before the International Court of Justice at The Hague but acquiesced in U.N. involvement. United Nations Resolutions 1497 and 1661—passed in 1960 and 1961, respectively—urged both Austria and Italy to resume negotiations so as to reach a final settlement of the dispute over the application of the Paris Agreement or, in case of failure, to accept third-party intervention.

The Report of the Committee of Nineteen

Upon the Italian initiative, a commission of nineteen members was set up in 1961. Composed of eleven Italians, seven Südtiroler, and one Ladin, it addressed itself to the numerous issues of controversy in the Alto Adige. Its work was facilitated by the Südtiroler Volkspartei declaration of August 2, 1962, that the party would no longer oppose the existence of the Regione Trentino–Alto Adige if the cultural and economic autonomy of Bolzano province would be fully guaranteed.[e]

After more than 200 meetings, the commission finally presented its report in April 1964. The findings and recommendations included three main sections dealing, respectively, with measures of linguistic parity, an extension of administrative powers for Bolzano province, and legal guarantees of minority rights. A supplementary section contained statements by various committee members, whose conflicting views showed that differences had not been overcome altogether. Of fifty-four issues taken up by the commission, nine could be only partially resolved and four not at all. Among them—according to the Südtiroler Volkspartei—were failure to extend provincial powers regarding industrial development, labor exchanges, credit controls, education, and last but not least, responsibility for public order.

The prolonged deliberations by the Commission of Nineteen and subsequent high-level talks between the Austrian and Italian governments on possible solutions were punctuated by an accelerating series of acts of violence. Throughout the 1960s, these acts coincided with rising tensions among the two major population groups in the area and an apparent stalemate in Austrian-Italian negotiations. Südtiroler extremists, soon labeled terrorists by international observers, at first confined their attacks to state property—mainly railroads, viaducts, and power lines. However, extremist agitation and militancy, furthered by Austrian and German neo-Nazis, soon led to loss of life. Moreover, terrorist activities expanded far beyond Bolzano province into Lombardy and even to Rome.

Between 1961 and 1963, about 150 acts of sabotage were recorded. Most of them were the work of members of the intransigent Befreiungsausschuss für Südtirol (BAS), with the support of such organizations in North Tyrol as the Berg-Isel-Bund. Casualties remained low until the mid-1960s. Between 1964 and 1967, however, a score of Italian soldiers, carabinieri, and customs and border police were killed.

The Italian Government's Response to Terrorism

The Italian authorities responded with increasing severity to these challenges and dangers. Several leading Südtiroler extremists died in police custody or in not fully explained circumstances at their hideouts. A far larger number of activists and suspects were rounded up and eventually tried. At two major trials in 1964 and 1966, 100 of those tried in Milan courts received prison sentences ranging from four to twenty or more years, the stiffest terms being imposed on those in absentia; another 45 were acquitted.[f] And in an effort to balance the scales of justice, at least one major trial of ten Italian police officers, charged with brutality, took place in Trento. Eight of them were acquitted, however, and two amnestied.

New Efforts at Conciliation

In the late 1960s, the widespread realization that the impasse of confrontation and spiraling violence had to be ended led to efforts at conciliation. Austrian, Italian, and Südtiroler leaders joined in these efforts. Some among the latter group—such as Südtiroler Volkspartei leader and provincial governor Silvius Magnago and Dr. Toni Ebner, a former SVP deputy in the Italian parliament—had rejected terrorism as a political instrumentality from the beginning. Other influential and moderate SVP leaders, however, took the view that the outrages by Südtiroler extremists had been useful, if indeed not necessary, in order to goad the Italian government into accelerated action and to draw international attention to the Südtirol problem.

Toward the end of the decade, contacts between the Italian and Austrian foreign ministers and between their deputies expanded, and differences over the Alto Adige situation lessened. On August 8, 1969, Italian Premier Mariano Rumor stated in parliament that his government would soon present proposals for the solution of the entire Alto Adige problem.

Shortly afterward, a settlement "package"—*il pacchetto*—was announced. It included many of the recommendations of the Commission of Nineteen. More than 100 changes in the special statute of 1948 were detailed, and other projected measures dealt with administrative ordinances and specific provincial laws. A so-called operations calendar accompanied the *pacchetto* and provided a schedule for its implementation.[10]

In a special convention in November 1969, the Südtiroler Volkspartei accepted the two documents by the narrow majority of 52 percent; and they were approved overwhelmingly by the Italian parliament on December 4, 1969, with only the neo-Fascist Movimento Sociale Italiano and a handful of monarchists in opposition. By contrast, the Austrian parliament assented with but a slim margin of four votes—its assent being required under Article 4 of the operations calendar. On the basis of the provisions of the settlement package, a revised autonomy statute came into force on January 20, 1972.

Strengthening the Autonomy of the Südtiroler

Like their 1948 predecessor and the initial Paris Agreement of 1946, the two new documents were expected to serve as the charter for a greatly improved partnership of the multiethnic components in the Trentino–Alto Adige. The revised statute went a long way toward meeting overall as well as specific demands by the German-speaking population. The administrative, cultural, and economic autonomy of Bolzano province was substantially strengthened.[11]

Moreover, a permanent commission at the premier's office in Rome would advise him on specific Südtiroler concerns and issues. And the head of the provincial government, the *Landeshauptmann,* acquired the right to participate in cabinet meetings dealing with Südtirol—a right previously granted only to the governor of the region.

On the always-sensitive linguistic issue, the settlement package and subsequent regulations offered further concessions. German was declared an equal with Italian, although the latter remained the sole official language, with the additional proviso that it alone had to be used in the military. Italianized first and family names in such documents as birth or death certificates could be changed back into German. The designation *Südtirol,* so long suppressed in official nomenclature, now became part of it. Street, traffic, and commercial signs could be in either language. And German films could be imported duty-free.

In economic matters, the provinces of Bolzano and Trento were empowered to pass legislation on industrial development, including foreign investments; on the exploitation of mines and minerals; on the regulation of commercial activities; and on the utilization of water resources, except for major hydraulic and hydroelectric undertakings. Public housing—long a bone of contention in the Bolzano municipality, as mentioned earlier—now came fully under provincial jurisdiction, as did transportation and communications systems of a local or provincial nature.

In cultural and educational matters, the German (and Ladin) schools were given full autonomy and equality with regard to teacher training and supervision, the building of new schools and kindergartens, and the appointment of a superintendent by the provincial government. German-language radio and television programs were to be expanded, and these programs were to be managed by members of the same ethnic group. Professional diploma equivalency pertained, at first, only to dentists who had graduated from Austrian or German universities, but it has been extended since.[g]

One of the most important sectors of the revised legislation dealt with employment in state services, such as railroads, post and telecommunication, customs and taxation, and social security. Although "equality of rights" in public office and on the basis of "appropriate proportion" had already been embodied in the Paris Agreement of 1946, much remained to be done in reality. As late as 1960, some 90 percent of state employees in Bolzano province reportedly were ethnic Italians.[12] Many of them knew little or no German, although bilingualism was a legal requirement for service in the province.

Under the terms of the settlement package and the revised statute, a gradual filling of more than 7,600 positions would ultimately lead to an employment ratio of two to one in favor of the German-language minority.[h] Moreover, out-of-province transfer of such employees could not exceed 10 percent.

Exempt from these stipulations were personnel of the security forces, civilians in the defense department, and the higher-level administration in the interior ministry.

Progress alongside Prolonged Südtiroler Militancy

In the decade and-a half since the promulgation of these charters, substantial progress in carrying out their provisions and promises has been acknowledged by Südtiroler spokespersons.[13] Yet from the late 1970s onward, acts of violence have recurred, and they have not been confined to one side only. The "war of the pylons" of the early 1960s became "the war of the monuments." In 1979, symbols such as the Hofer monument in Merano and the Alpini monument in Brunico were blown up in quick succession.

Attacks in the early 1980s took a more serious form, targeting military barracks, railroad stations or equipment, and even individual residences. On New Year's Eve 1986, a small bomb exploded outside the Merano hotel where the Italian foreign minister was staying. And in the early summer of 1987, another series of outrages occurred. They were thought to be related to the forthcoming national elections, but they continued at ever-shorter intervals through most of the remaining year. By November, nineteen bombing incidents had been reported for the whole of 1987, as against a total of thirty-four such incidents between 1979 and 1986.

A militant group named Tirol is most often directly involved in recent acts of violence. It has admitted to more than a dozen of them.[14] Leaflets found near the scenes of such acts—sometimes couched in vicious Nazi terminology—have called for the ouster of Italians from the Südtirol and its separation from Rome. Extremists have also frequently invoked or inscribed on their bombs the hallowed name of Andreas Hofer, an ever-effective sanctification of any movement or action in South Tyrol.

In some cases, the militants may have ties with the Heimatbund, a diehard separatist organization; knowledgeable foreign observers, however, assume that by no means all of its members support violence. The average age of the militant activists is reckoned to be between the mid-thirties and the mid-forties. It is important to note that the younger age groups have largely remained within the ranks of the Südtiroler Volkspartei.

General support for the *Bumser* (bombers) who are responsible for the outrages seems to be very limited and mostly passive, especially in the current setting of prosperity. An overwhelming majority of Südtiroler apparently has little time for and less interest in violence. One recent opinion poll showed an extraordinary high percentage (97 percent) as quite satisfied with their life.[15] Moreover, the Roman Catholic local clergy has, on occasion, spoken out strongly against terrorism.

The terrorism that continues feeds on its own momentum. Südtiroler militants can hardly claim that brutal Italian repression is a major stimulant to their current activities. Although instances of manhandling and even torture were reported during and after the big confrontation of the early 1960s, no such ill treatment has been mentioned recently. On the contrary, Italian local and, even more so, national officials have criticized stronghanded measures by the judiciary. In August 1987, seventeen Südtiroler activists were taken into custody, having demonstrated for secession earlier in Vienna. As might be expected, protests from both Südtiroler Volkspartei leaders and the Austrian government followed quickly. But Italian politicians voiced the strongest displeasure. Within five days, the examining magistrate ordered the release of all but one of those arrested.

Cooperation between the provincial authorities and the national security forces to counteract extremist violence is reported to be good. In May 1987, the minister of internal affairs chaired a meeting of high officials in the security services at Bolzano. Under new guidelines, these services were to keep all potentially militant activists, including ethnic Italians, under surveillance. And fuller cooperation by Austrian officials in preventing violence or tracking down suspects was requested.

In spite of the increase of bombing or small-arms attacks, no casualties have resulted as yet in this latest series of militant actions. For the time being, it is more demonstrative than destructive in character. The primary objectives of Südtiroler extremists apparently are to keep the province in a state of agitation, to attract more supporters to their intransigent policies, and perhaps to frighten ethnic Italians into leaving.

Although there has been a slight downward trend of about 5 percent among the resident Italian population in the past two decades, a substantial reduction in numbers—barring an unlikely economic slump in the Alto Adige—is thought improbable. Prolonged Südtiroler militancy may, in fact, cause a hardening of Italian nationalism and extremism in the area, as is already evident in the spectacular electoral gains of the Movimento Sociale Italiano (MSI).

The February 1987 Resolution

Partly to undercut MSI growth potential and partly to head off a new round of escalation of violence, the five-party government of then-premier Bettino Craxi passed a resolution in February 1987. It offered to implement still outstanding measures concerning the region, and Bolzano province in particular, before the end of the year. Inter alia, the resolution called for adjustments in the hiring of personnel in the state services, bilingual training in all public schools in the area, and a reassessment of the distributive structure of revenues for the region and its component provinces.

More irksome to the Südtiroler was the proposal in the same resolution to expand the existing census categories, which up to then had been based on compulsory inclusion into one of the three ethnic groups in the region. Under the expansion proposal, all inhabitants of the region would be free to opt out of their group and into a new category of "unaffiliated." Such a crossover presumably would weaken Südtiroler claims to proportional quotas in state services, public housing, revenue sharing, and the like.

Equally objectionable to them was a suggested change in the present residency requirements for voting purposes in Bolzano province. Currently, voters there must be residents of the province for at least two years and of the region per se for two more years.[i] As a shortening of residency requirements would benefit the more-transient Italian population in the province, rather than the sedentary Südtiroler, objections by the latter could be expected.

Not surprisingly, therefore, the Südtiroler Volkspartei opposed the February resolution. So—for very different reasons—did the Movimento Sociale Italiano, the self-proclaimed champion of Italian interests in the Alto Adige. The primary goal of the resolution was to lessen tensions in the region, but if it also aimed at undercutting MSI voter appeal, that goal was obviously missed in the June 14–15 elections. The MSI overtook the Christian Democrats, the largest Italian party on the national level; and now, next to the SVP, the MSI is the strongest party in the Alto Adige. Its main strength is in Bolzano City, with its heavy Italian majority.

Italian neo-Fascists have managed to capitalize on their resurgence in the Alto Adige. An MSI deputy was elected, for the first time in postwar years, from Bolzano province to the national parliament, and a meeting of the MSI national leadership was held there for the first time in October 17–18, 1987. On that occasion, MSI deputy Franco Franchi summed up the feelings of his fellow Fascists and the voters behind them when he declared: "It is no longer possible to tolerate a situation where Italians feel like strangers in their own home."[16]

The Südtiroler Volskpartei, in turn, made only marginal gains over the last national elections in 1983 because of competition with the Heimatbund. In 1979, the Heimatbund, motivated by ideological intransigence and extremist inclinations, split off from the SVP. Its major theme in the 1987 elections was the creation of a Südtirol "free state." Even though the Heimatbund increased its vote to nearly 4 percent, the SVP leadership seems more irked by than concerned about this rival.

The Desire for "Ultimate Integration"

The real concern is with an entirely different group. The Alternative Liste für das Andere Südtirol (ALFAS) was organized less than a decade ago for the primary purpose of putting multiethnic relations in the area on an entirely new basis. Deliberately seeking a break with the troublesome past, the ALFAS favors a discontinuation of ethnic census categories and a mingling of people, including mixed marriages and cultural integration. Much of its ideology and program resembles that of the "Greens"—the West German ecological and peace party—and in the June 1987 elections, a joint Grüne Liste/Lista Verde, which included ALFAS, won slightly over 4 percent of the provincial vote, equaling the results of the 1983 elections.

Ultimate integration is also the desire and design of various Italian parties, from the Christian Democrats to the Communists. In 1986, the minister for regional affairs in the national government called for "a breakout from the fortress mentality and the buildup in South Tyrol of one society in which the ethnic groups will work toward ultimate integration."[17] The same note was struck by Flaminio Piccoli, one of the leaders of the Christian Democrats, in August 1987. In connection with his criticism of the arrests of Südtiroler demonstrators, referred to earlier, he spoke of "the cause of peaceful integration in the Alto Adige" as leading to "a tranquil solution of its problems."[18]

Yet most Südtiroler remain basically opposed to that solution. Eva Klotz, the leader of the Heimatbund, warned against "a deadly fraternization,"[19] and important Südtiroler Volkspartei leaders have taken similar positions. The head of the provincial cultural and education department stated in 1980 that "the more we separate, the better we understand each other."[20] And the most authoritative Südtiroler personality, Governor Silvius Magnago, declared in September 1986 that "a linguistic minority can only be protected by a special status, not by parity."[21] Even the moderate Dr. Friedl Volgger, who sometimes is at odds with his party, has proposed that the young generations in the Alto Adige should live "next to one another, with each other, for one another—but not mixed together."[22]

Unless a breakthrough along the lines envisaged by the ALFAS and moderate Italians occurs within the next generation or two—which at present seems unlikely—solutions will have to be worked out through the existing constitutional and institutional framework. Italian government flexibility and the pragmatism of the majority in the Südtiroler Volkspartei have made possible the considerable progress in the restructuring of that framework. Extremism on either side is likely neither to undo it nor to change the delicate balance of interests decisively.

Undeniable Progress

Relations between the provincial and central governments have been facilitated over the years by the ideological similarities of the Christian Democrats and the Südtiroler Volkspartei. Except for a break in the early 1960s, the SVP has generally supported the Christian Democrats, which have led all but five of Italy's forty-nine postwar governments. In 1987, however, the SVP was withholding support for the Giovanni Goria government pending passage of promised measures, approved the previous year by the provincial and regional authorities and expected to be promulgated before the end of 1987.

Delay in this enactment—as in earlier instances—has been partly due to the frequent changes of government in Rome. The government of Ciriaco De Mita, however, lost little time in committing itself to full implementation of the still outstanding reform measures. In April 1988, a majority in the Chamber of Deputies approved rapid passage of all but three measures and the Senate concurred in the spring of 1989. Approval already has been voted by the majority of parties in the South Tyrol.

Moreover, the Austrian government—in its continuing if self-proclaimed role as the "protective power" for the Südtiroler—has expressed satisfaction with the indicated progress. Foreign Minister Alois Mock stated in a meeting with SVP leaders on April 30, 1988, that before the end of the year, his government might issue a declaration to the effect that Austria considered the dispute with Italy over the South Tyrol settled. He did mention one condition, however, when he pointed out that prior to such a final step, the Austrian government would have to check the effectiveness of the 137 implementation regulations.

Despite future uncertainties and the recurrence of acts of violence[j] or the hardening of confrontational positions, undeniable administrative and legislative progress has been made in four decades toward the accomplishment of a satisfactory majority–minority relationship in the Alto Adige. Linguistic near-equality, educational and cultural autonomy, extensive administrative and judical powers,[k] and equal opportunity for employment in state services have been achieved. Among the remaining Südtiroler demands, only a couple are of major importance: bilingualism in the courts and among the police and the extension of provincial authority, mainly in fiscal and economic matters. Implementation is sought for degree equivalency, school registration, and the Germanization of place names.

Regardless of how long that implementation process will take or what measures may be enacted to quiet uneasiness over such looming new issues as census categories or voting requirements, even the most conciliatory legislation must remain limited in its effects. It can do little to bridge deep-seated attitudinal, emotional, historical, and social cleavages. That formidable dichotomy, long ago succinctly circumscribed by the French as the difference between *pays légal* and *pays réel*, is very likely to continue in the Alto Adige for a long time to come. It is accentuated there by the historic memory of the 1809 uprising against foreign dominance, a memory much alive among the Tyroleans on either side of the Brenner frontier.[23] Any complete and lasting settlement of multiethnic relations in the area would have to take that factor into consideration.

Notes

a. Article 116 of the Italian constitution of December 1947 established Friuli–Venezia Giulia, Sardinia, Sicily, Trentino–Alto Adige, and Valle d'Aosta as regions with special status. Article 131 listed them together with fifteen administrative regions.

b. One councillor was to be elected for every 15,000 inhabitants. According to the 1981 census, the last available, the region has just under 875,000 inhabitants, of whom about 290,000 belong to the German-language group.

c. Some 150,000 Südtiroler neither emigrated nor received German citizenship, and only 15,000 were granted German citizenship.

d. By 1961, ethnic Italians constituted 34.3 percent of the population of the autonomous province of Bolzano. Twenty years later, that percentage had dropped by more than five points. These figures are taken from the official *Südtirol Handbuch*, 5th (enlarged) ed. 1986, pp. 168–69.

e. In January 1959, the Südtiroler Volkspartei, as a sign of protest, ended its eleven years of cooperation with the Christian Democrats, the largest Italian party.

f. A moderate and important Südtiroler political leader, Dr. Friedl Volgger, called the Milan judgments "mild" in his autobiography, *Mit Südtirol am Scheideweg*, p. 253 (cited in note 7.)

g. Südtiroler studying at Austrian universities numbered about 2,770 in 1985–86. That figure included all linguistic groups in the Alto Adige, but it is safe to assume that most of the students belonged to the German-language group. About an equal number studied at Italian universities.

h. This increase is to take effect over a span of thirty years, but it has already resulted in very substantial changes. Of almost 5,000 filled positions in state employment in 1986, nearly 45 percent were held by members of the German-language group. During the preceding three years, some 760 positions had been added, and all were filled by Südtiroler, except for 39 Ladins. By contrast, there was a slight drop in the number of ethnic Italians in government jobs for the province. These data were made available by courtesy of the provincial government.

i. On the day that the February 1987 Resolution was passed in the Italian parliament, the Constitutional Court in Rome ruled that the residency requirements for Bolzano province were unconstitutional.

j. In mid-May 1988, several explosions heavily damaged Italian facilities in Bolzano.

k. After a prolonged legal contest, the superior administrative court for the Regione Trentino–Alto Adige now has an autonomous German-language section for Bolzano province. Thus, judicial appeals can be taken directly from that section to the Italian Constitutional Court, rather than being channeled through the regional court structure.

References

1. The text of the treaty provided under Article 4, inter alia, that Italy should receive, upon the conclusion of peace, "Cisalpine Tyrol with its geographic and natural frontier (the Brenner frontier) . . . " Reprinted in Great Britain, *Parliamentary Papers,* Cmd. 671 (1920).

2. On the policies and role of Tolomei, see Antony E. Alcock, *The History of the South Tyrol Question* (London and Geneva: Michael Joseph, 1970). The book is an outgrowth of a doctoral dissertation and contains much useful source material.

3. Karl Heinz Ritschel, *Diplomatie um Südtirol* (Stuttgart: Seewald Verlag, 1966), p. 149. The title page of Hitler's *Die Südtiroler Frage und das Deutsche Bündnisproblem* (1926) has been reprinted in this book.

4. One of the most comprehensive and objective treatments of this "devils pact" may be found in Mario Toscano, *Alto Adige–South Tyrol,* English edition by George A. Carbone [hereafter cited as Toscano-Carbone] (Baltimore: Johns Hopkins Press, 1975), ch. III, pp. 1–4. This monograph remains the best available study in English on both the domestic and the international aspects of the South Tyrol issue.

5. Conrad F. Latour, *Südtirol und die Achse Berlin–Rom, 1938–1945* (Stuttgart: Deutsche Verlags Anstalt, 1962), Annex IV, quoting German figures. The author states that about 195,000 people opted for Germany, but that figure excluded German-speaking voters in the Bozen Unterland area, which had been incorporated into Trento province since 1927. Italian figures put those who opted for Italy at 82,000—considerably higher than the corresponding figure of 22,000 given, for obvious reasons, by the German side.

6. Figures listed in Alcock, *The History of the South Tyrol Questions,* p. 501, chart A.

7. This resistance movement was led by Canon Michael Gamper and Dr. Friedl Volgger. The latter gave a convincing and interesting account of it in his autobiography, *Mit Südtirol am Scheideweg* (Innsbruck: Haymon Verlag, 1984), pp. 63ff.

8. There are numerous reprints of the Paris (De Gasperi–Gruber) Agreement. The one quoted here is taken from Alcock, *The History of the South Tyrol Question,* pp. 473–74. The original text of the agreement is in English.

9. Erich Amonn statement of February 25, 1948; quoted in Toscano-Carbone, *Alto Adige–South Tyrol,* p. 136.

10. The *pacchetto*'s text in English translation may be found on pp. 434–48 and that of the operations calendar on pp. 448–49 of Alcock, *The History of the South Tyrol Question.* For a comprehensive summary and the German text, see Heinrich Siegler, *Die Osterreichisch–Italienische Einigung über die Regelung des Südtirolkonfliktes* (Bonn, Vienna, and Zurich: Verlag für Zeiterchive, 1970).

11. The text of the revised *statuto* is contained, inter alia, in *Il Nuove Statuto di Autonomia* (Bolzano: Ufficio Stampa della Giunta Provinciale, 1985).

12. For these figures, see *Memorandum on the South Tirol,* submitted by the Austrian United Nations Association in 1958. Alcock, *The History of the South Tyrol Question,* gives a slightly higher figure of about 26 percent of Südtirol and Ladins in state services, based on the 1961 census.

13. See, for instance, the introduction to *Das Neue Autonomie-statut,* 4th (enlarged) ed. (Bozen: Athesia Druck, 1985), where in the Landeshauptmann and the chairwoman of the Landtag express their satisfaction with institutional progress.

14. As reported by Foreign Broadcasting Information Service (FBIS/WEU), September 30, 1987.

15. Cited in Hansjakob Stehle, "Los von Rom?" *Die Zeit,* October 9, 1987. This article is one of the most comprehensive and objective among numerous recent journalistic pieces on South Tyrol problems.

16. Quoted in a *Times* (London) article, "Neo-Fascists thrive on the fears of Italians," October 23, 1987. The same MSI deputy had asserted in December 1986 that the Südtiroler were "the most pampered majority-minority in the world." Quoted in Stehle, "Los von Rom?"

17. Stehle, "Los von Rom?"

18. Quoted in *la Repubblica,* August 9–10, 1987.

19. Stehle, "Los von Rom?"

20. Quoted by Erich Brunner in *Profil* (Vienna), January 1980.

21. Stehle, "Los von Rom?"

22. Volgger, *Mit Südtirol am Scheideweg,* p. 311.

23. On the lasting importance of the uprising of 1809, symbolized in the person of Andreas Hofer, see F. Gunther Eyck, *Loyal Rebels: Andreas Hofer and the Tyrolean Uprising of 1809* (Lanham and London: University Press of America, 1986), especially ch. XII.

III
Sri Lanka in the Southern Asian Context

Perhaps the most complex of the three "hot" conflict situations, Sri Lanka demands extensive study. Although it can be said that Northern Ireland and Sudan share with Sri Lanka the experience of British colonialism, Sri Lanka and its predecessor, Ceylon, have a much older burden of conflict history to plumb, not least the competition of Hinduism and Buddhism, interwoven with the tapestry of ethnic and linguistic battles for hegemony in the subcontinent and Indochina.

Bryan Pfaffenberger and Marshall Singer make permanent contributions to the understanding of Sri Lankan complexity with descriptive narratives, historic analyses, and assessments of conflict among classes, castes, and age cohorts.

Richard Stubbs's chapter on Malaysia provides extremely useful information on the ethnic conflict management technique of centrist coalition-building, to keep ethnic extremists on the sidelines. Malaysia is one of the most popular countries with students of peacemaking in multiethnic societies.

Few people in the world can match Selig Harrison's knowledge of Pakistan and its fractious tribal history. He describes a balancing act by Islamabad that has been relatively successful but could obviously benefit from much of the conflict resolution knowledge and sensitivity revealed in this volume. Since this essay was written, President Zia has died, but the background Harrison provides should have a long shelf life.

Of the hundreds of ethnic and linguistic groups jockeying for respect and status in an India also heir to ancient, complex history, the Assam settlement, effectively described by Walter Andersen, was chosen by the comparative multiethnic conflict experts of this volume as one of the most illuminating and manageable to present. As in so many other cases, there is constant stress and anxiety on the part of the Assamese at the thought of being overwhelmed by Bengali immigrants. Andersen explains how the parties limited violence in the past through a great deal of dialogue, negotiation, and attention to detail.

15

Ethnic Conflict and Youth Insurgency in Sri Lanka: The Social Origins of Tamil Separatism

Bryan Pfaffenberger

On its independence from Great Britain in 1948, the island nation Sri Lanka (formerly Ceylon[a]) was widely thought to have the best prospects of any Asian nation for prosperity and civil order as an independent country. It possessed a high rate of literacy (approximately 65 percent of the population over five years)[b] and a well-developed tradition of democratic political participation. Indeed, Sri Lanka was the first Asian country to introduce universal adult suffrage. Four decades later, however, the dream of a bright future lay shattered amid the hatred and ruin of a protracted ethnic conflict. Many Sri Lankans have come to believe that the island's two major ethnic communities—the predominant Sinhalese and the principal minority, the Sri Lanka Tamils—will never be able to live together again in communal amity. The following pages endeavor to explain how it is that Sri Lanka has come to this impasse.

The Tamil–Sinhalese Conflict: A Brief Overview

When the first European explorers reached Sri Lanka in the early sixteenth century, they found a population that was far from homogeneous. In the Jaffna peninsula, Sri Lanka's northernmost region, a Hindu king ruled a settlement of Tamil-speaking folk, the descendants of South Indian immigrants who began settling the peninsula in the thirteenth century. In the central highlands and the southwest, two Buddhist kingdoms divided a population of Sinhala-speaking peoples, whose residence on the island predated the Christian era. Between the two lay a huge gulf of dense, dangerous, and sparsely populated jungle. Along the eastern coast were to be found a series of independent, Tamil-speaking chiefdoms; the population there was evenly split between Hindus and Muslims (quaintly called Moors to this day in Sri Lanka).

The colonial period added to the island's heterogeneity. The Portuguese

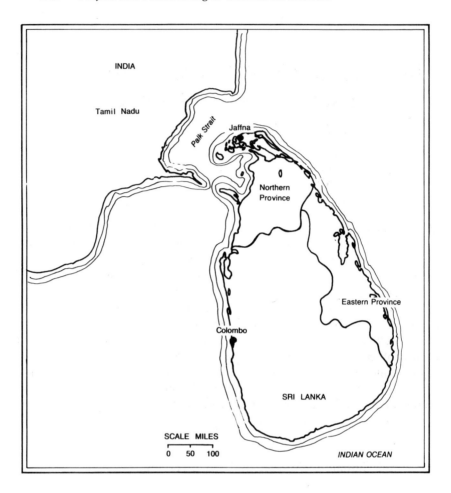

Figure 15–1. Sri Lanka

(1505–1658) converted some Tamil and Sinhalese coastal peoples to Catholicism. The Dutch (1658–1796) left behind a small community of mixed Sri Lankan and European ancestry called Burghers, most of whom are now English-speaking Christians, and a smaller community of Indonesians and Malayans (now called Malays). The British (1796–1948) brought Tamil Hindus from the poorer regions of South India to work in the central highland tea plantations. The descendants of these immigrants, called the Indian Tamils to distinguish them from the indigenous Tamil Hindu population (now called Sri Lanka Tamils), have little in common with the Tamil Hindus of the north and east, and their citizenship has been the subject of protracted and often acrimonious negotiations with India.

These ethnic divisions left their mark on Sri Lankan politics throughout the first half of the twentieth century. As Sri Lankans came to contemplate independence from Great Britain, questions were raised about the status of minority ethnic groups, languages, and religions. Some pointed with fear to the specter of communalism—the attitude that society is composed of separate and competing communities, which will always put their own interests above those of the nation as a whole, and that it is therefore necessary for the members of a community to act in concert to defend their rights and privileges. And there was indeed something to fear: Sinhalese Buddhists would be overwhelmingly predominant in the electorate of an independent Sri Lanka, suggesting that a frankly communalist Sinhalese Buddhist government could, if it were so inclined, abuse the rights of religious or ethnic minorities. Yet communalism had only rarely led to communal violence prior to independence.[c] On the whole, what one colonial governor called "a large measure of fellowship and understanding" prevailed among Sri Lanka's ethnic populations prior to independence, at least at the level of the masses.[1] And even though the period from 1921 to 1948 saw much debate among the Western-educated Tamil and Sinhalese politicians over the status of the Tamil minority in an independent Sri Lanka, the debate was "strikingly peaceful and orderly."[2]

The 1956 Elections and the Sinhala-Only Policy

The tensions that would later tear Sri Lanka apart emerged in full force, however, after independence. A 1956 election brought to power precisely the communalist organization that Tamils had feared: a Buddhist-backed coalition that favored the imposition of Sinhala as the "sole official language of government affairs." The coalition reflected the frustrations of a non-Westernized Sinhalese Buddhist majority, which saw itself subordinated to a Western-oriented, English-speaking elite. This elite, in the view of many Sinhalese, contained a disproportionately large number of Tamils.[d] Owing to the construction of an excellent school system in Jaffna by American missionaries in the nineteenth century, the Tamils of that northern region had ready access to English-medium instruction—and because the colonial government decided in 1885 to leave English education to private schools, such instruction was difficult to obtain elsewhere (except in Colombo). Knowledge of English gave Jaffna Tamils an advantage over the broad mass of rural Sinhalese in the competition for ardently desired civil service positions, which required English skills. Yet very few Tamils speak Sinhala, so they would be at a great disadvantage if these positions were to require literacy in Sinhala rather than English. The victory of the Sinhala-only coalition, in sum, was not only a move against the vestiges of colonialism, but also an attempt to cancel the Tamils' perceived advantage in the competition for public service positions.

The 1956 election was, predictably, received with alarm by Tamil political organizations, which mounted a nonviolent civil disobedience campaign in protest. Soon afterward, tensions over the language issue erupted in the 1958 Tamil–Sinhalese riots, in which hundreds died. Since that time, Tamil political parties have met with little success in stemming the erosion of Tamil educational and employment opportunities in Sri Lanka. Subsequent government policies designed to reduce Tamil access to the universities led to a 30 to 40 percent decline in Tamil university enrollment, vastly increasing unemployment and career frustration among Tamil youth. A 1972 constitution not only reaffirmed the role of Sinhala as the sole official language of government affairs but also mandated special state protection for the Buddhist religion, a move that deeply alarmed Tamil Hindus. Increasing numbers of Tamils have come to believe that they have no future in a Sri Lanka dominated by Sinhalese political organizations. To be sure, Sri Lanka's leaders have, on occasion, tried to address Tamil concerns by devolving state power to the provinces (and thus to Tamils, who predominate in the northern and eastern provinces). Yet every time the devolution of power has been proposed, Sinhalese public opinion and organized opposition by Buddhist groups have strenuously opposed the proposals and have agitated to bring down the government that makes them.

The Rise of the Tamil Tigers

By the early 1980s, Sri Lanka found itself in the midst of what can only be termed a civil war of secession, as several militant Tamil organizations, led by the youthful Liberation Tigers of Tamil Eelam (LTTE), resorted to violence as a way of remedying the Tamil plight. The war has its origins in the late 1970s. In May of 1976, several Tamil political parties formed the Tamil United Liberation Front (TULF) and issued a call for the union of the northern and eastern provinces as Tamil Eelam. (Eelam is the Tamil name for Sri Lanka.) The TULF called for the creation of Eelam through peaceful negotiations; however, this call was widely interpreted in Sri Lanka not as a call for actual secession, but rather as a ploy to force further concessions from the government and to appease Tamil youth organizations, which were showing increasing impatience with their elders' politics. The youth, however, did not seem to have been appeased: The TULF manifesto was followed in short order by LTTE efforts to force partition through the use of political violence. In a series of daring bank robberies and assassinations during the late 1970s and early 1980s, the Tamil militants—called "the boys" in Sri Lankan parlance—showed that they were quite capable of posing a serious challenge to the existing political order. Prominent among the militants' victims were moderate Tamils and those who had forged bonds with Sinhalese political parties. By 1982, the LTTE had effectively eliminated the moderate element in Tamil politics, including the TULF itself, few of whose members dared remain in Jaffna or the east.

Security Forces in Jaffna

In an attempt to control the Tamil militants, the Colombo government sent what amounted to an army of occupation to Jaffna, the northernmost city of Sri Lanka and the center of Tamil civilization in Sri Lanka. The security forces, which are overwhelmingly Sinhalese, found the Tamil population uncooperative as attempts were made to track down the militants; for instance, no witnesses could be found to bank robberies the militants carried out in broad daylight. Tamil civilians were doubtless fearful of reprisal from the militants themselves, but the security forces interpreted the public's unwillingness to cooperate as a sign of broad Tamil support for the militants. Such attitudes led to attacks on Tamil civilians, replete with cordoning operations, "disappearances," and other gross abuses of human rights.

For all their efforts, the security forces experienced little success in identifying and apprehending the militants, mainly because after the robberies or assassinations, the militants fled across the Palk Strait to their havens in the southern Indian state of Tamil Nadu. The Tamil Nadu state government, for its part, gave tacit support to the militants, a fact that greatly aggravated Indian–Sri Lankan diplomatic relations. By early 1983, Sinhalese frustration had reached the boiling point; and after the LTTE assassinated thirteen Sinhalese security personnel in Jaffna, Sinhalese mobs took to the streets in a systematic attack on Tamil homes, shops, and industries in the south. In reply, Tamil militants drove the government forces back to their bases in much of the Tamil north and set up the rudiments of an administrative and judicial system in areas they controlled.

After a major government offensive in the spring of 1987, the security forces recaptured much of the Jaffna peninsula, but only at the cost of inflaming public opinion in India. In a pointed violation of Sri Lanka's air space, India ferried a large cache of food and medical supplies to the besieged Tigers via an air convoy, which Sri Lanka was helpless to repel. Weeks later, however, India and Sri Lanka announced a major accord, which brought in thousands of Indian peacekeeping forces in exchange for the Colombo government's promise to push through legislation devolving power to the provinces. The LTTE opposed the accord, however, and the Indian troops found themselves fighting the Tigers, just as the Sri Lankan security forces had done.

Although the Indian forces managed to drive the LTTE out of Jaffna eventually, the Tamil militants retreated to the north-central jungles and the east, where they continued their activities. And soon after the accords, the Janatha Vimukthi Peramuna (JVP)—"People's Liberation Front"—launched a violent campaign against the accords—which, ironically, was consciously modeled on the Tigers' successful war on the political middle. By mid-1988, the situation in the south had deteriorated to the point that any Sinhalese person who advocated a solution to the conflict had reason to fear violent retaliation.

Applying Theories of Ethnic Conflict to Sri Lanka

Why did the promise of 1948 lead to the dismal reality of 1988? There is no shortage of theories that purport to explain why ethnic conflict occurs; as will be seen, however, the standard theories cannot be squared with the facts.

Primordial Antagonisms and Divisions

One theory explains ethnic conflict as a stubborn vestige of traditional antagonisms and divisions. On the surface, this theory seems readily applicable to Sri Lanka—a culturally heterogeneous country created by the colonial powers, rather than any indigenous notion of unity. Sri Lanka, in other words, resembles what Furnivall called a "plural society": an inherently unstable and disunified society, which consists of historially distinct and geographically separate linguistic, racial, or ethnic groups. These groups are brought together in a single polity only by the exogenous imposition of colonial authority.[3] When such societies become independent nations, the task of government is to "domesticate" the "primordial sentiments" of language, race, and ethnicity,[4] building the shared national culture that is vital to civil order.[5] The tragedy of Sri Lanka, or so one would argue using this approach, is that no shared national culture exists, and the sad events since independence have done little to build one.

A major problem with this explanation is that despite the country's divisions of language and religion, a substantial degree of shared culture does exist in Sri Lanka. The ruling families of the Sinhalese and Tamil kingdoms were close relatives and shared a single ideology of legitimate rule. Underlying similarities between the Tamil and Sinhalese cultures, moreover, testify to many long centuries of interaction and intermarriage. The kinship systems of the two peoples are so similar that they readily enable intermarriage, which was doubtless more common in the past than it is today. Sinhala has been described as a language with an Indo-European vocabulary and, testifying to long centuries of contact with South Indian peoples, a Dravidian grammatical structure. And within the sphere of popular religion, away from the Brahmans and Buddhist monks, there is remarkable similarity in Tamil and Sinhalese religious thought and practice. Although the twentieth century has witnessed growing cleavages between the Tamil and Sinhalese communities, it is reading history backward to suppose that those cleavages have always existed.

It is more accurate to say—despite the notion in Sri Lanka today that ethnic identity is ascriptive and even racially defined—that the Tamil and Sinhalese identities have persisted throughout history *despite* a considerable flow of persons across ethnic boundaries. In fact, many people who now call themselves Sinhalese are of South Indian (and perhaps Tamil) origin, having migrated to the island from the thirteenth to the eighteenth centuries. That the flow of persons across the Tamil–Sinhalese boundary is continuing seems evident from the changing proportions of those who have identified themselves as Tamils and Sinhalese to census interviewers during the past century; from 1871 to 1981, the proportion of Tamils (Indian and Sri Lankan) in the population fell from 24.9 to 18.2 percent, while the proportion of Sinhalese rose from 66.9 to 74 percent. To be sure, these trends are partially explained by differential rates of reproduction and the repatriation of some Indian Tamils to India. Yet it is likely that the old tradition by which South Indian peoples became assimilated into Sinhalese culture still continues today. For this reason, it is utterly false to claim that there are two "races" in Sri Lanka.

A second and related criticism of this explanation of Sri Lanka's ethnic conflict is that the so-called primordial sentiments of race in Sri Lanka are, arguably, not primordial at all. On the contrary, they are demonstrably quite modern in origin, having resulted from the nineteenth-century Sri Lankan appropriation of Western concepts of race and nationalism. These concepts have their origin in the 1788 publication of William Jones's theory of the ancient historical kinship of Indo-Aryan languages, a theory that Hegel called "the great discovery of history."[6] Jones's theory set the stage for a new, and value-laden, perspective on South Asian history, which was advanced by Muller and other Orientalists: The Aryan civilizations of South Asia, now in decay, were once great, and this greatness testified to the inherent superiority of the non-Semitic German and Indian peoples. This thesis, which found ready adherents among anti-Semetic elements in Europe at the time, depicted the classical period of ancient Indo-Aryan civilization as an idyllic golden age, an age to be set apart from the inferiority of India's "darker" Dravidian peoples of the south.[7] Sri Lanka's colonial masters found ready application for these racialist notions in Sri Lanka: Sinhala is an Indo-Aryan tongue, so the Sinhalese were of the "Aryan race"; likewise, Tamil is a Dravidian term, so the Tamils were of the "Dravidian race."

However inappropriate the concept of race might be to Sri Lankan history, it was nevertheless appropriated by the Sinhalese themselves in the late nineteenth and early twentieth centuries. For the Sinhalese, the Aryan ideology had much appeal: "It provided a section of the colonial peoples of South Asia with a prestigious 'pedigree'; it elevated them to the rank of their rulers, even though the relation was a distant and tenuous one."[8] The ideology fit in well, moreover, with Sinhalese Buddhist attempts to stave off the twin onslaught of Christian missionaries and Westernization. For Sri Lankan Buddhists of the late nineteenth and early twentieth centuries, the ancient Pali chronicles—the Culuvamsa and Mahavamsa—testified to the ancient and enduring existence of Lanka as an isle set apart for the preservation of a great civilization, one based on Buddhism, the Sinhala language, and the Sinhalese race. Ironically, the Sinhalese attempt to ward off Westernization made use of (and inculcated) what is clearly a Western concept: the notion of race.

The Sinhalese appropriation of European racialist ideology was convenient, as well, for the internal competition against Tamils, who had gained for themselves what many Sinhalese saw as a disproportionate share of public service positions. And here again, history was reinterpreted to suit political purposes. The ancient chronicles castigate the South Indian Tamils who periodically invaded the island in antiquity, and modern Sinhalese writers came to interpret these ancient conflicts in ethnic terms—that is, as the clash between the superior Aryan race and its ancient corrupter, the dark Dravidians. Especially suited to such interpretations is the tale of the Sinhalese King Dutthagamani's defeat of the Tamil King Elara, who had usurped the Sri Lankan throne.[9] Yet the Sinhalese identity of that time was fundamentally a political rather than a racial concept. What is more, "Elara and Dutthagamani were participants in a feudal power game and not in a racial war fought between the Sinhalese and the Tamils."[10] To attribute nineteenth- or twentieth-century notions of "race" to the events described in these chronicles is to make a fundamental historical error; it is to "present a view of the past molded by contemporary ideology."[11] In short, the sentiments that bedevil the politics of contemporary Sri Lanka are far from primordial; they are of quite recent origin.

The Modernization Theory

In confrontation with such facts as these, a more persuasive theory of ethnic conflict has emerged in the work of Karl Deutsch and others. This theory, which we can call modernization theory, does not see ethnic conflict as a recrudescence of ancient and enduring tradition. On the contrary, this theory views ethnic conflict as an outgrowth of modernity itself: Specifically, it results from the mobilization of ethnic ties in the competition for scarce political and economic resources.[12] An explicit assumption of modernization theory is, as Robert Bates put it:

> Ethnic groups persist largely because of their capacity to extract goods and services from the modern sector and thereby satisfy the demands of their members for the components of modernity. Insofar as they provide these

benefits to their members, they are able to gain their support and achieve their loyalty.[13]

Modernization theory fits the Sri Lankan facts well enough, at least up to a point. Consider, for instance, the Sinhala-only tactics of the 1956 coalition, which clearly sought to pry public service positions away from the hands of an English-speaking (and disproportionately Tamil) elite and place it in the hands of Sinhala-speaking Buddhists. The presecessionist Tamil parties, for their part, sought to guarantee Tamil access to state-distributed wealth at the levels prevailing prior to independence.

Modernization theory also helps to explain why the conflict has worsened with time: As the pie gets smaller, competition for the slices becomes more intense. And, in a word, Sri Lanka's economic performance since independence has been poor. Furthermore, efforts at economic expansion have met with little success. In the wake of the Korean war boom, the weaknesses of Sri Lanka's export-based economy became apparent, as did the country's inability to develop a growing industrial base: Indeed, during the 1970s, Sri Lanka actually experienced a significant amount of deindustrialization, reversing the trend experienced by most Third World countries during that decade. By 1981, it was obvious, as L. Piyadasa has remarked ruefully, that Sri Lanka was "economically behind most of the countries she had been ahead of 35 years previously."[14] To be sure, efforts by the government of President Junius R. Jayewardene to expand the economy led to improved economic growth from 1978 to 1984. Yet deficit spending and indebtedness to international lending agencies, coupled with unfavorable market conditions and huge increases in defense expenditures, have since combined to slow the economy's expansion.

What modernization theory does not explain, however, is why Sinhalese and Tamils have pursued ethnic conflict beyond the point that it could confer any real economic advantage. To put it baldly, Sinhalese and Tamils—like ethnic groups in other world areas—have frequently been willing to sacrifice economic gains for the sake of purely symbolic gains in the realm of ethnicity. Two cases in point: The 1983 riots in Colombo, which may have been organized with the assistance of some sections of the Jayewardene government, led to the destruction of more than 2,000 Tamil-owned businesses and factories, most of which employed Sinhalese workers and made vital contributions to the country's economic development effort. And the LTTE effort to create Tamil Eelam may well succeed in creating only a desperately impoverished nation with an inadequate economic base—not to mention that it would strand more than one-third of the Sri Lanka Tamil population, and most of its managerial and professional expertise, outside the borders of Eelam. The point here can be simply put: Ethnic conflict in general, and particularly ethnic conflict in Sri Lanka, is not rational behavior. Any theory that seeks to explain the ethnic violence in Sri Lanka must recognize that some of the parties to the conflict are willing to pursue it to the point of self-destruction.

The Social Psychology Theory

As Donald Horowitz has written, "the sheer passion expended in pursuing ethnic conflict calls out for an explanation that does justice to the realm of the feelings."[15] Horowitz's explanation, as will be seen, does a good (but not perfect) job of accounting for the Sri Lankan case. Citing a variety of experimental and anthropological studies, Horowitz argues that we learn in-group versus out-group distinctions easily: Favoritism toward in-groups and discrimination against out-groups is a prominent characteristic of social life. A major reason for this penchant for differentiation is psychological: We seem to have a deep need to evaluate ourselves (that is, our own group) favorably in comparison to other groups in the environment. Summing up this point of view, Horowitz has noted: "If the need to feel worthy is a fundamental human requirement, it is satisfied in considerable measure by belonging to groups that are in turn regarded as worthy."[16]

For Horowitz, the colonial experience is decisive in focusing attention on ethnic groups as reference groups for comparative evaluations of self-worth. The colonial incursion "clears the field" for comparison and, what is more, sets up new standards for recruitment into new roles. Frequently, the use of such standards leads to the differential incorporation of ethnic groups into the colonial order. In Sri Lanka, for instance, Tamils and Burghers were able to win public service jobs out of proportion to their numbers in the population because they were adept at English. As a result, a new standard of group evaluation emerged, a standard that was founded on perceptions of a group's success or failure in the competition for public service jobs. This standard, as Horowitz has predicted, persists long after the colonial powers depart. To win a government-salaried white-collar job is widely considered in Sri Lanka to constitute the be-all and end-all of life, a fact that frequently astonishes visitors to that country. Viewed in this context, it is hardly surprising that the most significant structural change in Sri Lanka from 1965 to 1981 was the growth of employment in service occupations at the expense of agriculture.[17]

The colonial experience does not merely establish a ranking criterion; it also produces perceptions that certain groups are advanced or backward in the competition for group worth. "To be backward," Horowitz has asserted, "is to feel weak *vis-à-vis* advanced groups"; it is to have failed in the competition for self-worth, and to judge oneself accordingly. Stereotypes of backward groups emerge in which they are described (and sometimes describe themselves) as "poor, lazy, traditional, inefficient, ignorant, leisurely, indolent, docile, easygoing, feudal, polite, submissive, unintelligent, lacking in initiative, proud, dependent, [and] spendthrifty." To be advanced, in contrast, is to be viewed as "enterprising, aggressive, ruthless, money-hungry, industrious, shrewd, successful, stingy, arrogant, cunning, intelligent, energetic, resourceful, serious, clannish, nepotistic, tribalistic, progressive, crafty, frugal, avaricious, pushy, efficient, thrifty, ambitious, coarse, miserly, [and] clever."[18] As anyone who has spent some time in Sri Lanka knows, these stereotypes perfectly describe the views that Sinhalese and Tamil people hold of each other, even though these lists of adjectives are derived from comparative studies of worldwide scope.

From this perspective, the passions that have animated the broad mass of Sinhalese Buddhists in the electorate become quite clear. The Sinhalese masses, like backward groups elsewhere, have been deeply troubled by invidious comparison with the advanced Tamils; and the disparaging evaluation of self-worth has manifested itself in anxiety, hostility, and violence. Backward groups, for instance, typically display an inordinate fear of cultural extinction; the advanced group is seen as a dire threat to the survival of the group's customs and language. In Sri Lanka, Sinhalese fears of cultural extinction are multiplied because of the presence of tens of millions of Tamil-speakers in neighboring South India, so that the Sinhalese—overwhelmingly the majority group in Sri Lanka—actually see themselves as a minority in the wider regional context. In such a context, the Tamil threat is sure to be exaggerated far out of proportion to the actual danger. During the 1983 riots, for instance, an absurd rumor that the Tamil Tigers were attacking Colombo led to a mass panic in Colombo's business district, from which thousands of Sinhalese office workers fled on foot.

The threat the Tamils pose, however, is not real but subjective; it is a threat to self-worth, and it quite naturally engenders hostility toward the outgroup. It is hardly surprising, then, that the backward group is frequently the initiator (and advanced groups are the targets) of ethnic riot behavior, as is clearly the case in Sri Lanka. By far the greatest number of victims of ethnic conflict in Sri Lanka are Tamils, not Sinhalese.

Just as the invidious judgment of self-worth promotes the display of hostility toward the advanced group, so, too, does it fuel the backward group's quest for legitimacy, preferably in terms defined by the colonial order. The colonial power, after all, set up the terms of the comparative contest, and if the battle for self-worth is to be won, it must be won in these terms and no others. It should now be clear why Sinhalese Buddhists adopted the Aryan racialist ideology of Orientalist (and mainly British) scholars with such enthusiam. This ideology concedes the backward group's deficiencies in modern times, but it holds open the promise of greatness once the glory of the past is recaptured. That it also denigrates the advanced group, the "Dravidian" Tamils, makes it utterly irresistible. Sinhalese politics since 1956, then, has been a symbolic politics of ethnic legitimation, in which the political structure has been made to revolve around the twin poles of Sinhalese greatness in antiquity, the Sinhala language, and the Buddhist religion.

What Horowitz's theory does not completely explain, however, is the rise of a violent and passionate Tamil secessionist movement, spearheaded by the Liberation Tigers. Advanced groups in backward regions such as the Tamil homelands, according to Horowitz, are likely to be "reluctant secessionists": They attempt secession "only when the advantages of remaining in the unified state are much reduced and the costs of remaining seem perilously high."[19] To be sure, Tamils may have already reached precisely this threshold. Between the human rights abuses of the army and the riots in the south, many Tamils may find the cost of remaining in a unified Sri Lanka too great. Yet secession would have no advantage for the one-third of the Tamil population that dwells outside the northern and eastern provinces. And despite the increase in acts of violence against Tamils in the south, the proportion of Tamils living outside the northern and eastern provinces has actually increased—and increased steadily—since independence. Horowitz's theory, in short, explains the passions of the Sinhalese very well, but it does not suffice to explain the passion with which the LTTE and allied groups are now fighting for Tamil Eelam. To grasp the Tamil secessionist movement, an additional (and complementary) theoretical perspective is needed, one that focuses squarely on the role of youth politics and youth insurrections in rapidly growing populations.

The LTTE and the Politics of Youth Insurrection

Youth movements have bedeviled civilization since its inception, a fact revealed by a 4,000-year-old tablet found at the Biblical city of Ur: "Our civilization is doomed," the tablet reads, "if the unheard-of actions of our younger generations are allowed to continue."[20] Yet comparative historical studies have shown that certain generational and historical forces are likely to fuel youth movements. Such movements are organized and conscious attempts by young people (typically, men and women in the fifteen- to twenty-four-year age group) to bring about (or resist) social change.

A generational factor that contributes to the rise of a youth movement is the existence of an unusually large and self-aware cohort of young people, one that results from an unprecedented "baby boom." A precipitating historical factor is "a perceived discrepancy between the individual needs and aspirations of young people and the existing social and political conditions."[21] And, as will be seen, both factors were at work in Sri Lanka during the 1970s and 1980s.

Unemployment and Political Disillusionment

Sri Lanka experienced a period of explosive population growth between 1946 and 1971, when the population nearly doubled. Causative factors were an abrupt drop in mortality rates after 1945 and an increase in birth rates, which peaked at 39.8 births per 1,000 individuals in the population in 1951 and declined sharply thereafter. From 1946 to 1963, the largest increase in population occurred in children under age fifteen. Between 1963 and 1971, however, the largest increase occurred in the age group fifteen to twenty-nine as the 1946–63 cohort ascended up the age pyramid. This cohort, therefore, was very prominent in the population and, like the "baby boom" generation of the United States, was aware of itself as a generational unit. Unlike the United States, however, in Sri Lanka the economy could not accommodate the huge numbers of young people who came into the job market in the 1960s, when Sri Lanka's economy, measured by per capita increases in gross national product, was all but stagnant.

By the early 1970s, youth aspirations for employment combined with Sri Lanka's poor economic performance created an explosive situation. Many youths had believed, following the older generation's earnest advice, that education was the pathway to success in obtaining employment. The youth of Sri Lanka took this advice seriously; for instance, between 1960 and 1970, the number of university graduates increased sevenfold. Yet the advice, however well intentioned, was at best misleading; the jobs were not there. In 1969–70, for instance, unemployment among persons aged fifteen to twenty-four with secondary educations was about 70 percent. Worse, unemployment rates among youths rose with educational attainment. Among males aged fifteen to twenty-four, for instance, the rate of unemployment for those who had completed a secondary education was twice that of those with no schooling or only primary schooling. For Sinhalese youth, the lack of employment opportunities was especially galling. The promise of the 1956 Sinhala-only legislation was that government jobs would finally be available for educated rural Sinhalese youths who knew little English. The reality in the late 1960s was that access to highly valued public service positions really was not a matter of educational attainment, as thousands of youths had learned to their misfortune. It was a matter of having the right political connections. By 1970, the public service had become so politicized that virtually all public service positions, no matter how trivial, were allocated by members of Parliament—and largely to their kinsmen and political retainees.

Not surprisingly, Sri Lankan youths during the late 1960s and 1970s came to feel that their interests were not being looked after by the existing political leadership, the politicians of the established political parties, who were increasingly viewed as utterly corrupt—indeed, irredeemably corrupt. Not only had this leadership failed to provide rural Sinhalese youth with jobs, but also it was significantly older than the population as a whole, a mark of suspicion in the eyes of youth. Kearney noted that the age group from forty to sixty-four years of age was at this time markedly overrepresented in Parliament, for instance, while the population under thirty-five was just as markedly underrepresented. For Sri Lankan youth in the early 1970s, however, the problem was not merely that the politicians were too old; the problem was that they were politicians, interested only in playing the political game rather than carrying out the needed reforms. This belief led naturally to a rejection not merely of the politicians in office but of the entire existing political order.

The 1971 Sinhalese Insurgency

The frustrations of educated but unemployed youth, coupled with a widespread conviction that the existing political system was unjust, laid the foundation for the 1971 insurgency among rural Sinhalese youth. More than 10,000 insurgents, mostly armed with shotguns and homemade bombs, attacked seventy-four police stations simultaneously across the island and very nearly succeeded in toppling the Colombo government. The insurrection was put down after several weeks of bitter fighting, resulting in an officially estimated 1,200 deaths and 14,000 arrests. Unofficial estimates placed the death toll at 6,000 or more. Planned and executed by the JVP, the insurgency threw the problems of youth into dramatic relief. About 90 percent of the insurgents were under thirty years of age; almost three-quarters were under twenty-five.

The JVP's ideology was an unsophisticated and utopian version of ultraradical Marxism, and it called for a complete rejection of the existing political and social order. Also prominent was a penchant for heroic romanticism: The JVP youths imposed austerities on themselves and took almost unbelievable risks in battle. In practice, however, the JVP seems to have succeeded only in reproducing, rather than changing, the system it sought to challenge. Its leaders squabbled over caste issues, for instance, and it is quite clear that the group's objective was not so much to abolish the existing system of political and bureaucratic offices as it was to install themselves in these offices. In areas that the insurgents briefly controlled, the youths gave themselves high-sounding titles, such as "judge" and "prime minister."

The Insurrection of the Tamil Tigers in Jaffna

The LTTE insurrection in Jaffna is virtually a repeat performance of the 1971 insurgency, except that the youths involved are Tamil instead of Sinhalese. That difference is a crucial one, to be sure, as in this case, the youth insurrection is also an ethnic confrontation. Yet the similarities are compelling. The Tamil militant groups are known to have grown out of several Tamil student organizations, including the youth wing of the Tamil United Front, the TULF's predecessor, and the Unemployed Graduates' Union, a Tamil youth organization composed of disgruntled university and secondary school graduates. Like the JVP militants, the Tamil youths were deeply frustrated by their inability to find public service jobs, and they repudiated the older political leadership that had failed to address their needs. (Indeed, Tamil militants have assassinated two former TULF members of Parliament, and the LTTE has published a death warrant for its leader, A. Amirthalingam.) Also prominent is the dimension of heroic romanticism, replete with self-imposed austerities and astounding acts of courage. And like the JVP, the Tamil militant leaders have squabbled over caste issues and have adopted a simplistic, unsophisticated version of Marxist ideology.

Troubling Trends

Two conclusions follow from looking at the Tamil separatist campaign in the theoretical terms provided by Horowitz and comparing it to the 1971 insurgency. The first, suggested by Horowitz's analysis, is that the broad majority of Sri Lanka Tamils have been, and probably will remain, "reluctant secessionists." The interests of most Tamils are too closely tied to the rest of the island for Eelam to offer much appeal, except as a way of staving off the murderous activities of the undisciplined security forces. The second conclusion, suggested by the comparison to the 1971 insurgency, is that the LTTE movement—like the insurgents of 1971—represents only a tiny fraction of the population whose interests it purports to defend. Even more troubling, the Tamil militants, like the JVP, may well prove themselves incapable of governing should their movement succeed. According to Richard Braungart:

> Youth movements pose a threat to society when they are so strongly committed to total change or the radical transformation of a given society . . . that they become incapable of diagnosing existing conditions and offering practical and workable solutions. . . . Their contact with reality tends to be abstract and pure rather than tempered or conditioned by experience. . . . Political extremists project and distort reality in such a way that they may be unable to function effectively as leaders in a political system that has a tradition of pragmatism, compromise, and relative tolerance for competing ideologies and points of view.[22]

The LTTE's leadership shows ample sign of this penchant for abstraction and unwillingness to compromise. The organization has repeatedly refused to negotiate with the Colombo government, which it regards with absolute distrust. Admittedly, most Tamils would probably agree that this distrust is amply deserved. Yet the LTTE's leader, Veluppillai Prabhakaran, has staked out a position so radical that it virtually rules out any form of negotiation or compromise. Reportedly, Prabhakaran—like the 1971 insurgents—draws a firm distinction between "revolutionaries," who do not compromise, and "politicians," who have no integrity. Obviously, his attitude will have to change if he is to become an effective leader of the Tamil community, which is internally stratified and in which there are conflicting interests. To ask Prabhakaran to become a "politician," however, is to ask him to forgo the dubious brand of integrity that he had risked his life to achieve.

What is starkly apparent in both the Tamil and Sinhalese communities today is a disturbing trend toward authoritarianism and away from democracy. The LTTE demonstrated its authoritarian penchant in 1987, when it wiped out rival Tamil militant groups in a series of bloodbaths.[e] Its leader speaks openly of a "one-party government," modeled on Eastern European regimes.[23] The Jaffna population fears the militants, and many Tamil refugees in Europe and the United States privately concede that they are fleeing the LTTE as much as the Sinhalese. The Jayewardene government, meanwhile, continues its suppression of Sinhalese dissent in an attempt to garner the power needed to make meaningful concessions to the Tamils; indeed, the president threatened to cancel the 1989 elections if the Tamil problem was not solved. Although this strategy has helped to silence the Sinhalese political opposition, it has also energized the radical left, which just five years ago was all but moribund. Some observers of Sri Lanka—and increasing numbers of Sri Lankans themselves—are beginning to doubt that the present political system can survive the stresses to which it is now being exposed. Sri Lanka's long tradition of representative democracy may well prove to be the next victim of the island nation's descent into the politics of ethnic conflict.

Notes

a. Ceylon's name was changed to Sri Lanka in the Constitution of 1972. For the sake of consistency, Sri Lanka will be used to refer to the country both before and after its name change, except in quotations that use the old name.

b. According to the Ceylon Department of the Census, literacy was defined as "the ability to write a short letter and read the reply to it" in the individual's mother tongue.

c. The major exception was the 1915 Sinhalese–Muslim riots, which reflected Sinhalese Buddhist antagonism toward profiteering Muslim traders.

d. The Tamil advantage was frequently overstated, however. See S.J. Tambiah, "Ethnic Representation in Ceylon's Higher Administrative Services, 1870–1946," *University of Ceylon Review* 8, no. 2-3 (1955): 113–34.

e. For example, in April 1986, the LTTE exterminated a rival organization—the Tamil Eelam Liberation Organization (TELO)—causing some 300 deaths.

References

1. Sir Andrew Caldecott, quoted in Great Britain, Colonial Office, *Correspondence Relating to the Constitution of Ceylon* (London: His Majesty's Stationery Office, 1938), p. 8.

2. Robert N. Kearney, *Communalism and Language in the Politics of Ceylon,* (Durham, NC: Duke University Press, 1967), p. 40.

3. J.S. Furnivall, *Netherlands India: A Study of Plural Economy* (Cambridge: Cambridge University Press, 1939).

4. Clifford Geertz, "The Integrative Revolution: Primordial Sentiments and the New States," in Clifford Geertz, ed., *Old Societies and New States* (Glencoe, IL: Free Press, 1963), pp. 105–57.

5. Karl W. Deutsch, *Nationalism and Social Communication* (Cambridge, MA: MIT Press, 1953).

6. Cited in R.A.L.H. Gunawardena, "People of the Lion: Sinhala Consciousness in History and Historiography," in Social Scientists' Association, *Ethnicity and Social Change in Sri Lanka* (Colombo: Karunaratne and Sons, 1984), p. 33.

7. Kumari Jayawardena, "Class Formation and Communalism," *Race and Class* 26 (1984): 59.

8. *Ibid.,* p. 37.

9. W.I. Siriweera, "The Dutthagamani–Elara Episode: A Reassessment," in Social Scientists' Association, *Ethnicity and Social Change in Sri Lanka,* pp. 54–73.

10. *Ibid.,* p. 56.

11. Gunawardena, "People of the Lion," p. 2.

12. Karl Deutsch, "Social Mobilization and Political Development," *American Political Science Review* 55 (1961): 493–514.

13. Robert Bates, "Ethnic Competition and Modernization in Contemporary Africa," *Comparative Political Studies* 6 (1974): 481.

14. L. Piyadasa, *Sri Lanka: The Holocaust and After* (London: Marram Books, 1984), p. 42.

15. Donald Horowitz, *Ethnic Groups in Conflict* (Berkeley and Los Angeles: University of California Press, 1985), p. 140.

16. *Ibid.,* p. 185.

17. World Resources Institute and the International Institute for Environment and Development, *World Resources 1986* (New York: Basic Books, 1986), p. 231.

18. Horowitz, *Ethnic Groups in Conflict,* p. 167.

19. *Ibid.,* p. 244.

20. Quoted in Richard G. Braungart, "Historical and Generational Patterns of Youth Movements: A Global Perspective," *Comparative Social Research* 7 (1984): 12.

21. *Ibid.,* p. 4.

22. *Ibid.,* pp. 55–56.

23. Quoted in an interview published in *India Today,* June 30, 1986.

16

Prospects for Conflict Management in the Sri Lankan Ethnic Crisis

Marshall R. Singer

Sinhalese and Tamils

The Sinhalese comprise about 71 percent of the population of Sri Lanka, now a country with a population of nearly 16 million people.[1] They are overwhelmingly Theravada Buddhist and consider themselves the "true defenders of the faith." The bodhi tree in Anuradhapura is a sapling of the original one under which Buddha obtained enlightenment more than 2,500 years ago. Although the Sangha (the Buddhist priesthood) was ignored and more or less left to its own devices for 450 years of colonial history, it persisted, and the hold of Buddhism on the population is very strong today.

Although other Theravada Buddhist societies exist in Burma, Thailand, and elsewhere, the Sinhalese, as a linguistic and ethnic group, exist nowhere else in the world.[a] Thus, much as with the Israelis and the Afrikaners, there is a feeling that there is nowhere else for them to go. They have to defend their homeland—and in the Sinhalese mind, their homeland is the entire island of Sri Lanka.

Although Buddhism does not recognize a caste system, there is a strong one among the Sinhalese; the highest caste, the Goyigama, or farmer caste, is the largest. Every head of state in Sri Lanka until now has been Goyigama.

The Tamils comprise almost 22 percent of the population of Sri Lanka. They can be divided up in several significant ways. Most important is the distinction between the Tamils who are the descendants of those from South India who started invading Sri Lanka in about the tenth century A.D. and the Tamils who are the descendants of those who came in the nineteenth century.

Material for this chapter was taken from interviews conducted in Sri Lanka and India with more than 300 individuals who were directly involved in the ethnic conflict in the summer of 1985, 1987, and 1989, including the president, the prime minister, and other members of the government; opposition party leaders; military personnel; Buddhist priests; and lawyers, doctors, and academicians. It also includes material from interviews in India with spokesmen for various militant groups fighting the government, as well as with some of "the boys" actually doing the fighting. This was written in 1987 and revised in February 1991; this is important for the reader to know, because events on the island change so rapidly.

The early invaders settled mainly in the Jaffna peninsula, in the north of Sri Lanka, and along the east coast. They are sometimes called Jaffna Tamils or Ceylon or Sri Lanka Tamils. The other major group of Tamils in Sri Lanka consists of the offspring of the tea estate workers who were brought to the island by the British in the late nineteenth century to work in the coffee and tea plantations of the upper Kandyan hills around Nuwara Eliya. The Jaffna Tamils have traditionally been very conservative; the Hindu caste system is even more important to them than caste is to the Sinhalese. That may be changing among the younger Tamils. However, the Estate Tamils or Indian Tamils, as they are called, are exclusively of very low caste, and that has always been a major division between the two groups. Numerically, the two groups are about the same size, with each numbering more than a million and a half people.

Until July 1983, about 500,000 Tamils lived in or near Colombo. Their perceptions of the world were quite distinct from those of the other two groups of Tamils. The Colombo Tamils were much more a part of mainstream Sri Lankan life. Many of the most educated spoke English in preference to Tamil (as many older, educated people did in Colombo, whether they were Sinhalese or Tamil). Since that time, many of the Colombo Tamils have fled either to India or to the United States, Canada, or other Western countries.

The Sri Lanka Muslims are, in fact, a religious rather than an ethnic group in the true sense of the word, but they see themselves as a separate community and thus behave as though they were. The Muslims comprise about 7 percent of the population. The largest proportion of the Muslims, descendants of early Arab traders who are now called Ceylon Moors, have been living on the island the longest; the Malays are descendants of East Asian traders who are reported to have arrived mostly during the Dutch period; and the so-called Indian Moors are the descendants of Arab traders who lived in India for several centuries before settling in Sri Lanka. Although some of the more religious know the language of the Koran, the vast majority of them speak the Tamil language. Although Muslims are scattered all over the island, the majority of them live on the east coast.

Whereas the northern province is overwhelmingly Tamil, the eastern province is divided almost equally among Tamils, Muslims, and Sinhalese. This is important to a settlement of the conflict, because the Tamil militants have insisted that the northern and eastern provinces together form the traditional "Tamil homeland" and must be reunited under Tamil control. The Sinhalese are relative newcomers to the east coast, having come in large numbers only since independence, as colonizers on land schemes developed by the government—hence the recent efforts of Tamil militants to drive the Sinhalese out of the eastern province. As the Muslims speak the Tamil language, the militants claim them as "one of us." It is not at all clear as of this writing, however, whether the Muslims want to be claimed. Traditionally, they have sided with the group in power, and because the Sinhalese were usually in power, they have tended to side with the Sinhalese.

When President Jayewardene agreed to a temporary union of the northern and eastern provinces in the July 1987 Accords, he did so only on the stipulation that there would be an election in the newly created province to decide its future. He was counting on the Muslims voting with the Sinhalese against the union of the provinces so that they would continue to play a pivotal role—sometimes siding with one group, sometimes with the other, depending on who offered more. What the Muslims do not seem to want is to become a permanent minority in a predominantly Hindu, permanently merged northern and eastern province.

The Origin and Nature of the "Tamil Problem"

Scholars and practitioners alike differ on when the "Tamil problem" started. Some Sinhalese extremists will tell you it started with the Tamil invasions of the tenth century and has been building since. Some will tell you it started under the British, when they gave the better jobs in the civil service to Tamils rather than to Sinhalese. Others point to geographic considerations. The land on the Jaffna peninsula is poor, and with only one monsoon, there is not much agriculture. Tamil men were forced to turn to business, the professions, and the civil service to make a living, and they did well in each. At the time of independence, the Tamils were overrepresented in all of the professions, the universities, and the civil service—a fact that was not lost on the Sinhalese.

One of the first things the newly independent government did in 1948 was to disenfranchise those Estate Tamils whom the government said were Indian and should not be allowed to participate in Ceylonese political life. They could apply for Sri Lankan citizenship—a process that was long and cumbersome—and could have the right to vote only after they became Sri Lankan citizens. About 400,000 have applied thus far, but perhaps 1 million more have not been able to aquire Sri Lankan citizenship. Several hundred thousand were supposed to be repatriated to India under various agreements that have been reached between the two governments, but nowhere near that number have actually gone.

In the 1956 election, S.W.R.D. Bandaranaike ran on a "Sinhala-only" platform; that is, Sinhala was to be the only official language of the country (at the time, English was the official language). He also promised to "restore Buddhism to its proper place in society." His overwhelming electoral victory showed that ethnic chauvinism pays off at the ballot box. No party has been able to forget that lesson since.

The move was clearly aimed, in part, to reduce the disproportionately large numbers of English-speaking Tamils in the civil service and to get more rural Sinhala-speakers into universities. Both goals were accomplished by the move. The latter goal was achieved by switching the language of university instruction to Sinhala. When it was found in the 1970s that a disproportionately high number of Tamils were still gaining entrance to the universities, a complex system of weighting grades from different regions was introduced, to make it easier for students from Sinhalese areas to gain university admission than it would be for Tamils.

The Tamils did not take very kindly to these moves against them, but every time their representatives were able to hammer out a compromise agreement with the Sinhalese government of the day, the Sinhalese opposition party invariably argued "sellout of the Sinhalese people," and the Sinhalese party that made the deal was forced to renege.

Essentially, what the Tamils have consistently been pushing for—at least since 1956—is greater autonomy for Tamil areas. But because *federalism* is a dirty word to the Sinhalese, every effort in that direction has been scuttled by Sinhalese chauvinists. Through the late 1950s and 1960s, the party that captured the northern Tamil votes was the Federal party, which favored some federal system. But the party could not deliver, and younger militants began saying that the older generation was wasting its time asking for partial autonomy—the Sinhalese would never grant it. The only alternative for Tamils was to secede from Sri Lanka and become a separate country. *Tamil Eelam* (actually meaning an independent Tamil country in Sri Lanka) became the buzzword, particularly among young northern Tamils. The idea became so popular that when the two major Tamil parties merged to form the Tamil United Liberation Front (TULF), they had to publicly demand a separate state, even though everyone knew privately that they would be perfectly happy to settle for some form of federalism. Indeed, when the District Development Councils system was created in 1982, the word *development* was put in specifically to disguise the fact that the system was actually a form of federalism. Unfortunately, the scheme was never fully implemented. Had it been, there is widespread belief—particularly among moderate Tamils—that it would have been a workable solution to the problem. But it was not, and the younger, more militant Tamils became increasingly violent.

The 1983 Riots

The main turning point was July 1983. Some militant Tamils killed thirteen Sinhalese soldiers in an ambush in the north. The bodies of the thirteen were brought back to Colombo for a mass funeral, despite a government prohibition on demonstrations. Needless to say, the funeral triggered an emotional outburst from the Sinhalese in Colombo. Their anger took the form of attacks on innocent Tamils in Colombo and elsewhere. Although the first night of rioting might have been understandable, it didn't end there. Indeed, it got out of hand and went on for five days, with the government doing nothing to stop it. Worse, there is some evidence that certain ministers in the government provided their private "thug groups" with voter registration lists and vehicles to go where Tamils lived and set their houses on fire—either with the residents having been given a chance to leave or, it is alleged, often with the residents sealed inside.[2]

Between 140 (official figures) and 600 (unofficial reports) Tamils were killed and thousands were made homeless by the riots, but the government did not protest this lawless behavior. Nor did any high-ranking government official visit the centers where the refugees of the rioting were being looked after. When government officials finally went before the TV cameras five days later, they blamed the riots on the "cumulative indignation of the Sinhalese people." This seeming lack of concern for Tamil human rights seemed so gross, even to moderate Tamils, that many became convinced that "the boys," as the young militants were called by Tamils, were right in believing that Tamils would be safe only if they had their own state.

At the time of the July 1983 riots, most experts agree that the militants numbered somewhere between 200 and 700. By June 1985, after two years of government efforts to stamp out the "terrorists" (as the militants were called by the Sinhalese) militarily, the number of militants had grown to between 2,000 and 10,000. The riots themselves—and the government's reaction to them—convinced many young Tamils that they had no choice but to fight for Tamil rights.

After the 1983 riots, thousands of Sri Lanka Tamils fled the country. Some went north, where they thought they could feel more safe, but thousands more fled to India or, if they could afford it, to Europe, Australia, or North America. At the same time, New Delhi and Madras allowed the militants to operate from bases in Tamil Nadu. They would strike in Sri Lanka and then flee across the Palk Strait back to safe sanctuary in India. In an effort to curb that cross-strait traffic, Colombo tried to clear a stretch of land along the Sri Lankan coast of all population and foliage. In that effort, they displaced thousands of innocent fishermen and farmers; some fled to India, and many of the younger ones became militants.

After the riots, the government followed a policy of locking up young Tamil boys and men and holding them in camps, just because they were young and Tamil. Some were released after they had been roughed up a bit and humiliated. Some were not. Amnesty International has claimed for some time that young Tamil men were being tortured in the detention camps, and although the Sri Lankan government has repeatedly denied the charges, it has also repeatedly refused to let the International Red Cross investigate. The government undoubtedly intended by these actions to warn the young men not to get involved with the terrorists, but the warning had the opposite effect and markedly increased the number of active militants.

The army, which up until then had been primarily ceremonial, reacted in a very undisciplined manner. In the early days of the insurgency, if a troop carrier hit a land mine and was blown up, the soldiers in the troop carrier behind it would dismount and spray the surrounding civilian population with bullets. Such outbursts were partly an expression of rage and partly borne of a conviction that the peasants were guilty of complicity.

All of the excesses on the part of the government contributed to the increase in the size of the militant forces.

The Sinhalese Actors in the Conflict

The United National Party

There are a number of actors on the Sinhalese side, but none is more important than the United National Party (UNP). A plurality of Sri Lanka voters—if not a majority—have usually given their allegiance to the UNP. Perceived to be the party of the Goyigama caste—which is the highest caste in the Sinhalese system and also the largest—and of Sri Lanka's wealthier people, the UNP has traditionally had a Western orientation. In 1977, the UNP experienced a landslide election victory in which it captured more than two-thirds of the seats in Parliament, thereby giving it the power to amend the constitution at will.

In 1978, the then president, J.R. Jayewardene took advantage of the UNP's two-thirds majority and had the form of government constitutionally changed from a parliamentary democracy on the Westminster model to a De Gaulle-type presidential system in which a vast amount of authority was vested in the president.[3] He won election to the newly created presidency in 1982; then, instead of holding an election for Parliament—as both the old and the new constitutions seemed to require—he held a refendum on extending the life of the old Parliament for another term. Thus, he maintained the UNP's two-third majority in Parliament, a percentage that certainly would have been eroded even if the UNP had won reelection.

In December 1988, amid great turmoil, the man who was prime minister throughout the Jayewardene years, Ranasinghe Premadasa, was elected president. President R. Premadasa is a self-made, low-caste man of the people who had made a reputation for himself by getting things done. Among the projects he launched, while still prime minister, was a scheme to build housing for the homeless. So successful has this project been that when it is finished, it will provide 1 million homes for Sri Lankans. At approximately five people per family, that means that almost one-third of the population will have benefited from the scheme.

President Premadasa has made no effort to hide his anger at India for not putting an end to the ethnic conflict from the very beginning. He, more than anyone else, has accused the Indians of being able to "turn it off" any time they wanted, just as he claims they "turned it on." After the Accords of July 1987, he emerged looking as though he had been correct all along. He is extremely popular within the UNP despite his humble origins. Although the wealthy, well-educated, and rather snobby "Colombo 7" wing of the party tends to look down on him because he is not from one of the "right families," there are many in the group who support him because they feel that as a "man of the people," he is the only member of the UNP who could have won the election for president. Although he is anti-Indian, some of the most militant Sinhalese and Tamil chauvinists believed that he would put an end to the conflict quickly.

The Sri Lanka Freedom Party

The other important political party on the Sinhalese side is the Sri Lanka Freedom party (SLFP). Before independence, S.W.R.D. Bandaranaike founded a Sinhalese nationalist group called the Sinhala Maha Sabha. At independence, this party joined the UNP but later broke with it before the 1956 elections and became the SLFP. In those elections, the newly formed SLFP, in coalition with the left opposition parties, soundly defeated the UNP on a platform of blatant Sinhalese Buddhist chauvinism.

The son of a highly Westernized, wealthy Sinhalese Christian, Bandaranaike spoke virtually no Sinhala before returning to Sri Lanka from Oxford University in England. Upon entering politics, however, he became a Buddhist, learned Sinhala and started dressing in what he called "national dress," rather than the Western clothes most politicians wore at the time. In the 1956 elections, he enlisted the overwhelming support of the Buddhist Sangha (priesthood), the vernacular teachers (who taught the Sinhala language) and the *ayurvedic* (traditional) medicine practitioners. In every town and village, these people commanded great respect, and their support for the SLFP was crucial. In addition, the smaller-town middle class and the lower-caste people joined the coalition against the more Westernized "better people." In a sense, Bandaranaike fundamentally changed Sri Lankan politics, in that he and his party proved how effective ethnic nationalism can be as a vote-getting platform. The only parties that resisted that bandwagon were the old left parties, which were trampled in the process.

As the appearance of being both devoutly Buddhist and staunchly Sinhalese nationalist is critical to winning elections, the UNP and the SLFP each tries to prove to the voters that it stands firmer on Sinhalese rights than the other. From the standpoint of ethnic conflict resolution, this poses a major problem. Jayewardene and the UNP screamed "sellout" when Bandaranaike concluded an agreement with the Tamils giving them a bit of autonomy in Tamil regions; and they did so again in the early 1970s, when Mrs. Bandaranaike (who took over the lead of the SLFP after her husband's assassination in 1959) tried it. On the other hand, Mrs. Bandaranaike and the SLFP have screamed "sellout" at every effort the UNP government has made to reach accommodation with the Tamils since they came to power in 1977. The SLFP opposed the District Development Councils scheme of 1982—which just might have solved the problem, once and for all, peacefully. They opposed giving some autonomy to Tamil areas, as proposed by the All-Party Conference in 1983–84 (which was called to try to find a peaceful solution to the problem). They opposed the Provincial Councils scheme proposed by President Jayewardene in the summer of 1986 and the July 1987 Accords, which do provide for a de facto federalism. In sum, the SLFP has opposed virtually every compromise agreement President Jayewardene has proposed. Accommodation with the Tamils will not be possible without "giving something to the Tamils," yet both Sinhalese parties have opposed accommodation when they were in the opposition.

The UNP and the SLFP collectively account for approximately 85 percent of all the votes cast in any election in Sri Lanka. If the two could agree to work together toward a solution to the problem, they could bring the bulk of the Sinhalese people along with them. The problem is that they generally refuse to work together. Rather than negotiate with each other, they both seemingly would rather negotiate with Veluppillai Prabbakaran—leader of the largest Tamil militant group, the Liberation Tigers of Tamil Eelam (LTTE)—whom both have called a murderer and a terrorist.

The Buddist Sangha

The Buddhist Sangha, or priesthood, is a very powerful force in Sri Lanka. It was one of the influential groups that lined up behind Bandaranaike in 1956 and helped to secure his election; and even though it was a Buddhist monk who killed Bandaranaike (for not moving fast enough to promote Buddhist rights after he was elected), the Sangha continues to play a major role in the political life of the country. From the Sangha's perspective, Sri Lanka is the home of the true Buddhist faith. Some monks view all of the island as sacred and indivisible Sinhalese soil that, over the centuries, has been under siege—

first by the Indians, then by the Portuguese, followed by the Dutch, who, in turn, were followed by the British and now by the Indians again. Some extremist monks consider the landing of Indian troops in Sri Lanka an invasion of Hindus against Buddhists. Others, even more extreme, view the separation of the north and the east as merely a first step toward the ultimate goal of Hindu subjugation of Buddhism.

Clearly not all monks share this view. In fact, there are some who have worked for years trying to achieve ethnic reconciliation. Many of the more moderate monks have been active in the search for peace. The problem is, of course, that a call for peace and national reconciliation rarely generates the public enthusiasm aroused by a call to resist a threat to national pride and ethnic identity. Indeed, there are those who would argue that it is not the monks who are the problem, but rather the Buddhist laity who are most vocal in their condemnation of the Indian–Sri Lankan peace accords. Certainly it is they, and the more chauvinist monks, who dominate the national media in Sri Lanka.

The Army

Prior to 1971, the Sri Lankan Army had been completely ceremonial. They marched at parades on Independence Day and other national holidays, but that was about it. They had never been called upon to fight and did not know how to. But in 1971, when a group of primarily unemployed Sinhalese youth, led by the ultra radical Janatha Vimukthi Peramuna (JVP)—"People's Liberation Front" staged an insurrection, the army put it down ruthlessly by killing thousands of the young boys involved in it.[b] The international community—including the Indians, the Americans, and the Russians—provided tactical material support. After the insurrection was over, the Sri Lankan forces reverted to being primarily a ceremonial army.

From 1983 to 1987, Jayewardene's government attempted to professionalize the army and turn it into a more disciplined fighting force. The government created a special task force as an elite, crack unit to fight the Tamil militants, in part because of international criticism of the Sri Lankan Army for repeatedly losing control and shooting Tamil civilians. By 1987, the army had been increased nearly threefold over its pre-1983 levels and had gained significant tactical experience in combatting Tamil guerrilla forces. By June 1987, the army came close to defeating the guerrillas militarily.

The top officers of the Sri Lankan Army are presumed by the government to be completely loyal. The highest ranking generals were put in by the UNP government, in part because of their loyalty. The SLFP supporters at the very top of the armed forces were more or less retired when the UNP government came to power after 1977. There are still a good number of SLFP supporters at the ranks of captain and lieutenant, but they, too, are presumed to be loyal to the government.

A coup might still be mounted, however, most likely by company-grade officers. They are thought to be both less disciplined and perhaps less loyal to the government than other strata of the military. They are the ones who have actually been involved in fighting the Tamil militants, and they feel that the government has put unnecessary restraints on the amount of force they are allowed to use. Although many Tamil groups have claimed that the Sri Lankan government was following a conscious policy of genocide, the government's *official* policy has been to restrain the troops from using excessive force against civilian populations wherever possible. Sinhalese soldiers resent Colombo's meddling with their "getting the job done" against Tamil militants and resent being asked to fire on rioting Sinhalese civilians who are protesting what the soldiers see as an Indian partition of the country. This situation greatly increases the danger of a coup.

Since its failed insurrection in 1971, the JVP has been consciously attempting to infiltrate the military. The JVP believes that had it infiltrated the military before that attempt, it might have been more successful. And although the military has known about the JVP attempts at infiltration for some time, it is not clear whether the military has been able to prevent them and at the same time rapidly recruit to meet the emergency caused by the Tamil militants.

When the war is going badly for the military, or when the militants humiliate the military by pulling off spectacular attacks in Sinhalese areas (such as the May 1985 killings of Anuradhapura, just a mile or two from a major military base, or the bombing of the bus depot in Colombo in 1987), there is more danger of a coup. Also, losses have not been light. Midlevel officers repeatedly say that they know how to take care of the terrorists, if Colombo would let them. They feel that they have not been given the freedom to "win," regardless of the cost in Tamil civilian lives, and they resent it.

The possibility of a military coup simply cannot be ruled out. The complexion it would take would depend on who made it. The higher the rank of the perpetrators, the less likely that a *major* shift in direction would take place. The lower the rank, the more violent both the coup and the repercussions of the coup are likely to be. Regardless of who makes it, if there is a coup, the likelihood is that it would be detrimental to the prospects for managing the conflict politically.

The People's Liberation Front (the JVP)

The JVP came to prominence in early 1971 with its nearly successful attempt to overthrow Mrs. Bandaranaike's government. The JVP is an ultraleftist party—so far left that its leader was kicked out of the university in Moscow for "left deviation." The JVP's attempted coup against the government of Sri Lanka, in 1971, occurred at a time when that government included Marxists of virtually every stripe, including the Communist party of Sri Lanka and the Lanka Sama Samaja Party (LSSP), a long-time Trotskyist party. Still, the JVP accused the government of "selling out to capitalists." The JVP ranks were made up largely of Sinhalese village boys who had managed to go to the university—thanks to the Sinhala-only language policy—but then could not get jobs when they graduated.

Since the 1971 insurrection, many JVP members have been successfully integrated into mainstream Sri Lankan society, but there is a hard-core leadership group that has remained underground and has continued to mobilize and recruit—particularly among university students. In recent years the politics of the universities have been dominated by the JVP. IN 1985 the JVP split into two groups. The original group is highly Sinhalese-chauvinist and wants to "give" nothing to the Tamils. The other group stresses class struggle and the proletarian revolution and believes that revolution will come to Sri Lanka only when Sinhalese revolutionary groups organize the Sinhalese and Tamil revolutionary groups organize the Tamils. This group believes that some of the militant Tamil groups fighting the government are sufficiently revolutionary to warrant cooperation, and there is some evidence that there actually has been some cooperation. One of the far-left groups—the Eelam Revolutionary Organization of Students (EROS)—reportedly had Sinhalese help—perhaps from the JVP—in blowing up the central bus depot in Colombo in 1987. Some have argued that it is unlikely that EROS could have brought the explosives into Colombo by itself.

After the government signed the Indo-Sri Lankan Accords in 1987, the JVP seized on their unpopularity, and began demanding that the Indian army leave the island. Instead of trying to contest the elections for president in December 1988, or parliament in February 1989, based on this position, however, the JVP followed its, by now traditional policy, of trying to overthrow the government by force. Although it was not able to totally disrupt those elections, in some districts it was so powerful that only 5 percent of the population took the risk of voting in the elections, after the JVP threatened to kill anyone who did.

Although they are leftist, and largely rural, the youth who support the

the JVP are also poor and mostly lower caste. This is a group whom President Premadasa sees as his natural constituency. Immediately after his election, and for several months thereafter, President Premadasa did everything he could to bring the JVP into the mainstream political process. The problem is that the JVP had no desire to become legal and take part in electoral politics. Indeed, it was formed precisely because it had no faith in the mainstream political process, and that situation had not changed. Finally, President Premadasa had no choice but to try to restore order to the country. In August 1989 the government began a brutal, but effective crackdown on the JVP. In five weeks more than 7,000 people were reported killed. Not all were JVP youth. Many were government policemen, soldiers and innocent families of soldiers and policemen, whom the JVP had started to kill in an attempt to intimidate. In any event the JVP was crushed, its leader was caught and killed, and quiet has returned to the south or Sri Lanka. At least for the time being.

As long as the JVP is on the outside of the political process (it is illegal), it is in its interest to encourage as much dissent and dissatisfaction with any central government as it can; hence, it is a danger to the peaceful management of the conflict. What would happen if the party were made legal remains to be seen. Some argue that the JVP must be brought into the mainstream political process; others argue that the JVP has no desire to become legal and take part in electoral politics. Indeed, it was formed precisely because it had no faith in the mainstream political process, and there is little reason to assume that this situation has changed.

The Tamil Actors in the Conflict

The Tamil United Liberation Front

Until the end of 1984, the Tamil United Liberation Front (TULF) was able to speak for the majority of northern Sri Lanka Tamils. In the 1977 election, it had won all of the seats in Parliament from the north. As the largest opposition party, its leader, Appapillai Amirthalingham, became leader of the opposition. The TULF represented the moderate Tamils, but its rhetoric was the rhetoric of a separate Tamil state—and that infuriated the Sinhalese.

After the breakdown of the All-Party Congress in 1984, which was an attempt to arrive at a negotiated settlement, the government passed an amendment to the constitution (Number 6) that said that all members of Parliament had to swear an oath to maintain a unified Sri Lanka. Obviously, the TULF could not take such an oath, and its members had to leave. Many also chose to leave the country, not because of the Sinhalese but because of the Tamil militants. They simply could not speak for the militants, and no matter what concessions they agreed to, there was not way they could force the militants to go along.

Prior to the 1983 riots, the TULF leadership had viewed "the boys" as a bit wild but understandably frustrated and angry. However, "the boys" presented a useful foil for the party. The TULF could say to the government, "For God sake, either give us what moderate demands we make, or you will have to deal with the far more radical demands of the militants." Unfortunately, the government did not give the TULF anything—in part, no doubt, because it was not able to "deliver" the militants and end the violence. Hence, the government eventually had no choice but to try to deal directly with the militants.

For their part, the militants saw TULF members as traitors, willing to sell out the rights of the Tamil people for their own personal gain. Several top TULF leaders in Sri Lanka were killed by the militants on just those grounds. With no place else to go, several TULF leaders, including Amirthalingham, fled to Madras, where they were given sanctuary by the Tamil Nadu state government. Removed from the scene in the north, the TULF was no longer able to claim to speak for Jaffna Tamils. The loss of the TULF as an active participant in Sri Lankan politics makes the prospect of a negotiated settlement less likely. No other Sri Lanka Tamil force is either able or willing to enter into negotiations for a peaceful settlement of the conflict. Indeed, when Mr. Amirthalingham returned to Colombo in 1989 to attempt to negotiate with the government, he was assassinated presumably by the militants.

The Militants

It is not necessary for the reader to know the names of the multitude of militant Tamil organizations fighting for an independent Tamil state. At the height of the militancy, there were five such major organizations and perhaps thirty splinter groups, some composed of only a few individuals. The first and last of the major groups is called the Liberation Tigers of Tamil Eelam (LTTE). It is because of its name that all militants are sometimes called Tigers. The LLTE leader is a young, lower-caste man named Veluppillai Prabhakaran. Some people consider him a charismatic nationalist leader; others consider him a common criminal and a murderer. He took credit for the killing in 1977 of the Tamil mayor of Jaffna; and since mid-1986, he has killed—or has had killed—several hundred young *Tamil* men who were members of other militant groups. Prabhakaran supporters say that to defend the

LTTE from being eliminated by these rival groups, Prabhakaran had no choice but to carry out the assassinations. Whatever the truth, by early 1987, the LTTE had virtually eliminated the People's Liberation Organization of Tamil Eelam (PLOTE), the Tamil Eelam Liberation Organization (TELO), and the Eelam People's Revolutionary Liberation Front (EPRLF).

Actually, the Tamil Tigers were less successful in eliminating the EPRLF (which was largely an eastern province—based group) than they would have liked to have been. Those EPRLF members who escaped the initial LTTE attack reportedly turned on the LTTE by showing the government forces where LTTE bases were located. Thus, the government was able to make heavy strikes against the LTTE. After the 1987 Indo-Sri Lankan Accords were signed, and the Indian army occupied the Northern and Eastern Provinces, the Indians tried very hard to build up the EPRLF as an alternative to the LTTE. Elections were held for Provincial Council in the newly merged Northeastern Province, and with Indian help, the EPRLF emerged victorious. (The LTTE and not contested, and had attempted to disrupt the elections, but they were held nonetheless.)

The only group to remain unscathed at the hands of the LTTE thus far is the Eelam Revolutionary Organization of Students (EROS), which specializes in spectacular bombings and which more or less recognizes the hegemony of the LTTE and is reported to work closely with it.

All militant organizations claim to be revolutionary Marxists. Some have received material aid from Libya and George Habash's wing of the Palestine Liberation Organization, but this support from the left is probably extended not for ideological reasons but to counteract the support that Western countries, included Israel, have provided. All of these groups would have liked to receive Western support, but barring that have taken whatever aid they could get.

It is reported that Mrs. Gandhi's government tended to support some of the militant groups with arms, money, and training, while the Tamil Nadu state government tended to support others. Such support gave the Indians some leverage with the militants; but when the militants recognized the dependent position they had allowed themselves to get into vis-à-vis both the Indian and the overseas Tamil groups that sent them financial support, they took steps to become more self-sufficient. For example, they apparently entered the drug trade. It was reported to me that in 1986 alone, ninety-six Sri Lanka Tamils were arrested in Europe for trafficking in drugs. Many more may have actually been involved. In addition, by early 1987, the LTTE had shifted virtually all of its men, material, and operations from Madras back to Sri Lanka. It became apparent that as long as they stayed in Madras, LTTE members were vulnerable to Indian pressure. In November 1986, hundreds of their men were arrested in Madras by Indian police, and several hundred million dollars worth of weapons and equipment were confiscated. (The men were released the next day and given back their weapons, but the incident shocked the militants.) Even Prabhakaran had returned to Sri Lanka by January 1987.

Moving back to their home territory put the LTTE members at more risk vis-à-vis the Sri Lankan Army, to be sure, but the LTTE probably felt that the Sri Lankan Army was less of a danger than the Indian police. That proved to be a wrong assumption. Once the LTTE was back in Sri Lanka, the Sri Lankan Army did so much damage to it that the Indians felt they had to intervene.

It is perhaps the ultimate irony that the Indian Army came to Sri Lanka in July 1987 to disarm the Tigers but also to save them from annihilation at the hands of the Sri Lankan Army. Within three months, the tables were turned: The Indian Army was trying to annihilate the Tigers, and the Tigers were accusing the Indian Army of committing excesses.

Some people argue that the situation is insolvable largely because, until now at least, the LTTE has not trusted the normal political process and has not wanted to join it. As with the JVP, the Tamil Tigers party formed because of its members' distrust of electoral politics, and nothing has given them a reason to be any more trusting than they were.

Overseas Tamils

Because South India is one of the poorest parts of India, its major export has always been Tamil men and women who were willing to do the low-skilled, of Indian origin—the Caribbean, Fiji, Malaysia, Africa, or Sri Lanka—the "Indians" are usually Tamils. But in terms of providing support to Sri Lanka's Tamil militants, the more important expatriates are the wealthier Sri Lanka Tamils who left Sri Lanka before the riots of 1983—or since—to settle, most frequently, in English-speaking countries. Many of these people are professionals or businessmen who are doing very well for themselves financially. They invariably send money back to their less well-to-do relations and to Tamil militants in Sri Lanka.

Clearly, most of these wealthier Tamil bourgeoisie do not approve of the professed Marxism of virtually all of the militant groups, but they tend not to take it too seriously. Marxist or not, these groups are seen by the overseas Sri Lanka Tamils as the only ones "doing anything" to help the Tamils. Although no one knows just how much is actually being funneled to these groups, the fact that the Indians were able to seize hundreds of millions of dollars worth of weapons and equipment in Madras alone indicates that the figure is very high indeed.

When the LTTE turned on the TELO and killed about 150 of its members in 1986, and when militants killed innocent civilians in attacks on a Sri Lankan tourist plane and the telecommunications offices in Colombo in May and June 1986, several overseas Tamil organizations are reported to have warned the LTTE and the EROS to stop, on the grounds that they could raise money for a "liberation movement" but not for terrorists.

Estate Tamils

The Sri Lankan estate workers have to be considered *potential* actors. Although they support Tamil rights, until now, at least, they have not supported Tamil Eelam. Estate workers are low-caste, very poor people who are able to endure the hardships of plantation work. As such, they have traditionally been treated with contempt by the Jaffna Tamils. No Jaffna Tamil wants his daughter to marry an estate worker. They are the wrong caste and the wrong class, and their social and historical roots—and even their dialect—are different.

Tamil political movements have also ignored or shunned the estate workers because of their low caste. But the leadership of some of the Tamil militant groups is predominantly lower caste; these groups have tried to capitalize on this similarity in status to win over the estate laborers, but it has not worked as yet.

Tamil Eelam holds nothing for the Estate Tamils. If the northern and eastern provinces were to become a separate country, they would be left out, and it is not likely that there would be jobs for them in a newly created country. In fact, they are much more likely to want to stay on the estates, although they certainly would like to see improvements in social services, wages, and political representation. Traditionally, Estate Tamils have shied away from national politics and political parties and, instead, have given total support to their trade union, the Ceylon Workers Congress and its political arm. V.E.K.R.S. Thondaman has been leader of the group since the 1940s. Always elected to Parliament, he makes deals with the other parties; depending on what they offer, he decides whether he can get more for his group by joining the government or opposing it.

The young estate workers could become a major force if they were to join or support the militants. Tea is the major foreign exchange earner for Sri

Lanka. If the estate workers do not pick it, Sri Lanka does not earn its major source of foreign exchange. If the government deported all of these "Indians," there would be no one to take their place. The climate is too inhospitable in those hills, the work too backbreaking—and Sinhalese culture finds plantation work unacceptable. That is why the British had to import foreign laborers in the first place. Political rhetoric about the Indians' taking a million jobs from the Sinhalese notwithstanding, Sri Lanka needs the Indian estate workers.

Foreign Actors in the Conflict

The Tamil Nadu State Government

Fifty-five to 60 million Tamils live in the South Indian state of Tamil Nadu. They are an integral part of the problem, because they see the Tamils living in Sri Lanka as their brethren. Any attack by a Sinhalese on a Tamil is perceived by a large number of Tamils in Tamil Nadu as an attack on all Tamils.

The Tamil Nadu state government has been supportive of the Tamil cause in Sri Lanka all along, and certainly since the riots of July 1983. Its position is somewhat analogous to the position of the Republic of Ireland vis-à-vis Northern Ireland—though not quite, of course, as Tamil Nadu is not a separate country, and it does not claim northern Sri Lanka as an integral part of itself. Yet the parallels are there. The people in Tamil Nadu believe that they belong to the same group of people as the Tamils in Sri Lanka. When the Sinhalese take oppressive action against the Sri Lanka Tamils, the Tamils of India feel that they have a responsibility to offer assistance.

The Dravida Munnetra Kazhagan (DMK), a political party in Tamil Nadu, has been calling for Tamil Nadu to secede from India, virtually since independence. At times, this party has been very powerful in the Tamil Nadu state. These is also a breakaway segment of the DMK called the All India Anna Dravida Munnetra Kazhagan (AIADMK), which, in coalition with the Congress I party, won a very healthy electoral victory in Tamil Nadu after the death of Mrs. Gandhi. The AIADMK was led, until his death in December 1987, by a very popular former actor named M.G. Ramachendran (commonly known as M.G.R.).

Because of the rivalry between the DMK and the AIADMK, each party wants to be perceived as supporting fellow Tamils more than its opponent. Each is motivated by genuine concern as well as by pure political pragmatism.

Each tries to appear to be more genuinely supportive of Tamil grievances than the other. And both have championed the Sri Lanka Tamil cause.

When the leader of the TULF fled Sri Lanka, the AIADMK-led Tamil Nadu state government put him up at the official guest house in Madras and has been doing so since. The hundred thousand-some Sri Lanka Tamils who fled Sri Lanka in the wake of the 1983 riots and the onslaught of the army are being put up in camps by the Tamil Nadu government.

Even though there had been a waning of popular support in India for the militants in 1985, 1986, and early 1987—as they engaged in shoot-outs among themselves on the streets of Madras and in smuggling and other illegal activities, and the finally in the fratricidal slaughter of other militants at the hands of the LTTE—public sympathy for their cause remained generally high. Tamil Nadu support counted enormously when the Sri Lankan government tried to crush the militants in a military offensive in May 1987; and when the Tamil Nadu goverment publicly announced that it was giving $4.5 million in supprt to the LTTE, it was roundly supported in Tamil Nadu. Tamil Nadu was sending the Sri Lankan government a very important message: The state was a direct actor in this drama; it could and would aid the militants directly and exert pressure on the Indian central government to back the militants. The Sri Lankan government may have overlooked these factors when it decided to try yet another military offensive in the north in June 1987. Since the LTTE turned on the Indian army in late 1987 and 1988, and since fights among militant groups have continued, support for the militant cause in Tamil Nadu has waned enormously. But Tamil Nadu should not be ruled out as a potential source of support, should large numbers of Sri Lankan Tamil civilians again begin to die at the hands of the Sri Lankan government.

The Central Government of India

The central government of India, because it is the dominant regional power, has always been in a position to play a central role in its neighbors' affairs when it chooses to. Just how central a role it has played in the Sri Lankan ethnic conflict became public knowledge only after 1985.

outside. They also had to agree not to reveal that India was aiding them and not to allow any Indians (other than those assigned the task) or foreigners to see the training or have access to information about Indian support.

It is thought that Mrs. Gandhi was motivated to support these groups because people in the Indian state of Tamil Nadu empathized with the plight of the Tamils in Sri Lanka—particularly after the riots in Sri Lanka of July

1983. Also, elections were scheduled for all of India. The separatist Tamil party in Tamil Nadu (the DMK) strongly supported the militants (even the more middle-of-the-road party gave at least lipservice to the Sri Lankan cause). By June 1985, however, the situation was totally changes. Mrs. Gandhi was dead and Rajiv Gandhi had become prime minister of India. The Congress I party (the faction of the Congress party that had supported Mrs. Gandhi after the party split years ago—hence I for *Indira*) not only had swept the elections throughout India but had done handsomely in Tamil Nadu as well. Tamil Nadu separatism was no longer perceived to be a threat to India. A far bigger threat was posed by militant Sikh separatists in the Punjab. Rajiv Gandhi apparently came to believe that he could not allow Sri Lankan separatists to prove that they could obtain a separate Tamil state through military action. If it became known that India itself was assisting the Sri Lankan insurgents, it would have been difficult for him to caution foreign powers not to intervene on behalf of the Sikhs. An independent Tamil Eelam could easily have become a "safe sanctuary" and staging area for Sikhs, Assamese, and other militant separatist groups in India.

In his first year of office, Rajiv Gandhi supported a peaceful settlement. It was he who was willing to pressure the militants to accept the first cease-fire in the summer of 1985, and it was he who forced them to go to Thimphu, Bhutan, to negotiate with the Sri Lankans. Apparently, however, the Indians became very disappointed when they realized that the UNP government was not offering enough at Thimphy, and they put pressure on the Sri Lanakans to offer more.

India continued to use its good offices to promote a peaceful resolution, from the breakdown of the Bhutan talks until April 1987. India seemed dismayed with the UNP government for not having made more concessions in order to get a peaceful solution and for launching a military offensive in the north in February 1987. When the Sri Lankan government started bombing the north again and launched another offensive on the Jaffna peninsula in April 1987 in retaliation for the militant strikes at civilians in the east and at the bus station in Colombo, India took a completely different stance and sent an airlift of "humanitarian aid" to the Tamil "civilians in the north."

There were many reasons for this sharp Indian government reaction. Elections were coming up in one of the states of India (the Congress I party had lost elections in several other states in the last four years). In addition, reports in the Indian press of the Sri Lankan offensive gave the impression that the Sri Lankan government was trying for a final military settlement. The *Hindu,* an otherwise very respectable newspaper in Madras, reported that the Jaffna peninsula was being "carpet bombed" and that innocent Tamil citizens were being killed by the hundreds and wounded by the thousands.[4] This information apparently came directly from the LTTE, and the *Hindu* reported it as factual. In reality, the Sri Lankan air force was incapable of "carpet bombing," and independent reports later confirmed that there probably were fewer than 200 deaths from the attack. On the basis of the outcry in India, New Dehli decided to send tons of food and "humanitarian aid" to the civilians of the Jaffna peninsula. Eventually, goods were airlifted, with fighter jets as protection. This move achieved nothing *by itself* in terms of moving the Sri Lankans and the Tamil militants closer together, but it did achieve two things for the government of Rajiv Gandhi. First, domestically, it was an extremely popular move, demonstrating to Indians that New Dehli could use its power when it wanted to. Second, it reminded the Sri Lankans that India had a great deal of power, that it would use its power in matters it deemed important, and that the Sri Lankan Tamil problem was deemed important.

Until the airlift, it was unthinkable that the Indian Army might invade Sri Lanka, the way Turkey invaded Cyprus, and "protect" the Tamils of the north and east—as at least some of the militants had been trying to force the Indians to do all along. Now it was no longer unthinkable. Provoked enough, the Indian central government let it be known that it might just do the unthinkable.

The United States and Other Donor Nations

Sri Lanka has been called the best beggar in the world. Colombo receives more aid per capita from foreign countries than any other countries except Israel and Egypt. This has been particularly true since 1977 and the election of the UNP government, which has been so friendly to foreign and domestic capitalists. Mrs. Bandaranaike's socialist government was quite hostile to private foreign investment, and the West reacted by snubbing it. When she was defeated at the polls, Western governments responded with enormous gifts and loans to the UNP government. Between 1977 and 1991, the donor countries contributed approximately $3 billion to Sri Lankan development. In addition, since 1977, there has been an inpouring of direct foreign investment of approximately $500 million.[5] These inputs have stimulated the economy; but at the same time, the donor countries have gained a certain amount of leverage over Sri Lanka. They can threaten to withdraw their support unless there is a peaceful solution. To some degree, Canada and a few other countries have already done just that.

None of the traditional donor countries has been willing to give Sri Lanka direct military aid (in part, because none wants to offend India), but the large amount of assistance to Sri Lanka has received enabled it to syphon off as much as $1 million *per day* to fight the insurgency. Colombo hired private British organizations to train its army; and to some degree, it would appear, the Israelis and the Pakistanis also were supplying some military assistance, although it is not presumed to be a great deal. Rather, the Sri Lankans were buying what they needed in the world armaments market, just as the Tamil militants were.

On the Sri Lankan issue, the U.S. government has taken a hands-off position. In the early years of the Jayewardene regime, the United States gave Sri Lanka a great deal of economic aid—cumulatively surpassing $1 billion—but it went mostly for work on a very large irrigation scheme that is being built on the island. By the time the ethnic conflict flared in 1983, the United States was already cutting back on the aid it was giving—not in reprisal for the ethnic conflict, but because the irrigation scheme was completed. Also, given the enormous budget deficits in the United States in the mid-1980s, it was inevitable that foreign aid would be cut back. But although the United States did not contribute any significant amount of military aid, because of the aid it *was* supplying, the Sri Lankans were able to divert money from other sources to the war effort. Some criticized the United States for not putting economic pressure on the Sri Lankans to reach a negotiated settlement by denying them economic aid. Certainly, the U.S. government constantly urged the Colombo government to be more forthcoming to the Tamil cause than it had been prior to June 1986, but the United States did not want to alienate a Western-oriented friendly government by applying too much pressure. Also, the United States recognized that Sri Lanka fell within India's "sphere of influence"—if that old-fashioned term may still be used—and did not want to appear to be meddling in the Indians' backyard.

When the Indians airlifted humanitarian aid in May 1987—against the Sri Lankan government's wishes—the United States did nothing to help the Sri Lankans, even though they had accommodated U.S. interests on some other matters. It was then that Sri Lanka realized that it had no choice but to come to terms with India.

The Indian Intervention

On July 24, 1987—to the surprise of virtually everyone familiar with the problem—the minister for lands and development announced at a meeting in

Sri Lanka that Rajiv Gandhi was coming to Colombo on July 29 to sign a peace accord with President Jayewardene that would end the ethnic fighting. As the terms of the agreement became known, there was even greater surprise and, in some cases, disbelief. Under the terms of the agreement,[6] Jayewardene agreed to merge tne Northern and Eastern Provinces into a single Provincial Council for one year, or until there could be a referendum on the merger in the old Eastern Province any time after December 31, 1988. (Note: That referendum has never taken place.) The Provincial Councils scheme was to be introduced into Parliament and passed, devolving considerable autonomy and power to the provinces. Elections to the new Provincial Councils were supposed to take place before December 31, 1987. They did not in 1988.

For their part, the Indians agreed to introduce a peacekeeping force onto the island to disarm the militants, maintain the cease-fire, and ensure fair elections. In addition, India agreed to deport all Sri Lankan separatists from India and provide training facilities and military supplies for Sri Lankan security forces.

In the exchange of letters that accompanied the accords, Jayewardene agreed, in effect, (1) to check with India on all foreign military and intelligence personnel allowed in Sri Lanka (an obvious attempt to get rid of the Pakistanis and Israelis); (2) not to allow Trincomalee (a port on the east coast) to be used for a military purpose by any country of which India did not approve; (3) to develop the Trincomalee oil storage facility jointly with India only (Sri Lanka had expected to develop the facility with an American company); and (4) to permit India to review Sri Lanka's agreement with the Voice of America and all future foreign broadcast facilities, to ensure that the facilities were not used for military intelligence purposes (India has always contended that these facilities were being used by the Central Intelligence Agency to spy on India). Clearly, Indian hegemony in the region was being officially recognized by Sri Lanka.

When the terms of the accords became known, all parties to the conflict were shocked. Jayewardene had agreed to a merger of the Northern and Eastern Provinces, even though most Sinhalese seemed to find this completely unacceptable. In addition, he had agreed to permit Indian troops to occupy those two provinces. Many Sri Lankans—Tamils as well as Sinhalese—wondered if India, once invited in, would ever leave. Indeed, the most anti-Indian Sinhalese saw the peacekeeping force as a prelude to India's taking over the entire country.

Whereas most Tamils recognized the accords as the best political solution they could likely get—and a step toward restoring civil order for the first time in four years—on the Sinhalese side, riots erupted in Colombo and elsewhere in the south, as Sinhalese by the thousands, led by Buddhist monks, protested "giving away too much to the Tamils." Nineteen were reported killed in the south—including a member of Parliament—during the first day of the accords, despite a twenty-four-hour curfew. Even within the government, the two most important ministers—Prime Minister Premadasa and Minister for National Security Athulathmaduli—publicly disapproved of the accords. Both had been out of the country when the agreement was announced and both canceled plans and returned to Colombo, presumably to try to prevent the president from signing it.

Despite all the protests, Rajiv Gandhi came to Colombo on July 29, 1987, as announced, and he and Jayewardene signed the agreement. Soon thereafter, some 10,000 Indian soldiers and paramilitary forces began arriving on the island to police the cease-fire, which came into effect forty-eight hours after the signing of the agreement.

It was not immediately clear that militant leaders would accept the accords. The Indian troops made it clear that Prabhakaran and the LTTE had to turn over their arms or the Indian Army would forcibly take them. Some weapons were turned in, to be sure, but many people believed that the militant groups withheld their most sophisticated weapons. Virtually all of my informants believed that a shoot-out between the rival groups would be inevitable as soon as the Indian Army left, and each of the groups wanted to be prepared. Moreover, the LTTE was being forced to accept the fact that there would not be Tamil Eelam—for the time being. When Prabhakaran finally made his speech to "the boys," tentatively accepting the accords in the first days after the Indians arrived, he said that they were not giving up the struggle for Eelam but were being coerced by overwhelming force to deal with a new reality, and that they would continue the struggle by other means.

For whatever reasons, the LTTE did not jump at the opportunity for a peaceful settlement in October 1987. Instead, LTTE members not only refused to turn over their weapons but used them to attack Sinhalese civilians in the Eastern Province. More than 200 Sinhalese civilians were killed in a number of different raids on Sinhalese villages in the Eastern Province in approximately a week of violence before the Indians finally attacked the LTTE. The LTTE says that it was the Indian Army and remnants of the other militant groups that conducted the raids, but virtually everyone else blames the LTTE for the attacks. What is more, the Sinhalese government said, in effect, "So much for the myth that the Indians had virtually completely disarmed the militants," and it revoked the amnesty it had granted the LTTE. Further, it threatened to send Sri Lankan troops to defend Sinhalese villages if the Indians could not do so. The Indians had virtually no choice but to move against the LTTE militarily or face the collapse of the accords. In so doing, they seem to have been stunned by how much sophisticated military hardware the LTTE still had at its disposal, how well dug in at Jaffna the LTTE was, and how difficult a time they had taking the city. The Indians had to increase their troop strength in Sri Lanka to over 100,000, and it took over 1000 Indian soldiers killed, and countless more wounded, before the LTTE militants were driven from Jaffna City.

There is some debate as to why the Indian army—then called the forth largest in the world—could not totally defeat the Tigers. Certainly the Indian army wanted to—their pride was at stake. There are some who believe that the central government in New Delhi ordered that the LTTE *not* be completely destroyed. The argument goes that if the LTTE were completely destroyed, the Sri Lankan government would not have gone ahead with the devolution of power to the provincial councils, and hence some new militant group would have emerged to continue the struggle for at least some autonomy for Tamil areas. Whatever the cause, the Indians did not destroy the LTTE. That fact was not lost on Mr. Premadasa. Having been suspicious of the Indians all along, and having been opposed to the accords that invited the Indian army into Sri Lanka in the first place, Mr. Premadasa ran for president in 1988 on a platform of promising to get the Indians to leave. Having been elected, one of the first things he did upon coming to office was to enter into a *de facto* truce with the Tigers, on the promise to get the Indians to leave. That was a very audacious tactic for Mr. Premadasa to have adopted at the time. He had his hands full trying to put down the JVP inspired chaos in the south. There was no way he could have taken on the LTTE in the north and east at the same time. But he gambled that much of the support for the JVP was coming from ordinary Sri Lankans who were opposed to having an Indian presence in Sri Lanka. His logic was that if he could get the Indians to leave, he would undermine one of the basis of support for the JVP.

His gamble proved correct. He insisted that the Indians had to leave, and although Mr. Gandhi dragged his feet somewhat there didn't seem to be much he could do about it. Actually, there are those in Sri Lanka who believed that had Mr. Gandhi won his election at the end of 1989, he would not have left. India watchers I know assure me that he would have. Whatever the case, Mr. Gandhi did lose the election, and the last Indian troops left in March 1990. However, by June of 1990 the truce between the LTTE and the Sri Lankan government was shattered, and the fighting between the two sides continued anew.

Prospects for Conflict Management

Where does all this leave the prospects for conflict management? Donald Horowitz argued in his *Ethnic Groups in Conflict*[7] that a country with two ethnic parties representing the same ethnic group would have a harder time trying to reach peaceful accommodation than would countries having only one party representing each group. Sri Lanka clearly falls into the former category. At least it did. Certainly the Sinhalese are now, and since independence, have been represented by two major Sinhalese parties, each claiming that the other is selling out Sinhalese interests every time they try to reach accommodation with the Tamils. For their part the Tamils have usually been represented by at least two parties, *de facto.* The TULF may have taken all of the Sri Lankan Tamil seats in parliament during the 1977 election, but the rise of the Tigers, and other militant groups thereafter certainly represented the existence of two parties among the Tamils—moderates and militants. As of this writing there does not seem to be a unified force among the Tamils to represent the moderate factions. The Liberation Tigers of Tamil Eelam have taken over the radical extreme, killing not only moderates who they viewed as traitors, but other militant groups as well. Whether the remnants can coalesce into a unified opposition to the Tigers remain to be seen. Certainly many of them have cause to hate the Tigers. On the other hand, even though severely hurt, the Tiger is not yet dead. Given the fact that the opposition is so divided, maybe the Tigers can remain the only credible spokesmen for the Tamils. But if there is to be a peaceful resolution of the conflict they will have to be willing to negotiate and to compromise. That is not something the Tigers either do well, or respect.

The Sinhalese for there part are in a strong position for the time being. Having put down the JVP in 1989, President Premadasa is in virtual complete control of the south. When the Indian troops left, Sinhalese troops replaced them in the east. Since the LTTE was never strong in the east, and since the Tigers have been severely damaged in all these years of fighting, they are in no position to take control of the east physically. They may be capable of staging hit and run raids on the east, to be sure but that is probably all they are capable of doing. As of this writing they are in control of much of the north, but that is where they have always been strongest.

The government is also in a strong position vis-a-vis India. Having intervened once, and gotten burned, India is not likely to intervene again. Even if Rajiv Gandhi comes back to power, as seems likely as of this writing, he is not likely to want to get involved in Sri Lanka again. Nor is the government of Tamil Nadu state likely to get directly involved again. There is too much ill will in Tamil Nadu toward the LTTE for killing Indian soldiers, and for killing so many other Tamils, for the state government to come to the aid of the LTTE in any big way.

Although the Sri Lankan government has shown a willingness to bomb LTTE strongholds in the north repeatedly—regardless of civilian losses—it has not shown a willingness to launch a land campaign to physically take the north. For the moment it seems contented to allow the *status quo* to continue to exist. The government will undoubtedly try to wear down the LTTE forces in the north, while the LTTE will undoubtely try to conduct some spectacular raids on Sinhalese and Muslim populations in the east—in order to try to drive them out. They may even try some spectacular raids on Sinhalese areas in the south, but clearly they can't win a land war with the government at this time. Since it is doubtful that the government is willing to pay the price it would take to win a land war in the north, the likelihood is that the stalemate will continue as it is for some time.

At some point the Tigers might decide that they have no choice but to settle for something less than complete independence. Or it could happen that the Tamil opposition to the Tigers might ultimately coalesce, and try to negotiate a solution within the Tigers. How much Mr. Premadasa can negotiate away without incurring the wrath of the Sinhalese chauvinists remains to be seen. There is no doubt that he would like to negotiate a solution. But the Tiger are demanding more than any Sinhalese party can give away. Since President Premadasa and the UNP are in a stronger position than the opposition Sinhalese parties are in a stronger position than the opposition Sinhalese parties are likely to be in form some time to come, Mr. Premadasa is clearly the Sinhalese party to deal with. Whether the Tigers will do so, however, also remains to be seen.

Notes

a. To be sure, there are small groups of expatriate Sinhalese in the United States, Britain, Canada, and Australia, but they are very small in number.

b. See Bryan Pfaffenberger's piece in this volume (chapter 15). Although the official figure is much, much lower, I have been told unofficially, by people within the government who were very much in a position to know, that as many as 20,000 JVP youth may have been killed in 1971, and that represented between one-third and one-half of their total numbers.

References

1. All population percentages used here are taken from James Manor, *Sri Lanka in Change and Crisis* (New York: St Martin'g Press, 1984).

2. See Manor, *Sri Lanka in Change and Crisis.*

3. A. Jeyaratnam Wilson, *The Gaullist System in Asia, the Constitution of Sri Lanka [1978]* (Londong and Basingstoke: Macmillan, 1980).

4. See *New York Times,* June 1, 1987, p. 9. The *Times* article does not cite the *Hindu* coverage, but I have seen the *Hindu* version.

5. Figures provided by knowledgeable sources at the U.S. Agency for International Development and the World Bank.

6. "Indo-Sri Lanka Agreement to Establish Peace and Normalcy in Sri Lanka," signed July 29, 1987 by His Excellency J.R. Jayewardene, President of the Democratic Socialist Republic of Sri Lanka, and Mr. Rajiv Gandhi, Prime Minister of the Republic of India.

3. A. Jeyaratnam Wilson, *The Gaullist System in Asia, the Constitution of Sri Lanka [1978]* (London and Basingstoke: Macmillan, 1980).

4. See *New York Times,* June 1, 1987, p. 9. The *Times* article does not cite the *Hindu* coverage, but I have seen the *Hindu* version.

5. Figures provided by knowledgeable sources at the U.S. Agency for International Development and the World Bank.

6. "Indo-Sri Lanka Agreement to Establish Peace and Normalcy in Sri Lanka," signed July 29, 1987 by His Excellency J.R. Jayewardene, President of the Democratic Socialist Republic of Sri Lanka, and Mr. Rajiv Gandhi, Prime Minister of the Republic of India.

17

Malaysia: Avoiding Ethnic Strife in a Deeply Divided Society

Richard Stubbs

Deep ethnic divisions within a Third World country may make widespread communal conflict more likely; however, as the Malaysian experience has so far demonstrated, they do not make it inevitable. Although it would be difficult to imagine a more deeply divided society than that of Malaysia, the different ethnic communities within the country have been fortunate in that they have been able to conduct their relations in such a way as to limit the possibility that ethnic tensions will get out of hand and engulf the population in open communal violence.

Ethnic Cleavages in Malaysia

The roots of Malaysia's multiethnic society are found in the late nineteenth and early twentieth century. With the formal involvement of the British in peninsular Malaya from the 1870s onward came the development of the tin and rubber industries and the expansion of trade and commerce. To provide the manpower needed to fuel the growing economy, the colonial administration encouraged the influx of Chinese and Indian labor. So successful was the economy and so large was the number of immigrants that by independence in 1957, only 50 percent of the population of 6.3 million were Malays, while 37 percent were Chinese, 11 percent were Indian, and 2 percent were "other."[1] Following the formation of Malaysia in 1963,[a] some minor changes in the ethnic distribution occurred; but even so, in 1986, the population of 15.8 million was still divided roughly evenly between Malays and non-Malays.[2]

The ethnic cleavages that divide Malaysia are compounded by language, religious, and cultural differences. The Malays speak Malay, or what is officially called Bahasa Malaysia; they are Muslims; and they have a shared system of traditions, beliefs, and values known as *adat,* which, together with Islamic tenets, governs their social relations. They also consider themselves *bamiputras*—"sons of the soil"—or the indigenous people of the region

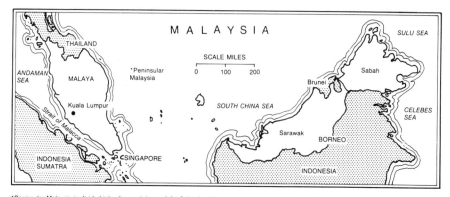

*Peninsular Malaysia is divided into eleven states and the federal territory: Johor, Kedah, Kelantan, Melaka, Negeri Sembilan, Pahang, Pinang, Perak, Perlis, Selangor, and Terengganu. In East Malaysia, there are two states, Sarawak and Sabah.

Figure 17–1. Malaysia

and, therefore, the rightful possessors of political power in Malaysia. The Chinese speak various dialects, and some now also speak Mandarin. They may be Buddhists, Confucianists, or Taoists or, more usually, some combination of the three. Essentially, it has been the legend and lore of Chinese history and religious literature and the observance of major Chinese festivals that have been most instrumental in binding the Chinese community together. Traditionally, the Chinese have dominated major sections of the economy. Most of the members of the Indian community are Tamils; they speak Tamil and are Hindus. Within the Indian community, there are also a few Muslims, a noticeable Sikh population, and a small group of Sinhalese. Overall, it is generally understood that the major ethnic division in Malaysia is between the Malays and the non-Malays.

Although Malaysia's ethnic communities have been relatively successful in avoiding widespread ethnic conflict, open communal violence has broken out a number of times in the past. The first set of incidents took place at the end of World War II in the weeks immediately after the surrender of the Japanese and before the British returned. Chinese guerrillas of the Malayan Communist party (MCP) clashed with Malays, whom they accused of being collaborators. The subsequent eight months or so saw more than 600 people killed and many thousands made homeless. A second set of incidents occurred during the guerrilla war between the MCP and the Malayan government, which was commonly referred to as the "Malayan emergency" and whish lasted from 1948 to 1960. Although it was very much an ideological conflict, the war clearly also had an ethnic dimension. On the one side, 90 percent of the MCP members were Chinese, and the "official" language of the MCP was Mandarin. The Malays even referred to the MCP as the "Chinese party." On the other side, the vast majority of the locally recruited members of the security forces were Malays. On a number of occasions, MCP guerrillas attacked Malay *kampongs* as they searched for food, and Malay special constables fired randomly into Chinese villages they were supposed to be guarding. But ethnically induced violence was not widespread. A third set of incidents was prompted by the elections of May 1969, the results of which were interpreted as a major setback for the Malay-dominated governing party—the Alliance. Demonstrations by the Chinese supporters of the opposition parties and counterdemonstrations by Malays ended in rioting. The violence continued sporadically for a few days before petering out. Estimates of the number of people killed varied from 178 to 800.[3]

Keeping Ethnic Violence in Check

Despite these incidents—as well as other, more minor ones—at no time did the ethnic conflict spread to such an extent that it threatened to embroil large sections of the country's population. In other words, although there have been any number of sparks, they have not so far started a major ethnic conflagration. An examination of the causes for the incidents that have taken place and of the reasons why they have not resulted in full-scale intercommunal conflict will provide a better understanding of ways in which ethnic violence may be kept in check.

Balancing Political Interests

In Malaysia, incidents of open conflict have occurred when a swing in the distribution of political power is anticipated. For Malays, the concern has always been that they have sufficient control over the levers of power, whereas for the non-Malays, the issue has been the need to have proper access to the levers of power. Both communities have recognized the important link between political power and the ability to ward off any threat to their core values. In each of the sets of incidents, the possibility of an immediate change in the distribution of power clearly contributed to the communal violence. For example, the clash that occurred in the months immediately after World War II was prompted not only by Chinese bitterness over the treatment they had received during the Japanese occupation, but also by the fear of the Malays that the MCP, as the self-proclaimed victor, would replace the surrendering Japanese as the governors of the country. Similarly, during the "emergency," communal feeling was heightened by the general sense among the Chinese community that the colonial administration did not listen to their views—a factor that contributed to the Chinese support of the MCP—and Malay fears that the MCP might replace the British if the guerrilla war proved successful. The May

1969 riots indicated most clearly how the perception of a sudden shift in political power can induce an increase in ethnic tensions. Once the election results were announced, the Chinese saw the shift in power going in their favor, whereas the Malays saw it going against them. The consequent mix of jubilation and fear sparked the ethnic violence.

In the years immediately after World War II, the responsibility for balancing the political interests of each ethnic community fell to the British colonial administration. The postwar ethnic violence was held in check by the general anticipation that the British would restore a semblance of order and would act in the best interests of all communities. The British, however, were unable to live up to these expectations fully. Indeed, Chinese disillusionment with the actions of the colonial administration contributed toward the growth of support for the MCP and was one of the reasons why the "emergency" lasted so long. However, as part of a strategy to counter the success of the guerrillas, the administration introduced elections in order to wean support away from the Communists. The result was the emergence of a vibrant party system, which quickly changed the political landscape in Malaya by giving all ethnic communities the opportunity to exert political influence.

At the center of this new political system was the Alliance party. A coalition of the United Malays National Organization (UMNO), the Malayan Chinese Association (MCA), and the Malayan Indian Congress (MIC), the Alliance party contained representatives of each of the major ethnic communities and managed to dominate Malayan and Malaysian politics from the first federal elections in 1955 onward. Its composition appeared to satisfy everyone. The British were persuaded that such a party met their concern that independence could not be granted until the various ethnic groups in the country were united. The Malays, through the UMNO, controlled the post of chief minister—later, prime minister—and had a majority in the cabinet; and the Chinese and Indian communities had access, through the MCA and MIC representatives, to the highest decision-making institutions in the country.

The ability of the Alliance party and its expanded successor after 1974, the National Front, to regulate ethnic and political relations in Malaysia has been a key element in the effort to avoid communal violence. The reasons for the rise and subsequent durability of the Alliance party were persuasively analyzed by Donald L. Horowitz.[4] He noted, for example, how quickly commitments to establishing the coalition were made once its vote-getting potential was demonstrated and how well the leaders coped with the changing political relations among the component groups. He also pointed out that there grew up around the Alliance a solidifying mystique, based on successfully negotiating a "bargain" between the ethnic communities, which was the basis for the country's constitution.[b] His most telling point, however, was that the Alliance and the National Front have been able to command the "ethnic center," forcing competing ethnically based parties out onto the political flanks. This configuration has tended to hem in the component parts of the Alliance and to make it difficult for any other multiethnic party to get established.[5] It is interesting that one of the ways in which the Alliance leaders dealt with the 1969 crisis and the seeming disenchantment with the representatives of the ethnic center was to broaden the base and to bring in those parties on the flank that could be accommodated. The three component parties of the Alliance that contested the 1969 elections thus became nine component parties when the National Front was formed in 1974 and thirteen component parties by the 1986 election.

Support for the Coalition Government

The ability of the Alliance party and the National Front to maintain their cohesion and to occupy the political high ground is clearly a significant factor in the relative absence of ethnic violence in Malaysia. Yet equally significant is the fact that the various ethnic communities have continued to support the centrally positioned coalition government. In general, Malaysian society has not polarized, nor has the bulk of public opinion vacated the center ground in favor of the more extreme communal parties, a move that undoubtedly would have increased the likelihood of widespread communal conflict. How have the Alliance and the National Front managed to keep the support of the major portion of the Malaysian public?

It must be emphasized that each of the component groups in the Alliance and the National Front has had to demonstrate its capability to represent the views of its ethnic community. Hence, each prime minister has had to establish his Malay nationalist credentials before being elevated to the top position by the UMNO. Only because each prime minister has been trusted by the Malays to advance their interests has he been able to maintain their support while balancing the interests of all communities. For example, Tengku Abdul Rahman, the first prime minister, was well known for his "Malaya for the Malays" stand, which he espoused before taking the UMNO into the Alliance. It is interesting that one of the reasons he was forced to resign after the May 1969 riots was that he was considered to have become too much of an arbiter and not enough of an advocate, and he had therefore lost the confidence of a significant segment of the Malay community.[6] Moreover, the current prime minister, Datuk Sri Dr. Mahathir Mohamad, won his pro-Malay spurs when, in the aftermath of the 1969 riots, he attacked Alliance policies as too pro-Chinese and, consequently, was temporarily expelled from the UMNO. Thus, the success of the major Malay flank party, the PAS (Malay-Arabic acronym for the Partai Islam Se Malaysia), which appeals to Malays on the basis of traditional Malay and Islamic values, has been limited by the ability of the UMNO's leaders to appear to match its pro-Malay stand on many issues.

Although the UMNO leaders have generally been able to retain the support of much of the Malay population, the MCA and MIC leaders have not been so successful. Forced to play a subordinate role to the UMNO, the MCA and MIC representatives—and since the formation of the National Front, the other non-Malay ethnically based party representatives—have found it much more difficult to portray themselves as unreservedly pro-Chinese or pro-Indian, as their communal backers would wish. As a result, the non-Malay components of the Alliance and the National Front have faced one crisis after another over policy choices. Moreover, Chinese and Indian voters have been more willing to flirt with the flank parties, the most successful of which has been the Democratic Action party. However, the voting system, inherited from the British, of first-past-the-post, single-representative constituencies—combined with a built-in bias against the urban, predominantly Chinese electoral districts and in favor of rural, predominantly Malay districts—has reduced the ability of the non-Malay flank parties to translate their popular support into seats and has thus limited their effectiveness and, to some extent, their appeal. Certainly, they have experienced major difficulties in mounting a serious challenge to the governing center coalition.

The Habit of Accommodation

Each episode of limited ethnic conflict has served to inoculate, for a period of time, the Malaysian body politic against widespread ethnic violence. In other words, the experience of suffering through incidents of communal conflict, in which all communities end up as losers, has made party leaders and the general public value ethnic cooperation as a means of avoiding, where possible, ethnic clashes that could lead to a serious breakdown in political and social order. At the level of party leaders, this has been translated into what can be thought of as a learned behavior of accommodation, which has developed over the years. At the level of the general public, it has meant that measures taken to reduce ethnic tensions—such as those to restrict the discussion of "sensitive issues" (primarily Malay privileges)—have been widely, if reluctantly, accepted. Moreover, the recognition of the need for maintaining stability has worked to the advantage of the Alliance and the National Front. For example, in the last election, in August 1986, the National Front was able to play on people's concerns about the return of ethnic violence as a means of overcoming the many problems they appeared to face in retaining voter support. Indeed, the National Front government conducted much-publicized antiriot "public order exercises" in a number of cities, and the prime minister publicly warned of the possible recurrence of the May 1969 troubles if "opposition propaganda" was heeded. Certainly, one of the reasons that the National Front was able to gain another resounding victory—148 of 177 parliamentary seats and 57.4 percent of the popular vote—was the general fear that a government weakened by an increasingly more powerful and ethnically chauvinist opposition would not be able to contain a rise in communal tensions and any resulting open conflict.[7]

Patronage Networks

The Alliance and the National Front have made excellent use of extensive patronage networks in order to deliver benefits to their supporters. Some of these networks cross ethnic boundaries and have proved to be an effective means for the government to bring together the leaders of the different ethnic communities. Moreover, with the implementation of the new economic policy, which was introduced in the early 1970s as a consequence of the May 1969 riots and which was designed to give Malays a greater role in the economy, the state has explained its business activities and, as a result, has had more benefits to bestow. Even the move toward privatization, begun in 1983, has occasionally worked to the advantage of those tied in to the governing coalition. Hence, whether it be at the elite level or at the level of the general public, flank parties have been unable to compete with the Alliance and the National Front in offering generous rewards to friends and supporters.

Economic Factors

Underlying each outbreak of ethnic violence in Malaysia since 1945 has been economic hardship. The incidents of communal conflict that occurred immediately after the surrender of the Japanese and during the early years of the "emergency" can be attributed, in part, to the economic dislocation caused by a combination of the "scorched earth" policy of the British, as they retreated down the peninsula in the face of the Japanese invading army, and the neglect by the Japanese regime of the country's economic infrastructure and its rubber and tin industries. Particularly frustrating for everyone in the peninsula was the severe shortage of rice. Plans drawn up in London for postwar Malaya estimated that the "minimum tolerable per diem rice ration was 12 ounces per capita" and that anything lower would cause "disease and unrest."[8] However, in the months immediately after the end of the war, the returning colonial administration could provide only 4.6 ounces per day, and this became a derisory 2.5 ounces by late 1946. Even by 1948, the average per capita daily ration of rice was a mere 7.6 ounces, and the price was many times prewar levels. Shortage of such a key staple exacerbated communal tensions. Similarly, in 1969, a sustained drop in the price of natural rubber during the preceding decade—from 310 cents per kilogram in May 1960 to 164 cents per kilogram in May 1969—provided an important backdrop to the tensions that were vented, particularly by the Malays who traveled into Kuala Lumpur from the surrounding rubber-growing areas, in the riots following the 1969 elections.[9]

Despite these problems with the Malayan/Malaysian economy and its cyclical boom-and-bust nature, the government has been successful in generating a consistently high growth rate. Since the Korean war boom of the early 1950s, the economy has performed remarkably well, with average annual growth rates of 6 to 8 percent per year recorded during the 1960s and 1970s.[c] Even when a couple of years of slightly negative growth are included, it can be argued that a modest level of success has been achieved during the hard times of the 1980s. Hence, although there have been occasions in the past when ethnic tensions have been increased by a shrinking economic pie and a government that could do little to help because of reduced revenues from falling commodity prices, the growth in the economy has generally allowed many of the material aspirations of each community to be met and has helped to forestall any major retreat into ethnic identity.

Over the years, the expanding economy has allowed for two major spurts of socioeconomic restructuring in answer to communal frustrations. The first occurred in the early 1950s, when the Korean war boom made possible the resettlement of more than 500,000 rural Chinese into new villages, many of which were provided with what now would be termed "basic needs." Partly as a result of this policy and the employment opportunities produced by the boom, the rural Chinese population's antigovernment sentiments were neutralized, and the Malayan Communist party lost much of its support. The second spurt was the New Economic Policy, which was introduced in the early 1970s as a result of an extensive evaluation by the government of the root causes of the May 1969 riots and which was originally scheduled to be completed by 1990. Among its objectives was an increase in Malay participation in the economy, so that an "ethnic balance" in the various economic sectors and occupations could be attained, more Malay entrepreneurs and managers would be created, and the share of capital held by Malays would be raised. The New Economic Policy has not necessarily reached the targets originally set, and the distribution of wealth still places a large number of Malays below the poverty line; nevertheless, the results of the policy have been impressive. As one analyst has noted: "There has been a more complete transformation of Malaysian society than most observers thought possible."[10] Moreover, the successes of the New Economic Policy have been achieved without antagonizing the Chinese and Indian communities to the point of precipitating a major ethnic confrontation. Although there have been a number of very contentious issues, particularly concerning educational matters, the Chinese have continued to dominate the private sector, and the general expansion of the economy has produced enough of what Milton Esman has called "unoccupied fiscal space" to accommodate a large measure of the economic expectations of Malaysians.[11]

Administrative Control

In examining the reasons for the first two sets of incidents of communal violence, it is important to note that they were made worse by the inability of the government to exert administrative control over all parts of the peninsula. It can also be argued that the May 1969 riots were contained as much as they were because the government could rely primarily on routine administrative and police measures in most areas of the country and was forced to resort to extraordinary coercive measures only in a few key places and for a relatively short period of time.

The Malayan government's experience during the "emergency" is instructive on this question of administrative control. Initially, the government employed a "coercion and enforcement" approach, in which the military and police used force—often excessive force—in an attempt to intimidate the Communists' supporters into withholding aid to the guerillas. The policy proved to be counterproductive, as it alienated many rural Chinese and quickly swelled the ranks of the MCP guerrillas. A reversal of fortunes did not come until 1952, with the introduction of a very different policy by General Sir Gerald Templer, the newly installed high commissioner. Templer sought to neutralize the population by addressing their major grievances and thus weaning them away from the MCP and leaving the guerrillas much more vulnerable to the security forces. In order to deal with the grievances, the government had to build up an extensive administration to deliver health care, sanitation, education, transportation, and community services. The result was that the Malayan bureaucracy grew from 45,000 in 1948 to more than 150,000 in 1960, and the government was able to regain administrative control of the rural areas. As Bernard Fall, among others, has argued, when a country is being subverted, it is "not being outfought, it is being outadministered. Subversion is literally administration with a minus sign in front."[12] This observation applies as much to ethnically motivated violence as to ideologically rooted subversion.

This experience left two important legacies. First, Malaya gained independence with a more developed administration than most newly independent countries have. Moreover, the education system, which the British had expanded and regulated as a means of countering Communist propaganda, provided enough trained manpower for the continued growth of the administration during the 1960s. For example, by 1965, the size of the administration had reached about 228,000 in West Malaysia, and the percentage of civilian public employees in the total labor force was "comparable to such countries as the United Kingdom and Denmark, double the rate for Japan, and four times the rate for India."[13] This has meant that when policies have been devised to counter ethnic frustrations, the government has had the administrative capacity to implement them—a capacity that not all developing countries have had the good fortune to possess. Second, Malaysian leaders have an example in the country's past of ethnically and ideologically rooted violence having been successfully countered by reform and administrative control, rather than by military repression. Hence, although the "emergency" laid the foundation for the strong authoritarian strain that still underpins the actions of the Malaysian government, it is an authoritarianism different from that found in many other developing countries, because the administrative aspects of the state generally outweigh its coercive aspects. In the past, the government has generally appreciated the value of using political forums to deal with communal tensions and has been able to keep most incidents of ethnic conflict in check through routine police operations and administrative measures, rather than by unpredictable and often counterproductive military actions.

Disturbing Trends

Since the end of World War II, Malaya and Malaysia have experienced a good deal of communal tension and a number of serious outbreaks of ethnic violence. To date, however, political, economic, and administrative factors have combined to ensure that each incident of open ethnic conflict has been localized and its consequences limited. But there is no assurance that this state of affairs will continue. Though unlikely, it is possible either that the central coalition will break down or that there will be a polarization of the population away from the coalition government and toward more extreme ethnically based organizations. If either or both were to occur, the factors that served to limit the expansion of ethnic conflict in the past might not be present or might not be sufficient to contain it in the future.

Certainly, some trends have emerged that suggest that the tradition of ethnic accommodation could be undermined. For the first time since independence, there is a distinct possibility that factionalism will overtake the UMNO. The prime minister, who is also the leader of the UMNO, has responded to the Supreme Court's ruling in early 1988 that his party is an unlawful society—because thirty of its branches were not registered under the Societies Act—by setting up a new party, called the UMNO Baru (New UMNO), and by refusing to admit those who have actively contested his leadership. His opponents have attempted to establish their own party, called UMNO Malaysia. The concern is that a divided UMNO could, in turn, divide the Malay vote; weaken, or even destroy, the ruling coalition; and create a situation in which political power could shift dramatically. This, of course, is precisely the set of circumstances that is most likely to heighten tension and produce outbreaks of ethnic violence.

There are also signs that non-Malay support may move to the more extreme flank parties. Certainly, the strains within the UMNO could spill over and affect non-Malays. Even if the UMNO avoids an open split, there is always the fear that increased competition for rank-and-file support within the organization might encourage leaders to expand Malay privileges, thus eroding non-Malay rights. Such a train of events would make it very difficult for non-Malay representatives in the National Front government to retain the confidence of the non-Malay voters. Other issues that may lead non-Malays to abandon the ruling coalition include the seemingly growing influence of Islamic revivalism and Malay nationalism; concerns about the continuing integrity of the Chinese education system and, thus, Chinese culture; changing demographic trends, which suggest that in a few years, the Chinese may be reduced to less than 25 percent of the Malaysian population; increasing doubts about the coalition government's ability to manage the economy efficiently; and fears about the erosion of the independence of the judiciary, which has been seen by some as a bulwark against seemingly arbitrary government actions.

Several of these issues were recently highlighted by the events of October 1987, when ethnic tensions approached a dangerous climax reminiscent of May 1969. The government's decision to try to defuse a potentially explosive exchange of rhetoric between ethnically based groups by detaining 106 people under the Internal Securities Act prompted much debate. Although some measure of intervention was viewed by many as necessary, the detention of individuals who were opponents of the prime minister but apparently not really a threat to ethnic harmony was questioned. Most particularly the government's action prompted some people to wonder whether present and future leaders will resort more and more to coercion and repression, rather than to accommodation, in dealing with issues likely to raise ethnic tensions. Such a policy, if it were adopted, could well backfire.

Yet the possibility of a divided UMNO, the events of October 1987, and the other issues noted here must all be set against a number of factors that continue to favor relatively stable ethnic relations. Obviously, the UMNO still has some time before the next election to resolve its internal battles, and there will be considerable pressure on all sides to present a united front to the electorate. The events of October 1987 demonstrated once again how quickly ethnic tensions can escalate and how important it is to actively seek out ways of minimizing the likelihood of a major ethnic confrontation. Indeed, it might be argued that the Malaysian body politic has been reinoculated against ethnic violence, at least for a short period. Further, the economy, which went through a two-year period of negative growth—causing a buildup of frustrations, which contributed to the October crisis—appears to be on the upswing. Prices have increased for Malaysia's main commodities, and the exports of manufactured goods are up markedly. For many Malaysians, and particularly for the Chinese community, the legitimacy of the government is tied, in part at least, to the performance of the economy, and a reasonable annual growth rate will do much to give moderate leaders the leeway to find solutions to ethnically based problems.

Overall, then, there can be little doubt that incidents of open, ethnically motivated conflict will continue to plague Malaysia. Despite this, however, and although there can be no guarantee either of continued ethnic accommodation or of containing any communal violence that may break out, these incidents are likely to remain relatively minor and not enmesh the general population. Malaysia's past experience suggests that ethnic tensions can be dealt with if the right combination of political, economic, and administrative circumstances prevails.

Notes

a. In 1963, the Federation of Malay was joined by Sabah, Sarawak, and Singapore to form the Federation of Malaysia. Singapore was expelled from Malaysia in 1965. The term *Malaya* will be used when referring to the country in its pre-1963 form, and *Malaysia* will be used for its post-1963 form. It should be noted that this chapter will concentrate exclusively on peninsular or West Malaysia. The present distribution of the population in West Malaysia is approximately 55 percent Malays, 34 percent Chinese, 10 percent Indian, and 1 percent "other."

b. A significant measure of solidarity had also been achieved somewhat in 1954, when the Alliance leaders staged a successful political strike. They resigned from councils and committees at all levels in order to force the British administration to ensure that one party in the 1955 election would be able to gain a majority of elected representatives in the Federal Legislative Council.

c. This has been done by expanding the number of export commodities to include not just rubber and tin but also palm oil, timber, coffee, and most recently and most importantly, petroleum and natural gas. Since 1975, Malaysia's manufacturing industry has grown very rapidly.

References

1. Gordon P. Means, *Malaysian Politics* (London: Hodder and Stoughton, 1976), p. 12.

2. R.S. Milne and Diane K. Mauzy, *Malaysia: Tradition, Modernity and Islam* (Boulder, CO: Westview Press, 1986), p. 66.

3. Means, *Malaysian Politics,* p. 397; John Slimming, *Malaysia: Death of a Democracy* (London: John Murray, 1969), pp. 29–48.

4. Donald L. Horowitz, *Ethnic Groups in Conflict* (Berkeley and Los Angeles: University of California Press, 1985), ch. 10.

5. *Ibid.,* pp. 405, 410–16, 420–24.

6. See Karl Von Vorys, *Democracy Without Consensus* (Princeton, NJ: Princeton University Press, 1975), pp. 164, 205, 343, cited in Diane K. Mauzy, "Malaysia," in Diane K. Mauzy, ed., *Politics in the ASEAN States* (Kuala Lumpur: Maricans, n.d.), p. 183.

7. See Diane K. Mauzy, "Challenges to Nation-Building: Political Issues Towards the 1990s," Paper presented at the Canada Malaysia Conference in Ottawa, October 7–9, 1986.

8. See Francis Kok-wah Loh, "Beyond the Tin Mines: The Political Economy of Chinese Squatter Farmers in the Kinta New Villages, Malaysia," Ph.D. dissertation, Cornell University, 1980, p. 71.

9. For rubber prices, see Colin Barlow, *The Natural Rubber Industry: Its Development, Technology and Economy in Malaysia* (Kuala Lumpur: Oxford University Press, 1978), pp. 440–43.

10. Gordon P. Means, "Ethnic Preference Policies in Malaysia," in Neil Nevitte and Charles H. Kennedy, eds., *Ethnic Preference and Public Policy in Developing States* (Boulder, CO: Lynne Riemer, 1986), p. 113. See, also, Milton J. Esman, "Ethnic Politics and Economic Power," *Comparative Politics* 19, no. 4 (July 1987): 401–6, 413–14.

11. Esman, "Ethnic Politics and Economic Power," p. 416.

12. Bernard Fall, "The Theory and Practice of Insurgency and Counter Insurgency," in M. Smith and C. Johns, eds., *American Defence Policy* (Baltimore: Johns Hopkins Press, 1965), p. 277, cited in O.P. Dwividi and J. Nef, "Crises and Continuities in Development Theory and Administration: First and Third World Perspectives," *Public Administration and Development* 2 (1982): 60.

13. Milton J. Esman, *Administration and Development in Malaysia: Institution Building and Reform in a Plural Society* (Ithaca, NY: Cornell University Press, 1972), pp. 70–71.

18
Ethnic Conflict in Pakistan: The Baluch, Pashtuns, and Sindhis

Selig S. Harrison

T he expanding horizons of social consciousness in newly awakening traditional societies can be likened to a series of concentric circles. Initially, social awareness is defined by the inner circle of identity; but clan, tribal, linguistic and regional perspectives gradually widen as rising economic expectations merge with a sharpening perception of the global environment.

Confronted by the subcontinental dimensions of the United States, the Soviet Union, and the European Economic Community, the new nation-builders of the Third World increasingly place a premium on size. The search for a satisfactory political expression of "national" identity often leads to the subordination of local particularisms within multiethnic states, which offer greater hope for economic progress than states based on a narrowly conceived nationalism. As experience has shown, however, the larger, multiethnic unit is likely to be viable only to the extent that the constituent groups concerned belong to a common communication universe delimited by broadly shared historical memories and sociocultural patterns. Where multiethnic states have been established without regard for such communication boundaries, disaffected ethnic groups with real or imagined grievances against dominantly situated rival groups are likely to take psychological refuge within their inner circle of identity and seek to develop a homogeneous nationalism.

The case of Pakistan presents a striking example of a multiethnic state in which three ethnic minorities have been struggling to define an appropriate concept of nationality and nationalism in the face of repressive rule by an overwhelmingly dominant ethnic majority. For the entrenched Punjabis, Pakistani nationalism subsumes and cancels out the ethnic identity of the Baluch, Pashtun, and Sindhi minorities. But the minorities, who see themselves as the victims of wide-ranging economic and political discrimination, are seeking the recognition of their identities as a necessary precondition for equitable federal, or confederal, constitutional arrangements in which their rights and autonomy would be respected. In the absense of such arrangements, Baluch, Pashtun, and Sindhi separatist movements are continuing to grow. Some of

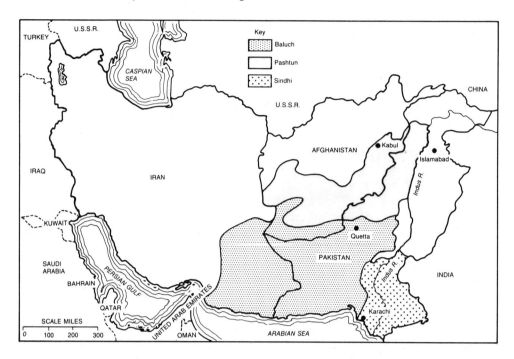

Figure 18–1. Baluch, Pashtun, and Sindhi Majority Regions in Iran, Afghanistan, and Pakistan

these movements advocate independent sovereign states for each minority, while others call for a confederation that excludes the Punjabis or for affiliation with neighboring India or Afghanistan.

The 1961 Pakistani census was the last one that contained a specific question concerning the mother tongue of individual respondents. For this reason, the ethnic arithmetic of Pakistan is a subject of controversy. In the 1961 census, Punjabis constituted 66.39 percent of the population of the areas that now constitute Pakistan.[1] This figure included speakers of Seraiki, a blend of Punjabi and Sindhi spoken in the border districts of Punjab adjacent to Sind. By contrast, the 1981 census, which posed a language question only to a random sample of 10 percent of the respondents, distinguished between Punjabi and Seraiki. The 1981 sample suggested that speakers of Punjabi constituted 48.17 percent of the population (40.31 million); Seraiki, 9.83 percent (8.22 million); Sindhi, 11.77 percent (9.85 million); Pushtu, 13.14 percent (10.99 million), and Baluchi, 4.21 percent (3.52 million).[2] In political terms, the distinction between Punjabi and its Seraiki variant is not a meaningful one,

especially in the eyes of the Baluch, Pashtuns, and Sindhis, who view Punjabi-
and Seraiki-speakers as a single bloc. More important, with the notable
exception of the Sind region, the minorities emphasize the alliance between
the Punjabis and elite elements of the Urdu-speaking refugees (Muhajirs),
numbering 7.60 percent (6.36 million), who migrated to Pakistan from India
after partition.

It is noteworthy that although the Baluch, Sindhis, and Pashtuns comprise
less than 30 percent of the population, they identify themselves historically
with ethnic homelands that constitute 72 percent of Pakistan's territory. To
the proponents of Pakistani nationalism, it is galling that the minorities
should advance proprietary claims over such large areas of the country despite
their numerical inferiority, and Islamabad deliberately seeks to stamp out
regional and ethnic identities in order to push modernization programs
addressed to what is viewed as the greatest good for the greatest number of
Pakistanis. But to most members of the minorities, the disparity between their
population and their territorial claims is irrelevant, since they equate "Pakistan" with the Punjabis and Muhajirs, who are perceived as having occupied
and annexed their territories forcibly as an imperial power.

This chapter will examine the potential for separatism in each of the
ethnic minorities, emphasizing the alienation of the Baluch, who, as a result
of their numerical weakness, see no hope for achieving significant power in
Pakistani politics, even under a democratic regime. Only the Baluch have carried on significant armed insurgencies against successive Pakistani central governments, and only the Baluch have produced a broadly accepted leadership
that is openly committed to winning independence from Pakistan. By contrast, the Sindhis, though seriously estranged from most regimes in Islamabad, have not yet organized a unified separatist movement; and the Pashtuns
are satisfied, for the present, to use separatism as a bargaining weapon to
maximize provincial autonomy and to exact economic and political concessions from the Punjabi-Muhajir elites. After discussing each of the three cases,
the chapter will suggest ways that ethnic conflict in Pakistan might be
resolved, assessing Punjabi and Muhajir attitudes toward the minorities and
their demands, especially with respect to the appropriate type of constitutional setup for Pakistan as a multiethnic state.

The Baluch

The Baluch tribal homeland is a vast area of desert and mountains, bigger
than France, stretching for nearly 900 miles along the Arabian Sea. A small
slice of the Baluch area reaches up into southern Afghanistan, but the majority
of Baluch are native to the Baluch areas of western Pakistan and eastern Iran,

though many have migrated in recent years from their arid homeland to seek jobs in other parts of Pakistan and Iran as well as in the Persian Gulf. Like the divided Kurds, with their dream of a unified Kurdistan, many Baluch nationalists dream of an independent Greater Baluchistan, where the Baluch would be in the majority and would not face what they regard as the indignities inflicted by Punjabis, Pakistan, and Persians, in Iran. Many of the older generation of Baluch leaders, however, would prefer negotiated settlements with Islamabad and Tehran, granting the Baluch regional autonomy within the existing Pakistani and Iranian political structures. Such settlements are preferred because they offer the potential economic advantages of identification with larger polities. In addition, these Baluch leaders fear that the movement for a Greater Baluchistan could all too easily become a focal point for destructive superpower conflict.

The size of the Baluch population remains a matter of sharp disagreement. Nationalist writers have attempted to support claims of 16 million, 18 million, and even 30 million. By contrast, official estimates in Pakistan, Iran, and Afghanistan would indicate a Baluch population of at most 3.2 million. My own analysis of these conflicting estimates suggests a rough provisional estimate of some 5 million, pending more definitive independent demographic studies. The overwhelming majority of this 5 million lives in Pakistan (3.52 million) and Iran (1 million).

Most estimates suggest a literacy rate among the Baluch of 6 to 9 percent—that is, 300,000 to 450,000 Baluch literates. This literate population provides the most volatile raw material for the organized Baluch nationalist movement. But the underlying strength of Baluch nationalism comes from a broad-based sense of Baluch cultural and political identity that cuts across the largely detribalized urban majority and the seventeen major Baluch tribes in the hinterland. Deeply rooted in history, Baluch political consciousness has been steadily sharpened in recent decades by the recurring military conflicts resulting from the forcible incorporation of the Baluch into Iran in 1928 and into the new state of Pakistan in 1947.

In seeking to mobilize a nationalist movement today, Baluch leaders can invoke powerful historical memories of a tortuous struggle for survival, stretching back for more than 2,000 years. The Baluch are passionately absorbed in their past and relive it endlessly in their books, magazines, and folk ballads. They debate where and when they originated; hark back to the "golden ages" of powerful rulers; and revel in the glories of thunderous battles against Persians, Arabs, Tartars, Hindus, and other adversaries.

A Distinctive, Vital Heritage

Politically, the Baluch record is a mixed one, marked by relatively brief interludes of unity and strong leadership amid centuries of fragmentation and tribal strife. In cultural terms, however, the Baluch have been remarkably successful in preserving their separate identity in the face of continual exposure to alien influences. Despite the isolation of the scattered pastoral communities in Baluchistan, a relatively homogeneous Baluch language, literary tradition, and value system have spread over the vast, 207,000-square-mile area reaching from the Indus in the east to the Persian province of Kerman in the west. It is the continuing vitality of this distinctive heritage that explains the strength and tenacity of the present demand for the political recognition of Baluch identity.

According to the "Daptar Shair" ("Chronicle of Genealogies")—an ancient ballad popular among most of the major Baluch tribes—the Baluch originally came from Aleppo in what is now Syria.[3] Western historians tend to dismiss the Aleppo theory as unsubstantiated by credible evidence, but it has widespread acceptance among contemporary Baluch writers, including the late Khan of Kalat, who ruled the largest Baluch principality until its annexation by Pakistan.

Whether or not historians will ever be able to trace the Baluch back to Aleppo, there is an increasing consensus among scholars both in Baluchistan and in the outside world that the Baluch were living along the southern shores of the Caspian at the time of Christ. This conclusion is based largely on linguistic evidence showing that the Baluchi language originated in a lost language linked with the Parthian or Medean civilizations that flourished in the Caspian and adjacent areas in the pre-Christian era. As one of the oldest living languages, Baluchi is a subject of endless fascination and controversy for linquists. Although it is classified as a member of the Iranian group of the Indo-European language family—consisting of Persian, Pushtu, Ossetic, Baluchi, and Kurdish—Baluchi is a distinctive language and is closely related to only one of the other members of the Iranian group, Kurdish. In its modern form, it has incorporated borrowings from Persian, Sindhi, Arabic, and other languages, but it retains striking peculiarities of its own.

Linguistic analysis offers one of the few means available at present for reconstructing the history of Baluch migrations in view of the paucity of historical records, the absence of significant archeological excavations, and the unreliability of Baluch legends. However, the limited historical evidence that does exist tends to confirm the view that the Baluch were living either along the southern shores of the Caspian or in the Kavir Desert until the end of the Sassanid dynasty in the seventh century A.D.

During the five centuries following the seventh century eclipse of the Sassanids, most of the Baluch gradually moved eastward into what is now Pakistani Baluchistan, where they made progressively more ambitious efforts to achieve political unity. A significant but smaller group that remained behind in Iran was to remain largely outside of the mainstream of Baluch political history.

Unification Efforts

In order to validate their demands today, Baluch nationalists focus on the unification efforts made by two Baluch monarchs who ruled during the three centuries preceding the British Raj. The first nation-builder cited in Baluch historical accounts is Mir Chakar Rind, who, in the fifteenth century, established a short-lived tribal confederacy reaching from the Makran coast to the present-day Marri tribal area south of Quetta.

After Mir Chakar's death in 1511, the Moghul Empire, based in Delhi, made several unsuccessful attempts to incorporate the Baluch, but they were able to cooperate militarily to preserve their independence. However, the Baluch tribes were not able to restore even a modicum of political unity until the Ahmadzai tribe established the Kalat Confederacy in 1666. Based in the Kalat highlands, southwest of Mir Chakar's former capital, the new confederacy gradually encompassed an area even larger than Mir Chakar's domain, under the leadership of the sixth Khan of Kalat, the dynamic Nasir Khan, who ruled for more than half a century, beginning in 1741. Nasir Khan's most notable achievement was the creation of a unified Baluch army of some 25,000 men and 1,000 camels, an impressive force by eighteenth-century Southwest Asian standards. For the first time in their history, most of the major Baluch tribes were rallied under the banner of an agreed system of military organization and recruitment.

At the height of his power, Nasir Khan asserted claims of sovereignty over the Iranian Baluch areas and sent occasional expeditionary forces to his western borderlands. Nevertheless, it should be emphasized that the freewheeling Iranian Baluch tribes were, for all practical purposes, a law unto themselves. Separated by geography from the main body of the Baluch tribes to the east and divided, themselves, into several distinctive regional subgroupings, the Iranian Baluch have been on the fringes of Baluch political life throughout history and continue to be so today.

For contemporary Baluch nationalists, Nasir Khan's achievements remain an all-important symbol, providing some semblance of historical precedent for the concept of a unified Baluch political identity. Why did the unity built by Nasir Khan collapse during the decades after his death in 1805? Was it, as most available evidence would suggest, simply because his successors succumbed to the centrifugal pulls of tribal strife?

"Divide and Rule" in Baluchistan

The issue is confused in that Nasir Khan's passing from the scene coincided with the beginnings of the "great game" between Britain and Russia in Afghanistan and British adoption of the "forward policy," designed to push the jurisdiction of the Raj to the Afghan frontier. When the British concluded that Afghanistan should become a buffer state to shield their Indian empire from Russia, Baluchistan, as a key area flanking Afghanistan, immediately acquired a new strategic significance. Determined to establish direct control over the access routes to Afghanistan, the British fought bloody battles with the Baluch for more than forty years. By 1876, they were able to subdue Kalat and obtain formal treaty rights to station troops there in return for handsome subsidies and guarantees of tribal autonomy. Playing off rival chiefs against each other during the closing decades of the century, Britain systematically proceeded to divide the Baluch area into seven parts. In the far west, the Goldsmid Line gave roughly one-fourth to Persia in 1871; in the north, the Durand Line assigned a small strip to Afghanistan in 1894; and in British India, the Baluch areas were divided into a centrally administered enclave (known as British Baluchistan) guarding a key mountain pass, a truncated remnant of the Kalat Confederacy, and three smaller puppet principalities.

In Iran, the shah's repression kept the Baluch largely under control (with the exception of a brief Iraqi-supported insurgency from 1968 to 1973) until the advent of the Ayatollah Ruhollah Khomeini in 1979 led to an erosion of the central authority and an outburst of long-sublimated nationalist feeling. In Pakistan, by contrast, Baluch insurgents have waged an intermittent guerrilla struggle ever since the departure of the British, culminating in the mid-1970s in a bloody confrontation with 80,000 or more Pakistani troops, in which some 55,000 Baluch were involved at various stages of the fighting. At the height of the fighting, in late 1974, U.S.-supplied Iranian combat helicopters, some operated by Iranian pilots, joined the Pakistan Air Force in attacks on Baluch camps. The Baluch, lacking any meaningful foreign help, were equipped only with bolt-action rifles and primitive grenades.

Significantly, when they launched their poorly prepared insurgency in 1973, the Pakistani Baluch were fighting not for independence but rather for regional autonomy within a restructured, confederal Pakistani constitutional framework. By the time the shooting stopped in 1977, however, separatist feeling had crystallized. The indiscriminate use of superior firepower by the Pakistani and Iranian forces, especially the air attacks on Baluch villages, left a legacy of lasting hatred. Since most Baluch felt the direct impact of Pakistani repression, the Baluch populace became politicized to an unprecedented degree.

There is still a chance to avert renewed conflict through negotiations, in my view, but the communication gap is rapidly widening between the Baluch and Pakistani leaders. Islamabad views the thinly settled expanses of Baluchistan as a haven for surplus population, as a source of critically needed raw materials, and above all, as strategic real estate over which the central government should rightfully hold undisputed control. For the ideologists of Pakistani nationalism, the Baluch and other minorities cannot be permitted to obstruct modernization programs that are designed to meet the overall development needs of the country.

My extensive conversations with General Muhammad Zia ul-Haq and his successors between 1978 and 1990 have led me to conclude that Islamabad is unlikely to make the concessions necessary to reach an accomodation with representative Baluch leaders. Dominated by Punjabi military and bureaucratic elites, successive authoritarian Pakistani regimes have identified their interests with the preservation of a unitary state and have thus resisted pressures for democratic government, which have been linked, inseparably, with demands for provincial self-rule.

Discrimination against the Baluch

There is an unmistakable note of ethnic arrogance in the Punjabi attitude—a desire to show the "primitive" Baluch tribesmen who is master and a feeling that the armed forces could suppress the Baluch once again, if necessary, as they did in the 1973–77 insurgency. This condescending posture is reflected in the almost-complete exclusion of the Baluch from the political, bureaucratic, and military power structure of Pakistan.

The Baluch charge that their area is neglected economically and that Punjabi-linked big business interests in Lahore and Karachi are milking Baluchistan of its resources. They point, in particular, to the natural gas deposits at Sui, which have been used until recently to build up industries outside Baluchistan. Evidence abounds to back up these allegations, as well as parallel charges that Punjabi settlers are grabbing the prime farmland in Baluch areas and that Punjabi real estate speculators are buying up properties in Quetta, the principal urban center in Baluchistan. The Zia regime responded to such criticism with increased economic development spending, especially on roads, and developed a gas pipeline from the Sui fields to Quetta. But Zia continued to channel development funds through the Punjabi bureaucracy, ignoring Baluch pleas for local control over development decisions.

For cosmetic purposes, Zia occasionally consulted several marginal Baluch politicians and businessmen, but at the same time refused to negotiate on the autonomy issue with the three Baluch leaders who have commanded the overwhelming support of the Baluch populace: the late Ghaus Bux Bizenjo, Ataullah Mengal, and Khair Bux Marri. These are the leaders who emerged triumphant in 1970 when the Baluch had their first—and last—opportunity to elect their own provincial government. It was the dismissal of this government by the late President Zulfiqar Ali Bhutto that touched off the 1973–77 insurgency. In the March 1985 elections to national and provincial assemblies, held under the aegis of Zia's martial law regime, military intelligence agencies controlled the screening of candidates, and political parties were banned. In Baluchistan, the elections produced an assembly dominated by Pashtun and Punjabi elements in the province, and Baluch tribes and nationalist elements had virtually no representation.

in the province, and Baluch tribes and nationalist elements had virtually no representation.

Despite Zia's refusal to hold representative elections and to negotiate on the autonomy issue, he sharply criticized Bhutto for "needlessly inflaming the passions of the Baluch" by summarily removing their elected regime. Zia said that he would be careful to avoid comparable frontal assaults on Baluch pride. Given the proper mixture of benign neglect and "nonprovocative" firmness, he maintained, the Baluch problem would gradually subside. Thus, he ordered army units in Baluchistan to maintain a low profile, but at the same time, he clamped down firmly on political activity in the Baluch areas and in the rest of the country as well, forcing most nationalist activity underground. Since Zia's death in 1988, the military intelligence agencies that he created have continued to be the ultimate arbiters of Pakistani politics, and Balunchistan has remained under effective central control through local collaborators despite a facade of provincial electoral politics in 1988 and 1990.

Confronted with firm Punjabi-Muhajir domination and fearful of arrest, Ataullah Mengal and Khair Bux Marri went into political exile during the Zia years, Mengal to London and Marri to Kabul, and both were still in exile in 1990. Mengal and Marri are both hereditary chieftans of large tribes that collectively number some 200,000 people, but they emerged during the 1973–77 insurgency as "national" leaders. Both openly advocate independence and have attempted with little success to obtain foreign help, whether from the Soviet Union, China, the United States, India, the Arab world or a combination of these.

Baluch Organizations

Mengal is the leader of the London-based Baluchistan Liberation Organization (BLO), formally launched in July 1982, which publishes a Baluchi-language monthly, *Azad Baluchistan (Free Baluchistan)*, the leading organ of the nationalist movement. According to Mengal, the BLO has underground units in Baluchistan that were organized more than forty years ago. Mengal describes the BLO as the heir to the Kalat national party, which campaigned for an independent Baluchistan in the 1930s and 1940s and opposed the forcible integration of the Baluch-majority princedom of Kalat and other Baluch areas into Pakistan in 1947. In its program, the BLO calls for "a completely independent and sovereign state of Baluchistan" in which "all patriotic classes and sectors of the populace" will have a voice. As for its foreign policy, said the program, the new state "will adopt an anti-imperialist and non-aligned stand, unequivocally supporting all those nations that are anti-imperialist and promoting friendly and neighborly relations with all neighboring countries."[4]

In contrast to the BLO, which carefully avoids ideological labels, Khair Bux Marri's Afghanistan-based Baluch People's Liberation Front (BPLF) espouses an exotic, Baluch brand of national communism that explicitly rejects the primacy of either Moscow or Peking and flies in the face of traditional Marxist-Leninist doctrine by embracing the "healthy" aspects of nomadic life. An outgrowth of guerrilla groups that opposed the regime of Muhammad Ayub Khan in the 1960s, the BPLF was formally launched during the 1973–77 struggle and now consists of some 8,500 guerrillas in organized combat units, plus a skeleton underground infrastructure in Pakistan and Iran. The organized guerrilla units are based in refugee camps in southern Afghanistan, where they were given sanctuary by the non-Communist regime of Muhammad Daud during the insurgency, in keeping with the tradition of Baluch–Afghan kinship dating back to the Nasir Khan period. Both the Khalq and Parcham regimes have continued to subsidize the camps since the 1978 Communist takeover. Many of the guerrillas are Marri tribesmen, and the group looks to Marri as its leader.

I spoke with Marri in Kabul in March 1984 and found that the BPLF had not formed a formal political alliance with the ruling People's Democratic (Communist) party of Afghanistan and was not receiving significant military support or training from the Soviet Union or the Communist regime in Kabul. Moscow appears to be wary of alliances with Baluch nationalist leaders—especially hereditary tribal chieftains, or *sardars,* such as Marri and Mengal—and is seeking to build a Baluch Communist party by indoctrinating young Baluch at Kabul University and, in selected cases, at Soviet institutions.

Next to the BPLF, the best organized nationalist group is the Baluch Student Organization (BSO), boasting some 6,000 members and fifty chapters, including several newly established branches in Iranian Baluchistan. The BSO leadership is divided between sympathizers of the BPLF and various Pakistani Communist factions but jealously guards its own organizational independence. Although the BSO's public declarations are circumspect, its underground publications make thinly veiled allusions to independence as the Baluch goal.

The Baluch Liberation Movement (BLM), a Soviet-inspired offshoot of the BSO, led by two of its former presidents, has been operating out of Afghanistan since 1984 and has had some success in organizing pro-Communist Baluch youth. An estimated 200 Baluch high school and college students recruited by the BLM had gone to Moscow for education by 1987. Mengal's BLO formed an alliance with the BLM in 1987, creating an underground grouping known as the Baluch National Liberation Front (BNLF). Mengal described the new alliance as a nationalist attempt to create greater operational unity among antigovernment Baluch in Pakistan. Significantly, however, Marri's BPLF, suspicious of the BLM's Soviet-sponsored origins, did not join.

Surprisingly, there have never been strong Soviet-oriented Communist parties in either Pakistani or Iranian Baluchistan, primarily because Moscow has vacillated over the years about the desirability of an independent Greater

Baluchistan. While defining the Baluch as a separate nationality and upholding their inherent right of secession, Yuri Gankovsky, the principal Soviet expert on South Asia, wrote in 1964 that the Baluch nation was still in its "early stages of formation" and that it would be premature to exercise the right of secession. Baluch progressives should work for broad united fronts with progressives throughout Pakistan and Iran, he said, avoiding "bourgeois nationalist" tendencies.[5]

In the case of Pakistan, the faction-ridden Communist movement has been controlled by urban, middle-class leaders who migrated at the time of the partition to Karachi and Lahore from areas now in India. These leaders lack local roots in any of the ethnic regions that now constitute Pakistan. They have built some Baluch cadres among students and unionists, but they have won few collaborators among nationalist leaders, with the exception of Bizenjo, whose concept of a loose federation is in tune with the current Communist line.

The Pakistani government dismisses the concept of Baluch nationalism, depicting Baluch society solely in terms of its traditional tribal character and organizational patterns. The government argument is that Baluch discontent is artificially promoted by the tribal *sardars* to protect their feudal privileges and that economic modernization will dampen Baluch unrest by gradually dissolving the *sardari* system. This argument has some validity, but it is exaggerated. Moreover, the central government has actively protected and enlarged the privileges of cooperative *sardars*. Most *sardars* have attempted to safeguard their privileges by avoiding direct identification with the nationalist movement, while keeping the door open for supporting the nationalist cause in time or armed conflict between the Baluch and the central government, as in the 1973–77 insurgency. The only exceptions are the chieftains of the two largest tribes, Mengal and Marri, who have followers in all of the major tribes.

It is important to recognize the strength of tribal loyalties and the monolithic power of the *sardar* in the hierarchical Baluch social structure to mobilize and discipline his tribes. It was the unified support of nearly every tribe, acting on a tribal basis, that made the Baluch insurgency during the 1973–77 period so effective. At the same time, it would be a mistake to underestimate the significance of the ongoing process of urbanization and education that is taking place as a result of the slow but steady impact of economic change. As already noted, out of a total Baluch population of some 5 million in Pakistan, Iran, and the Persian Gulf, 300,000 to 450,000 are literate in at least one of the languages found among the Baluch.[6] Many are politically conscious and active in the growing Baluch nationalist movement. Theoretically, education and economic modernization could lead to assimilation, but unemployment among the educated—aggravated by job discrimination against Baluch, especially in the civil service—fuels political discontent.

The Pashtuns

Independence versus Regional Autonomy

In contrast to the demand made by Baluch leaders for complete independence or, at a minimum, sweeping confederal powers, Pashtun leaders insist only on regional autonomy. It was this difference that led to the breakup of Baluch–Pashtun unity after a brief period in the mid-1970s during which the two minorities cooperated to oppose the Bhutto regime. When opposition leaders formed the National Democratic party in 1979 to supplant the banned National Awami party, the principal Pashtun leader, Khan Abdul Wali Khan, objected to moderate Baluch leader Bizenjo's proposed reference to "nationalities" in the party platform to describe the provinces of Pakistan, urging instead that they be characterized as "distinctive cultural and linguistic entities." On the issue of provincial autonomy, Bizenjo wanted the central government to control only defense, foreign affairs, communications, and currency, whereas Wali Khan advocated a variation of Bhutto's 1973 constitution, which accorded far-reaching powers to Islamabad.

In 1987, this issue continued to divide Baluch and Pashtun leaders. Wali Khan, muting regional demands, supported a "national progressive front" that sought to win control of the central government. Bizenjo advocated a restructured, confederal Pakistan, while his fellow Baluch leader, Ataullah Mengal, joined with Sindhi nationalists and marginal Pashtun leaders to form a "Sindhi–Baluch–Pashtun front." The front called for the creation of a confederation of the three minorities from which Punjab province would be excluded.

The Baluch feel much more alienated from the Punjabi-Muhajir establishment than the Pashtuns. The Baluch perception is that the Punjabis view them with condescension and contempt as "primitive," in contrast to a more complex Punjabi attitude toward the Pashtuns, especially toward the Pashtun aristocracy. More important, the Baluch have been almost completely shut out of the economic and political power structure in Pakistan, whereas the Pashtuns, albeit bitter over Punjabi-Muhajir dominance, do not feel a comparable sense of complete exclusion. During British rule, Pashtuns from the more aristocratic, urbanized families were given powerful posts in the army and bureaucracy. Pashtun officers constituted a significant bloc in the upper ranks of the army following partition, until many of them were pushed out in the late 1950s, when the Punjabis increased their power. Even today, however, there is still a significant number of Pashtuns in high places in Pakistan, and the expansion of Punjabi influence in the military and the bureaucracy during the Zia ul-Haq regime was not at the expense of Pashtun members of the establishment.

Geographically, the Pashtun areas are not as cut off from other parts of Pakistan as the Baluch areas, which partly explains why the Pashtun areas are better integrated with the overall Pakistani economy than the Baluch areas are. In Pashtun eyes, this integration has its disadvantages, in that it brings what is seen as excessive dependence on Punjab province and makes the Pashtun areas vulnerable to exploitation by big-business interests centered in Karachi and Lahore. Pashtun nationalism focuses, in large part, on alleged economic discrimination against the North-West Frontier province in allocations of development expenditures both in industry and agriculture. Among the standard charges leveled by Pashtun leaders is that Islamabad deliberately holds back on electrification of the Pashtun areas because it does not want them to become industrialized and that even the electricity produced there goes primarily to Punjab province. For example, Wali Khan repeatedly points to the fact that most of the tobacco and cotton grown in the North-West Frontier province is used to supply cigarette and textile factories located in other provinces. Islamabad even discriminates against the Pashtuns in agricultural development, nationalist spokesmen argue—channeling funds for the expansion of irrigation primarily to Punjab province or to areas in other provinces where Punjabi settlers will benefit most.

Political scientist Hamida Khuhro, a Sindhi, observed in an interview that "basically, the Pashtuns want a bigger share of the cake," while "the Baluch want something more—identity, self-respect, real autonomy." This distinction is important, but it does not necessarily follow that the possibility of a resurgent Pashtun separatism can be entirely dismissed. Even if one could assume that Islamabad will make the economic concessions necessary to temper Pashtun discontent, there is likely to be growing resentment in Pashtun areas if Punjabi civil servants continue to play a dominant role in provincial administration and if Islamabad continues to block Pashtun nationalist efforts to promote the Pushtu language in education. At present, Pushtu is the medium of instruction only up to the age of ten. Thereafter, Pashtun children not only must attend classes conducted in Urdu and use textbooks written in Urdu but must also use Urdu when competing in civil service examinations and in university and graduate school entrance examinations. The language issue is important in Baluchistan, Sind, and the North-West Frontier province alike, but it is more important in the Sindhi and Pashtun areas than in Baluchistan, because Sindhi and Pushtu are more standardized and better developed as literary languages than Baluchi and thus more readily adaptable for educational purposes.

As Pashtun refugees have poured into Pakistan from neighboring Afghanistan since 1979, the Jama'at-i Islami and other Islamic fundamentalist groups have been able to strengthen their position in the Pashtun areas of Pakistan. However, this growth in support for the Jama'at has been largely limited to Jama'at-oriented Afghan resistance groups. It has not altered Pashtun antagonism toward what is viewed as a hostile, Punjabi-dominated government in Islamabad. Anti-Jama'at Pashtun groups identified with Wali Khan and his revered father, the late Khan Abdul Ghaffar Khan, continue to claim widespread support among many of the same Afghan refugees who have been responsive to the Jama'at.

Against the background of the Soviet occupation and the resulting turmoil in Pashtun society, the idea of a unified "Pashtunistan," linking the Pashtuns on both sides of the Durand Line, has been relatively quiescent since 1979. By the same token, however, should the Pashtun refugees remain in Pakistan, pressures are likely to grow for an autonomous Pashtunistan within the framework of Pakistan. For this reason, the Punjabi-dominated regime in Islamabad has been seeking to resettle as many of the refugees as possible in Baluchistan, vitiating the strength of Baluch and Pashtun separatism at one stroke.

Pashtun Nationalism

Just as the Baluch blame the British Raj for impeding their achievement of a national identity, the Pashtuns, too, feel that colonialism robbed them of their birthright. Until the Raj, the Pashtuns (or Pakhtuns) were politically united for nearly a century under the banner of an Afghan empire that stretched eastward as far as the Indus River. It was traumatic for Pashtuns when the British seized 40,000 square miles of ancestral Pashtun territory between the Indus and the Khyber Pass, embracing half of the Pashtun population, and then imposed the Durand Line in 1893, formalizing their conquest. When they subsequently handed over this territory to the new, Punjabi-dominated government of Pakistan in 1947, the British bequeathed an explosive, irredentist issue that has perennially dominated the rhetoric of Pashtun-dominated Afghan regimes and has poisoned the relations between Afghanistan and Pakistan. At various times, Zahir Shah's monarchy, Muhammad Daoud's republic, and post-1978 Communist governments in Kabul have all challenged Pakistan's right to rule over its Pashtun areas, alternately espousing the goal of an autonomous Pashtun state to be created within Pakistan, an independent Pashtunistan to be carved out of Pakistan, or a "Greater Afghanistan" directly annexing the lost territories.

The Pashtuns today gloss over the internecine strife within the newly established Afghan monarchy, which opened the way for the intervention of the British and their allies in the early nineteenth century. Surveying the broad picture, however, there is more than enough evidence in the historical record to account for the emotive power of Pashtun nationalism. Long before the British arrived on the scene, the Pashtuns were struggling to preserve their identity against the onslaughts of advancing Moghul emperors, who ruled tenuously over the areas west of the Indus from their capital in Delhi. Pakistani nationalists exalt the memory of Akbar and Aurangzeb as the symbols of a lost Islamic grandeur in South Asia. For the Pashtuns, however, the Moghuls are remembered primarily as the symbols of past oppression.

Pashtuns on both sides of the Durand Line share an ancient social and cultural identity dating back at least to the Pakti kingdom mentioned in the writings of Herodotus and possibly earlier. When a Punjabi critic asked him in 1975 whether he was "a Muslim, a Pakistani, or a Pashtun first," Wali Khan gave a much-quoted reply that he was "a six-thousand-year-old Pashtun, a thousand-year-old Muslim, and a 27-year-old Pakistani."[7] Eighth-century A.D. inscriptions have been found in a precursor of the Pushtu language. By the eleventh and twelfth centuries, Rahman Baba and other poets were writing Pushtu folk ballads that are still popular today;[8] and by the mid-seventeenth century, Khushal Khan Khattak had begun to develop what is now treasured as the classic style of Pashtun poetry.

The total Pashtun population was estimated at some 20 million in 1987, consisting of about 10.99 million native to the Pakistan side of the Durand Line and 9 million native to Afghanistan, some 2.5 million of whom are currently living in Pakistan as refugees. There are from two to three dozen Pashtun tribes, depending on how one classifies them, generally divided into four major groupings: the Durranis and Ghilzais, concentrated in Afghanistan; the so-called independent tribes, straddling the Durand Line; and several tribes, such as the Khattaks and Bannuchis, centered in the North-West Frontier province of Pakistan. In addition, some 200,000 Pashtuns who live in urban or semiurban areas have become detribalized, but the tribal hold is still powerful throughout Pashtun society.

As Richard Tapper wrote:

> In spite of the endemic conflict among different Pashtun groups, the notion of the ethnic and cultural unity of all Pashtuns has long been familiar to them as a symbolic complex of great potential for political unity. Of all tribal groups in Iran or Afghanistan, the Pashtuns have had perhaps the most pervasive and explicit segmentary lineage ideology on the classic pattern, expressed not only in written genealogies but in territorial distribution.[9]

However, in contrast to Baluch society, with its hierarchical structure and its all-powerful *sardars,* Pashtun culture has an egalitarian mystique epitomized by the role of the *jirgah* (assembly). Moreover, as Akbar Ahmed has observed, although the tribal *malik* (village headman) is the most powerful single figure in tribal affairs per se, the *malik* shares local power with the *mullah* in a complex, symbiotic relationship that differs basically from the case of the Baluch.[10]

The Changing Ethnic Balance in Afghanistan

The Afghan state that Ahmad Shah Durrani forged in 1747 was frankly Pashtun in character. It was a Pashtun tribal confederacy, established for the purpose of uniting the Pashtuns and shielding their interests and integrity against non-Pashtun rivals. To be sure, even at its inception, the new state was not entirely homogeneous ethnically, but Afghanistan had an overwhelming Pashtun majority in the early nineteenth century. By contrast, the loss of the trans-Durand territories in 1823 and the consequent division of the Pashtuns left a truncated Afghanistan with a more tenuous ethnic balance. As the "great game" between Britain and Russia developed during the nineteenth century, the British egged on successive Afghan rulers, who gradually pushed the borders of Afghanistan northward to the Oxus River. The British goal was to make Afghanistan a buffer state, and the Pashtun rulers in Kabul had imperialist ambitions of their own. Extensive areas populated by Hazaras, Tajiks, Uzbeks, and other non-Pashtun ethnic groups were annexed by Kabul after long and costly struggles that left a legacy of built-in ethnic conflict.

Non-Pashtuns constituted at least 35 percent—possibly as much as 45 percent—of the population of Afghanistan during the decades preceding the Soviet occupation, and their relative strength has grown in the wake of the large-scale Pashtun refugee movement to Pakistan. As the ethnic balance has changed, the Pashtuns in Afghanistan have intermittently attempted to forge some form of political unity with the Pashtuns in Pakistan that would make possible a restoration of unchallenged Pashtun dominance in Kabul. By the same token, given the responsibility of the British for the division of the Pashtuns, it is not surprising that anti-British sentiment during the 1920s and 1930s sparked the emergence of a Pashtun nationalist movement on what was to become the Pakistan side of the Durand Line. Stephen Rittenberg, analyzing the origins of Khan Abdul Ghaffar Khan's "Red Shirts," has shown that this anti-British sentiment was directly stimulated by the economic conflict between the wealthy khans who were allied with the Raj and a coalition of Pashtun tenants, small landholders, and artisans.[11] At the same time, Ghaffar Khan appealed to the feeling of solidarity between the Pashtuns of the North-West Frontier and their brethren in Afghanistan, calling explicitly on the eve of partition for an independent Pashtunistan. In Ghaffar Khan's Bannu Declaration of June 22, 1947, he demanded that the Pashtuns be given a choice between joining Pakistan or establishing an independent Pashtunistan, rather than a choice limited to Pakistan or India.

The Red Shirts boycotted the referendum that was used by the departing British as their legal rationale for handing over the North-West Frontier province and the adjacent tribal areas to the new Pakistani state. As a consequence, when it fit their purposes, Ghaffar Khan and Wali Khan were able to cast doubt on the legitimacy of the incorporation of these Pashtun-majority areas into Pakistan. For their part, Pakistani leaders, questioning protestations of loyalty to Pakistan by Ghaffar Khan and Wali Khan, have frequently cited the Bannu Declaration.

Pakistan and Pashtun Separatism

Even though the two Pashtun leaders have reformulated the Pashtunistan demand since 1947 as a demand for provinicial autonomy within Pakistan, Islamabad has continued to doubt their allegiance to Pakistan. This distrust is rooted not only in suspicions of collusion with Afghanistan but also in the fact that Ghaffar Khan was openly opposed to the very idea of Pakistan and was actively identified with the Indian National Congress in its struggle against the British. As we shall see, Ghaffar Khan recognized clearly that the Pakistan movement was promoted mainly by Muslims in those provinces of undivided India where Hindus were in a majority. He contended that the formation of Pakistan would not serve the interests of the North-West Frontier province, with its Muslim majority, because the new Pakistani state would be dominated by the Punjabis and Muhajirs. By contrast, as we shall see, Sindhi leaders failed to anticipate the demographic changes that partition would bring to their homeland.

The Sindhis

Although Greek, Arab, Moghul, and British invaders have annexed Sind to their empires, Sindhi nationalist writings trace a continuous Sindhi identity in the Indus Valley dating back for more than 5,000 years to the Mohenjodaro and Harappa civilizations. Nationalist lore focuses on the persistent struggles waged against the invader and, above all, on the fact that Sind has been ruled, for the most part, by independent local Muslim dynasties. The exceptions were the period of Arab rule from the eighth through the tenth centuries, the brief interlude under Mahmud of Ghazni in the eleventh century, and the Moghul imperium during the seventeenth and early eighteenth centuries. The Sindhi golden ages spotlighted in nationalist works were the eleventh-century Soomro dynasty and the period of Kalhora rule that lasted for more than a century, between the expulsion of the Moghuls in 1738 and the British conquest of Sind in 1843. Sind has a national "poet-saint," Shah Abdul Latif (1690–1750), who chronicled Sindhi history in *Shahajo risalo* (*Book of Kings*) and patriotic epics such as *Umar Marin* (*The Prince and the Shephardess*). Latif's work, which marked the beginning of Sindhi literature, was the subject of an international literary conference in Karachi in October 1987, sponsored by Sindhi literary groups. Nationalists stress that the Sindhi language has retained its own distinctive flavor, despite the efforts of the Arabs and the Moghuls to infuse it with Arabic and Persian. The nationalist movement has focused much of its energy on the defense of Sindhi as the medium of local education and government in the face of pressures for the introduction of Urdu.

Origins of the Sindhi Nationalist Movement

The modern Sindhi nationalist movement began during the latter years of British rule with a campaign for the separation of Sind from the Bombay presidency. The formation of a separate Sind province in 1936, with Karachi as its capital, gave the Sindhi Muslims a majority in their province, but the Sindhi Hindus continued to dominate the business and professional life of Sind. Thus, in 1939, Sindhi Muslim leaders decided to support the Muslim League's demand for Pakistan, hoping to profit economically from driving out the Sindhi Hindus.

G.M. Sayed and some of the other Muslim leaders involved have acknowledged their failure to foresee that the majority of Muslim Muhajirs from Hindu-majority areas of India would settle in Sind following partition; that the Muhajirs would make expedient alliances with a newly entrenched Punjabi bureaucratic and military elite to rule over Sind; and that the central government would foster Punjabi and Pashtun immigration to Sind to reshape the demographic balance there.

One of the first acts of the new Pakistani government was to detach the city of Karachi and its environs from Sind, making it a federal district. In the eyes of Sindhi Muslims, this "dismemberment" symbolized the advent of Punjabi-Muhajir dominance. A Sindhi journalist charged that it had led to the abolition of Sindhi in city governmental affairs, the wholesale replacement of Sindhis in city jobs with Urdu-speaking employees, the shutdown of the Sindhi Department in Karachi University, and a ban on the use of Sindhi in the university as an examination medium.[12] Some of these measures were later reversed, but the memory lingered on. Another journalist, seeking to explain "the defeatism and despair which have prevailed among a large section of the Sindhis over the last 25 years or so," concluded in a 1978 *Dawn* article that "the beginnings of this feeling can be traced to Pakistan's early days when Karachi was separated from Sind." This malaise became "more and more pronounced," he added, when Sind and other provinces were subsumed under "One Unit," embracing all of West Pakistan, and it was during this One Unit period that G.M. Sayed's movement for a sovereign and independent Sindhu Desh (Sindhi homeland) began to catch hold.[13]

The dissolution of One Unit by Muhammad Yahya Khan in 1970 and the reestablishment of the provinces moderated Sindhi discontent, especially when a Sindhi, Zulfiqar Ali Bhutto, took over the leadership of what remained of Pakistan following the separation of Bangladesh. In 1972, Bhutto's People's party sponsored a successful drive to enact legislation in the provincial assembly making Sindhi the official language of Sind, and Bhutto became a Sindhi hero. Ironically, in view of the Punjabi-Muhajir support that had helped to bring him to power, Bhutto's removal at the hands of the military and his execution in 1979 made him a martyr to the Sindhi cause.

Weaknesses of the Nationalist Movement

The post-Bhutto atmosphere in Sind was marked by continuing tension, and the Zia ul-Haq regime kept a tight grip on the province, installing a more comprehensive network of local military rule there than in any other part of Pakistan. But the Sindhi nationalist movement has been poorly organized and divided, reflecting structural peculiarities in Sindhi society. One is the fact that the prepartition Sindhi middle class was entirely Hindu and that a Sindhi Muslim middle class has yet to replace it. Another factor weakening the nationalist movement is the confrontation between the powerful Sindhi *waderas,* absentee landlords with large holdings, and the *haris,* a rural lumpen-proletariat of some 3 million landless, nomadic farm workers. This conflict has driven the landlords into intermittent alliances with the Punjabis and Muhajirs, leaving the Sindhi nationalist movement mainly in the hands of a variety of leftist factions. Employing economic as well as religious appeals, Islamabad has also been able to make alliances with some of the tightly organized local Muslim sects that have grown up under the leadership of powerful *pirs* (saints) in the feudal environment of rural Sind.

Nationalist Demands

An index of the supercharged political climate in Sind during late 1982 was the fact that thirty-six Sindhi periodicals were banned. It was thus no surprise to objective observers that antigovernment upheavals erupted in Sind when Zia threw down the gauntlet in August 1983, serving notice that political parties would not be permitted to contest the "elections" projected for 1985 and that all candidates would have to be certified by an "Islamic ideology council," to be appointed by the incumbent military regime. The Sindhi response to Zia's declaration demonstrated an unprecedented unity, spanning leftist Sindhi nationalist groups and conservative elements that have long dominated the feudal environment of rural Sind, including powerful *pirs.* At least 300 Sindhis were killed in clashes with some 45,000 Punjabi troops, leading to a consolidation of Sindhi nationalist sentiment and a rapid growth in underground political activity.

Sampling Sindhi underground literature, one finds vacillation between demands for a sovereign Sindhu Desh, restructuring of Pakistan as a loose confederation, and merger with India. Moderates in nationalist ranks argue that confederal autonomy would enable Sindhis to achieve many of their demands—notably, greater civil service and educational opportunities—and that a struggle for independence would entail enormous bloodshed. Advocates of independence respond that Sindhis can win economic control of their province from the Muhajirs and Punjabis, develop the economic potential of Sind, and end its exploitation by other provinces only by struggling for full sovereignty, with help from India or the Soviet Union, or both. Independence, it is argued, would give Sind increasing bargaining power in dealing with the Punjab over the key issue of the Indus River waters; as part of Pakistan, Sind is helplessly dependent and has been cheated of its fair share of the waters, whereas as a sovereign state, controlling Punjab's outlet to the sea, it would be able to safeguard its rights.

This argument was carried a step further by G.M. Sayed, who declared in a 1987 book—published in New Delhi and banned in Pakistan—that merger with India would maximize Sind's bargaining leverage in dealing with the vital waters issue.[14]

Demographic Factors and Sindhi–Baluch Unity

Demographic factors greatly complicate the Sindhi effort to forge a nationalist front against Islamabad. Of the total population of 19 million in Sind in the 1981 census, only 8.5 million were "original" Sindhis,[a] with the balance split among some 6 million Muhajirs and Punjabis, 4 million Baluch, and 500,000 Pashtuns.

Initially allied with the Punjabis, the Muhajirs reacted to the continuing growth of Punjabi economic power in Sind by forming, in 1985, a tightly knit political organization known as Muhajir Quami Mahaz (MQM), or Muhajir National Front. The MQM swept a series of local elections in 1987 and emerged as a pivotal force in Sind politics, alternately allying with Sindhi and Punjabi groups as opportunity dictates.

The Baluch in Sind subdivide into some 2 million relatively recent Baluchi-speaking migrants, mainly in Karachi, and 2 million earlier migrants. Most of these 2 million earlier migrants have assimilated into Sindhi life and can speak Sindhi, which accounts for the 9.85 million figure for Sindhi speakers in the 1981 sample. They speak Baluchi at home and operate as a monolithic ethnic bloc in local politics. However, this Baluch bloc has generally joined with the "original" Sindhis in intraprovincial rivalry with the Muhajirs, the Pashtuns, and the Punjabis.

The concept of a Sindhi–Baluch federation has a strong appeal for both groups, especially on economic grounds. Baluchistan has more natural resources than Sind, and Sind has an industrial base that Baluchistan lacks, together with a thriving, established port in Karachi. The case for a federation is also based on the overlap of Sindhi and Baluch populations in the border districts and their resulting interpenetration. Moreover, given the infusion of Baluch, Pashtuns, Punjabis, and Muhajirs throughout Sind, supporters of a federation contend that the idea of a separate Sindhi political identity is unworkable. In this view, the absence of ethnic homogeneity in the province makes it difficult in practical terms to establish a Sindhi-majority province within Pakistan or an independent Sindhi-majority state, just as it is difficult to create a separate Baluch-majority state in the complex, multiethnic environment of Baluchistan, with its continuing influx of Pashtun and Punjabi settlers. The federation proposal is depicted as a way for Sindhis and Baluch to neutralize the power of their ethnic adversaries in some form of common legislature. Such a federation, it is argued, is a more practical objective than the proposed "Confederation of the Indus," uniting Pashtuns with Sindhis and Baluch.[15]

Elements of a Constitutional Compromise

American interests in Pakistan would be served best by a compromise—between moderate leaders of the minorities, who favor the continuance of Pakistan but wish to see it restructured along the lines of a confederation or a looser federation, and moderates in the Punjabi-Muhajir elites, who recognize the need for constitutional adjustments to forestall Balkanization. Is such a compromise possible, and if so, what would be its essential elements?

Federation or Confederation?

Proposals for a looser federation were advanced by the influential Sindhi leader G.M. Jatoi, a former Bhutto confidante, who rejected a confederation as "unworkable" but called for the devolution of more powers to the provinces than those stipulated in the 1973 constitution. When I interviewed him in 1984, Jatoi said that the provinces should have all powers except defense, foreign affairs, foreign trade, railways, post and telegraph, and currency. Taxes collected by the central government should not be allocated as at present—solely on a population basis, which favors Punjab; instead, only half should be allocated on a population basis, while the rest should be distributed in accordance with the amount collected in each province. As the provinces have equal representation in the Senate, even under the 1973 constitution, he argued, the upper chamber should be given greater powers. For example, he said, the Senate, rather than the president or prime minister, should have the power to dissolve a provincial legislature or declare an emergency. But he bemoaned the fact that separatism is "growing very fast." He went on:

> People who see things the way I do, who stand for the continuance of Pakistan, are losing out. A new generation of leadership will take over based on provincial nationalism. The onus lies on the Punjabi bureaucracy and the army to show greater vision. The survival of Pakistan depends on parliamentary democracy and greater autonomy.

The most articulate advocate of confederation, A. Hafeez Pirzada—former law minister in Bhutto's cabinet and also a Sindhi—sharply criticized Jatoi's taxation proposal. He said that the minority provinces could not have justice unless they had the power not only to determine which taxes would be levied but also to collect them. Another leading proponent of confederation, Baluch leader Ataullah Mengal, has demanded complete parity for Baluch, Pashtuns, Sindhis, and Punjabis in both chambers of the National Assembly as well as in civil service and military recruitment, irrespective of population disparities. Dissenting from this position, the late moderate Baluch leader Ghaus Bux Bizenjo called for parity only in the upper chamber, which suggests that Mengal's approach to the parity issue may prove to be negotiable. At the same time, all factions among the minorities give priority to radically upgraded representation in the civil service and the armed forces and view the Punjabi concessions made in this respect to date as tokenism.

Constitutional Safeguards

Jatoi's suggestion that the power to dissolve provincial assemblies should rest with the Senate reflects a widespread desire for constitutional safeguards to prevent the central government from arbitrarily removing an elected provincial government, as Bhutto did in 1973. In a 1980 memorandum to the Zia government, Bizenjo urged reinforcement of the articles providing for equal representation of the four provinces in the Senate and a concomittant strengthening of the Senate's powers, as the precondition for an effective federalism in Pakistan. By balancing the control exercised by the more populous provinces in the lower chamber of the National Assembly, the memorandum said, such a reform would make central intervention acceptable under specified circumstances. It suggested that Islamabad could then be empowered to take over a province if "expressly authorized to do so for a specified and limited purpose, and for a specified and limited period of time" by a two-thirds Senate majority.

Room for Bargaining

In my view, the issue of safeguards against arbitrary central intervention is a nonnegotiable one for the minorities, although there is room for bargaining concerning the precise division of powers between Islamabad and the provinces. What the minorities are seeking is both the substance of autonomy and the feeling of autonomy. The psychological factor explains their emphasis not only on the safeguards issue but also on the need for a linguistic redemarcation of provincial boundaries—which would give each minority majority control over a specific territory—together with constitutional recognition of their respective ethnic identities. Most minority leaders demand recognition of four distinct "nationalities" in Pakistan—a concept that is repugnant to many Pakistanis, who believe in a monolithic Pakistani nationality. However, some minority leaders go further, demanding that the constitution include the right of secession. These leaders cite the 1940 Lahore Resolution, in which the Muslim League had foreshadowed its demand for Pakistan. Envisaging two Muslim states in the subcontinent following the departure of the British, the resolution called for a regrouping of "geographically contiguous . . . areas in which the Moslems are numerically in a majority, as in the northwestern zones of India . . . to constitute independent states *in which the constituent units shall be autonomous and sovereign.*[16]

For many Punjabi and Muhajir moderates, minority demands for greater representation in the civil service, the armed forces, and the National Assembly are relatively easy to accept. Increased autonomy for the provinces and safeguards against arbitrary central intervention are more controversial issues, and even the moderates are greatly disturbed by the extent of minority demands for economic autonomy. It is in the economic sphere that a constitutional compromise is likely to be most elusive, regardless of Pakistan's future political coloration. The issue of economic autonomy comes to a focus on two key minority demands: for larger royalties on natural resources and for limitations on the role of outside entrepreneurs and central government corporations in exploiting these resources. Compromise may be possible over the terms of royalty arrangements and over proposals for joint development ventures in which the provinces and the central government share the profit. But is is unlikely that any Islamabad regime would surrender the residual authority of the central government over the exploitation of natural resources in all parts of Pakistan.

In the final analysis, the possibility of a constitutional compromise in Pakistan is inseparably linked with the overall course of the struggle for democratization. The 1985 elections gave the Zia ul-Haq regime a limited civilian base and resulted in significant liberalization of the press and political activity for a three-year period. In early 1988, however, when Prime Minister Mohammed Khan Junejo attempted to challenge Zia's power on foreign policy and defense issues, Zia nullified the election by dissolving the National Assembly and reasserting unlimited personal authority. His successor as president, Ghulam Ishaque Kahn, inherited both Zia's arbitrary executive powers and the powerful military intelligence machinery that underpinned Zia's rule. The 1988 and 1990 elections were conducted under the auspices of the same quasi-authoritarian power structure that had governed the country during the Zia decade, with the Army exercising decisive residual power behind the scenes. Thus, when Benazir Bhutto, like Junejo, transgressed the bounds of civilian authority acceptable to the Army, she was removed.

As in the Zia period, the Army in Pakistan is prepared to share power with cooperative civilian political forces, permitting meaningful parliamentary debate on most issues and a significant degree of press freedom. But the Punjabi and Muhajir elites that dominate both the Army and allied civilian political groups remained firmly opposed in 1990 to constitutional revisions that would give recognition to minority ethnic identities or to minority ethnic demands for provincial autonomy.

Note

a. Including the Sindhi-speaking Baluch, domiciled in Sind for centuries and largely absorbed into a composite Sindhi bloc socially and politically, this figure becomes 9.85 million—that is, 11.77 percent of the total population of Pakistan, cited earlier.

References

1. For 1961 data, covering the areas then constituting West Pakistan see *Census of Pakistan: Population 1961* (Karachi: Ministry of Home and Kashmir Affairs, 1961), Statement 7-B, p. IV-46.

2. *Main Finding of 1981 Population Census* (Islamabad: Population Census Organization, Statistical Division, Government of Pakistan, December 6, 1983), p. 13, table 4(c).

3. For the best historical discussion of the "Daptar Shair," together with textual extracts, see M. Longworth Dames, *Popular Poetry of the Baloches,* Vol. 1 (London: Royal Asiatic Society), pp. 2ff. See, also, Mir Khuda Bakhsh Bijarani Marri Baloch, *Searchlight on Baloches and Baluchistan* (Karachi: Royal Book Company, 1974), p. 58.

4. *Azad Baluchistan,* London, July 1982, p. 1.

5. Yuri V. Gankovsky, *Narody Pakistane: Etnicheskai Istoriia* [*The Peoples of Pakistan: An Ethnic History*] (Moscow: Nauka Publishing House, 1964), p. 225. An English edition was issued by the same publisher in 1971. See, also, Yuri V. Gankovsky, *Natsionl'nyi Vopros i Natsional'nye Dvizhenii v Pakistane* [*The National Question and National Movements in Pakistan*], reprint of the 1967 edition (Moscow: Nauka Publishing House, 1977), pp. 206, 250.

6. Robert G. Wirsing found that the highest literacy rate in eight of the nine districts in Pakistani Baluchistan was 7.7 percent. See his "South Asia: The Baluch Frontier Tribes of Pakistan," in Robert G. Wirsing, ed., *Protection of Ethnic Minorities: Comparative Perspectives* (New York: Pergamon, 1982), p. 18. Alvin Moore, South Asia specialist of the Library of Congress, estimated that there were 123,000 literates in Baluchi in 1981. See his "Publishing in Pushto, Baluchi and Brahui, Part 2," in *South Asia: Library Notes and Queries* (Chicago: University of Chicago Library, South Asia Reference Center, March 1980), p. 3. *Census of Pakistan: Population 1961,* Vol. 2, p. IV-94, reported 87,000 literates in Baluchistan province. The 1972 census did not contain comparable tables.

7. Affidavit to the Supreme Court of Pakistan, 1975, p. 133.

8. A.R. Pazhwak, *Pushtunistan* (Kabul: Foreign Ministry, 1956), pp. 48, 50.

9. Richard Tapper, "Tribal Society and Its Enemies," *Royal Anthropological Institute News* (London), October 1979, p. 6.

10. Akbar S. Ahmed, *Millenium and Charisma Among Pathans: A Critical Essay in Social Anthropology* (London: Routledge and Kegan Paul, 1976), pp. 52–55. This is addressed, in part, to Frederik Barth, *Political Leadership Among Swat Pathans* (London: University of London, Athlone Press, 1959), especially pp. 18–28, 133–34.

11. Stephen Rittenberg, "Agrarian Change and the Rise of Nationalism in the Peshawar Valley," Paper submitted to the Southern Asia Seminar, Columbia University, New York, March 10, 1981.

12. Fazul Sulleman, "Sind's Agony," *Frontier Guardian* (Peshawar), August 26, 1972, p. 15.

13. Mazhar Yusuf, "Political Undercurrents in Sind Today, *Dawn,* November 22, 1978.

14. G.M. Sayed, *Pakistan Hani Tuttan Ghurqi* [*Time for Pakistan to Cease to Exist*] (New Delhi: Lajpat Rai, Sindhu Nagar, 1987). This is cited in a useful survey of the Sind scene in early 1987 in Dastgir Bhatti, "Sind Scenario" (a three-part series), *The Muslim* (Islamabad), June 22, 23, 24, 1987.

15. For the "Confederation of the Indus" proposal, see Sindhi–Baluch–Pashtun Front, *Declaration,* London, April 18, 1985, signed by Khalid Leghari, A. Hafeez Pirzada, Mumtaz Ali Bhutto, Ataullah Mengal, and Afzal Bangash. See, also, an earlier proposal for a confederation embracing Punjab: Mumtaz Ali Bhutto, *Confederation,* London, January 1983.

16. Significantly, this was cited in Zulfiqar Ali Bhutto, "Pakistan Builds Anew," *Foreign Affairs* 51, no. 3 (1973): 545. See, also, Muhammad Iqbal's 1930 proposal for a "loose federation of all India," in Sir Reginald Coupland, *India: A Restatement* (London: Oxford University Press, 1945), p. 189.

19
Multiethnic Conflict and Peacemaking: The Case of Assam

Walter K. Andersen

On August 15, 1985—India's Independence Day—Prime Minister Rajiv Gandhi announced, during his message from the Red Fort in Dehli, the signing of an accord ending seven years of antiforeigner agitation in the northeastern state of Assam. This was the second major accord (the first was in the state of Punjab a month earlier) that he had worked out to defuse the ethnic crises he had identified as his major domestic problem when he assumed power after his mother's assassination in October 1984. Problems have appeared in both accords, because neither fully resolved the fundamental causes of discontent. The antiforeigner stir in Assam was fueled by fears that the Assamese would become a minority within their own state, but the accord did not provide for a mechanism to identify illegal immigration, and almost no one has been deported since the accord was signed. In the long run, the Assamese still face the prospect of becoming a minority in their own state because of the potential for continued emigration from overpopulated Bangladesh.[1]

The Background of an Agitation

India is one of the world's most ethnically diverse countries, and ethnic agitation in India is not a new development. An upsurge of such agitation in the 1950s led the government of Jawaharlal Nehru in 1956 to create linguistic states to satisfy language groups that felt disadvantaged by being linked administratively with other language groups. However, Nehru's administrative reforms did not eliminate the problem of ethnic discontent. Along the margins of several states remained areas with overlapping linguistic groups, such as the Marathi-speaking population in the Belgaum district of the state of Karnataka. Migration to India's expanding urban centers has resulted in substantial linguistic minorities in almost every major city. Moreover, continuing migration from neighboring countries, as occurred in the case of Assam, has created growing linguistic minorities in contiguous Indian states.

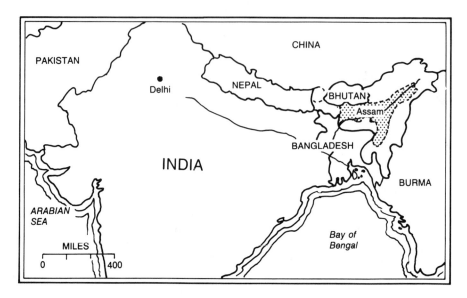

Figure 19–1. India: The State of Assam

Although Nehru's reforms were successful in defusing tensions in most places, in Assam, the new arrangement did not assuage the fears of the Assamese-speakers, who barely formed a majority in the ethnically diverse state. They were afraid of continuing migration from the neighboring Indian state of West Bengal and from Bengali-speaking East Pakistan (now Bangladesh). For almost a century, the Assamese have struggled to assert their political control over the Brahmaputra Valley and the surrounding highland area, and they feared that continued illegal immigration threatened their political domination of Assam.

The Brahmaputra area has always been ethnically complex. When the British took control of it in the 1820s, it was a patchwork of tribal groups ruled over by the Ahoms, an ethnic group of Thai origin that adopted the Sanskritic culture of the Gangetic plains. They spoke an Indo-Aryan language and had adopted the major tenets of Hinduism. The Ahom kingdom straddled the Brahmaputra River, and by the early nineteenth century, the population along this river was already beginning to think of itself as a separate people. However, in the surrounding highlands, tribal groups were not assimilated, and the British, like the earlier Ahom rulers, barely exercised control over these areas. Sanskritic culture had only weakly penetrated there, and a major competitive influence came from the West—through Christian missionaries, many of them American Baptists. The British were apprehensive that the missionary societies might weld members of the tribes into cohesive and perhaps politically troublesome groups. They sought to restrict the entrance of missionaries and even refused permission for them to work in certain areas.

The British Raj added to the ethnic complexity of Assam by employing Bengali-speaking caste-Hindus to staff the lower levels of the bureaucracy. Moreover, Bengalis, both Muslim and Hindu, began to migrate to Assam to take advantage of new business and professional opportunities and to farm new tracts of land cleared from the forests. At the end of the century, the development of tea estates attracted laborers from Nepal and the Hindi-speaking areas of British India, far to the west. But the bulk of migration from the outside continued to come from the province of Bengal. Only about 40 percent of the people living in what is today Assam listed themselves as Assamese-speakers at the time of the last census prior to independence in 1947. No other area in India has experienced a similar surge of migration from other places.

When independence came, the Assamese were already worried about being dominated by Bengali-speakers, the next largest ethnic group. A disproportionately high percentage of businesses and administrative posts was controlled by Hindu Bengalis who had earlier migrated to the state. Between 1947 and 1950, several hundred thousand Hindu Bengalis left what was then East Pakistan and came to Assam in the wake of the partition of British India.

The Assamese political elite, drawn from the small but growing urban middle class, sought to expand the Assamese-speaking population by assimilating other groups into their ethnic pool. Indeed, the Assamese in the nineteenth and twentieth centuries have demonstrated considerable success in assimilating tribesmen who lived in the Brahmaputra plains as well as many Bengali-speaking Muslim peasants who moved from their overpopulated homeland to the relatively open spaces of Assam. The largely low-caste Muslim peasantry had little in common with the caste-Hindu Bengalis, and they had no important symbolic reason to remain loyal to the Bengali language. A major political proposal on the Assamese political agenda, therefore, was insistence that Assamese be the sole language of administration and education—a demand vehemently resisted by Hindu Bengalis.

This effort at enlarging the Assamese population was also resisted by tribal groups living in the mountains around the Brahmaputra Valley. Christian missionaries had introduced education to these tribal areas, and the educated elites among some tribal groups began to demand separate states of their own. Since 1947, three tribal states have been carved out of Assam: Meghalaya, Mizoram, and Nagaland. Other areas of the northeast—Arunachal Pradesh, Manipur, and Tripura—which were recommended for inclusion in Assam by the States Reorganization Committee in the mid-1950s, have become separate political entities. Even now, some tribal groups in Assam continue to demand their own states.

The Bengali-speakers, especially caste-Hindu Bengalis, were the largest and most politically sophisticated ethnic minority, and they resisted assimilation. They had taken a leading role in organizing the Congress party, the country's major political institution, in the state, and they were a major part of the ethnic coalition within the party that ruled Assam from independence in 1947 to 1977, when the Congress party lost power at the national level. This coalition included the Ahoms, the traditional Assamese aristrocacy, Assamese Muslims, members of tribal groups, and illegal Bengali-speaking migrants—mainly Muslim peasants—from what is now Bangladesh. At the time of partition, Assamese Hindus looked at Bengali Hindus as allies in the effort to remain outside a Muslim-majority Pakistan.[a] But after partition, these two Hindu groups increasingly became estranged. The Assamese demanded the exclusive use of their language in education and administration, whereas the Bengali Hindus supported a policy according equal status to both languages.

The Congress party governments in the state tried out a series of compromises affirming the rights of both language groups, but the growing Assamese Hindu middle class, who increasingly perceived these compromises as endangering the cultural future of the Assamese, began to desert the Congress party. The issue that mobilized them politically was the continued illegal migration from Bangladesh. They feared becoming a minority within their own state.

Although those who migrated from Bangladesh after 1951 were technically illegal, the dominant Congress party leadership came to look on them as a vote bank of considerable importance. The number of illegal migrants since 1951 from what is now Bangladesh is subject to much debate, but a commonly used figure is 3 million to 5 million (out of a total population of about 20 million in 1981). The organizations backing the antiforeigner movement estimate that there are 4.4 million to 5 million illegal migrants, or about one-fourth of the population.[2] Whatever the precise figure, the numbers were significant enough to make illegal migration a burning political issue.[b] The Assamese were infuriated that no real effort had been made to remove the illegal migrants—except in 1965, when expulsions were carried out in the wake of the 1965 war with Pakistan.

A Time of Troubles

The continued migration from Bangladesh after 1971 convinced many Assamese that they would soon become a permanent minority in their own state. Indeed, they were already a minority in the state's southern Cacher district and in many of the urban areas along the Brahmaputra River. The migration was sufficiently large and concentrated so that there was often little need for the migrants to abandon their own language. In addition, the predominance of non-Assamese in the state's economy hindered assimilation. The Assamese were not the only "native" group that was concerned by the continued migration into the state. Various tribal groups also became alarmed as more of the land they considered communal tribal land was taken over by the enterprising Bengali-speaking peasantry.

The magnitude of what the Assamese and Assam's tribal groups see as a problem only partly shows up in the census statistics. The ethnic division by language, according to the 1971 census,[3] was as follows:

Assamese, 60.89 percent

Bengali, 19.71 percent

Hindi, 5.42 percent

Bodo (tribal), 3.65 percent

Nepali, 2.39 percent

The remaining 8 percent consists mainly of various small tribal groups.

The Assamese figure is inflated because a substantial part of the Muslim Bengali-speaking migrants from Bangladesh tend to list themselves as Assamese-speakers. They have done so for two reasons: (1) to protect themselves from possible deportation and (2) to reject identification with the Hindu-dominated Bengali-speaking group. If this is taken into consideration, the Assamese figure drops—perhaps as much as 10 to 12 percent—whereas the Bengali total rises to 30 to 32 percent. Of the approximately 50 percent estimated to be genuinely Assamese-speaking, some 7 to 8 percent are Muslims, almost all of whom were originally Bengali-speaking and assimilated in varying degrees into the Assamese ethnic population. The Assamese consequently look with trepidation at the prospect of continuing migration from Bangladesh, with its population of 100 million and growth rate of over 2.5 percent a year. They observe that the neighboring Indian state of Tripura, one-third Bengali-speaking in 1947, was by the late 1970s about two-thirds Bengali-speaking and dominated politically by the Bengalis.

The Assamese fears were voiced most effectively by the large Assamese student population, the product of Assamese-language universities established after independence to satisfy the demand for entry into the middle class. However, there have not been enough white-collar jobs to absorb the growing number of Assamese graduates from secondary schools and colleges. The problem of unemployment has been exacerbated because few Assamese seek jobs outside their own state. Indeed, Assamese have one of the lowest rates of migration to other states of any ethnic group in India.

The students increasingly blamed the lack of job opportunities on the overrepresentation of Hindu Bengali-speakers in the bureaucracy and the professions. They demanded job quotas, like those that commonly have been granted in India to other groups considered historically underprivileged. The students also wanted to restrict the rights of outsiders to own land and to establish businesses. But both sets of demands require political power, and many middle-class Assamese fear that their political power is being diminished because the large Bengali populations to the west and south are attracted to Assam. The student activists—unlike the youthful Sikh radicals in Punjab—did not advocate secession, even during the most violent phase of the agitation in the early 1980s. Instead, they demonstrated for causes that were within acceptable political parameters: constitutional issues involving illegal immigration and the principle of linguistic states, which had earlier been accepted as the norm in India. They utilized Mahatma Gandhi's tactics of nonviolent disobedience.

The language issue erupted after the 1972 decision of the Academic Council of Gauhati University to permit students to take their examinations in English and Bengali as well as in Assamese. In response, the All Assam Students Union (AASU) held demonstrations. (The AASU was to play a major role in mobilizing support during the early 1980s to remove the names of illegal immigrants from the electoral rolls. It had widespread support from ethnic Assamese and members of tribal groups residing on the Brahmaputra plains.) The late Prime Minister Indira Gandhi intervened personally to get the state leaders of her party to come up with proposals to defuse the tension. As a result, the state's chief minister promised that Assamese would be a compulsory subject in all non-Assamese secondary schools. The demonstrations were called off, but Assamese militants were not completely satisfied. Some militants interpreted the promise as the first step in creating the feared multilingual state. Some non-Assamese also had misgivings with the decision; they saw it as a move toward the forced adoption of Assamese culture.

After a period of comparative quiet, in June 1979, the AASU sponsored a twelve-hour general strike to demand the "detection, disenfranchisement, and deportation" of illegal aliens. The disintegration of the national Janata government in mid-1979 provided the students with an opportunity to address the problem more forcefully. Still more opportunities were provided by the collapse of the state's Janata party government in September 1979; the catalyst was the prospect of new elections using old electoral rolls. The political uncertainty of late 1979 thus revived the effort to remove illegal voters from the rolls. A protracted series of strikes and demonstrations gripped the state. Central rule (that is, Indian government control) was declared just prior to the December 1979 general elections that were necessitated by the collapse of the Janata party government in New Delhi.

Unable to get the government to purge the electoral rolls—the Congress party had benefited from vote banks of illegal immigrants—the students called for a boycott of the December 1979 general elections. The boycott was far more successful than they had anticipated; only two of the fourteen parliamentary seats, both from Bengali-dominated districts, were able to elect representatives to the central parliament.

The AASU utilized still another, more politically powerful tactic to achieve its goal: It called for a strike to cut off the local oil production that provides India with about 20 percent of its domestic production. With widespread support from Assamese workers in the oil fields and Assamese members of the bureaucracy and police, the strike was a success. The government's decision to call in troops to break up the strike only intensified support for the AASU.

The growing Assamese support for the boycott and the strike also touched off a reaction among the large Hindu Bengali-speaking population. Recognizing a threat to their position, Bengali-speaking students organized the All Assam Minority Students Union (AAMSU) to oppose the AASU demands. Clashes between the two groups further polarized the political situation in the state.

Attempts at a Resolution: Negotiations and Politics

The second government of Indira Gandhi, which came to power in January 1980, adopted a two-track approach to cope with the Assam problem: negotiate with the AASU (and the AAMSU) and cobble together a Congress government in the state that might reunite the traditional coalition that had ruled Assam since independence (that is, Bengali-speaking Hindus, some Assamese Muslims, illegal migrants, Ahoms, and some plains tribal groups).[4] Even without the Assamese Hindus, these various minority groups had sufficient votes to retain power if they remained together. The student leaders of the AASU, who had maintained control of the Assamese movement, sought to undermine this coalition by seeking allies outside the Assamese Hindu group, a tactic that was relatively successful. This was possible because illegal immigration was considered a threat to several of the constituents of the traditional political coalition that had supported the Congress party.

Defining precisely who is an illegal immigrant was the key issue in the drawn-out negotiations initiated by Prime Minister Gandhi. The AASU leaders demanded that all illegal migrants who had arrived after 1951 be deleted from the electoral rolls and deported. The government argued that this was impossible, because on March 24, 1971, the Indian government had signed an agreement with Mujib Rahman, leader of the movement for an independent Bangladesh, in which India promised to accept all immigrants who had come to India prior to that date. Prime Minister Gandhi was head of the government that had signed the agreement.

The Indian and Assamese student negotiators quickly agreed to accept those immigrants who had come between 1951 and 1961 as legal residents. They also agreed that those who had arrived after March 24, 1971, would be defined as illegal and thus subject to being removed from the electoral rolls and deported. However, they could not agree on the fate of those who had come between 1961 and March 24, 1971. Twenty-three inconclusive meetings on this subject were held between 1980 and 1982. Neither side seemed ready to compromise on the contested ten-year period.

While these negotiations were taking place, the Gandhi government in New Delhi tried to put together a state government for Assam that would reestablish the traditional governing coalition. In late 1980, a Congress I government,[c] led by Anwara Taimur, an Assamese Muslim, was patched together with defectors from other parties, but it fell apart the next June. After a spell of central rule, another Congress I government was formed in January 1982 under an Assamese Hindu. He belonged to the Ahoms, a group that was a potential weak link in the traditional ruling coalition that had politically dominated the state since India's independence. This government lasted two months. There was a second spell of central rule, and in late 1982, new Dehli dissolved the assembly and called for new state elections.

These political moves not only failed to achieve Gandhi's goal of defusing the anti-immigrant stir but they also further polarized the situation. The series of short-lived state governments removed officials suspected of helping the AASU. The Assamese saw this purging as a veiled attempt to reduce the role of the "sons of the soil"—as the Assamese are often called—in their own government.

In this charged atmosphere, the militants were infuriated by the refusal to revise the contested electoral rolls. The decision to base the February 1983 state elections on the 1979 electoral rolls—which had not been purged of illegal migrants—was perceived as a challenge to the central demand of the Assamese. The rolls were also flawed because they did not include voters who had come of voting age after 1979. Violence mounted, straining the viability of the Congress coalition in the state as well as the coalition of groups that the AASU had put together.

Arun Shourie, one of India's leading investigative journalists, toured Assam at the time and noted that the almost-total breakdown of order set groups against each other.[5] He reported, for example, that in the town of Nelli, where more than a thousand people died, Lalung tribesmen had killed Bengali Muslims; in Kokrajbar, plains Boros fought Bengali Hindus; in Gohpur, Boros fought Assamese Hindus. His litany of interethnic conflict covered almost every ethnic group in the state.

The violence made a farce of the 1983 elections. In 78 of the 126 constituencies, one-third or less of the people voted; the vote was so negligible in 14 constituencies that the results had to be voided; and in some strongly Assamese constitutencies, the polling was below 1 percent.[6] The Congress I party won control of the state assembly again, but it was a hollow victory. The new government of Hiteshwar Saikia, another Ahom, lacked credibility.

The AASU also had its problems. The intercommunal fighting strained the coalition it had tried to put together. Assamese Muslim supporters charged that the AASU was beginning to show a definite Hindu bias, pointing to the disproportionate number of Muslims killed during the rioting. The Bodos, the largest plains tribal group, demanded separate autonomous districts and wanted their own language to be written in Roman script. This demonstration of separateness from Assamese culture not only undermined the likelihood of assimilation into Assamese culture but also, of more importance over the short term, undermined the political ties of the Bodos with the Assamese coalition. In an obvious effort to weaken the student coalition, the government patronized the major Bodo cultural organization.

In the wake of the 1983 elections, the AASU sought to hold together its coalition of groups by calling for a statewide convention. Assamese Muslims and tribal groups were given a more prominent role in the movement. In an effort to appeal to Nepalis and Hindi-speaking Bihari tea estate workers, the AASU did not call for the tea estate workers to join its strike calls in the state. The government of Chief Minister Saikia also sought to attract Assamese support by (1) announcing plans to stop the continued movement of illegals from Bangladesh (for example, the construction of a fence along the border); (2) changing the official spellings of place names, to make them correspond more closely with Assamese pronunciation; and (3) creating new districts, to provide more administrative jobs to the Assamese middle class. But this was not enough to defuse the crisis, because the core demand—the removal of illegals from the electoral rolls—was not addressed. Hence, the leaders of the antiforeigner movement refused to consider the Saikia government legitimate. It had been elected on the basis of the flawed electoral rolls.

In 1984, Prime Minister Indira Gandhi resumed negotiations, and they were continued by her son Rajiv when he came to power after her assassination in late 1984. A compromise on the key question of who was an illegal migrant was successfully negotiated by Rajiv Gandhi in the August 1985 accord.[d] The major provisions of the compromise were as follows:

All those who had immigrated prior to January 1, 1966, would be considered legal entrants, with full voting and residency rights.

Illegal migrants who came between January 1, 1966, and March 24, 1971, would be deleted from the electoral rolls but would retain residency rights, so that the 1971 Gandhi–Rahman agreement would not be violated. Parliament passed legislation revising the 1955 Citizenship Act so that this unusual arrangement would be legal. After a ten-year period, this group would be permitted to register to vote.

Those who had arrived after March 24, 1971, would be deleted from the electoral rolls and deported.

The state assembly would be dissolved, and new elections would be held in December 1985.

The Gandhi government quickly moved to honor the agreement. As already mentioned, special citizenship legislation was passed, and almost 700,000 people were reportedly deleted from the electoral rolls. The AASU closely monitored the steps taken to modify the electoral rolls, and the process was a kind of celebration. However, no real effort was made to deport immigrants defined as illegal in the accord.

A New Party Is Established

The AASU, which had not functioned as a political party, had to decide how it would approach the forthcoming state assembly elections. The long-dominant Congress party was discredited in the eyes of the AASU. Rather than joining any of the other existing national parties, AASU leaders began laying the groundwork for a separate regional party in late 1984, several months before the accord was signed. After the signing of the accord, a new party, the Asom Gana Parishad (AGP)—the Assamese People's party—was established by the AASU's student leaders. By taking this step, the AASU joined a growing trend to regionalize political parties in India. The large Assamese student community quickly established a grass-roots organization and employed Assamese symbols to mobilize support. Like the modification of the electoral rolls, the campaign was a festival of ethnic pride.

Another new party—the United Minorities Front (UMF)—sought to unite all "minorities"—immigrant Muslims, Bengali Hindus, Assamese Muslims, Nepalis, and tribal groups—to oppose the implementation of the accord. The results suggest that it succeeded only in attracting significant support from immigrant Muslims and some Assamese Muslims. Most Bengali-speaking Hindus stayed with the Congress I party, and the tribal groups split their votes among the AGP and various small tribal parties.

There had never before been such a high turnout as there was in the December 1985 state elections;[7] over 85 percent of the electorate voted. The AGP won 64 of the 126 seats in the assembly (though only 35.17 percent of the vote). The Congress I party won 25 seats, with 23.43 percent of the vote. The UMF won 17 seats, with 11.09 percent of the vote. The victory of the AGP owes much to its ability to elicit support from Assamese Muslims and various tribal groups, besides the core Assamese Hindu constituency. It even scored some victories in constituencies dominated by Bengali Muslims, suggesting that Bengali Muslims might be reverted to their traditional pattern of aligning themselves with the dominant political party as a way of enhancing their interests.[8]

As the results demonstrate, a reuniting of immigrant Muslims with the Congress I party would virtually put it on a par with the ruling AGP if the Congress I party could maintain the support it received in the December 1985 election. Consequently, if the AGP lost some of its ethnic support, the traditional political coalition that governed the state between 1947 and 1985 could reassert itself. In turn, that might revive the historical Assamese fear of losing control of their own state.

The Deportation Question

Of more immediate danger to the accord is its silence on how to identify illegal immigrants who are subject to deportation. The central government committed itself only to strengthening the administrative machinery to achieve this objective. Not surprisingly, almost no illegal immigrants have been deported. Even if illegal immigrants had been identified, it is doubtful that India would deport them. Bangladesh says that there are no illegal immigrants and refuses even to consider taking any back. India is not likely to try to push them across the border and is clearly reluctant to apply pressure on Dacca to change its mind—a step that would surely cause major bilateral problems and would be upsetting to India's other South Asian neighbors. Moreover, other Indian states will not accept large numbers of migrants, most of whom are poor farmers. West Bengal itself is already overcrowded, and other states would be reluctant to accept people of a different cultural background. The Asom Jatiyababi Yuva Chattra Parishad (Assamese Youth Student Organization), the student wing of the AGP, organized demonstrations in April 1987 that pointed the accusing finger at both the center and the state for not carrying out the intent of the accord.[9]

Perhaps in response to the demands to carry out the accord, the new Assamese chief minister, Prafulla Kumar Mahanta, called a meeting of the leading regional parties of the northeast in April 1987, and the group proposed that the colonial British "inner line" restrictions be applied to the whole northeast.[10] That is, acquisition of land by nonresidents would be prohibited, business and employment opportunities of nonresidents would be restricted, and all nonresidents would be required to register.

These recommendations reflect a fear generally felt throughout the northeast of being swamped by Bengali-speakers. In short, the "sons of the soil" of the northeast all fear going the way of Tripura, which now has a Bengali-speaking majority and is dominated politically by the Bengalis. Perhaps the only lasting solution would be to promote the economic development of Bangladesh so that there would not be such an incentive for Bangladeshis to migrate to the relatively underpopulated areas of northeastern India.

Nonetheless, the new AGP leadership has shown that it is willing to work out compromises within India's constitutional framework; this enhances the possibility of an accommodation among the various ethnic groups of the state. Furthermore, accommodation builds on the traditional Assamese effort to reach beyond itself to integrate different ethnic groups. India's democratic political system thus provides a framework for the Assamese leadership to seek ways of creatively integrating the demands of cultural survival with the imperatives of a culturally diverse society. However, the accommodative effort might be sidetracked if there is another surge of illegal immigration that threatens to alter the present ethnic distribution.

Notes

a. The Muslim League of prepartition India demanded inclusion of Assam within the new state of Pakistan.

b. Myron Weiner noted that had the Assamese population grown at the same rate as the rest of India between 1901 and 1971, the population in 1971 would have been 7.6 million instead of 15 million. It is likely, he suggested, that immigrants make up for the difference. Based on a projection using the 1891 census, Weiner proposed that immigrants and their descendants likely constitute a majority of Assam's population. See his *Sons of the Soil: Migration and Ethnic Conflict in India* (Princeton, NJ: Princeton University Press, 1978), p. 80.

c. Since the second split of the Congress party in 1978, the segment led by Indira Gandhi has been referred to as the Congress I (for Indira) party.

d. Not all constituent units of the AASU backed the accord. Moreover, some political groups that opposed the AASU's activities were also disturbed by the accord. For example, India's Communist Party of India-Marxist, which governs the neighboring Indian state of West Bengal, argued that the accord violated New Delhi's March 1971 agreement with the leadership of the movement fighting for an independent Bangladesh.

References

1. For discussions of the problems regarding the implementation of the Assam accord, see the *Hindu* (Madras), March 5, 1987; and *Times of India* (Bombay), May 5, 1987.

2. Figures noted in Sanjib Baruah, "Immigration, Ethnic Conflict and Political Turmoil—Assam, 1979–1985," *Asian Survey* 26, no. 11 (November 1986): 1189.

3. *Census of India, 1971, Series 3: Assam, Part 1-A, General Report* (New Delhi: Government of India, Controller of Publications, 1979), p. 80.

4. For a comprehensive discussion of New Delhi's negotiating tactics, see Sanjib Baruah, "State Responses to Ethnic Demands: Exacerbation and Resolution of the Assam Conflict," Paper presented at the President's Forum of the University of Pennsylvania on Ethnic Conflict in India and Sri Lanka, December 8, 1986.

5. See Arun Shourie, "Assam Elections: Can Democracy Survive Them?" *India Today,* May 31, 1983, p. 57.

6. Jaswant Singh, "Assam's Crisis of Citizenship," *Asian Survey* 24, no. 10 (October 1984): 1067.

7. For a review of the December 1985 state elections in Assam, see Sanjib Baruah, "Lessons of Assam," *Economic and Political Weekly,* February 15, 1986, pp. 282–84. A good statistical analysis of the elections may be found in *India Today,* January 15, 1986, pp. 22–35.

8. Baruah, "Immigration, Ethnic Conflict and Political Turmoil," pp. 1204–5.

9. For an account of the growing discontent regarding the implementation of the accord, see *Times of India* (Bombay), May 5, 1987.

10. *Ibid.*

IV
Sudan in the
African Context

The Sudan section is unique in that its lead essay is by one of the most thoughtful and enlightened statesmen ever produced in that country. Francis Mading Deng worked intimately with former President Nimeiri to develop concepts, language, and policies that would respect and reflect the basic human worth and rights of all Sudanese—northern and southern, Arab and black, Muslim, Christian, and animist. Tragically, the same Nimeiri who had the wisdom to appoint the outstanding black Sudanese Dinka moved under what he perceived as intense Muslim fundamentalist political pressure to outdo the fundamentalists in demogogic extremism. Deng now lives in the United States but remains, as his essay will show, a significant leader for Sudan.

Nelson Kasfir and John Voll easily match the excellence of their colleagues in this volume in knowledge, sensitivity, and erudition—Kasfir from the pan-Sudan and also southern perspective and Voll with his special expertise in Islam and Muslim politics in the north.

John Paden provides great detail on Nigeria's experience with the redistribution and redirection of actual and potential ethnic conflict in that huge country—which, like Malaysia, is a favorite laboratory for the academic specialists in this volume. His essay is of permanent value.

The Zimbabwe case, reviewed by Barry Schutz, has many of the elements of conflict combined with imaginative constitution drafting that are seen in other cases in this book. The case also reveals a great deal of continual "negotiation" between Robert Mugabe and Joshua Nkomo, who—to their and Zimbabwe's credit—have managed to overcome their ethnically based differences.

20

The Identity Factor in
the Sudanese Conflict

Francis Mading Deng

Most people who are familiar with the war that has been raging intermittently in Sudan since independence think of it in terms of the warring factions: the Arab Muslim north, two-thirds in land and population, and the remaining southern third, which is more indigenously African in race, religion, and culture, with a Christianized modern elite. What precisely do these labels mean? What factors count in determining the substantive content of an identity? In what ways do these identities influence the status of parties in political, economic, social, and cultural processes? And what changes could bring about a more equitable distribution of political and institutional power?

It is my thesis that the conflicting identities in Sudan are largely based on myths that have distorted the subjective and objective realities of Sudanese identities. These distortions have acquired a superficial form of reality, but probing more deeply into what the Sudanese really are, racially and culturally, shows that despite a diversity of subnational characteristics, there is a common national identity. That common identity could offer all Sudanese a sense of national belonging—a pride in being Sudanese of equal status—and could bring about commitment to that which unites and away from that which divides.

Promoting a common Sudanese identity implies an a priori commitment to unity, which some are beginning to question, both within and outside Sudan. But quite apart from the desirability of unity, the forces favoring the preservation of the colonial borders still seem overwhelmingly dominant within Africa and in the world at large. Until the obstacles to unity prove insurmountable and the political predisposition changes substantially in favor of revising the borders, intellectual and political energies have to be vested in finding ways that would foster the processes of unity, development, and nation-building within the present borders.

In the case of Sudan, this effort should begin with a critical reexamination of the prevailing notions of identity. Dividing Sudan into the Arab Muslim north and the African animist (and Christian) south, though valid as a rough generalization, is widely recognized as an oversimplification that can no longer be sustained.

Sudan is an example of a country in transition on matters of identity. Tribal or ethnic and religious identities still count for much, yet considerable changes have been made to diffuse these exclusive identities into a wider political concept of an inclusive national identity. Often, the exclusive and inclusive concepts coexist in varying degrees according to the context. In the north, being a Jaali, a Dongallawi, or a Shaigi has less significance in practical terms than being a Baggari, a Furrawi, or a Nubawi, whereas in the south, being a member of a tribal group remains considerably more significant. Depending on the context, the level of participation, and the issues at stake, one set of identifications may be viewed as either critical or insignificant. Thus, in north–south relations, internal differences among factions within the north or the south may be deemphasized to foster the greater unity of the group, whereas in internal conflicts, tribal differences become the dominant factor.

Sudan is clearly a nation at the crossroads, torn between the forces of secular democracy, modeled after Western concepts and institutions of government, and those that favor a more religiously based, racially and culturally hegemonic, and subnationally relativistic political system. At the crossroads, the nation is confronted with critical choices, which could lead to either national disintegration or unity and nation-building. Sudan arrived at this critical juncture as the result of a long history of racial and cultural stratification and discrimination, which has only begun to be challenged.

The Evolution of Identities in Sudan

The Advent of the Arabs

The seeds of the present division in Sudan between south and north were planted several thousand years before Christ, when the Egyptians and the Arabs began to expand southward, looking for slaves, gold, ivory, and revenue from taxation. Christianity entered the scene in the sixth century and was able to establish three kingdoms, which survived for a thousand years. But the impact of Islam, which intervened in the seventh century, set in motion a process of gradual decline for Christianity, culminating in the eventual overthrow of the Christian kingdoms in 1504 by an alliance of the Arabs and the Islamized kingdom of the Funj, whose origin remains obscure.

With a status enhanced by horses and cattle wealth, sophistication in trade, and the might of conquest, the Arabs began to spread throughout the north, marrying into prominent families, integrating themselves, and gradually taking over from within. There was dignity in being a Muslim and an Arab, contrasted with the indignity of being a Negro, a heathen, and a potential slave. For this reason, there was a tendency for people to convert to Islam,

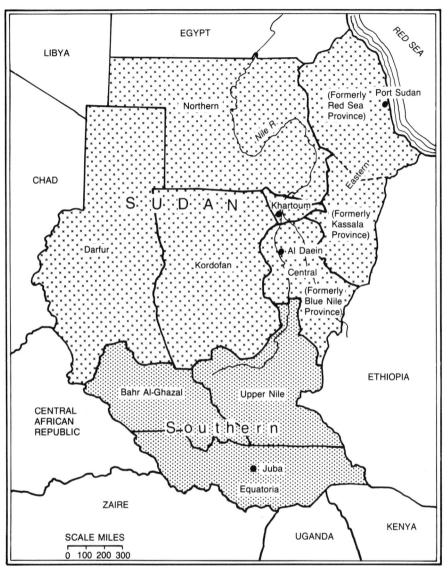

Figure 20–1. Sudan: Regional Divisions

adopt the Arabic language, and in due course refer to themselves as Arabs. This was possible because Islam fostered a "liberal" assimilationist attitude, which permitted the black animists and even the Christians to adjust their identity and join the favored Arab-Muslim mold. In due course, Arabization swept the north, eventually overshadowing the preexisting Sudanese and Christian elements.

However, although the north has largely been Islamized and Arabized, there is a considerable non-Arab element there, too. Many of the tribes of Darfur region are conspicuously Negroid. The Nuba of southern Kordofan region were barely touched by Arabism and Islam. Even the Nubians, with the longest history of contact with Arab civilization and Islam, have retained their language. The same is true of the Beja tribes to the east.

Southern Resistance

For reasons now attributed to the inhospitable environment and the forbidding resistance of the warrior Nilotic tribes, the south was never penetrated by the Arabs, but it remained a hunting ground for slaves. Paradoxically, despite this seeming isolation and the darkness of their skin, Nilotic racial and cultural features are said to reveal evidence of non-Negroid elements. Studies show that Dinka and Nuer religions bear a striking resemblance to the Middle Eastern religions, especially to the ancient Judaic tradition.

Dinka myths of creation contain such familiar bibical themes as God molding man from clay and creating woman from the man's rib, the woman succumbing to the temptation of the serpent in the lush garden of life, and a Christ-like prophet possessed with the spirit of Deng, the deity closest to God in might, descending to redeem man from evil and suffering.

Despite the ancient contacts with Egypt and the Middle East, which these similarities would tend to indicate, a long history of hostilities and deep-rooted animosities has so conditioned the peoples of both the south and the north that they cannot see that they have anything in common. Indeed, although both the Arabs and the Nilotics have been liberal in assimilating those they captured as slaves from either side, their prejudices against intermarriage and social mixing are profound and mutual. What gives the prejudices of the Arabs a greater profile is that they are sanctioned by Islam, which permits only men to marry outside the faith. Although the laws of many southern peoples, particularly the Dinka and the Nuer, prohibit intermarriage among those related by blood or within certain degrees of affinity by marriage (contrasting with the Arabs, who favor the marriage of cousins), those Nilotic peoples with agnatic (paternal) lineage systems discourage their people, especially the women, from marrying outside the tribe. As this prejudice against mixed marriage is regarded as mere convention or tradition, it is not given the degree of recognition or significance accorded the religiously ordained prejudice of the Muslim communities.

But the traditional Nilotic attitudes on marriage—as on other matters of race, culture, and religion—are based on feelings of distinctiveness as a people, rather than on assumptions of superiority over others, except insofar as they take themselves as the standard of what is normal in God's creation of man and his dignity. Having been dominated and ruled by others and having seen the technological superiority of others over them, their sentiments of human worth are more in the realm of moral than material values.

The threat of assimilation from the north has had the added effect of strengthening the Nilotic sense of identity, ethnic pride, and resistance to Arab Islamic influence. Of course, the people of the south have, over the centuries, adopted some cultural traits from the north, but they have tended to integrate and assimilate these traits into their own cultural mold.

Turko-Egyptian Rule

The racial and cultural division between the south and the north has been formalized and reinforced by more recent political interventions. The Turko-Egyptian rule of the Ottoman Empire, which entered the scene in 1821 and continued until 1885, was Islamic; and although it could not extend effective control over the south, except for a flourishing trade in slaves and a succession of terrorizing expeditions, its policies in the north reinforced the Arab Islamic identity and, therefore, the south–north dichotomy. However, being corrupt, oppressive, and alien, the Turko-Egyptian administration was deeply resented by the Muslim north and was characterized as a government of infidels.

The Mahdist Revolt

The situation exploded in 1882 when the nationalist leader, Muhammed Ahmad ibn Abdalla, who soon became known as the Mahdi—the Islamic Savior—mobilized the Sudanese people against the Turks. The spontaneous, nationwide support that the Mahdi aroused cut across the south–north dividing line. Initially armed with only spears and swords, the Mahdists won battle after battle, becoming increasingly zealous and confident in the process, until they miraculously succeeded in overthrowing the Turkish regime in 1885. General Charles George Gordon, the British hero who was then in the service of the Turko-Egyptian administration as governor, was killed, Khartoum fell, and Sudan became independent.

The response of the Dinka to the Mahdi, for example, is a good illustration of the selective manner in which they have tended to adopt Arab Islamic elements but have assimilated them to the point where they eventually lost their Arab origin. So captivated by the holy message of the Mahdi were the Dinkas that they composed hymns about him, conceiving him as a manifestation of the spirit Deng and praying to him to save them from their long suffering from invaders, who, ironically, would include Mahdists. Mahdi, as a symbol of that power, became known as the son of Deng, while Muhammed Ahmad, on whom the spirit of Deng was believed to have descended, continued to be viewed as an Arab.

The Mahdi died shortly after independence; and for thirteen years, his successor, Khalifa Abdullahi Muhammad, ran a theocratic state with an iron hand that devastated the country. For the south, it was a continuation of the northern incursions that had afflicted their world for as long as anyone could recall. Although the Mahdists, like the Turks before them, never succeeded in controlling the south, that whole phase of the nineteenth century is remembered by the Dinka as "the time when the world was spoiled," a total destruction of the world as they knew it.

Condominium Rule

Ironically, the Anglo-Egyptian reconquest in 1898 restored Sudan to a colonial status but brought relief to the peoples of both the north and the south. The Condominium Rule, as it became known, was unique in colonial history. A government headed by a British governor-general was to be established—not under the Colonial Office, but under the advisory jurisdiction of the foreign offices of the condominium powers, Britain and Egypt. No settlers were to be allowed in Sudan, nor were Europeans or Egyptians to be entitled to any special privileges on account of race. The Sudan political service was to be a distinguished club of an elite recruited from the best British universities, mostly Oxford and Cambridge.

To avoid repeating the mistakes of the Turko-Egyptian administration, the British recognized and respected the Arab Islamic sensibilities of the north and even characterized the government as Muslim. At the same time, however, they viewed the south as pagan and primitive, requiring only protection and tutelage. Although Christian missionaries were excluded from the north, in the south they were licensed and encouraged to play a civilizing role over defined "spheres of influence" to avoid denominational rivalry and conflict. Although the medium of instruction in northern schools was Arabic, replaced by English at the secondary level, teaching in southern elementary schools was in the vernacular languages, replaced by English from the intermediate level and on to the secondary level. For trade, the government preferred Greek merchants to the Arabs of the north, who, it was feared, were prone to exploiting the vulnerable peoples of the south. By law, the Southern region was regarded as "closed districts," and contact between the south and the north was regulated and severely restricted. What became known as the southern policy was intended to allow the people of the south to evolve along their own indigenous lines, insulated and protected from the supposedly corruptive materialism of modernity or the unscrupulous exploitations of the Arab north. Although carefully selected members of the political service who ruled the north were gradually extended to the south, the initial administrators there were military men with considerable autonomy, whose task, paradoxically, was both to silence the resistance of the unruly tribes and to provide paternalistic protection.

In both the north and the south, the British adopted indirect rule, leaving the administration of the tribes to their chiefs, with only an occasional visit by the district commissioner. The number of British administrators in Sudan in relation to the population is said to have been by far the smallest in the British Empire. As a result, the tribes did not feel the oppressive presence of an outside ruler. And yet, through indirect control, the British established peace, security, and a system of justice and civic order that contrasted sharply with what had prevailed. Seen from this perspective, it was indeed a golden era, unlike what had come before and what would come after independence.

Although Britain was the first to give meaning to Sudan as a unified nation-state, the northern Sudanese condemned its policies as having deepened the north–south division and having made it an obstacle to national unity. The southern Sudanese resented the preservative policies, however well-motivated, that relegated them to a position of inferiority vis-à-vis the north. Apart from the religiously oriented missionary education, the first efforts by the government to promote secular education in the south did not begin until the mid-1940's, when the British belatedly realized that they were about to leave; they wanted to help the south catch up with the north, so that it would be able to stand on its own in a united and independent Sudan in which the North would be dominant. They even came to accept the principle of formulating programs of accelerated development for the south.

Sudanization and Independence

The pressures from Egypt and the northern Sudanese forced the British out of the country before they could adequately prepare the south to catch up with the north. So wide was the gap that when Sudanization came, of the 800 posts that had been occupied by the colonial powers, only four junior positions went to the south. In August 1955, southern fears of a possible return to the "spoiled world" of the nineteenth century and of Arab domination triggered a mutiny that was initially localized to a battalion in Equatoria province but soon spread throughout the south. It was eventually contained only because of the intervention of the British governor-general, who, though at the tail end of his regime, promised justice for the rebels.

The Southern Sudanese joined the northern Sudanese in the declaration of independence on January 1, 1956, with the understanding that the southern call for a federal relationship with the north would be given full consideration. But it never was considered, and the dissatisfaction of the south led to a civil war that continued for seventeen years and brought to Sudan a great deal of human suffering and political upheaval and instability. Elected governments came and went on account of the problem. General Ibrahim Abboud seized control in 1958 and tried his military muscles for six years, but he also failed and was forced out of power by an unprecedented popular uprising in 1964. Although the brief period of the interim government of

Prime Minister Sirr al-Khatim al-Khalifa flashed some promising signs by initiating a round-table conference, the political parties that returned to power in 1965 only aggravated the problem, and most observers began to predict another military takeover.

Recent Dynamics of Identity Formation

Nimeiri Takes Over

The predicted change occurred on May 25, 1969, when General Jaafar al-Nimeiri led a successful coup, in alliance with the Communists, and declared Sudan a Socialist Democratic Republic. Within two years, ideological tensions developed among the various factions in the alliance, and the Communists were gradually phased out of power and finally routed in 1971, when they staged an abortive coup against the regime.

Having alienated both the right and the left, Nimeiri saw the south as the political force that offered the greatest potential as an ally. He immediately entered into negotiations with the southern movement and concluded the Addis Ababa Agreement of 1972, which ended the war by granting the south regional autonomy. The rebel forces were absorbed into the national army, and refugees and displaced people were resettled and rehabilitated with assistance from international organizations and friendly countries.

Politically, the country was reorganized around the Sudan Socialist Union, the official political party—conceived as "an alliance of the working forces" that included industrial workers, farmers, youth, women, the intelligentsia, professionals, national capitalists, and, of course, the army. A people's national assembly was established in which geographic areas and the various elements of the alliance were represented through both elections and presidential appointments. A new constitution was adopted that tried to strike an equilibrium between the main political forces in the country. Islam was recognized as the religion of the majority, while Christianity and other religious beliefs were also acknowledged. Arabic was made the official language, while English was accepted as the working language of the south. And by virtue of the provisions of the Addis Ababa Agreement, local languages, cultures, and customary laws were also acknowledged and accommodated.

On the basis of these domestic achievements, Sudan began to move regionally and internationally as an advocate for the peaceful settlement of disputes, taking or supporting initiatives for peace and reconciliation. Sudanese diplomacy was effectively mobilized to foster Afro-Arab solidarity and international cooperation in the development of the country. As an Arab country—and given the abundance of petrodollars that the oil boom of the early 1970s made available for recycling—Sudan's vast potential in agriculture and animal wealth made it ideally suited for trilateral cooperation involving Western technology and Arab money. The country was projected as a potential breadbasket for the Middle East and Africa. In addition to bilateral aid from Arab countries, a number of Arab funds became active in the country, and the Arab Authority for Agricultural Development was created, with its headquarters in Khartoum and Sudan designated as the first country of concentration.

Despite the ruthlessness with which he had destroyed his rightist and leftist adversaries, Nimeiri quickly developed, in the eyes of most of the world, the image of a statesman who was committed to the ideals of peace, reconciliation, development, and nation-building. He was able to do all this not so much through long-term strategic thinking but, rather, through the influence of key members of his government, whose ideas he followed or rejected, depending on their usefulness to his short-term tactical maneuvers for political survival, for which he had an instinctive talent.

Opposition to the Nimeiri Regime

The northern opposition groups, operating from bases in Libya and Ethiopia, continued to be a source of insecurity for Nimeiri and his regime. In 1976, they waged a ferocious attack, which, despite its failure to overthrow the government, inflicted heavy damage and demoralized the regime. Barely a year later, President Nimeiri met secretly with the opposition leader, Sadiq al-Mahdi, and agreed on a national reconciliation that resulted in the appointment of opposition members in the government, including Hassan al-Turabi, the leader of the Muslim Brotherhood, who occupied a succession of key positions, including attorney general, presidential adviser on legal affairs, and subsequently, adviser on foreign affairs.

For a while, reconciliation seemed to broaden the bases of national consensus and promote peace and stability, but significant differences soon developed between Sadiq al-Mahdi and President Nimeiri over what they had, in fact, agreed upon. Sadiq was particularly adamant that democratization of the system and respect for fundamental rights had been cornerstones of his agreement with the president, whereas Nimeiri insisted that all he had agreed to was the involvement of the opposition in the government, to promote its own objectives through existing institutions. In due course, while those members of the opposition who had been involved in government retained their positions, Sadiq became openly opposed to the regime.

Meanwhile, whether because of genuine religious persuasion or for political reasons—such as the desire to undermine the opposition leaders and the Muslim Brotherhood, whose alliance he recognized as mutually suspicious, uneasy, and precarious—President Nimeiri increasingly leaned toward the application of *sharia* (Islamic law) and the eventual creation of a theocratic Islamic state, with himself as the imam. This move was strongly opposed by

Sadiq al-Mahdi and other prominent religious figures as political exploitation of Islam and a misrepresentation of *sharia*. Nonetheless, President Nimeiri proceeded with his program of Islamization with the cooperation of the Muslim Brotherhood and in 1983 promulgated the so-called September Laws. Criminal justice, as elaborated in these laws, led to frequent floggings and amputation of limbs, most of the victims being poor Muslims from the west and destitute non-Muslims from the south.

Sadiq openly criticized the September Laws and was detained. The leader of the Muslim Republicans, Mahmoud Muhammad Taha, an elder in his seventies highly revered for his humanistic and progressive ideas on Islam in the pluralistic context of the modern world, also opposed the laws and was accused of apostasy. In a version of justice that shocked Sudan and the world, he was tried, convicted, and executed.

North–South Tensions

Meanwhile, tensions in south–north relations had begun to grow with Nimeiri's shift in policies, from his accommodation of the northern opposition parties to his alliance with the Muslim fundamentalists. These tensions were aggravated by the general deterioration in the economic situation, with concomitant hardships in the less-advantaged areas, of which the south was the worst. Sudan had struck significant oil reserves, most of which were in the south; but ironically, even the oil find became a source of friction. To alleviate the heavy debts of the country, the central government decided that oil should be refined in those areas where the infrastructure would facilitate quick returns. This meant the north. Later, it was decided that the crude would be pipelined to the Red Sea for export. These measures were viewed by the south as evidence that the north was enriching itself at the expense of the south. The mammoth Junglei Canal, which was designed to save the Nile waters from evaporation and retrieve valuable land from the swampy Sudd, was also viewed with disfavor, as benefiting the north and Egypt while destroying the natural environment and dislocating the human and animal life cycles of the region.

The more the south began to assert itself as a separate cultural entity and to make demands for a more equitable share of power, national wealth, and development opportunities, the more the president saw its autonomy, within a constitutionally guaranteed liberal democracy, as anathema in the context of the presidential system that governed Sudan. Political rivalries and ambitions for positions within the south also levied their toll. On the basis of alleged complaints by minority tribes in Equatoria province about alleged Dinka domination, President Nimeiri decreed that the south should be divided into three regions, with regional governments whose constitutional powers were reduced to put them on a par with the newly established regions of the north.

Reading the restless mood in the south, the government began to transfer the absorbed southern forces to the north, ostensibly to consolidate the integration of the army, but in the eyes of the southerners, aimed at weakening the capacity of the south to resort to military action against the government's southern policy. Although some units reluctantly obeyed the orders, the unit at the Bor Garrison resisted, triggering the renewal of organized hostilities in 1983. President Nimeiri added fuel to the fire by imposing Islamic laws on the country, virtually turning it into an Islamic state in which the non-Muslim population would be inevitably relegated to second-class citizenship. The reaction was a spontaneous return to the conditions of the seventeen-year-old war and the establishment of the Sudan People's Liberation Movement (SPLM) and the Sudan People's Liberation Army (SPLA), both under the leadership of Colonel John Garang, a Dinka officer who had earned all his degrees in the United States, including a Ph.D. in economics, and who had also received military training in a U.S. academy. With the sophisticated arms now available to both sides and the level of outside support that the southern movement was receiving from Ethiopia and Libya, the war soon proved far more devastating than the seventeen-year war had been. As a result of the war, Sudan's plan for the production and export of oil and the construction of the Jonglei Canal came to a standstill.

Nimeiri is Overthrown

The more the regime felt threatened, the more repressive and unpopular it became. Even the Muslim Brotherhood eventually fell prey to Nimeiri's political whims, and its leader, Hassan al-Turabi, left his executive position under arrest and was detained.

These developments were aggravated by mounting economic problems. Sudan had been carried away with borrowing at a time when the outside world was eager to lend money, particularly to countries with visible development potential, in order to circulate the rapidly accumulating petrodollars. To compound the problem, the concept of development the masses had in mind was not so much growth-oriented as it was geared toward the provision of services and the establishment of schemes or projects with a visibility that promised and symbolized a significant economic takeoff. The imagination of the nation was captured and engrossed in a grandiose and lavish notion of development that was more political than economic. When the debts began to mature, the oil bills began to soar, and severe drought in the west and the east began to afflict the country with an acute shortage of food (aggravated by the influx of refugees), then aspirations and realities became unbridgeable, and the stability of the system was severely threatened.

On April 6, 1984, a popular uprising, spearheaded by professionals—doctors and lawyers—and the trade unionists, forced the army to overthrow Nimeiri while he was visiting the United States. A transitional military council, headed by General Abdul Rahman Siwar al-Dahab, who had been Nimeiri's minister of defense, and a civilian cabinet headed by Dr. al-Gizouli Dafalla, who had played a prominent role in the popular uprising, was formed to coach the country back to parliamentary democracy within a year—an undertaking they carried out with meticulous loyalty and conformity.

During the transitional period, both the military council and the cabinet felt too constrained to do much more than the routine running of government and preparing the country for the elections. Even the infamous September Laws remained valid, though they were enforced more leniently. Turabi, by then out of detention, intensified his advocacy of *sharia* and, paradoxically, succeeded in widening his political base under the banner of the National Islamic Front. His fundamental appeal antagonized many, even those within his faith, and the country became sharply divided on the sensitive issue of religion. As might be expected, perhaps the most formidable challenge to national unity came from the south, where Nimeiri's overthrow did not seem to have helped the situation significantly. The leadership of the SPLM/SPLA saw in the membership of the Transitional Military Council and the continuation of the September Laws a form of continuity with the ousted regime. Besides, although the transitional government had abrogated Nimeiri's decree dividing the south, the three southern provinces continued to function as regions, and the newly formed unitary southern regional government remained redundant in Khartoum—unable to assume its duties in the south, allegedly because of the continued opposition of the minority tribes in Equatoria province that had called for the division of the south in the first place.

The SPLM's Strategic Shift

Although the SPLM/SPLA was initially identified with the Dinka, against whom Nimeiri's divisive policies had primarily been targeted, the leaders of the movement have repeatedly stated that they are not concerned with "the so-called southern problem," but rather with the liberation of Sudan as a whole—the ultimate objective being the establishment of "a new Sudan" free of all vestiges of racial, tribal, religious, and other forms of discrimination, in which all citizens will enjoy genuine democracy, civil liberties, and full equality.

In more practical terms, these lofty ideals tend to be viewed as favoring the disadvantaged areas—primarily the south, the west, and the east, where the majority of the non-Arab population of the country is to be found—for it has become increasingly obvious that the political, economic, social, and cultural disparities, and even the racial and religious inequities that the south has suffered, also affect other regions. The initial tendency toward separatism has therefore been replaced by the desire to foster national alliance against disparities and discriminatory practices in the country as a whole.

Whatever the motivations or calculations behind this strategic shift, it is subject to ambiguous interpretations. One is that it is a way of highlighting the intrinsic linkage between the local dimensions of the problem and the controlling instruments of power at the center. Another characterizes the problems as purely national. That approach appeals to patriotic sentiments and adheres to the African bias for preserving the boundaries inherited from colonialism; but it could ultimately be counterproductive, because it tends to obscure the racial, cultural, linguistic, and religious dimensions that have thus far characterized the south–north dichotomy. A third interpretation, which combines aspects of the first two, is that if the fundamental issues are addressed at the national level, the problems at the regional level will necessarily be addressed.

Perhaps the most significant aspect of the strategic shift is that whatever interpretation one adopts, it implies a commitment to national unity that is likely to win greater support within Sudan and in Africa than past movements were able to win with separatist or regional strategies. If it is sustained by both sides, this new strategy may prove to be a major step forward in the process of nation-building, but it will be worthless unless both sides can accommodate each other and find a mutually acceptable basis for ending the war in the south. In this, the positive aspects of the Nimeiri regime offer some useful guidance.

There is a tendency in Sudan today to paint the Nimeiri era as nothing but a dark page in the country's modern history. This is an understandable reaction to the authoritarian rule of one man, which was out of tune with the egalitarian and democratic spirit of the Sudanese people. But quite apart from being a grossly negative oversimplification of a complex mixture of positives and negatives, it does not do justice to the many Sudanese people who supported the system and worked diligently and with moral conviction within it. And indeed, many did so not for reasons of occupational opportunism or political ambition, but precisely because they believed the system provided a positive basis for guiding their country toward the dream of building a united Sudanese nation. The Addis Ababa Agreement that ended the war in the south was the most significant factor in this positive turn of events.

"National reconciliation," which later brought the rightist northern opposition parties into the government, also promised to broaden the basis of national consensus behind the emerging nation, the new Sudan. Furthermore, the extension of regional autonomy to the provinces of the north, albeit with less power than was given the southern region, showed that the positive lessons learned in the south were being applied to the benefit of the whole country. The fact that the most significant achievements of the revolution in the south were later reversed, with the result that the country plunged back into the tragic state of war, may be more the outcome of the compromises Nimeiri had to make with the rightist opposition groups than of an inherent shortcoming in the system at its best. The broad-based commitment to national unity, combined with the sharpened awareness of the regional disparities that this unity must realistically address, can be said to be the by-product of the legacy of the Nimeiri era.

Indeed, the Sudanese would do well not to persist in the blanket condemnation of some sixteen years of national experience; instead, they should be selective in more constructive criticism of that page in Sudanese history. The Nimeiri regime allowed the peripheral areas of the country to see what power and national resources they had been previously denied. Now it is impossible for them to accept the status quo—far less a return to the past, which the present system appears to represent. The present leadership must recognize this dilemma and address it realistically.

External Dimensions

The formation of internal Sudanese identities was affected by Sudan's external involvements and foreign interests. These influences continue to reinforce or undermine the Sudanese symbols of identity and the process of nation-building. For desperately poor people suffering from deprivations of a basic material nature, even small amounts of external resources can go a long way toward corrupting and distorting the character and the integrity of the individual citizen and thus, unfortunately, of the nation itself. In the 1960s and the early 1970s, the Sudanese were well into the process of uncovering their hidden or distorted national identity. They were beginning to see themselves united by certain attributes in their national character that differentiated them from their kindred in other Arab and African countries. Then, suddenly, dramatic developments on the world scene brought about waves of racial, cultural, and religious revival in the Arab world and reversed the progress in discovering the Sudanese identity. The process of reversal continues, but the forces of self-recognition and self-identification should not be underestimated; they could ultimately prevail over the obstacles of external intervention and the lures of material advantages accruing from external associations.

Foreign ideological and strategic interests have also become involved in Sudan, with the result that the conflict has become increasingly internationalized. As the forces of extremism become pronounced on both sides, the prospects of wider regional and international involvement become greater, and finding a national solution to the problem becomes far more difficult.

Internal Dilemmas

Whatever the degree of external involvement in the Sudanese conflict, the root causes are, nonetheless, domestic and have much to do with how people identify themselves and are indentified by others, what disparities attach to these identities, and how people react to the inequities. Although regional and international cooperation is obviously needed to support and reinforce any national solution the Sudanese might eventually adopt, it is up to the Sudanese themselves to bring about peace. The role of foreign powers or interests is a matter of only secondary importance.

Paradoxically, the simplistic labels of identity that have divided Sudan into north and south on racial, religious, and cultural lines are being challenged at the same time that they are being sharpened and highlighted. Sudan is Arabic-speaking, Islamic, and by and large identified with the Arab world. But in reality, most if not all northern Sudanese are of mixed racial backgrounds, and many of them, including their leaders, come from families in which languages other than Arabic are spoken, the Islam they practice is a fusion of pre-Islamic Christian and even pagan practices, and exclusive "tribal" labels of identity compete with the uniting concepts of Arabism, Islam, and "the north." Likewise, the south, though labeled as a racial and cultural unity, is emerging as internally diversified and by no means clearly distinguished from the north—racially, culturally, or even religiously. All this makes Sudan a country of surprising paradoxes. Most people would agree that it is anomalous and peripheral to the mainstream of Arabism and Islam in global terms. Yet the more the foundations of Arab-Islamic identity become questioned, the more their manifest symbols become reinforced by both internal and external supporters, and the more the clash of identities is heightened. The increasingly unified forces of nationhood thus confront the counterforces of fundamentalist revivalism that tend to be nationally divisive.

Northern Skepticism about Southern Ideals

In this paradoxical process, whereby barriers are being broken down while, at the same time, they are being reinforced with even greater zealousness, the quest for unity is being challenged for the first time by some northerners who—whether for ideological or practical reasons or merely as a bluff—are beginning to call for separation between the north and the south. They argue that the country has suffered too much from war, that it has been distracted from development and nation-building for far too long, and that the south should be let go so that the north can begin to focus on its own priorities. Of course, the assumption here is that the south really wants to separate, despite the unionist rhetoric of its leaders. But whatever the reasons—whether they have to do with idealism or pragmatism—the leadership in the south has decided that the country as a whole belongs to all the Sudanese and that southerners—even more than the northerners, who can claim external labels of identification—have a national duty to preserve the unity of the country and to create a new framework of equality for all races and religions. The message is clearly incongruous to the northerners, a people for whom the south has always been peripheral and on the receiving end of national generosity.

This fundamental shift in strategy has clearly created considerable confusion in northern thinking. The question often posed in the north is: What does Colonel Garang want? This question, which emphasizes the individual leader rather than the movement as a whole, shows that the lofty ideals of equitable unity postulated by the SPLM/SPLA are not believed by most northerners. Indeed, most northerners believe that the SPLM/SPLA secretly aims at separating the south from the north or at imposing its terms of unity on the country through military means. The distress of northerners is obvious in other questions often associated with the main question of what Garang wants: Does he want to come and rule the Sudan? Who does he expect to rule? These questions do not merely challenge the capacity of the SPLM/SPLA to impose its will on the nation but also betray ethnocentric sentiments.

And yet this skepticism is warranted to some extent, for it is widely accepted that the war is not winnable by either side. Even the leaders of the SPLM/SPLA would concede that they do not intend, nor do they have the means, to overrun the country and seize national power. Why, then, does the war go on?

In the north, there is currently a wide recognition of the ethnic, cultural, and religious differences between the north and the south, an acknowledgment of the political and economic disparities between the regions, and a willingness to address them through the democratic process. The dominant view in the north is that there can be no justification for the SPLM/SPLA to continue the war, since Nimeiri has been overthrown and replaced with a democracy. The only explanation, therefore, is that its leadership is not free but is being held hostage by the Ethiopian government to secure its own strategic interests.

What this argument misses is that the SPLM/SPLA leaders merely represent a broad-based movement with an even wider constituency in the south. Whatever degree of influence outside forces might exert on the leaders, they are ultimately accountable to the fighting men and the masses, whose grievances are deep-rooted and who have been alienated and place little if any faith in the prevailing system of democracy. Unless these grievances are addressed, there can be no prospect for lasting peace, whatever short-term concessions the leaders of the movement might be prepared to make. Nor is the northern argument that Sudan is a democracy accepted without serious qualifications in the south. What is meant by democracy and the concepts of majority and minority when they are applied to a pluralistic state that is still in search of an acceptable constitution? Is political power determined by sheer weight of numbers a reliable indicator of the democratic choice in a country where racial, cultural, and religious diversities challenge the very foundation of common nationhood?

The leaders of the SPLM/SPLA argue that the government and the dominant political parties inside Sudan are not sincerely committed to the peaceful resolution of the conflict. For example, they argue that the government has failed to implement the convening of a constitutional conference, one of the terms of the Koka Dam Declaration of March 1986. In the SPLM/SPLA view, the leaders of Sudan are in no way prepared to negotiate a just peace; they wish to remain dominant politically, economically, and culturally and therefore will concede only a small measure of participation to the marginalized regions. Just as they are accused of foreign dependency, the SPLM/SPLA leaders also see behind the dominant political forces in the north the involvement of foreign interests whose financial support is being mobilized and used to influence the political and even the military balance of power in pursuance of certain racial, cultural, and religious objectives.

And so, both sides profess to be interested in a negotiated settlement and accuse each other of intransigence. Paradoxically, the result is that they reinforce the vicious cycle of violence.

The Search for a Solution Acceptable to Both Sides

What are the options in this stalemate? If the mutually acceptable goal is a negotiated settlement between the forces that are currently dominant on both sides, then certain alternatives can be ruled out as not negotiable. The goal of the SPLM/SPLA is to liberate the whole country and create a "new Sudan"—free of any racial, religious, or cultural discrimination. Such a goal is clearly incompatible with the position and role of the present leaders of Sudan and would naturally be unacceptable to them. For their part, the present leaders in the north intend to maintain the main features of the prevailing political structures and processes and will concede only a measure of corrective remedies to the south and other disadvantaged regions or groups, through regional autonomy and other forms of affirmative action. Such an alternative will hardly appeal to the movement, and both sides are thus destined to fight on.

What, then, can be conceptualized and formulated as a possible meeting ground, a solution acceptable to both sides? Perhaps the most critical question is whether the two systems that are at loggerheads—one a parliamentary democracy and the other an armed liberation movement—are reconcilable. The answer given by both sides is that mutual accommodation is possible. Both sides further agree, in principle, that accommodation can be achieved through dialogue and negotiations. It would seem that the only outcome that could reconcile them is one that would permit the SPLM/SPLA to translate its gun power into a significant political power—primarily within the south, but with an assured southern participation on an equal par with the north at the center. This implies the acceptance of fundamental principles that would permit the evolution of the country toward the ideal postulated by the SPLM/SPLA, viewed in a long-term perspective. However, in the short run, it should not threaten to destroy the pillars of the power structure and constitutive process at the national level.

In specific terms, what principles could provide a foundation for the evolution of a united, democratic, and egalitarian Sudan? From the perspective of identity and its implications for the sharing of political power and national resources, the critical issues that have generated controversy are race, religion, and culture. Is Sudan an Arab or an African country? Should it be governed by an Islamic or a secular constitutional system? What should the official language or languages be? How should the resources of the country be shared between the center and the regions? And to what extent should the system be centralized or regionalized?

The answers to these questions must be based on the premise that because the process and consequences of identity formation have been inequitable, remedies must adjust past imbalances. On the issue of racial and cultural identification, Sudan must be more genuinely Afro-Arab in its self-perception than it has been in the past. This is more than a matter of labels, for it can have serious substantive implications for educational policy, cultural programs, and international relations.

The language dimension requires putting Arabic and English on a par, for although Arabic has increasingly become accepted as the lingua franca throughout the country, there is still a tendency to see English as the modern language of the educated southerner. English provides a counterbalancing force against Arabic, which is viewed as the symbol of northern identity and dominance. The fact that younger generations in the south may speak Arabic more than English does not invalidate this perception; it merely adds another myth to the folklore of Sudanese multiple identities. To balance the language equation, the Sudan should adopt Arabic and English as the official or working languages. The development of the local languages can then be left to the policies and resources of the communities concerned—with national assistance as feasible and appropriate.

With respect to religion, the argument that Islam does not separate religion and the state may be valid in homogeneously Muslim communities, but it cannot be sustained in religiously pluralistic societies, where applying one religion must of necessity imply inequality before the law. Nor would it help matters to devise a system of legal pluralism in public matters, as that is also bound to entail an unacceptable degree of inequity, encourage disunity, and perhaps lead to disintegration. A compromise that was successfully applied under British rule was for the state to be neutral on religious matters, ensuring freedom of religion for all and creating an overall political climate that was respectful of religious values without partiality to any one religion. Secularism does not mean being antireligion, nor does it necessarily imply a negation of moral and spiritual values, which are central to all religions and essential to the health of any community.

On the issue of the disparities in economic and social development, it is widely accepted that some form of affirmative action is necessary to bridge the gaps between the north and the south and among the regions of the North. It may indeed be necessary to reserve a percentage of the national budget to assist the relatively more backward areas until they can stand on their own. The utilization of such funds should fall within the jurisdiction of the areas concerned.

These issues raise the broad question of an effective constitutional framework for meeting the needs of the country. Both centralization and limited regional autonomy have been tested and found defective. Federalism, however—which the south first called for as a condition to the declaration of independence—has so far not been tested. It is, indeed, widely agreed that a federal constitution is best suited for a country as large and diversified as Sudan. Federalism would enable the various provinces, regions, or states to exercise effective control and management of their internal affairs within a national framework that would allow mobility, interaction, and a harmonious evolution toward national unity and integration.

What is now known of the SPLM/SPLA strategy tends to conform with this conceptual framework. The strategy divides the country into two war zones. "War zone one" is a euphemism for the south, and "war zone two" comprises the rest of the country. When war zone one is liberated and the authority of the SPLM/SPLA is established there, the movement will then continue to work for the liberation of the rest of the country by operating in close cooperation with like-minded forces in other regions of Sudan. This is a clear answer to those who wonder about the intentions of the SPLM/SPLA leaders. Their goals are by no means as grandiose or as impractical as they may sound.

The movement is already operating on the basis of a dualistic approach to the regional and national contexts of the problem. It would seem, therefore, that a solution that recognizes the full control of southerners over southern affairs while establishing a system of government at the national level that permits full participation without discrimination ought to be in relative harmony with the declared objective of the movement. Such a solution would promote the evolution of the nation toward its stipulated ideals, without generating change that would be considered too radical by the establishment.

Conclusion

Although there are many facets to the complex problems that have afflicted Sudan since independence, a central theme has been the issue of racial, religious, and cultural identity, largely viewed in terms of the south–north dichotomy. For the same reason, Sudan has been described as Afro-Arab, a microcosm of Africa, and the bridge between the continent and the Middle East, formulations that imply a positive strategic regional and international role but have also given rise to tension and confrontation. Since independence, and except for the brief period of the Addis Ababa Agreement, Sudan has been more of an embarrassment in Afro-Arab relations than the constructive intermediary it was envisaged to be. Worse, internal strife and internecine warfare have persistently threatened the stability of the country, retarded its economic and social development, and frustrated the process of nation-building.

Although the south continues to be the battlefield and therefore the most afflicted by the war, the damage is becoming increasingly felt throughout the country. Not only is the financial cost unaffordable and the economic burden unbearable, but even worse, the mushrooming of tribal militias and the spread of sophisticated weapons now threaten to turn the country into another Lebanon. Despite the consensus that the war must end and the national committment to democratic ideals that has twice culminated in popular uprisings against military dictatorships, the country seems enveloped in a consuming war psychosis.

It is quite obvious that only a solution that recognizes the need for a substantial change in the system and the manner in which diversities and disparities are managed stands any chance of success. The SPLM/SPLA has chosen to challenge the system through armed struggle, and whatever the differences within the south, the movement is widely recognized as the only force that can obtain significant concessions from the system. The military and political credibility of the movement can no longer be seriously questioned.

By the same token, the movement cannot impose its will on the whole country through military means. Nor can it expect the established leadership in the north to negotiate its own doom. Mutual accommodation must therefore be the art of the possible for the government as much as for the movement.

The solution, it would seem, is to adopt a system of government that would relax the pressures for centralized unity by giving a wide measure of regional self-rule while also establishing the framework for a harmonious evolution toward the ideals of genuine unity, democracy, and equality for all—without unduly traumatizing the establishment or threatening the system with destruction. Although the precise details of such an arrangement would have to be expanded and negotiated, the elements for such a compromise already exist in the declared objectives, policies, and strategies of the principal parties to the conflict.

21
Peacemaking and Social Cleavages in Sudan

Nelson Kasfir

hen the Addis Ababa Agreement ended the civil war in Sudan between the national government and southern dissidents in 1972, it was widely recognized as a rare success in bargaining. Here was an agreement negotiated between combatants locked in a violent stalemate. The negotiations produced a genuine compromise, which kept the peace for eleven years, despite the divisions that characterize Sudanese society. The agreement did not solve any of the problems created by those divisions, but it did provide a breathing space in which fundamental shifts in identification might have been promoted. But the opportunity was not grasped. Instead, soldiers, politicians, and office seekers used social divisions to advance their personal fortunes, both economic and political. When it came to political survival, significant political actors were prepared to violate the agreement. Civil war resumed in 1983. Consequences stemming from the failure of the Addis Ababa Agreement made it impossible to end the war in 1988, despite heartfelt desires by political leaders on both sides.

The extraordinary difficulties of achieving peace were epitomized by the refusal of opponents in the civil war even to agree whether they were fighting to solve the problem of the south or the problem of Sudan. The Sudan People's Liberation Movement (SPLM), though representing a largely southern army, insisted that negotiations must produce unprecedented changes in the national government, and it carried the war into the north to make that point. The national government, on the other hand, adhered to the long-held conventional Sudanese understanding of the south as an ethnically and religiously different region and to the more recent idea that this difference required a separate political solution. In short, the national government wanted to base new negotiations on the model of the Addis Ababa Agreement, which meant that southerners would regain political control of the south, while the SPLM insisted on negotiating national power-sharing, which meant that all peripheral regions would play a more important political role in the center.

Behind these positions lay opposed and intensely felt beliefs regarding the proper role of ethnicity, region, and religion in Sudanese politics. The main opponents in the second civil war searched for allies from each other's "home" areas, further complicating the political dispute. Some important southern notables accepted the approach of the leaders of the national government, while some northern professionals sympathized with the perspective of the SPLM. If the original impact of the Addis Ababa Agreement was to deemphasize ethnicity and religion in national and local politics, the reversal of this trend, ironically, could also be traced in part to the kind of politics encouraged by the agreement itself. Meanwhile, the imperatives of war exacerbated the politicization of these divisions among the Sudanese.

Documenting the heterogeneity of the peoples of Sudan is a simple matter. With more than a hundred separate languages spoken and perhaps forty different cultures practiced, there are differences galore. But the overriding question is which of these differences matters politically? For the sake of which differences were people twice willing to go to war after Sudan received its independence in 1956? And as those differences did not always evoke violent conflict, what other factors caused them to become so great that national politics could no longer be contained within existing political structures? In short, when and why did certain differences become the cleavages that made Sudan a deeply divided society?

The answers to these questions are rooted in the history of Sudan. In particular, during the condominium period, a pattern of political and economic inequalities was established that, after independence, enabled a small group of well-placed individuals to take control and use their power to enrich themselves. The two military regimes appear to have broadened this group without significantly altering its social composition. However, by demanding power-sharing, the SPLM forced consideration of how broad the governing group should be. In challenging the right of the existing elite to perpetuate its dominance, the SPLM necessarily raised the question of whether its members should continue to be considered "natural" leaders of the whole nation or should be redefined as one ethnic, religious, and regional group among many. Thus, the civil war focused attention on the connections between political and economic dominance and the social divisions of Sudanese society.

This question was not raised in the negotiations that ended the first civil war. The Addis Ababa Agreement accepted the existing pattern of dominance, on the condition that the privileged group of leaders be marginally expanded. The national government's failure to fulfill even this condition provoked the new and far more radical insistence of the SPLM that the second civil war could be settled only by removing the dominance of the ruling group and introducing power-sharing on a multiethnic, multiregional, and multireligious basis. (If the war were to be settled simply by admitting the leaders of the present rebellion to the national ruling group, the system of patronage would be maintained and the old understandings would remain in place.)

The relationships among Sudanese social forces are both responsive to significant political changes and constrained by basic elements of the political economy. On the one hand, the political salience of ethnic, regional, and religious concerns decreased noticeably in response to the imposition of the Addis Ababa Agreement but increased again with its breakdown. On the other hand, long-standing structural features of the Sudanese political economy, particularly the entrenched economic advantages of certain northern strata, guaranteed that these concerns would certainly be central issues once a second civil war began. Francis Deng captured something of both aspects in the introduction to his political novel, *Seed of Redemption,* when he expressed his "profound conviction that what divides the Sudanese people along racial and cultural lines is largely a myth, nurtured and perpetuated by a long history of stratification and discrimination."[1] But not even a peace agreement was sufficient to dissipate the political force of myths that turned the Sudanese into enemies. The larger task here is to learn how myth and politics nurtured each other as peace was negotiated and then broke down.

The argument has four parts, each developed in a separate section of this chapter. The first part considers how deeply rooted were the basic cleavages that led to civil war. The second explores the dramatic, if limited, impact of the Addis Ababa Agreement in reducing the political uses of underlying ethnic, regional, and religious feelings. The third argues that the breakdown of the Addis Ababa Agreement, the second civil war, and the immobility of the national government sharply intensified the salience of ethnicity, region, and religion in Sudanese politics. And the fourth part demonstrates that settling the second civil war has been made far more difficult by the central demand of the liberation movement that the pattern of political dominance be totally changed.

The Creation of Northern and Southern Identities

In the process of becoming a single political state, Sudan emerged as a deeply divided society in which ethnicity, region, and religion were frequently used to organize political competition. Uneven opportunities to accumulate wealth reflected differences in ethnicity, region, and religion and thus reinforced these three factors as the bases for forming the identities of different groups. Over time, particularly during the past century and a half, these opposed identities became embedded as markers for dominant and peripheral groups in Sudan's social structure. The specific question considered in this section is the degree to which these factors contributed to the construction of northern and southern identities so deeply opposed that civil war became inevitable, but not so deeply entrenched that a freely negotiated peace agreement was impossible.

Ethnicity is the most complex of the three factors. It encompasses all forms of identity that have at their root the notion of a common ancestor—

race as well as "tribe." As markers of identity, religion and region are quite different notions from ethnicity, even though they are sometimes also taken as stereotypical indicators of common ancestry. In Sudan, any individual will have many available social identities. Which identity or combination of identities applies depends on the particular situation, not merely on the individual's preference. For example, a person who is perceived as a southerner by northern residents of Khartoum may also be identified as a member of the Dinka "tribe" by non-Dinka living in Juba *and* as an Ngok Dinka from Abyei (located in what is typically considered "northern" Sudan) by other Dinka.

Mistakes in objective identity are an important consideration in the politicization of ethnicity. Though objective ethnic characteristics (race, language, culture, place of birth) usually provide the possible limits, subjective perceptions of either the identifier or the identified—whether objectively accurate or not—may turn out to be decisive for that social situation. Aspects of the social structure may have dramatic and long-lasting effects in stabilizing this identification process. Probably the most significant consideration is social power, especially when it amounts to political and economic dominance defined by participants in ethnic terms. The same logic explains how region and religion become politicized. The more the three factors were simultaneously used to identify the same groups at a particular moment, the more deeply divided and prone to conflict was Sudanese society. By the same token, steps that reduced the political impact of these factors made peaceful coexistence more feasible—at least temporarily.

Thus, the changing political role of ethnicity, region, and religion must be understood as the consequence of the social history of Sudan—the product of changing patterns of dominance and subordination of different groups responding to the articulation of the Sudanese political economy. The evolution of attitudes over many years tends to create habits of identification that are difficult to change because they are taken as self-evident—if they are thought about at all. Nevertheless, dramatic new patterns, sometimes created by singular events, may have a powerful impact in either creating or reversing habits of identification. For example, the slave trade in the nineteenth century was one such pattern. For a few years, the Addis Ababa Agreement appeared to be a singular event that could provide a fundamental opportunity to introduce new political structures that might reverse some of those identifications.

The Influence of the Slave Trade

Linguistic and cultural Arabization and Islamization of the northern part of what is now Sudan occurred slowly, unevenly, and incompletely over the past millennium. But the sheer physical difficulties of penetrating the Sudd and the arid clay plains, plus the absence of trade opportunities, insulated the southern part of the country from sustained contact with outsiders until the middle of the nineteenth century. The slave trade, which began not long after the first explorers traveled the Nile through southern Sudan in 1841, provided a powerful and lasting image of differences between northerners and southerners. The trade, though also involving some Europeans, was largely the work of a small number of Muslims who were also Arabs. Because southerners were not Muslims, enslaving them on the pretext that they were captured in war did not violate the Koran.

The indigenous and fundamentalist northern Islamic revolt against Ottoman rule in the 1880s—led by Muhammed Ahmad ibn Abdalla, known as the Mahdi, or "expected one"—was originally supported by at least some Southern peoples. However, the Mahdi's followers encouraged the slavery of "infidels" more widely and more ruthlessly than before and thus deepened the sense of ethnic division expressed in terms of region and religion. Slavery was never so rigid a social category in Islamic society as it was in the West, but the violence of the original contact of people from the north with those from the south made race, religion, region, and ethnicity markers of social stratification long after slavery was prohibited.

Christianity, English, and Western Culture

Over the next century, these markers contributed to the construction of regional identities that were perceived differently by those in dominant groups than by those in subordinate groups. Southerners—especially the educated—constructed a perception of an aggressive and threatening north, associated with Islam and Arabic language and culture, set off against a weak and vulnerable south, associated at first with traditional religions and African languages and cultures but later, also, with Christianity and English. Northerners—particularly intellectuals—tended to perceive Islam and Arabic as the substance of a superior culture now available to southerners who were willing to take advantage of it. What Christianity, English, and Western culture did to Sudan, as they saw it, was to drive a wedge that further separated northerners and southerners and made a single nation that much more difficult to achieve.

European missionaries and British officials played important roles in the construction of these separate identities. Once Condominium Rule was declared in 1899, Christian missionaries, who had arrived in the south as early as the ivory and slave traders, were given responsibility for Western education. By independence, however, only a small percentage of southerners had become Christians and thus had been educated in English. Though few in number, they displaced traditional chiefs as leaders of southern opinion—particularly as the implications of the withdrawal of British officials at independence became apparent.

British Rule

To establish their dominant position in Sudan, nominally a condominium in which rule was shared with Egypt, British officials had originally allied themselves with the Khatmiyyah—for many years the largest Islamic brotherhood in the area—in order to conquer the Mahdi and his followers, who formed a second brotherhood known as al-Ansar. Their success, therefore, gave a "tilt" to the political economy that British officials then consolidated. By the eve of World War I, however, British officials had begun to admit to official favor the posthumous son of the Mahdi and his family. In order to speed economic growth that would make Sudan self-supporting and to avoid sectarian politics, British officials opened extraordinary economic opportunities to the notables controlling both brotherhoods. Their families rapidly became extremely wealthy, permitting them to use patronage to strengthen their positions in their movements, which eventually became important, and competitive, political forces. The result was to create a tiny group of families with almost complete control over economic investment and development and to give the north a crucial head start in the production of wealth as well.

Early economic decisions by condominium authorities resulted in significant regional inequalities in wealth and economic development, which further reinforced the social perceptions of the differences between north and south. The low-level officials required to staff the civil service were first recruited from schools that drew students from Nubians and Arabized peoples along the Nile in the north. In addition, export earnings were needed from the start of the condominium to support administrative, military, and social welfare expenses. The British were also anxious to reduce Sudan's reliance on Egypt, the other condominium authority. The huge Gezira cotton-growing scheme in the north became the core economic area. Capital investment was concentrated on its development, at the expense of other areas, in the hope that its profits would later support development projects in other parts of the country. But by the time the Gezira showed a profit in the late 1930s, its tenant farmers had become sufficiently entrenched to prevent diversion of its income. Eventually, the Gezira provided over half of Sudan's export earnings, but the wealth it created remained concentrated in the northeast. Large parts of the north became peripheral to the national economy.

The south became peripheral for equally fortuitous but nonetheless decisive reasons of condominium policy. After 1918, condominium authorities introduced a policy that gave administrative support to a separate identity for the south, in order to protect its local cultures from Islamic influences. One result was to retard the economic development of the south. The policy was reversed in 1946 by the Sudan government, which determined that Sudan should be administered as one country. But by then, mistrust had reinforced perceptions of differences. To the profound misgivings of many in the south, southern chiefs agreed to this reversal in a conference called in Juba to assure southern leaders that southern rights would be safeguarded in a unified Sudan. What bothered the first generation of educated southern nationalists was the lost opportunity—implicit in the chiefs' acquiescence—to convert the separation that the condominium authorities had imposed on the south thirty years earlier into a federal status that might have better protected southerners after independence. The creation of a separate status for the south became the core of southern nationalism until 1981, when southern unity foundered on ethnic rivalries.

Civil War

Uncertainty grew as plans for self-government went forward after 1953. Southern fears of northern domination sharpened when the Sudanization Committee gave only 6 of 800 posts to southerners. Southern soldiers in the Equatoria Corps mutinied in 1955. By 1963, the northern-dominated military government's policy of imposing Islamization and Arabization on the south led to the formation of an armed secessionist movement that continued until the Addis Ababa Agreement was negotiated. Though the civil war was intermittent, it destroyed much of the southern infrastructure and most of the government development schemes and schools. The leading southern secondary schools were simply transferred to the north. The lack of education and investment and the destruction of war meant that southerners who needed to earn cash to pay taxes or school fees or to buy consumer goods had to migrate and become unskilled laborers in northern cities, particularly the capital. Some were able to work for northern merchants who dominated trade in the south.

For northerners, the war was a peripheral issue in national politics, just as the south was peripheral to the economy—except that the southern issue had provided the occasion for toppling national governments in 1964 and 1969. Northern nationalism expressed the ideological correlates of the economic core: that the nation corresponds to the boundaries of the state and reflects the social characteristics of those who control it. Southern nationalism expressed the ideas of the periphery: that the nation consists of those exploited on the basis of their race, religion, and culture within a distinct region.

The new political economy of Sudan and the dominant nationalism to which it gave rise were both based on the creation of a core area focused on the northeast, particularly on the capital city. Those originally given access to the rewards that created this core achieved sufficient political power to vest their interests and successfully defend the ensuing inequalities in regional investment. In a short time, it became rational for any profit-seeking entrepreneur, local or foreign, to invest in enterprises in the northeast core area.

This potent combination of regionally concentrated economic investment and education meant that patrons among the riverine peoples of the north consolidated decisive advantages in controlling wealth and policymaking, which they exercised after independence. Though the British intended their policy only to produce wealth for Sudan quickly, its consequences and the civil war that followed turned the south into a peripheral area, discontinuously integrated into the national economy—principally as a source of labor and secondarily for trade in agriculture and animal products for consumer goods. Though not disrupted by war and sharing Islam to a greater degree, eastern and far western areas of the country were similarly linked to the northeast core of the national economy.

Thus, significant but limited early nineteenth century differences in social stratification were turned into decisive relations of political and economic dominance and subordination by the time Sudan received its independence a century and a quarter later. Ethnicity, region, and religion became the metaphors expressing these seemingly irreversible structural relationships.

Dampening the Salience of Social Cleavages: The Addis Ababa Agreement

For a regrettably short time, the 1972 Addis Ababa Agreement committed northern and southern leaders to cooperate on initiatives that reduced political reliance on ethnicity, region, and religion. But the agreement did not alter any of the basic parameters of the political economy that had made those social identifications salient for the maintenance of political power of northern and southern leaders. On the one hand, the agreement called for all leading public figures to abandon the confrontational politics of ethnicity, region, and religion in favor of joint efforts for peaceful development. On the other hand, the incorporation of southern politicians into the existing system of patronage ensured that relations with the center would depend fundamentally on ethnicity, region, and religion. Eleven years later, these contradictory streams of incentives had definitively crippled the prospects for using the agreement to transform the long-standing social cleavages that deeply divided Sudan.

Though the first civil war had been conducted intermittently and without much overall direction, it had strongly reinforced southerners' distinctive sense of region and African culture. However, the growing belief in a southern nationality had not replaced the older patchwork of more localized ethnic identifications by the time the agreement was signed. Meanwhile, the successful coup d'état in 1969 that made Jaafar al-Nimeiri head of state created confusion within the Northern nationalist movement that was not resolved until he was overthrown sixteen years later. In large measure, the agreement was negotiated by leaders on both sides who were responding to the same predicament—the lack of acceptance by presumptive supporters.

The southern guerrilla movement, called the Anya-Nya, consisted of many small groups that organized violent resistance, starting in the early 1960s. It failed on numerous occasions to create a unified organization that was widely accepted by southerners. Ambitious civilian and military southern leaders, often relying on ethnic bases, frequently attacked each other rather than engaging the national army. Though the Southern Sudan Liberation Movement (SSLM), led by Joseph Lagu, was the most successful and best organized of these groups, it had been created only three years before the negotiations and was still, even as it engaged in the bargaining, in the process of achieving recognition among southerners active in the liberation movement.

The military government not only had recently seized power but also had adopted a radical stance, allied itself with the Sudanese Communist party (SCP), and attacked the patrons of both of Sudan's large religious movements—even sending soldiers to oust Imam al Hadi al-Mahdi, grandson of the original Mahdi. Shortly afterward, Nimeiri denounced the SCP and was then briefly overthrown by army units that supported the party. Loyal army units returned him to power six months before the negotiations, but the absence of public support on the right and the left could not have been more conspicuous.

A Solution for the Southern Problem

On taking office in 1969, Nimeiri had agreed to a long-standing SCP policy calling for regional autonomy for the south on the basis of its cultural and historical differences. Though this was regarded as a radical policy—reversing earlier northern expectations for the progressive Islamization and Arabization of the south—it remained, in 1971, a cornerstone for the negotiations. By the time the negotiations actually got under way, however, the radicals had been replaced by middle-of-the-road politicians and technocrats—both southerners and northerners—who rejected both the radical left and the Islamic right. These political figures had very limited popular support in either the north or the south, but they did have the commitment of the military government. They intensified the series of contacts initiated before the abortive SCP coup. Led by Abel Alier, Nimeiri's new minister for southern affairs, a group of southern leaders who had worked throughout the war with the national government, rather than with the liberation movement, were given the responsibility by Nimeiri for developing the government's negotiating position. Meanwhile, Lagu also named a team of negotiators. Most had recently been appointed by the SSLM and did not occupy critical positions in the organization. Both Lagu and Nimeiri may have felt that an agreement would consolidate their own positions. More likely, they believed that the negotiations would founder.

The manifest rationale for the negotiations was to end the civil war by finding a solution for the southern problem—a political framework in which southerners could be confident that they could achieve security and prosperity within a united Sudan, which all the participants inevitably assumed would be run by northerners with close links to the northeast core of the national economy. This required the negotiators to dispense, somehow, with the long-standing contradictions between northern and southern nationalisms. The pragmatic solution chosen was to ignore these contradictions by proclaiming a new nationalism in which the government explicitly recognized that Sudan was an African country in which unity was created out of diversity.

The agreement had two principal features. First, it created a single autonomous southern region, combining the three southern provinces (Equatoria, Bahr al Ghazal, and Upper Nile) in a parliamentary system that, because it was accountable to the national government, fell short of a federa-tion. Second, it integrated 6,000 dissident soldiers into the national army and limited the national government's troops in the south to the same number. The agreement could succeed only so long as the head of state did not exercise his prerogative to reverse decisions made by southern region officials. That he would not was, of course, an informal understanding among the negotiators. To outmanuever northerners or southerners who might try to kill the agreement at the last minute, Nimeiri declared the agreement to be law in advance of the date set for ratification. As it happened, SSLM officials did reject the agreement, and they sent Lagu to the ratification ceremonies bearing unacceptable new conditions. However, he was persuaded to abandon these conditions, to ratify the agreement, and even to fly to Khartoum to celebrate the end of the war with Nimeiri.

For additional protection, southern politicians managed to entrench the agreement in the new "permanent" constitution adopted by the national government in 1973. In addition, despite strong opposition in the Constituent Assembly, southerners introduced restrictions into the constitution limiting the use of *sharia* (Islamic law) as the basis for legislation. Nimeiri took special pains to support southern aspirations. He made Abel Alier a national vice-president and Lagu a major-general. He welcomed a detachment of southern troops, recruited into the national army from Anya-Nya ranks into his presidential guard. He opened his formerly radical vanguard movement, the Sudanese Socialist Union (SSU), to all southerners, whether or not they sup-ported his government.

Promoting a New National Ethos

The most obvious consequence of the successful negotiations was to turn southerners, despite lingering doubts, from rebels to outspoken supporters of national unity. The government took advantage of the triumph to promote a new national ethos—stressing a secular state, democracy, national unity, and a commitment to Africa. In each case, it explicitly repudiated the social cleavages of ethnicity, region, and religion in its efforts to build widespread support for a "new Sudan" and, in the bargain, some sorely needed legitimacy for itself.

Nimeiri was quite direct about this:

> We are talking about a fact of life in the new Sudan; a reality that the whole world can see. To get to where we are now, we had first of all to liberate the Sudanese man and woman from administrative, tribal and sectarian tyrannies, thus creating the logical climate for resolving the Southern question.[2]

In the political language of Sudan, this was a rejection of the leadership of the religious movements and ethnic notables. A few months after the agreement was adopted, Nimeiri stressed the government's commitment to recast Sudan's international image more as an African nation and, thus, less as an outpost of the Middle East—an image that had reinforced the social cleavages of both religion and region: "By consolidation of her National Unity, she created an example for the Unity of North and South on the African Continent. The Sudan is, in fact, a miniature model of Africa."[3]

The intellectual framework for the government's position was officially articulated in *Peace and Unity in Sudan,* a revisionist history of Sudan prepared by the Ministry of Foreign Affairs to celebrate the Addis Ababa Agreement and chart the government's future course: "Our country is an amalgam of complex diversities which the passage of history has brought into clashes and mergers."[4] The agreement meant, the government insisted, that "Sudan is better placed to play the role of a link between the two parts of Africa, the Negro part and the Arab part," while also providing "a first step in tackling problems of ethnicity." This is possible because

> . . . the labels of identification are not rigid, but are dynamic. . . . We in the Sudan today are not striving to deny the diverse realities of our identifications whether those be tribal, religious, ethnic, racial or cultural. But we are resolved to build our common national identity on those factors which unite us and give us common pride in our country.

In other words, according to the official theory, the Addis Ababa Agreement created the social momentum that enabled the government to begin to change the situation so that existing social cleavages would no longer deeply divide Sudanese society.

The government's theory was entirely plausible, but would it actually account for subsequent Sudanese politics? The precise theoretical issue was whether the existing economic domination of the state, or the coercive force available to the military, or the legitimacy of the regime was sufficient to create the desired social situation in which hitherto fundamental cleavages would no longer determine political response. In hindsight, it must be judged a brave and imaginative as well as probably a desperate and self-interested gesture that did not succeed. Whether this was a failure of nerve and public duty, as prominent southern defenders of the agreement insisted, or a failure preordained by the structure of the political economy, as the SPLM argued, is crucial to the question of peaceful settlement of the second civil war.

The Breakdown of the Addis Ababa Agreement and the Revival of Social Cleavages in Sudanese Politics

The failure of the Addis Ababa Agreement to refocus social identification was due, in large part, to the unwillingness of both northern and southern political leaders to incur the political risks involved in supporting it and in working within its rules. Nevertheless, just carrying out an agreement between distrustful national and regional officials kept alive regional, religious, and ethnic cleavages. Factional competition within southern politics weakened southern unity and allowed the national government to intervene in regional disputes in violation of the agreement. Nimeiri's desperate search for a secure northern political base led him to cast aside his southern loyalties and then to violate the terms of the agreement. When large oil reserves were discovered in the south, northerners were motivated to undermine the agreement for fear of future secession, and southerners expressed frustration with the agreement because it did not protect mineral rights for the south. As the agreement crumbled, the underlying social cleavages once again became explicit bases for political action.

By creating a single southern region, the Addis Ababa Agreement gave administrative expression to southern nationalism for the first time, even though the extent of independent control by southerners remained in question. The new working relationships created by the agreement provoked issues that raised further distrust between southerners striving to protect regional autonomy, but essentially without the economic resources to do so, and northerners intent on preventing the quasi-autonomous south from making a bid for a more distinct separation. As the issues created conflict, regional, religious, and ethnic cleavages once again rose to the surface. Had these issues been successfully resolved in the same spirit as the negotiation of the Addis Ababa Agreement, the net effect might have been to reduce, even further, their importance for Sudanese political conflict. Instead, the implementation of the agreement, combined with other political issues—some not even closely related to north–south disputes, others not even anticipated when the agreement was signed—destroyed the social momentum for building a "common national identity."

Political and Military Issues

Sorting out the military relationships imposed by the agreement provided the greatest threat and, consequently, the deepest temptation to focus political issues on regionalism and thus seriously to challenge the government's invitation to refocus social identifications. The agreement not only limited the number of northern troops in the south but also called for the absorption of the ex–Anya-Nya soldiers into the national army under the same field command as the northern troops, whom they had formerly been fighting. Southern nervousness over the number, arms, and activities of northern military forces stationed in the southern region led to accusations and several mutinies in the first years after the agreement. Nevertheless, according to Alier, the phased integration of former combatants was surprisingly successful during the first four years.[5] It was not until 1983, when Nimeiri ordered southern troops to serve in the north, that the Bor mutiny touched off the second civil war—just as a similar order in 1955 had caused the insubordination of the Equatoria Corps, generally taken as the beginning of the first period of southern armed resistance.

Political issues that erupted between the center and the south further entrenched the political cleavage between regions of the country. Southerners deeply resented Nimeiri's use of his presidential office to manipulate the choice of the head of the regional government. The Addis Ababa Agreement gave Nimeiri the right to appoint the president of the southern region upon recommendation of the regional assembly. This was one of the powers that both sides at Addis Ababa had understood to be symbolic, not substantive. When Alier, who did not have widespread political support in the south, was challenged for the regional post, Nimeiri issued an official decree declaring that the SSU, the official party, endorsed Alier's candidacy. That violated no rules, but it aroused resentment among southern politicians, who felt they could not publicly oppose the president's wishes, though one of them attacked his intervention from the regional assembly floor.

That incident could be explained away as a manipulative but legal maneuver. Later, however, Nimeiri clearly disregarded the agreement's rules by dissolving the regional assembly and replacing the head of the regional government in February 1980 and again in October 1981. In both cases, he was careful to gain the support of some (though not the same) southern politicians, but by this time the southern politicians had become sharply divided by ethnic considerations. For those southern politicians on the losing side (first one faction, then another), Nimeiri seemed ready to revive the confrontation between the national government and the southern region.

Administrative disputes further deepened this sense of regional confrontation. There had been jostling between the center and the region over the right of the national president to expect his provincial commissioners in the south to inspect and report on activities of the regional civil service, particularly the police and teachers. (The southern region was still divided into three provinces for administrative purposes.) More significantly, Nimeiri divided the three southern region provinces into six in 1976—a clear but unchallenged violation of the agreement. Far more serious was the attempt by the national parliament in November 1980 to change the boundaries of the southern region to incorporate into the north a part of the area where oil had recently been discovered. This time the south erupted in demonstrations, and Nimeiri eventually instructed the parliament to pass the bill with the old boundaries intact.

Finance for the South and the Discovery of Oil

The oil issue was one of two different economic conflicts between the southern region and the national government that also intensified regional identification as the basis for political loyalty. The other was the south's overwhelming dependence on northern finance for any economic activity at all. The south counted on the national government for 75 to 90 percent of the revenue for its annual budget, but usually received much less.[6] Left to its own resources, the south could neither pay its civil servants or ministers nor invest in either maintenance or development. Indeed, it was never able to repair the few revenue-producing schemes that had been damaged in the first civil war, and therefore it had only a tiny tax base.

The two issues cut in opposite directions, though both exacerbated the sense of regional identification. Financial dependence on the north is a direct reflection of the extraordinarily peripheral relationship of the southern region to the core of the Sudanese political economy—exacerbated by the destruction of civil war. The presence in the south of at least 70 percent of the oil discovered so far creates the possibility of a new core, or at least a new southern economic growth pole.[7] The agreement had clearly awarded control over natural gas and minerals to the central government, perhaps because the negotiators had not dreamed of the possibility of any such discoveries (Chevron's first strike occurred in 1979) and thus had not thought to protect the south.

The presence of oil increased northern fears of southern secession—as demonstrated by the crude ploy of trying to move the border southward—and southern fears that the benefits of oil would be bottled up in the north. The issue was fought over the location of an oil refinery expected to stimulate local economic development. Southern regional politicians pushed for a site in Bentiu near the oil fields; but in 1981, the national government ultimately decided, on cost-efficiency grounds, to locate it in Kusti, a growing industrial northern town on the Nile. The decision was greeted with much bitterness and strong feelings of regional betrayal throughout the south. It readied southerners and northerners to interpret Nimeiri's next moves as abandoning Addis Ababa Agreement in favor of the old politics of regional identification.

Nimeiri's Measures to Gain Support

Meanwhile, Nimeiri faced desperate problems in finding a secure base of political support. Though the Addis Ababa Agreement made him genuinely popular throughout the south, that was a small fraction of the population and the most subordinate part of the political economy. The dominant social forces in the political economy had been attacked by Nimeiri's soldiers and had had some of their assets confiscated. With the rupture occasioned by the abortive 1971 Communist coup d'état, Nimieri attempted to use the Addis Ababa Agreement as a formula to build a new political base. He reckoned without the staying power of existing patronage relations, however. So in 1977, he took the first steps to create an alliance with the conservative notables who led the largest northern religious movements and the fundamentalist Muslim Brotherhood, despite the narrow failure by some of these very leaders to overthrow him only one year earlier. They entered the government, but they refused to pay more than lip service to Nimeiri. Thus, after a few years, it was clear that this overture had failed. Nevertheless, it had restored the economically powerful proponents of Islam—as well as their agenda—to the national government.

In response, Nimeiri took the desperate step of proclaiming that he would adopt his own version of the *sharia,* in which he himself would become the imam. Once again, he attempted to outflank the leadership of the established movements by attracting notables from smaller brotherhoods and those who preferred a more fundamentalist orientation for the government. He was immediately criticized publicly by Sadiq al-Mahdi—a leader of al-Ansar, whom he clapped into prison—and privately by most other respected Sudanese Islamic authorities. From the perspective of the southerners, he had reintroduced the religious and regional cleavage in the most emphatic way he could. To them, *sharia* could only mean that southerners had once again become second-class citizens, whose political rights were now reduced to the same level as their economic weaknesses.

Paradoxically, however, it was political maneuvering by one southern faction seeking to displace another that led to the public rupture of the agreement. The issue reached a climax a few months *before* Nimeiri declared his support for *sharia.* Politicians who had lost electoral control of the southern regional government proposed to redivide the south into the three regions that had existed as separate provinces before the Addis Ababa Agreement was adopted. They claimed that fear of perceived Dinka domination over all other ethnic groups could be resolved only by such an administrative separation. This proposal explicitly reintroduced ethnicity as a political cleavage in southern public life and played directly into Nimeiri's desparate search for northern political support. It provided the national government with enough southern allies to achieve the redivision, effectively destroying the Addis Ababa Agreement and triggering the outbreak of the second civil war.

The Politics of Patronage and Ethnic Divisions

A closer look at southern politics is essential to understand this astonishing reversal. With the introduction of elections in 1953, southern politics was organized on the basis of factional competition. In the south, holding a political post was one of the few ways to earn a cash income. It was no wonder, therefore, that Lagu once observed that "the problem of the south is inherent in the position of the southern intellectuals. . . . Every intellectual wants to hold an important post."[8] The negotiators of the Addis Ababa Agreement took it for granted that patronage was an important way to integrate various factions into the political system.

The agreement had simply introduced new southern patrons into a well-understood system. Nimieri, for example, appointed the chief southern figures on both sides of the negotiating table to crucial roles in the army and the new regional government. They, in turn, appointed their trusted lieutenants to regional cabinet and civil service positions and controlled the recruitment into the new southern units in the national army. No one raised any questions about this—who, after all, could better implement the new agreement? But continuation of patronage laid emphasis on the resources of patrons to maintain a following. In southern Sudan, these followings were constructed first and foremost on the basis of ethnicity and were maintained through the provision of official positions and the perquisites that went with them. Ethnicity was as important a resource for factional leaders in the south as religion was for leaders in the north. Other factional bonds—former political party membership, inside or outside status during the first civil war, and provincial residence—also provided ties between patrons and clients, but none of these was as significant as the links of ethnicity. As James Tombura, the last head of a single southern region, admitted, "If you look critically, you will find the cabinet is composed of different tribes. It is a United Nations by itself."[9]

Over the decade after the agreement was signed, ethnicity became ever more salient as factional competition among southern politicians became more fierce. The competition for control over the regional government crystallized into a battle between factions led by Alier and Lagu in 1977. At the time, Lagu's faction, though including more outsiders than Alier's, represented all parts of the south. But after displacing Alier as head of the south, Lagu ran into difficulties, and his government was removed from office in 1980. Shortly thereafter, he championed the smaller ethnic groups of Equatoria province by calling for redivision.[10] By raising this issue as a question of "Dinka dominance," he turned ethnic identification into a legitimate political question within southern politics. That split the unity of southern politicians in support of the Addis Ababa Agreement, making it much easier for northern politicians to break up the south. Shortly afterward, following time-honored patronage practices, Nimeiri made Lagu second vice-president of Sudan in place of Alier.

Nevertheless, the immediate cause for the resumption of civil war was the order given to southern soldiers stationed at the Bor Garrison to proceed to a new station in the north. With this command, the national government made explicit its belief that it could no longer trust southern military units. That recognition put the north–south regional cleavage, complicated by internal southern political disputes, back at center stage. The formal prohibition negotiated in the agreement against rotating southern troops to the north had officially lapsed, but up to 1983, an informal understanding and growing mutual suspicion had sustained the policy. The order produced a mutiny. Lieutenant-Colonel John Garang, by coincidence on vacation leave at his home in Bor, was asked by the soldiers to assume command. He chose the occasion to form the Sudan People's Liberation Army (SPLA) and go into rebellion. But he did not carry the support of all southerners. As a Dinka, he was particularly distrusted by politicians who represented the ethnic groups of Equatoria region (the old provinces became regions after redivision). That was the last part of the south to which the SPLA carried the war.

By September 1983, all remaining momentum to redefine the Sudanese political situation in terms that excluded ethnic, regional, and religious cleavages between north and south as well as within the south had utterly disappeared. The Addis Ababa Agreement, once the ideological foundation of the national government, had become a dead letter. A pattern of governmental immobility emerged. For the next five years, all political initiatives—attempted by three distinctly different governments—foundered on the *sharia,* the civil war, and the disunity among southern politicians. The familiar deep divisions within the Sudanese political economy set extremely narrow policy limits, and the interaction of the main antagonists worked increasingly to reduce room for maneuvering. The intertwining of all three cleavages sharply separated north from south and, at the same time, fragmented the south.

The End of the Nimeiri Regime

In the last two years of his regime, Nimeiri became increasingly isolated and thus erratic in his search for political support that would sustain his regime. The repression that accompanied the introduction of *sharia* tainted it for northern Muslims. Not only did Nimeiri imprison his critics, but he was also willing to countenance harsh Islamic penalties—flogging and amputation—thus dismaying his erstwhile supporters. Perhaps the most shocking sign of Nimeiri's weakness was his execution in January 1985—for heresy—of Mahmoud Mohammed Taha, leader of the Republican Brothers, a small sect that had formerly been a strong supporter of the president. Eventually, only weeks before the overthrow, even the Muslim Brotherhood, which had supported Nimeiri's version of *sharia,* was banned, and its leader, Hassan al-Turabi, was put in prison.

Meanwhile, the SPLA, which had rapidly organized itself with military assistance from Ethiopia and Libya, soon proved capable of disrupting the peace with impunity in Upper Nile. However, it was challenged by Anya-Nya II, another guerrilla group, perceived as made up largely of Nuer. This led to a disturbing new pattern. To take advantage once again of southern disunity and bring pressure on the SPLA, which was perceived as a predominantly Dinka force, the national government formed an opportunistic alliance with Anya-Nya II and supplied it with weapons. This was the beginning of a new national government policy of arming southerners on an ethnic basis. In this way, ethnicity within the south became a murderous and increasingly entrenched factor in the new civil war.

The removal of Nimeiri eventually returned Sudan to surprisingly open, though flawed, democratic civilian rule. But the effect of transitional military rule and the democratic regime that followed—given the specific political conjuncture inherited from Nimeiri—served only to reinforce the government's promotion of all three cleavages, despite its evident desire to moderate them. Just as in 1964, the overthrow of Nimeiri was precipitated by civilian demonstrators on the streets of Khartoum, organized by professional associations and joined at the last moment by the army. But this time, the generals did not return to their barracks and let the civilians organize the government. Instead, they formed the Transitional Military Council (TMC), under which a civilian cabinet functioned. The SPLA, which had declared a cease-fire as soon as Nimeiri was overthrown, denounced the assumption of power by "Nimeiri's generals" and refused to stop the civil war. Though the TMC immediately decreed the reunification of the south in a vain effort to placate the SPLA, continuation of the war forced it to administer each of the three former regions separately—within the increasingly narrow limits of national governmental power in the south.

Social Cleavages as the Basis for Fighting the Civil War

The elements of continuity with Nimeiri's policies outweighed any attempted changes—particularly in relation to the south. Perhaps the most desperate example was the TMC's expansion of Nimeiri's policy of arming militia among ethnic groups. To have southerners, instead of northern soldiers, fighting the SPLA may have been a short-run rational response for an army that was demoralized by the loss of most of its battles with the SPLA and the progressive loss of control of the countryside, even in Equatoria. But in the longer run, it could only destabilize the south on an ethnic basis. In the Reverend Clement Janda's eyes:

> When military activity is carried out by militia of an ethnic group, the memory will linger on for years, and one cannot rule out the wish of the aggrieved party to organize revenge. . . . Is the government deciding to turn the Sudan into another Lebanon where each political group owns an army or militia?[11]

For example, by May 1985, the Mundari people in Equatoria had been armed to resist the SPLA. During the last few years of the Nimeiri regime, automatic weapons from the national army's arsenals found their way into the hands of members of Muslim Baggara nomadic groups living in the southern Kordofan and Darfur regions. But these groups have intermittently feuded with their southern Dinka neighbors for centuries. The opportunity and desire for vengeance was too much to resist, and they immediately engaged in a wave of murderous attacks on nearby Dinka. Meanwhile, the SPLA attacked targets in the Kordofan and Blue Nile regions as part of its strategy of demonstrating that the civil war was national, not regional. The shock of SPLA attacks in northern Sudan led to the sharply increased distribution of arms and the formation of militia among Muslim groups, which wreaked far more devastation among their southern neighbors.

Because the TMC declared itself an interim administration dedicated to retiring from politics after holding elections within one year, all substantive changes in response to criticism of Nimeiri's policies were held in abeyance. The elections in April 1986 put Sadiq al-Mahdi into power at the head of a delicately balanced coalition government of the parties representing the two leading religious movements. But the momentum generated by overthrowing Nimeiri had disappeared, which meant that religious, regional, and ethnic cleavages were progressively deepened. Most important, despite promises to eliminate the September Laws—as Nimeiri's version of *sharia* was popularly referred to—the TMC insisted on maintaining them, while agreeing that they would have to be cleansed of the "impurities" imposed in Nimeiri's version. But nothing was done during the TMC's year in power, aside from suspending the worst excesses in the enforcement of the *sharia* punishments. Nor was the coalition government under Sadiq able even to introduce the legislation it continually promised, which in any event was intended to modify Nimeiri's version, not eliminate it. Meanwhile, the SPLA emphatically refused to negotiate an end to the war and a new constitution until the national government removed the *sharia*. Thus, the religious cleavage continued to make peace impossible.

The shocking al-Daein massacre in March 1987 sharply revealed the degree to which these three social cleavages had deepened political divisions beyond anything previously imagined and thus had made the prospects of a peaceful settlement so much more daunting. Reportedly, more than a thousand unarmed Dinka civilians living in al-Daein, Darfur region, were slaughtered by armed Rezeigat militiamen, mostly at the railway station, where they were waiting for trains to take them to safety.[12] Sadiq, the prime minister, claimed that the militiamen were taking revenge for an attack on them by the SPLA a week or two earlier. But that battle had been between two armed groups and had taken place in the context of a series of exchanges, in at least some of which the Rezeigat had been the aggressors. Furthermore, it had taken place in the Safaha marshes 158 miles south of al-Daien. Apparently, no public commission was appointed to inquire into the massacre, nor was any effort made to discipline the perpetrators.

In Mahmud and Baldo's analysis, the roots of the massacre can be traced to the breakdown of the 1976 Babanusa Accord, which stopped the intermittent but long-standing feuds between the Rezeigat and the Dinka over water rights for cattle. The success of that accord can be traced to the momentum in changing social identifications created by the Addis Ababa Agreement and supported by both the national and the southern regional governments. In 1985, famine in Kordofan had forced some Rezeigat south, and they had been given land in areas acknowledged to be Dinka. Because the members of the national government perceived the SPLA in ethnic terms, and thus as a predominantly Dinka force, they encouraged the formation of the Rezeigat militia and armed them, as well as providing more powerful weapons to their neighbors, the already armed Miisseiriya *marahillin*. The government's purpose, Mahmud and Baldo argued, was to foment attacks that would undermine Dinka support for the SPLA. The government, it ought to be recognized, was badly unsettled by a string of military losses in the south as well as by the SPLA attacks in the North.

In any event, the escalating violence that followed affected both soldiers and civilians. It apparently involved not only raping, killing, and looting in the heat of battle, but also the seizure of Dinka men, women, and children, who were forcibly taken back to Rezeigat areas as slaves. Mahmud and Baldo substantiated these claims with personal reports from some who escaped or whose relatives had been taken as slaves. They believed that new economic needs among Rezeigat in some areas provided the incentive for taking slaves. The Rezeigat and other northern Muslim Arab groups, such as the Miisseiriya and the Ruf'aa, could carry out their plans because the government's policy was to arm militias in areas with a history of ethnic, regional, and religious strife, without making any effort to control them.

The consequences of these attacks are worth noting because they frame the meaning of the civil war for the participants. Creating militias universally perceived as ethnic in both the north and the south, whether or not that was the government's intention, unavoidably entrenched ethnic identification as the basis for war and thus the problem for peace. Because the Rezeigat and the Miisseiriya were also perceived as northerners and as Arab Muslims and the Dinka were regarded as southerners following their own religion or Christianity, the long-standing social cleavages were seen as the basis for the civil war. Peace negotiations could not be organized other than on the terms of these cleavages. Consequently, a settlement was all the more unlikely, despite pronouncements on both sides of a desire to negotiate.

The New SPLM Challenge to Conventional Peace Formulas

Since its founding in 1983, the SPLM has explicitly insisted that the solution to the breakdowns caused by the revival and intensification of social cleavages required nothing less than the reorganization of the political economy of a united Sudan. The movement put forward neither a demand for secession nor a proposal for a separate "southern" solution along the lines of the Addis Ababa Agreement. Instead, it called for genuine power-sharing between the center and the periphery. Its proposals threatened the unchallenged domination of those northern groups whose privileged position stemmed from the formation of the economy of the condominium. Because the SPLM quickly gained military control of the southern countryside and demonstrated the capacity to hold *northern* towns for lengthy periods, its rationale had to be taken seriously. Though some northern progressives supported the SPLM, they represented a tiny fraction of northern public opinion. All northern power-holders from Nimeiri forward have responded to the SPLM's demands with peace proposals based on the conventional parameters of Sudanese politics. Each of these proposals was emphatically rejected. Consequently, the prospects for a peaceful settlement appeared highly unlikely, despite a continuous flurry of initiatives from private and governmental actors.

The SPLM theory of social cleavages was not explicitly spelled out in the speeches and documents it published, though its demands for immediate policy changes were quite specific. In essence, the theory asserted that political and economic rule by one core group led to domination of all peripheral groups. Social cleavages in Sudanese society, it argued, marked the boundaries and described the relations between these groups—not only in the south, but also in equally poor areas in the west, the east, and the center. The cleavages were the product of uneven development, which led to domination by a privileged group. Once in existence, the cleavages both supported the pattern of domination and provided widely shared popular explanations that helped to sustain it. Therefore, the political salience of these cleavages could be reduced only by making changes at the center, not by tinkering with regional governance. The thrust of the argument was democratic and populist, but not majoritarian. It called for decentralization of power, not just deconcentration of administration. The theory radically widened the argument beyond anything contemplated at the Addis Ababa negotiations and, of course, utterly ruled out the notion—still entertained by certain powerful northern politicians—that peace in Sudan could follow from an imposed cultural policy of Arabization or a religious policy of Islamization.

The only point on which the SPLM agreed with the national government was Sudan's territorial integrity—which is why the S in SPLM stands for *Sudan* not *Southern*. The divergences began with the SPLM's interpretation of its fundamental premise "that Sudan is multiracial and multireligious."[13] Though Muslims are in the majority, "a Sudan based on a sectarian majority cannot be viable." For the SPLM, that also ruled out political arrangements based on either the African or the non-Arab majority. "Dictatorship by one racial group or by one religious group over the others is clearly a recipe for disaster and explains why the Sudan has been at war within itself for 21 of her 32 years of political independence." Peaceful resolution depended on "a national consensus on the fundamental problems of the Sudan: the economy, power sharing at the center; the nationality question; the religious question, et cetera." A national constitutional conference of all political forces in the country was the only way to develop solutions for these issues. Thus, the SPLM rejected the Addis Ababa Agreement, because it was based on the assumption that the south was a peripheral region in a system dominated by certain northern groups. By the same logic, the SPLM rejected those southerners who formed alliances with Khartoum in opposition to its own program.

Unlike the at least official consensus that stemmed from the Addis Ababa Agreement, the SPLM approach did not suggest that a new identity would arise to take the place of ethnicity, religion, and region. It expected to maintain existing social identities while removing cleavages by increasing the power of the disadvantaged regional groups all over the country. Presumably, the absence of dominance would encourage groups to live together peacefully.

Because they lacked economic and social power, the SPLM appealed to the disadvantaged in all parts of the county, plus the progressives in the center. Together, these groups probably amounted to a majority of the population. But Sudanese politics, at least since the formation of the condominium, had never created direct links among them. It was particularly significant that progressive forces, for which Garang had evident appeal, had succeeded in overthrowing two Sudanese military governments—in 1964 and 1985. But the last-minute success of Nimeiri's generals in taking over the interim regime emasculated the power of the National Alliance for the Salvation of the Country (NASC), a loose grouping of professional associations that had organized the popular meetings that conclusively demonstrated Nimeiri's lack of popular support. These professionals, and almost all of the political parties that had joined them in overthrowing Nimeiri, sent representatives to meet with the SPLM in Koka Dam, Ethiopia, in March 1986.[14] The declaration that emerged from that conference—which, with the exception of one point, followed the SPLM rationale—demonstrated that there was northern support for the SPLM theory.

However, the NASC had steadily lost its legitimacy, energy, and professional support during the transitional year, particularly as the parties prepared themselves for the national elections that were organized by the interim government only one month after the Koka Dam meeting. Though some notables representing disadvantaged groups in other parts of the country, particularly the leaders of the Nuba, expressed support for the SPLM, most were quite guarded. Finally, the consternation in the north caused by the SPLA's attacks in northern Sudan—and particularly by SPLA occupation of northern towns such as Kurmuk for several months—demonstrated that most northern political leaders were not willing to take the SPLM argument seriously.

From the day it took office, the government of Sadiq al-Mahdi seemed almost entirely consumed with unending consultations to balance the demands of notables from different parties in order to form a cabinet that could govern. Meeting the most important programmatic demand of the SPLM—the elimination of Nimeiri's September Laws—was beyond the national government's political capacity and was never its intention, even though it finally introduced legislation revising the *sharia* laws in late 1988. It simply did not have a sufficiently secure political base to consider any aspects of the SPLM rationale on their merits, which forced it to act to entrench the regional, religious, and ethnic cleavages more deeply. Thus, despite the exhaustion and utter impoverishment of the national economy, the second civil war remained firmly in deadlock at the end of 1988, even with the best efforts of would-be peacemakers.

Conclusion

The Sudanese case demonstrates the immense difficulties in finding a path to peace for a second time. The pattern of social stratification that developed in the nineteenth century was sharply focused and then entrenched by northern groups, which were able to vest great economic advantages during the condominium and then dominate the political economy after independence. Further economic development perpetuated the pattern of inequality. The resulting social cleavages of region, religion, and ethnicity marked the inferior status of peripheral regions, heightened the political salience of the deep divisions in Sudanese society, and led to the first civil war.

Unexpectedly, a peaceful end to that war was negotiated, and both the southern and the national governments devoted considerable energy to creating a new Afro-Arab Sudanese identity. But those whose economic and political dominance rested on maintenance of the long-standing social cleavages could not be so easily overcome. The military regime under Nimeiri never acquired adequate support to maintain the agreement, and eventually it disintegrated. The position of the SPLM in prosecuting the second civil war was to demand that regions disadvantaged by unequal development be given effective power in future governance. Enormously weakened by the war, the national government was unwilling to consider this demand, unable to defeat the SPLM, and virtually incapable of governing the country. In 1988, no one knew how to untie this Gordian knot.

References

1. Francis M. Deng, *Seed of Redemption* (New York: Lillian Barber Press, 1986), p. viii.

2. Democratic Republic of Sudan, Ministry of Culture and Information, *Unity Day Speeches by President Nimeiri and Vice-President Abel Alier, Juba, 3rd March 1973* (Omdurman, 1973), p. 4.

3. Quoted from a speech by Nimeiri on May 25, 1972, in Democratic Republic of Sudan, Ministry of Culture, Information, Youth and Sports, Southern Region, *President Nyerere's Visit to the Southern Region, 1974* (Juba, 1974), p. 11.

4. The quotations in this paragraph are from Democratic Republic of Sudan, Ministry of Foreign Affairs, *Peace and Unity in the Sudan: An African Achievement* (Khartoum: Khartoum University Press, 1973), pp. 99, 94–95, 102.

5. Abel Alier, *Peace and Development in the Southern Region* (Khartoum: Ministry of Culture and Information, 1976), pp. 41–51.

6. See Democratic Republic of Sudan, Southern Regional Ministry of Finance, *Regional Budget 1974/75* (Juba: Publications Bureau, 1974), p. 1; and Abel Alier, "Policy Statement to the Third People's Regional Assembly, 7th July, 1980" (mimeographed copy of an official, but unpublished statement from the author's files), pp. 1, 3.

7. Nagi Saliem Boulis, "Everything's Oil Right," *Sudanow,* March 1983, p. 11. Estimates of how much oil Sudan had ran from 1 billion to 10 billion barrels—enough to cover domestic consumption and exports for a few years, but not enough to finance any grandiose schemes.

8. Interview in *al-Sahafah* (Khartoum), September 1, 1982, translated in Joint Publications Research Service, No. 82-227, November 15, 1982, p. 107.

9. Quoted in *Sudanow,* July 1983, p. 13.

10. Joseph Lagu, *Decentralisation: A Necessity for the Southern Provinces of the Sudan* (Khartoum: Samar Press, April 1981).

11. Clement Janda, in *The Guiding Star* (Khartoum), May 29, 1986, p. 5, reprinted in Joint Publications Research Service, *Near East and Africa,* No. 86-094, August 1, 1986.

12. Ushari Ahmad Mahmud and Suleyman Ali Baldo, *Human Rights Violations in the Sudan 1987: Al Diein Massacre, Slavery in the Sudan* (Khartoum, July 1987); and Alfred Logune Tabar, "Danger in Darfur," *Sudanow,* May 1987, pp. 28–29.

13. "Highlight on the Civil War in the Sudan: Why the War Continues," Radio of the SPLA, July 27, 1987, in Foreign Broadcast Information Service, Southeast Asia and North Africa, No. 150, August 5, 1987, p. G1. All the quotations from this paragraph are taken from this press statement. Earlier elaborations of essentially the same position may be found in John Garang, *John Garang Speaks,* Ed. and Intro. Mansour Khalid (London: KPI, 1987).

14. "The Koka Dam Declaration, March 24, 1986 (A Proposed Programme for National Action)," in Garang, *John Garang Speaks,* p. 74.

22
Northern Muslim Perspectives

John O. Voll

T he civil war in Sudan is usually seen as a conflict between the north and the south, but this identification may obscure the complexities of the situation. Northern Sudan is itself a complex multiethnic society, with its own internal rivalries and dynamics. There is not a single unified "northern perspective" with regard to the north–south conflict. As a result, it is important to see both the differences and the common features of the northern Sudanese perspectives on the national conflict.

The Nature of the North

The geographic area that is referred to as northern Sudan is, in fact, a heterogeneous collection of different groups. There are many different northern Sudanese languages and a variety of northern Sudanese political traditions. *Northern* is, properly speaking, an adjective relating to the political, social, and cultural elements found in the northern part of what is now called the Sudan. When *the north* is used as a noun to represent a specific entity, it implies a contrast with *the south,* which, by inference, helps to define the North. It may not be too extreme to say that without the concept of the south, there is no "north" in Sudan. As a result, although the north–south conflict in Sudan reflects tensions within multiethnic Sudanese society, northerners, as northerners, cannot be considered a distinctive ethnic group. They do, however share some views on the nature of the north–south conflict and hopes for the future of Sudan.

The Role of Arabic

One shared characteristic of the peoples in Northern Sudan—that is, the area between Egyptian Nubia and the Nilotic homelands—is in the realm of language. The region contains significant linguistic diversity, but there is one language that tends to dominate society: Arabic. Regardless of the language that most northern Sudanese speak at home, in private family life, or in local ethnic activities, most northern Sudanese use Arabic as the medium for discussion of topics that educated people discuss. Arabic tends to be the language of formal education and the public language of people who are considered, or would like to be considered, intellectual.

This does not mean that these people are Arabs, nor does it necessarily mean that they come from Arabized groups. It only means that for discussions of certain types of subjects, Arabic is the language that is usually chosen as the medium of communication.

In this region, the vocabulary of nationalism, socialism, economics, and especially religious exegesis and world-view expression is Arabic. The vocabulary of the marketplace, of childraising, and of many other activities may be drawn from distinctive local language traditions. This presents an important shared characteristic: The language of regionwide affairs and of "great tradition" activities tends to be Arabic in northern Sudan.

It is in this relatively restricted sense that northern Sudan can be called Arabic. A significant proportion of northerners speak Arabic but are not identifiable as Arabs. For example, the first census after independence, in 1956, indicated that only about 55 percent of the population of the northern provinces were Arabs, even though a much larger proportion spoke Arabic. In the context of contemporary Sudan, "it should be emphasized that the increasing acquisition of Arabic as a second language does not necessarily lead to the assumption of Arab identity."[1] This is a continuation of the long-term historical evolution of northern Sudanese society. There had been interaction between Arabs and the inhabitants of the Sudan for centuries, with a significant cultural Arabization taking place. However, as a result of this process, even with regard to premodern times, it is possible to state that "the term Arab was progressively being emptied of nearly all its ethnic significance."[2]

The Arabic language thus provides a common element for people in northern Sudan but does not represent the basis for a northern ethnic identity. It is, instead, a common medium of communication for expressing disagreement as well as agreement among northerners.

Islam

A second feature in this broad cultural umbrella in northern Sudan is Islam. The overwhelming majority of the people in the region can be identified in some way as Muslims. However, this identification is not the basis for a single, simple group identity. The fact of diversity among Muslims everywhere, not just in northern Sudan, has long been recognized.

The shared dimensions among Muslims involve the belief in direct revelation from God to Muhammad, as preserved in the Koran, and a sense that this revelation provides the proper basis for human life. However, within this broad framework, many different traditions have emerged. Scholars such as Clifford Geertz and Michael Gilsenan have provided helpful analyses that "emphasize that seemingly similar Islamic institutions, prototypical figures and even concepts can resonate with contrasting meanings and serve strikingly different purposes from one community to another."[3]

The perspectives involved in the different Islamic traditions are shared. "It is the relations between them and the stress on a particular interpretation of a given element that are significant for the distinctions between movements and groups."[4] Talal Asad, an anthropologist who has done important studies of northern Sudanese groups, explained how Muslims share discursive traditions: "Islam is neither a distinctive social structure nor a heterogeneous collection of beliefs, artifacts, customs, and morals. It is a tradition." In Asad's conceptualization, there is not one discursive tradition but many: "An Islamic discursive tradition is simply a tradition of Muslim discourse that addresses itself to conceptions of the Islamic past and future, with reference to a particular Islamic practice in the present."[5] Within northern Sudan, a number of significant Islamic discursive traditions are the basis for the different northern Muslim perspectives with regard to the past, present, and future of Sudan.

Although northern Sudan can be described in a meaningful way as Arab and Islamic, or as Arab-Muslim, this does not mean that the north–south conflict can be described simply as a war between Muslims and non-Muslims or between Arabs and non-Arabs. Within the north, the Arabic language and Islam provide the means for discourse and the basis for perceptions, but they do not provide the basis for a unique group within the multiethnic society of Sudan. At the same time, the Arab-Muslim traditions of northern Sudan do provide a basis for distinctions between the north and the south in the country.

Perceptions of Sudanese Pluralism

The pluralist nature of Sudanese society has been viewed and described in various ways, depending on how the basic social units are identified and how relationships among those units are perceived. National and large-scale regional identities—such as "Sudanese" or "Southern" or "Northern"—are relatively recent. Some of the older features of identification have become more exclusive in their nature.

The Mosaic Metaphor

Historically, one of the major dynamics in northern Sudan has been the gradual introduction of Arabs and Arabic cultural elements. Along with this was the similarly gradual introduction of Islamic concepts and traditions. In general, new groups and cultures assimilated and adopted the existing ones. The processes of Islamization and Arabization in northern Sudan tended to be integrative, with a high degree of continuity. As the Sudanese anthropologist and diplomat, Francis Deng, has noted:

> That the North has maintained its previous group identities illustrates the way Islamization and Arabization built upon the pre-existing system. . . . By recognizing and building upon the traditional order, Islam became identified with the local community and rapidly ceased to be regarded as alien.[6]

According to one perception of Sudanese pluralism, diversity and heterogeneity are recognized and accepted, but the separate units are viewed as having the potential for being integrated rather than being destroyed. Accordingly, it is possible to maintain clear ethnic autonomy within a broader pattern of social interaction and identification. This tendency has often been noted about Muslim societies in the Middle East. It has been said, for example, that the "most conspicuous fact about Middle Eastern civilization is that in each country the population consists of a mosaic of people."[7] This mosaic metaphor does "little more than indicate the fact of significant internal regional differentiation" in a manner that is not unique to the Middle East,[8] but such a metaphor does help to identify one form of social organization within a multiethnic society and can, to some extent, be applied to northern Sudan.

As a description of northern Sudanese society, the mosaic metaphor has its limits. It is probable that the boundaries of the mosaic in premodern Sudan were defined by the Arab-Muslim traditions of discourse. In the modern era, in addition to these limits, it appears—at least in conceptual terms—that the "old mosaic system and modern nationalism are clearly incompatible."[9] What Francis Deng proposed in his earlier studies and in his recent novel is the creation of a national sense of unity while maintaining respect for Sudan's ethnic and cultural diversity—that is, maintaining the mosaic within a national sense of identity.[10]

Ranked and Unranked Pluralism

Many Sudanese would accept Deng's proposal as an ideal. However, an important question arises: How would the separate pieces of the mosaic relate to one another?

Donald Horowitz suggested two different patterns of relations among ethnic groups in a multiethnic society. In what he called "ranked ethnic systems," the ethnic groups "are ordered in a hierarchy, with one superordinate and another subordinate;" whereas in "unranked systems . . . parallel ethnic groups coexist, each group internally stratified." In terms of the whole society, Horowitz noted that ranked ethnic groups "are ascriptively defined components of a single society," whereas parallel groups in unranked systems "are themselves incipient whole societies and indeed may formerly have constituted more or less autonomous whole societies."[11]

It is helpful to try to place Sudan within this typology. Sudan seems to be a curiously mixed system or grouping of systems. The Sudanese themselves differ on whether or not Sudanese society is ranked, and their differences provide an important basis for proposed solutions to existing ethnic or regional conflict.

Actual relations between northerners and southerners tend to be dominated by a feeling that Sudan is a ranked society. It is felt that "northern" is a dominant identity and that southerners are subordinate and of lower status within a single Sudanese ethnic system. In discussions of ethnic group relations in Sudan, there are frequent references to mistreatment of southerners by northerners. It is often stated, for example, that northerners tend to call southerners *abid* (slaves), as a reflection of the historical experience of the slave trade and the existence of a substantial southerner slave population in northern areas in earlier periods. Traditional north–south relations in the northern region thus reflected, and may continue to reflect, a ranked structure of intergroup relations.

In national terms, however, Sudan possesses many of the characteristics of an unranked society. The geographic labels of north and south reflect the fact that there is a significant geographic concentration of different groups within Sudan. Those groups that are in some way identified by the broad Arab-Muslim conceptual umbrella are concentrated in the northern region and are not a demographically significant element in the south. In contrast, most of the major Sudanese groups that are not covered by the Arab-Muslim conceptual umbrella are concentrated in the southern region. There they present a picture of a more or less autonomous whole society.

When northerners and southerners interact on a national basis, they tend to operate as separate groups within an unranked ethnic system. In politics, for example, there have regularly been southern parties that have bargained and competed in the national assemblies as southern parties. When there was a major respite in the north–south conflict in the 1970s, it came as a result of the Addis Ababa Agreement of 1972, which was based on a perception of Sudan as an unranked system within which the incipiently autonomous south was recognized as a separate but participating element. The fact that the 1972 agreement succeeded in bringing an end to large-scale and overt conflict for almost a decade would indicate that it was, to some significant degree, based on the realities of Sudanese society.

These two different perceptions reflect an important ambiguity in northern Muslim perspectives on north–south relations. Within northern society, northern and southern groups appear to interact within a ranked system, with southerners in a clearly subordinate position. However, in terms of national politics, the perception is often of two incipiently autonomous groups inter-acting in what is a relatively unranked system. Northern leaders, who must act in both arenas, often find it difficult to reconcile the two different per-spectives.

This problem of ambiguity is manifested in a number of areas. Within the Arab-Muslim conceptual paradigm, there are strong elements that emphasize equality and thus are opposed to the idea of a ranked system of social inter-actions. Yet however many individuals within a given group are seen as equals, there is a strong tendency for ranked patterns of action to emerge. For example, in the Mahdist movement in the late nineteenth century, social rank, wealth, and tribe or clan affiliation did not, in principle, affect the standing of the individual follower of Muhammad Ahmad ibn Abdalla—the Mahdi. Yet the attempts of the family of the Mahdi to become a special leadership group within the Mahdist state after the Mahdi's death—and the emergence of the family of the Mahdi's successor, Abdallahi ibn Muhammad—reflect the tendency toward some form of ranked hierarchy of ethnic groups within Mahdist society.

In general, this ambiguity is found within Muslim groups in Sudan. The Islamic world view stresses the equality of all believers; yet in the most char-acteristic Sudanese Muslim organizations, ranked systems have emerged. In the brotherhoods as well as among the Mahdists, special clans or "holy families" have provided the leadership. Among the brotherhoods, or Sufi *tariqahs,* this came to be explained in terms of an inherited spiritual power, or *baraka,* which characterized the family of the *tariqah* founder and subse-quent leaders.[12] Thus, within brotherhoods such as the Khatmiyyah, there is a ranked order of participants, with the Mirghani family providing the leadership.

Policy Implications

The national policy implications of whether Sudanese society is ranked or unranked are significant. If Sudanese society is inherently ranked and the sub-ordinate groups are now in conflict with the dominant groups, then the solu-tion has to be a transformation in some way of the whole social system. In terms of the present conflict, this is the view of John Garang, leader of the Sudan People's Liberation Army (SPLA), and it provides the basis for the pro-gram of the Sudan People's Liberation Movement (SPLM). The SPLM artic-ulates this view in socialist terms, rejecting the southern separatism (which is based on a perception of Sudan as an unranked society). A 1983 statement of the objectives of the SPLM makes this clear:

> The immediate task of the SPLM is to transform the Southern Movement from a reactionary movement led by reactionaries and concerned only with

the South . . . into a progressive movement . . . dedicated to the socialist transformation of the whole Sudan.[13]

The SPLM program, then, is based on the assumption that Sudanese society is ranked. As Horowitz noted,

> Because the boundaries of ranked ethnic groups largely coincide with class lines, conflict in ranked systems has a class coloration. When warfare occurs, it takes the form of a social revolution.[14]

If Sudanese society is basically unranked, this appeal to the subordinate peoples of the country in both north and south will have no audience.

However, the Addis Ababa Agreement, the round-table conference in 1965, and other power-sharing negotiations assume that Sudanese national society is closer to an unranked ethnic system. Resolution of conflict in such a system involves bargaining and compromise, along with a recognition of the autonomy of the participating units.[15] If Sudan is basically an unranked society, solutions would lie in rebuilding an agreement similar to the Addis Ababa Agreement, in which the special autonomy of the various ethnic groups would be given special recognition. Resolution of the conflict would come through a balanced compromise rather than a social revolution.

In general, the perspectives of northern Sudanese leaders tend to be mixed on this issue. As part of an existing elite, they tend to draw back from solutions that require a revolutionary transformation of their society and opt for creating greater recognition for the potentially autonomous ethnic groups within Sudan. However, this may be more than simply an elite trying to protect its own interests. Groups that appeal to class identities or other more national and homogeneous principles have not been able to develop significant mass followings in independent Sudan. However, with the emergence of important and powerful groups such as the SPLM and the Muslim Brotherhood, this situation may be changing.

Northern Muslim Perspectives

Many elements shape the views of northern Sudanese toward the north–south conflict. Individual experience and family background play a role, as do regional origin, northern ethnic affiliation, and economic class or status. Each of these influences a northerner's attitude toward southerners. However, it is worth examining the different types of Islamic perspectives in the north to see how they help to shape the different northern attitudes. Islam is important both as a significant factor in the northern conceptual paradigm and as an issue in the conflict. (For example, the potential role of Islam in the definition of Sudanese law is a major source of disagreement both within the north and in north–south relations.)

Among the great diversity of perspectives among Muslims in northern Sudan, it is possible to identify at least four distinct, but often overlapping, explicitly Islamic clusters of concepts and perceptions. (In addition, it should be noted that there are also clusters that represent non-Muslim perspectives.) These four perspectives, which have provided the foundations for Sudanese Muslim experiences in the realms of national policies and politics, not only reflect a part of the dynamic diversity among Muslims in Sudan but also suggest the main alternatives visible in the present situation.

In concrete terms, each perspective is identified with a different group of Islamic tradition within the Sudan: (1) the Mahdist movement in Sudan, which, at present, is most publicly identified with the ideas and policies of the prime minister, Sadiq al-Mahdi; (2) the Khatmiyyah Tariqah, whose leadership has historically been provided by the Mirghani family and which, at present, is led, along with the political party it supports, by Muhammad Uthman al-Mirghani; (3) the Muslim Brotherhood of Sudan, whose most prominent leader and major spokesperson is Hassan al-Turabi; and (4) the Republican Brotherhood, a small but visible group whose programs are based on the teachings of Mahmoud Muhammad Taha, who was executed by President Jaafar al-Nimeiri in January 1985.

It is possible to suggest that these four perspectives also reflect the logical and historical options that have developed within the Islamic experience in Sudan. One pair of options is between direct involvement or more indirect, but still active, political influence. A second pair of options is between the historical style associated with the long-established Islamic organizations and the more contemporary and newer type of association.

Using these two pairs of options, it is possible to create a matrix that suggests how the four different concept clusters are related (see figure 22–1). It might also be used as the basis for a broader typology to help describe the many different experiences within the Islamic community.

The Mahdist Perspective

It is often said, in many different ways, that there is no separation of church and state or of religion and politics in Islam. This generalization is widely

	Direct political involvement	Indirect political influence
Historical establishment style	Mahdists	Khatmiyyah
Contemporary style	Muslim Brotherhood	Republican Brothers

Figure 22–1. **Matrix of Logical and Historical Options in Sudan**

accepted, but it is implemented in various ways. The most direct way occurs when an individual with overtly Islamic authority assumes a position of direct political leadership, either in a political system that is identified as Islamic or in a movement that is actively working to create such a system. In Sudan, the Mahdist movement and tradition exemplify this style of direct political involvement.

In the late nineteenth century, a respected Islamic teacher organized and led a successful revolt against the existing government. This leader, Muhammad Ahmad, claimed to be the divinely guided leader for humanity, the Mahdi. Although the state that he created was finally brought to an end with the Anglo-Egyptian "reconquest" in 1898, the Mahdist movement continued to be an important force within Sudan.

The Mahdist tradition of direct political involvement continued, first in the form of support for one style of Sudanese nationalism and then, later, as patronage for one of the major Sudanese political parties, the Umma party. Prime Minister Sadiq al-Mahdi is a great-grandson of the Mahdi, the current head of the party.

Although, in principle, Mahdist teachings are universally applicable, in practical political terms, they are identified with modern Sudan:

> To many modern Sudanese, . . . [the Mahdi] is *Abu'l-Istiqlal,* "The Father of Independence," a nationalist leader who united the tribes of the Sudan by an Islamic ideology, drove out the alien rulers, and laid the foundations of a nation-state.[16]

In this vision, the Mahdi was the "first Sudanese nationalist," and his son, Abdal-Rahman al-Mahdi (1885–1959) was the "father of modern Sudanese nationalism." In other words, the very emergence, existence, and nature of the modern Sudanese state is directly tied to the history of Mahdism. Contemporary leaders of many political persuasions have felt obliged to identify with the "nationalized" tradition of the Mahdi. In the early days of his rule, for example, Nimeiri stated that the Mahdist heritage "is part of the Sudanese heritage upon which the May Revolution stands," and leaders of the leftist group that attempted to overthrow Nimeiri in 1970 listed the Mahdist movement among the great revolutions in Sudanese history, in whose tradition their own movement participated.

For some people, such statements may simply be necessary political formulas, part of the rhetoric of competition for support; but formulas or not, their use indicates the continuing vitality of Mahdist symbols and concepts. For others, such statements reflect their actual conceptualizations and positions. This is especially true of the Umma party in general and Sadiq al-Mahdi in particular. He regularly identifies modern Sudan with the Mahdist tradition. For him, the Mahdiyyah is the beginning of popular Sudanese resistance to oppression. In his major address on policy to the newly elected Constituent Assembly in July 1986, for example, he began by listing those great events that had brought international attention and significance to Sudan. He stated that "the first of those times was when our people by their armed waves of humanity challenged the British Empire at the peak of its glory, defeated it and dispersed its forces in 1885."

Those who believe that the Mahdist tradition is a basic aspect of Sudanese identity naturally assume that Islam will also be an important and overt part of the identification of the Sudanese state. The emphasis on the Mahdi as a nationalist revolutionary has a corollary in the minds of people like Sadiq al-Mahdi—that a Sudanese or authentically local government (as opposed to an imperialist or foreign-inspired government) will in some significant way be Islamic. In speaking of Islamic societies in general, Sadiq al-Mahdi has stated that the "masses have always regarded Islam as the basis of their identity."[17] Although Sadiq knows, in practical political terms, that this is not true of all of the people in Sudan, there is a real sense in which his basic political conceptualizations include this feeling.

From the Mahdist perspective, Sudan is an unranked society in terms of the structure of its ethnic interactions, for the social order of Islam is seen as relatively comprehensive and inclusive. Non-Muslim groups that are geographically separate are viewed as autonomous units to be dealt with in a variety of ways, either in rivalry or in cooperation. Since Sudanese independence, this has meant that Mahdist politicians have considered the south a distinctive part of Sudan. (However, they have not been especially active in advocating separate, autonomous institutions for the South.)

These characteristics of the Mahdist perspective are reflected in Sadiq al-Mahdi's political career. Despite his support for Islamic teachings, he has opposed governmental policies that seemed to involve the forced Islamization of the south. He and his father before him were opponents of the regime of General Ibrahim Abboud, which initiated forced programs of southern Islamization. After the overthrow of Abboud in 1964, Sadiq took part in the negotiations to bring an end to the civil war. In these discussions, he was able to work closely with William Deng, the leader of the largest southern political organization at the time, the Sudan African National Union (SANU). The key to this cooperation was a willingness to consider some recognition of southern autonomy in ways suggested in the round-table conference of 1965, in which both Deng and Sadiq participated.

In Sadiq's view, the problem of national unity in Sudan is to provide a broad umbrella under which the two (or more) relatively complete social orders in Sudan can find protection and a common national identity. It is not easy, however, to find an umbrella that is conceptually acceptable to the Mahdists. For Sadiq, in some way, the national integration mechanism must be identifiable as Islamic. In his first address to parliament as prime minister in 1966, for example, he stated that the "dominant feature of our nation is an Islamic one . . . and this Nation will not have its entity identified and its prestige and pride preserved except under an Islamic revival."[18] A similar implication can be found in his address as prime minister in July 1986, when he spoke of the "Muslim majority's desire to make Islam the arbiter of their private and public lives in conciliation with the civil, human and religious rights of others."

The key to the Mahdist perspective is its identification of Sudanese identity with Sudan's special Islamic experiences and history. Pluralism in Sudan as a whole is seen within the framework of a Muslim majority, which determines the character of the state and in which conflicts are resolved through a bargained recognition of the rights of various minorities, whose security can be ensured without threatening the Islamic identity of the whole. This may involve utilizing new interpretations of Islam; nonetheless, the approach must remain authentically Islamic. Sadiq al-Mahdi stated the position clearly:

> We have always advocated the application of Islam according to an interpretation which suits the present age, taking into account the modern nation-state, relations with religious minorities and international relations. Islamic principles do allow for this new concept.[19.]

The Khatmiyyah and Mirghani Perspectives

Historically, the popular Muslim devotional brotherhoods (or *tariqahs*) preceded the Mahdist movement as an important element in Sudanese Islamic experiences. The *tariqahs,* which vary widely in organization, social roles, and conceptual frameworks, are an important aspect of "popular" Islam among the general population. The earliest orders were already an important part of Islamic life during the Funj sultanate in the sixteenth century.

The early orders in Sudan were focused on individual figures and their families in particular localities. However, at the beginning of the nineteenth century, *tariqahs* with a more integrated, regional type of organization were established. Ultimately, the largest of these was the Khatmiyyah Tariqah, which was introduced to Sudan in the first half of the nineteenth century by Mohammad Uthman al-Mirghani and his descendants. Since that time, that *tariqah* has been led by the Mirghani family and has spread throughout northern Sudan, with its largest concentrations in the eastern and north-central regions.

Because of its size and the abilities of its leaders, the Khatmiyyah came to be a significant political force in the region. However, members of the Mirghani family tended to avoid direct involvement in politics—acting, instead, as mediators and power brokers. This was a political style that was established early in the order's history in Sudan.

During the nineteenth century, much of present-day Sudan was subject to Turko-Egyptian control, which had been established when Muhammad Ali, the Ottoman governor of Egypt, conquered a significant part of modern Sudan in the 1820s. The Mirghani family established effective working relations with the Turko-Egyptian regime and became one of its most visible supporters. On occasion, for example, members of the family acted as mediators between the government and local Sudanese groups that had revolted. However, even though in those times the Turko-Egyptian government appointed Sudanese notables to government positions, members of the Mirghani family did not choose to hold administrative or governmental posts. The Mirghani mode was to maintain influence but not to be directly or openly involved in the political arena.

The Mirghani family were prominent opponents of the Mahdi in the 1880s, and the major members of the family were forced into exile. When the British established the government of Anglo-Egyptian Sudan, the Mirghanis returned and continued their role as influential mediators. The head of the family, Ali al-Mirghani, was widely recognized as a major spokesman for Sudanese opinion. Later, he became the acknowledged patron, first of the nationalists who sought the unity of Sudan with Egypt and then of the major non-Mahdist political parties.

Sayyid Ali made it clear, however, that he was not interested in assuming a position of formal political leadership. Later Khatmiyyah descriptions of the history of nationalism in Sudan report that the British offered the throne of Sudan to Ali, who turned it down, saying that he did not want political authority because he was of a house that carried the message of religious reform and spiritual enlightenment.[20] Even after independence—when a Khatmiyyah party, the People's Democratic party (PDP), was formed—members of the Mirghani family were active patrons but not formal leaders in the organization.

This aloofness from direct political involvement cannot be taken as an indication of a secularist approach to politics. Khatmiyyah leaders did not believe in the separation of religion from politics. They simply found their most effective mode of political operation to be indirect and through mediation and influence. The parties supported by the Khatmiyyah have relatively consistently supported some kind of Islamic identification for the state in the Sudan.

In the period since the death of Ali al-Mirghani in 1968, there has been a trend toward more active involvement by the Mirghani family in politics. In 1968, for example, Muhammad Uthman, Ali's son and successor as leader of the *tariqah,* became a member of the executive committee of the Democratic Unionist party (DUP), which was created by the union of the PDP and the National Unionist party (NUP) in that year. The revolution led by Nimeiri in 1969 brought an end to open party politics, but following the overthrow of Nimeiri in 1985, the DUP reemerged, with Muhammad Uthman al-Mirghani as its head. In the coalition politics after the elections of 1986, the DUP became a partner in the government of Sadiq al-Mahdi, and Mohammad Uthman's brother, Ahmad, became chair of the Supreme Council, which functions as head of state. This reflects a much more direct involvement in the political process than had been customary for the Khatmiyyah in the past. There remains, however, a sense of a lesser overt involvement than the Mahdists had.

The Khatmiyyah has historically expressed a concern for establishing and maintaining a state sensitive to Islamic issues. It has been flexible enough, however, to allow Khatmiyyah-supported parties to ally themselves with old rivals, such as the Mahdists, or even with modern ideological and non-Islamic parties, such as the Communist party. However, there has always been an Islamic dimension to the Khatmiyyah political identification. As a result, like the Mahdists, the Khatmiyyah has viewed the Sudanese civil war as a problem within an unranked society, in terms of ethnic pluralism. Khatmiyyah leaders have been willing to consider special arrangements for non-Muslim minorities in Sudan, but their own power base and identification do not allow these considerations to include modification of the state so that it would not have at least some Islamic identification. Where the Khatmiyyah politicians have, at least on occasion, been flexible has been in the form that identification might take.

The Muslim Brotherhood Perspective

During the twentieth century, a number of groups have emerged that have developed special Islamic perspectives different from those of the large-scale historical establishments just described. These movements have started from the premise that the Sudanese Muslim establishments have become rigid and unable to cope authentically with the contemporary problems and opportunities of the Sudanese. The best-known of these groups is the Sudanese Muslim Brotherhood (or Ikhwan), discussed in this section, and the Republican Brothers, discussed in the next.

In the twentieth century, groups that actively advocate a more rigorous adherence to the message of the Koran have arisen in Muslim communities in many places. Such groups have often been called Islamic fundamentalists because of their call for a return to the fundamentals of what they identify as pristine Islam. Increasingly, however, these groups represent a postmodern reaction to the problems of "modern" Islamic societies and go beyond a conservative or reactionary perspective.

In Sudan, such groups began to emerge in the years following World War II and drew most of their support from students and younger professionals. In the early 1950s, the Sudanese Muslim Brotherhood was formed from these groups. For many years, the brotherhood had limited appeal in the face of the popularity of Arab nationalism and Arab socialism, as articulated by President Gamal Abdel Nasser of Egypt. By the late 1960s, the brotherhood had gained growing support and had emerged from the Nimeiri era with a significantly broadened base of support. During the 1986 elections, the Muslim Brotherhood won seats both among those specially reserved for secondary school and college graduates and in regular territorial constituencies. It became the leading opposition party in the Constituent Assembly. Many who are not formal members of the brotherhood express sympathy or support for its aim of creating an authentically Islamic society in Sudan.

Muslim Brothers have been actively involved in politics to achieve this goal. Parties that are identified as the political arm of the organization have contested many elections; and Hassan al-Turabi and other Muslim Brotherhood leaders have held cabinet and other political posts. The program that they have advocated involves the long-term transformation of society and state in Sudan.

For the brotherhood, the primary community is the Islamic community. Turabi knows that there are non-Muslims in Sudan, but he stresses that the majority are Muslims and asserts that a proper understanding of Islam will provide a suitable place for the non-Muslim minorities. Because the brotherhood is the group most clearly identified with the Islamization of law, state, and society, its program is most often cited as arousing the fears of non-Muslims. The Muslim Brotherhood perspective is clearly shown in al-Turabi's responses in 1980 to questions about non-Muslims' fears about the implementation of Islamic law:

> I think the fear of our brothers the Christians is attributable to the fact that they see this issue in Western terms. The intention to apply the Sharia in the Sudan is an authentic expression of what people want. . . . If they [Christians] look into these laws carefully, they will see that they conform to their national interests as religious people.[21]

The Muslim Brotherhood perspective regarding the nature of ethnic pluralism in Sudan is thus mixed. Al-Turabi views non-Muslims as separate and distinct groups within Sudan. Special arrangements are needed to preserve their rights. In this sense, Sudanese society is seen as unranked. At the same time, the brotherhood articulates its programs in terms that describe Sudan as a single social unit, with a majority and minorities who act and live together. Ranking is involved, for the Muslims are identified as the majority and non-Muslims as minorities. This identification is assumed to be permanent. The charter of the Islamic National Front (INF)—the political organization of the Muslim Brotherhood, spells out the implications relatively clearly:

> The Muslims are the majority among the population of the Sudan. . . . The Muslims, therefore, have a legitimate right, by virtue of their religious choice,

of their democratic weight and of natural justice, to practice the values and rules of their religion to their full range—in personal, familial, social or political affairs.

The state is described as a place where "none shall be legally barred from any public office only because of his adherence to any religious affiliation. But religiousness in general may be taken into consideration as a factor of the candidates integrity."[22]

One might note that the relatively ascriptive character of the brotherhood's definition of the majority creates a situation that Horowitz has called a "majority in perpetuity."[23] The brotherhood perspective remains tied to a perception of Sudan as a Muslim society, whose structures should preserve the rights of participating minorities but whose basic nature must continue to be defined by the identity of the majority.

The Republican Brothers

The Republican Brothers and Sisters are those who accept the interpretations of Mahmoud Muhammad Taha, a Sudanese engineer and intellectual. The movement gained some international visibility in January 1985, when Taha was executed for heresy by Nimeiri's regime. Even those who had objected to the content of his teachings spoke of his execution as another sign of the oppressive nature of the Nimeiri government. For some years, the Republican Brothers have had a relatively high level of visibility, even though it is a small organization. The Republican Brothers and Sisters were active in public preaching, and for many years Taha himself had been a controversial speaker.

The organization was founded right after World War II, when Taha formed the Republican Party, a small and electorally unsuccessful group. Gradually, Taha became more concerned with matters of faith than day-to-day political activity. He began to speak out on the need for a revival of Islam based on a total rethinking of the message contained in the Koran. For leaders in Muslim establishments in Sudan, Taha appeared to go so far beyond the mainstream of Islamic traditions that he was preaching the abrogation of Islam itself. However, some students and educated Sudanese believe that the message of Mahmoud Muhammad Taha reveals how Islam can survive in the contemporary world.

Taha emphasized the difference between the Islamic teachings of the early period of the Prophet Muhammad's ministry (in Mecca) and the later period of his life and work as leader of a full community in Medina. Taha's fundamental thesis was that Islam "was offered first in tolerant and egalitarian terms in Mecca, where the Prophet preached equality and individual responsibility between all men and women without distinction on grounds of race, sex, or social origin."[24] The historic Islamic law is not directly the product of that experience, however, but arises out of the time when Muslims had their own community in Medina. It reflects the adjustments that were necessary under the particular conditions of that time. Taha preached that the twentieth century is the time in which it is possible and necessary to return to the original, primary message of Islam, free of the adaptations to the specific conditions of the seventh century. This basic approach and program has appeared radical to most Muslims in Sudan, although its emphasis on the need to rethink and reshape the traditional structures is shared by people as different from Taha as Sadiq al-Mahdi and Hassan al-Turabi.

The teachings of Taha have a direct bearing on the possibility of resolving the major ethnic tensions in the Sudan, at least in an Islamic context. Regardless of how it is qualified by contemporary analysis, the historic *sharia*, or Islamic law, protects but discriminates against non-Muslims. Taha and the Republican Brothers maintain that it is now necessary to go beyond the historic *sharia* and recognize the primary principles of Islam. Included in these is full equality for both Muslims and non-Muslims in a truly Islamic society (and they also stress similar full equality of male and female). Islam, understood in this way, would not, for example, require that the head of state be a Muslim. In fact, Republicans will say that such a restriction would be contrary to the primary teachings of Islam.

The Republican perspective sets a goal of providing social equality in a diverse society. Mahmoud Muhammad Taha was a strong critic of the discrimination that he saw in Sudan, based on many different inequalities—social, economic, political, and religious. His critique of contemporary Muslim society, based as it was on his personal experience in Sudan, assumed an ethnically ranked society.[25] His solution was to reorient the world view of Muslims so that those features by which people are ranked would not cause harmful discrimination. In Islam, as he reinterpreted it, the emphasis is on individuals in society and on their equality regardless of race, sex, or faith.

The Republican Brothers and Sisters organization remains small, and its future is unclear. Most Sudanese who find Taha's message appealing remain outside the formal group of followers. Their position tends to be similar to that of Murwan Hamid el-Rashid, the chairman of the committee formed in 1986 to commemorate the "trial and martyrdom" of Taha: "Although I don't agree with some of Mahmoud's ideas, I highly respect him as a thinker and a philosopher."[26]

Basic Issues

These four prominent Northern Muslim perspectives present some contrasts but also indicate certain common, critically important themes. This can be seen directly in terms of how they perceive the problems of ethnic pluralism in Sudan and also in what seems to be their approach to resolving tensions arising from that pluralism.

Contrasting Perceptions

The two historical establishment perspectives, although they differ on many fundamental issues, share a perception of Sudan as an ethnically pluralist society of an unranked nature. The north is viewed as basically an Islamic society and the south as basically non-Muslim. In that situation, resolution of tensions can come from bargaining and negotiation. The "solution" would be in terms of a formal arrangement recognizing southern autonomy within Sudan.

Because these historical establishments have dominated much of the political history of modern Sudan, it is not surprising that most attempts at resolving the civil conflict in Sudan have been based on their concept of the problem. The early discussions of a federal structure for Sudan in the 1950s (ultimately rejected by northern establishment leaders) and the round-table conference of 1965 aimed at this type of solution. Even during the military government of Nimeiri, this seemed to be the most effective policy; the Addis Ababa Agreement of 1972 was based on this "unranked" concept.

In contrast, the contemporary perspectives share a sense that the society needs to be transformed. The Muslim Brotherhood has a mixed image of Sudanese society, at least to the extent that its leadership shares the feeling that there should be special arrangements for southern autonomy. However, both Hassan al-Turabi and Mahmoud Muhammad Taha's followers believe that a major transformation of Sudanese society is necessary if any of Sudan's major problems are to be solved.

Both groups are aware of problems of inequality and discrimination, even within the Muslim communities of Sudan. Both advocate a transformation of Muslim life and reject the structures and programs of the historical establishments. For both Turabi and Taha, the important first steps are an independent reexamination of the Islamic tradition and a return to the fundamental principles of the Koran. These two teachers represent dramatically different viewpoints in terms of specific interpretations, but they both urge a social and religious transformation of Muslim life that will cause the discrimination that gives rise to ethnic tensions to disappear.

It is this sense of discrimination within the Muslim sectors of society that makes it possible to say that, at least in terms of general perspective, the Muslim Brotherhood and the Republican Brothers see Sudan as a ranked society in which discrimination must be eliminated. In their programs, the two groups advocate a transformation of the social order, not a bargained "treaty" among the various groups.

Common Issues

It must be emphasized that although their interpretations differ, all four of these groups are grounded in and loyal to the Islamic fatih. None advocates the removal of Islam from the social or political arena in Sudan. This is most clear in the case of the two that are actively and directly involved in the political processes. The Mahdist tradition cannot be separated from the political arena without ceasing to be Mahdist, and the Muslim Brotherhood has as a primary goal the further Islamization of all aspects of society.

It must be emphasized, however, that the more indirect involvement in politics of the Khatmiyyah tradition or the Republican Brothers does not imply support for a secular state. The DUP now and other Khatmiyyah-related parties in the past have consistently supported some formal, constitutional recognition of Islam. The Republican Brothers' position was made clear by Abdullahi Ahmed an-Na'im, translator of Taha's *The Second Message of Islam*. In his view, "the religious obligation of Muslims to conduct every aspect of their public as well as private life in accordance with Islamic teachings would not permit" the establishment of a secular state.[27]

There are a few northern Sudanese Muslims who articulate their vision of the future in terms of a secular state. It is advocated, in principle, by the Sudan Communist party and by a small number of northern intellectuals, such as Mansur Khalid, who are part of the SPLM. In general terms, it is difficult for any of the major northern groups, whether historical establishment or contemporary, even to conceive of the possible objections to an Islamic state if that state is organized in accord with what they believe to be a correct or authentic Islam. These Sudanese have the same problem as people in the United States have in imagining why anyone would object to a "democratic" state, even though some peoples in the world see American concepts of democracy as involving culture-bound assumptions of Western capitalism or Christianity.

Faced with the choice between an Islamic or a secular state, Mahdists, Mirghanis, Muslim Brothers, and Republican Brothers agree on the desirability of an Islamic state. Yet most non-Muslims in Sudan feel that a secular state can be the only choice. Francis Deng has presented the argument for the latter position clearly:

> If national unity is the top priority, then we must be uncompromising in setting aside those elements of identity that divide us. . . . In the face of religious diversities and potentials for conflict, the Founding Fathers of the post-colonial Sudan wisely chose to accept the principles of mutual respect, tolerance, and understanding represented by the slogan of "Religion to God and the Nation to All." The need for a secular state is as pertinent today as it was then.[28]

The SPLM and others are resolute in their demands for a secular state, whereas for most northern Sudanese Muslims, Islam remains an integral part of their definitions of politics and the state. This clash of perspectives was made more complicated by the policies of Nimeiri. In the fall of 1983, Nimeiri instituted a program of Islamization that represented a significant attempt to impose a particular interpretation of Islamic law onto all of Sudanese society, Muslim and non-Muslim alike. Almost immediately after the initiation of this program, Sadiq al-Mahdi spoke against it and was imprisoned as a result. The Mirghanis were less public in their opposition to the September Laws (as Nimeiri's program came to be called), but they stated clearly that the Nimeiri program did not represent an authentically Islamic policy. Mahmoud Muhammad Taha vigorously opposed the program and was executed for it. Even the Muslim Brotherhood, which was identified with the program in the eyes of many, argued—even before the overthrow of Nimeiri—that his program was not legitimately Islamic. Its criticism of the September Laws may have been a factor in its final suppression by Nimeiri in 1985. However, despite the fact that all of these groups publicly expressed their opposition to the September Laws during the election campaign of 1986, none has yet been able to act effectively to abrogate these laws formally, because none wants to appear to weaken the identification of the state with Islam. If leaders pledged to eliminate the September Laws have difficulty in accomplishing that task, it is not surprising that the ideal of a secular state has very limited appeal.

Conclusion

The contradiction between northern Muslim perspectives on the need for an Islamic state and the belief of other Sudanese citizens in the necessity for a secular state must be resolved if civil strife in Sudan is to come to an end. There are a number of possible ways of resolving the tensions, but all will require either significant compromise or reconceptualizations. The task for northern Muslims who are committed to some type of Islamic political system will be to persuade their fellow Sudanese that non-Muslim autonomy can be preserved with justice and equality or that a transformed Islam will ensure a nondiscriminatory pluralist society.

Sudanese pluralism will not disappear. However, the old Western ideal of an ethnically homogeneous society is itself no longer seen as realistic, even in Western societies. As a noted world historian, William McNeill, has observed:

> The ethnically unitary European nation-state never existed except as an ideal. Since the world wars of this century, it has plainly become obsolete in the place of its birth. It can scarcely be taken as a viable model any longer. Polyethnicity in some form or other is preferable, despite all its drawbacks and difficulties.[29]

The challenge for contemporary Sudan is not to create a homogeneous society but, rather, to create an effective pluralist society.

References

1. Harold D. Nelson, *Sudan: A Country Study* (Washington, DC: U.S. Government Printing Office, 1982), p. 89.

2. Yusuf Fadl Hasan, *The Arabs and the Sudan* (Edinburgh: Edinburgh University Press, 1967), p. 176.

3. Shaul Bakhash, "Reinventing Modern Civilization," *New York Times Book Review*, May 8, 1983, p. 9. See, for example, Clifford Geertz, *Islam Observed* (Chicago: University of Chicago Press, 1968); and Michael Gilsenan, *Recognizing Islam* (New York: Pantheon Books, 1982).

4. Gilsenan, *Recognizing Islam*, p. 15.

5. Talal Asad, *The Idea of an Anthropology of Islam*, Occasional Paper Series (Washington, DC: Georgetown University, Center for Contemporary Arab Studies, 1986), p. 14.

6. Francis Mading Deng, *Dynamics of Identification* (Khartoum: Khartoum University Press, 1973), pp. 16–17.

7. Carleton S. Coon, *Caravan: The Story of the Middle East,* rev. ed. (New York: Henry Holt, 1958), p. 2.

8. Dale F. Eickelman, *The Middle East: An Anthropological Approach* (Englewood Cliffs, NJ: Prentice-Hall, 1981), p. 4.

9. Coon, *Caravan*, p. 5.

10. Deng, *Dynamics of Identification* and *Seed of Redemption: A Political Novel* (New York: Lilian Barker Press, 1986).

11. Donald L. Horowitz, *Ethnic Groups in Conflict* (Berkeley and Los Angeles: University of California Press, 1985), pp. 22–23.

12. P.M. Holt, *Studies in the History of the Near East* (London: Frank Cass, 1973), pp. 121–22.

13. "Background and Manifesto of the Sudan People's Liberation Movement (SPLM)," *Horn of Africa* 7, no. 1 (1985): 43.

14. Horowitz, *Ethnic Groups in Conflict*, p. 30.

15. *Ibid.*, p. 31.

16. P.M. Holt and M.W. Daly, *The History of the Sudan*, 3rd ed. (Boulder, CO: Westview Press, 1979), p. 87.

17. al-Mahdi, al-Sadiq, "Islam-Society and Change," in John L. Esposito, ed., *Voices of Resurgent Islam* (New York: Oxford University Press, 1983), p. 231.

18. Quoted in Abel Alier, "The Southern Sudan Question," in Dunstan M. Wai, ed., *The Southern Sudan: The Problem of National Integration* (London: Frank Cass, 1973), p. 24.

19. "Interview: Mr. Sadiq El Mahdi—No Going Back," *Sudanow*, October 1978, p. 18.

20. Ali Abd al-Rahman al-Amin, *The Role of al-Murghani in the National Struggle* [in Arabic] (Khartoum: Sawt al-Sudan, 1961), p. 10.

21. "Interview: Dr. Hassan El Turabi—An Equal Place for All," *Sudanow*, February 1980, pp. 14–15.

22. "Sudan Charter," in Francis Deng and Prosser Gifford, eds., *The Search for Peace and Unity in the Sudan* (Washington, DC: Wilson Center Press, 1987), pp. 79. 80.

23. Horowitz, *Ethnic Groups in Conflict,* p. 86.

24. Abdullahi Ahmed an-Na'im, "Translator's Introduction," in Mahmoud Mohamed Taha, *The Second Message of Islam* (Syracuse, NY: Syracuse University Press, 1987), p. 21.

25. Taha, *The Second Message of Islam.*

26. "One Year On," *Sudanow,* February 1986, p. 42.

27. an-Na'im, "Translator's Introduction," p. 23.

28. Francis Mading Deng, "Myth or Reality in Sudanese Identity," in Deng and Prosser Gifford, eds., *The Search for Peace and Unity in the Sudan,* p. 68.

29. William H. McNeill, *Polyethnicity and National Unity in World History* (Toronto: University of Toronto Press, 1986), p. 84.

23
National System Development and Conflict Resolution in Nigeria

John N. Paden

T he national system in Nigeria has been evolving into a modern nation-state since about the time of World War II, when major changes occurred throughout the colonial world. This chapter relates the broad outlines of this long-term process of national system development to conflict resolution processes.

Throughout, the chapter will try to raise issues of appropriate *context* and *time frames,* as an attempt to correct the tendency of social scientists to take things out of context and to utilize inappropriate or unrealistic time frames in analyzing change. Another underlying issue is the degree of permeability–impermeability (or transformability) of the boundaries of the subnational *units* that are being linked into a national system, whether such units are characterized as linguistic, ethnic, religious, regional, kinship, historic, class-based, gender-based, political, or administrative. Ideally, the individual would be the unit of analysis, but in practice, this is often not possible. It should also be noted that direct discussion of ethnic politics and identities in Nigeria is widely regarded as ill-mannered at best and potentially destabilizing at worst. An elaborate vocabulary of surrogate identities has emerged, the most important of which are state identities and location-of-origin identities.

About a quarter of the population in sub-Saharan Africa is located in Nigeria, which is characterized by relatively high population densities. The country, which takes its name from the river Niger, stretches across several ecological zones, from rain forest along parts of the Atlantic coast to subdesert along parts of the northern border. The country is English-speaking at an official level but is surrounded on three sides by French-speaking national states—Benin, Niger, and Cameroon (although Cameroon is technically bilingual). Estimates of the number of language groups in Nigeria range from about 200 to 400, with the ten major groups accounting for about 90 percent of the population. Nigeria is one of the few countries in Africa to experiment successfully with federalism; hence, this case study may have wider significance.

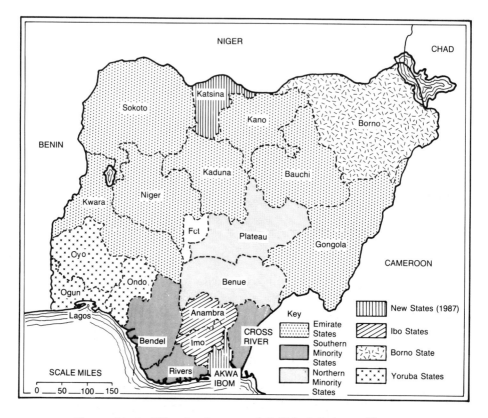

Figure 23-1. Nigeria: States and Political Culture Clusters

Structural and Distributional Issues, with Special Reference to Federalism

With more than 100 million people, Nigeria is a large and complex national system. The theory and practice of federalism has helped to accommodate this scale and complexity. One argument of this chapter is that over time, federalism has shifted in practice from providing linkages between vertical levels of society—that is, national, state, and local—to providing a balance between horizontal segments of society—that is, the various regional and subregional interests, most often expressed through the state system. At present, with Nigeria actively planning for a return to civilian rule in 1992, a central issue is the way in which horizontal and vertical aspects of federalism will relate to each other.

By way of brief review, the national system in Nigeria stems from the amalgamation of the Protectorate of Northern Nigeria and the Protectorate of Southern Nigeria in 1914 by the British governor-general, Frederick Dealtry Lugard. (Lugard also developed the idea of indirect rule in Northern Nigeria and then extended it throughout Nigeria.) Yet the attempt to integrate these two states or regions was not undertaken until after World War II. By 1948, the Macpherson Constitution began to involve Nigerians in constitutional discussions, and regional assemblies were designed that would choose from their members to participate in a central House of Representatives in Lagos. Political parties were formed, and elections were held during late 1951 and early 1952. By 1952, the party system was in place, and the basic elements of an indigenous Nigerian state were being worked out. The primacy of regional bases to national politics was established at this time. The elections of 1959 set the stage for the postindependence state, with a national coalition of northern- and eastern-based parties.

During this early period, local-level politics directly influenced regional politics, which determined national politics. This bottom-up approach, whatever the arguments for or against its democratic base, was soon replaced by a more top-down model in both the civilian and the military periods. In short, there was a continuous shift of power from the local level to the state and national levels in a three-tiered system. As the pendulum swung between civilian and military regimes, there was little serious consideration of returning power to the local level, and the ambiguity of the role of the third tier permeated all of the postindependence regimes. During 1987–88, there was active discussion and experimentation regarding the possible strengthening and utilization of local government authority units in the process of returning to civilian rule. (The percentage of federal funds allocated to local government was doubled.) It is this discussion, in part, that invites a closer examination of the structural and distributional aspects of the relationship between vertical and horizontal federalism in Nigeria.

The structure and process of *vertical federalism* is, essentially, part of a classical model based on concepts of decentralization, democratic input, accountability to the people, states' rights, and so forth. It may range from situations in which the national-level decision makers are severely restricted in the scope and categories of their functions (for example, defense, monetary systems, foreign affairs) to situations in which the national-level authorities have wide latitude, with only specified residual functions being performed at the state or local levels. The essence of the model is that powers and functions are divided among levels of government. The exact division of such functions varies and, even within a single federal system such as Nigeria, has changed considerably over time.

Horizontal federalism is a system that recognizes the political reality of various forms of subnational cleavages and establishes state structures to accommodate, alleviate, or crosscut them. The concepts of "federal character" and "balance of rewards" are central to the notion of equality of treatment of the component states in the federal system. The criteria for inclusion or exclusion in the units of a horizontally balanced federal system are crucial to its intended or unintended consequences and, in practice, range from criteria based on ethnicity or nationality to mixed or crosscutting criteria.

In a preintegrated nation, the balance between vertical and horizontal federalism may take various forms, depending partly on the threats to unity that various subunits may pose. In some ways, the horizontal issues are more critical to the nation-state than the vertical issues, because without horizontal linkages, the nation-state may fracture into its component parts. At the same time, because of the international basis of the national system and the diverse nature of the local indigenous political systems, the gap between modern and traditional, or mass and elite, or grass-roots and national, may increase to the point where the legitimacy of both levels is always in serious question by some constituencies in society, and conflict and tensions remain unresolved. Different elements in the Nigerian political system may emphasize the primacy of different levels and linkage issues, but ultimately, the smooth functioning of the country probably requires a resolution of both horizontal and vertical issues. Currently, the twenty-one-state system in Nigeria (plus the Federal Capital Territory at Abuja) is the framework for this mix of horizontal and vertical structures.

National-Level Federalism

Balancing Horizontal Units. With regard to horizontal linkage politics, a basic north–south regionalism has characterized the Nigerian system since its inception. Yet during the period of political development in Nigeria (1952–present), a further clustering of subregionalisms has emerged, to a large extent reflecting a reassertion of vibrant local-level political culture zones. These, in turn, often become incorporated into the dynamics of regional coalition-building at the national level, to the point where the original cultural bases may be obscured. Six basic subnational political culture clusters may be identified, using both practical politics and abstract culture cluster coding schemes as criteria: (1) the emirate states (Bauchi, Gongola, Kaduna, Katsina, Kano, Kwara, Niger, Sokoto); (2) Borno; (3) the northern minorities (Plateau, Benue); (4) the Yoruba states (Lagos, Ogun, Ondo, Oyo); (5) the Ibo states (Anambra, Imo); and (6) the southern minority states (Bendel, Rivers, Akwa Ibom, Cross River). Much of Nigerian political history is a result of relations among these six basic clusters, although it is equally important to recognize that all of the formal federal experiments in Nigeria (that is, the two-state, three-state, four-state, twelve-state, nineteen-state, and twenty-one-state models) have tried to crosscut these clusters. Indeed, it would be inaccurate to assume that referring to the components of the clusters by current state designations implies cultural homogeneity within those areas.

The current twenty-one-state system in Nigeria is the obvious way in which the horizontal units are balanced within the constitutional and political framework. The debate over the creation of new states—which reached its zenith during the Second Republic (1979–83), when serious demands were heard for as many as fifty states—involved a variety of cultural, historical, economic, and political considerations. Having a separate state became something of a luxury consumer item, as it clearly enhanced the prospects for the inflow of federal government revenues. In the austerity period (1984–present) that followed the oil-boom period (1970–83), this became impractical. Although the Political Bureau had recommended six new states, only two were created (Katsina and Akwa Ibom) in September 1987.

In any case, the "federal character" arguments that have predominated at least since the time of the civil war (1967–70)—that is, that the distribution of human and material resources across the various horizontal units should be fair and should be seen to be fair—have become a central political fact of the Nigerian nation-state. Even military regimes, with their unified command structures and their control of appointments throughout the state and federal levels, have held sacred the principle of a balance of rewards (including national decision-making appointments), and there is no sign that it is losing its salience.

Fluctuations of Vertical Relationships. Vertical relationships (between national-level activities and state and local governments) have fluctuated more than horizontal relationships, depending on political and economic circumstances. The five major political periods under consideration are as follows:

Civilian: the First Republic (1960–66) and its precursors (ca. 1952–60).

Military: the first military period (1966–79), including the four separate regimes of Generals J.T.U. Aguiyi Ironsi (January–July 1966); Yakubu Gowon (1966–75); Murtala Muhammad (1975–76); and Olusegun Obasanjo (1976–79).

Civilian: the Second Republic (1979–83), including the first regime of Alhaji Shehu Shagari (1979–August 1983) and the second Shagari regime (September–December 1983).

Military: the second military period (1984–present), including the regimes of Generals Muhammadu Buhari (1984–August 1985) and Ibrahim Babangida (August 1985–present).

Civilian: a transition to civilian rule (the Third Republic), scheduled for completion in 1992. It commenced in December 1987, with direct elections to the 301 Local Government Authority units, which served as grass-roots local governments.

During the First Republic, national power was more clearly derived from regional or provincial power bases, which in turn drew on local political realities. During the first military period, Nigeria was faced with a threat to the cohesion of the state by the civil war and, later, with the transformation of the state through the highly centralized oil revenues. These developments led to a shift of powers from local and regional to national. The regions were abolished, and a twelve-state system, later modified to a nineteen-state system, was promulgated.

During the Second Republic, although political power reverted to civilians—with the requirement that they develop a national political base—the oil revenues still provided the basic logic for centralization. That is, national-level power was enhanced through the use of oil revenues, even though some of these revenues were reallocated to the states.

During the second military period, oil revenues fell sharply, and the economic logic was to reduce the role of the national government—and lower political expectations—but at the same time continue the military chain of command from top to bottom. In some cases, a sole administrator was appointed to run local governments (until the process of returning to electoral representation was initiated in 1987).

Military federalism is probably a contradiction in terms when it is used to refer to vertical federalism, but it is more accurate when it is used to refer to horizontal linkages. The issues facing the current military regime as it prepares for a return to civilian federalism may revolve in significant measure around the question of vertical federalism and, in particular, the role of local government. Yet this is where some of the ambiguities and countervailing pressures begin to reemerge.

Local-Level Federalism

Local government and/or indigenous political culture in Nigeria does not correspond exactly to the ethnolinguistic-linguistic heterogeneity of Nigeria. The basic issue of local government is the recognition that Nigeria is a nation of nations and that the transformational or revolving nature of the subnational nations—before, during, and after the colonial period—often puts them in direct competition for political loyalties with the modern nation-state. The predominant characteristic of these subnational systems is that they are diverse in their political cultures, ranging from small-scale segmental societies with high degrees of popular participation to large-scale transethnic federations with limited participation. This diversity of political cultures may present the major obstacle to understanding the relationship between local government and national government in the postindependence period. Overall, the efforts of postindependence Nigerian states have been to try to *standardize* local government procedures and to modernize the processes of local government from their presumed premodern nature. Yet the evolution and adaptation of local government institutions, both formal and informal, has become a political factor of considerable importance, as Nigeria faces the task, in the post–oil-boom era, of trying to encourage development and self-sufficiency through the mass mobilization of people at the grass-roots level.

The Process of Local Government Reform. During the late colonial and early independence period, power was shifted from the native authority units to the regional or provincial levels. Most notably, judicial powers of the local state systems were limited to family matters, and criminal and corporate law became a matter for larger political units. Likewise, local legislative powers were severely curtailed by including new constituencies in decision making, limiting the roles of local traditional rulers, and transferring certain key portfolios to higher-level bodies. Executive powers were shifted, sometimes in an outright manner (for example, the control of police) and sometimes through the system of regional and native authority joint control over certain functions. Still, taxation remained primarily a local government function, with revenues flowing up, rather than down.

During the first military period, which coincided with the oil boom, most development projects and most revenues were generated from above, rather than from below. The major local government reforms in 1975–76 resulted in the virtual emasculation of traditional legislative, executive, and judicial functions. Traditional state leaders were to be "fathers of their people," with ceremonial functions only. Many of these elected to the new local government councils were from the business classes and could provide some linkage with the new, centralized sources of wealth.

At the same time, with the formal abolition of the established political class during the military period, the military regimes often dealt directly with the traditional leaders of the states, as access points to the local populations. It was clear that to be appointed to traditional office, it was necessary to have a Western education and some access to the modern nation-state. Yet the alliance between military and local leaders, even if only for ceremonial and efficiency reasons, created what amounted to a national coalition of forces, which were the power center in the nation-state—that is, the military, the new business classes, and the traditional leadership classes. The stripping of local powers was less painful to the local traditional leaders, because they had direct access to national power. The marriage and kinship systems also provided increasingly close links among military, business, and traditional leaders.

With the return to civilian rule in the Second Republic, the political classes reemerged, and in many cases, this meant the end of the direct access to power by the traditional local-level leadership. Although traditional leaders were expected to abstain from partisan politics, they were clearly locked into state and national politics and informally had considerable influence. Yet they were now in direct competition with politicians at the state level for access to influence at the grass-roots level. Elections, for whatever level, often hinged on questions relating to the role of the traditional leaders; hence, such leaders has a stake in the outcomes of these elections. Nor was it clear that the grass-roots voters were so enthralled by the political and military classes, with their uncertainties and shifting alliances, that the long-term stability of traditional leadership, with its common characteristic of lifetime tenure, was not a psychological counterbalance to the apparent chaos of elections and coalition reformulations. Because of the outright purchase of local support by the political classes (at a time when oil revenues were dwindling and the major source for purchasing local political support was looting the public treasury), the intervention of the military at the end of December 1983 was welcomed by many at the grass-roots level.

This second military period was characterized by austerity. The high price of political participation at all levels was cut off by the official abolition of political parties and the subsequent loss of influence of many political interest groups and individuals. The traditional leaders were once again left with considerable influence, if not power, because local government councils, state councils, and national assemblies were all proscribed. Again, the military turned to the traditional leadership class, if only for stability to maintain law and order. Yet with popular expectations rising and economic reality falling, the frustration gap began to increase. Some elements in society began to take desperate measures to make money, including trafficking in drugs, and the military reacted with extremely harsh penalties. Religious millenarian movements arose, and when they took an antisocial form, the military responded with brute strength. Yet the use of sheer military power seemed inadequate to the larger tasks of governing and resolving conflicts in a large and diverse society that was going through one of the most rapid economic downturns in recent times. Oil revenues dwindled, and most foreign credit was cut off. The modern sector was reeling, but at the grass-roots level, where the expectations had not been so high, traditional ways began to reemerge. Again, the pendulum swings of the modern economy and the political arena seemed to give a special legitimacy to both religious and traditional forms of perspective and assurance.

Reassessment of the Role of Local Government. While the second military period (including the Buhari and Babangida phases) witnessed shifts of power within the horizontal federal structure, the reassessment of the role of local government—seen as the basis for stability in Nigeria—was also under way.

In 1987–88, the national government articulated ways of strengthening local governments—by providing them with direct access to federal funds and adjusting the timing of the electoral process—while at the same time sounding a cautionary note to traditional leaders in terms of their political roles. The question of the allocation of local community land and the ambiguous role of traditional leaders has not been finally resolved, and the debate over these issues sometimes takes on a symbolic quality that goes to the heart of some of the conflicts involved in social change and national development.

Essentially, the debate is between a Westernized elite (including university senior staff, students, journalists, labor leaders, and urban professionals) who are articulate and influential, and the less vocal (in English) but equally influential cadre of administrators and community leaders who live and work at the local level. Military and business elites at the national level appear to be trying to mediate between these two positions to come up with pragmatic solutions. Although the debate is sometimes cast in terms of premodern (or feudal) versus "modern" forms of government (whatever that may mean)—or perhaps Burkean versus Rousseauist perspectives on how to change society— it is clear that marriage and mobility patterns and the impact of Western education have created Nigerian political elites, at all levels and in all sectors, who combine "premodern" and "modern" perspectives. There are very few successful modern-sector influential individuals, in business or in politics, who have not been bestowed traditional titles or who are not tied by kinship or marriage with traditional forms of leadership. Nor are there many traditional leaders who do not sit on the boards of modern corporations.

Religious Roles of Traditional Leaders. Perhaps an additional dimension in the debates over the role of traditional leaders at the local level has to do with their religious roles. Modern-sector spokesmen may argue that Nigeria is a secular state—at all levels—and that religion has no place in such a state. Others argue that the Nigerian state should not establish any one religion over another but should provide a context in which a variety of religions may flourish. They may further argue that Nigeria is not a secular state but a multireligious state, in which Islam, Christianity, and traditional animism exist side by side.

Still others may argue that Nigeria is predominantly a Muslim society—if only by a slight majority or plurality—and that the separation of church and state that has evolved in the Westernized concept of the nation-state has been at the root of the moral collapse of society. Although a minority may call for the creation of a truly Islamic state—perhaps even at the cost of the preservation of the state of Nigeria—others argue that Islamic principles, including cordial relations with Christians, can serve Nigeria in a future civilian state in which consensus, rather than coercion, is the basis of the social contract.

The politics of local government in Nigeria is not dissociated from the role of the emirate states in Nigeria. These states constitute a plurality of the twenty-one states and, with Borno added, nearly half of all states. Yet the historic Islamic political culture in these areas has not remained static. There have been important revitalization trends, which have resulted in an increasing, rather than decreasing, saliency of religion in many areas, whether at the official or the unofficial level. Likewise, many of the traditional leaders in other parts of Nigeria have become Muslims, especially in the Yoruba states, and the question of the role of traditional leaders and local-level political cultures has become partially linked to the question of the role of Islam in society.

However the issues of local government are resolved in the Third Republic, it is likely that the 301 (later, 304) Local Government Authority (LGA) units will be an integral part of the new system and will provide a vital link between national and state levels of political life and the lives of individual citizens at the grass-roots level.

State-Level Federalism

Between the national and the local levels in Nigeria, the role of the state is crucial in the political process, whether the number of states remains at twenty-one for convenience and efficiency or is increased to reflect local political pressures or matters of national balance. At present, the subnational states in Nigeria approximate the size of many other African countries, and there is a sense in which Nigeria as a "nation of nations" may more accurately be called a "federation of federations." The intent in state formation in Nigeria has never been to create ethnic or national states. Although some of the states are ethnically or linguistically homogeneous, there is no state that contains all of the members of a particular ethnolinguistic community to the exclusion of all others. This has been true from the period of colonialism, when the three regions prevailed, to the early independence experiment with four regions, to the military creation of twelve, nineteen, and then twenty-one states. Although state identity may be used as a surrogate for other types of ethnolinguistic identity—and the whole concept of federal character is based on the notion of equal access to basic resources by the citizens of each state— the basic function of the states evolved as a counterbalance to the powers at the *local* government levels. That is, the power of the states was an extension of higher-level powers. (During the colonial era, higher-level power was extended through the provinces.) The fact that the states were not coterminous with particular ethnolinguistic groups or precolonial states meant that the state level was one at which the issues of heterogeneity could be mediated, without necessarily escalating to the national level. In short, the states were mini-arenas for national concerns.

Dramatic Changes in the Functions of States. During the First Republic, the provinces, which became the basis for many of the subsequent states, took over the major local government powers, reflecting the general shift of power from local to regional. Yet the shift of powers was not abrupt, and, in most cases, the traditional leaders were enticed into according legitimacy to the changes involved.

With the first military regime (Aguiyi Ironsi) and the abortive attempt to centralize all powers, the shock was so great that local governments felt they had been eclipsed. Military rulers and the civil services were responsible for most executive (and legislative) functions. Even though the military regime of General Gowon returned many functions to local initiative, the military–civil service coalition persisted, and the state level was the most obvious reflection of this power. During the civil war effort and the subsequent spurt of development fueled by the oil boom, the military–civil service team came to dominate the political landscape. The military governors were directly appointed by the federal government, and each new state developed its own civil service, which was responsible to the governor. The state civil services were parallel to the federal civil service and worked in close cooperation with federal structures. Local governments were being reformed during this period, and as newly elected local councils were being set up, the more highly educated state-level civil services led the rush to modernization. Tensions were often high between state and local authorities, but the basic transformations meant that the return to civilian rule in 1979 allowed the political class to fill the military vacuum at all levels, as local leaders had been essentially neutralized.

During the Second Republic, some of the more radical governors tried to eliminate traditional forms of local political culture and influence; but in so doing, they often appointed their own people to fill newly created "traditional" roles or districts. Hence, there was a dual pattern of strengthening and weakening. Although the constitution of the Second Republic specified how many local government authorities there should be, in practice, no limit was placed on the number of local government authorities that were created, and there was no agreement as to which incumbents had legitimacy. In short, many political machines at the state level tried to consolidate power by undermining traditional authority.

With the demise of the Second Republic and the temporary incarceration of many members of the political class for corruption, the state level became more neutral on the question of balance of powers with the local level, as the military regime again needed local authorities to support its programs and, indeed, to give it an air of legitimacy. Although state powers were still an extension of federal military powers, there was no attempt to undermine further the authority or legitimacy of the traditional leaders. Instead, some efforts were made to recognize them as having a legitimate role within the Nigerian state.

Yet since the Local Government Authority unit elections in December 1987, the national (and state) military leaders have a new local base for linkage. More important, however, is the prospect that as the number of states has increased over time, a long-term pattern is emerging whereby state-level political life will become more closely linked to local community politics and to local-level administration.

Structural and Distributional Issues

As already mentioned, military rule and the centralization of oil revenues resulted in the gradual weakening of the institutions and authority of local-level government. At the same time, in the changes back and forth from civilian to military regimes, the general status of local authorities probably increased during military rule, when the political class was put on hold. As centralized oil revenues began to decline after 1981, and despite a transition based on heavy external borrowing, a series of national-and-state-level military regimes took responsibility for structural adjustments in the economy and for presiding over austerity programs. A fundamental reassessment of the division of labor, within both the public and the private sectors and across levels within the public sector, began to occur. Yet the symbolism and power allocation inherent in rebuilding from the bottom up (in the post-oil boom era) has produced some ambiguity regarding what to do with local-level units. Although it may not be possible to reverse the long-term trend toward removing power from the traditional institutions at the local level, the utilization of local-level structures for constitutional and developmental purposes may reopen the question of how to balance both vertical and horizontal forms of federalism. Figure 23–2 shows how the four major variables under discussion have evolved over time: (1) approximate strength of local-level authorities; (2) approximate levels of oil reveneus; (3) patterns of civilian and military rule; and (4) patterns of state creation.

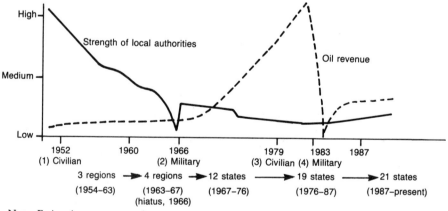

Note: Estimations are approximate.

Figure 23–2. Nigeria: Strength of Local-Level (Relative to National-Level) Authorities in Relation to National Oil Revenues, Military–Civilian Patterns, and Creation of States

Processes of Conflict Resolution

During the decade of oil-fueled, fast-paced economic growth (1971–81), when Nigeria had one of the highest economic growth rates in the world, a number of projects and programs were undertaken that were intended to facilitate national unity as well as economic development. Within the public sector, Nigeria undertook massive infrastructure projects: road building to link up the major cities in the country, expansion of internal rail and air facilities, improvements in telephone and postal services, television and radio programming, and so forth. In addition, the government established a new federal capital, which was intended to incorporate the most desirable features of "central place theory." It was located in the center of the country, approximately equidistant from the three main regional growth poles: the north (Kaduna-Kano), the west (Lagos-Ibadan), and the east (Enugu). Furthermore, massive investments were made in education at all levels, including expanding the number of universities to twenty-seven in anticipation of the consequences of universal primary education.

During this same period, there was considerable private sector investment in housing construction and education. The beginnings of a middle class, complete with homes, education, and cars, began to emerge—in addition to some industrial giants—as the "indigenization" decree created more opportunities for local business people. The distributional issues associated with income levels is not a focus of this chapter, but clearly, as new stratification patterns began to emerge, the upward mobility patterns were so strong as to make room for almost anyone who happened to be in the right place at the right time. The right place was the cities, and the rate of urbanization in Nigeria during this period was believed to be the highest in the world. Agriculture was scorned as old-fashioned, and even unskilled jobs (for example, in construction) were bringing unprecedented wealth to those at the lower income levels. Urbanization and job mobility brought about new patterns of contact between previously rural people, often from different ethnolinguistic backgrounds.

At the level of the emerging educated elite, the rapid expansion of university facilities created places outside the established universities, and university students often found themselves outside their state of origin—just as many able secondary school students found themselves in federal schools outside their areas of origin. Furthermore, after graduation, these educated elites were required to serve for one year in the National Youth Service Corps, usually in an area outside their state of origin. Basically, education was free at all levels, and staff development programs within the universities allowed able graduates to continue their educations, often abroad, through to terminal professional degrees (often to the Ph.D. level). Jobs were assured, because such graduates were already on salary and were merely on study leave to pursue higher degrees. By about 1981, Nigeria had the third largest contingent of students in the United States of any country in the world.

In short, the distributional issues within and among the areas and segments of Nigerian society were decided within the context of a political formula of national character that had emerged out of the civil war experience and within an economic context in which scarcity of financial resources was not the major problem. Distributional issues had to do with equity of access to the mainstream of opportunities. Nigeria's possibilities for experimenting in nation-building were unparalleled in Third World experience.

Then, in about 1981, the price of oil fell from about forty dollars to about ten to fourteen dollars per barrel. Nigeria found itself in competition with British North Sea oil, which further undercut its price. The revenues that had fueled the Nigerian economic and political system fell sharply, although the borrowing powers of the nineteen states were virtually unrestricted in terms of outside sources, and many of the previous expenditure patterns continued until the military intervention in December 1983. From that point, distributional issues took on a different dimension, as expectations were expanding and economic reality was contracting.

As frustration levels increased and economic plans were put on hold, the issue of equity, especially at the horizontal level, became even more crucial. Was each area getting its share of the diminishing pie or, conversely, was each area suffering equally in the austerity programs that necessity mandated? How could the tide of rapid urbanization be turned? How could agriculture be reinvigorated? How could public sector unemployment be transformed into private sector initiative? Would unemployed construction workers stay in their new locations or return to their areas of origin? What was the role of states in preferential treatment of indigenes? How could the traditionally strong family ties in Nigeria serve as a safety net for those who were in need? Would a younger generation become disillusioned with Western ways and seek salvation in nonsecular ways? Would Nigerian professionals (established or in training) seek to leave the country? What was to be the role of the military in all of this? Could the military withstand the stress and, at the same time, keep the legitimacy it had earned in earlier periods, during the civil war and the infrastructural development of the 1970s? Would old political scripts be employed in the struggle for power, or could new scripts be devised that would be appropriate to new challenges? Would the return to civilian rule, with its system of inputs from all sectors and its mediating function as allocator of resources, serve as the major mechanism for conflict resolution? Would the process of constitution-drafting itself resolve or exacerbate conflict? How would religious issues and demands—such as the ten-point communique by the Nigerian Supreme Council for Islamic Affairs in April 1988—be treated? (Issues such as the status of Islamic family law would be considered later by the Constitutional Drafting Committee.) Was there anything in the indigenous political cultures of Nigeria that could contribute to the experience needed to weather this test of the national system? What are the processes of conflict resolution in Nigeria? These and many smaller questions were posed in the wake of a contracting economy.

Traditional Conflict Resolution: The Emirate Example

Traditional cultural patterns in Nigeria are important to understand, not least because in times of stress, the learned behavior and attitudes of early socialization may resurface as the more modern rules of the game seem to be inadequate. However, there is such a wide variation in Nigeria's cultural traditions that analyzing them might be seen as reinforcing a sense of diversity, rather than a sense of unity. Also, from an intergenerational perspective, perhaps "time makes ancient good uncouth." Yet the alternative is to ignore a potential resource of experience and a hidden dimension in the real expectations of ordinary people. One example, which may serve to illustrate traditional patterns of conflict resolution, may be drawn from the emirate paradigm, which is part of the shared experience of a plurality within the country.

In ordinary civil disputes between people, not including criminal matters such as murder or theft, emirate culture has encouraged working within the broad framework of values and beliefs that characterize its jurisprudential system. Within emirate culture, the role of law is central to an understanding of the purposes of the state, the legitimation of power, and the role of teachers and scholars. The central purpose of government is felt to be to provide justice, which implies equal treatment before the law. No one is regarded as above the law, and legal principles and procedures are well known in society.

Yet the prevailing trend in emirate society is not to utilize legal channels, except as a last resort. It is not a litigious society. People look to the courts not as a place to get real justice but as a threat, a place to go if there is no other alternative. In cases of a dispute between people, there are three choices: (1) go to court; (2) submit to mediation; or (3) leave it to God.

Without delving into the details of structure and process, the basic process of conflict resolution between individuals involves the informal process of deference to mediation by elders and the formal process of rule of law, in which the central executive authority is the equivalent of a supreme court judge, bound by a framework of legal precedents and traditions. The elders, both official and unofficial, may include learned people, general leaders, or simply anyone who is older than the disputants. The process also includes consultation with specialists and elders before a final decision is made, and even a final decision may be appealed in the "court of public opinion" in the open streets. Hence, no judgment is ever immune from review.

Perhaps the most notable part of the informal process is the role played by the elders. It is this feature that is picked up in the modern sector process of conflict resolution. (It is also fair to note that emirate culture is better equipped to handle conflict resolution between disputants who identify with the emirate system than situations that include disputants from mixed systems.)

Within the emirate system, the importance of intergenerational relations is central to understanding deference patterns in conflict resolution and mediation. As those from the emirate cultural tradition go into national public life, the relations among elder statesmen (often in their sixties and seventies), retired politicians (perhaps in their fifties), military generals (often in their forties), and young men (perhaps in their twenties or thirties) become salient, because, as in other hierarchically organized cultures (such as Japan), everyone knows who is senior and who is junior in terms of general deference patterns. The special role of teachers, as persons who are knowledgeable about values, also warrants emphasis.

Intercultural Conflict Resolution

The aforementioned emirate society is multiethnic but more or less monocultural. That is even the predominant ethnic identity group in emirate culture is signified with a hyphen (that is, Hausa-Fulani), and there are many other ethnolinguistic groups in emirate society (for example, Yoruba, Nupe). Those members of ethnolinguistic groups who identify with emirate culture are welcome to do so. Those who do not are still able to live and work within the society. In the late colonial period, new towns were established within each of the emirate city-states to accommodate such strangers. Inevitably, as conflicts arose between communities, some process of conflict resolution was needed. The challenge became more pressing when the colonial power left and cultural differences had to be mediated locally.

There have been a number of interethnic and/or intercultural crises in the period since the Kano crises of 1953, in which Hausa and Ibo urban populations clashed, ostensibly over the timing of independence but also over issues of economic competition. The most notable, perhaps, were the riots in May 1966 in various northern cities. More recently, in March 1987, there were intercultural crises in Kafanchan, Kaduna, Zaria, and other cities in Kaduna state. The number of intercultural crises that have developed in Nigeria— apart from the civil war itself—have been relatively limited. Indeed, the potential crises that have been averted would probably make a more impressive list. The question, perhaps, is how the potential crises have been averted.

The Role of Traditional Authorities. Although there is no simple answer to this question, it can be said that mutual interdependencies have been created in which virtually the entire establishment has a vested interest in avoiding direct confrontation. For every communal group A that is at risk as part of a stranger community in area B, there is a corresponding group from communal group B at risk in area A. But how are clashes actually avoided? The answer lies partly in the reconstituted role of traditional authority throughout Nigeria.

When military regimes turn to traditional authorities to reinforce law and order and to appeal for calm, they are articulating publicly what is known privately: that traditional authorities hold themselves—and are held by others in national power—responsible for resolving local conflicts that involve more than one community. The standard way of mediating such crises is for the central authority (with or without the aid of counselors) to meet with the constituted authority from the "stranger" community. Hence, it becomes imperative to identify and/or generate legitimate representatives from each significant community within a multicultural urban area or district. In times of impending crisis, a crisis management committee is available immediately to try mobilize all human and other resources to avert the crisis. This may require extensive discussions of grievances, patience, additional ad hoc committees of representatives, and a full use of political and financial pressures to restore or maintain peace. The most dramatic instances of the breakdown of urban peace in recent years have been not interethnic or intercultural conflicts but *intra*cultural conflict when a portion of the dominant society has broken away and has denied itself the usual access to constituted authority. In December 1980, the Maitatsine religious community in Kano, by defying all constituted authority, provoked a situation in which thousands died. (The adherents of this religion, mainly poor young men from the rural areas, took over mosques and homes in a portion of Kano City and resisted police and army units until the massive use of force was employed.)

Indeed, the legitimacy of traditional authority, in the minds of many modern sector educated elites, rests not on traditional claims of dynastic and/or cultural symbolism but on the practical grounds that traditional authorities—especially in the more recent periods in which almost all traditional leaders have had access to relatively high levels of Western education—have a truly impressive track record of crisis management under conditions of rapid change. Traditional leaders are increasingly selected for their diplomatic skills as much as for any other characteristics. This makes it difficult for most national governments—civilian or military—to confront the traditional leaders openly. Indeed, many traditional leaders are former schoolmates and colleagues of those in power.

The argument is not that traditional leaders alone are engaged in crisis management or that all traditional leaders are equally effective. Rather, the argument is that the long practice of traditional leaders in the process of intercultural crisis management has set a model or standard by which those in other sectors define the general process of conflict resolution. As many politicians also carry traditional titles, and even many of the younger generation of radical thinkers are from the families of traditional leaders, it is not difficult to see a general pattern of crisis aversion and crisis management.

Networking and the Family System. The key to the process is to be able to identify community or social networks and to identify gateways—persons with internal legitimacy and communication skills—before they are needed. Such social networks are not necessarily ethnic. Indeed, the term *ethnic* has always been a dynamic concept in Nigeria, rather than a set of static categories. Any social criteria can be used to identify a community: language, religion, occupation, politics, and so forth. Even when political coalitions are built on such communities, those excluded from the inner coalition are still included in the broader communication network. Political party leaders have always had close communication links with opposition party leaders, even when they were not speaking to each other publicly.

The family system reinforces this networking pattern. Marriages are often arranged to cement political or social alliances, and the children of such marriages become the heirs to a joint legacy. The family system links not only horizontal groups in Nigerian society but also sectoral groups, such as the military, the law, education, commerce, and politics. Families provide the basic communication network and metaphor in Nigerian society. Marriages also have been a way of reconciling previously warring parties. After the civil war, a number of northern military men married eastern region women. Such behavior has a long tradition in Nigeria.

The ultimate recourse when stranger communities, or dissident political groups, cannot remain within a particular area is flight—that is, emigration. This pattern of exodus has been a classic way of avoiding direct and/or violent confrontations. The underlying assumption is that immigrants have some place to resettle—which in the past has often been the case.

To preempt conflicts, the standard cultural model is for constituted authority to set up an advisory council that includes members of all the various camps. This was done in northern Nigeria during the First Republic to dissipate the tension between the Tijaniyya and Qadiriyya Brotherhoods within the Islamic community. It has been done more recently at the federal level to involve spokespersons from the Muslim and Christian communities in Nigeria in dialogue on matters of mutual concern.

Constitutional Processes and Human Rights

The recurrent debates over the rules of the game in Nigerian constitutional life since the 1950s reveal an overall pattern of concerns. The initial struggle to find a formula to accommodate horizontal federalism was achieved, by and large, before the time of the Second Republic constitutional discussions, although the formal criteria for state creation continued to be a matter of some debate. The idea of regular electoral cycles (as in the presidential system), rather than periodic elections (as in the parliamentary system), seems to have been accepted by all as a way of minimizing the already large advantage of incumbency. Indeed, the basic features of vertical and horizontal federalism are probably well accepted.

Four constitutional issues are of continuing concern to the resolution of potential community conflict: (1) procedures for amending the constitution; (2) the delineation of fundamental rights and enforcement mechanisms; (3) multiple legal systems and appeal procedures; and (4) the constitutional role of the military. Other issues may be controversial—such as the procedures for a population census or the mechanisms to enhance fair elections—but the principles are well accepted. The idea of cutting back on the size and scale of legislative bodies is also well accepted in the austerity era.

Amendment Procedures and Fundamental Rights. The issue of amendments was never clearly delimited in the constitution of the Second Republic and is of concern as it relates to the fears of minorities in a hypothetical situation in which a majority decides to change the rules to its own advantage. This issue is closely related conceptually to the issue of fundamental rights, especially in the areas of freedom of speech, assembly, press, and religion. In allaying the fears of minorities (to paraphrase the designation of the preindependence British commission that explored the subject), the provisions of the constitution may be of less importance than the procedures for interpreting and enforcing the provisions. Apart from minorities that might harbor such fears, there is the still largely unexplored issue of how courts have interpreted U.S. First Amendment types of freedoms in the Nigerian context. Does freedom of the press extend to cartoons that stereotype religious or ethnic groups and may incite to riot? Does freedom of religion or assembly extend to campus parades that may be confrontational? Under the constitutional civilian regimes—as distinct from military regimes—the political interpretations of such freedoms often had more to do with constituency-building than with jurisprudential propriety. In fact, because the courts were least effective in drawing an appropriate set of boundaries in these areas, the fears of groups that do not feel themselves in the mainstream are magnified. The consequences of these fears may result, at worst, in a partition mentality—as in Biafra—or, at best, in a continual sense of not having full citizenship rights. The issues of freedom of religion and press are perhaps best dealt with at a constitutional level but, for various reasons, are difficult to fine-tune through legal means because of the widespread preference for nonlegal settlements of such matters.

Multiple Legal Systems. The question of multiple legal systems in Nigeria is part of the transition to a workable political system, and the issue is not likely to go away soon. Questions of appeal procedures in civil cases—especially marriage, divorce, and inheritance—in mixed cases, or in cases in which those in minority status in a particular area demand access to their own legal tradition will probably continue to be resolved by muddling through, as very few participants in the constitutional debates want the whole constitution to stand or fall on this issue.

The Role of the Military. The issue of the constitutional role of the military continues to be salient in considering conflict resolution, because for more than twenty years, the military has regarded itself as the ultimate guarantor of the Nigerian nation. When political means fail to resolve conflict, and when the system appears near breakdown—a likely situation in times of extreme stress—the military is apt to take power and suspend portions of the constitution. How this long precedent can be protected from abuse is more than a constitutional issue, but it is also a constitutional issue. When a supreme court cannot mediate conflict between high-level political opponents, what should be the role of the military? What checks and balances can be built into these procedures? Military regimes may be better at conflict settlement than at conflict resolution, but the Nigerian military has played a crucial role in the development of a national system, and the internal composition of the military seems, in many ways, to reflect the national consensus with regard to national character. But the role of the military, even under noncrisis conditions, is probably a matter that should be incorporated in the formal rules of the game.

Informal Conflict Resolution

Although much of the focus of this chapter has been on structure and process at all levels within the public sector, this does not mean that informal, or nongovernmental, linkages, transactional flows, and social mediating facilities are not of crucial importance. Many examples of these processes are available in the complex interweaving of the strands of Nigerian life. It is beyond the scope of this chapter to do justice to the social fabric that gives saliency to these patterns, except to reinforce the notion that age groups and family linkages are important communication nodes within and among cultural communities. In addition, the key role of teachers, in both traditional and modern Nigerian society, as gateways to societal paradigms and as people who are trusted generally makes this occupation particularly salient in the mediation processes.

A theme that might also be pursued is the idea of catharsis for past grievances—real or imagined—within complex cultural contexts in which the common tendency is to ritualize events as a way to forgive and forget. The ritualization process is widely alluded to in Nigerian literature but has less often been the focus of social science inquiry related to contemporary multicultural contexts.

Conclusion

This chapter has suggested that structural and distributional issues continue to be of central importance to the general process of national system development in Nigeria. Such issues have tended to revolve around horizontal balance, at a time when vertical issues were superseded, in theory, by the practical effects of centralization inherent in an oil-centered economy and in military-led regimes. With the increased incentives to diversify the economy and, in particular, to restore the agricultural sectors at the grass-roots level, many issues of local government reemerge. But they reemerge at a time when a neoclassical return to tradition has attracted the hearts of many ordinary people throughout the world who appear frustrated with the demands of modern life. Whether a revitalization of the grass-roots economy and an involvement of local people in the political process can be achieved without exacerbating relations in a multicultural society remains a central challenge to the Nigerian national system.

Facing this challenge in an era of austerity, Nigerians are drawing on their long experience with indigenous cultural processes of conflict resolution, with the use of traditional authorities in crisis prevention and management, with the nature of constitutional debates, and with the informal processes of conflict resolution. Within this context, perhaps the family system is the basic ingredient, both in dealing with adversity and in providing nodes in larger communication networks that, at their best, work to resolve conflict.

24
Political Change and the Management of Ethnic Conflict in Zimbabwe

Barry M. Schutz

The political reconciliation of Robert Mugabe and Joshua Nkomo suggests that Zimbabwe[a] is one Third World country that takes ethnic conflict management seriously. The Mugabe–Nkomo antagonism epitomized a political conflict between the Zimbabwe African National Union (ZANU) and the Zimbabwe African Peoples Union (ZAPU), which, in turn, articulated an enduring ethnic conflict between the nearly 80 percent Shona and 20 percent Ndebele groups. The reconciliation of these two nationalist leaders brings a hopeful mood to ethnically divided Zimbabwe, opening up prospects for economic development and political clout for the conflict-laden Matabeleland provinces in southwestern Zimbabwe.

However, the reconciliation of Mugabe and Nkomo also threatens to redirect the dynamic of ethnic conflict. Indeed, the Ndebele–Shona conflict has been only the most salient of multiple ethnic cleavages in Zimbabwe. White–black and intra-Shona divisions have also disturbed political unity in the white Rhodesia of the past and the black Zimbabwe of the present. It could also be the wave of ethnic conflict in the future.

Ethnic Conflict in Zimbabwe's History

Zimbabwe has learned to live with the ebbs and flows of ethnic conflict. Ethnic conflict and change have been characteristic of a plethora of epochs in Zimbabwe's history.

The Monomotapa and Rozwi kingdoms reigned from the seventeenth to the early nineteenth centuries. These kingdoms reflected the apex of early Shona dominance in what is now northern, central, and eastern Zimbabwe. The Rozwis were more likely a distinct ruling elite than a self-contained ethnic group, and their descendants are now predominant in the various Shona-speaking subgroups.

The Ndebele incursion into southwestern Zimbabwe derived from the Zulu explosion in South Africa. In 1823, Mzilikazi, a lieutenant of the Shaka

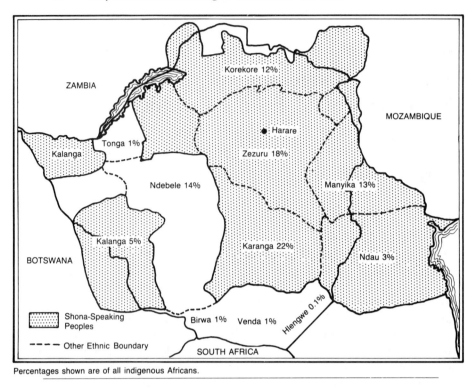

Figure 24–1. Zimbabwe: Ethnic Groups

Zulu, led a variegated group of people, called Ndebele into an arid, hilly region, sparsely populated by Kalanga, a Shona subgroup. The Ndebele conquered and absorbed the Kalanga while raiding livestock in contiguous Shona territory.

In 1889, whites colonized both Shona and Ndebele peoples through the British South African–based Pioneer Column under the leadership of Cecil John Rhodes. The imposition of white colonial rule and, later, white settler minority rule engendered an 1896–97 coordination (but not quite cooperation) between the Shona and Ndebele who were resisting white rule.[1] White-ruled Rhodesia "pacified" intra-African ethnic conflict by mobilizing collective anticolonial attitudes among Shona and Ndebele elites. The emerging leader of Zimbabwe African nationalism in the 1950s and early 1960s was Joshua Nkomo, a leader with Ndebele origins, who remains a vital force in Zimbabwe ethnic conflict and cohesion today.

Since independence, the stage has been set in Zimbabwe for overt Ndebele–Shona ethnic conflict and covert intra-Shona political competition. The retreat of white–black hostility into nonpolitical realms has reintroduced the Ndebele–Shona conflict and has generated a number of intra-Shona conflicts through competition for postcolonial political and economic resources.

White Rule and Ethnic Conflict

The "civilizing" rationale for white rule in Rhodesia distorted healthy ethnic bargaining by suppressing incipient intrablack competition and conflict. Ironically, whites saw their own ethnic hegemony as serving nonethnic purposes. Warning against rampant black "tribalism," white Rhodesians argued that their "civilized" rule would permit black entry into participatory politics at a rate consistent with "their own social evolution." This presumably meant that blacks could gain the vote when they abandoned their own ethnic identities and acted like the ostensibly nonethnic (that is, nontribal) whites. Whites focused on policies that would maintain the British, English-speaking character of the settler community and saw themselves as the conciliators of black tribal conflict.[2] Thus, white-ruled Rhodesia was a period of zero-sum ethnic policy, wherein white rule equated with black subordination. This zero-sum approach to ethnic conflict management, though efficient in controlling ethnic violence, distorted the emerging political interplay of distinct black ethnic groups.

The 1979 Lancaster House Agreement focused on reversing the zero-sum configuration of white Rhodesia—that is, implementing black majority rule over the then 3 percent white minority. This development brought into play a number of aspects of the rich panoply of black ethnic politics. The first was the establishment of rival ethnic party movements—namely, the ZANU, broadly representing the political interests of the 80 percent Shona culture group, and the ZAPU, led by Joshua Nkomo and representing Ndebele culture as well as other interests. This was accomplished by intra-Shona jockeying for positions and economic resources with the ZANU. In addition, in late 1987, ZANU leader Robert Mugabe established a formal one-party state. This arrangement brought ZAPU chief Joshua Nkomo into Mugabe's ZANU government and formally folded the Shona–Ndebele cleavage within the ZANU.

Ethnic Groups and Subgroups

Geographic mobility, intermarriage, and pervasive urbanization make it difficult to obtain precise percentages for Zimbabwe's ethnic groups. Nevertheless, the following tally, by broad culture group, gives an approximate notion of Shona ethnic preponderance:[3]

Shona, 78%

Ndebele, 17%

Whites, 2%

Others (Africans, Asians, "coloreds"), 3%

Shona are divided into what can be called clans or subgroups, although these descriptors are somewhat misleading, as the subgroups are based on geography. They identify specific geographic regions in Zimbabwe that have had distinct historic experiences. The percentage of Shona who belong to each of the subgroups is as follows:

Karanga (Masvingo and central/south-central region), 27%

Zezuru (Harare and environs and north-central region), 22%

Manyika (Mtari and east/northeast border region), 16%

Korekore (Chinoi and northern region), 15%

Ndau (southeast border region), 3%

Rozwi (historical rather than geographic entity)[4], 11%

Kalanga (southwestern region), 6%

The primary competition for ethnic political ascendancy within the ZANU—the Shona vehicle for political rule—is between the more numerous Karanga and Zezuru subgroups. Because Zezuru and Manyika perceive the Karanga as the largest Shona subgroup, they tend to ally against the Karanga in the context of Zimbabwe politics. The Ndau tend to identify with their Manyika neighbors to the north, while the Korekore identify similarly with their Zezuru neighbors to the south. These alliances and coalitions are neither automatic nor overt. Certain elites from these subgroups tend to be more committed in their ethnic solidarity than others. Karanga, on the other hand, have occasionally been linked to Ndebele as "natural" political partners, although this connection exists more often in the minds of outside observers than among Zimbabwe political actors themselves. (Some of Nkomo's fiercest ZANU opponents were, and are, Karanga—indeed, quite visible Karanga in the ZANU cabinet.)

Ethnic Perspectives

A number of ethnic groups in Zimbabwe have a historical basis for claiming to be "the core" to their competitors' "periphery." Two Shona subgroups—the Rozwi and the Karanga—identify themselves as the historical core of Shona tradition. The Rozwi Changawire Kingdom of the seventeenth through early nineteenth centuries dominated northern and central Zimbabwe. The ruling elites of that kingdom were the ancestors of the Rozwi subgroup of Shona people. The Karanga were a part of that kingdom and are the descendants of the rulers of the earlier Monomotapa Kingdom. The Karanga are numerous and are keenly aware of their historical role as the guardians (and perhaps even builders) of Great Zimbabwe, whose ruins are located near Masvingo. (Great Zimbabwe was constructed between the twelfth and seventeenth centuries.)

Perhaps as a consequence of inhabiting the core area of white settlement, Harare/Salisbury, the Zezuru are the most Europeanized and urbanized of the Shona subgroups.[b] Their sense of "being there" for Zimbabwe is both conscious and existential, manifested in the leadership of their own Robert Mugabe. The Zezuru's relative numerical inferiority to the Karanga has led to their quiet coalition with the less numerous Manyika, Ndau, and Korekore subgroups.

The culturally distinct Ndebele, with their history of conquest and apparent independence from the Shona, harbor a contrary claim to being at the core. Their own kings—Mzilikazi, who reigned from 1837 to 1871, and Lobengula, who took over after Mzilikazi's death and reigned until 1897—established their *kraal* (royal court) in Bulawayo. For the Ndebele, the Shona were the periphery. The emergence of the towns of Harare/Salisbury and Bulawayo generated a fundamental geographic conflict with ethnic-cultural overtones. The ZAPU leader Joshua Nkomo—culturally Ndebele and from Bulawayo—ultimately deepened this cleavage rather than modifying it.

Whites came to identify with Harare/Salisbury as their center of a larger Central African Federation.[c] Under white rule, the Salisbury–Bulawayo cleavage endured in the form of civic political and economic competition. That Harare/Salisbury predominated suggests that whites and Zezuru share a common sense of "centeredness" that transcends the fall of white Rhodesia and the emergence of African Zimbabwe in 1980. This line of geographic continuity has likely engendered much of the reciprocal goodwill between Zimbabwe's remaining whites and the Robert Mugabe government, in which Zezuru predominate.

As a result of the challenge of the Mozambique National Resistance (RENAMO) to the government ruled by the Front for the Liberation of Mozambique (FRELIMO) in Maputo, the Shona-speaking Manyika and Ndau may now be emerging as a core zone of conflict in Zimbabwe. Much of what exists of RENAMO's indigenous support derives from Mozambique's Shona population, who are the kith and kin of the Manyika and Ndau of Zimbabwe. Since Zimbabwe sent troops into Mozambique in 1986 to protect its vital rail and road corridor to the Mozambican port of Beira from RENAMO sabotage, RENAMO has retaliated by carrying out operations against Zimbabweans inside Zimbabwe's eastern borders. This focuses attention on the loyalty of the Manyika and Ndau of Zimbabwe to the Mugabe government in Harare. Manyika loyalty is not a major issue at this time, but its divisive potential for the ZANU government is considerable.

Ethnic Competition

Historical "Fragments"

Historical perspectives often can explain much about the development of ethnic competition. This is clearly true in Zimbabwe, where successive foreign incursions have helped to shape the context of ethnic relations. The theoretical perspective used here is borrowed from the theory of "fragment," as expounded by the late Louis Hartz.[5] The fragment framework focuses on the migration or transplantation of a distinct ethnic entity into a foreign geographic and cultural setting. The impact of this transplantation on the indigenous population pervasively shapes the context of ethnic relations far into the future.

Zimbabwe's past contains two major historical fragmentations. The Ndebele migration from the South African Transvaal was the first. The Ndebele, a fragment of Zulu society that broke away from the Zulu in 1821 under Mzilikazi, moved from Natal to the Transvaal in 1825 but were pushed across the Limpopo River into Zimbabwe in 1838. Ndebele warriors mated with Shona speaking Kalanga women, thus establishing domination over that Shona subgroup.

From 1840 through the 1880s, Ndebele warriors extended their impact on Shona society by raiding cattle and, occasionally, women among the contiguous Karanga subgroup. These persistent incursions did nothing to endear the Ndebele to the Shona in general nor to the Karanga in particular. Indeed, the impact of the Ndebele on Shona society extended as far as central and southeastern Zimbabwe, an area inhabited today mostly by Zezuru and Ndau. These historical clashes between two distinct cultural groups have left a legacy of considerable suspicion and mistrust.[d]

The second fragmentation comprised an entirely different racial and physical group—the (European) whites. Although the European settlement ostensibly brought British settlers and culture to Zimbabwe, in fact the intruding Pioneer Column was primarily British in culture but South African in geographic derivation. This South African connection was later to have an enormous effect on the organization of ethnic groups and attitudes in white Rhodesia.

The character of subsequent white migration to Rhodesia reinforced the British South African imprint. The early settlers during the 1890–1920 period left a distinctly Natalian imprimatur on Rhodesian society and political institutions.[e] The dislocations wrought by World War II brought some new white elements into Rhodesia: British Conservative refugees from Labour rule; British South African escapees from newly ensconced Afrikaner rule; and some Greeks, Italians, and Portuguese. After topping out at about 4 percent of the total Rhodesian population in the early 1960s, white emigration began to outpace white immigration. Only after the black disturbances in South Africa in 1984 did whites begin to return from South Africa to black Zimbabwe, apparently concluding that the South African future could only be worse than the Zimbabwean past and present.

Today, Zimbabwe's 100,000 or so whites represent what Horowitz identified as an "unranked" ethnic group.[6] (Unranked ethnic groups embrace multiple classes.) The status of whites depends, of course, on black policy choices. But white expertise, experience, and even support has been deemed essential to Zimbabwean national interest. Indeed, there is even a hint of a ZANU (especially Zezuru)–white coalition, particularly in dealing with ZAPU-Ndebele violence in the southwestern periphery. Nonetheless, white interest in black (ZANU) politics is nearly nil. Whites remain political only when the protection of their economic assets is at issue.

Ndebele–Shona Cleavage

The Ndebele–Shona ethnic conflict remains despite the ZANU's apparent cooptation of the ZAPU. The Ndebele language and culture derive from South Africa. Inklings of future ethnic conflict appear in the form of the Super-ZAPU, South Africa's attempt to build, support, and deploy a dissident guerrilla movement in Zimbabwe, similar to the National Union for the Total Independence of Angola (UNITA) in Angola and the RENAMO in Mozambique. The Super-ZAPU is not now a serious threat to the ZANU government, but neither was the RENAMO a threat to the FRELIMO government in 1979. The Zulu-Ndebele historical connections could also have meaning in a future South African government with some black representation. That sort of development could seriously inflame the Shona–Ndebele split in Zimbabwe.

Intra-Shona Cleavage

Events in Zimbabwe since the Lancaster House Conference and Agreement in 1979–80 demonstrate the dynamic fluidity of ethnic definition in plural societies. From 1895 until 1979, the primary ethnic conflict pitted the superordinate whites against the subordinate blacks, both Shona and Ndebele. After 1979, ethnic conflict burgeoned among blacks.

First, the ZANU–ZAPU cleavage flared into open warfare in southwestern Zimbabwe between ZAPU-Ndebele bands and essentially Shona (heavily Karanga) troops. Second, the ZAPU leader, Joshua Nkomo, continued to challenge the legitimacy of Robert Mugabe's authority. It was a personal challenge with ethnic overtones. In a like manner, Mugabe perceived Nkomo as a real threat. As has become fashionable among African rulers, Mugabe labeled the challenger, Nkomo, a "tribalist." Third, the Karanga–Zezuru cleavage in the ZANU became more pronounced. Although Robert Mugabe's regional origins make him Zezuru, he has no feeling of attachment to this subgroup. But again, ethnic conflict is as much a product of perceptions as of reality. The Karanga know that Mugabe is not one of them and so are acutely sensitive regarding the allotment of scarce political and economic resources. They object to the use of Karanga-filled Zimbabwe military forces in operations designed to protect the Beira Corridor against RENAMO attacks—operations that subject the forces to great risks of death and injury. Some Karanga militants call it "a Zezuru scheme to spill Karanga blood in a Manyika war."

Zezuru militants within the ZANU understand that their hold on power is fragile vis-à-vis Karanga aspirations. In response to these concerns, a secret "Committee of 26" Zezuru was reportedly formed from Zezuru ministers in the ZANU government. The Karanga, in the meantime, have always tended to have one or two cabinet ministers as their spokesmen.

However, these ostensible cabals within the ZANU-Shona culture group are not as deleterious to the ZANU government as might be expected. Mugabe is an assertive nontribalist whose political realism leads him to recognize the pervasive ethnic (and other group) factions within the ZANU. While discouraging ethnic factions and affections, he nevertheless remains attentive to ethnic fears and aspirations. These little subgroup formations provide cues for Mugabe to move toward a policy or personnel choice that might "satisfice"[f] the subgroup's concern.

Managing Ethnic Conflict

The ZANU versus the ZAPU

Robert Mugabe had to confront the contradiction of maintaining his own rule while accommodating the fears and interests of diverse ethnic groups—a problem not atypical in African politics. This dilemma required force and cooptation in proper measures. Because neither Mugabe nor the two Zimbabwe liberation movements openly accepted ethnicity as an issue in the organization of a Zimbabwe government, the problem aquired greater complexity. Mugabe and his former adversary, Joshua Nkomo, also rejected the notion that either the ZANU or the ZAPU was an ethnically anchored movement. How did these movements become so ethnically identified?

The ZAPU was the parent organization, deriving from the banned Democratic party of Southern Rhodesia in 1961 (which, in turn, had risen from the African National Council of Southern Rhodesia and the Harare Youth League in the late 1950s). Its leader, Joshua Nkomo, an Ndebele-Kalanga, was testimony to the ZAPU's transethnic foundation. However, Nkomo's "boss rule" style was abrasive to the polished Shona intellectuals on the ZAPU's executive committee (Mugabe, Ndabaningi Sithole, and others). Tensions between Nkomo and the executive committee built up in 1962–63. However, it was Nkomo's decision-making style and extensive external travel that engendered the opposition. Finally, in 1963, while Nkomo was in Tanzania, the executive committee malcontents voted to remove him from leadership. Subsequently, the Reverend Sithole assumed leadership of an entirely new movement, the ZANU. Nkomo maintained control over the ZAPU but most of the ZAPU Shona transferred allegiance to the ZANU during the 1963–73 period. Violence between ZANU and ZAPU youths, primarily over the allegiance of Shona-speakers, ensued during this period. Ultimately, such violence helped to bring to power Ian Smith and the Rhodesian Front and accelerated Rhodesia's declaration of independence. The Unilateral Declaration of Independence (UDI) came in 1965. Some old Nkomo supporters who were Shona remained in the ZAPU, and the ZAPU–ZANU schism was not clearly ethnic at first. However, during the late 1960s and into the 1970s, the split did, indeed, become pervasively ethnic. By the time of the 1980 general election for the first Zimbabwe government, regional voting patterns showed that the ZAPU and the ZANU reflected clear ethnic identification. The second general election in 1985 revealed even more striking evidence of this trend.

Confronted by the perceived threat of being overthrown by Nkomo ("an ethnic putsch") or trying to govern an ethnically cohesive but dissident population group on Zimbabwe's periphery, Robert Mugabe tried to attract ZAPU elites with ZANU carrots—that is, ministerial and subministerial positions in his government. He had some success. One major ZAPU official, Callistus Ndlovu, and several lesser ZAPU figures joined the ZANU. However, the big fish was Nkomo. Without an accommodation with this successor to the Ndebele kings of the past, Mugabe had no chance to successfully manage ethnic conflict between the Ndebele and the Shona.

In late 1987, Mugabe and Nkomo finally came to terms. Nkomo was to accept Mugabe's offer to serve as minister of rural development in the ZANU government. The ZAPU would renounce its autonomy, and Zimbabwe would enter a new constitutional phase as a formal one-party government. The terms of this agreement were officially met on January 1, 1988.

The Ndebele challenge is not over, however. Rebel guerrillas—some of them bandits, some ethnic militants—remain in the southwestern countryside. The South African connection to the Super-ZAPU persists and could generate a serious, externally assisted movement if life in the Matabeleland countryside does not improve for its residents. In any event, the entry of Ndebele elites into the ZANU government will not have a significant impact on current ZANU office-holders. The number of available posts for ZAPU elites is not infinite.

It is important to note, however, that the Shona–Ndebele cleavage has been overemphasized. An external threat such as a South Africa–supported Super-ZAPU guerrilla force would more likely divide the Ndebele than create a violent conflict between united Ndebele and Shona. The imposition of British South Africa Company rule in the 1890s helped to engender a simultaneous and committed Ndebele and Shona resistance to that rule. Historical relations between Ndebele and Shona have not been exclusively conflictual. Intermarriage, linguistic commonality (English), and common educational, economic, and social situations have brought together Ndebele and Shona, especially in and around Harare. The Shona–Ndebele ethnic cleavage should be one that can be managed unless external forces try to manipulate the situation.

The Single-Party State

Multiparty systems in Africa and other Third World states have tended to founder on the rocks of ethnic conflict. In fact, in the context of African politics, the primary utility of the single-party system has been to aggregate diverse ethnic interests into a single political unit. Thus, the ethnic group's vital interests and grievances can be aired within the party before threatening the state. This is the *ideal* functional manifestation of the single-party system for resolving or managing ethnic conflict. Reality points to a more imperfect arrangement between ethnic groups and single-party systems.

Robert Mugabe's primary influences have been Julius Nyerere's Tanzania and Kwame Nkrumah's Ghana. However, neither of these cases approximates Zimbabwe's ethnic configuration. Tanzania's single party, the Chama Cha Mapinduzi (CCM)—previously the Tanzania African National Union (TANU)—comprises a myriad of numerically nonthreatening ethnic groups. Ethnic conflict has never been a major problem for Tanzania, where Nyerere's idealism and visionary politics have created what Mugabe sees as a model political system.

During the late 1950s, Mugabe was a young schoolteacher in Kwame Nkrumah's newly independent Ghana. Indeed, Mugabe's wife, Sally, is an indigenous Ghanian. The Zimbabwean leader's search for a structural coincidence of state, party, and ideology was probably a seed first implanted in him in Ghana. Ethnic conflict contributed to, but did not cause, the failure of Nkrumah and his Convention Peoples party (CCP) to survive in Ghana.

However, some African single-party systems have effectively aggregated ethnic group interests. The Kenya African National Union (KANU) is the most visible case, having managed the Kikuyu–Luo conflict, intra-Kikuyu disputes, the Kenya–Somali grievances, and the burgeoning Kalenjin aspirations in a generally effective manner. Kenya's current political problems are more the fault of President Daniel arap Moi's leadership than of any structural deficiency in Kenya's system.

Although Zimbabwe's newly declared single-party state is, in many respects, an anachronism on the African scene, Robert Mugabe may be using the wrong model for the right reasons. If the single party is to be the beacon for political vision, economic progress, and ideological unity, then Mugabe's ZANU will likely fail. But if the single party is to be the collector of interests and the articulator of ethnic grievances, then the ZANU might be the best of a problematic set of institutional choices—at least for this particular stretch of Zimbabwean history. Although the single-party system might not "sell" to South African whites, it may, on the other hand, "buy" enough Ndebele to head off even more divisive violence inside Zimbabwe.

The Threat from Mozambique

Zimbabwe's most serious threat during the late 1980s, and perhaps beyond, lies in its eastern border with Mozambique. At first glance, the conflict with the RENAMO appears an external problem: a Mozambique-based dissident movement with covert South African assistance. However, the ultimate impact of a dissident movement in a neighboring country conducting cross-border raids into Zimbabwe might be a destabilizing ethnic conflict inside Zimbabwe itself. These RENAMO incursions are in retaliation for the 10,000-plus Zimbabwe forces operating inside Mozambique to protect the Beira Corridor (that is, railroad, highway, pipeline) against RENAMO attacks. As the RENAMO increasingly includes civilian targets in its attacks, popular discontent in this region of Zimbabwe will also grow. As the region is inhabited by the Manyika and Ndau subgroups, and as the RENAMO is supported by some Manyika and Shangaan (Ndau kin) inside Mozambique, ethnic dilemma looms for the Zimbabwe government. Because these Manyika and Ndau are important allies in Zezuru attempts to assuage Karanga grievances within the ZANU, their unhappiness with Zimbabwe policy in Mozambique could be politically significant. If these eastern-border Shona were to condemn Mugabe's policy toward Mozambique and the RENAMO, a major ethnic conflict would likely erupt within the newly single-party state. Shona could be combatting Shona in eastern Zimbabwe as Shona had battled Ndebele in southwestern Zimbabwe. The continuing threat of South African sponsorship of such anti-Harare ethnic upsurges intensifies the potential threat to Zimbabwe's fragile unity and security.

Six Keys to Ethnic Conflict Management

Zimbabwe's social and historical conditions have engendered ethnic conflict; but at the same time, several elements of success can be found in its management of ethnic conflict. Six of these successful elements are identified and elaborated here.

1. *History and tradition have provided links among ethnic groups.* First, as Ranger[7] and others have argued, religious and other links between Ndebele and Shona led to their coordinated resistance to British rule and settler occupation in the 1896–97 Shona and Ndebele resistance. Second, white rule necessarily established social, economic, and political ties between whites and blacks that persist today in contemporary Zimbabwe. Third, overriding cultural and linguistic cohesion have always connected the geographically diverse Shona subgroups.

2. *British colonial rule left institutions that promote interethnic cooperation.* First, the settlers introduced an economic system that was primarily Rhodesian and, therefore, inclusive of (even if discriminatory toward) blacks. Second, the imposition of a zero-sum native policy by ruling whites over ruled blacks sparked a unifying anticolonial sentiment among ethnically diverse black elites. Third, diverse religious missions and churches introduced a plurality of church denominations that cut across ethnicity. Thus, Methodist mission schools brought together, for example, Manyika, Karanga, and Ndebele, while Catholic schools drew in Zezuru, Ndebele, and so on. Finally, the survival of white residence and influence in black-ruled Zimbabwe has helped to temper the Shona–Ndebele and intra-Shona ethnic rivalries.

3. *State and party institutions have taken ethnicity into account in selecting their personnel.* Most obviously, Robert Mugabe, as state executive (prime minister through 1987, president in 1988), publicly eschews ethnic criteria in selecting his cabinet, his military staff, and the Politboro and Central Committee for the ZANU. In fact, he consciously attempts to choose the most politically reliable and efficient people for these posts, but he keeps ethnic factors in mind. He tries not to "load" too many Zezuru and purposely chooses less ethnically conscious Karanga and whatever politically reliable Ndebele might be available. In addition, efforts are being made to diversify recruitment into the military forces and police. Until recently, Karanga have apparently been overrepresented among military troops.

4. *Mugabe has brought about a political reconciliation through bargaining with his principal ethnic rival.* This belated cooptation of Mugabe's enduring nationalist adversary from the ZAPU, Joshua Nkomo, succeeded, whereas a previous coercive approach had failed because it had contributed to an even greater hostility between Ndebele and Shona. So long as Nkomo

remained in opposition, the prospects for an Ndebele–Shona understanding—let alone consensus—remained dim.

5. *Structural reorganization of the government has been used to minimize ethnic conflict.* The Lancaster House Agreement brought forth a transitional system in which the 1 percent whites received 20 percent of the legislative seats. This brought on black rule but fell short of one man, one vote. Then, in December 1987, Mugabe announced the formation of a one-party state. This development followed the bargaining with Nkomo to join the government.

6. *External threats have brought ethnic groups together.* The most visible external threat is in the very real form of forcible intervention from South Africa. Mugabe's legitimacy hinges on Zimbabwe's sovereignty; and to the extent that Mugabe demonstrates effectively that Zimbabwe's survival depends on internal unity, the divisive impact of ethnic conflict can be reduced. Another threat looms in the RENAMO's operations inside eastern Zimbabwe. Zimbabwe's internal unity can be enhanced in proportion to the demonstrability of the RENAMO's political and military links to South Africa. Finally, Zimbabwe's enthusiastic espousal of Third World status and its role as a leading Third World advocate project the image of a hostile world order, manipulated especially by the United States and the capitalist West. By this reckoning, South Africa is the visible extension of these threatening interests.

Zimbabwe as a Role Model for Ethnic Conflict Management

Zimbabwe has only a limited ability to influence other states with problems of ethnic conflict, although the traditional links between its two major ethnic groups suggest some comparison with Sudan, where the Arab north and the black south have oscillated between conflict and anticolonial consensus.

The settler tradition in Zimbabwe was perceived by subordinated blacks as a vicious curse, but since independence, it has proved to be a stabilizing source of economic expertise and productivity. Whites have economically and politically supported national efforts to protect the Beira Corridor, although their support has been grudging. Finally, whites in Zimbabwe, as in Kenya, provided blacks with a viable legislative system—indeed, a legacy of functional politics. Sudan and other ethnically conflicted states lack the mixed blessing of the settler experience and presence.

When states such as Zimbabwe attempt to balance ethnicity without publicly announcing such a policy, they create an appearance of fairness—an obvious conflict-inhibitor. However, for ethnic balancing to be successful over time, there must be constant reshuffling of personnel in government and party positions. During his tenure, President Jaafar al-Nimeiri of Sudan intermittently carried out such balancing, but without the adroitness and consistency of Robert Mugabe. In the end, Nimeiri rejected such balancing out of hand—and it spelled his downfall.

Mugabe's feud with Joshua Nkomo seemed endless, especially since the ZANU achieved power in 1980. However, with a policy of sticks, then carrots, Mugabe finally convinced his primary ethnic opponent to join his government. Sudan's president, Sadiq al-Mahdi, lacks Mugabe's base of support and political experience, but perhaps a long-term "sticks and carrots" approach to John Garang, leader of the Sudan People's Liberation Movement (SPLM), would be as successful for him as it was for Mugabe.

The single-party option in Zimbabwe bears some elements of rationality, but its ultimate success is not assured. It is unlikely that such a single-party development would be successful in Sudan, where Nimeiri's attempt to organize a single-party system was not the reason for his longevity of rule.

Zimbabwe, although landlocked, is an integral state in southern Africa. Its ability to hold a large share of the white population while inclining toward leadership of the Southern Africa Development Coordinating Council provokes South African concerns. Sudan, although a large and strategically important state, is peripheral to both the Horn and the Maghreb and really has no neighbor (Libya or Ethiopia) that threatens it as much as South Africa threatens Zimbabwe.

Thus, Zimbabwe ironically serves as both a typical example of an ethnically Third World state and a model for a type of ethnic conflict management. The irony extends to the fact that a leader who claims to eschew ethnicity uses covert ethnic balancing and bargaining as a major source for his own authority. It is unlikely that the single-party state will provide an answer for Zimbabwe. Having to survive and develop in the shadow of the ethnically riven behemoth to its south reduces the prospects for Zimbabwe's success in its experiment in single-party ethnic togetherness.

Notes

a. The Republic of Zimbabwe was named Southern Rhodesia, Rhodesia, and the Central African Federation while under white rule. I shall refer to the country as Zimbabwe as a political entity in past, present, and future unless the context is specifically focused on white Rhodesia as a historical entity.

b. This is similar to the Kikuyu–Nairobi linkage in Kenya and the Baganda–Kampala connection in Uganda. In each of these former British African colonies, the ethnic people residing in and around the urban center of British colonial (or Asian) settlement modernized more rapidly than did other ethnic peoples in the peripheral areas. This uneven development tended to exacerbate ethnic tensions and conflict between the core group and those on the periphery.

c. The Central African Federation, created in 1953, consisted of Southern Rhodesia, Northern Rhodesia (present-day Zambia), and Nyasaland (present-day Malawi). It was intended as a counterweight to newly Afrikaner-dominated South Africa.

d. The enduring hostilities between Ndebele and Karanga seem to have escaped some U.S. observers of ethnic conflict in Zimbabwe, who apparently see common political interests between the two groups.

e. It can be noted that Natalian "liberalism" also helped to give birth to apartheid through Shepstone's establishment of "native reserves" in 1881. Rhodesian "native policy" followed suit.

f. The term *satisfice* (a blending of *satisfy* and *suffice*) describes the desired outcome of political compromise or accommodation. The term was coined in the classic study of organizational political behavior by James March and Herbert Simon, *Organizations* (New York: Wiley, 1958).

References

1. This thesis has been effectively argued by T.O. Ranger. See his *Revolt in Southern Rhodesia, 1896–1897* (London: Heinemann, 1967).

2. See Martin Loney, *Rhodesia: White Racism and Imperial Response* (Baltimore: Penguin, 1975), especially p. 74.

3. Taken from Michael F.C. Bourdillon, *The Shona Peoples* (Gweru, Zimbabwe: Mambo Press, 1976).

4. Most summaries of Zimbabwe's Shona ethnic subgroups do not include the Rozwis. For an impressive history of these kingdoms, see D.N. Beach, *The Shona and Zimbabwe 900–1850* (London: Heinemann, 1980), especially pp. 220–78.

5. Louis Hartz, *The Founding of New Societies* (New York: Harcourt Brace, 1964). See, also, Barry M. Schutz, "The Concept of Fragment in Comparative Political Analysis," *Comparative Politics* 1 (1968): 111–25.

6. Donald L. Horowitz, *Ethnic Groups in Conflict* (Berkeley and Los Angeles: University of California Press, 1985), pp. 21–36. Horowitz explained that "unranked" ethnic groups are cross-class; that is, they embrace multiple classes.

7. Ranger, *Revolt in Southern Rhodesia.*

V
Lessons to Be Drawn for Ethnic Conflict Management

The authors in this part constituted the panel of "wise men" who participated in all of the case study presentations, drew on their previous knowledge, and—enlightened by the new information and analysis—sought to draw some conclusions that would be useful to policymakers in the U.S. Department of State and other chanceries—and universities—around the world. Their essays speak for themselves. The quasi-encyclopedic Horowitz presents another treasure trove of comparative analysis and simply good ideas for peacemakers to consider and try out.

Although Milton Esman is clearly at an early stage of the massive task of empirical research he has set for himself to deal definitively with the relationship of economic factors to multiethnic conflict, even a review of his working hypotheses and preliminary findings makes a significant contribution to the subject.

Arend Lijphart, whose influence has permeated this volume, finally appears in his own right to make a fresh, strong plea for the power-sharing approach, taking into consideration the limitations and criticisms his colleagues have offered. His work must surely continue to have a prominant place in the tool kit of the peacemaker in multiethnic conflict.

As the last formal essayist, William Zartman does an excellent job of putting the diplomatic peacemaker's agenda and timetable into a realistic framework. The special attention he gives to prenegotiation reflects an important new development in conceptualization in the formal diplomatic process.

I hope my chapter—the Epilogue—also speaks for itself.

25

Making Moderation Pay:
The Comparative Politics of
Ethnic Conflict Management

Donald L. Horowitz

There is no guarantee that any three cases of a given phenomenon will adequately represent the range of variables that go into the making of that phenomenon. This is particularly so when the three cases are selected to represent yet another variable: geographic distribution. Consequently, the attempt in this volume to extract some recurring principles of conflict and conflict reduction from a European case, an African case, and an Asian case of "hot" ethnic conflict is problematic. The geographic criterion intrudes into a selection strictly according to theoretical preconceptions and makes the institution of even rudimentary controls in case selection difficult. Similarly, the other cases that are intended to serve as controls—because they manifest low levels of ethnic conflict at the moment—have also, of course, been selected because they possess ethnic conflict potential or history, and that renders them vulnerable to the possibility that they are not, in fact, controlled-conflict cases. Indeed, it can be asserted for Pakistan and Kenya, as we shall see, that the current tranquility is subject to change. Without the most careful matching of experimental and control cases to hypotheses, the effort to extract propositions from case studies is fraught with difficulty.[1]

Still, the strategy of this kind of comparison is by no means always futile. Not all of the control cases are miscast as controlled-conflict cases. Malaysia is assuredly more tranquil than Sri Lanka, Belgium and Canada are both in a more controlled state than Northern Ireland, and Nigeria has more effective restraints on conflict than Sudan. Close examination of these comparisons reveals that some portion of the difference between hot and cool ethnic conflict is a function of raw conflict conditions—the structure of cleavages, the history of group encounters, and so on—and some portion is attributable to measures deliberately undertaken to reduce conflict. It is difficult to say which is the more powerful explanation for reduced conflict worldwide. In the Western cases—particularly, Canada, Belgium, and Northern Ireland—a good case can be made that favorable raw conflict conditions have played a bigger role in moderating ethnic conflict than political engineering has. To put it differently, the West has been more fortunate than Asia and Africa in the givens of its ethnic conflict. Asian and African leaders have had to be more inventive in meeting problems that emerge from relatively unfavorable conditions. Some have met the challenge. Many have not. For most leaders, most of the time, there are greater rewards in pursuing ethnic conflict than in pursuing measures to abate it. One of the great challenges of political engineers is to make moderation rewarding and to penalize extremism.

I shall say more about these themes as I proceed. At the outset, however, I want to note a few regularities in the high-conflict cases, some of which happen to be shared by the low-conflict cases; then I intend to identify what distinguishes the hot cases from the cool ones. Thereafter, I shall pursue in detail a paired comparison between Sri Lanka and Malaysia, in order to show that ethnic conflict is not just a function of the raw materials of cleavage and antipathy (though they are surely necessary conditions) but is also a function of the institutional structure in which conflict and restraint find expression. That institutional structure is amenable to change—it is willed and not merely given. In conclusion, I shall return to the predicament of the three states that find themselves in the midst of hot ethnic conflict.

Common and Uncommon Elements in Ethnic Conflict

Before I pinpoint some of the regularities in the cases, a more general observation is in order. It has to do with the relations between ethnic groups and the modern state.

The system of state sovereignty that emerged between the sixteenth and eighteenth centuries in Europe has spread all over the globe in the nineteenth and twentieth.[2] To be sure, some governments do not control all of their territory. Some undertake more functions than others. The penetrative power and practice of states vary enormously. But virtually all states aspire in principle to control all their territory at some level of activity, and that control is what passes for sovereignty—in principle, the power to exclude the control of others. The matter of ethnic conflict needs to be viewed in the light of worldwide norms of sovereignty, for ethnic groups often find themselves in control of states, and others aspire to put themselves in that position or to escape from the control of others. Because the principle of sovereignty is qualitative—sovereignty is possessed or it is not—that principle becomes an obstacle to interethnic accommodation. That is why the joint participation of the Irish Republic and Great Britain in Northern Ireland, following the Anglo-Irish Agreement, is so novel. It seems to divide the indivisible, to grade the precipice. The recent Meech Lake Agreement between Quebec and the other provinces of Canada appears equally novel. It divides sovereign responsibilities in new ways.[3] That is also why various forms of devolution, including federalism and regional autonomy, are so often resisted by central governments, although devolution is often well suited to reduce ethnic conflict. Devolution appears to be a partial concession of what can only be given whole, and as such, it is usually believed (often erroneously) to be but a step toward complete secession. So some part of the problem of ethnic conflict is a matter of finding ways around the stumbling block of contemporary conceptions of sovereignty.

One of the elements common to ethnic conflict in the modern world, therefore, is its highly focused relation to the state. Parties in conflict make demands of the state and, in severe cases, demands for some reconstitution or recomposition of the state. This particular uniformity is a remarkable tribute to the rapid worldwide spread of the modern state and its acknowledged power in conferring recognition of ethnic status and other satisfactions that ethnic groups seek.

The cases dealt with in this volume share a number of characteristics, the first of which is that their conflicts involve not merely the state but also the land. They involve the relation of people to territory, raising the question of who really *belongs* to the land and, hence, to the political community. In Sri Lanka and Northern Ireland, as well as in Malaysia and Assam, there is a sense of priority for some groups by virtue of earlier migration. The Sinhalese have a myth of their early arrival from North India that persists despite the fact that considerable numbers of Sinhalese actually came from South India, many in recent centuries, more recently than most Tamils did.[4] In Northern Ireland, the Protestant migration of the seventeenth century introduced what Catholics regarded as an alien element into Ireland and began a debate over whether the Picts had actually preceded the Irish, who could thus not be regarded as properly indigenous. In Malaysia and Assam, the term "sons of the soil" is used for the Malays and Assamese vis-à-vis non-Malays (especially the Chinese) and non-Assamese (especially the Bengalis) who share the land, despite the fact that Malays and Assamese are both recent amalgams of subgroups. In the 1985 Assam accord, the Indian government agreed to strike some 700,000 names from the electoral rolls and to deport a somewhat lesser number of Bengalis, who arrived in the state after March 24, 1971. In all of these cases, political claims and a variety of ethnic policies are justified—and disputed—on grounds of indigenousness.

Related to concepts of indigenousness in the whole country are notions of localized priority. If the Sinhalese claim all of Sri Lanka, the Sri Lankan Tamils claim the north and east as their "traditional homelands." They want power over those areas, and they want Sinhalese settlers, largely sponsored by government colonization schemes, kept out. The same applies to the southern Sudanese, who fear that the Jonglei Canal scheme will bring in an influx of northerners. In 1974, there were riots in Juba after a rumor circulated among southern Sudanese that large numbers of Egyptian peasants would be settled near the canal.[5] In Canada, Québécois made it a condition of their assent to the new constitution that Quebec be given some control over immigration into the province. And the one portion of Belgium's regionalization agreement that has not been implemented concerns the status of Brussels, lodged as it is in Flanders but possessing a French-speaking majority. Whose territory this is and who will live in each part of the territory are contested issues.

Several of the most serious conflict cases lie along a great divide between even larger categories of people. Sudan, like some other divided African societies, straddles Arab Africa and black African Africa. Northern Ireland is part of the "Celtic world" and the "Anglo-Saxon world," although most of the Protestants originally came from yet another part of the Celtic world, Scotland. The Tamil areas of northern and eastern Sri Lanka are seen as a southern extension of the Tamil-Dravidian world of Madras, and the Sinhalese see themselves as Aryans, rather than Dravidians, whatever historians and anthropologists may say about their actual origins. The Malays partake of a much larger Malay world—certainly many have affinities to and ancestral origins in Indonesia—and although very few Malaysian Chinese have any concrete attachments to China, there is a keen awareness in Malaysia of the proximity and power of China. There is an equal awareness among Assamese of the proximity of Bengalis, in both West Bengal and Bangladesh, who outnumber the Assamese at least fifteen-fold. Although none of these cases is really irredentist in the way the South Tyrol is (potentially, at least), there is a strong sense of external affinity.

There is an even stronger apprehension of external affinity felt by the groups that do not share the affinity. The Sinhalese have long sensed ties between Jaffna and Madras that were not very close until recently. The Malays have tended to believe that the Chinese were attached to China long after they were, and the Chinese have often discerned greater Malay kinship with Indonesia than exists, ignoring the ambivalence and occasional hostility that is expressed, especially toward the Javanese. Southern Sudanese have feared that the northerners might be more willing to be closely connected to Egypt, when many northern Sudanese were actually wary of the attachment. So the effect of external affinity is magnified by anxiety.

Underlying virtually every severe case of ethnic conflict is a fear of competition. The Malays, the Sinhalese, the Assamese, the southern Sudanese, the Pakistani Baluch and Pashtuns and Sindhis, the Québécois, the Catholics in Northern Ireland, several non-Kikuyu groups in Kenya, and the Nigerian Hausa-Fulani all have a sense that their antagonists—respectively, the Chinese, the Tamils, the Bengalis, the northern Sudanese, the Punjabis and Muhajirs, the English-speaking Canadians, the Ulster Protestants, the Kikuyu, and the Ibo—are, in some important ways, better equipped to deal with the world they confront.[6] They are often better educated and are seen to be more energetic or well organized or more hard-working or clever.[7]

Where such sentiments are overlaid with an experience or fear of domination, the prospect of severe conflict is considerable. In 1966, what appeared to be an Ibo military coup was followed by a number of administrative measures, such as the unification of regional civil services and then the complete abolition of the regions. It looked as if an Ibo regime was bent on controlling the whole country. The northern reaction was violent—anti-Ibo riots, an anti-Ibo coup, and then the even larger scale riots that paved the way for the Biafra war. Likewise, when the northern Sudanese imposed a measure of Arabization and Islamization on the south—and even more when they sent northern civil servants to administer the south, virtually excluding southerners from succeeding to senior positions vacated by the British—southern Sudanese regarded this as a new colonialism that had to be resisted.

In most of the serious conflict cases, ethnically based political parties pervade civilian politics. That has been true in all three of the hot cases—Northern Ireland, Sri Lanka, and the Sudan—and in a good many of the others as well. It has certainly been true of Zimbabwe, where Shona and Ndebele are fairly well divided by party. In Kenya, the Kikuyu–Luo cleavage found its way into very clear party divisions until the Luo party was outlawed in favor of a single-party state in which Kikuyu and now Kalenjin domination is only thinly disguised. In the Nigerian First Republic (1960–66), parties were coextensive with the three main ethnic contestants. In Pakistan and Assam, there is some correlation between party and ethnicity, but it is not perfect; and in Malaysia, ethnic parties flank a dominant multiethnic coalition. In Belgium and Canada, there is a relation between party and ethnicity, albeit a changeable one, but party politics does not resolve exclusively around ethnic conflict.

Distinguishing High-Conflict Cases from Low-Conflict Cases

To take a first cut at differentiating the three severe cases—Sudan, Sri Lanka, and Northern Ireland—from the others, several of the elements just discussed make a considerable contribution. All three of the hot cases have strong elements of external affinity that produce apprehensions—of being Arabized, or swallowed up by the South Indian and Tamil worlds, or submerged by the more fecund Catholics to the south. All three cases possess powerful, emotive group juxtapositions and stereotypes. All have a concrete experience of ethnic domination, ranging from tight Protestant control of Ulster, to the history of the Arab slave trade and the postcolonial administration of southern Sudan, to the progressive exclusion of Tamils from the public life of Sri Lanka and the occasional invocation of slogans such as "Sinhalese from Dondra Head to Point Pedro" (from the extreme south the extreme north). All have had ethnically based parties, with sharp lines between them, and no significant interethnic parties or coalitions.

In all three cases, moreover, there has been significant intraethnic party competition, which has excerbated interethnic tensions. As I shall show later, the two main Sinhalese parties have competed in outdoing each other at being anti-Tamil. Until their merger in 1972, the two Sri Lankan Tamil parties competed in being more resistant to Sinhalese pressure. After their merger and the emergence of armed Tamil movements, the Tamil guerrillas have been far more resistant to negotiations than the Tamil party has. The same intraethnic competition was present among both northern and southern Sudanese in the 1960s, as moderates were outbid by extremists. In the Northern Ireland of today, the Catholic, Social Democratic Labour party has had to contend with growing support for the Sinn Fein (and with the Irish Republican Army, the IRA), and the Unionists have been almost as seriously divided. Where ethnic hostility is reinforced by the exigencies of intraethnic party competition—and particularly by the vulnerability of ethnic parties to being accused of being too moderate—ethnic conflict is likely to take a nasty turn. And so it has in these three countries.

Does this suffice to distinguish the three from the states that have been asserted to be cooler (or at least more controlled) in ethnic conflict? In considerable measure, it does; and to the extent that some of the low-conflict cases resemble the high-conflict cases, it can be argued that the former are misclassified as controlled conflicts.

The cases from the Western world are the easiest. In Canada and Belgium, external affinities may be strong, but they are not threatening. Neither the recently rediscovered sentimental attachment of Quebec for France nor even the affinity of the Western provinces for the United States poses any dangers comparable to Unionist loyalty to Britain or Republican loyalty to Ireland. Likewise, Belgian independence is more than a century and a half old, and Flanders is as unlikely to rejoin the Netherlands as Wallonia is to join France. There certainly was an emotive content to Francophone–Anglophone relations in Quebec, but never enough to create majority support for separatism. Rather, the economic costs of even the "sovereignty-association" at stake in the 1980 referendum were quite sufficient to overcome Québécois nationalism. Comparable costs have not been enough to overcome a good many uneconomic ethnic separatisms around the world in countries that are more severly divided.[8] In Belgium, interethnic antipathy has been at a still lower level. The fear of domination and even a sense of being colonized have been present at times for the Québécois and the Flemings, but political relations have been negotiable in a way that they most conspicuously have not been in Northern Ireland, where they have had a distinctly zero-sum quality.

Finally, in neither Canada nor Belgium has party politics been coextensive with ethnicity, and in neither has party politics revolved only around ethnicity. In Belgium, social class and religious issues have alternated with ethnicity. In Canada as a whole, social class and regional issues have alternated with ethnicity, and even French–English ethnic issues are not the only important ones. Canada is bilingual but multicultural, and the other groups (Ukrainians, Italians, Inuits, and so forth) pose important challenges as well. Even in Quebec, the rise of the Francophone Parti Québécois (PQ) did not end the career of the provincial Liberals, although they were linked to Anglophone Canada. Instead, the Liberals and the PQ competed in Quebec for the Francophone vote. This situation is hardly typical of politics in ethnically aggrieved regions, where parties with extraregional, transethnic connections tend to be ousted. In Canada and Belgium, the major national parties have, in some measure, had to compromise ethnic claims within party councils as well as outside. On all of these dimensions, Northern Ireland looks more like Sri Lanka and the Sudan than like Belgium and Canada.

The southern Sudan resembles the Nigeria of the First Republic but not the Nigeria of the Second Republic (1979–83) or even the Nigeria of the current military regime. When Nigeria went back to civilian rule in 1979, it did so after dramatic changes in its institutional structure had greatly lessened the possibility of ethnic confrontation that could divide the whole country.[9] Nigeria's new federalism, with nineteen states, fractionated its overarching ethnic cleavages and set up alternatives to them. Its new constitution created a president elected separately from the legislature through an electoral system that placed a premium on interethnic appeals by presidential candidates and on the formation of parties that, in some measure, transcended ethnic divisions. Ethnic differences persisted, to be sure, but they had lost their ability to bifurcate the state. Chastened by a bitter civil war and determined not to return to the political system that produced it, Nigerian leaders consciously embarked on a program of ethnic engineering that bears study and emulation.[10] Many of its effects seem to have been carried into the period of military rule that began on the last day of 1983.

Much less persuasive is the case for regarding Kenya and Zimbabwe as low-conflict or controlled-conflict countries. Kenya's single-party regime long covered over but did not obliterate or even mitigate severe tensions while the Kikuyu were at the pinnacle of power. Now that the regime of Daniel arap Moi seems determined to create a new ethnic base of Kalenjin, Luhya, Luo, and some dissenting Kikuyu, it seems highly likely that it will trigger a massive Kikuyu response. Much the same general observation applies to Zimbabwe, deeply divided between Shona and Ndebele and now a one-party state. Contrary to what was once conventional wisdom, the single-party regime is typically not a particularly supple or effective vehicle for interethnic accommodation. There is nothing in Kenya or Zimbabwe that compares to the Nigerian determination to avoid protracted ethnic conflict and to create conflict-reducing institutions.

A case can be made that the raw material of Nigerian ethnic conflict is at least as potent as the raw material of the Sudanese conflict. How a conflict develops, however, is a function not only of raw materials but also of measures devised and implemented to reduce conflict. I shall argue shortly that Malaysia's considerable conflict potential has been reduced by the creation of an interethnic center, almost in spite of itself—that is, an interethnic coalition that occupies the middle ground and that, whatever the actual beliefs and sentiments of its members and leaders, fosters interethnic accommodation. Sri Lanka has no such center, just as Northern Ireland and the Sudan have no such center. In all three, moderation has few institutional supports and is largely unorganized.

The same may be true of Pakistan, held together partly because the large Punjabi majority can affort to make concessions to the minorities at the periphery and partly because, for those minorities, the alternative to staying within Pakistan is likely to be not independence but rather absorption into Iran or Afghanistan, both much less desirable prospects. In 1971, when the East Bengalis, who were very much harder to propitiate, saw that the alternative to political exclusion was independence, they took it.

There are few reasons to consider Assam a well-controlled case of ethnic conflict and no reason at all to think of it as a low-conflict case to begin with. What Assam has in its favor is India, a large state with a greater number of ethnic conflicts—some more serious, some less serious—scattered all over its territory, a state that can afford to make concessions to ethnic groups in localized conflicts. Nevertheless, it seems unlikely that concessions of that sort can, over the long term, reduce the Assamese–Bengali conflict. The Assamese have a powerful sense of indigenousness, a powerful fear of being displaced in their own state, and a powerful sense of the Bengali ability to displace them. As Sri Lanka discovered with the large number of Indian Tamils it agreed in 1964 to "repatriate" (really, expel) to India, having disenfranchised them in 1949, it is easier to disfranchise people than to deport them and easier to agree to deport them than actually to send them on their way.

Although some of the control cases may be less controlled than we might wish, some really are controlled. It is possible to articulate differences that separate Northern Ireland from Canada and Belgium, the Sudan from Nigeria, and Sri Lanka from Malaysia. Those differences pertain both to raw conflict conditions and to the institutions that arise or are devised to reduce the conflict. Although raw conflict conditions and institutional setting relate to each other in subtle ways, they also have a degree of independent variation. Severe conflict can be reduced by deliberate action, whereas relatively moderate conflict—left unattended or, worse, nurtured under unfavorable political institutions—can grow into very serious ethnic problems. In support of these propositions, I offer two of the cases now rightly regarded as hot and cool: the contrasting cases of Sri Lanka and Malaysia.

Conflict Prospect and Retrospect:
Sri Lanka and Malaysia

If we were to go back to the time of their independence and ask which of these two countries was likely to have the more serious ethnic conflict in the decades ahead, the answer would have been unequivocal. Any knowledgeable observer would have predicted that Malaysia (then Malaya) was in for serious, perhaps devastating, Malay–Chinese conflict, whereas Sri Lanka (then Ceylon) was likely to experience only mild difficulty between the Sinhalese and Tamils. Certainly, that is what British officials thought, for in Ceylon they rebuffed attempts to secure special constitutional protection for minorities, whereas in Malaya they encouraged interethnic compromise and approved a constitution with many ethnically protective provisions. These views were based on a sense that conditions in Ceylon were more propitious for the containment of ethnic conflict.

First of all, the Ceylon Tamils comprised a mere 11 percent of the Ceylonese population. A small minority, its aspirations could easily be met, even if they entailed, for example, some modest degree of overrepresentation in the civil service. The Chinese were well over a third of the population of the Federation of Malaya and might reasonably have been thought indigestible; especially if the 10 percent Indian minority were added to the Chinese, the Malays were scarcely a majority and were not at all as securely placed in the Malayan economy as the Sinhalese were in the Ceylonese economy.

Second, the Ceylon Tamils arrived in Sri Lanka, on the average, close to a thousand years ago. The Chinese and Indians, by contrast, were relatively recent migrants to Malaya. The Ceylon Tamils were citizens; the Malayan Chinese and Indians, by and large, were not. The Ceylon Tamils were legitimate participants in the political system. Some of the early Ceylonese nationalists, such as Ponnambalam Arunachalam and his brother, Ponnambalam Ramanathan, were Tamils. The Malayan Chinese were not yet accepted as legitimate participants in politics. Around the time of independence, segments of the Malay press were advocating the return of the Chinese to China. The contrast between indigenous Malays and immigrant non-Malays was far more developed than was any comparable contrast between Sinhalese and Ceylon Tamils.[a] To be sure, the Indian (or Estate) Tamils, who had migrated to Ceylon some decades earlier, were disfranchised in 1949; however, it is not they, but the Ceylon Tamils, who are involved in the current conflict, and no one would have dreamed of disfranchising or deporting the Ceylon Tamils.

Third, events before and at independence were especially unconducive to peaceful ethnic relations in Malaya. The Chinese guerrillas who had fought the Japanese occupation forces during World War II had also fought Malay villagers who resisted their exactions of food and supplies. After the war, the guerrillas emerged from the jungle, proclaimed the abolition of the Malay sultanates, and claimed control of the country. Until the British completed the reoccupation of Malaya, there were bloodbaths up and down the peninsula. Thereafter, the guerrillas returned to the jungle to fight the British and the largely Malay armed forces in a war that lasted officially from 1948 to 1960. Again, the hostilities had, de facto, an ethnic character, and they succeeded in undermining the Chinese political position in Malaya at a crucial period. There was nothing remotely comparable in Sri Lanka, which remained entirely peaceful. Sinhalese and Tamils had both joined the Ceylon Defense Force during the war and the Ceylon Army that succeeded it after independence. Tamil leaders had proposed a form of ethnically balanced representation for the postindependence parliament, but the British had rejected it. Independence nonetheless found the Tamils with ministerial portfolios.

Fourth, where Malay and Chinese elites had been divided by the structure of educational institutions in colonial and postcolonial Malaya, Sinhalese and Tamil elites had been brought together by the educational system in Ceylon.[11] Although common, English-medium education was available for Malays and Chinese, the Malay leadership class was disproportionately channeled to the Malay College at Kuala Kangsar, an institution self-consciously designed along British public school lines. No comparable monoethnic elite institution existed in Ceylon. Instead, a number of elite colleges were established, largely in Colombo, where both Sinhalese and Tamils were educated. The result was that, in countries of approximately the same population, Malay and Chinese political leaders were not on intimate terms, whereas Sinhalese and Tamil leaders, having been to school together, frequently knew each other well. It is fair to describe the Ceylonese elite at independence as a genuinely intercommunal elite, sharing many common values. The same description would not hold for the Malayan elite at independence.

Fifth, whereas Malay politicians were quite discriminating and cautious about whom they would deal with—and before independence, some Malay newspapers were urging "no diplomacy with the Chinese"[12]—the Ceylonese had what could only be described as a bargaining political culture. No agreement was automatically foreclosed. Tamil parties dealt with several Sinhalese parties, and vice versa. The question "What are your terms?" was frequently heard, and party discussions often revolved around whether a better deal could be obtained from a competitor of the party that had made the last offer. For purposes of interethnic negotiation, it would be reasonable to assume that such a bargaining political culture would be more advantageous than one that put a premium on personal relations, was hesitant to deal at arm's length, and had a set of unwritten rules governing interethnic negotiation.[13]

Despite all these favorable conditions, Sri Lanka is now in the midst of an ugly ethnic war. Despite all its unfavorable conditions, Malaysia has been at peace. Its last serious episode of ethnic violence occurred in May

1969, when riots followed national and state elections. This contrast is not wholly fortuitous, and it does not vitiate the contrasting conflict conditions to which I have just called attention. Malaysia *has* had the more difficult problem, but it has also had better conflict management.

The outcomes of ethnic politics depend on the interplay of conflict-fostering conditions and conflict-reducing processes and institutions. As I noted earlier, Nigeria's ethnic problems have been at least as serious as the Sudan's, but whereas the Sudan is now in its second civil war, Nigeria seems far from the experience of its one civil war, the Biafran war of 1967–70. Again, the difference is attributable to the conflict management systems of the two states. And Northern Ireland, which admittedly has more intractable problems than either Belgium or Canada, also has practically no political institutions of conflict reduction in place. It is on the interplay of conflict conditions and institutions that I shall focus. For such an inquiry, there can be no more instructive material than the Sri Lanka–Malaysia contrast.

Vote Pooling and Multiethnic Coalitions

Without any doubt, the most important contrast between Malaysian and Sri Lankan ethnic politics has been the role of multiethnic political coalitions in the two countries. The dominant parties in the Sri Lankan system have all been ethnically based, whereas the dominant party in the Malaysian system has been the multiethnic Alliance and National Front.

The Ceylon National Congress, formed in 1919, was originally a multiethnic national movement, modeled on the Indian National Congress. Within two years, however, most Tamils had left the Congress in a dispute over the future mode of representation, and Sri Lanka settled into a pattern of representation by ethnically based political parties. Although there were still some Tamils in the mainly Sinhalese United National Party (UNP), which took power at independence, by the mid-1950s virtually all politically active Sri Lanka Tamils had opted for either the Tamil Congress or the Federal Party, leaving the UNP, the Sri Lanka Freedom Party (SLFP), and the various parties on the left to the Sinhalese. Consequently, Sri Lanka's party system revolved around the competition of the two main Sinhalese parties for Sinhalese votes and the two main Tamil parties for Tamil votes until the two Tamil parties merged in 1972. With the exception of a brief period from 1965 to 1968, when a UNP-led coalition government included the Tamil parties, the dynamics of intraethnic competition, particularly for the Sinhalese vote, have pushed the parties toward meeting ethnic demands and have limited their leeway to make concessions across ethnic lines.

The rise of the SLFP as a competitor to the UNP in the 1950s went hand in hand with appeals to Sinhalese ethnic sentiment. After the resounding victory of an SLFP-led coalition in 1956, Sinhala-only legislation was passed, and Tamil civil servants were discriminated against on linguistic grounds. Rebuffed at the polls, the UNP responded by becoming as ethnically exclusive as the SLFP was. When Prime Minister S.W.R.D. Bandaranaike attempted to cool Sinhalese–Tamil tension by a compromise agreement with the Federal party leader, S.J.V. Chelvanayakam, the UNP campaigned against it, and the compromise was abandoned. After Bandaranaike's assassination in 1959, his wife, Sirimavo Bandaranaike, became prime minister. Under her regime, from 1960 to 1965, there was an acceleration of favoritism toward Sinhalese Buddhists. Tamil protest was met with harsh measures, including an armed occupation of the Tamil areas from 1961 to 1963. Following the victory of the UNP-led coalition in the 1965 elections, concessions were made to redress some Tamil grievances, but a modest devolution to district councils was thwarted by SLFP opposition and the fear of UNP backbenchers that they would lose their seats to SLFP candidates if they went along. The Federal party left the coalition over this issue. Interethnic compromise was strictly limited by intraethnic competition.

Mrs. Bandaranaike's second regime, from 1970 to 1977, was characterized by an even more virulent anti-Tamil strain. In 1972, a new constitution was promulgated that gave Buddhism a "foremost place" and virtually ignored the Tamil presence in the country. A scheme for "standardizing marks" was implemented; its effect was to reduce the grades achieved by Tamil students on examinations that determined university entrance, thereby depriving large numbers of Tamil students of the university education for which they were plainly more qualified than many of the Sinhalese who were admitted.[14] By such measures, a half-generation of recruits for Tamil separatist organizations was created. By the time the UNP came to power in the 1977 elections, Sinhalese-dominated governments, always with an eye on Sinhalese political competition, had managed to plant the seeds of guerrilla warfare that the UNP government was later to reap.

The structure of political competition made it incumbent on each of the major Sinhalese parties to champion the cause of Sinhalese ethnic assertion against Tamil interests, and segments of each party were militantly chauvinist. The anti-Tamil riots that followed the elections of 1977 and did much to encourage a Tamil resort to arms, and the anti-Tamil riots of 1983, which accelerated the armed warfare, were both alleged to have been organized, at least in substantial part, by activists associated with the UNP.[15]

Underlying this process of bidding and outbidding for the Sinhalese vote was an electoral system that translated small swings in popular votes into large swings in seats. The system was first-past-the-post in mainly single-member constituencies. With multiparty competition in the Sinhalese south, it was often possible to win a parliamentary majority on a plurality of 30 to 40 percent of the vote. In every parliamentary election between 1952 and 1970—in fact, six times—there was alternation in office. In the south, the vast majority of constituencies was Sinhalese-dominated. As a result, parties derived rich rewards from appealing to Sinhalese ethnic sentiment and conspicuously opposing government proposals to conciliate the Tamils. The combination of largely homogeneous constituencies, plurality elections in mainly single-member constituencies, and a competitive party configuration on the Sinhalese side that produced two main contenders for power and two plausible contenders for nearly every seat created a system that was exceedingly sensitive to Sinhalese opinion and inhospitable to interethnic accommodation.

Several of these conditions were later altered. In 1978, the UNP government promulgated a new constitution that made some important electoral changes. In a major departure from the parliamentary system, a separately elected presidency was instituted. The president is elected by a system of preferential voting that accords weight to voters' second choices in a way that they are not weighted in plurality parliamentary elections. Tamil second preferences might, under some circumstances, actually provide the president his margin of victory. Prudent presidential candidates could hardly ignore Tamil interests under such conditions. In parliamentary elections, first-past-the-post in mostly single-member constituencies was changed to a party list system of proportional representation in multimember constituencies. Small swings in votes should no longer produce large swings in seats. Under normal conditions, Tamil candidates might also find a place in Sinhalese party lists in constituencies with Tamil minorities, and parties might be more moderate in ethnic appeals now that every vote in each constituency counts. In short, under normal conditions, the new electoral system might produce a change in the character of the party system.

Soon after these changes came into effect, however, conditions were anything but normal. The Tamil United Liberation Front (successor to both the Federal party and the Tamil Congress) had been excluded from parliament, separatist violence had begun in earnest, and Sinhalese and Tamil opinion had so polarized that, in the short term at least, no electoral system could foster moderation. In addition to accommodative arrangements, therefore, timing must be taken into account. Thus far, the new arrangements have had no impact on moderating the conditions fostered by the old.

It is necessary to emphasize the *combination* of conditions in Sri Lanka that made ethnic extremism so profitable and interethnic moderation so costly. Very few conditions were different in Malaysia, and yet the results have been dramatically different. Like Sri Lanka, Malaysia has had first-past-the-post elections, entirely in single-member constituencies. Like Sri Lanka, there has been a good deal of party competition on both the Malay and the non-Malay sides, much of it revolving around attention to mutually exclusive ethnic claims and demands. Unlike Sri Lanka, however, interethnic compromise has also had a claim on party attention, and moderation, as well as extremism, has paid some dividends.

Three differences between Malaysia and Sri Lanka have produced a different balance of incentives. The three relate to timing as well as to structure. The first, which in some measure was fortuitous, is that the Malaysians began working on interethnic accommodation early in relation to independence. They had had a bitter taste of ethnic violence during and after World War II and did not wait, as the Sri Lankans had, until accumulated grievances again reached the threshold of widespread and sustained violence.

The second difference is that there have been significantly more ethnically heterogeneous parliamentary constituencies in Malaysia than in Sri Lanka. This was not always the case. In 1955, more than 84 percent of the registered voters for the Malayan parliamentary elections were Malays. But, largely because of compromises reached by the multiethnic coalition that I shall cite presently as the third difference from Sri Lanka, the composition of the parliamentary electorate changed quickly. By 1959, the electorate was already more than one-third Chinese; and by 1964, it was 38 percent Chinese and 8 percent Indian.

As the electorate as a whole was heterogeneous, so were individual, single-member constituencies. By the early 1960s, 40 percent of the parliamentary constituencies had Chinese pluralities and, in toto, non-Malay majorities of registered voters. An additional 20 percent had a registered electorate that was at least 30 percent Chinese, and in only about 20 percent of all constituencies did registered Chinese voters comprise less than 10 percent. (The constituency delimitation of 1974 effected considerable changes, to the disadvantage of non-Malays,[16] but this was long after the structure of party politics was established.)

The Sri Lankan figures are in marked contrast. In only 11 percent of all parliamentary constituencies were Ceylon Tamils a plurality as late as 1976 (based on 1971 census figures), and in all but one of those (where they comprised 49.8 percent), they were actually a majority, usually an overwhelming majority. In only one additional constituency out of 160 did Ceylon Tamils comprise between 30 and 50 percent, and in only another 8 percent were they between 10 and 30 percent of the constituency. In 81 percent of all constituencies, Ceylon Tamils were less than 10 percent, usually far less. The comparable figure for Malaysian Chinese was that in only 18 percent of all constituencies did they comprise less than 10 percent.[17]

It is important to underscore that these figures reflect not merely that Malaysian Chinese were three times as numerous as Ceylon Tamils in proportion to the total population of the country, but that the Tamils and Sinhalese are much more regionally concentrated than the Chinese and Malays are. This point is easily demonstrated by noting that in ten of the eighteen constituencies in which Ceylon Tamils were a plurality or majority, they were actually a majority of more than 90 percent.

What difference does regional concentration make? It has a bearing both on party positions and on the prospects for interethnic coalitions based on the exchange of votes. In first-past-the-post elections, if the Sinhalese comprise 70, 80, 90, or even 95 percent of the voters—as they did in a large number of constituencies—and two main Sinhalese parties compete for those votes, there is hardly any restraint on the anti-Tamil positions than can be taken. The 1 or 2 percent of Tamil voters in such constituencies can offer nothing to the party that is more moderate on ethnic issues. The same is true at the party level nationwide: where constituencies are largely homogeneous, a Tamil party has little to offer a Sinhalese party that is inclined to moderation on ethnic issues but fearful of the loss of Sinhalese votes as a result of its moderation. There were many more Sinhalese votes to be had by being extreme than there were Tamil votes to be had by being moderate. Likewise, no Sinhalese party had very much to offer Tamil candidates to help them win marginal seats. For the Tamils, there were no such marginal seats. Tamil candidates either won overwhelmingly, or they did not win at all. With constituencies and electoral rules structured as Sri Lanka's were until 1978, interethnic coalitions based on the exchange of votes between the partners—the most durable and important kind of interethnic coalition—were highly improbable and indeed, with the one short-lived and partial exception referred to earlier, did not come into being.

Malaysia's heterogeneous constituencies made ethnic calculations more complex. In many constituencies, Chinese voters could punish Malay extremists and reward moderates. There were not always more Malay votes to be gained than Chinese votes to be lost by taking extreme positions. By the same token, Chinese and Malay parties could exchange votes profitably at the constituency level and come out ahead. Where there were more Malays than Chinese, a Chinese party could urge its supporters to vote for a friendly Malay candidate—and vice versa when there were more Chinese than Malays. Parties might still evolve along wholly ethnic lines, but—especially if there were more than one party per ethnic group—there would be countervailing incentives fostering an interethnic coalition. Such incentives are now also built into Sri Lankan electoral arrangements, especially in presidential elections, whereby the whole country is one large heterogeneous constituency and Sinhalese divisions make it likely that the election will be decided on second preferences, including Tamil second preferences. But in the formative period of Sinhalese exclusiveness and Tamil separatism, all of the incentives were the other way.

The third difference between Sri Lanka and Malaysia, which relates closely to the first two, is that a permanent multiethnic coalition in Malaysia, established before independence, occupied the center of the ethnic spectrum. Whereas the main Sinhalese parties were driven by electoral logic to espouse ethnically exclusionary positions, the leading Malay party found itself impelled by coalition logic to moderation and compromise, albeit without altogether foreclosing extreme claims. The Malaysian Chinese, who at independence had neither assured citizenship nor full acceptance in the country, did not have their presence in the country delegitimized and devalued, as the Sri Lankan Tamils did.

The formation and persistence of the Alliance party is a complicated story. The principal motivation for its formation was the fact that town council elections, in which electorates were heterogeneous, preceded the first national elections, in which they were not. Both sets of elections took place before independence. The town council elections, conducted in 1952–53, were regarded as a kind of trial heat, and it was important to win them. The multiethnic Independence of the Malaya party (IMP), led by Dato' Onn bin Ja'afar, was well organized all over the peninsula. Dato' Onn had resigned in 1951 as leader of the United Malays National Organization (UMNO), the leading Malay party, because UMNO had refused to accept non-Malay members. As a result, Onn's multiethnic credentials were very much in order. The vast majority of the urban population and the majority of the town council electorates consisted of non-Malays. To compete with Onn's IMP, it made sense for UMNO to align with a non-Malay party. Malay votes alone could not win town council elections. As it happened, the local leader of the Malayan Chinese Association (MCA) in Kuala Lumpur was opposed to the IMP, so the MCA made an agreement with UMNO, later replicated in other towns, to run candidates on a joint "UMNO-MCA alliance" slate against the IMP. The slate was successful in Kuala Lumpur and elsewhere, and the local alliances ripened into a national multiethnic coalition—the Alliance Party—which later won all but one of the parliamentary seats in the 1955 elections. For interethnic accommodation, there could hardly be a more convincing demonstration of the power of formal incentives to induce informal arrangements.

The 1955 parliamentary elections preceded the grant of citizenship to most Chinese and Indians, and, as I mentioned earlier, Malays comprised an 84 percent majority of the national electorate. Had these national elections preceded the town council elections, UMNO would not have found the formation of a multiethnic coalition to be in its interest. Instead, it would have responded exclusively to Malay demands; and the independence constitution of 1957, which consisted of an elaborate package of carefully negotiated compromises, would not have been possible. Malaysian politics would have looked more like Sri Lankan politics. The liberal citizenship provisions for the non-Malays that were part of the independence bargain would not have been enacted. Fewer non-Malays would then have become citizens, and the electorate, which by 1964 had become only 54.1 percent Malay, would have remained overwhelmingly Malay, as it was in 1955. Malay parties would have competed with each other, as Sinhalese parties did, by pursuing the interests of their own group at the expense of the other half of the population.

What happened was quite different. Committed to a permanent coalition and to interethnic compromises, the Alliance (and later the National Front) created opportunities for parties representing Malays and non-Malays to line up on the flanks and accuse the ruling coalition of selling out the rights of the Malays and the rights of the non-Malays, respectively. Once this happened, the Alliance was locked into place in the middle of the ethnic spectrum. All alternatives looked worse than the status quo. For the MCA, UMNO was, on ethnic issues, the most moderate Malay party with which to form a coalition. Even if the other Chinese parties had been agreeable to a coalition with the MCA (which they were not), no combination of non-Malay parties alone could control a majority of seats to form a government. For UMNO, the MCA was likewise the most accommodating Chinese party. The only plausible Malay coalition partner in a possible all-Malay government was the Pan-Malayan Islamic party (PMIP), which most UMNO leaders, secular as they were, regarded with deep suspicion. Moreover, the raison d'être of the PMIP was opposition to UMNO's compromises with the Chinese. On the other hand, neither the MCA nor UMNO could form a government alone. The two together controlled about half the popular vote. Although UMNO controlled many more votes than the MCA did, it could still not count on forming a government by itself. The MCA candidates received more Malay votes from UMNO supporters than UMNO candidates received from MCA supporters, but the heterogeneous nature of more than half the parliamentary constituencies made it impossible for UMNO to count on going it alone. Although relations between UMNO and the MCA were not always cordial, each side knew very well that electoral arithmetic made the other the lesser evil by far. The Alliance coalition had created opposition that divided the party system into three blocs: non-Malay opposition, Malay opposition, and the Alliance. Redivision was not practicable, so the coalition, however unsatisfactory, was self-perpetuating.

Party Systems and Ethnic Policies

The exchange of votes thus formed the underpinning of compromise, as it might have done in Sri Lanka if the present electoral system had been in force earlier. To see the difference in ethnic effects, one needs only to contrast the Sinhala-only legislation of 1956 with the Malaysian language act of 1967 or the 1972 Sri Lankan constitution with the 1957 Malaysian constitution and the 1971 amendments to it. The Sri Lankan language policy and state religion provisions symbolically wrote the Sri Lanka Tamils out of the polity. The Malaysian language act, by contrast, provided for the continued "liberal use" of English, Chinese, and Tamil—much to the chagrin of Malay language extremists. The Malaysian constitution safeguarded a "special position" for the Malays, subject to the "legitimate interests" of the other groups. After the

1969 riots, the constitution was amended to preclude any challenge to the special position of the Malays and also to preclude any challenge to the citizenship of the Chinese. These amendments were enacted in an environment that could only be described as unfavorable to the non-Malays. Despite that, the potentially tenuous citizenship of the non-Malays was solidified permanently, at the same time as the Sri Lanka Tamils, unquestionably citizens, were increasingly being regarded as and treated like aliens in their own land.

The explanation for the course Malaysian ethnic politics took lies in a combination of incentives, leadership, and chance. The future coalition partners responded to electoral incentives in the early 1950s and, by their action in agreeing to non-Malay citizenship, changed the composition of the electorate in a way that created new electoral incentives to compromise. Of course, it was sheer good fortune that the local elections preceded the national ones. And it was equally fortunate that the main competitor of UMNO was the multiethnic IMP. Had a militantly pro-Malay competitor party existed, UMNO would surely have hesitated to make a lasting arrangement with the MCA. Fortunately for both, the strength of the PMIP grew as a reaction to the Alliance, rather than antedating it. Not heterogeneous constituencies alone, but heterogeneous constituencies plus no serious intraethnic competition, made the coalition possible. It also took good leadership, particularly on the part of Tengku Abdul Rahman, the national UMNO leader. The leadership recognized the long-term utility of the Alliance format and decided both to approve it locally and to pursue it nationally, even though the composition of the national electorate was initially radically different. Once again, therefore, it was not any particular condition—not incentives, not chance, not political will alone—but a combination that governed the choices that were made and the effects they had.

Still less was it a matter of goodwill or interethnic tolerance that was determinative. Goodwill was not always present in Malaysia; at most times before the recurrent Sri Lankan violence began in earnest, there was probably more interethnic tolerance in Sri Lanka. Rather, the course of Malaysian politics was determined by a series of responses to constraints that hemmed the decision makers in at any given moment. To say this is to denigrate the part played by heroic action for ethnic harmony and to elevate the role of simple good judgment and rational response to the predicament in which decision makers find themselves. Implicit in this assessment is the possibility for still other decision makers, working within the constraints that impinge on *their* choices, to alter the predicaments that will face future decision makers—to alter them in such a direction that they, too, will respond in ways conducive to interethnic accommodation.

It might be thought that an ethnically balanced coalition, even one slanted somewhat more toward the interests of one group than another would tend to immobilism, that such a coalition could not institute policies that might impinge on vested ethnic interests. The only policy it could have would be a predictable compromise. There were some tendencies toward immobilism in the Malaysia of the 1960s, although even then not everything was compromise and not everything was predictable. In the 1970s, however, there were dramatic departures in ethnic policy regarding language, education, and the economy. On some subjects, Malaysian ethnic policy went in the same direction as Sri Lankan policy; on others, Malaysian policy was even more ethnically exclusive. But in virtually every case, Malaysian policy appeared to be more carefully planned and implemented in a more controlled and less threatening way.

In language policy, Malaysia moved to make Malay the medium of instruction in nearly all the schools, one grade level at a time, beginning in 1969, soon after the Kuala Lumpur riots. This was a ministerial decision, not contemplated by the previous policy—and it went much beyond the Sri Lankan two-stream policy of education in Sinhala and Tamil—but it was implemented without very much difficulty and was widely accepted. What was by no means accepted—and therefore not implemented—was the abolition of the Chinese primary schools, broached from time to time by Malay extremists.

In higher education, the Malaysian policy of the 1970s resembled the Sri Lankan policy, but again it was put into effect—and altered—in a more orderly and confident way. In the early 1970s, there was a sense that the Malaysian Chinese and the Sri Lankan Tamils, respectively, were overrepresented as students in higher education. As the Sri Lankans adopted standardization of marks, the Malaysians also altered admission criteria to universities, so that many more Malay students were admitted and more Chinese and Indians were refused admission. In both Malaysia and Sri Lanka, the policy precipitated strong reactions from the groups that suffered the exclusion.

Once again, the action taken as a result illustrates the blend of chance and structure in determining outcomes in the two systems. The Malaysian Chinese, with considerably higher average incomes than the Sri Lanka Tamils, responded, first, by sending students in the thousands abroad for higher education. Many fewer Sri Lanka Tamils were able to go even to India, much less to Britain, Australia, Canada, or the United States. Beyond this, however, in 1978, the MCA—its electoral fortunes then at one of many low points in recent years—made it clear that it could no longer accept declining quotas in higher education at home. The MCA and UMNO jointly agreed that university admission quotas for non-Malays would be revised upward in stages until they reflected the ethnic composition of the population as a whole. In Sri Lanka, the UNP committed itself in 1977 to abolishing standardization of marks. Upon assuming office, it attempted to do so but provoked a Sinhalese backlash. The result was a series of partial amendments that have opened university admission to more Tamils than were enrolled under standardization but many fewer than before standardization. The Malaysian agreement, a product of the coalition, was implemented as planned. The Sri Lankan policy repeal was implemented only in part. Both because of the Malaysian Chinese ability to absorb higher educational costs and because of the way the respective policies were put in place and amended, the Sri Lankan educational preferences have been far more damaging to national unity than the Malaysian preferences have been.

In ethnic restructuring of the economy, the Malaysians have gone much further than the Sri Lankans. Following the riots of 1969 in Malaysia, a consensus developed within the government that the source of the violence lay in Malay economic grievances. In 1971, an extensive program, called the New Economic Policy (NEP), was put into place to achieve ethnic proportionality in employment and 30 percent Malay share ownership by 1990. Policies were also devised to increase loans, government contracts, licenses, and franchises available to Malays. As the NEP was put in place at a time of Chinese political weakness, it would have been difficult to oppose. But in fact, most Chinese political leaders shared the view that augmenting Malay economic resources was necessary. Moreover, the stated policy was that the changes would be accomplished without expropriating existing business—only future opportunities would be affected—and the policymakers were flexible about implementation. Strict employment quotas were not enforced. Well-connected Chinese found ways to profit from the new policies. Although the full balance sheet on the NEP remains to be drawn up, dramatic changes in economic power were achieved without major disruptions of the economy or the polity.

As this was happening, the multiethnic coalition was also undergoing enlargement, to embrace all of the peninsular Malaysian parties except one party on the Malay flank (the PMIP, which joined the coalition briefly) and one on the Chinese flank. The MCA—and the Chinese voice in general—became somewhat weaker in the National Front than it had been in the Alliance, but Chinese votes were still important to victory, and the coalition was unwilling to dispense with any of the Chinese political parties. Beginning in 1983, a protracted leadership battle in the MCA was endured in the coalition in a way that demonstrated the strongly held sentiment that, even in bad times, the coalition was better than any alternative.

The Rewards of Moderation

Taken together, Malaysia and Sri Lanka show that small differences can produce big differences; that, once a multiethnic coalition gets going, multiethnicity can become a habit; that interethnic accommodation does not preclude major structural changes in ethnic relations; and that in the absence of accommodative arrangements, governmental actions that could otherwise have been either endured or modified can be so provocative as to produce violent responses. The Malaysians took no chances with ethnic conflict in the 1950s, and the structures they established could later be modified to take account of changed conditions. The Sri Lankans were reckless with their milder ethnic conflict in the 1950s, and their failure to establish sound structures left them defenseless later, when conflict became more serious. Contrast what followed the Malaysian postelection riots of 1969 with what followed the Sri Lankan postelection riots of 1977. The Malaysian response to the riots was to tilt toward Malay economic aspirations. Within a year of the Sri Lankan riots, the UNP government had enacted a constitution likely to provide Sri Lankan Tamils with more political influence than they had ever previously enjoyed. At worst, little harm, in terms of ethnic conflict, came out of the Malaysian response. At best, little good has come, so far, out of the Sri Lankan response. By then it was well established that interethnic moderation pays in Malaysia, whereas extremism pays in Sri Lanka.

Conciliation, Early and Late

It is all well and good to learn that the arrangements made by the Malaysians thirty-five years ago saved them many difficulties that the Sri Lankans have experienced because they lacked such arrangements. One way to read this comparative experience is simply to conclude that earlier is better. There are a good many aphorisms—about an ounce of prevention, for example—that attest to the same general lesson. That particular lesson is not very helpful, however, to those countries for which it is not only no longer early but in fact very late. What are the Sri Lankas, Northern Irelands, and Sudans to do when they are already *in extremis*?

The first thing they might do is read the Malaysian (and Nigerian) lesson more broadly. Above all, the Malaysian arrangements made moderation pay, and by now it is hardly a secret how one goes about doing this. *The most reliable way, under conditions of democratic elections, is to make politicians reciprocally dependent on the votes of members of groups other than their own.* In the Malaysian case, as I have shown, highly heterogeneous constituencies (plus some unusual early conditions—namely, multiethnic rather than ethnic-flank competition) were the main vehicle for facilitating interethnic vote exchange. In post-1979 Sri Lanka, alternative voting was another way, especially suitable for countries where territorially demarcated constituencies are likely to be homogeneous. In the Nigerian Second Republic, electoral distribution requirements for the winning presidential candidate were yet another. Neither the wishful abolition of ethnic parties nor a solemn admonition to politicians to think of national rather than ethnic interests is a good substitute for providing concrete incentives to multiethnic behavior. Pure heart is not the issue—decent behavior is. And heterogeneous constituencies, together with incentives to vote pooling across ethnic lines, are the key to moderate behavior. Where territorial constituencies are homogeneous, it remains possible, as in the Sri Lankan and Nigerian presidential elections, to turn the whole country into a single, heterogeneous constituency.

Where groups are territorially separate, of course, arrangements for devolution may also be in order, especially if separatist organizations have arisen and are fighting. Here the obstacles to agreement are formidable. Federalism has a bad name in many countries that could benefit from it. Sovereignty, as I argued earlier, seems, in principle, to be indivisible, and it requires a substantial modification of conventional thinking in a world of putatively sovereign states to envision the benefits of dividing up territory. The potential costs come much more readily to mind. In particular, it is widely thought that devolution paves the way for separatist independence. On this, there is good evidence that the way to prevent the loss of a region to which power is devolved is to keep some substantial portion of the population of that region occupied in rewarding roles outside the region, particularly at the center. In the case of the Sri Lanka Tamils, nearly one-third of whom have customarily resided outside the north and east of the island, this should be easy to arrange, provided that their security can be assured. The case of the Ibo, who returned to northern Nigeria after the civil war—and remained undisturbed—provides one of many models of sustained group interests outside the group's home region. The Pathans of Pakistan provide another such example, for they are heavily employed outside the North-West Frontier province.

Beyond this, it is insufficiently recognized how much intraethnic and interethnic conflict is likely to arise—and, with it, how much resistance to independence—within self-governing regions that appear homogeneous from the outside. This is the way to think about whether there should be one or two Tamil territorial units in Sri Lanka and one or three, or more, southern Sudanese territorial units—and what powers they should have. In states such as Sri Lanka and the Sudan, there will be a good many counterincentives to separatism once devolution is accomplished. The southern Sudan from 1972 to 1983 illustrates precisely this point.

If we know roughly what incentives to build in—and I believe we do—what we assuredly do not know is what incentives to dangle before the parties to the conflict to secure their assent to the requisite arrangements once the conflict has gone as far as the Sri Lanka, Northern Ireland, and Sudan conflicts have gone. For in a sense, we have come full circle. Interests in pursuing the conflict—even intraethnic interests—outweigh interests in reducing it. The non-Vellala caste composition of the leadership of the Liberation Tigers of Tamil Eelam is a good example. For the Tiger leadership, normalization probably conjures up images of renewed Vellala dominance, for the Vellala have dominated Tamil political parties since independence. Fighting may seem preferable to anything resembling the status quo ante. At the same time as interethnic issues are addressed in a negotiation, therefore, intraethnic issues must be considered and proposals developed that appeal to the specific interests of the relevant actors, not just to the group as a whole.

Unfortunately, the leading examples of accommodative arrangements following warfare are not very helpful. The Nigerians decided on accommodation after fighting a thirty-month war to a military conclusion. The Sudanese in 1972 agreed to end their nine-year war because both sides had become significantly weaker at roughly the same time. Even laying aside the fact that the Sudanese agreement was later abrogated, it would take an unusual concatenation of circumstances to replicate the occasion for agreement in 1972. And pushing a bloody civil war to a decisive victory—in order to achieve a widespread Nigerian-type desire not to repeat the bloodshed—would be self-defeating.

One hopeful general circumstance is that external actors rarely wish, by their assistance, to bring into being the events most feared by central governments in power. The Indian government would scarcely benefit from a Tamil secession from Sri Lanka that made the ex-Sri Lankan Tamils poor dependents of India or, worse, that incited a comparable secessionist movement among the 50 million Tamils of Tamil Nadu. The Irish Republic would presumably not be keen to absorb a Northern Irish segment that was significantly more heterogeneous and conflict-prone than Protestants and Catholics now in the Republic are. Ethiopia and other black African states that assist the Sudan Peoples Liberation Movement and Army would not likely take comfort in a dismemberment of the Sudan that would provide a nearby example of success for dissident minorities that have already taken up arms in Ethiopia. If, then, the interests of states that are offering assistance do not lie in the most extreme results, there is room for actions to induce them to abandon their assistance.

These actions are of two types. First, when the help of the assisting state is based on some political interest other than ethnic affinity, there is room for state-to-state negotiation to induce a change in policy. The abruptness with which Iran ended its support to the Kurds in Iraq in 1975 when it received an unrelated quid pro quo provides an apt illustration. Despite some trans-border affinities, Uganda ended its assistance to Anyanya rebels in the southern Sudan in 1972 when Idi Amin's Muslim and Arab connections increased. Ethiopia's support for the Sudan Peoples Liberation Army is not based on ethnic affinity and is therefore susceptible to state-to-state negotiation. Second, when the help of the assisting state is based on ethnic affinity—as in occasional, if unofficial, Irish indulgence toward the Irish Republican Army or the former Indian support for the Sri Lankan Tamil guerrillas—domestic opinion in the assisting state will be moved only by concessions on the outstanding ethnic issues.

Such concessions, however, are subject to the constraints of domestic opinion in the state affected by the ethnic violence. Or, to put the point differently, this is a matter of foreign policy that is coterminous with domestic ethnic politics. Groups that have a history of dominating others or anxiety about the capacities and aspirations of others—and some combination describes the Ulster Protestants, the northern Sudanese, and the Sinhalese—are unlikely to be able to reach the requisite determination to settle. This is particularly true if their governments continue—as all three do—to be subject to intraethnic competition that is alert to any signs of concession, such as that embodied in Mrs. Bandaranaike's anticoncession "movement for the defense of the nation." Even so, the increasing concessions offered at virtually every stage of the armed conflict—concessions that easily would have conciliated their antagonists at earlier stages—will be insufficient to placate the determined leaders of armed movements or the outraged public opinion among the relevant segment of the assisting state. Only when disaster is impending are the parties likely to be brought to new ways of thinking. Although it is too late in such cases for the Malaysian ounce of prevention, it still needs to be driven home just how serious are the costs of ignoring some such prophylaxis in a severely divided society. After protracted armed conflict, if the lessons are widely enough understood, it will not necessarily be too late for the survivors to apply the Nigerian pound of cure.

Note

a. The indigene–immigrant dichotomy had been reinforced by recent colonial policies and policy reversals, at the time of the Malayan Union (1945–46) and Federation of Malaya (1948) schemes, which had incorporated radically different notions of the relations of the various ethnic groups to the country.

References

1. For the most careful discussion of the choice of case studies, see Harry Eckstein, "Case Study and Theory in Political Science," in Fred I. Greenstein and Nelson W. Polsby, eds., *Handbook of Political Science,* Vol. 7 (Reading, MA: Addison-Wesley, 1975), pp. 79–137.

2. See, generally, Charles Tilly, ed., *The Formation of National States in Western Europe* (Princeton, NJ: Princeton University Press, 1975).

3. The draft text of the Meech Lake Agreement appears in the *Toronto Globe and Mail,* May 2, 1987.

4. For the common South Indian roots of Sri Lankans, see S.J. Tambiah, *Sri Lanka: Ethnic Fratricide and the Dismantling of Democracy* (Chicago: University of Chicago Press, 1986). For the relatively recent South Indian origin of certain Sinhalese castes, see Bryce Ryan, *Caste in Modern Ceylon* (New Brunswick, NJ: Rutgers University Press, 1953).

5. Ann Mosely Lesch, "Confrontation in the Southern Sudan," *Middle East Journal* 40, no. 3 (Summer 1986): 410–28, at p. 414.

6. For the role of intergroup comparisons in ethnic conflict, see Donald L. Horowitz, *Ethnic Groups in Conflict* (Berkeley and Los Angeles: University of California Press, 1985), pp. 141–84.

7. For examples, see Harold Jackson, *The Two Irelands—A Dual Study of Inter-group Tensions* (London: Minority Rights Group Report No. 2, 1971), p. 9; Myron Weiner, *Sons of the Soil: Migration and Ethnic Conflict in India* (Princeton, NJ: Princeton University Press, 1978), pp. 47,113.

8. See Donald L. Horowitz, "Patterns of Ethnic Separatism," *Comparative Studies in Society and History* 23, no. 2 (April 1981): 165–95.

9. I have described some of these changes in my earlier chapter in this volume (chapter 8) and in *Ethnic Groups in Conflict,* pp. 602–13, 635–38.

10. The Nigerian constitutional process and the sentiments that underlay it are described in Donald L. Horowitz, "About-Face in Africa: The Return to Civilian Rule in Nigeria," *Yale Review* 68, no. 2 (Winter 1979): 192–206.

11. See B.H. Farmer, *Ceylon: A Divided Nation* (London: Oxford University Press, 1963), p. 51.

12. *Utusan Melayu* (Singapore), September 2, 1955.

13. For the unwritten rules of the Malaysian coalition, see Horowitz, *Ethnic Groups in Conflict,* pp. 416–20.

14. For the Sri Lankan schemes and their effects, see C.R. de Silva, "The Politics of University Admissions: A Review of Some Aspects of the Admissions Policy in Sri Lanka, 1971–1978," *Sri Lanka Journal of Social Science* 2, no. 1 (June 1979): 85–123.

15. See Tambiah, *Sri Lanka,* p. 32.

16. Sothi Rachagan, "The Development of the Electoral System," in Harold Crouch, Lee Kam Hing, and Michael Ong, eds. *Malaysian Politics and the 1978 Election* (Kuala Lumpur: Oxford University Press, 1980), pp. 271–79.

17. Computed from *Report of the Delimitation Commission, 1976,* Sessional Paper No. 1 of 1976 (Colombo: Government Publications Bureau, 1976), pp. 12–238.

26
Economic Performance and Ethnic Conflict

Milton J. Esman

It has become an article of conventional wisdom that economic growth mitigates ethnic conflict. Simply put, when there is more to go around, everybody benefits, thus relieving material grievances and reducing incentives for conflict. To a great many people, this would seem to be grass-roots common sense.

In the wake of the disastrous ethnic riots of May 1969, the government of Malaysia, prompted by prestigious foreign advisors, launched the New Economic Policy (NEP), designed to eliminate the identification of race with economic function.[1] Its strategy was to enhance participation by the politically dominant but economically depressed Malays in the modern economy by large-scale government intervention; sustained economic growth would make this possible without penalizing non-Malays. Both communities would benefit, though at different rates. By removing the main obstacle to national unity, the achievement of economic equality would substantially reduce the propensity for ethnic conflict.

More recently, opponents of economic sanctions against the government of South Africa have made similar, if somewhat more modest claims for the efficacy of economic growth. As stated by the distinguished long-time enemy of apartheid, Helen Suzman, "the most effective instrument for change [in the apartheid system] is economic expansion"; since international sanctions may limit economic growth, they are likely to exacerbate interracial tensions and are therefore counterproductive.[2] Such statements continue to be made in the face of incontrovertible evidence that the principal nonwhite beneficiaries of economic growth to date have been among the most militant protesters and that acknowledged spokespersons for South Africa's majority insist that they will not be satisfied with anything short of fundamental political changes.

It was immediately after World War II that the intellectual basis was laid for the optimistic faith that economic growth could be the main solvent for all social conflicts. Economic theory, stimulated by the seminal writing of John Maynard Keynes, had developed prescriptions that seemed to work for achieving sustained economic expansion. H.W. Arndt, the Australian economist, has traced how the idea of economic growth became the central core of contemporary economic policy, essential to the achievement of such goals as full employment, improved living standards, and the defusion of class conflict:

> Perhaps no other argument appealed more to thoughtful people on the left as on the right, than that economic growth may, in Galbraith's paraphrase, prove to be "the great solvent of the tensions associated with inequality."[3]

This view was summed up neatly by the late Walter Heller in these words: "When the social pie grows even bigger, there is less room to quarrel over who gets the biggest slices."[4]

Originally, the idea that economic growth was a useful, even a necessary solvent for conflict was meant to apply to class tensions between owners and workers. It was soon extended, however, to a wider range of conflicts. By the late 1960s, when ethnic and racial differences appeared to be matching and even overshadowing class as a threat to social order—both in Western societies such as the United States and Canada and in a great many developing countries—economic growth was conveniently available as the solvent for these conflicts as well.

But although the utility of economic growth for the management of ethnic conflict is frequently asserted and has become an article of faith for both scholars and laymen, it has never been convincingly demonstrated. I am at the very beginning of a research effort that will examine the master proposition that national economic growth mitigates ethnic conflict and, conversely, that economic stagnation or decline exacerbates and intensifies these struggles. Where such relationships can be established, an effort will be made to identify the particular conditions under which these relationships hold. The collection and analysis of data from many sources is just getting under way, and it would be premature to report these raw, preliminary findings at this time. But the underlying intellectual base for this inquiry, some of the possibilities that are anticipated, and their implications for public policy may, even at this preliminary stage, be of interest to students of ethnic politics and conflict management.

The Context for the Debate

Before laying out specific propositions, it may be useful to define the context in which these competing ideas are intended to apply. That context is the contemporary territorial state. Throughout the modern world, the state—notwithstanding basic differences in constitutions, methods of governance, effectiveness of administration, and relations with citizens and subjects—has become the main institutional allocator of values. In the most fundamental sense, it is the state that determines who gets what.[5] It is the state that lays down and enforces the rules for access to employment in the civil, military, police, and judicial establishments of government and even in private enterprises. The state determines who can vote and who can hold office; who is eligible for loans, licenses, and public contracts; who can qualify for higher education; and what languages enjoy official status in government operations and in education. Market institutions by which economic values are allocated in most societies are sanctioned and their specific rules are frequently modified by the state. Because the state establishes and enforces these rules, its institutions become the arenas of competition and conflict between groups that seek to gain and maintain favorable treatment or to redress what they perceive to be unfavorable or oppressive conditions.

In this competitive struggle, ethnic communities have become conspicuous participants, to the surprise and disappointment of many observers, some of whom have difficulty reconciling themselves to this reality. Liberal thought has been committed to the principle that with enlightenment and progress, the individual would and should become the main actor in public affairs. Individuals should be accorded equal status; opportunities and rewards should flow to individuals according to competitive performance and achievement, irrespective of race, religion, ethnicity, or other forms of ascriptive group membership. Ascriptive affiliations were regarded—and continue to be regarded by many—as residues of a primitive and less enlightened past that will inevitably be assigned to the ash heaps of history.[6]

The principal opponents of the liberals, the Marxists, have also been convinced, though for different reasons, that ethnicity is doomed to disappear. According to Marxist theory, in capitalist economies, the objective basis for common interest and thus for group conflict is membership in one of two antagonistic classes: the bourgeoisie and the proletariat. Ascriptive solidarities, the detritus of earlier stages of historical development, continue to be exploited by the bourgeoisie to create a "false consciousness" among the working class. Lenin taught that expedient concessions must be made to ethnic and national loyalties and that these might even be turned to useful and progressive purposes in the revolutionary struggle. Such tactical gestures should be minimized, however, in order to speed the inevitable and desirable emergence of class solidarity and a higher stage of civilization, embodied in international proletarian brotherhood and a classless society.[7]

Perhaps the most influential paradigm in contemporary social thought— modernization theory—joined the liberals and the Marxists in the confident prediction that ethnic solidarity would decline as a significant factor in societal development. This theory taught that technological advancement, secularization of values and beliefs, the imperatives of urban life, and the speed of communications systems would combine to minimize social differences.

Living in similar societies, aspiring to the same goals, and earning their liveli-hoods in similar social structures, people were bound to value achievement above all. Ascriptive group loyalties would be superseded and would no longer be functional in modern societies. These socioeconomic trends would be reenforced, in turn, by the political processes of "nation-building," designed to supplant parochial (ethnic) identities with more cosmopolitan allegiances associated with a more homogeneous culture promoted by the state.[8]

This optimistic expectation has not been realized. Instead, modernization has stimulated and politicized ethnic solidarity. Allocations by the modern state, by design or by inadvertence, have had differential impacts on ethnic communities. The prevailing rules of competition have affected their oppor-tunities and rewards differently and unequally. Individuals have found that they are treated not as disembodied atoms but as members of an ethnic com-munity; they have discovered that the most natural way to promote and defend their security and economic prospects is through ethnic associations. Ethnic groups whose members feel blocked or disadvantaged by the prevailing rules have been readily mobilized by aspiring political entrepreneurs to pro-claim their common grievances and advance their collective claims in ethnic terms; those who are advantaged have been mobilized defensively to protect their perceived group interests. Thus, economic development and modern statehood have not eliminated ethnicity. Instead, they have invested it with new functions.[9]

Ethnicity has become politicized in the competitive struggle for relative power, cultural status, and economic opportunities and rewards, in which the state and its organs are the principal arenas of conflict. Of course, ethnicity is not the only important cleavage in modern politics, and in some situations it is irrelevant. But in those policies where it is the dominant cleavage, it sur-faces in many guises, and it engages the anxious attention of political elites. It is there elites who shoulder most of the responsibility for regulating or managing ethnically based conflicts. It is in the framework of highly mobilized and politicized ethnic solidarity groups operating in and about the institutions of the modern state that the debate on economic performance becomes rele-vant. In what ways, if any, can the performance of the national economy af-fect interethnic relations? Does it provide a policy resource for the managers of the state or for sympathetic outsiders in their efforts to maintain the polity in peace?

Three Propositions

Three major propositions attempt to explain the relationship between eco-nomic performance and ethnic conflict. As these are incompatible proposi-tions, they highlight the contradictory perspectives on this relationship.

Economic Growth Facilitates Ethnic Conflict Management

The first proposition is that economic growth facilitates and may even be a necessary condition for the successful management of ethnic conflict. By increasing the material resources of society, economic expansion makes it possible to provide material benefits to members of all ethnic groups. Everyone benefits in this positive-sum game, and no individual or group need be harmed or deprived. Grievances and claims can be accommodated at no real cost to any of the participating ethnic parties. Economic gains need not be distributed equally or even proportionately among ethnic groups. Indeed, this is the very point. More can be provided—in job opportunities, business licenses, credit, housing—to the relatively disadvantaged, mitigating their grievances and satisfying their aspirations for material improvement and greater justice without penalizing the economically advantaged. Thus, economic expansion and only economic expansion provides the means to benefit all, though at different rates.

Though material conditions may not, according to this perspective, be the sole issue dividing ethnic groups, they are inevitably at the root of much societal conflict. Material scarcity generates severe struggles for shares, as the benefits that accrue to one competitor necessarily come at the expense of others. Conditions of economic stagnation or slow growth, not to mention decline, are inauspicious for the management of any kind of societal conflict. Vigorous economic growth, on the other hand, creates a social climate of satisfaction, optimism, and generosity that can generate intergroup trust, facilitate mutual accommodation, and enhance prospects for the peaceful and consensual management of ethnic conflict.

Economic Growth Aggravates Ethnic Conflict

The second proposition predicts that economic growth, especially in the short run, will accentuate and aggravate, rather than diminish, ethnic conflict. Whatever the other benefits that economic growth may bring to society, reducing ethnic conflict will not be one of them. This pessimistic assessment is drawn from the celebrated sociopsychological concept of relative deprivation.[10] Although economic expansion may produce real improvements in material conditions, its more important effect is to shift aspiration levels. Persons who once acquiesced in deprived economic conditions because they could visualize no practical alternatives now begin to reassess their prospects and possibilities. No longer are they content to compare their improved circumstances with their previous experience and be grateful for the improvement. Instead, they now compare their present conditions and opportunities with those of groups that are materially better off than they, asking by what right the others should be more privileged. So perversely, as their conditions improve, they become more dissatisfied because their aspiration levels have moved faster than their accomplishments.

As their grievances mount, so does the stridency of their demands. When the target of these demands is a competing or hostile ethnic group—as is likely to be the case in an ethnically divided society—these demands are readily perceived by their ethnic competitors as a threat to the latter's fully deserved and hard earned economic and occupational status. They then mobilize to protect their position, thus inflaming preexistent ethnic antagonisms and increasing the likelihood of conflict. Advocates of the relative deprivation school regard as simply naive the notion that economic growth is likely to mitigate ethnic or any other form of societal conflict. Even if there were enough growth to go around—to make a significant difference—its distribution would be problematical and probably conflictual. Moreover, the hypothesis that growth promotes satisfaction seems to ignore the main psychological consequences of economic expansion—the shifts in aspiration levels and in reference groups that generate fresh dissatisfactions and grievances in the wake of economic growth. These dissatisfactions breed hostility, not positive-sum contentment, and they diminish the individual and collective propensity for accommodation and compromise. Thus, in ethnically divided societies, economic growth is more likely to exacerbate than to mitigate group conflict.

Economic Growth Does Not Affect Ethnic Relations

The third proposition, essentially agnostic on this relationship, argues that economic growth is essentially irrelevant to the management of severe ethnic conflicts. The foundations of ethnic conflict, proponents of this proposition hold, are not economic but cultural and, especially, political: Whose country is it? Which group shall control the central government? How shall minorities be represented and participate in national politics? How much autonomy shall be conceded to regionally based minorities? Which language or languages should enjoy official status in education and in government operations? These are the critical political issues about which some contending parties adopt uncompromising, nonnegotiable postures. On such issues, men and women are prepared to put their lives on the line under conditions of intense ethnic hostility, as in Sri Lanka, Sudan, Cyprus, Northern Ireland, South Africa, Israel's West Bank, the state of Punjab, and the other cases examined in this volume.

Although economic issues are not insignificant, they are, according to this line of argument, usually derivative of these more basic political issues. Neither economic growth nor economic stagnation can fundamentally affect the course or the outcome of intense conflicts that are waged for different stakes.

Of relevance to this argument is a tendency among contemporary Western social scientists to transmute political to economic issues. This tendency is due to one of two equally erroneous beliefs, both of which reflect the intellectual sin of economism: that most societal controversies are at their base economic, behavior being actuated primarily by material needs and motives; or that whatever the multiple causes and occasions of group conflict may be, difficult and often impossible as they are to disentangle, economic rewards are the most available and the most effective means for controlling and eventually resolving such conflicts. While conceding that economic growth, combined with the astute distribution of its increments, may be helpful in mitigating moderate disputes between ethnic parties—where neither the boundaries of the polity nor control of the central or regional state apparatus are at stake—the proponents of this proposition see little if any significant relationship between economic performance and successful management of emotionally intense and violent ethnic conflicts. The core of this perspective, simply put, is that economic performance seldom explains and economic means are seldom available to resolve the more dangerous and violent instances of ethnic conflict. Economic factors are irrelevant to the management of conflicts that originate from other, mainly political, causes.

Distributing the Benefits of Economic Growth

Further complicating these contradictory theoretical perspectives is the difficult question of interethnic and intraethnic distribution of the benefits of economic growth. What are the various possibilities?

Interethnic Distribution

Assuming two competing ethnic communities, the increments of growth can be distributed by one of three patterns: disproportionately to the already advantaged; proportionately to both groups; or disproportionately, through "affirmative action" policies, to the disadvantaged group.

Market processes of distribution are likely to direct wealth and income disproportionately to the already economically advantaged. They have the skills, the connections, the financial resources, and the self-confidence that enable them to capitalize on fresh opportunities and to earn, through competitive performance, the lion's share of the increments of growth. The economically weaker ethnic group may benefit through trickle-down processes as growth increases the demand for labor, especially skilled labor, but the main benefits accrue to those who are initially better endowed to compete. It is for this reason that Malay political elites, though committed to capitalist patterns of ownership, have been unwilling to rely entirely on market processes to distribute the increments of macroeconomic growth. Predictably, the better-endowed Chinese would sweep the boards in this kind of competition, and Malays would be reduced to the structurally inferior status of the native Hawaiians or the "Red Indians of North America" in their own country. As market-regulated growth increased existing interethnic disparities, the ground would be prepared, according to this perspective, for further grievances, which would readily be exploited by ethnic political entrepreneurs. The predictable result would be aggravated grievances, polarization, and violence. Interethnic harmony and the maintenance of a consensual polity depend critically on balancing growth with interethnic distributional fairness. Those who argue this position find it hard to visualize how growth distributed primarily by market criteria could have any but negative effects on interethnic tensions in seriously divided societies.

What if growth were distributed proportionately among ethnic competitors? Each group would be rewarded in proportion to its initial share in the distribution of wealth and income, so that its relative status would remain unaltered. Leaving aside the practical question of what mix of economic policies and programs could produce this kind of outcome, the results might indeed approach the optimum of the proponents of economic growth: Every group would benefit in real, absolute terms without disturbing preexistent patterns of interethnic economic relationships. It is not obvious how such evenhanded distribution would affect interethnic relationships; the optimistic expectation would be that mutual benefits within a familiar pattern of distribution would produce generalized satisfactions, thereby attenuating the struggle for shares. Skeptics might ask how long the disadvantaged party, despite improvements in its economic circumstances, would be willing to accept without protest an originally inequitable relationship once the disturbing processes of economic growth had been set in motion.

The third pattern is the disproportionate distribution of increments of wealth and income to the originally disadvantaged ethnic group in order to arrive at a more equitable outcome. This requires the displacement or limitation of market competition by public policies or administrative allocations that deliberately skew the flow of resources and economic opportunities in favor of the disadvantaged group. Despite claims that such programs negatively affect economic efficiency and thereby jeopardize future growth, and despite a rankling sense of reverse discrimination, the economically privileged group is asked to accept such measures—at least temporarily—as its contribution to building a more just and stable society, in which the economic basis for ethnic grievances will have been eliminated. In the long run, it is argued, this protects and secures the position of the economically privileged group. Economic growth makes possible a positive-sum game. The originally advantaged group is not deprived; its economic welfare continues to improve, but at a slower rate than that of the "have-not" group.[11] Once the have-nots have caught up, the policy would no longer be needed. As members of both groups would be able to compete economically in the market on relatively equal terms, affirmative action measures could be abandoned.

This was the official rationale for the Malaysian New Economic Policy, initiated after the ethnic riots of 1969 with the objective of "eliminating the identification of race with economic function." (On a much more modest and less interventionist scale, this has been the objective of affirmative action in the United States.) This policy has been in effect in Malaysia for nearly two decades—time enough to permit at least a provisional evaluation of its impact. It has produced significant shifts in the ownership of assets and in the distribution of income and employment in the modern sectors of the economy. Its consequences for interethnic relations and for the management of ethnic conflict have not yet been carefully assessed. This case will be examined in our current research. It provides an important empirical test of the ability of compensatory allocations in an environment of rapid and sustained economic growth to mitigate deep-seated ethnic tensions.

Intraethnic Distribution

Ethnic communities are far from homogeneous, of course. They usually contain their own internal cleavages, based on economic class, occupation, ideology, kinship and regional rivalries, personal ambitions, and other factors. In some situations, they may be uneasy coalitions of clans that harbor long-standing animosities. Interethnic politics are further complicated by intraethnic competition and struggle. Assuming economic growth, its distribution within ethnic groups may be as important as its interethnic distribution in determining its consequences for ethnic conflict.

An example can be drawn from the occupied West Bank of Palestine. There the poorest, least-educated, lowest-status, proletarian elements among the Palestinians have, because of opportunities to work in Israel, achieved material standards of consumption far beyond any level previously attained or even contemplated in their society. The effects of this material prosperity on Israeli–Palestinian relationships—dependent as this prosperity is on the performance of menial tasks in the Israeli economy—is itself an interesting subject for investigation. Even more interesting are its effects on two other groups of Palestinians. The first is the traditional landed gentry, whose education, political connections, and control of employment had long ensured them a dominant position in Palestinian society. With the loss of control over the most significant economic resources, they have also lost status and political clout. The second group of Palestinians comprise students and the young educated class; they find their professional opportunities totally blocked both in Israel and in the dependent economy of the West Bank. Not sharing in the newfound economic prosperity of the West Bank, they have become the most militant fighters for Palestinian nationalism, the most active supporters of the

Palestine Liberation Organization, and the most determined opponents of the Israeli occupation. The differential distribution of the benefits of economic growth among Palestinians has directly affected the intensity of ethnic conflict on the West Bank, and in unexpected ways. It seems to have pacified its direct, lower-class beneficiaries; demoralized the gentry class, which some Israelis hoped would tacitly support the occupation; and radicalized those who have been excluded from the new prosperity.

On the other hand, the main benefits of Malaysia's New Economic Policy has accrued to a relatively small number of Malays, who have enjoyed access to higher education and thereby preferential eligibility to jobs and a middle-class life-style in government and industry. It has especially benefited persons with political and governmental connections that enabled them to acquire substantial wealth. Many Malays remain in poverty, especially in rural areas. Dissident Malay politicians, often combining populist rhetoric against the political-economic establishment with Islamic fundamentalism, have campaigned for support among rural Malays who have been bypassed by economic growth. Their targets are the Malay elites, charged, among other offenses, with abandoning their own people and favoring the immigrant, infidel Chinese. To protect their standing among their Malay constituents, the government elites must be perceived as taking a firm line, not conceding too much to the Chinese. Thus, in any ethnically divided society, the unbalanced distribution of the benefits of growth *within* an ethnic community—in the Malaysian case, in favor of the upper class, in the Palestinian case, in favor of an upstart lower class—has important repercussions for interethnic relations and for the ability of government to manage ethnic conflict.

The Effects of Economic Decline

A related theme is the effects of economic stagnation or recession on ethnic conflict. If an expanding pie creates opportunities for intergroup accommodation—all groups benefiting, none at the expense of the others—then should not economic decline have the opposite effect? The struggle for shares presumably intensifies; no group benefits; all are penalized, though at different rates; and bitterness and hostility spread and intensify as each group blames its reduced share on the machinations of the others. In a defensive climate of mutual recrimination, it might be expected that no group would be prepared to concede anything to the others, and all might blame the state and its leadership for their plight. Poor economic performance would thus set the stage for more intense ethnic conflict.

There are those who blame the outbreaks in the urban black townships in South Africa in 1984 less on the exclusion of blacks from the new constitutional arrangements (the three-chamber parliament) than on the stagnation of the economy. By blocking the occupational aspirations of young blacks, the economic slowdown, it is believed, channeled their frustrations into anti-regime protests and violence. The only healthy way to reverse this cycle of frustration and aggression in South Africa, according to this view, is by the resumption of vigorous macroeconomic growth that could promise fresh hope for decent livelihoods and improved quality of life for young black men and women.

The commonsense notion that economic trouble means ethnic trouble has not been empirically tested in South Africa or elsewhere. And there appears to be some evidence that just the opposite may be the case. As the Canadian economy began to turn down in the early 1970s, it seems that much of the original enthusiasm for independence among French-Canadians in Quebec began to recede. As economic growth had encouraged the belief that Quebec could go it alone, an economic slowdown induced a contrary mood of caution and prudence, a feeling that the benefits of independence might not be worth the costs of achieving it and, especially, the subsequent economic risks. Except among the youth and those safely ensconced in government employment, the mood shifted from confrontation to accommodation as the economy weakened. The same phenomenon was observed in Scotland at about the same time; support for Scottish independence or even regional autonomy (devolution) diminished as economic prospects dimmed. Similarly, black militancy in the United States, which escalated in the wake of vigorous economic expansion in the 1960s, lost its momentum in the 1970s as the economy slowed down. More prudent and patient tactics seemed to be called for. In each of these cases, however, factors other than the performance of the economy probably affected the course of ethnic protest. In the United States, for example, the Nixon administration was committed to aborting the war on poverty and repressing militant and violent protest by black and other dissident groups. How to sort out the relative influence of economic and non-economic trends and events as explanations of changes in the direction and intensity of ethnic conflicts is one of the problems in this kind of inquiry. To deal with this problem, my research will attempt a form of nonquantitative factor analysis, as pure economic cause and effect are seldom likely to be present in real-world events.

Identifying Significant Factors

This discussion has outlined the range of hypothetical relationships between macroeconomic performance and the incidence and intensity of ethnic conflict. These hypotheses included the possibility that economic performance may be irrelevant to ethnic conflict; they range from the contradictory propositions that growth may facilitate or impair conflict management to the more refined notion that what is critical is the distribution of economic gains between ethnic groups and, indeed, even within their ranks. There seems to be some commonsense plausibility in all these possibilities, indicating the need to search out the specific *conditions* under which any of them is likely to apply. For example, measures that satisfy the demands of immigrant or diaspora communities may not be useful or acceptable to groups that claim native status in territorial homelands.

There are also more subtle possibilities. Perhaps the original or evolving *intensity* of hostility determines which kinds of conflict-regulating measures are likely to be effective. Or perhaps there are *thresholds* before which one pattern may hold for a limited period of time or until such factors as real growth, psychological expectations, or political mobilization reach a certain point, after which a fresh logic may take over, which may require different explanations or new policy measures. There are many variable factors that may affect these relationships. These need to be identified before they can be analyzed and evaluated.

The process of identifying and sorting out the significant factors calls for inductive empirical analysis. This is the strategy that will inform my research effort. I have selected for preliminary analysis three cases that I have previously examined in other research. In all three cases, ethnic conflict has been sufficiently intense and persistent to constitute a major macropolitical problem for the society and its political leadership. The first of these is the Anglophone–Francophone conflict in Canada, focusing especially on Quebec and its status in the Canadian polity. This is an example of moderate conflict fought mostly by civil means within the rules of the system and with relatively little violence. The second case, the Malay–Chinese confrontation, is a more intense and bitter conflict, including serious episodes of violence in an environment of chronic hostility. Although there have been periods of relatively peaceful coexistence between the two groups, the potential for overt conflict is a continuing preoccupation of all members of the political class in Malaysia, especially those responsible for government. The third case is South Africa, where racial polarization and conflict are overt, persistent, and violent, and the polity is sustained by sheer coercion in the face of a mounting challenge from internal and external sources. I may also trace these relationships in Israel and the Occupied Territories, another case of intense and escalating conflict accompanied by antagonistic, nonnegotiable claims in an environment of unremitting hostility and violence.

In each of these countries, there have been stretches of sustained and impressive economic growth, succeeded by periods of stagnation. In each of these cases, I shall attempt to trace the performance of the economy during the past forty years or so, since about 1950, and to relate economic performance to the incidence and intensity of ethnic conflict. I shall then attempt to determine the degree to which periods of relative relaxation of tensions between ethnic groups can be explained plausibly by economic causes. This kind of events analysis unavoidably encounters the problem of multiple causation—more than one possible factor influencing behavior and outcomes. Nevertheless, the tracing and sorting out of these relationships over extended time periods should yield sufficient information to permit reasonable inferences about the effects of economic performance on ethnic conflict.

Preliminary Expectations

What do I expect this research to yield? I expect it to reveal that macroeconomic performance has only marginal effects on ethnic conflict—quite insufficient to confirm the crude expectation that growth, however vigorous and sustained, has beneficial consequences for interethnic relationships. The more polarized the initial conflict, the less I expect that these relationships can be influenced by macroeconomic performance. But although the crude growth-diminishes-conflict proposition cannot be sustained, it would not surprise me if the *distribution* of the increments of growth—both between and within ethnic communities—were to yield some general statements about the course of ethnic conflict, at least in the short run. More likely, I think, would be a finding that vigorous and equitably distributed economic growth might be instrumental in reenforcing or protecting the settlement of underlying political or cultural issues among contending parties. However, these essentially political agreements will probably not be found to be dependent on the experience of economic growth. Although they might include procedures for allocating economic values—such as educational opportunities, jobs in the governmental, parastatal, and private sectors, government contracts, and housing—both the process and the substance of such agreements are essentially political. They are not the consequence of economic performance, and in the absence of such agreement, economic growth cannot serve as a substitute, nor can it finesse failure to achieve political accord. Economic growth may reenforce political agreements, fostering conditions that favor and strengthen the hand of moderates against ultras within ethnic communities who might resist compromise agreements, even violently.

External agencies that wish to support political accords among conflicting ethnic communities may find in economic assistance a practical vehicle for contributing to and implementing such agreements. The main point, however, is the primacy of politics in the management of ethnic conflict. Economic performance can facilitate and reenforce but never substitute for political measures; even in that instrumental role, the distribution of the benefits of economic growth or of externally provided economic resources is likely to be far more consequential than the fact or the rate of growth.

These are, of course, empirical questions. The data and the inferences from the data will, no doubt, modify, refine, and perhaps even reverse these preliminary expectations. Nevertheless, they represent our intellectual point of departure.

References

1. The origins of the New Economic Policy are traced in Donald Snodgrass, *Inequality and Economic Development in Malaysia* (Kuala Lumpur: Oxford University Press, 1980), pp. 56–61. The logic and specific provisions of the NEP are fully laid out in *Second Malaysia Plan* (Kuala Lumpur: Government Press, June 1971).

2. Helen Suzman, "Sanctions Won't End Apartheid," *New York Times*, October 4, 1987.

3. H.W. Arndt, *The Rise and Fall of Economic Growth* (Melbourne, Australia: Longman Cheshire Press, 1978), p. 73.

4. Walter Heller, "Economic Growth, Challenge and Opportunity," Unpublished speech, delivered on May 18, 1961.

5. Harold Lasswell, *Politics: Who Gets What, When, How* (New York: McGraw-Hill, 1936).

6. Vernon Van Dyke, "The Individual, the State, and Ethnic Communities in Political Theory," *World Politics* 29, no. 3 (April 1977): 343–69.

7. Walker Connor, *The National Question in Marxist-Leninist Theory and Strategy* (Princeton, NJ: Princeton University Press, 1984).

8. Karl W. Deutsch and William Foltz, eds., *Nation Building* (New York: Atherton Press, 1963).

9. Robert Melson and Harold Wolpe, "Modernization and the Politics of Communalism: A Theoretical Perspective," *American Political Science Review* 64, no. 4 (December 1970): 112–30.

10. Robert K. Merton, *Social Theory and Social Structure* (Glencoe, IL: Free Press, 1957).

11. Milton J. Esman, "Ethnic Politics and Economic Power," *Comparative Politics* 19, no. 4 (July 1987): 395–418.

27
The Power-Sharing Approach

Arend Lijphart

The Ubiquity and Strength of the Ethnic Factor

In the discussion of the power-sharing approach as a solution to ethnic conflict in this chapter, I shall use the twelve cases treated in earlier chapters as my main—but not exclusive—examples; but I should like to emphasize that although these are especially interesting cases, they are not special in the sense of being exceptional or deviant. It is very important to realize that most countries in the world are ethnically divided. This is sometimes not immediately apparent, because ethnic cleavages may superficially look like religious, ideological, or some other kind of divisions. The clearest case in point is Northern Ireland, where the groups in conflict are commonly referred to as Protestants and Catholics; the labels are religious, but the two communities are true ethnic groups. This does not mean that their religious differences are unimportant but, rather, that religion is only part of the distinctive set of characteristics that define the groups. Another example is Lebanon, which is usually described as being divided between Muslims and Christians or fragmented into a larger number of "sects." Here again, the true picture is not just a religiously divided society but a multiethnic one. A recent analysis aptly applies the term "religious ethnicity" to the Lebanese case.[1] And in Colombia, the labels liberal and conservative sound like political or ideological ones, but in fact also designate ethnic—and strongly antagonistic—communities.[2]

Saying that *most* countries in the world are ethnically divided may in fact be an understatement. It is more accurate to state that *almost all* of them belong to the multiethnic category. That this is so becomes especially clear when we try to think of examples of countries that are completely homogeneous and that have no ethnic diversity at all. The Western European countries are often regarded as homogeneous "nation-states," with the exception of obviously heterogeneous countries such as Belgium, Switzerland, and Finland. In recent years, however, we have become more aware of ethnic divisions in other Western European countries, too. For example, Richard Rose formulated the consensus of scholarly observers when he wrote in 1964:

"Today politics in the United Kingdom is greatly simplified by the absence of major cleavages along the lines of ethnic groups, language, or religion."[3] But six years later, he corrected himself when he published a monograph about the United Kingdom as a "multi-national state," with particularly important Scottish and Welsh minorities in addition to the minorities of Northern Ireland.[4]

Similarly, other superficially homogeneous nations in Western Europe are, in fact, not homogeneous at all but are dominated by a large national majority inhabiting the same country with one or more relatively small ethnic minorities: the South Tyroleans in Italy, the Frisians in the Netherlands, the Danish-speaking minority in Germany, the Lapps in Sweden, and so on. Furthermore, the *Gastarbeiter* in Western Europe represent important ethnic minorities, many of whom are not just temporary "guests" but permanent residents. Portugal and Iceland are probably the only Western European countries that can properly be regarded as *not* multiethnic.

The same pattern prevails in the Third World. Here it is even harder to find monoethnic societies. Botswana may be the only example in Africa. The twelve cases in this book are all taken from the First and Third Worlds. It is worth emphasizing, however, that the ethnic factor plays a role of great importance in the Second World of Communist states, too. The Soviet Union itself, in which the national minorities constitute about half of the total population, is the prime example.

The ubiquity of the ethnic factor does not imply that ethnicity is permanently fixed and unchangeable. On the contrary, we find an extraordinary range of variation in this respect: from the sharp linguistic boundary in Belgium, which had remained virtually frozen since the Middle Ages, to the great fluidity of ethnic distinctions in the Sudan and Nigeria. Indeed, recent scholarship has moved away from the primordial view, which sees ethnicity as an unalterable given, and toward an instrumental or situation approach that instead sees ethnicity as taking shape only when it is manipulated by political elites: Instead of a "given" it is more like a "taken" or a "chosen."[5] In my view, both approaches are valuable, and they do not exclude or contradict each other. In particular, the instrumentalist approach does not mean that ethnic divisions are artificially created by political leaders for their own ulterior purposes or that they can simply be ignored by the elite. On the other hand, the way in which political leaders respond to and "use" ethnicity is by no means fixed. For this reason, ethnic division does not necessarily spell ethnic conflict—a crucial assumption underlying the power-sharing approach.

It is also important to emphasize that although ethnicity may be manipulated, it is not completely manipulable—and certainly not in the sense of being easily manipulated out of existence. Walker Connor's work has been especially enlightening in making us aware of the enormous strength, tenacity, and resilience of ethnic differences. In the 1950s, both statesmen and scholars were much too optimistic in thinking that multiethnic societies could be homogenized by deliberate nation-building efforts.[6] One of the foremost experts on nationalism and ethnicity, Karl W. Deutsch, has estimated, on the basis of historical evidence, that the full assimilation of different ethnic groups requires between 300 and 700 years.[7] Eliminating ethnic groups by trying to forge them into a homogeneous nation is therefore not a practical approach to peacemaking in multiethnic countries.

There are two ways in which ethnic tensions may significantly decrease, at least for short periods of time. One occurs in situations where ethnic groups are united because they are threatened by a common enemy. This was the fortunate condition—but unfortunately only a temporary one—in which many Third World countries found themselves in the period before and immediately after achieving their independence. The other is the forcible suppression of ethnicity, which can be effective in the short run but does not work—apart from being morally repugnant—in the long run.

Hence, the only solutions to the problems of ethnic division and strife that remain are power-sharing and partition or secession. My conclusion is that in the vast majority of cases, partition or secession cannot be a practical solution. At the same time, I strongly disagree with what appears to be the consensus of contemporary statesmen and scholars that partition should be completely ruled out. As Samuel P. Huntington has correctly pointed out:

> The twentieth-century bias against political divorce, that is, secession, is just about as strong as the nineteenth-century bias against marital divorce. Where secession is possible, contemporary statesmen might do well to view it with greater tolerance.[8]

In particular, two common arguments against partition are quite unconvincing: that the process of partitioning a state is usually attended by violence; and that once a partition has been completed, hostilities do not always cease. My response to the first argument is that most of the violence that takes place in the process of partitioning is the result not of partition itself but of the efforts to prevent it. The answer to the second argument is that the level of postpartition violence should be compared not with a theoretical—and probably quite unrealistic—ideal of complete peace, but with the level of violence that occurred prior to partition and that is likely to have occurred without partition.

On the other hand, I wholeheartedly concede that partition has very serious disadvantages. The biggest problem is that ethnic groups are usually geographically intermixed to a considerable extent. As a result, it is usually not possible to draw clear and clean boundary lines between them, and partition has to be accompanied by a large-scale exchange of populations—a process that is very costly in both economic and human terms. Another drawback is the difficulty of effecting a partition that divides the land and natural resources fairly among the contending groups.

Consequently, it is almost always better to accommodate different ethnic groups in the same state with proper guarantees of political influence and autonomy—the power-sharing approach—than to assign them to separate territorial states. The most useful function that partition can perform is as a solution of last resort in case power-sharing fails. Moreover, it can be very helpful if, in the process of reaching a power-sharing solution, the possibility of partition is not precluded. This is one of the important lessons to be learned from the case of Quebec's near-secession from Canada. The fact that it was clear from the beginning that the Canadian government would not oppose or prevent Quebec's secession—if that would turn out to be Quebec's choice—was a very important moderating influence. The best way for a government to prevent secession is a pledge not to resist it, accompanied by an offer of fair and effective power-sharing.

Power-Sharing: Possibilities and Probabilities

The Characteristics of Power-Sharing

Power-sharing can be defined in terms of four characteristics. The two primary characteristics are the participation of the representatives of all significant groups in the government of the country and a high degree of autonomy for these groups. The secondary characteristics are proportionality and the minority veto.

The term *power-sharing* is obviously derived mainly from the first of these characteristics: jointly exercising governmental—particularly executive—power.[a] This may take various institutional forms. The most straightforward form is that of a grand coalition cabinet in a parliamentary system. In presidential systems, it is more difficult but not impossible to arrange. One way is to distribute the presidency and other high offices among the different groups. In both parliamentary and presidential systems, these arrangements may be strengthened by broadly constituted councils or committees with important advisory or coordinating functions.

The secondary characteristic of power-sharing is group autonomy. It complements the principle of joint rule: On all issues of common concern, decisions should be made jointly by the different groups or their representatives; on all other issues, decisions should be left to be made by and for each separate group. If the groups have a clear territorial concentration, group autonomy may be institutionalized in the form of federalism. If the groups are intermixed, autonomy will have to take a nonterritorial form or a combination of territorial and nonterritorial forms.

Proportionality, the third characteristic of power-sharing, serves as the basic standard of political representation, public service appointments, and allocation of public funds. Its great advantage is that it is widely recognized as the most obvious standard of fair distribution. In addition, it facilitates the process of decision making because it is a ready-made method that makes it unnecessary to spend a great deal of time on the consideration of alternative methods of distribution. With regard to political representation, proportionality is especially important as a guarantee for the fair representation of ethnic minorities.

The minority veto—the fourth characteristic of power-sharing—is the ultimate weapon that minorities need to protect their vital interests. Even when a minority participates in a power-sharing executive, it may well be outvoted or overruled by the majority. This may not present a problem when only minor matters are being decided, but when a minority's vital interests are at stake, the veto provides essential protection. The veto power clearly contains the danger that the entire power-sharing system can be undermined if one or more minorities overuse or abuse their veto power. It works best when it is not used too often and only with regard to issues of fundamental importance.

Examples of How Power-Sharing Can Work

Among the twelve cases on which this book focuses, I regard two as clear examples of power-sharing systems: Belgium and Malaysia. These two cases serve as instructive examples of the different ways in which power-sharing can work. In Malaysia, it operates mainly by informal arrangements, particularly the grand coalition of ethnic parties that was originally called the Alliance and is now called the National Front. The coalition distributes the candidacies in the different electoral districts among its parties and, hence, achieves a high degree of proportionality of representation without formally using the method of proportional representation. It has won all elections held in Malaysia so far, and it has always formed governments that have included representatives of all the significant groups. Belgium, on the other hand, has formally incorporated power-sharing principles in its constitution. For instance, the constitution specifies that the cabinet has to be a power-sharing body composed of equal numbers of Dutch-speakers and French-speakers; decision making on cultural and linguistic matters is delegated to two cultural councils; the electoral system is proportional representation; and the French-speaking minority has a constitutionally guaranteed veto power with regard to issues that affect its cultural autonomy.

In addition to these two clear examples of power-sharing, three of the twelve cases can be described as partially power-sharing systems: Canada, India, and Nigeria. Their strongest power-sharing feature is ethnic-cultural autonomy; and in all three cases, this autonomy takes the form of federalism. In bilingual Canada, the province of Quebec contains most of the French-speaking minority, and the degree of provincial self-government is so high that linguistic autonomy is largely assured. In multilingual India, federalism is completely based on the principle of making the states as linguistically homogeneous as possible. This principle was violated in the first constitution with which federal Nigeria began its independence in 1960: There were three very large and ethnically heterogeneous states, officially called regions. However, these regions were subdivided in later years, and by 1976, nineteen states were in existence, providing much more effective autonomy to Nigeria's many ethnic minorities.

The principle of joint rule is less consistently present in these three cases, although the Canadians do have an informal understanding that federal cabinets should contain both Anglophone and Francophone ministers if at all possible and although, in India, the almost perennially governing Congress party is a multilingual movement that has some of the qualities of an inter-ethnic grand coalition. But it would be misleading to compare the Indian Congress party to the Malaysian National Front, which is an ethnically power-sharing alliance in much more explicit terms.

Even though the foregoing examples support the proposition that power-sharing can be a practical and effective solution to ethnic differences and conflict, skeptics may still raise the objection that although power-sharing can work in some instances, it cannot be applied in other, more difficult, situations. This claim has been made particularly with regard to Northern Ireland. In his chapter on Northern Ireland in this volume (chapter 9), Richard Rose writes that the problem is that "there is no solution." I must admit that I *almost* agree with Rose, because there is no doubt that the Northern Ireland problem is an unusually difficult one for several reasons. One big problem is the clear majority status of the Protestants. It is always much harder for majorities than for minorities to seek or to accept a power-sharing solution. This problem is compounded by the fact that the Protestant majority in Northern Ireland fears the minority status they would have in a united Ireland. Their fear is similar to that of the Sinhalese majority in Sri Lanka, who are acutely aware that in the wider region, including South India, they are the minority and that the Tamils are the minority in Sri Lanka but a majority in the broader regional perspective.

An additional problem in the Northern Ireland case is that the British government has made the error of promising the Protestant majority that no change in the constitutional status of the province will be made without the approval of the majority of the voters in the province. This gives the Protestants what they want most—a guarantee that they will not have to join the Republic of Ireland—without obligation on their part to make a system of power-sharing work within Northern Ireland. In other respects, the British government has followed the correct approach: It has reintroduced proportional representation for all elections in Northern Ireland (with the exception of the elections to the House of Commons in London, but including the election of the Northern Ireland representatives to the European Parliament in Strasbourg), and it has insisted that self-government in Northern Ireland will be restored only if the government is a power-sharing government that includes both Protestants and Catholics. This British policy must be credited as especially farsighted and commendable in view of the fact that proportional representation and coalition government run counter to the strong majoritarian traditions in Britain and are firmly rejected by the British government for the United Kingdom as a whole.

The danger of complete pessimism in the case of Northern Ireland, as well as other difficult cases, is that it tends to become a self-fulfilling prediction: If everyone is convinced that power-sharing cannot be applied, nobody will even try to introduce it, and consequently it will certainly not be adopted. Or if it is introduced in a particular multiethnic society, the conviction that it is bound to fail will kill any effort to make it succeed—and that will surely cause it to fall. It is vastly preferable to think of success and failure in terms of probabilities rather than absolutes. For instance, my view of the Northern Ireland case, contrary to Rose's, is that the probability of successful power-sharing is low but not nil.

Factors That Favor Power-Sharing

Approaching the problems of multiethnic societies and of the application of power-sharing solutions in terms of probabilities prompts the question: Which factors are favorable and which are unfavorable to power-sharing? In my previous writings, I have identified nine factors that make it more likely that power-sharing will be adopted and that it will work well.[9] The two most important of these factors are the absence of a majority ethnic group and the absence of large socioeconomic differences among the ethnic groups. I have already discussed the former in the context of the Northern Ireland and Sri Lanka cases. Other examples among our twelve cases of the unfavorable situation of a majority ethnic group facing one or more minorities are Zimbabwe and its Shona majority, Pakistan and its Punjabi majority, Belgium and its Dutch-speaking majority, and Canada and its English-speaking majority. The contrasting, much more favorable situation in which all ethnic groups are minorities is exemplified by India and Kenya. Socioeconomic equality among ethnic groups does not exist anywhere, but the degree of inequality can range from severe, as in Malaysia, to relatively mild, as in India, in Zimbabwe, and even—contrary to the frequently heard Marxist interpretations of the conflict—in Northern Ireland.

The seven other favorable factors are (1) that the ethnic groups are of roughly the same size, so that there is a balance of power among them; (2) that there are not too many groups, so that the negotiations among them will not be too difficult and complicated; (3) that the total population is relatively small, so that the decision-making process is less complex; (4) that there are external dangers that promote internal unity; (5) that there are overarching loyalties that reduce the strength of particularistic ethnic loyalties; (6) that the ethnic groups are geographically concentrated, so that, among other things, federalism can be used to promote group autonomy; and (7) that there are prior traditions of compromise and accommodation. Concerning these factors, there is a great deal of variation among the twelve cases, as well as in other multiethnic countries. The greatest contrast exists with regard to population size: India, the world's second most populous country, versus Northern Ireland, with its mere million and a half people.

I should like to emphasize that the most important aspect of these favorable factors is they are not *decisive:* They are neither necessary nor sufficient conditions for the adoption or success of power-sharing. They are merely *helpful* factors. This means that even when all or most of the conditions are favorable, the success of power-sharing is by no means guaranteed. And even when many conditions, or the most crucial ones, are unfavorable, success is still possible. For instance, power-sharing has generally worked out well in Belgium and Canada despite the presence of ethnic majorities in both instances.

It is also in this respect that the Malaysian case is particularly significant and instructive: Its largest ethnic group, the Malays, is a near-majority in Malaysia as a whole and a clear majority in peninsular Malaysia, and the socioeconomic differences between the ethnic groups are extreme. In spite of the unfavorable nature of both of these crucial conditions, power-sharing has worked for a long time. Critics of Malaysian democracy often point out that the democratic system is not perfect, in that certain fundamental constitutional provisions cannot be openly challenged, and that power-sharing is not ideal either, in that the Malays tend to have a larger than proportional share of political power that is only partly counterbalanced by the preponderant economic power of the Chinese. However, these are relatively minor blemishes on a largely successful power-sharing system. The main conclusion is that the Malaysians have been remarkably good power-sharers, in spite of formidable obstacles. Therefore, they provide a hopeful model to other multiethnic societies.

One final point with regard to these background conditions must be considered here in the light of David D. Laitin's criticism. He wrote:

> if conditions are favorable, Lijphart's theory leads him to propose a consociational [power-sharing] system; if conditions are unfavorable, he proposes the same. The status of the conditions is questionable if the score [of the

favorable versus unfavorable conditions] does not alter the recommendation.[10]

My answer is that a distinction must be made between power-sharing theory as an empirical theory and as a normative or prescriptive theory. The empirical theory tries objectively to explain and predict where power-sharing has been or is likely to be adopted and how well it has worked or is likely to work. The normative theory advocates power-sharing for multiethnic societies because it is the optimal—indeed, usually the only—solution, regardless of whether the background conditions are favorable or unfavorable. To aspiring power-sharers who find themselves in an unfavorable situation, it does not say: "Give up." Instead, it counsels: "Be aware of the obstacles you face, and try extra hard."

Adapting Power-Sharing to Special Circumstances

I shall devote the remainder of this chapter to a different aspect of what I have just called power-sharing as a normative theory: How can power-sharing be adapted to the special circumstances of particular countries, and which specific rules and institutions are optimal for power-sharing? This section will deal with four special situations that challenge the creativity of power-sharing engineers: ethnic dividing lines that are diffuse and fluid, the presence of a majority ethnic group, ethnic groups that are geographically dispersed, and the presence of very small minorities.

Diffuse Dividing Lines between Ethnic Groups

As the Sudanese case makes especially clear, it is possible for a society to be multiethnic where the boundaries between the ethnic groups are highly diffuse and fluid. This situation presents a problem for power-sharing, because the ethnic groups normally serve as the basic building blocks. It is much easier when the ethnic groups can be identified without any ambiguity, when it is known how many people belong to each group, and when the ethnic groups manifest themselves in ethnic political parties and other ethnically based organizations. Then it is possible to design a system in which each of these groups is given a share of executive power, cultural autonomy, seats in the legislature, and a veto power on specified issues. This cannot be done if the groups in a particular society cannot be identified.

The only solution in such a situation is to let the ethnic groups define themselves. The main methods are proportional representation, multiparty coalition government, and cultural councils. It is a well-known fact that proportional representation permits and encourages the election of parties on the basis of whatever social cleavages happen to be the most salient in a society, regardless of whether these groups are large or small. In multiethnic countries, ethnicity may be diffuse, but it is still likely to have the strongest appeal for most voters. Consequently, without predetermining the groups and their relative sizes, proportional representation allows them to define themselves and gives them parliamentary representation according to the shares of votes that they manage to attract. Next, instead of stipulating that particular, explicitly named ethnic groups be included in the executive, the constitution can simply state that all parties of a specified minimum size will be invited to join the cabinet. The veto power can be granted—with regard to vitally important matters—to groups of legislators that exceed a certain minimum percentage. And cultural autonomy can be introduced by giving any group that wishes to have it a cultural council responsible for legislation and administration in the area of culture and language.

In my view, the foregoing self-defining types of power-sharing arrangement has many advantages, even when most of the members of a multiethnic society and objective observers of the society have no great difficulty in identifying the constituent ethnic groups. Three positive points stand out. First, the relative strengths of the groups may change over time; proportional representation then provides for a continuous flexible adjustment of their political representation. Second, a group may be distinct now, but it may gradually become more diffuse or it may develop internal splits; again, proportional representation takes care of providing the appropriate political translation of these changes. Third, there may be a sizable number of voters who cannot identify themselves with any major ethnic group or who reject ethnicity as a proper basis for electoral politics; as proportional representation is completely neutral among all parties, ethnic or nonethnic, it provides for the expression of this kind of preference, too. The same kind of flexibility is inherent in the cultural councils: Groups that want them can have them, but no group is forced to have them, and no individual is forced to join them.

The Presence of a Majority Ethnic Group

As mentioned earlier, one of the two most serious unfavorable factors for power-sharing is the presence of a majority ethnic group. However, this is not an insuperable obstacle; there is a method to overcome it, but considerable caution should be exercised before the method is adopted. It consists of majority underrepresentation and minority overrepresentation or, in its most far-reaching form, parity of representation for all ethnic groups. For instance, a group comprising 80 percent of the population might be given only 70 or 60 percent of the seats in parliament and the ministerial positions in the cabinet or even, in the case of parity, only 50 percent; and the representation of the minority or minorities would be increased correspondingly. An empirical example of such an arrangement among the twelve cases is the overrepresentation of whites in Zimbabwe's postindependence parliament: This minority of less than 3 percent was given 20 percent of the seats.

The obvious advantage of majority underrepresentation is that it makes minorities feel more secure. But the several disadvantages of this arrangement must be considered, too. First, it constitutes a disincentive for majorities to join a power-sharing system or to feel a commitment to it. As I have indicated before, majorities tend to be reluctant to accept power-sharing in the first place; underrepresentation quite understandably increases their reluctance. The Belgian system of parity in the national cabinet and in the Brussels executive appears to be an exception, but it was possible only because it entailed a bargain between different majorities: The Dutch-speaking majority in the country as a whole accepted parity in the cabinet—that is, underrepresentation—in exchange for parity in Brussels—that is, overrepresentation—for the Dutch-speaking minority there.

The second disadvantage is that minority overrepresentation requires the prior determination of which groups are entitled to particular shares of representation. I have argued earlier that it is preferable to let the groups define themselves rather than being predefined. As a choice has to be made between the incompatible goals of self-defined groups and minority overrepresentation, the advantages of the former outweigh those of the latter.

A third disadvantage is that it seems far preferable for minorities to rely on the normal protection devices of power-sharing than on the somewhat illusory benefits of overrepresentation; after all, unless the majority's representation is reduced to 50 percent, the reduced majority is still a majority. The true protection of minorities rests on their ability to be active participants in central decision making, to enjoy cultural autonomy, and if necessary, to use their veto power.

The final consideration is that proportional representation entails a dual advantage for minorities: Not only does it guarantee their own fair representation, but it also encourages splits within the majority group. This advantage is lost in the minority overrepresentation/majority underrepresentation arrangement. In Northern Ireland, for instance, the split between Official Unionists and Democratic Unionists might well have occurred even if plurality elections had continued, but the introduction of proportional representation certainly facilitated this development.

Geographically Dispersed Ethnic Groups

If the ethnic groups are geographically intermixed, it is impossible to use federalism and decentralization as devices for providing group autonomy. Consequently, autonomy must be based on nonterritorial arrangements. Even though there are not many empirical examples of such alternative arrangements, they are, at least in principle, not usually difficult to conceive. The crucial question is the definition of who belongs to an autonomous community. If this community is a state in a federation, membership is defined in terms of residence within the state. But membership can just as easily be defined in terms of other objective characteristics of the individual or, preferably, in terms of the individual's voluntary affiliation with the community in question.

In practice, the geographic relationships of ethnic groups vary not from complete territorial concentration to complete intermixture but between different degrees of intermixture. This means that group autonomy should usually take a combination of territorial and nonterritorial forms. Belgium is an example of an intermediate situation between ethnic concentration and intermixture: Flanders and Wallonia are linguistically almost homogeneous, but Brussels contains both language groups. Very appropriately, the Belgian constitution prescribes a combination of territorial and nonterritorial autonomy. There are three autonomous regions, comparable to states in a federation (Flanders, Wallonia, and Brussels), and two autonomous cultural communities that are partly defined in nonterritorial terms and that are governed by cultural councils: The Dutch-speaking community comprises Flanders plus the Dutch-speakers in bilingual Brussels, and the French-speaking community consists of Wallonia and the francophone Bruxellois. Given the fact that most multiethnic societies are characterized by an intermediate degree of ethnic concentration and dispersion, an appropriate general model of group autonomy with wide applicability would be a combination of territorial federalism, in which the states are reasonably but not perfectly homogeneous, and a system of cultural councils, which ethnic groups have the option of establishing and with which individuals can freely affiliate themselves.

Very Small Minorities

The final special situation to be addressed in this section is how very small minorities—such as the Baluch in Pakistan, the Christians in Malaysia, the South Tyroleans in Italy, and the German-speakers in Belgium—can be accommodated in a power-sharing system. The basic problem is that for a small minority of, say, 1 to 2 percent of the population, it is difficult to claim a permanent share of executive power; power-sharing cabinets would become unweildy if they had to include representatives of all such small groups. The Baluch, with 4 percent of the population of Pakistan, are near the lower limit of a minority that can be included in a power-sharing executive.

There are two ways to address this problem. One way is to take care of the interests of small ethnic groups more by means of group autonomy than through participation in central decision making. If the small minority is geographically concentrated, the creation of an autonomous region appears to be the logical solution. If not, a cultural council—such as the German cultural council in Belgium—may be established for them.

The other way is to introduce a degree of shared power (without full power-sharing) at the highest executive level. For instance, if a small minority is geographically concentrated to some extent, it may constitute a sufficiently large minority at the regional and local levels to participate in power-sharing executives there. At the national level, minority representatives may be asked to serve as advisory members of cabinets, with the right to participate in cabinet decisions only on issues that are of special importance to them and perhaps without having a formal vote. Also, committees or councils may be set up by cabinets in order to give advice on matters that especially concern minorities; and even very small minorities may be given permanent representation on these councils. Finally, if they use a fully proportional system of representation, legislatures are usually large enough to give representation even to small minorities. For instance, in a 100-member legislature elected by full proportional representation, a minority of 1 percent can elect its own representative, and a minority of half that size can elect its representatie in a 200-member parliament.

Power-Sharing as a Multimethod System

Power-sharing has been defined in terms of four characteristics or methods: the participation of all significant groups in the government, a high degree of autonomy for the groups, proportionately, and the minority veto. Here, I should like to emphasize the inseparability of these four characteristics: Power-sharing is not complete unless all four are included, and it cannot work well—and certainly not optimally—if one or more are missing. In particular, I want to warn against two proposals that look like power-sharing but that rely mainly or exclusively on just one of its four methods: the Kendall-Louw plan for an extreme form of federalism and the view of some enthusiasts that proportional representation is the panacea for all societies, including, in particular, multiethnic ones.

Frances Kendall and Leon Louw's proposal focuses on the South African problem, but it is really a general model for peacemaking and stable democracy in multiethnic societies, which they apply, as an extended example, to their own country. The authors say that they were inspired by the power-sharing system in Switzerland, but they misread the Swiss case and used its evidence in a highly selective fashion. The essence of their plan is to divide a multiethnic society into a large number of small cantons and to concentrate virtually all power in the cantonal governments. In their concrete example, the average population of the cantons is only 80,000—approximately a third of the average size of the Swiss canton. The great advantage of such a federal system is that it results in units with a high degree of ethnic homogeneity. In general, the more units a federation has and the smaller these units are, the easier it is to draw them in such a way as to make them virtually monoethnic. In addition, Kendall and Louw count on voluntary mobility to make the cantons even more homogeneous.

Vesting almost all power in the cantonal governments means that there is very little central power—and, hence, very little power to share at the central level. In Kendall and Louw's own words, "The national constitution should be based on two main principles: maximal devolution and strict limitation of central government power." The question of joint decision making—the first characteristic of a power-sharing system—is a "nonissue, since central government in a canton system would be so limited that at the national level there would be little power to share."[11]

Kendall and Louw appear to favor proportional representation for the election of one house of their national bicameral legislature when they propose a "formula of one house with proportional representation and another based on equal representation" of the cantons. However, their concept of proportional representation is rather unorthodox. They argue that there are two main forms of proportional representation. One is "for representation to be based on population density. In the canton system, this would mean that a canton with a million voters would have twice as many representatives as one with 500,000, ten times as many as a canton with 100,000, and so on." The second form, as they see it, is "for each political party to have proportional representation based on the number of votes cast nationwide in its favor."[12] The second form is proportional representation, but the first is not. It is simply the kind of rule that governs the allocation of seats in the U.S. House of Representatives to the several states; the subsequent election of these representatives is, of course, not by proportional representation but by the plurality method. What Kendall and Louw end up proposing is a combination of the first form with an option for the cantons to use either the second form—which would be proportional representation—or whatever electoral system they would prefer. In short, their plan falls far short of elections based on proportional representation

Finally, their proposal does not include a provision for a minority veto power over national legislation. Because there is so little power at this level, a veto may indeed by unnecessary. On the other hand, they propose an extreme veto with regard to constitutional amendments. Amendments would require the unanimous consent of the cantons; that is, each small canton would have a veto. This goes far beyond the Swiss system, in which constitutional amendment is difficult—both popular and cantonal majorities are required—but not virtually impossible. Kendall and Louw's system would be an extremely rigid one.

The viability of such a complete decentralized system, headed by an extremely weak central government, appears very doubtful. For one thing, there would be no way of dealing with economic inequalities among groups and regions, and these inequalities are often severe in multiethnic societies. Moreover, the Kendall-Louw plan would be much less likely to be accepted by the leaders of ethnic groups than a more balanced, multimethod, power-sharing arrangement. The latter can be a good compromise solution, because it promises everyone a share of political power; but if there is virtually no power to be shared at the national level, the only incentive is that everyone loses equally.

The second single-method approach that I want to take issue with is the reliance on proportional representation without the other elements of power sharing. To be sure, the claim that proportional representation has a vital role to play in multiethnic societies is extraordinarily strong. That system was adopted in Europe in the late nineteenth and early twentieth centuries principally to accommodate ethnic diversity and meet the demands of ethnic minorities. In the words of the late Stein Rokkan:

> It was no accident that the earliest moves toward proportional representa-
> tion . . . came in the ethnically most heterogeneous countries: Denmark in
> 1855; the Swiss canton in 1891; Belgium in 1899; Moravia in 1905; Finland
> in 1906. In linguistically and religiously divided societies majority elections
> could clearly threaten the continued existence of the political system. The
> introduction of some element of minority representation came to be seen as
> an essential step in a strategy of territorial consolidation.[13]

Moreover, a survey of the comparative politics literature dealing with democratic political institutions reveals strong empirical relationships among electoral systems, party systems, and types of cabinet coalitions: Proportional representation is conducive to multiparty systems, which, in turn, are conducive to broad multiparty governing coalitions. From the point of view of those who favor majority rule, these are negative effects, but they must be regarded as positive from a power-sharing perspective. As Nobel laureate Sir Arthur Lewis stated, "The surest way to kill the idea of democracy" in a multiethnic society is "to adopt the Anglo-American system of first-past-the-post." As Lewis saw it, "one of the advantages of proportional representation is that it tends to promote coalition government."[14]

However, although proportional representation is empirically associated with and encourages a broadly inclusive coalition government, it does not guarantee it. Hence, it is necessary to make a separate provision for it. Furthermore, there is no logical or empirical link between proportional representation and group autonomy or between proportional representation and the minority veto, and these two elements of power-sharing should therefore also be explicitly introduced as part of the total power-sharing system.

Zimbabwe can serve as a good example of the insufficiency of proportional representation unaccompanied by the other power-sharing devices. Proportional representation has given the Ndebele minority a fair share of seats in the national legislature—and, as discussed earlier, the much smaller white minority has been greatly overrepresented by a special constitutional arrangement—but this has not prevented the Shona majority from capturing the majority of legislative seats, from giving the Ndebele little or no role in cabinet decision making, and from opposing the wish of the Ndebele for more autonomy in their own areas. In short, proportional representation is an important ingredient of power-sharing, but it cannot establish or maintain a power-sharing system by itself. Multiethnic societies need proportional representation, but that is not *all* they need.

Two Negative Recommendations

Power-sharing is compatible with a wide variety of institutional alternatives. It consists of a set of general principles, not specific rules and institutions. There is no detailed blueprint for a power-sharing constitution. On the other hand, not all institutional alternatives are equally effective power-sharing devices. On the contrary, some are only barely compatible with and certainly not helpful to power-sharing. In this section, I shall strongly recommend against two alternatives: presidential government and "mixed" electoral systems.

There are two main ways in which democratic states organize the relationships between executives and legislatures. In parliamentary systems, the executive is a cabinet that is selected by the legislature and is dependent on the legislature's confidence; the latter characteristic means that the legislature has the right to dismiss the cabinet. In presidential systems, the executive is a directly or indirectly elected president who is independent of the confidence of the legislature. The advantages and disadvantages of parliamentary and presidential systems have been debated for a long time, but most of this debate does not concern us here. The important question for multiethnic societies is: If we want to use a power-sharing system, is parliamentarism or presidentialism to be preferred?

In the presidential form of government, executive power is concentrated in the hands of one person, who, in a multiethnic society, is inevitably a member of one ethnic group. Power-sharing prescribes joint rule by the representatives of the different ethnic groups, and such joint rule requires a collegial decision-making body. Hence, although a cabinet in a parliamentary system can easily be a power-sharing vehicle, a president lacks this advantage. This drawback may be partly alleviated in two ways. One is to consider the presidency as one of a series of high offices in a country and to divide these offices among the different ethnic groups. This is exemplified by the Lebanese system, which reserves the presidency for a Maronite, the prime ministership for a Sunni, the speakership of parliament for a Shiite, and so on. The other way is to introduce rules that make the president less the exclusive representative of only one group. For instance, the 1979 constitution of Nigeria stipulated that to be elected president, a candidate had to win a plurality of the total nationwide vote plus at least 25 percent of the votes in at least two-thirds of the nineteen states.

These kinds of special provisions are merely palliatives, however. If a new power-sharing system is to be created, the presumption should be clearly in favor of parliamentary rather than presidential government.

The same kind of unambiguous recommendation can be made with regard to the choice of an electoral system from the three main types of electoral systems: proportional representation, plurality and majority systems, and "mixed" systems that combine elements of proportional representation and plurality. I strongly recommend proportional representation, for reasons that I have already given. The other types of electoral systems have clear disadvantages, although it is obviously not impossible to use a nonproportional representation system and still have power-sharing. Malaysia, a prime example of power-sharing, uses the plurality method. And the same plurality method is also used by Canada and India, which I have cited as countries with significant power-sharing attributes. Where there is a relatively high degree of ethnic concentration in particular areas, as in India and Canada, the plurality rule in single-member districts can yield a reasonably proportional outcome. Where this is not the case, as in Malaysia, a reasonable degree of proportionality can be achieved by a prior agreement of the ethnic parties participating in an electoral coalition. In other words, only in special circumstances or as the result of special agreements can plurality produce the proportionality that power-sharing requires. Again, when a new power-sharing system is being engineered, it would be hard to find a good argument to favor plurality over proportional representation.

The choice is not only between proportional representation and plurality, of course. Especially for multiethnic societies, various mixtures of the two have been proposed and, in a number of countries, actually instituted. I cannot discuss all of these possibilities here, but one deserves to be singled out for analysis: the Lebanese "mixed" system, which is often praised not only for being proportional but, in addition, for promoting interethnic cooperation. In Donald Horowitz's words, "Rarely in a divided society has there been a system that placed as high a premium on . . . interethnic cooperation."[15] The Lebanese system used the plurality rule in multimember districts, with the special provision that candidates had to be elected according to the ethnic ratio of the district. To give a hypothetical example, in a five-member district with a 60 percent Sunni, 20 percent Shiite, and 20 percent Maronite population, three seats would be reserved for Sunni candidates, one of a Shiite, and one for a Maronite. Several ethnically balanced slates with this predetermined 3:1:1 ratio would compete with each other. Voters could either vote for one of these slates or pick individual candidates, as long as they respected the 3:1:1 ratio. The advantages of this system are that it is a basically proportional one and, further, that it encourages politicians of different groups to work together because interethnic slates have to be formed.

Nevertheless, the Lebanese system had serious disadvantages as well. First, it required a predetermination of the ethnic groups—which, as I argued earlier, is very undesirable. The second and more serious drawback is that it violated the basic principle of representation: Being the representative of a certain group means not just belonging to that group but being chosen by the group. In my hypothetical example, the Shiite and Maronite "representatives" were, in fact, chosen by the Sunni majority instead of by their own people. This violation of the principle of representation also entailed a serious practical problem. As Pierre Rondot has pointed out about the Lebanese system:

> Each elected person is above all the representative of communities other than his own. . . . To be elected as a deputy, a man must be a compromise candidate. The typical champions of each community run the risk . . . of being passed over in favor of tamer individuals.[16]

As a result, the Lebanese deputies were not the true spokesmen of their ethnic groups, and the chamber as a whole was not an effective representative and decision-making body.

Conclusion

Because I have just expressed my disagreement with one specific judgment by Donald Horowitz—one of the contributors to this volume—I should like, by way of conclusion, to cite and endorse the final sentence of his book *Ethnic Groups in Conflict:* "Even in the most severely divided society, ties of blood do not lead ineluctably to rivers of blood."[17] And I am convinced not only that peacemaking in multiethnic societies is a realistic objective but also that the power-sharing approach is the optimal means for achieving that objective.

Note

a. In my previous writings, I have used the terms *consociational democracy* and *consociation* in the same sense as I use *power-sharing* here.

References

1. Hanna E. Kassis, "Religious Ethnicity in the World of Islam: The Case of Lebanon," *International Political Science Review* 6 (1985): 216–29.

2. On the Colombian case, see, especially, Robert H. Dix, "Consociational Democracy: The Case of Colombia," *Comparative Politics* 12 (April 1980): 303–21.

3. Richard Rose, *Politics in England: An Interpretation* (Boston: Little, Brown, 1964), p. 10.

4. Richard Rose, *The United Kingdom as a Multi-National State,* Occasional Paper No. 6 (Glasgow: University of Strathclyde, Survey Research Centre, 1970).

5. See Sammy Smooha, "Ethnic Groups," in Adam Kuper and Jessica Kuper, eds., *The Social Science Encyclopedia* (London: Routledge and Kegan Paul, 1985), pp. 267–69.

6. Walker Connor, "Nation-Building or Nation-Destroying?" *World Politics* 24 (April 1972): 319–55.

7. Karl W. Deutsch, "Space and Freedom: Conditions for the Temporary Separation of Incompatible Groups," *International Political Science Review* 5 (1984): 135.

8. Samuel P. Huntington, "Foreword," in Eric A. Nordlinger, *Conflict Regulation in Divided Societies,* Occasional Papers in International Affairs, No. 29 (Cambridge, MA: Harvard University, Center for International Affairs, 1972), p. vii.

9. Arend Lijphart, *Power-Sharing in South Africa,* Policy Paper in International Affairs, No. 24 (Berkeley: University of California, Institute of International Studies, 1985), pp. 119–28.

10. David D. Laitin, "South Africa: Violence, Myths, and Democratic Reform," *World Politics* 39 (January 1987): 265.

11. Frances Kendall and Leon Louw, *After Apartheid: The Solution for South Africa* (San Francisco: Institute for Contemporary Studies, 1987), pp. 143, 189.

12. *Ibid.,* pp. 146–47.

13. Stein Rokkan, *Citizens, Elections, Parties: Approaches to the Comparative Study of the Processes of Development* (Oslo: Universitetsforlaget, 1970), p. 157.

14. W. Arthur Lewis, *Politics in West Africa* (London: Allen and Unwin, 1965), pp. 71, 79.

15. Donald L. Horowitz, *Ethnic Groups in Conflict* (Berkeley and Los Angeles: University of California Press, 1985), p. 633.

16. Pierre Rondot, "The Political Institutions of Lebanese Democracy," in Leonard Binder, ed., *Politics in Lebanon* (New York: Wiley, 1966), pp. 132–33.

17. Horowitz, *Ethnic Groups in Conflict,* p. 684.

28

Negotiations and Prenegotiations in Ethnic Conflict: The Beginning, The Middle, and the Ends

I. William Zartman

T here are only two ways in which multiethnic conflict can be handled by a government—unilaterally and bi- or multilaterally. Unilateral strategies can involve either defeat of the insurgency or accommodation through measures that remove the grievances. But short of those methods, the only path left is through negotiation between the government and the ethnic group.

Although distinctions are never as sharp in reality as in concept, negotiation is *joint* rather than *unilateral* decision making and therefore involves the other party (the contesting ethnic group) in both constructing and accepting the decision. There is thus a measure of equality involved in negotiation that governments find inherently distasteful and that puts heavy requirements on insurgents. The ethnic group must be strong enough to confront the government, to make compromises, and to hold to an agreement. These considerations mean that negotiation cannot be either studied or practiced out of its context. Negotiating strategies are related to the evolution of the conflict they seek to resolve.

Appropriate measures to reduce or resolve the conflict are as varied as the grievances themselves but fall into a limited number of categories. To begin with, solutions are either internal or external—that is, secessionist. Internal solutions involve a greater role for the ethnic groups either in the center or on the periphery. External solutions have fewer ramifications; the seceding portion can either go it alone or join a neighboring state. In either case, the solution is related to the negotiating strategies.

Less obvious is the choice of negotiating partners available to governments. As long as ethnic troubles are fully internal, the parties to the negotiation are all members of the body politic, including its institutions of authority. But as the conflict progresses, it is the nature of the dissenting groups to seek to borrow power from outside, thus bringing foreign (usually neighboring) states into the picture. If a neighboring state shares the same ethnic group or if the ethnic insurgents turn to their neighbor for sanctuary, then that neighbor becomes a full party rather than just a supporter, and the constellation of relations is profoundly changed. Two of the parties are now states, with a whole spectrum of issues between them, of which the ethnic rebellion is only one; and as states, they are on the same status level. Now three sets of strategies are involved—between state and insurgency, between neighbor and insurgency, and between neighboring states—with a geometric increase in complexity.

Finally, ethnic conflict and negotiation, like other conflicts and negotiations, can be enough of a threat to peace and stability to warrant a watchful outside eye and may even evoke attempts at helpful as well as disruptive intervention by an outside party. However, helpful intervention is more difficult by its nature than intervention that supports one side or the other. As ethnic conflict is an internal matter by definition (even if it is not exclusively so in fact), governments are loath to regard external intervention of any kind as friendly—all the more so because mediatory intervention necessarily implies some compromise on the part of the government (as well as the dissidents) and some criticism of government practices. Therefore, mediators have to develop their own strategies, and even more problematically, they often have to develop strategies of positioning so as to be able to take advantage of an appropriate moment for mediation later on down the line.

All of these elements—when, what, who, and how—are involved in strategies of negotiation and prenegotiation. As a result, it is impossible to lay out a single linear strategy for negotiations, or even for mediation. Instead, the effects of each of these elements must be examined to make available the full richness and creativity that is needed to prepare bilateral solutions when a government can no longer handle the problem by itself.

When to Begin Negotiation

The determination of when to negotiate is related to the life of the ethnic conflict. It is usually impossible to tell when a conflict begins; and frequently, the conflict involves the resurgence of latent feelings or dormant grievances when a group perceives itself as deprived of some social benefits because of its ethnic identity. The sense of deprivation may be direct, as in South Africa or southern Sudan, or it may be relative to others in society or even to expectations, as in Biafra, Northern Ireland, or the Kabyle region of Algeria.[1] But for deprivation to turn into ethnic conflict, it must be seen as arising from discrimination against the deprived as an ethnic group. There are also situations in which two minority groups of the periphery carry on a feud between themselves, like the Hatfields and McCoys, but usually the Hatfields are in charge of the government and the McCoys carry on the feud from the deprived periphery—as the Shona and Ndebele in Zimbabwe or the Kikuyu and Luo in Kenya. The appropriate response to groups that feel deprived—in a responsible and responsible political system, whether democratic or not—is a process of petition and remedy. The problem is brought to the attention of the authorities, and benefits and opportunities are distributed better. That action in itself often involves some exercise of negotiation and lies in the gray area between unilateral and bilateral solutions to grievances.

But if, at any point, the "change-absorbing institutions" of government do not or cannot handle the grievances,[2] ethnic groups find themselves in need of new strategies. They face three imperatives: They must attract government attention, constrain negative responses, and mobilize and consolidate their own support. Blocking one government measure may be a good way to get attention and at the same time to mobilize support, but things may not fall into place in order, and it may be necessary to mobilize support under unfavorable conditions of repression in a way that means passing up chances for positive attention. Frequently, once the political system has had a chance to respond and there are no satisfactory results, the dissatisfied group must go through a period of "solidarity-making" before it can begin the problem-solving process.[3]

Elements of the Conflict Life Cycle

Needs. One element of the conflict life cycle has to do with the needs of the protest movement. In the first phase, the movement is a petitioner, seeking to bring its grievances to the attention of government, but as a subordinate. Negotiations among unequals are possible in this phase as part of the *petition-and-response* process. But if this phase fails, the second phase is one that requires the dissidents to oppose the government more fiercely, attracting its displeasure and even inviting repression. This is a phase of *consolidation,* in which the dissidents need to strengthen their ranks and representativeness, assert their legitimacy, and back up their claim to be an equal negotiating partner with the government. Only when this consolidating phase is over can the dissidents move on to phase three, which takes them back to problem solving and *negotiation* again, but on a new footing. Obviously, there is a lot of movement back and forth between the second and third phases, as the government tries to weaken the dissidents' cohesion and support and contest their legitimacy so as to get an upper hand in the negotiations. However, if the government is too successful in its efforts, it can push the conflict back into phase two, where neither side is willing to negotiate and where the conflict is further from any resolution. From the consolidation phase, where the government will try to break up the protest into manageable splinter groups, the government will try to push the protest further back into phase one, where it can handle the petitions of the tractable splinters and isolate the intractable ones. Thus, government and protesting groups try to push the protest back and forth across the successive phases, with the middle, or consolidation, phase being the main battlefield across which the protest ebbs and flows.

Unity. The question of the dissidents' unity is another element of the conflict life cycle. In the early, petition phase of the ethnic conflict, there are likely to be several organizations representing different aspects of ethnic activity and, therefore, various parts of the ethnic group. As the dissidence enters into the consolidation phase, the group is under pressure to bring this diversity under one roof so that it can exert maximum pressure on the government and assert its legitimacy and representativeness on behalf of the protest. But as the conflict bogs down in phase two, this unity is likely to come under severe strains and eventually fall apart. Parts of the group will challenge its leaders for their inadequate policies and offer their own prescriptions as a better way out of the impasse. Failure also encourages dreamers and, therefore, more pluralism. Only when one of the new groups starts making progress again in furthering its cause does it have a claim on the exclusive allegiance of the dissidents. Yet, as already seen, this moment is ambiguous, in that the movement needs solidarity in order to compel the government to provide it with some success, and it needs success to attract solidarity. These conflicting needs and pressures tend to keep the conflict in phase two, where it is not ready for resolution.

Paradoxically, there is another moment when the dissidents' unity is threatened—at the end of the process. The closer the ethnic protest moves toward success, the greater its need and efforts to maintain unity and the greater the temptation for rivals and splinter groups to cut loose and try to make deals on their own. Such splinter groups seek to turn the group effort to their own advantage by offering a slightly better deal to the government. If they succeed (and the arrangement holds), they have provided a better, mutually satisfactory outcome for the two sides. If they fail and are swept aside, they may well have helped clear the way for a more lasting solution by eliminating an option that at least seemed attractive to some. This was the case of Abel Muzorewa in Zimbabwe in 1979 and Tahar ben Ammar in Tunisia in 1955, both cases of the "disposable moderate" on the road to independence. Of course, all is not positive: Splinter groups may also so shatter and enfeeble the protest in the process that the conflict is again thrown back into the second, or consolidation, phase, with the loss of a potentially appropriate moment for resolution.

Goals. A third element in the life cycle of a conflict has to do with its goals. Ethnic protests are a search for appropriate outcomes, so that "resolution" also depends very much on when the solution is negotiated. Much literature points to the fact that initially, members of a protest seek to attract the attention of the government to their existence and their insufficient share in the benefits of society.[4] They want more, not less, government attention—but attention of a positive, not an intrusive, nature. During this phase, the government's role and primacy are not contested but, rather, are appealed to. This is the usual condition of North African Berbers and Native Americans. If the period of petition is prolonged, the protesters eventually realize that they cannot depend on the goodwill of others and must make procedural as well as substantive demands. The protesters demand greater participation in the distribution of benefits. At this stage, protesters are calling for collaborative control of their own destiny. This is the stage that Tamils and southern Sudanese are in today.

But if participation is not enough to assure satisfaction, the protest moves on to the third phase, secession. At this point, the protesters have reached the conviction that they cannot get redress of grievances from collaboration with others but must take their entire destiny into their own hands, despite the cost or danger of reduced resources. This was the story in Biafra. "More of less" is calculated to be greater than "less of more," although the logic of the phase may even carry further, to indicate that self-determination is better in and of itself, even if the material benefits are not greater. Both "greater" and "better" give different insights into the famous statement by Sékou Touré, Guinea's first president: "It is better to have poverty in freedom than richness in slavery."

Of course, these phases do not describe neat and clear divisions. Not all protesters reach the same conclusion at the same time, and the conservative, non-risk-taking tendency in human nature indicates that many will not dare petition when the leaders are in the petitioning stage, many will want to petition and will not dare to participate when the leaders are in the participating stage, and many will not dare to secede but will be willing only to petition and participate when the leaders have reached the stage when they see secession as the sole solution. Similarly, not all leaders will reach the same conclusions at the same time. Furthermore, governments, too, have a conservative, status-quo tendency, responding to considerable pressure only by finally adopting the option that would have satisfied the previous stage. That is why "too little, too late" is frequently the judgment on government responses to ethnic protest. As the government finally comes to the reluctant conclusion that a given outcome is necessary, the protesters have similarly learned that it is not enough and have moved on to the next outcome stage. Because this learning process often involves not only the conversion of some leaders but also the replacement of others, backtracking becomes difficult.

Means. Finally, the conflict life cycle can be thought of in terms of means. The protest begins with the normal activity of *articulation* of demands, in which individuals bring requests and grievances to the attention of the authorities on behalf of their constituents. This is a totally political phase, calling, above all, for skills of expression and persuasion. If it fails, there is pressure to move to a mobilization phase. Mobilization is still a political exercise, but it calls for actions that provide a visible backup to the demands. The people are used in marches, campaigns, and demonstrations, but in an expressive rather than an instrumental role: They are seeking not to tear down the walls of government but merely to impress those inside. There is, however, an element of threat in this exercise, in that the mass could turn into a mob if not heeded. In the third phase, it does so, and the means become those of violence, exercised as a guerrilla movement. At that point, the mobilization and articulation leaders become less necessary and are pushed aside in favor of confrontation leaders, who can mobilize small groups.

Often, class as well as ethnic values are thrown into the protest at this stage, accentuating the shift from the previous leadership. If this phase fails—or, curiously, if it moves toward success—a fourth phase may be necessary—that of conventional military violence. This, too, requires different tactics and different leadership.

Each of the four ways of carrying out the protest—articulation, mobilization, confrontation, and war—involves different persons to lead and different relations between leaders and their followers. The passage from one phase to another is often accomplished, therefore, by changes in leadership and by internal political conflict. Yet contrary to the opinions of those involved and also to the judgments of some analysts, negotiators are needed at each phase. Even in the last phases, it is rare that a military victory is so complete that some negotiation is not necessary. But it is at the middle two elements of mobilization and guerrilla activity that it is hardest to combine the requirements of the means of protest with those of negotiation.

Stalemate. It would be analytically neat if these various elements in the conflict life cycle had nicely synchronized phases; unfortunately, the fact that each runs on its own time and logic makes for the richness of opportunities and the elusiveness of possibilities in conflict resolution.

These life cycles have one thing in common, however. Even though the passage from one phase to another is never crystal clear, it is generally triggered by a stalemate in the current phase. As long as there is hope in the present course, there is no need to change. But when a given goal or means is blocked, it causes people to rethink what they are doing and reevaluate the situation. This is true internally, within the protest movement, and externally, between the movement and its opponent, the government. Stalemate is the key to both the escalation process and the shift of ends, means, tactics, and leadership. The internal and external elements are intimately related. When a movement sees itself blocked in its achievement of an important goal, it is faced with the decision either to raise or to call, to change and intensify its attack or to seek accommodation at the present level. (It can also fold, of course, either retreating to the previous level or giving up entirely. That decision is often likely to lead simply to a takeover of the protest in different forms by others—that is, to the same escalate-or-accommodate decision as was previously posed.) Thus, stalemate marks a particularly important moment for negotiation.

Testing the Patterns

It would take a large number of cases to test these patterns. Unfortunately, not only do cases of ethnic protest vary widely, but cases of negotiated settlements are very few. Indeed, one may well ask what happens to ethnic protests. Except for anticolonial protests—which in the post–World War II era have generally been resolved through the independence of the territory as colonially constituted—ethnic protest generally appears to rise and fall, in most cases, without any attempt or success at resolution. Its declines and revivals are marked by incidents, often accidental or circumstantial in nature, that have more to do with a learning or socialization process, opportunity-cost calculations, and arousal and fatigue than with a conscious attempt to analyze and resolve. Indeed, even scholarship follows these waves, turning attention to the phenomenon when it forces itself on public attention, but content to let well enough alone, as if ethnic conflicts will never return, in times in between.

The anticolonial movement illustrates again and again the notions of blockage and relative deprivation as the sources of ethnic protest. The contribution of World War II, with both its evidence of the weakness of colonial powers and its proclamation of the goals of anticolonial liberation, has frequently been noted.[5] What has been less noted has been the economic element. The Korean war boom in demand for raw materials meant a sudden increase in the economic fortunes of colonial economies, contrasted with an exclusion of colonial populations from benefiting from that boom for ascriptive reasons. Economically, the anticolonial movement was a redistributive movement of ethnic protest.

Other cases can help identify specific triggers of the same nature. The southern Sudanese revolt began in 1955 as a protest against the prospects of continuing discrimination under the impending new circumstances of independence. The Tamil protest in Sri Lanka began with the Standardization of Marks measure in 1972, which discriminated against the educational achievements of Tamils. The Kabyle rebellion of 1980 in Algeria occurred because Kabyles took the new liberalization spirit of President Chadli Ben Jedid literally and thought it applied to them. In all of these cases, ethnic awareness was present for a long time and conflict was latent, but it took a specific incident—often not directly related to ethnicity, as in Sudan—to start the protest. In terms of conflict resolution and negotiation, it would have been best to recognize the problem immediately and deal with its current manifestation. That was a small order in Algeria and a tall order in Sudan, and in Sri Lanka, it touched on intentional measures that were the source of the problem.

Many conflicts, including those in Northern Ireland and revolutionary Algeria, illustrate the conflict between the need for solidarity and the need for resolution, with the former preventing the latter from being pursued. South Africa today also provides an example of a situation in which the weaker side must build up its organization and mobilization before it can allow its representatives to talk with the government. Of course, in all these cases, the governments have helped the consolidation process either by refusing negotiations or by offering to negotiate only under acceptable conditions. Agreeing to negotiate without conditions, this analysis suggests, would have been wiser from the governments' point of view and would have been no worse from the dissidents' point of view. French and British decolonization experiences elsewhere show the wisdom of negotiating early, when some consolidation has been accomplished and the identification of an *interlocuteur valable* serves to legitimize an appropriate negotiating partner.

An equally eloquent reason for negotiating early in the course of an ethnic protest is found in the escalation of goals. Ethnic rebellion to attract greater positive (and less intrusive) attention from the government was the characteristic of the postindependence rebellion of the Berbers in Morocco, where the phenomenon was identified, and also of the Berber (Kabyle) rebellion in Algeria. The rebellions died in 1959 and 1963, respectively (after being put down militarily), when the Berbers achieved representation of their own interests in politics. Similarly, Tamils and Eritreans, having seen the government backtrack on their previously acquired status, came to feel that only by taking their destiny into their own hands through self-determination of independence or something close to it could they be guaranteed a fair result.

Southern Sudan offers an interesting case in the evolution of goals. Originally calling for greater benefits, the southern Sudanese turned to a call for participation and then, when that proved illusory, finally called for independence. When a federal solution collapsed in 1978 after having been negotiated to mutual satisfaction in 1972, the new ethnic movement in 1983 called for a revolution of the whole Sudanese polity, including the north. The example shows that negotiations are possible at any time, or at least at any phase, but must be organized and conducted in good faith. Once again, however, it takes more and more to satisfy the movement as each phase ends in disillusionment over the limitations on current goals (not the reverse, as some might suspect and as governments often hope).

The effect of pluralistic tendencies on the course of negotiation is more problematic. In the beginning, pluralism does not appear to be an obstacle, as long as the government negotiates with a group that is large enough to claim some representativeness. Perhaps radical splinters can puncture a potential agreement; they seem to have done so in regard to the Palestine Liberation

Organization (PLO), although at a later stage of conflict, but they failed in Tunisia and Morocco in 1955. Indeed, such splinter groups are useful as bargaining ploys for more moderate majorities seeking to get the best early deal from a government, although they are not without counters: The government may try to chide the majority for paying attention to the splinters, although it may not get far on that tack.

Stalemate-induced pluralism is a trap rather than an opportunity. Competing groups render potential negotiating partners vulnerable to criticism and one-upmanship from their rivals, as the PLO case demonstrates. Because splits in an ethnic movement tempt the government to make a lesser deal with weaker parties, the dynamic does not favor the elaboration of a resolving agreement. If the government has no incentive to deal with a united movement that can speak for its constituency, splits do not give it an incentive to resolve the problem with partial groups. The history of the Rhodesian negotiations for the first twelve years after the unilateral declaration of independence provides eloquent examples.

Rhodesia also gives a good example of the problems and advantages of splintering. By 1977, after the attempt by Secretary of State Henry A. Kissinger and the joint initiative of U.S. Representative to the United Nations Andrew Young and British Foreign Secretary David Owen, the end was in sight, although it was not clear when or where it was. The internal settlement marked the attempt of some nationalist leaders to take advantage of the moment to grab the benefits of a solution for themselves or, in other words, to split. They failed not so much because the internal agreement was intrinsically unworkable but because the regime of Rhodesian Prime Minister Ian Smith could not bring itself to implement it wholeheartedly. In the process, too, the government had shown itself to be ready for a deal and thus was weakened for its final encounter with the real nationalists at Lancaster House.

The effect of the escalation of means on negotiations is also ambiguous. The guerrilla and perhaps mobilization phases are less conducive to negotiation than are the articulation phase or the last phase, out-and-out war, as studies of succeeding political generations in Algeria have shown[6] and contrasting studies of Tunisia have supported.[7] Yet, as noted, at some point even warriors must negotiate, as they did in Zimbabwe and the south Philippines (the Moros rebellion in 1976), even though it splits their ranks, as it did in Sri Lanka and Sudan. Once violence has been tried, it probably must be played out to a stalemate for the ripe moment for negotiations to appear. Warriors have to carry their investment in violence to the point at which major escalation is needed to get out of the deadlock before they can try the other track. It is interesting that they are often willing to try negotiations at that point because it enables them to stay in control, whereas major escalation poses the danger of a new leadership, as all four of the aforementioned examples indicate.

With Whom to Negotiate

After the first question, when to begin negotiations, comes a more unsuspected query, with whom to negotiate. Usually, and certainly at the beginning of the ethnic protest, the protesters are citizens—albeit deprived citizens—of their country. At this point, negotiations are only internal and bilateral, but as the conflict goes on, the dissidents need to seek and gain outside supporters, sources of power, and sanctuary. Once the insurgency establishes a physical presence in a neighboring country, the nature and particularly the structure of the negotiations change. Negotiations become trilateral, goals and dynamics become more complex, and results become more difficult to achieve.

From Bilateral to Trilateral

It is in the interest of both the government and the dissidents to keep negotiations bilateral, if negotiations are indeed taking place. A complication arises, however, if negotiations are not taking place. In that case, it is in the interest of the dissidents to bring in a third party as a source of power, but such an intrusion is definitely not at all in the interest of the government. Nevertheless, governments often push dissidents to seek external support and sanctuary, because the governments think that they can and should win rather than talk; and by trying so hard to win, they make things worse for themselves.

In such a situation, the insurgents are presumed to be in a coalition with the third party (which will be called the *host* in the following discussion), whereas negotiation implies that a coalition will be built between the insurgents and the government. Behind this tug-of-war over the alliance possibilities of the insurgency lies the possibility of an alliance between the two states—the government and the host—on the backs of the insurgents; this occurred between Iran and Iraq against the Kurds in 1975 and between India and Sri Lanka about the Tamils in 1987. But even if a coalition is not envisaged on that side of the triangle, the interstate relations will be the dominant influence on the relations between the government and its ethnic opposition.

Each of the three parties has its own interests within this triangle. The government has a choice between winning the insurgency away from its host or using the host to influence the insurgency. Also, the government has a wider choice of seeking an accommodation with the neighbor-host on a broad range of issues that concern neighboring states or of seeking accommodation with its ethnic insurgents, often against the advice and interests of the host. To make these choices, the government will have to decide whether the neighbor-host state is interested in improving bilateral relations or is just using the insurgency as a cause and excuse for bad relations, just as it will have to judge whether the insurgency is interested in a settlement or is still focusing on the needs of consolidation.

Similarly, the host-neighbor will have to choose between good or bad relations with its neighbor, a question that may override the earlier, independent matter of whether or not to offer support and sympathy to the ethnic issue. If the host wants good neighborly relations, it is in the perfect position to act as mediator; with potentially good ties with both sides and a motive for mediation, it can deliver the side it is closest to—the insurgents. If it wants bad relations, it can support the insurgents as a surrogate, either to keep neighborly relations bad or to use as a bargaining chip when the time comes. The host-neighbor must decide how hard it can press the government, because it can conceivably draw the government into an agreement that will cause its overthrow at the hands of domestic hard-liners, thus giving the host a worse government as a neighbor. It must also decide how attractive it would find an agreement between the government and the ethnic opposition that would provide precedents for the host-neighbor's own ethnic problems.

Finally, the insurgency has its own choices and strategies to decide. Although it is the ally-presumptive of the host state, it must face the problem of closeness in that relationship. Specifically, is it an autonomous actor—even though it is a prisoner of the host state in its sanctuaries—or is it only a puppet of the host? At the same time, it must decide whether it is ready for accommodation or only for consolidation. The fact that it has fewer choices open to it shows its greater vulnerability and the consequent vulnerability of negotiations.

These multiple questions clearly show the crucial importance of the change from bilateral to trilateral relations and its effect on the possibilities of negotiation. In general, it is in the interest of the government and the insurgency to negotiate, assuming that they want a solution to the mutual problem. And in the same general-interest sense, it is not in the interest of the host-neighbor to see negotiations between the government and the insurgency, as such negotiations would remove its own bargaining chip. Thus, the trilateralization of relations worsens the situation for negotiations, requiring new efforts to reverse the balance of interests. To negotiate successfully in a trilateral situation, the government has to pay a higher price, in that it has to satisfy two parties, with divergent interests, instead of just one.

There is one salient way to change the host-neighbor's calculation of what is in its interests: to render the hosting of the insurgency costly and offensive to the host-neighbor. Only then does it develop a direct interest in resolving the problem with which it otherwise is not directly concerned. Once this shift in interest has occurred, another latent role can come into action. The host-neighbor is the party best placed to act as a mediator in the conflict. Mediation is difficult when the conflict is only internal and when no party has any direct leverage over the two opponents. But when the conflict has been externalized, the host-neighbor can legitimately take on the role of mediator. It has leverage over the insurgency, by virtue of its sanctuary, and over the government, by virtue of its ability to produce a solution. But the road to this impasse is long and hard, and subjective animosity and historic feuding may block progress. The host-neighbor may just not want to play its natural role, whatever its objective interest.

Examples of Trilateral Ethnic Disputes

The record is full of illustrations of these dynamics. In the southern Sudanese rebellion, as the continued warfare threatened to embroil neighboring Ethiopia, it was brought in as a backup mediator. Once the insurgency actually moved to Ethiopian territory as its sanctuary—after the 1972 Addis Ababa Agreement had collapsed (and once the imperial regime had been replaced by the Communist regime of Mengistu Haile Mariam)—Ethiopia became a restraining force rather than a mediator, and relations between the Sudanese People's Liberation Army/Movement and Ethiopia tightened considerably. Efforts by the new Sudanese government—first of General Abdel Rahman Siwar al-Dahab of the Transitional Military Council and then of Sayed Sadiq al-Mahdi of the civilian government—to reopen negotiations stumbled not only against the substantive obstacle of the Islamic legislation in Sudan but also against the procedural obstacle of Ethiopia's greater interest in keeping the sore open than in reviving the mediatory possibilities.

In the Algerian nationalist challenges to colonialist France, Tunisia—considerably inconvenienced by the occupation of a part of its territory by the National Liberation Army—tried to mediate with the French. But it was in no position to deliver the agreement of the Algerian National Liberation Front, and French attacks against Tunisian territory serving as sanctuary weakened its mediatory role. Nonetheless, Tunisia played an important part in softening Algerian opposition to negotiation and in facilitating contacts. More recently, Algeria has resisted entering negotiations over the western Sahara even as a negotiator, claiming, instead—at most—a role as a disinterested friend, while Morocco has shunned negotiations with the Sahrawi dissidents and, instead, has insisted on negotiations with the host-neighbor.

In southern Africa, both Angola and Mozambique have been brought into direct negotiations with South Africa over the fate of the dissidents in neighboring territories, defined as ethnic rebels by South African law. In Namibia, Angola moved from a mediator to an active party in the negotiations, ending up with the Lusaka Agreement for the control of the ethnic rebellions of both parties and with direct negotiations with South Africa over implementation of UN Resolution 435. At the other end of the battle line, Mozambique negotiated a similar accord with South Africa at Nkomati, providing for control of the ethnic rebels of both parties, in order to avoid direct negotiations of their own with their own respective dissidents, the National Resistance Movement (RENAMO) and the African National Congress. Obviously, none of these arrangements solves the issues behind the rebellion.

In the Middle East, the ethnic Arab revolt against Israeli rule over all or some of Palestinian territory has brought neighbor-hosts into a variety of relationships. Jordan and Egypt have tried to act as mediators between the Palestinians and Israel, while also urging direct negotiation between the two parties. Israel has preferred to deal directly with the host-neighbors and not to talk with representatives of its ethnic minority. In Syria, bilateral relations have completely dominated relations between the Israeli government and the minority being given sanctuary, and neither mediation nor direct negotiation is possible.

The same is true of relations between Ethiopia and its Somali minority. No negotiation has taken place between the government and the ethnic group, and only the most timid beginnings of negotiations have begun between the government and the host-neighbor. For the most part, the ethnic rebellion of Ethiopian Somalis has been dealt with as a subject of political control and repression domestically and as a subject of international conflict and hostility in Ethiopia's relations with Somalia. It has taken a long time and a good deal of interpretative optimism to see any chance for resolution or negotiation in this situation.

In Sri Lanka, trilateralization of the conflict has led to different possibilities. Because the Tamil population is a minority on an island, the case of sanctuary is not posed as acutely as it would be in the absence of a water boundary. Nonetheless, Sri Lanka Tamils enjoy the full range of support both from Tamils in southern India and from the Indian government. As the conflict continued, in the mid-1980s, India moved in as a mediator and failed. It then took a more active role, moving militarily to force the ethnic rebels to acquiesce in a solution close to the Tamils' own demands. In the terms used in the previous discussions, India delivered the agreement of the ethnic rebels to their own, not to the government's, solution. However, because the agreement was not a total victory for the rebels, their acceptance—even enforced—was not total either. Yet without Indian participation, neither side could have reached even the imperfect agreement at hand, because neither side was strong enough to make or to hold an agreement against its own internal critics. By escalating the conflict and thereby putting pressure on the neighbor, India was able to play a positive role.

Lessons Learned

Despite the wide variety of cases, some broad conclusions for negotiation are clear. First, entrance of a third party—especially a sovereign-state third party—into a conflict between a government and its ethnic dissidents complicates relations mightily. It brings in a whole new gamut of issues and interests, in that it places the hitherto internal conflict within the new context of neighbor-state relations; and it places the conflict on a new level, because it involves sovereign states.

Second, this complication hinders negotiations. The dyadic interests of the parties line up in such a way as to work against negotiations rather than for them and, more specifically, to reduce the interest of the rebels in solving the conflict by accommodation rather than by continued conflict.

Third, like any escalation, trilateralization can act as a threat—a riser in the stairway of escalation. As trilateralization is in no party's intermediate interest—that is, it may serve a very short-term purpose and a long-term purpose, but it makes things worse all around in the middle run—it is something that everyone can agree to avoid if they think carefully and rationally. That is, of course, a major and perhaps even unreal condition.

Fourth, for the trilateralization to turn from a negative to a positive effect, the entire conflict must escalate beyond the initial trilateralization itself to the point at which it is no longer useful but, to the contrary, begins to hurt the host-neighbor. Only then can the host envisage a helpful role in negotiations.

Fifth, the potentially useful role that the host-neighbor can play is that of a mediator, whereby the host-neighbor helps find a solution and then delivers the agreement of the ethnic rebellion to which it has given support and sanctuary. Alternatively, the host-neighbor can join the rebellion to topple the government, directly or indirectly. Although it may take a new government to make an agreement with the insurgency, that is usually a poor bet. As opposed to governments overthrown by the pressures of an internal conflict, governments overthrown by the pressures of external conflict tend to dig in their heels and harden their line against the foreign enemy, unless the latter has actually imposed its own candidate.

The Ends: What to Negotiate

The third question about negotiations with ethnic rebellions concerns what to negotiate or how to end negotiations. The options are undoubtedly limitless. Categorization has to be conducted along a number of crosscutting dimensions, because a spectrum of outcomes along a single variable does not cover all of the useful and creative typologies that are needed for imaginative negotiations and formulas for solutions.

Denying Ethnicity

At one end of a multiple-dimension spectrum are outcomes that solve ethnic problems by denying ethnicity, as opposed to those at the other end, which rely on ethnic compensation. Nonethnic solutions include assimilation and integration. Assimilation refers to the incorporation of ethnic minorities into a dominant national ethnicity. Amharization in Ethiopia, Wolofization in Senegal, Gallicization in France, and Anglicization in the United States have been tried as ways of creating a single nation—although when the solution does not work, by definition, it becomes the cause for the very ethnic problems that it seeks to cure. Yet this is probably the most successful approach. It involves equal opportunity for all under a dominant culture, regardless of race, creed, or color. It is particularly effective at the outset of ethnic protest, when its promise has credibility behind it and when the enforcing government or change-absorbing institution is in a dominant position. This type of solution can be obtained by negotiation combined with petition or by political pressure and threats of greater protest.

In integration, minorities are brought together into a new, rather than an old, dominant culture. Assimilation and integration are often hard to separate. For example, it is difficult to tell whether the resolution of ethnic problems in the United States involves assimilation into an Anglicized culture or integration into an American culture, or whether the solution in Ivory Coast involves assimilation into a Baoulé culture rather than integration of all groups into a Franco-African Ivorian culture. Integration has also been claimed as the operative solution in India, in Israel, and in other countries where modernization and the leftovers of colonial culture are ingredients in a new national culture. Minorities are asked not to become like someone else but, rather, to contribute to a new identity to be taken on by all. The outcome is hard to negotiate, because it does not exist until integration has devised the new culture; and when the new culture is in place and other groups seek to join, the result is harder to distinguish from assimilation.

Ethnic Compensation

Compensation, or affirmative action, is a third outcome for deprived minorities. When, as a result, minorities become no longer deprived but pampered (in the eyes of the majority)—like the pre-Nasserite Copts in Egypt, the Tamils in Sri Lanka, or the Asians in Kenya—then the old solution becomes a new problem. But until that occurs, compensation is an enlightened solution, imposed by a minority in revolt on a majority with a conscience. Compensation can be negotiated, as it has been in the United States, but the necessary conditions of conflict and conscience do not make it a very common solution. Moreover, compensation must be seen as a way for a minority to catch up with the majority, not as a way to overtake it. Therefore, it must be a temporary measure, to be discarded when quotas can be filled naturally. It would seem that compensation can no longer be considered as a solution once the possibility of secession has been raised, as it depends on an inextricable sense of community and obligation.

Separate Collective Status

In addition to the denial–compensation spectrum, there is a whole range of solutions of separate collective status, based on different ways of combining communal participation in central power with some degree of self-management. One such solution, known as power-sharing, refers to a central governmental coalition of ethnic (or other) group representatives, in which decisions are collective (hence, each group has a veto) and ties are tight between the representatives and their constituencies.[8] Such a solution depends on specific and sometimes elaborate rules and, hence must be preceded by negotiations. The Netherlands and Switzerland are often cited as examples, but there are also looser cases. The Berber "seat" in the Algerian council of ministers, the southern Sudanese vice-president in the 1972 Addis Ababa Agreement (while it lasted), and the proportional representation system in the executive according to the Lebanese National Pact are also approximations of power-sharing. Only the Algerian example was the result of explicit negotiations. Yet the conditions for power-sharing are also precise and limiting. The ethnic group must be cohesive, and it must be a solid supporter of its representatives. Because, as seen in the discussion of the conflict life cycles, consolidation is a passing phase that requires much effort, the conditions of power-sharing are likely to be fulfilled only temporarily. Negotiations, therefore, must not only put a solution in place but must also cover the ongoing mechanisms of maintaining it. Lack of consolidation dogged the Addis Ababa Agreement. It eventually fell apart because there were ethnic subdivisions within the southern Sudanese minority on which the politics of the north could play. It would have taken even greater statesmanship on the part of President Nimeiri to maintain the agreement than to negotiate it.

Competition, or regional bargaining, is another solution, but competitive relationships are subtle and are more difficult to negotiate explicitly. Competition is the local version of power-sharing. Instead of being based on collective decisions among ethnic leaders at the top, it is based on competition among ethnic regions at the bottom, before arbitration by national (presumably, nonethnic) leaders at the top. Dependence on the top is maintained; as in power-sharing, there is a high degree of local group and leader–follower cohesion, and allocations are made by the top according to some fair and independent criterion. Ivory Coast practices such a system, although it was never set up explicitly or by negotiation. The system works as long as there is no constant winner and as long as local groups (such as the Bété) can get some extra attention and extra benefits when they come to feel that they are being discriminated against. However, because of its serious preconditions, competition can only evolve rather than be created; and often, the breakdown of completion—for reasons of perceived unfairness—causes ethnic conflicts.

An alternative outcome that is at the same time more standard and more suspect is that of regional autonomy. Self-government for minority areas has been the path to successful solutions in Italy, where the five regions that enjoy a special status—Sicily, Sardinia, Val d'Aosta, Alto Adige, and Venezia Giulia—all suffered ethnic unrest until they were granted cultural and administrative autonomy. The fact that ethnic unrest has not been completely abolished in Italy does not diminish the effectiveness of regional autonomy. It should be compared not with an ideal situation, such as assimilation or integration, but with alternative possibilities of ethnic conflict. Negotiations over regional autonomy in Italy have been long and recurrent, to the point at which negotiation itself appears to be part of the solution, as autonomous arrangements and relations are repeatedly readjusted. A comparable situation, in which autonomy was part of the solution and its abolition part of the problem, was the Ethiopian "federation"—in reality, a decade of autonomous status for Eritrea. Over a quarter of a century of Eritrean rebellion began when plans became known for abolishing regional (federal) autonomy.

Yet state leaders fear autonomy, anticipating that the region will break off along the dotted lines if a separate territory is defined and given self-rule. In fact, history shows the reverse: With home rule, the population becomes preoccupied with its own issues; as in many other instances, responsibility tempers demands. Yet home rule is not enough, as can be seen in the initial analysis of ethnic demands: Ethnic rebellions arise only secondarily because minorities want to be left alone but primarily because they have not been accorded their fair share of national benefits. Therefore, regional autonomy must involve not merely setting minorities adrift in their own boat but also providing for their regular and equitable supply from the central storehouse. Central allocation and regional suballocation are the two components of regional autonomy, under conditions that involve intensive and continuous negotiations. Regional autonomy differs from power-sharing in that it does not require a specific coalition of group representatives at the center but leaves local allocation in the hands of the local group.

Another creative use of regionalism is regional breakup—that is, the use of regional organization to include several ethnic groups, or to break up a single ethnic area into several regions, or to mix and cut up ethnic areas into regions that bear no relation to any ethnic criteria. The first is hallowed in political annals as gerrymandering, which can serve either to drown one ethnic group in a multiethnic (or nonethnic) seat or to give an ethnic group a larger population to dominate. The second was the solution in Nigeria in preparation for the Second Republic, although it allows larger ethnic groups to be seen through the smaller provincial boundaries. The third is the basis of the Kendall-Louw proposal for a South African government based on 301 judicial districts.[9] For these solutions to work, there must be enough attraction in the new units to reorient attention away from ethnic solidarities; more specifically, goods for allocation must be made available exclusively within the new units to an extent that overcomes the benefits, psychic as well as material, of pursuing ethnic exclusiveness. Such measures may not solve the ethnic problem, but they are likely to have an effect—usually of reducing the scope of ethnic dissidence by fracturing it, so that the new groups either have a new focus or become submerged in the conglomerate. These measures may be too clever to work; they may well spur the pressure for unity, as occurred in the Tamil regions of Sri Lanka, or they may increase resentment with the submerged minority. Again, the result depends on the combination of positive and negative measures—the government's willingness and ability to co-opt or buy out the components of the fractionated ethnic group.

It is not always possible to negotiate such solutions because of the very ambiguity in their nature. Most frequently, measures of regional breakup are adopted and imposed by a government to deal with its ethnic groups and then are enforced as a less direct use of power than simple ethnic suppression. Yet negotiation can be used, probably under one of two conditions: either in hierarchical bargaining, whereby—as often occurs—the government decides but nonetheless has to bring its constituent groups along by horsetrading and consultation, or in a "national convention," whereby parties see the need for a common solution to defend the higher order in the last throes of disruption. Providing a sudden awareness of an overarching common good where it has been previously challenged by local (ethnic) nationalisms is difficult and is rarer than providing an overarching common authority.

Classical Solutions

The last three solutions are classical forms that lie beyond the possibilities already mentioned—federation, confederation, and secession. Federations have existed historically, but always as a devolution of power. The Central African, Cameroonian, Malaysian, Tanzanian, and American federations all brought their components together into a conglomerate in which the parties jealously combined the maintenance of their own home rule with the added benefits of a larger sovereignty. Even in the case of the Nigerian and Libyan federations, existing divisions were maintained within the larger framework, rather than handing down new powers from on high. Federation is an act of coming or staying together, not a way of handling ethnic fissiparous tendencies. Leaders tend to fear federation as much as they fear regional autonomy, and for the same reasons. Yet there is not a federation in the newly independent Third World that has not evolved into a more centralized government within a short time, rather than the reverse, and almost all of the federations (except Nigeria) have simply been abolished in the process. Federation then becomes part of the process of constitution-making—the setting up of the compromise rules by which the body politic pledges to govern itself; it is therefore always the result of negotiation at some level.

Confederations, on the other hand, are the figment of a legal imagination, found nowhere in contemporary reality. The stark necessity of locating sovereignty somewhere and respecting its overwhelming exercise means that a confederation is really a federation, as in Switzerland, or else it is only an alliance of sovereign states, as in Senegambia.[10] Confederations have never been successful in providing solutions for ethnic problems, probably because ethnic disputes that arrive at the point of contesting sovereignty require a clearer outcome than confederation can present.

The final solution is provided by secession, when ethnic groups feel that the only way to obtain their just deserts is through their own control of their destiny. Colonial situations—in which the conflict is defined in ethnic terms, whatever the ideological overtones that may accompany it—are an example of this phenomenon; and subsequent rebellions—such as the Eritrean, the Bengali, the Katangan, the southern Sudanese, the western Saharan, the western Somali, the Assam, the Tamil, the Pashtun, Baluch, and Sindhi, and many other minority disputes—all are cases in which the formerly colonized is then accused of attempting to colonize its own component ethnic groups to the point at which secession seems to be the only answer. By the time secession is called for, the protest movement is so desperate that it ignores the fact that the seceding unit would have real problems with its viability. The form, transition, and conditions of secession and independence are all subjects necessarily subject to negotiation; and if they are not, the aftermath of a unilateral declaration leaves many unresolved questions that need to be negotiated.

In reality, secession has succeeded in only a few cases in modern times. Bangladesh, with its unusual noncontiguous relation to the mother country, and Singapore, seceding from its federation, are unique postwar examples. A few other cases, such as the breakup of the Mali Federation or that of the United Arab Republic, concerned unions too short-lived to be significant. There are, of course, plenty of other cases in which secession has been posited by ethnic minorities as a solution, but they have not yet got their rebellion to the point of strength at which negotiations are imposed. Beyond the decolonizations, therefore, experience tells very little about how to negotiate secession. One element is sure and important, however: Dissident minorities that are bound on secession refuse to enter negotiations until the goal of independence is admitted by the other side, rather than letting it emerge from the negotiations. Negotiations then turn to the ways of defining and implementing secession—although, in the process, the type of secession and the nature of postsecession relations are still important aspects of the formula phase of negotiations.

The Range of Outcomes

In sum, the outcomes of negotiations cover a wide range of possibilities, and some outcomes are unlikely subjects of negotiation. Outcomes translate power relations and the evolution of the conflict. Some outcomes—such as regional breakup, assimilation, and integration—depend on a strong government position vis-à-vis the ethnic groups. Others—such as affirmative action, power-sharing, regional autonomy, and federation—presuppose a strong ethnic commitment to the higher unity and identity of the state, alongside a concern for management of their own affairs. Outcomes may evolve from negotiations themselves, although they are best prepared by a crystallizing consensus before negotiations actually begin. Some radical outcomes—notably, secession—can only be settled before negotiations open.

Conflict is a process of eliminating possible outcomes until the salient and agreed solution stands out amid the conflict. If that outcome proves unworkable, however, the search goes back to the battlefield, and the attempt at a solution can be considered merely a way of testing and rejecting an ostensibly prominent alternative. Negotiated outcomes can prove unworkable if they are not applied, if they do not function when applied, or if they leave out of their ambit some opposing groups that are powerful enough to disrupt them. These potential problems should be considered carefully during the negotiation process. If the conflict is costly enough and the negotiated outcome attractive enough to the parties, it will be implemented; but the threat of renewed conflict must be sufficiently perceived that the implementor (the government) does not simply bank the end of the conflict and throw away the agreement. Concerning leaving out a powerful player, it is never clear whether it is better to negotiate with the moderates, isolating the extremes, or to negotiate with the extremes, jumping and "enclosing" the moderates. The obvious key to the choice is the strength of the moderates versus the radicals, but other elements enter as well: the vulnerability of the radicals to co-optation even if they are strong, the distance that separates the radicals from the moderates, and the elements available for exchange and side payments to sweeten the argument, among others.

Mediation

It can be seen that the beginning, middle, and end of negotiation depend in different ways on the course of the ethnic conflict. Paradoxically, the same force that tears groups apart creates the conditions for bringing them together; but the tragedy of the paradox is that the forces of conflict are generally more powerful than the counterforces of conciliation. Even when conflict provides the conditions for its own end, its internal dynamic and the need to justify past efforts and mistakes keeps those ripening moments from being seized. Negotiation often needs help. Yet the ultimate irony is that internal conflicts such as ethnic disputes are more difficult to mediate than international disputes, because any would-be conciliator from the outside has little standing. In domestic disputes, mediation is meddling. It is important, therefore, to develop internal private agencies for dispute resolution and to foster a domestic view of their legitimacy, so that they can act as "marriage counselors" without challenging state sovereignty from without. When such domestic agencies are not available, foreign or transnational private agencies may have an easier time of providing good offices than foreign states would.

The problem of moving to conciliation and finding a mediator to help the process along also underscores a major theme that has run through the preceding discussion: It is better to handle ethnic problems early rather than late. If there are ripe moments for dealing with ethnic problems, they come not just at the end of the conflict but at each step of the escalation. Therefore, there are many moments to seize, and the conflict and the solutions are less jarring when the early moments are used instead of the ultimate stalemate.

Although much that is useful could be said about the tactics of private agencies, whether domestic or international, there are also some characteristics to be noted about the role of states as conflict managers. Unlike private agencies, third-party states do not enter a conflict with the object of reducing it merely for humanitarian reasons. States are motivated by their interests, and states generally have one or both of two interests in ethnic conflict resolution: because the conflict threatens to escalate and bring about national and regional destabilization or because it is damaging their own relations with the parties involved. Mediators therefore seek to keep out destabilizing side-takers and to maintain their own good relations—interests that can often be attained only by mediations.

But, as has been seen, the mediator is basically illegitimate and usually unwanted. If both the parties saw that they needed help out of their mess, the mediator's job would be greatly facilitated, but this is rarely the case. More than other parties to a negotiation process, a mediator must build leverage; and this, too, comes in only two forms. Either the mediator can use side payments and sweeteners, although they tend to be costly and are often delegitimized by an aura of bribery. Or the mediator can make itself needed by the very act of providing an attractive solution—a difficult thing to do—and, beyond that, by bringing to each side the other party's likely agreement to a peaceful solution. Mediators are thus caught in a vicious circle. Their leverage depends largely on finding an attractive solution, and their conveying a solution depends on their leverage.

The best way to ease this dilemma is to prepare for mediation through positioning and prenegotiation. Positioning is merely the conduct of good diplomatic relations with an eye to the growing ethnic problem. A number of actions are available. A potential mediator should maintain contacts with all parties. Denying contacts with ethnic representatives does not contribute to resolution of the problem, and it makes it difficult to collect useful intelligence and to build a base for a later, helpful role. A potential mediator should seek to promote legitimate discussion of the problem, at whatever level it may exist. Opposition groups are symptoms of a problem, even though their own particular view of the problem may be neither appropriate nor representative. Potential mediators can emphasize the need to handle the problem early, rather than letting it grow worse. Handling does not mean giving in to every demand of the opposition, but it does mean undercutting the basis of its demands in some way. Finally, positioning means paying careful attention to the tactics of pluralism within the ethnic dissidence. Although it is best to preserve the unity and representativeness of the movement, it is also good to avoid rewarding the extremism of the fringes; and although it is good to isolate the irrecuperables, it is best to do so without leaving them with a cause or the means to continue the conflict and upset a potential agreement. As these counsels are obviously contradictory, careful attention to tactics is important.

In prenegotiations, potential mediators can also take a number of concrete steps. They can foster discussions among the sides, by hosting meetings at the official, unofficial, and *officieux* level—the last being groups of well-placed private citizens who keep in touch with the official parties both before and after the discussions. Potential mediators can build up and often even legitimize moderate groups and leaders on both sides and help them develop a common sense of the problem and of its solution. An interesting device to be encouraged unofficially is an expression by each side of the measures and statements that it would consider to be confidence-building on the part of the opposite party, coupled with an appreciation (or nonappreciation) of these requests to prevent their becoming elements of further escalation. The efforts of mediators should be directed at producing these and other measures that serve to call but not raise the conflict and facilitate the process of ethnic satisfaction and integration and of state consolidation.

References

1. Ted Robert Gurr, *Why Men Rebel* (Princeton, NJ: Princeton University Press, 1970).

2. Shmuel Eisenstadt. *Modernization: Protest and Change* (Englewood Cliffs, NJ: Prentice-Hall, 1966), p. 38.

3. Herbert Feith, *The Decline of Constitutional Democracy in Indonesia* (Ithaca, NY: Cornell University Press, 1962).

4. See, for example, Jeanne Favret, "Traditionalism Through Ultra-Modernising," in Charles Micaud and Ernest Gellner, *Arabs and Berbers* (Lexington, MA: Lexington Books, 1973): 307–24.

5. Rupert Emerson, *From Empire to Nation* (Cambridge, MA: Harvard University Press, 1960); Immanuel Wallerstein, *Social Change* (New York: Wiley, 1966).

6. William B. Quandt, *Revolution .ind Political Leadership* (Cambridge, MA: MIT Press, 1970).

7. Charles Micaud, Clement Henry Moore, and L. Carl Brown, *Tunisia: The Politics of Modernization* (New York: Praeger, 1964).

8. Arend Lijphart, *Power-Sharing in South Africa,* Policy Paper in International Affairs, No. 24 (Berkeley: University of California, Institute of International Studies, 1985); David D. Laitin, "South Africa: Violence, Myths, and Democratic Reform," *World Politics* 39, no. 2 (January 1987): 258–79.

9. Frances Kendell and Leon Louw, *South Africa: The Solution* (Berkeley: University of California, Institute for Policy Studies, 1987).

10. Claude Welch, *Dreams of Unity* (Ithaca, NY: Cornell University Press, 1966).

29

Epilogue: The Human Factor Revisited

Joseph V. Montville

Vamık D. Volkan's chapter, "Psychoanalytic Aspects of Ethnic Conflicts" (chapter 5), seems like a brief flash in the sky against the
landscape of rich and stimulating historical background portraits,
lucid case studies, and insightful sociopolitical-institutional analyses that
make up the bulk of this volume. But it would be inappropriate to conclude
this work on political conflict and peacemaking without further reference to
some of the most recent findings in political psychology on the specifically
psychological tasks in ethnic conflict resolution. These findings are particularly important for cases of protracted and chronically violent ethnic conflict, as exemplified by the unresolved "hot" cases of Northern Ireland, Sri
Lanka, and Sudan.

John W. Burton, one of the true giants in political conflict resolution
theory building and practice, has laid the entire foundation of his work on the
recognition of the ontological needs of individuals and groups of individuals
for security, identity, and human development. These are needs that cannot
be compromised, bargained away, or negated by legal judgments, constitutions, electoral systems, or treaty language. They are needs that individuals
and groups will pursue with all means at their disposal, subject to limits only
they themselves impose. Failure by would-be peacemakers to understand
these needs and provide for them in conflict resolution strategies assures
failure of the process. Burton, a former diplomat and professor of international relations, has developed a body of work on facilitated conflict resolution that should be required reading for anyone seriously engaged in the
process.[1]

With an academic and professional background somewhat similar to Burton's, I have also been struck with the human needs aspect of political conflict
resolution, and I have developed a concept called "track two diplomacy"
to deal with the needs-specific tasks in conflict resolution that are usually
ignored in official, track one diplomacy.[2] The question, then, is what should
a student from any discipline or profession know about the human factor in
ethnic conflict and peacemaking?

As Volkan suggests in his chapter, the issue of individual and collective needs merits volumes itself and, indeed, rests on extensive research into the concepts of the individual and collective self derived from developmental and self psychology. Professor John E. Mack, a psychiatrist and academic director of Harvard's Center for Psychological Studies in the Nuclear Age, has a major study under way, tentatively entitled "Nationalism, Ideology and the Self," which examines the complex relationships among the self, ideologies (seen as cognitive-affective links between individuals and groups), and nationalism or intense ethnic self-consciousness. But for our purposes in understanding some of the challenges to peacemakers in "hot" ethnic conflicts, a few more thoughts on basic human needs and vulnerabilities are necessary. These include, but are not limited to, the continuing individual requirement throughout life for a strong sense of self, in the absence of which is the potential for depression and reactive violence; the special role of historical victimhood; and the need for collective mourning, as Volkan notes, before serious, violent ethnic conflict can be reduced and ultimately resolved.

The story begins, as Volkan indicates, in infancy, when all humans become aware of their weakness and dependency on others for survival. Babies soon learn ways to manipulate their caregivers into satisfying their needs for food, comfort, warmth, and physical contact. But regardless of the levels of "power" the infant achieves, he is continually aware of his helplessness. He thus attempts to acquire the ability to influence his primary caregivers through the development of affiliative bonds. These ties are gradually extended to the family as a whole, and it is this basic nuclear alliance system that becomes a model for later nurturing and protective alliances such as schools, communities, and corporations. As Mack has written:

> Our identification with those groups or institutions which serve functions of survival and protection, such as the military and the church, and, above all, the nation state, are especially profound and resemble quite dramatically the connection with our own families. It should not surprise us, therefore, that we may be willing to die or kill for the nation state should we be told its identity or survival is threatened. The violent uprising of threatened peoples all over the world attests to the supreme power of ethno-national identifications.[3]

Very closely related to the basic need for affection and belongingness is the human need for self-respect or self-esteem and the respect or esteem of others. As Abraham Maslow described it in his theory of psychic evolution, esteem needs are related to the desire for strength, mastery, achievement, a sense of independence, and freedom to act.[4] The esteem of others would be reflected in recognition (critically important), attention, prestige, and status. To measure the importance of these characteristics, one need only consider their opposite—that is, lack of recognition, no status, indifference, degradation. These are attitudes within in-groups that anticipate potential increased dehumanization of, and aggression against, out-groups.[5]

In more familiar psychological terms, negative self-esteem results in a growing sense of despair in everyday life. One feels debased, abandoned, denied any supporting love, basically unwanted. The socially dangerous aspect of this state is the potential rage it generates in the individual. Sometimes, the resulting aggression is directed inward, in the form of substance abuse or other self-destructive behaviors. Often, the aggression is directed at external objects—for example in the recent American experience, in the murder of a banker or a judge in his courtroom or an assembly of nine-year-old students in a California classroom.

What each of these examples has in common is the alienation of the aggressor from social mores and values, let alone concepts of law and order. The man of violence, seemingly rejected by society and a real or self-perceived victim of its "structural violence," in Johan Galtung's term, in turn rejects society's rejection of him. In the individual, such acts of violence are considered aberrations. When members of an identity or ethnic group engage in such violence, it may be called terrorism. For the alienated group, active violence is seen as a defense of life. Or as Menachem Begin, militant combatant for Israel's independence, put it, "We fight, therefore we are."[6]

It is important to note that the loss of or failure to achieve self-esteem is not a phenomenon restricted to urban, modernized, postindustrial people who are experiencing civilization and its discontents. Erik Erikson documented the phenomenon dramatically in his field work with Sioux and Dakota Indians on their reservations.[7] And in *Identity, Youth and Crisis*, Erikson chastised social scientists and historians for neglecting the individual's and the group's very personal form of developmental interaction with history made and in the making:

> Students of society and history . . . blithely continue to ignore the fact that all individuals are born by mothers; that everybody was once a child; that people and peoples begin in their nurseries; and that society consists of generations in the process of developing from children into parents, destined to absorb the historical changes of their lifetimes and to continue to make history for their descendents.[8]

Making history and absorbing historical change is one way of describing ethnic conflict over time. As the several case studies and analyses in this volume seem to indicate, there is a direct correlation between the intensity, scope, and continuity of interethnic violence—the absorption of history—and the difficulty in making peace between the ethnic groups involved. In other words, the higher the level of victimhood felt by aggrieved groups, the harder it is to get the conflict resolved. A situation is particularly difficult if both ethnic groups in conflict feel victimized—that is, if there is a competition of victimhood, over which group has suffered more.

The late political psychologist Jeanne Knutson developed a conception of the psychology of victimhood based on hundreds of interviews with people who had participated in and/or been hurt by ethnic or sectarian violence. Her understanding of the phenomenon as a political analyst was enhanced by her appreciation of the basic human needs for identity, affiliation, affection, self-esteem, and the esteem of others. (She had separate, earned Ph.D.'s in political science and clinical psychology.) These needs, taken together, were components of a sense of safety and security humans require for normal development—from infancy through old age—for getting through the life cycle with, it is hoped, only an average level of anxiety. By maintaining ties to family and expanding them in other social institutions, including the protection of laws, people develop material psychological defenses against the predictable traumas in life—death of a loved one, job loss, disability, riot, and even war. Victimization shatters the sense of safety provided by identity and affiliation. The victim is never the same after the first blows are struck.

Victimization is based on at least three components: It is the personal experience of stunning violence that creates a powerful sense of loss; there is no way that the violence can be seen as just and deserved; and the threat of further violence and loss at the hands of the aggressor continues into the future. Once a victim has been terrorized, he simultaneously grieves over his lost sense of personal safety and fears intensely for his future. Based on the interviews with men of political violence in prison and at large—in the United States, Northern Ireland, Cyprus, and the Middle East—Knutson concluded that the victim's intense anxiety over potential losses in the future is driven by an inner sense that passivity ensures victimization. The roots of political violence and terrorism—at least in ethnic and sectarian conflict—come from the conviction that only continued activity in the defense of one's *self,* including one's group self, can reduce the threat of further aggression against the self.[9]

From this level of analysis of conflict in multiethnic societies—and with a professional diplomatic background in the politics of peacemaking—I have drawn deeply from the works of psychoanalysts such as Freud, Erikson, George Pollock, and Vamık Volkan to understand the importance of a completed mourning process by which a victim or victim group "lets go" of its losses from historic or contemporary violence and reintegrates and adapts to a new, reasonably secure status so that it can get on with the business of life. For the mourning process to occur, however, requires that the victimizers accept responsibility for their acts or those of their predecessor governments and people, recognize the injustice done, and in some way ask forgiveness of the victims. In many cases, the contrition may have to be mutual where victimizers have themselves been victims. For example, a wise and insightful former Israeli general once proposed in a "track two diplomacy" problem-solving workshop with Palestinians that as part of a peace agreement, Israel and a new Palestinian state jointly build a memorial to the victims of both peoples who had died in their struggle.

I have dealt elsewhere in some detail on the mourning process, averring that the Franco–German reconciliation after World War II is a prime example of a successful mourning process in a protracted ethnic conflict.[10] However, recognizing that the concept is at least unorthodox in traditional political analysis, we shall apply it to a contemporary case.

Poland and the Soviet Union, including prerevolutionary Russia, have a historical relationship burdened with violence and accumulated grievances, the balance of which seem to be on the Polish side. One of the most significant responses of the Polish intelligentsia and population at large to the invitation by Soviet President Gorbachev to participate in *glasnost* and *perestroika* in the bilateral relationship has been the insistence that the Soviet Union acknowledge responsibility for the murder of 4,443 Polish officers whose bodies were found in mass graves forty-five years ago in the Katyn Forest near Smolensk in the Soviet Union.

The Soviets have always admitted that the Poles found at Katyn were part of a contingent of 15,000 reserve officers seized by the Red Army in 1939, when the Soviet Union absorbed eastern Poland under the Molotov-Ribbentrop pact. But Moscow insisted from the beginning that the massacre was carried out by Hitler's troops in 1941, after the German Army overran the Soviet camp where the officers were interned. Successive Communist governments in Warsaw have backed the Soviet story, but accumulating evidence indicates strongly that the NKVD, predecessor to the KGB, did the killings at Stalin's order. The other 10,000-plus reserve officers whose bodies were not found at Katyn have never been traced, and Polish opinion is that Stalin deliberately destroyed Poland's young leadership class as a prelude to establishing his hegemony in the country.

In 1987, General Wojciech Jaruzelski announced that a joint Soviet–Polish commission was being established to examine the "blank spots" in the history of the bilateral relationship. Also to be studied were the 1939 Soviet–German treaty dividing Poland and the 1944 Warsaw uprising, in which many Polish and Western observers believe the Soviets paused to let the Nazis finish off the pro-Western Polish leadership before occupying the city. At this writing, the Soviet side of the commission is still studying its archives. But on March 7, 1989, the Polish government officially announced its belief that the Soviets were responsible for Katyn.

Although political observers and journalists tend to believe that the Jaruzelski government is trying to legitimize itself in Polish public opinion by embracing a great patriotic issue, there is much more to Katyn than meets the traditionalist's eye. There has been a genuinely positive response by Polish intellectuals to the Gorbachev revolution and the official Soviet desire to improve the quality of the bilateral relationship. But the Katyn massacre symbolizes for the Poles the critical need to address all three aspects of victimhood: the stunning, terrorizing violence; the patent injustice of it, and the potential for more violence in the future. The only way the Katyn loss can be mourned by the Poles is through the Soviets' acknowledgment of Stalin's crime and asking forgiveness of the Polish people. Only with this action can the Poles begin to believe that they can "let go" of the lost victims and begin to believe that a new humanized, mutually respectful relationship with the Soviet Union is possible and that "it won't happen again."

Such, in essence, is the nature of the psychological tasks involved in resolving long-standing ethnic conflict. Peacemaking strategies will surely depend on the extraordinarily rich store of existing comparative knowledge of constitutions, electoral systems, and power-sharing schemes exemplified in this volume in the work of Donald Horowitz and Arend Lijphart, among others. They will benefit greatly by the historic and sociopoliticoeconomic wisdom and perspectives of the historians and country specialists we have read. But somewhere along the line, Britain will have to make amends to the Irish people; the Sinhalese and Tamils will probably both have to accept responsibility for the crimes of political oppression and reactive violence each group has committed; and the Muslim governments and peoples of Sudan will have to accept responsibility for the violations of human and civil rights of non-Muslim blacks in the south before a stable, mutually respectful pluralism can be established in any of these "hot" countries.

Only the participants in the multitude of ethnic conflicts around the world can know how the effective mourning of losses can be accomplished. And it will probably require various forms of nontraditional, supplemental, or track two diplomacy to reveal the critical psychological tasks in potentially successful peacemaking strategies. This is, in truth, the essential business of the pre-negotiation stage of any true resolution of a conflict, before formal negotiations focus on the essentials of political institution-building.

It is the fervent hope of the authors of this volume that they have made a meaningful and lasting contribution to the art and science of peacemaking, which still has enormous, but perhaps now more comprehensible, tasks ahead of it.

References

1. See John W. Burton, *Conflict and Communication: The Use of Controlled Communication in International Relations* (New York: Free Press, 1969); *Deviance, Terrorism and War: The Process of Solving Unsolved Social and Political Problems* (New York: St. Martin's Press, 1979); *Global Conflict: The Domestic Sources of International Crisis* (London: Wheatsheaf Books, 1984); and *Resolving Deep-Rooted Conflict: A Handbook* (Lanham, MD: University Press of America, 1987).

2. See Joseph Montville and William D. Davidson, M.D., "Foreign Policy According to Freud," *Foreign Policy* 45 (Winter 1980–81): 145–57; Joseph V. Montville, "The Arrow and the Olive Branch: A Case for Track Two Diplomacy," in

John W. McDonald, Jr., and Diane B. Bendahmane, eds., *Conflict Resolution: Track Two Diplomacy* (Washington, DC: Foreign Service Institute, U.S. Government Printing Office, 1987), and "Transnationalism and the Role of Track Two Diplomacy," in Scott Thompson, ed., *Toward the Twenty-First Century: An Investigation of the Roads to Peace* (Washington, DC: United States Institute of Peace), forthcoming.

3. John E. Mack, M.D., "Reflections of Two Kinds of Power," *Center Review* 3, no. 1 (Winter 1989): 1.

4. Abraham Maslow, *Motivation and Personality* (New York: Harper and Row, 1954).

5. See Viola W. Bernard, P. Ottenberg, and Fritz Redl, "Dehumanization: A Composite Psychological Defense in Relations to Modern War," in Milton Schwebel, ed., *Behavioral Science and Human Survival* (Palo Alto, CA: Science and Behavior Books, 1965).

6. Menachem Begin, *The Revolt: Story of the Irgun* (Jerusalem: Steimatzky, 1951), p. 46.

7. See Erik H. Erikson, *Childhood and Society* (New York: W.W. Norton, 1950, 1963).

8. Erik H. Erikson, *Identity, Youth and Crisis* (New York: W.W. Norton, 1968), p. 45.

9. Joseph V. Montville, "The Psychological Roots of Ethnic and Sectarian Terrorism," in Vamık D. Volkan, M.D., Demetrios Julius, M.D., and Joseph V. Montville, eds., *The Psychodynamics of International Relationships,* Vol. II, (Lexington, MA: Lexington Books, 1991.

10. Montville, "The Arrow and the Olive Branch"; and Joseph Montville "Psychoanalytic Enlightenment and the Greening of Diplomacy," *Journal of the American Psychoanalytic Association* 37, no. 2 (1989).

Bibliography

General

Annals of the American Academy of Political and Social Science: Ethnic Conflict in the World Today, 433 (September 1977).

Armstrong, John A. *Nations Before Nationalism.* Chapel Hill: University of North Carolina Press, 1982.

Ashworth, Georgina, ed. *World Minorities in the Eighties.* Sunbury, England: Quartermaine House, 1980.

Banton, Michael. *Racial and Ethnic Competition.* Cambridge: Cambridge University Press, 1983.

Barth, Fredrik, ed. *Ethnic Groups and Boundaries: The Social Organization of Culture Differences.* London: Allen and Unwin, 1969.

Bell, Wendell, and Walter E. Freeman, eds. *Ethnicity and Nation-Building: Comparative, International, and Historical Perspectives.* Beverly Hills, CA: Sage, 1984.

Brass, Paul, ed. *Ethnic Groups and the State.* Totowa, NJ: Barnes and Noble, 1985.

Buchheit, Lee C. *Secession: The Legitimacy of Self-Determination.* New Haven, CT: Yale University Press, 1978.

Cohen, Ronald. "Ethnicity: Problem and Focus in Anthropology." *Annual Review of Anthropology* 7 (1978): 379–403.

Connor, Walker. "Self-Determination: The New Phase." *World Politics* 20, no. 1 (October 1967): 30–53.

———. "The Politics of Ethnonationalism." *Journal of International Affairs* 27, no. 1 (1973): 1–21.

Coser, Lewis. *The Functions of Social Conflict.* New York: Free Press, 1956.

Enloe, Cynthia H. *Ethnic Conflict and Political Development.* Boston: Little, Brown, 1973.

———. "Police and Military in the Resolution of Ethnic Conflict." *Annals* 433 (September 1977): 137–49.

———. *Ethnic Soldiers: State Security in Divided Societies.* Athens: University of Georgia Press, 1980.

Esman, Milton J., ed. *Ethnic Conflict in the Western World.* Ithaca, NY: Cornell University Press, 1977.

Esman, Milton J. "Two Dimensions of Ethnic Politics: Defense of Homelands, Immigrant Rights." *Ethnic and Racial Studies* 8, no. 3 (July 1985): 438–40.

Esman, Milton J. "Ethnic Politics and Economic Power." *Comparative Politics* 19, no. 4 (July 1987): 395–418.

Freeman, Gary F. "Migration and the Political Economy of the Welfare State." *Annals* 485 (May 1986): 51–63.

Gans, Herbert J. "Symbolic Ethnicity: The Future of Ethnic Groups and Cultures in America." *Ethnic and Racial Studies* 2, no. 1 (January 1979): 1–20.

Geertz, Clifford, ed. *Old Societies and New States.* Glencoe, IL: Free Press, 1963.

Gelfand, Donald E., and Russell D. Lee, eds. *Ethnic Conflicts and Power: A Cross-National Perspective.* New York: Wiley, 1973.

Glazer, Nathan. *Affirmative Discrimination: Ethnic Inequality and Public Policy.* New York: Basic Books, 1975.

——. *Ethnic Dilemmas, 1964–1982.* Cambridge, MA: Harvard University Press, 1983.

Glazer, Nathan, and Daniel P. Moynihan, eds. *Ethnicity: Theory and Experience.* Cambridge, MA: Harvard University Press, 1975.

Hall, Raymond I., ed. *Ethnic Autonomy: Comparative Dynamics.* New York: Pergamon Press, 1979.

Heisler, Barbara Schmitter. "Immigrant Settlement and the Structure of Emergent Migrant Communities in Western Europe." *Annals* 485 (May 1986): 76–86.

Heisler, Barbara Schmitter, and Martin O. Heisler. "Transnational Migration and the Modern Democratic State: Familiar Problems in New Form or a New Problem? *Annals* 485 (May 1986): 20.

Heisler, Martin O., ed. *Politics in Europe: Structures and Processes in Some Post-industrial Democracies.* New York: David McKay, 1974.

——. "Transnational Migration as a Small Window on the Diminished Autonomy of the Modern Democratic State." *Annals* 485 (May 1986): 156–58.

Heisler, Martin O., and Barbara Schmitter Heisler, eds. "From Foreign Workers to Settlers? Transnational Migration and the Emergence of New Minorities." *Annals* 485 (May 1986).

Heisler, Martin O., and R.B. Kvavik. "Patterns of European Politics: The 'European Polity' Model." In Martin O. Heisler, ed., *Politics in Europe: Structures and Processes in Some Postindustrial Democracies.* New York: David McKay, 1974.

Heisler, Martin O., and B. Guy Peters. "Scarcity and the Management of Conflict in Multicultural Polities." *International Political Science Review* 4, no. 3 (September 1983): 327–44.

Henderson, Gregory, Richard Ned Lebow, and John G. Stoessinger, eds. *Divided Nations in a Divided World.* New York: David McKay, 1974.

Hewitt, Christopher. "Majorities and Minorities: A Comparative Survey of Ethnic Violence." *Annals* 433 (September 1977): 150–60.

Horowitz, Donald L. "Patterns of Ethnic Separatism." *Comparative Studies in Society and History* 23, no. 2 (April 1981).

——. *Ethnic Groups in Conflict.* Berkeley and Los Angeles: University of California Press, 1985.

Lijphart, Arend. *Democracies: Democracy in Plural Societies.* New Haven, CT: Yale University Press, 1977.

——. *Democracies: Patterns of Majoritarian and Consensus Government in Twenty-One Countries.* New Haven, CT: Yale University Press, 1984.

Mack, John E. "Nationalism and the Self." *Psychohistory Review* 2, nos. 2–3 (Spring 1983): 47–70.

Manor, James, ed. *SRI Lanka in Change and Crisis*. New York: St. Martin's Press, 1984.

McKay, James. "An Exploratory Synthesis of Primordial and Mobilizational Approaches to Ethnic Phenomena." *Ethnic and Racial Studies* 5, no. 4 (October 1982).

McNeill, William H. *Polyethnicity and National Unity in World History*. Toronto: University of Toronto Press, 1986.

Nevette, Neil, and Charles H. Kennedy, eds. *Ethnic Preference and Public Policy in Developing States*. Boulder, CO: Lynne Rienner, 1986.

Nordlinger, Eric A. *Conflict Regulation in Divided Societies*. Occasional Paper No. 29. Cambridge, MA.: Harvard University, Center for International Affairs, 1972.

Novak, Michael. *The Rise of the Unmeltable Ethnics*. New York: Macmillan, 1971.

Powell, G. Bingham, Jr. *Contemporary Democracies: Participation, Stability, and Violence*. Cambridge, MA: Harvard University Press, 1982.

Ra'anan, Uri. *Ethnic Resurgence in Modern Democratic States*. New York: Pergamon Press, 1980.

Race 12, no. 4 (1970–71) (on race and pluralism); 13, no. 4 (1971–72) (on race and social stratification); 14, no. 4 (1972–73) (on the politics of race).

Rogers, Rosemarie, ed. *Guests Come to Stay: The Effects of European Labor Migration on Sending and Receiving Countries*. Boulder, CO: Westview Press, 1985.

———. "The Transnational Nexus of Migration." *Annals* 485 (May 1986): 34–50.

Rokkan, Stein. "Dimensions of State Formation and Nation-Building: A Possible Paradigm for Research on Variations in Europe." In Charles Tilly, ed., *The Formation of National States in Western Europe*. Princeton, NJ: Princeton University Press, 1975.

Rose, Richard. *Governing without Consensus: An Irish Perspective*. Boston: Beacon Press, 1971.

Rothschild, Joseph. *Ethnopolitics: A Conceptual Framework*. New York: Columbia University Press, 1981.

Rudolph, J.R., Jr., and R.J. Thompson. "Ethnoterritorial Movements and the Policy Process." *Comparative Politics* 17, no. 3 (April 1985): 292.

Sahlins, M.D. "The Segmentary Lineage: An Organization of Predatory Expansion." In R. Cohen and J. Middleton, eds., *Comparative Political Systems: Studies in the Politics of Pre-Industrial Societies*. Garden City, NY: Natural History Press, 1967.

Simmel, George. *Conflict and the Web of Group Affiliations* (Trans. Kurt H. Wolff and Reinhard Bendix). New York: Free Press, 1955.

Simon, Gildas. "Migration in Southern Europe: An Overview." In *The Future of Migration*. Paris: Organization for Economic Cooperation and Development, 1987, p. 266.

Singer, Marshall R. *Intercultural Communication: A Perceptual Approach*. Englewood Cliffs, NJ: Prentice-Hall, 1987.

Smith, Anthony D. *The Ethnic Revival in the Modern World*. New York: Cambridge University Press, 1981.

Steinberg, Stephen. *The Ethnic Myth: Race, Ethnicity and Class in America*. New York: Atherton Press, 1981.

Steiner, Jürg. "Decision Modes towards Separatist Movements: Some Conceptual and Theoretical Considerations." In Edward A. Tiryakian and Ronald Rogowski, eds., *New Nationalisms of the Developed West*. Boston: Allen and Unwin, 1985.

Stephens, Meic. *Linguistic Minorities in Western Europe*. Llandysul, Wales: Gomer Press, 1976.

Suhrke, Astri, and Leila G. Noble, eds. *Ethnic Conflict in International Relations*. New York: Praeger, 1977.

Tiryakian, Edward A., and Ronald Rogowski, eds. *New Nationalisms of the Developed West*. Boston: Allen and Unwin, 1985.

Van Dyke, Vernon. "Justice as Fairness: For Groups?" *American Political Science Review* 69, no. 2 (June 1975): 607–14.

———. "The Individual, the State, and Ethnic Communities in Political Theory." *World Politics* 29, no. 3 (April 1977): 343–69.

Volkan, V.D. *The Need to Have Enemies and Allies: From Clinical Practice to International Relationships*. Northvale, NJ: Aronson, 1988.

Von Vorys, Karl. *Democracy without Consensus*. Princeton, NJ: Princeton University Press, 1975.

Wallace, Anthony F.C. "Revitalization Movements." In Barry McLaughlin, ed., *Studies in Social Movements: A Social Psychological Perspective*. New York: Free Press, 1969.

Young, Crawford. *The Politics of Cultural Pluralism*. Madison: University of Wisconsin Press, 1976.

Alto Adige/South Tyrol

Alcock, Antony Evelyn. *The History of the South Tyrol Question*. London: Michael Joseph, 1970.

Eyck, Gunther. *Loyal Rebels: Andreas Hofer and the Tyrolean Uprising of 1809*. Lanham, MD, and London: University Press of America, 1986.

Rusinow, Dennison I. *Italy's Austrian Heritage 1919–1945*. Oxford: Clarendon Press, 1969.

Toscano, Mario, and Carbone, George A. *Alto Adige/South Tyrol: Italy's Frontier with the German World*. Baltimore: Johns Hopkins University Press, 1975.

Assam

Baruah, Sanjib. "Immigration, Ethnic Conflict and Political Turmoil—Assam, 1979–1985." *Asian Survey* 26, no. 11 (November 1986).

Cantlie, Audrey. *The Assamese: Religion, Caste, and Sect in an Indian Village*. London: Curzon Press, 1984.

Gupta, Shekhar, *Assam: A Valley Divided*. New York: Advent Books, 1984.

Phukom, Girin. *Assam: Attitude to Federalism*. New York: APT Books, 1984.

Singh, Jaswant. "Assam's Crisis of Citizenship: An Examination of Political Errors." *Asian Survey* 24, no. 10 (October 1984): 1056–68.

Weiner, Myron. *Sons of the Soil: Migration and Ethnic Conflict in India.* Princeton, NJ: Princeton University Press, 1978.

———. "The Political Demography of Assam's Anti-Immigrant Movement." *Population and Development* (June 1983): 279–92.

Belgium

Fitzmaurice, John. *The Politics of Belgium: Crisis and Compromise in a Plural Society.* London: Hurst, 1983.

Heisler, Martin O. *Political Community and Its Formation in the Low Countries.* Ann Arbor, MI: University Microfilms, 1970.

———. "Institutionalizing Societal Cleavages in a Cooptive Polity: The Growing Importance of the Output Side in Belgium." In Martin O. Heisler, ed., *Politics in Europe: Structures and Processes in Some Postindustrial Democracies.* New York: David McKay, 1974.

———. "Managing Ethnic Conflict in Belgium." *Annals* 433 (September 1977): 32–46.

———. "Ethnic Division in Belgium." In Daniel J. Elazar, ed., *Self Rule/Shared Rule.* Ramat Gan, Israel: Turtledove, 1979.

———. "Belgium: Stability and Progress from Division." In Robert Rinehart, ed., *Global Studies: Western Europe.* Guilford, CT: Dushkin, 1989.

Heisler, Martin O., and B. Guy Peters. "Comparing Social Policy across Levels of Government, Countries, and Time: Belgium and Sweden Since 1870." In Douglas E. Ashford, ed., *Comparing Public Policies: New Concepts and Methods.* Beverly Hills, CA: Sage, 1978.

Laurent, Pierre-Henri. "Divided Belgium Walks a Tightrope." *Current History* (April 1984): 169–72.

Lijphart, Arend, ed. *Conflict and Coexistence in Belgium: The Dynamics of a Culturally Divided Society.* Berkeley: University of California Press, 1981.

———. "Proportionality by Non-PR Methods: Ethnic Representation in Belgium, Cyprus, Lebanon, New Zealand, West Germany, and Zimbabwe." In Bernard Grofman and Arend Lijphart, eds., *Electoral Laws and Their Political Consequences.* New York: Agathon Press, 1986.

Lorwin, Val R. "Belgium: Religion, Class, and Language in National Politics." In Robert A. Dahl, ed., *Political Opposition in Western Democracies.* New Haven, CT: Yale University Press, 1966.

McRae, Kenneth D. *Conflict and Compromise in Multilingual Societies.* Vol. 2: *Belgium.* Waterloo, Ontario, Canada: Wilfrid Laurier University Press, 1986.

Ridder, Martine de, and Luis Ricardo Fraga. "The Brussels Issue in Belgian Politics." *West European Politics* (July 1986): 376–92.

Zolberg, Aristide R. "Splitting the Difference: Federalization without Federalism in Belgium." In Milton J. Esman, ed., *Ethnic Conflict in the Western World.* Ithaca, NY: Cornell University Press, 1977.

———. "Belgium." In Raymond Grew, ed., *Crises of Political Development in Europe and the United States.* Princeton, NJ: Princeton University Press, 1978.

Canada

Bell, David V.J. *The Roots of Disunity: A Look at Canadian Political Culture.* Toronto: McClelland and Stewart, 1979.

Cannon, G.E. "Consociationalism vs. Control: Canada as a Case Study." *Western Political Quarterly* 37 (1982).

Desbarats, P. *René: A Canadian In Search of a Country.* Toronto: McClelland and Stewart, 1976.

Juteau-Lee, Danielle, ed. "Ethnic Nationalism in Canada." *Canadian Review of Studies of Nationalism* (Fall 1984): 189–270.

Latouche, Daniel. *Canada and Quebec, Past and Future: An Essay.* Toronto: University of Toronto Press, 1986.

McRoberts, Kenneth, and Dale Posgate. *Quebec: Social Change and Political Crisis.* Toronto: McClelland and Stewart, 1976.

Meekison, J. Peter, ed. *Canadian Federalism: Myth or Reality.* Toronto: Methuen, 1971.

Morf, Gustave. *Terror in Quebec: Case Studies of the FLQ.* Toronto and Vancouver: Clark, Irwin, 1970.

Morin, Claude. *Quebec v. Ottawa: The Struggle for Self-Government, 1960–1972.* (Trans. Richard Howard). Toronto: University of Toronto Press, 1976.

Pletsch, Alfred, ed. *Ethnicity in Canada: International Examples and Perspectives.* Marburg, West Germany: Geographisches Institut, 1986.

Quinn, Herbert F. *The Union Nationale: A Study in Quebec Nationalism.* Toronto: University of Toronto Press, 1979.

Vallières Pierre. *Choose!* (Trans. P. Williams). Toronto: New Press, 1972.

Verney, Douglas V. *Three Civilizations, Two Cultures, One State: Canada's Political Traditions.* Durham, NC: Duke University Press, 1986.

Wardhaugh, Ronald. *Language and Nationhood: The Canadian Experience.* Vancouver: New Star Books, 1983.

Malaysia

Barraclough, Simon. "The Dynamic of Coercion in the Malaysian Political Process." *Modern Asian Studies* 19 (October 1985).

Enloe, Cynthia H. *Multi-Ethnic Politics: The Case of Malaysia.* Berkeley: University of California Press, 1970.

Esman, Milton J. *Administration and Development in Malaysia: Institution Building and Reform in a Plural Society.* Ithaca, NY: Cornell University Press, 1972.

Klitgaard, Robert, and Ruth Katz. "Overcoming Ethnic Inequalities: Lessons from Malaysia." *Policy Analysis and Management* (Spring 1983): 333–49.

Mauzy, Diane K. "Malaysia." In Diane K. Mauzy, ed., *Politics in the ASEAN States.* Kuala Lumpur: Maricans, n.d.

Means, Gordon P. *Malaysian Politics.* London: Hodder and Stoughton, 1976.

———. "Ethnic Preference Policies in Malaysia." In Neil Nevitte and Charles H. Kennedy, eds., *Ethnic Preference and Public Policy in Developing States.* Boulder, CO: Lynne Rienner, 1986.

Milne, R.S. "The Politics of Malaysia's New Economic Policy." *Pacific Affairs* 49, no. 2 (Summer 1976).

———. *Politics in Ethnically Bi-Polar States: Guyana, Malaysia, Fiji.* Vancouver: University of British Columbia Press, 1981.

———. "Ethnic Aspects of Privatization in Malaysia." In Neil Nevitte and Charles H. Kennedy, eds., *Ethnic Preference and Public Policy in Developing States.* Boulder, CO: Lynne Rienner, 1986.

Milne, R.S., and Diane K. Mauzy. *Politics and Government in Malaysia.* Vancouver: University of British Columbia Press, 1978.

———. *Malaysia: Tradition, Modernity and Islam.* Boulder, CO: Westview Press, 1986.

Rachagan, Sothi. "The Development of the Electoral System." In Harold Croch, Lee Kam Hing, and Michael Ong, eds., *Malaysian Politics and the 1978 Election.* Kuala Lumpur: Oxford University Press, 1980.

Stubbs, Richard. *Hearts and Minds in Guerrilla Warfare: The Malayan Emergency 1948–60.* Singapore: Oxford University Press, 1989.

Nigeria

Achebe, Chinua. *The Trouble with Nigeria.* Exeter, NH: Heinemann, 1984.

Adekson, J. 'Bayo. *Nigeria in Search of a Stable Political-Military System.* Boulder, CO: Westview Press, 1981.

Horowitz, Donald L. "About-Face in Africa: The Return to Civilian Rule in Nigeria." *Yale Review* 68, no. 2 (Winter 1979).

Nnoli, Okwudiba. *Ethnic Politics in Nigeria.* Enugu, Nigeria: Fourth Dimension, 1978.

Oyoubaire, S. Egite. *Federalism in Nigeria: A Study in the Development of the Nigerian State.* New York: St. Martin's Press, 1985.

Zartman, I. William, ed. *The Political Economy of Nigeria.* New York: Praeger, 1984.

Northern Ireland

Aunger, Edmund A. *In Search of Political Stability: A Comparative Study of New Brunswick and Northern Ireland.* Montreal: McGill-Queens University Press, 1981.

Barritt, Denis P., and Charles F. Carter. *The Northern Ireland Problem: A Study in Group Relations.* London: Oxford University Press, 1972.

Bell, J. Bowyer. *The Secret Army.* Dublin: Academy Press, 1979.

Bell, P.N. "Direct Rule in Northern Ireland." In Richard Rose, ed., *Ministers and Ministries.* Oxford: Oxford University Press, 1987.

Birrell, Derek, and Alan Murie. *Policy and Government in Northern Ireland.* Dublin: Gill and Macmillan, 1980.

Bruce, Steve. *God Save Ulster: The Religion and Politics of Paisleyism.* New York: Oxford University Press, 1986.

Bukland, Patrick. *Ulster Unionism and the Origins of Northern Ireland.* Dublin: Gill and Macmillan, 1973.

Carlton, Charles, ed. *Bigotry and Blood: Documents on the Ulster Troubles.* Chicago: Nelson Hall, 1977.

Darby, John. *Dressed to Kill: Cartoonists and the Northern Irish Conflict.* Belfast: Appletree Press, 1983.

———, ed. *Northern Ireland: Background to the Conflict.* Syracuse, NY: Syracuse University Press, 1983.

Finnegan, Richard B. *Ireland: The Challenge of Conflict and Change.* Boulder, CO: Westview Press, 1983.

Flackes, W.D. *Northern Ireland: A Political Directory.* London: BBC Publications, 1983.

Fraser, Morris. *Children in Conflict.* New York: Basic Books, 1977.

Harris, Rosemary. *Prejudice and Tolerance in Ulster.* Manchester, England: Manchester University Press, 1972.

Hepburn, A.C. *The Conflict of Nationality in Modern Ireland.* New York: St. Martin's Press, 1980.

Hickey, John. *Religion and the Northern Ireland Problem.* Totowa, NJ: Gill and Macmillan, 1984.

Jackson, Harold. *The Two Irelands: A Dual Study of Inter-Group Tensions.* Report No. 2. London: Minority Rights Group, 1971.

Lijphart, Arend. "The Northern Ireland Problem: Cases, Theories, and Solutions." *British Journal of Political Science* 5, no. 1 (January 1975).

MacEoin, Gary. *Northern Ireland: Captive of History.* New York: Holt, Rinehart and Winston, 1974.

Mallie, Eamonn. *The Provisional IRA.* London: Heinemann, 1987.

Milnor, Andrew. *Politics, Violence, and Social Change in Northern Ireland.* Occasional Paper No. 5. Ithaca, NY: Cornell University Press, Western Societies Program, 1976.

Munck, Ronaldo. *Ireland: Nation, State, and Class Conflict.* Boulder, CO: Westview Press, 1985.

Nelson, Sarah. *Ulster's Uncertain Defenders.* Belfast: Appletree Press, 1984.

O'Malley, Padraig. *The Uncivil Wars: Ireland Today.* New York: Houghton Mifflin, 1983.

———. *The Hunger Strikes in Northern Ireland: A Study in the Psychology of Entrapment.* New York: Houghton Mifflin, forthcoming

O'Sullivan, Tadhg. "Reconciling the Diverse Irish Identities." *World Affairs Journal* (Fall 1983): 1–6.

Rea, Desmond, ed. *Political Cooperation in Divided Societies: A Series of Papers Relevant to the Conflict in Northern Ireland.* Dublin: Gill and Macmillan, 1982.

Rose, Richard. *Governing without Consensus: An Irish Perspective.* Boston: Beacon Press, 1971.

———. *Northern Ireland: A Time of Choice.* Washington, DC: American Enterprise Institute, 1976.

———. *The Territorial Dimension in Government: Understanding the United Kingdom.* Chatham, NJ: Chatham House, 1982.

Schmitt, David E. "Bicommunal Conflict and Accommodation in Northern Ireland." *Terrorism* 9, no. 3 (1987): 263–84.

Stewart, A.T.Q. *The Narrow Ground*. London: Faber and Faber, 1977.
Townshend, P. *Political Violence in Ireland*. New York: Oxford University Press, 1983.

Pakistan

Ahmen, Akbar S. *Millenium and Charisma among Pathans: A Critical Essay in Social Anthropology*. London: Routledge and Kegan Paul, 1976.
Barth, Fredrik. *Political Leadership among Swat Pathans*. London: University of London, Athlone Press, 1959.
Bhutto, Zulfiqar Ali. "Pakistan Builds Anew." *Foreign Affairs* 51, no. 3 (1973).
Harrison, Selig S. *In Afghanistan's Shadow: Baluch Nationalism and Soviet Temptations*. New York: Carnegie Endowment for International Peace, 1981.
———. *The State, Religion, and Ethnic Politics: Afghanistan, Iran, and Pakistan*. Syracuse, NY: Syracuse University Press, 1986.
Hussain, Asaf. "Ethnicity, National Identity, and Praetorianism: The Case of Pakistan." *Asian Survey* 16 (October 1976): 918–30.
Khuhro, Hamida, ed. *Sind through the Centuries*. Karachi: Oxford University Press, 1982.
Wheeler, Richard S. *The Politics of Pakistan: A Constitutional Quest*. Ithaca, NY: Cornell University Press, 1970.
Wirsing, Robert G. "South Asia: The Baluch Frontier Tribes of Pakistan." In Robert G. Wirsing, ed., *Protection of Ethnic Minorities: Comparative Perspectives*. New York: Pergamon Press, 1982.
Ziring, Lawrence, Ralph Braibanti, and W. Howard Wiggins, eds. *Pakistan: The Long View*. Durham, NC: Duke University Press, 1977.

Sri Lanka

Ames, Michael. "Ideological and Social Change in Ceylon." *Human Organization* 22 (1963).
Bienen, Henry. "Religion, Legitimacy, and Conflict in Sri Lanka." *Annals* 483 (January 1986).
Carter, John Ross, ed. *Religiousness in Sri Lanka*. Colombo, Sri Lanka: Marga Institute, 1979.
de Silva, Lynn. *Buddhism: Beliefs and Practices in Sri Lanka*. Colombo, Sri Lanka: Wesley Press, 1980.
Farmer, B.H. *Ceylon: A Divided Nation*. London: Oxford University Press, 1963.
Fernando, Tissa, and Robert N. Kearney, eds. *Modern Sri Lanka: A Society in Transition*. Syracuse, NY: Maxwell School of Citizenship and Public Affairs, 1979.
Jayewardene, C.H.S., and H. Jayewardene. *Tea for Two: Ethnic Violence in Sri Lanka*. Ottawa: Crimcare, 1985.
Kearney, Robert N. "Sinhalese Nationalism and Social Conflict in Ceylon." *Pacific Affairs* 37 (1964).
———. *Communalism and Language in the Politics of Ceylon*. Durham, NC: Duke University Press, 1967.

Kearney, Robert N. *The Politics of Ceylon (Sri Lanka)*. Ithaca, NY: Cornell University Press, 1973.

———. "Language and the Rise of Tamil Separatism in Sri Lanka." *Asian Survey* 18 (1978).

———. "Tension and Conflict in Sri Lanka." *Current History* (March 1986): 109–12.

Manor, James, ed. *Sri Lanka in Change and Crisis*. New York: St. Martin's Press, 1984.

Mason, Philip K., ed. *India and Ceylon: Unity and Diversity*. New York: Oxford Unversity Press, 1967.

Pfaffenberger, Bryan. *Caste in Tamil Culture: The Religious Foundations of Sudra Domination in Tamil Sri Lanka*. Syracuse, NY: Maxwell School of Citizenship and Public Affairs, 1982.

———. "Sri Lanka in 1986: A Nation at the Crossroads." *Asian Survey* 37, no. 2 (1987).

Piyadasa, L. *Sri Lanka: The Holocaust and After*. London: Marram Books, 1984.

Ponnambalam, Satchi. *Sri Lanka: National Conflict and the Tamil Liberation Struggle*. Totowa, NJ: Tamil Information Center, 1983.

Roberts, Michael, ed. *Collective Identities, Nationalisms and Protest in Modern Sri Lanka*. Colombo, Sri Lanka: Marga Institute, 1979.

Ryan, Bryce. *Caste in Modern Ceylon*. New Brunswick, NJ: Rutgers University Press, 1953.

Singer, Marshall. "Report on the Pressures and Opportunities for a Peaceful Solution to the Ethnic Conflict in Sri Lanka." *Journal of Developing Societies* 2 (1986).

Smith, Bardwell L., ed. *Religion and Legitimation of Power in Sri Lanka*. Chambersburg, PA: ANIMA Books, 1978.

Tambiah, Stanley J. *Sri Lanka: Ethnic Fractricide and the Dismantling of Democracy*. Chicago: University of Chicago Press, 1986.

Wriggins, W. Howard. *Ceylon: Dilemmas of a New Nation*. Princeton, NJ: Princeton University Press, 1960.

Yalman, Nur. *Under the Bo Tree: Studies in Caste, Kinship, and Marriage in the Interior of Ceylon*. Berkeley: University of California Press, 1971.

Sudan

Alier, Abel. "The Southern Sudan Question." In Dunstan M. Wai, ed., *The Southern Sudan: The Problem of National Integration*. London: Frank Cass, 1973.

Bechtold, Peter. "The Contemporary Sudan." *American-Arab Affairs* (Fall 1983): 88–101.

Deng, Francis M. *Africans of the Two Worlds: The Dinka in Afro-Arab Sudan*. New Haven, CT: Yale University Press, 1978.

———. *Seed of Redemption: A Political Novel*. New York: Lillian Barber Press, 1986.

Deng, Francis M., and Prosser Gifford, eds. *The Search for Peace and Unity in the Sudan*. Washington, DC: Wilson Center Press, 1987.

Gurdon, Charles. *Sudan in Transition: A Political Risk Analysis*. London: Economist Intelligence Unit, 1986.

Hasan, Yusuf Fadl. *The Arabs and the Sudan.* Edinburgh: Edinburgh University Press, 1967.

Holt, P.M. *The Mahdist State in the Sudan, 1881–1898,* 2nd ed. Oxford: Clarendon Press, 1970.

Holt, P.M., and M.W. Daly. *The History of the Sudan,* 3rd ed. Boulder, CO: Westview Press, 1979.

Kasfir, Nelson. "Southern Sudanese Politics Since the Addis Ababa Agreement." *African Affairs* 76, no. 303 (April 1977).

Lesch, Ann Mosely. "Confrontation in the Southern Sudan." *Middle East Journal* 40, no. 3 (Summer 1986).

Malwal, Bona. *The Sudan, A Second Challenge to Nationhood.* New York: Thornton Books, 1985.

Voll, John O., and Sarah Potts Voll. *The Sudan: A Profile in Unity and Diversity.* Boulder, CO: Westview Press, 1985.

Wai, Dunstan M. *The African-Arab Conflict in the Sudan.* New York: Africana, 1981.

Switzerland

Daalder, Hans. "On Building Consociational Nations: The Cases of the Netherlands and Switzerland." Reprinted in Kenneth D. McRae, ed., *Consociational Democracy.* Toronto: McClelland and Stewart, 1974.

Lehmbruch, Gerhard. "A Non-Competitive Pattern of Conflict Management in Liberal Democracies: The Case of Switzerland, Austria, and Lebanon." In Kenneth D. McRae, ed., *Consociational Democracy.* Toronto: McClelland and Stewart, 1974.

McRae, Kenneth K. *Conflict and Compromise in Multilingual Societies. Vol. 1: Switzerland.* Waterloo, Ontario, Canada: Wilfrid Laurier University Press, 1983.

Schmitter, Barbara E. "Immigrants and Associations: Their Role in the Socio-Political Process of Immigrant Worker Integration in West Germany and Switzerland." *International Migration Review* 14, no. 2 (Summer 1980): 179–92.

Zimbabwe

Beach, D.N. *The Shona and Zimbabwe, 900–1850.* London: Heinemann, 1980.

Bendahmane, Diane B., and John W. McDonald, eds., *Perspectives on Negotiation* (includes section on Zimbabwean independence negotiations). Washington, DC: U.S. Department of State, Center for the Study of Foreign Affairs, 1986.

Hitchens, Christopher. *Inequalities in Zimbabwe.* London: Minority Rights Group, 1981.

Loney, Martin. *Rhodesia: White Racism and Imperial Response.* Baltimore, MD: Penguin, 1975.

Mungazi, Dickson A. *The Cross between Rhodesia and Zimbabwe: A Racial Conflict in Rhodesia, 1962–1979.* New York: Vantage Press, 1981.

Ranger, T.O. *Revolt in Southern Rhodesia, 1896–1897.* London: Heinemann, 1967.

Schutz, Barry M. "The Colonial Heritage of Strife: Sources of Cleavage in the Zimbabwe Liberation Movement." *Africa Today* (January–March 1979): 3–27.

Miscellaneous Country-Specific Works

Adam, Heribert. *Ethnic Power Mobilized: Can South Africa Change?* New Haven, CT: Yale University Press, 1979.

Anwar, Muhammad. *Race and Politics: Ethnic Minorities and the British Political System.* London: Tavistock, 1986.

Bertsch, Gary K. *Value and Community in Multi-National Yugoslavia.* Boulder, CO: East European Quarterly, 1976.

Burks, R.V. *The National Problem and the Future of Yugoslavia.* Santa Monica, CA: Rand, 1971.

Coyle, Dominick J. *Minorities in Revolt: Political Violence in Ireland, Italy and Cyprus.* Rutherford, NJ: Fairleigh Dickinson University Press, 1983.

Gordon, David C. *Lebanon: The Fragmented Nation.* Stanford, CA: Hoover Institution Press, 1980.

Haley, P. Edward, and Lewis W. Snider, eds., *Lebanon in Crisis: Participants and Issues.* Syracuse, NY: Syracuse University Press, 1979.

Hechter, Michael. *Internal Colonialism: The Celtic Fringe in British National Development, 1536–1966.* Berkeley and Los Angeles: University of California Press, 1975.

Lijphart, Arend. *Power-Sharing in South Africa.* Berkeley: University of California, Institute of International Studies, 1985.

Montville, Joseph V., ed., "A Notebook on the Psychology of the U.S.-Soviet Relationship." *Political Psychology* 6, no. 2 (special issue) (June 1985).

Payne, Stanley. "Catalan and Basque Nationalism." *Journal of Contemporary History* 6, no. 1 (January 1971).

———. *Basque Nationalism.* Reno: University of Nevada Press, 1975.

Reece, Jack E. *The Bretons Against France: Ethnic Minority Nationalism in Twentieth-Century Brittany.* Chapel Hill: University of North Carolina Press, 1977, pp. 227–28.

Safran, William. "Islamization in Western Europe: Political Consequences and Historical Parallels." *Annals* 485 (May 1986): 98–112.

Sanders, Thomas G. "Portuguese Migrants: International and Domestic." In *UFSI Reports, 1985/18—Europe.* Indianapolis: Universities Field Staff International, 1985, pp. 3–8.

Steiner, Jürg. "Consociational Democracy as a Policy Recommendation: The Case of South Africa." *Comparative Politics* (April 1987).

Svensson, Frances. "Liberal Democracy and Group Rights: Individualism and Its Impact on American Indian Tribes. *Political Studies* 27, no. 3 (September 1979): 421–39.

Volkan, V.D. *Cyprus—War and Adaptation: A Psychoanalytic History of Two Ethnic Groups in Conflict.* Charlottesville: University Press of Virginia, 1979.

Wriggins, W. Howard. "Sri Lanka and South Asia: Conventions, Perceptions, and Policy." *Bangladesh Institute of Strategic Studies* (January 1985).

About the Contributors

Walter K. Andersen is a research specialist at the United States Department of State, Washington, D.C.

Remi Clignet is Professor of Sociology at the University of Maryland.

John Darby is Professor of Social Administration and Policy and Director of the Centre for the Study of Conflict at the University of Ulster. His most recent book is *Intimidation and the Control of Conflict in Northern Ireland* (Syracuse University Press, 1987).

Francis Mading Deng, a native of Sudan, is Senior Fellow in Foreign Policy at the Brookings Institution, Washington, D.C. He has previously served as Sudan's Ambassador to Canada (1980–83), Minister of State for Foreign Affairs (1976–80), Ambassador to the United States (1974–76), and Ambassador to the Scandinavian countries (1972–74). He is the author of twelve books, among them *The Search for Peace and Unity in the Sudan* (with Prosser Gifford; Wilson Center Press, 1987), *The Man Called Deng Majok: A Biography of Power, Polygyny, and Change* (Yale University Press, 1986), and *Seed of Redemption: A Political Novel* (Lillian Barber Press, 1986).

Milton J. Esman is the John S Knight Professor of International Studies, Emeritus, at Cornell University.

F. Gunther Eyck is Distinguished Adjunct Professor in Residence of the School of International Service, American University, Washington, D.C. He is the author of *Loyal Rebels: Andreas Hofer and the Tyrolean Uprising of 1809* (University Press of America, 1986).

Selig S. Harrison, a Senior Associate of the Carnegie Endowment for International Peace, Washington, DC, has specialized in South Asian Affairs and American Policy problems in South Asia for thirty-five years as a foreign correspondent and author. He is the author of *In Afghanistan's Shadow:*

Baluch Nationalism and Soviet Temptations (Carnegie Endowment for International Peace, 1981.

Martin O. Heisler is Associate Professor of Government and Politics at the University of Maryland.

Donald L. Horowitz is Charles S. Murphy Professor of Law and Professor of Public Policy Studies and Political Science at Duke University. Before joining the faculty of Duke, Dr. Horowitz was a Senior Fellow at the Smithsonian Institution's Research Institute on Immigration and Ethnic Studies.

Nelson Kasfir is Professor of Government at Dartmouth College. Previously, he taught for four years at Makerere University in Uganda. He has made several trips to Sudan.

Arend Lijphart is Professor of Political Science at the University of California, San Diego. He is the author of *Democracy in Plural Societies: A Comparative Exploration* (Yale University Press, 1977).

Kenneth D. McRae is Professor of Political Science at Carleton University in Ottawa. From 1964 to 1969, he was a research supervisor on the Canadian Royal Commission on Bilingualism and Biculturalism. He is the author of *Conflict and Compromise in Multilingual Societies: Volume 1, Switzerland* and *Volume 2, Belgium* (Wilfrid Laurier University Press, 1983, 1986).

Padraig O'Malley is editor of the *New England Journal of Public Policy,* Senior Associate at the John W. McCormack Institute of Public Affairs of the University of Massachusetts at Boston, and author of *The Uncivil Wars: Ireland Today* (Houghton Mifflin, 1983).

John N. Paden is Clarence J. Robinson Professor of International Studies at George Mason University. Previously, he was Professor of Political Science and Director of the Program of African Studies at Northwestern University. He has spent many years teaching and conducting research in Nigeria.

Bryan Pfaffenberger is Associate Director of the Center for South Asian Studies and Assistant Professor of Humanities in the School of Engineering and Applied Science at the University of Virginia.

Uri Ra'anan is University Professor in the University Professors Program and Director of the Institute for the Study of Conflict, Ideology, and Policy at Boston University.

Richard Rose is Director of the Centre for the Study of Public Policy at the University of Strathclyde, Glasgow. He has published widely about comparative politics and government in advanced industrial societies. On Northern Ireland, he has written *Governing without Consensus: An Irish Perspective* (Beacon Press, 1971), *Northern Ireland: A Time of Choice* (American Enterprise Institute, 1976), and *The Territorial Dimension in Government: Understanding the United Kingdom* (Chatham House, 1982).

Barry M. Schutz is Professor at the Defense Intelligence College and Adjunct Professor in the National Security Studies Program at Georgetown University. He formerly served as resident African specialist at the Rand Corporation. Dr. Schutz is an expert on southern African affairs, especially on Zimbabwe, where he has taught and conducted research.

Marshall R. Singer is Professor of International and Intercultural Affairs at the University of Pittsburgh. He is also President and Vice-Chairman of the Board of the U.S. Association for the Cultural Triangle of Sri Lanka.

Jürg Steiner is Professor of Political Science at the University of North Carolina at Chapel Hill. He also has a teaching appointment at the University of Bern, Switzerland.

Richard Stubbs is Associate Professor of Political Science at McMaster University and Associate Director of the Joint Centre for Asia Pacific Studies, University of Toronto—York University. He is the author of *Hearts and Minds in Guerilla Warfare: The Malayan Emergency, 1948–60* (Oxford University Press, 1989.

Vamık D. Volkan is Professor of Psychiatry, Director of the Division of Psychoanalytic Studies and Director of the Center for Study of Mind and Human Interaction at the University of Virginia. He is a member of the editorial boards of *Political Psychology, Psychoanalytic Study of Society,* and *The Yearbook of Psychoanalysis.*

John O. Voll has been teaching history at the University of New Hampshire since 1965. His primary areas of research expertise are cultural-religious developments in the modern Islamic world and the modern history of Sudan and Egypt. He is the author of *The Sudan: A Profile in Unity and Diversity* (with Sarah Potts Voll; Westview Press, 1985).

I. William Zartman is Jacob Blaustein Professor of Conflict Management and International Organization and Director of African Studies at the Johns

Hopkins University School for Advanced International Studies. He is the author of *Ripe for Resolution: Conflict and Intervention in Africa* (Yale University Press, 1989) and many other books and articles on African affairs and international negotiation.

About the Editor

Joseph V. Montville, a former career diplomat, is senor consultant on conflict resolution at the Center for the Study of Foreign Affairs, Foreign Service Institute, Arlington, Virginia. He is also a founding member of the International Society of Political Psychology.